Understanding WMI Scripting

Understanding WMI Scripting

Alain Lissoir

Digital Press
An imprint of Elsevier Science
Amsterdam • Boston • London • New York • Oxford • Paris • San Diego
San Francisco • Singapore • Sydney • Tokyo

Digital Press is an imprint of Elsevier Science.

 Recognizing the importance of preserving what has been written, Elsevier Science prints its books on acid-free paper whenever possible.

Library of Congress Cataloging-in-Publication Data

Lissoir, Alain.
  Understanding WMI scripting / Alain Lissoir.
    p. cm.
  Includes bibliographical references and index.
  ISBN 1-55558-266-4
    1. Microsoft Windows (Computer file) 2. Operating systems (Computers) 3. Programming languages (Electronic computers)   I. Title.

  QA76.76.O63 L5548 2002
  005.4'469--dc21   2002035109

British Library Cataloguing-in-Publication Data

A catalogue record for this book is available from the British Library.

The publisher offers special discounts on bulk orders of this book.
For information, please contact:

Manager of Special Sales
Elsevier Science
200 Wheeler Road
Burlington, MA 01803
Tel: 781-313-4700
Fax: 781-313-4882

For information on all Digital Press publications available, contact our World Wide Web home page at: http://www.digitalpress.com or http://www.bh.com/digitalpress

10 9 8 7 6 5 4 3 2 1

Printed in the United States of America

I dedicate this book to my friends and my family who didn't get the chance to see me a lot throughout these twenty months of hard work. Things will change now!

Contents

Foreword

No matter how hard they try, history teaches us that software engineers never manage to develop products that do everything that people need. This is the fundamental reason why application programming interfaces and scripting languages are so important. Closed software restricts creativity and stops people doing a complete job.

I never thought Windows NT was completely finished. Windows NT is a good file and print share operating system, but it exhibits some defects as systems scale up within large enterprises. All enterprise operating systems allow administrators some freedom to tailor their environment; think of JCL for IBM operating systems or DCL for OpenVMS. Windows NT had all manner of utilities and add-on programs such as the Resource Kit, but lacked real scripting, a common way for applications to provide or consume management data, and only had a primitive scheduler. This didn't matter so much in a world where most Windows NT servers ran one application or supported small user communities, but it certainly became an issue as servers scaled and began to host multiple, increasingly complex, applications.

Windows 2000 is a huge step forward and deserves recognition as an enterprise operating system. The gaps in functionality and flexibility are narrowed (some work remains to be done) and the combination of a common API for management data (WMI) and Windows scripting allows administrators to tailor systems to meet their needs. Knowledge remains an issue. By themselves, WMI and scripting don't do anything—they have to be applied and combined to do real work and before you can do that, you need to know what's possible and how to approach problems.

I don't have much time for those who insist on recreating the wheel. Use the knowledge and the code examples contained here to solve common management problems and to provide the foundation for tailored solutions to your own specific system administration needs. I think you'll find that you can do much more than you realized to understand what's really happening on your servers, and get real work done as you dip into the knowledge contained here.

I know Alain has worked very hard to bring this book together. It's hard to appreciate that this is only the first volume and there could be more to say on the topic of WMI, but the second volume that covers providers, security, and applications has even more to discover.

Enjoy the unique collection he has assembled, the code he has written, and the depth of knowledge he demonstrates. Above all, don't leave this book on the shelf as it will solve some real-world Windows system administration problems for you.

Enjoy!

Tony Redmond
Chief Technology Officer,
HP Consulting and Integration

Preface

This book is the first of two dedicated to Windows Management Instrumentation (WMI). Why two books about WMI scripting instead of one? When I started this project, I decided to produce a book to help people take advantage of the WMI power for their day-to-day work. Unfortunately, WMI is not a simple technology and covers a huge area of technologies like Simple Network Management Protocol (SNMP), Windows Group Policies (GPO) or Active Directory replication to name a few. This becomes even more complex when the goal is to cover Windows XP and Windows.NET Server as these two last operating systems from Microsoft contain loads of WMI features when compared to the implementation in Windows NT 4.0 and 2000. Last but not least, the field of applications for WMI can vary widely. WMI can be used to develop applications (i.e. tools like scripts) or can be used in Enterprise management software solutions like HP Open-View Operations for Windows (HP OVOW) or Microsoft Operations Manager (MOM). To get the benefit of WMI through these Enterprise Management solutions, a basic understanding of the WMI mechanisms is more than helpful. Next, the level of experience that some people may have regarding WMI can vary widely. Writing a too basic book about WMI was more than likely missing the spot for the gurus. On the other hand, writing a too complex book about WMI didn't offer a chance for beginners to start with WMI.

In order to address all fields of application and people expectations about WMI, I decided to organize the huge amount of information that WMI offers in two different books entitled:

Understanding Windows Management Instrumentation (WMI) Scripting (ISBN 1555582664)

Leveraging Windows Management Instrumentation (WMI) Scripting (ISBN 1555582990)

There are two important points to note about these two books. The first point concerns the scripting aspects. Although both books contain the word "scripting" in the title, the WMI mechanisms discovered and illustrated via scripts can be useful to non-scripters as well. Actually, people working with WMI applications like WMIC or Enterprise Management Software consuming WMI information will find loads of interesting information to monitor their Enterprise Windows Environment. The second point concerns the concept of the books. Both books are developed with one concept in mind: "The practice". A far as possible, I always tried to avoid long theoretical descriptions to prioritize the practical discovery. Therefore, each time a new feature, a new concept or a new script is developed, it is very important for the reader to play with the technology involved to make sure that the piece of information is perfectly understood. This is an important aspect of the books because each step we go through is a building block reused further when learning new concepts or features. Finally, from a usage perspective, both books are double-sided. On one hand, they guide you in the WMI discovery; on the other hand, once you have completed your WMI learning, they can be used as references completing the Microsoft SDK information.

For people interested to start with WMI from ground up or willing to get a more solid basis with this technology, they can start with this first book, *Understanding Windows Management Instrumentation (WMI) Scripting* (ISBN 1555582664). The goal of this book is to setup the foundation of the WMI knowledge required to develop solutions on top of WMI. The information contained in this book is organized in six chapters:

Chapter 1 covers everything that is related to Windows Script Host (WSH) since version 1.0 up to version 5.6 included in Windows XP and Windows.NET Server. As all WMI scripts developed throughout the two books make use of the WSH environment, it is useful to explore the features it offers. For the readers already working with WSH today, this chapter will bring you up to speed as you will discover the brand new features that WSH 5.6 includes like digitally signed scripts or the XML command line parsing.

Chapter 2 covers everything related to the Common Information Model (CIM) extensively used by WMI. It also covers the WMI-specific terminologies and concepts, the tools available to work with WMI (like WMIC or WBEMTEST). To remain practical and avoid too much theory, this chapter also proposes two discovery exercises with the WMI tools to understand the WMI mechanisms in place.

Chapter 3 covers everything related to the WMI Query Language (WQL). This pseudo-SQL language is of primarily importance when searching some specific management information or when monitoring management events. In this chapter you will see how you can perform queries and the possibilities offered by WQL to extract information and monitor events in different ways.

Chapter 4 covers the basic WMI scripting techniques. It explains how a coded-logic can be developed on top of the WMI COM objects to perform some basic management operations. By reading this chapter, you will understand the WMI COM object model and how to retrieve management information with it. This chapter is the foundation of the WMI scripting.

Chapter 5 covers the advanced WMI scripting techniques. For example, in this chapter you will discover how some WMI information can be retrieved asynchronously or how WMI data can be represented in XML.

Chapter 6 covers everything that is related to WMI events and its related scripting techniques. The material discovered is the foundation to build WMI monitoring applications. You will see how to catch events by combining some WMI scripting and WQL statements. You will also see how you can trigger actions at fixed time or at regular time intervals.

Last but not least, this first volume contains more than 150 script samples. They can be downloaded for free from http://www.LissWare.Net.

That's it for this first book. Once you have completed reading and practicing the first part, you will be ready to discover and apply your WMI knowledge to any technology that WMI interfaces with. This may include things like managing SNMP devices, monitoring Active Directory replication or configuring the security in a Windows environment. This is the purpose of the second book, *Leveraging Windows Management Instrumentation (WMI) Scripting* (ISBN 1555582990).

This second book addresses the most advanced WMI topics to put WMI in practice and therefore requires a good WMI and Windows platform experience. If you are one of these persons or if you just completed reading *Understanding Windows Management Instrumentation (WMI) Scripting* (ISBN 1555582664), this is the logical step for you to complete your WMI background. Based on the information learned in the first volume (or in your existing WMI experience), you will see how you can exploit the features brought by various WMI interfaces (called the WMI providers) to manage the real-world environment components. Note that if you are used to work with WMI, this second book can be used on a standalone basis as well. Nothing forces you to start with the first book if you already have a good WMI experience.

Let's begin our first step in the world of management, scripting and automation by starting with the first Chapter dedicated to WSH.

Acknowledgments

In 1997, when I joined Digital Equipment Corporation (DEC), I never imagined that one day I would complete a two volume book covering any area of technology. Like many other IT consultants, I was busy delivering IT solutions based on Microsoft technologies for various customer projects. Life has many surprises and the IT world is constantly changing—each change offering its own opportunities and challenges. In 1999, Compaq (which had taken over DEC and has since itself merged into HP) embarked on their Windows 2000 Academy program, and allowed Compaq consultants a great chance to meet colleagues from all over the world and learn a new set of Microsoft technologies. This time was also a great opportunity to share knowledge and increase our experience. In this context, Micky Balladelli and Jan De Clercq provided great motivation for me to start writing my first official publication for Compaq. I'm really grateful to them for supporting me and giving me the guts to start my first white paper. The first publication is always the hardest. In this context, I would also like to acknowledge Tony Redmond, Vice-President and Chief Technology Officer of HP Consultancy & Integration (HPCI), for all the support he has given me since 1999 when I was still working as a local consultant in Belgium. His trust, his support and all opportunities he gave me, such as working at Microsoft in Redmond during the Exchange 2000 development phase and being part of his team, the HPCI Technology Leadership Group (TLG), have built my confidence and my experience for a book project.

Working with a team like TLG is great. It is a team of talented people, a team implicitly showing you the way to follow and helping you to express capabilities that you never imagined you had. Today, I'm proud to be part of such a great team and I owe a great debt to each of my team mates for their support in creating this book on Windows Management Instrumentation. In this regard, I want to acknowledge each of the TLG members who worked with me at Compaq and HP. More specifically, I want to acknowl-edge the contribution of Aric Bernard (US) for giving me the marvelous chance to rebuild my lab almost every month with the new Windows.NET Server builds, Pierre Bijaoui (FR) for providing me some hardware resources and his advice about the book publishing and editing process, Jerry Cochran (US) for acting as a bridge between Microsoft in Redmond and myself in Brussels, Jan De Clercq (BE) for showing me the way to approach writing white papers, articles, and, last, a book, Olivier D'hose (BE) for his constant support, his carefulness, and the delicious northwest smoked salmon strips, Dung Hoang Khac (FR) for his help with the Chinese mafia, Kevin Laahs (SCO) for his thorough reviews, sharing loads and ideas about my ADCchecker project, Donald Livengood (US) for saving my life in a road bend in Lexington, Massachusetts, Kieran McCorry (IR) for the good laughs we had in Orlando, Emer McKenna (IR) for her thorough reviews and carefulness she gave me, Daragh Morrissey (IR) for sharing his insights about Microsoft clusters, John Rhoton (AT) for saving my life (once more!) in an incredible hailstorm in Nice on a beautiful day in September. All these people gave me, sometimes without even knowing it, invaluable help in completing this work.

I also want to acknowledge the TLG management for their support and for the understanding they always demonstrated during twenty months of work. Being part of TLG involves you in many activities, such as customer projects and workshops, knowledge-sharing activities, and delivering pre-sentations at major IT industry events, such as Microsoft Exchange Confer-ence (MEC), IT Forum, TechED, or DECUS, to name a few. This doesn't leave much time to write a book during normal work hours, so most writ-ing is done during weekends, vacations, and airplane travels. Having man-agement support is a great asset when you are trying to balance everything that's expected of you. Therefore, I want to acknowledge Don Vickers, Todd Rooke, and Tony Redmond for their trust and continuous support.

Of course, the people of TLG were not the only ones who contributed to this project. My colleagues around the world helped in many ways, too. Some people helped me simply by asking technical questions and exposing their problems in our technical discussion forums. This type of knowledge sharing represents an invaluable source of information for a book writer, as it brings to your desk the real-world problems and situations that people are trying to solve in the field around the world. The practical and concrete approach I tried to bring to these WMI books is inspired by these contribu-tions. In this respect, I want to acknowledge Lyn Baird (US), Eric Bidonnet (BE), Andy Cederberg (US), Warren Cooley (US), Michel Cosman (NL),

Henrik Damslund (DK), Vincent D'Haene (BE), Mike Dransfield (AU), Ian Godfrey (UK), Guido Grillenmeier (DE), Gary Hall (CA), Juergen Hasslauer (DE), Ken Hendel (US), Mike Ireland (US), Henrik Joergensen (DK), John Johnson (US), Lasse Jokinen (FI), Andy Joyce (AU), Richard Joyce (IR), Patrick Kildea (US), Missy Koslosky (US), Ales Kostohryz (CZ), Stuart Ladd (US), André Larbière (BE), Carey Lee (US), Paul Loonen (BE), Paul Marshall (US), Susan McDonald (BE), John McManus (UK), Kim Mikkelsen (DK), Brendan Moon (US), Joseph Neubauer (US), Gary Olsen (US), Ken Punshon (UK), Ben Santing (IR), Rudy Schockaert (BE), Terry Storey (UK), Peter Struve (DK), Jason Trimble (CA), Peter Van Hees (BE), Marc Van Hooste (BE), Michael Vogt (CH), Filip Vranckx (BE), Raymond Warichet (BE), Randy Warrens (US), and Mats Weckstrom (FI).

It's hard to write a book about Microsoft technologies without the support of the Microsoft designers, program managers, and developers in Redmond. Again, in this respect, I'm more than grateful to many Microsoft people for their interest, their support, and their contribution to this project by sharing and reviewing information despite their other commitments. People who gave me help come from various development and service teams at Microsoft, such as the Exchange team, the WMI team, the Programmability team, the MOM team, the Support Server group team, and Microsoft Consultancy Service, to name a few. In this respect, I want to acknowledge Muhammad Arrabi, Jim Benton, J. C. Cannon, Andy Cheung, Max Ciccotosto, Andrew Clinick, Andi Comisioneru, Ahmed El-Shimi, Clark Gilder, Mary Gray, Keith Hageman, Andy Harjanto, Russ Herman, Vladimir Joanovic, Pat Kenny, Stuart Kwan, Eric Lippert, Jonathan Liu, Andreas Luther, Sergei Meleshchuk, Arun Nanda, Sasha Nosov, Ajay Ramachandran, Paul Reiner, Arkady Retik, Jan Shanahan, Barry Steinglass, Greg Stemp, Sanjay Tandon, Patrick Tousignant, Deun Dex Tsaltas, and Céline Van Maele.

I want to give very particular thanks to Mary Gray and Sergei Meleshchuk from Microsoft who supported me for more than 15 months via e-mail despite the heavy load of work they had. I'm even more grateful when I think that we didn't get the chance to meet for the first time until September 2002. They helped by answering questions and reviewing some of the chapters without even knowing each other. I really appreciate the trust they gave me throughout these months.

Reviewers are very important and they bring an enormous value to a book. I admire the commitment they demonstrated by reading carefully all chapters and correcting my English and technical mistakes in these two books despite their availability. I want to acknowledge Mary Gray, Kevin Laahs, Susan McDonald, Emer McKenna, and Sergei Meleshchuk for their thorough reviews. I know they suffered a lot during the readings.

Beside the Microsoft people, I also want to thank some people of the HP OpenView team for their support in sharing the information related to HP OpenView Operations for Windows (OVOW) and WMI. I want to acknowledge Viher Bogdan (SI), Jonathan Cyr (US), Drew Dimmick (US), Jerry Estep (US), Angelika Hierath (DE), Roland Hofstetter (DE), Wilhelm Klenk (DE), Siegfried Link (DE), Reinhard Merle (AU), Juergen Riedlinger (DE), and Pradeep Tapadiya (US).

In the same way, I also want to acknowledge some people from the Compaq Insight Manager team who shared information about the Compaq Insight Management Agents. Thanks to Kevin Barnett (US), David Claypool (US), Brian R. Matthews (US), Mike Mckenna (US), Alan Minchew (US), Rich Purvis (US), Merriam Rudyard (US), Scott Shaffer (US), and Bernardo Tagariello (US).

Creating a book is not only about writing the technical content. The production of a book is also a long and tedious task. Having the full support of a publishing house like Digital Press is a very important aspect of the success of a book project. In this respect, I want to acknowledge Pam Chester, Theron Shreve, and Alan Rose—with particular thanks to Theron Shreve for his support when we decided to change the initial one book project to a two book project. I really appreciate his commitment and support in all the decisions we made during these twenty months.

Even if a book about Windows Management Instrumentation is purely technical, there is another form of contribution, which is almost as important as the technical contribution. In this respect, I want to acknowledge all my friends and family who supported me throughout these 20 months of hard work despite the frustration they had of not seeing me as much as they wanted. I spent weekends, vacations, and most evenings working on this project when I was not traveling for my TLG job. Without their support, their interest, and their understanding, I would never have been able to complete this long writing effort. During twenty months of hard work, having friends and family give you their best support "to get some rest" is a great asset. First of all, I want to acknowledge my mother who didn't see me a lot during these two last years. Despite the difficult moments, she always demonstrated courage and understanding with regard to the too small amount of time I dedicated to her. I also want to acknowledge all my friends: Elisa Araya for showing me how you can spend years writing a book between Louvain-La-Neuve in Belgium and Santiago de Chile, Caroline Bonami for her discrete presence, her tenderness, carefulness, and interest in what I do, Véronique Burguet for her constant commitment of getting news from me, Pascale Caloens for her listening and close tenderness for so long, Christian Cambier for always bringing me a realistic view in life and his interest in what I do for 20 years, Isabelle Cliquet for her support, her listening, and carefulness she gave me despite her busy life, Caroline Criquilion for her complicity and tenderness combined with a great sensitivity and understanding during the long talks we had together, Paul Crompton for chasing down the funniest DVDs on the market for me while I was writing, Serena De Palo for constantly asking news about me from Italy, Angélique Deprez for acting like a sister, Olivia Deroux for acting like a mother, and Eric Henrard for showing me that you can have loads of stupid (not always that stupid, actually!) and annoying problems at work, Thierry Devroye for his friendship, his carefulness, and for cooking me the best French fries and T-bone steak meals from all over the world, Paul-Marie Fouquet who is my best hardware advisor and supplier, Nathalie and Emilio Imparato for showing me how to prepare a delicious salad when I was following a diet and didn't have sufficient time to prepare meals due to my writing commitment, Philippe Liemans for his constant support and interest despite the difficult moments he was living, Sophie Lowagie for her years of friendship, Benoît-Michel Morimont for his interest in what I do, Nathalie Pinet for her friendship and complicity for 30 years, France and Ivan Syemons for their interest in this project and the nice evenings we spent together.

The last category of people I would like to acknowledge are the people I was working with before I joined Digital Equipment Corporation (DEC) in 1997. Their continuous interest, support, and friendship for years were a great asset to my motivation. I want to thank Jean-Pierre Aerts, Philippe Foucart, Emmanuel Limage, André Mathy, Ounis Rachiq, Rudy Vanhaelen, and Jean-Michel Verheugen.

For twenty months, I had so many contacts with so many people around the world that I do apologize to people I inadvertently omitted. If you fall into that category, then please accept my apologies and know that I am eternally grateful for your contribution.

Without all these people behind me, it would have been impossible to complete these two books on Windows Management Instrumentation. I'm very grateful to them for being what they are to me and for simply been present before I started this, during these twenty months of work, and after.

If you have any comments or question about the material in this book, I would be happy to hear from you. You can contact me at the following email address: alain.lissoir@hp.com

Alain Lissoir
December 2002

List of Figures

Chapter 2: Starting with WMI

List of Samples

Chapter 2: Starting with WMI

Chapter 3: The WMI Query Language

Chapter 4: Scripting with WMI

Chapter 5: Advanced WMI Scripting Techniques

List of Tables

Windows Script Host

1.1 Objective

In this chapter, we will review what Windows Script Host (WSH) actually is. As WSH will be used throughout this book, this first chapter provides the necessary foundation required to understand subsequent script samples. Those of you who are new to WSH or who are interested in a WSH refresher and an overview of its new features under Windows.NET should not skip this chapter!

WSH is a language-independent scripting host that allows you to run scripts from both the Windows desktop and the command prompt. Reviewing WSH does not involve a review of scripting languages; therefore, it is expected that the reader is familiar with WSH-compatible scripting languages, such as VBScript or JScript. It is also important to note that WSH is often used in combination with other COM objects provided by the Windows system. For instance, it is typical to find WSH samples using Active Directory Service Interfaces (ADSI) to perform some tasks. Reviewing all other COM object models that can be used with WSH is a huge undertaking that contains enough material to produce more than one complete book. This chapter focuses on the WSH COM object model and its associated features, so that you will be prepared to use WSH with Windows Management Instrumentation (WMI) in subsequent chapters.

1.2 Some scripting history

Since the introduction of the PC to the world in 1981–1982, there has been a need to automate certain system functions. From the simple .bat (batch file) up to the most complex tasks, administrators and software developers have always wanted a way to describe and automate common tasks. In 1982, the need may have been to automate the simple compilation of a program developed in IBM/Microsoft Basic 1.0 or to simply make a safe copy of files located on the 10MB hard disk to the famous 180K/360K 5 ¼-inch floppies.

The evolution of the PC operating system has consistently proven that the interpreted batch file from the COMMAND.COM was really not enough to address all the needs. During all those years, due to this lack of support in the operating system, third-party vendors have developed many initiatives to solve the scripting problem. One of the best examples is the adaptation of Unix tools to DOS (i.e., GNU Utilities, Perl Scripting). This was a great help to many administrators and developers. But the challenge was to choose the right tools, and sometimes the right script interpreter.

One important initiative came from IBM with the arrival of OS/2 in 1988. IBM delivered an established scripting language called REXX. As part of the OS/2 operating system, REXX offered all the functions required to perform common tasks, such as automating a full operating system setup, installing applications, creating icons, calling 32-bit API DLLs, and so on. IBM developed a DOS version of REXX that was available in PC DOS v7.0.

In addition to the "classical" .bat extension, OS/2 added a new file type for native OS/2 command files and REXX script files. The extension was called .CMD (Command File). Of course, under Unix, such scripting capabilities were certainly not new. The Korn Shell, Bourn Shell, and C Shell had all offered similar features for quite some time.

More or less in parallel with OS/2 came the arrival of Windows 3.1. Windows 3.1, which was still based on DOS, offered no real scripting language, and the REXX support under Windows 3.1 was not well integrated. Scripting continued to be neglected in the DOS world. Most people expected many new scripting features with the arrival of the first Windows NT version. In fact, there were some new built-in features available in Windows NT 4.0 Service Pack 3 through the use of .CMD files. Unfortunately, those new features fell far short of the capabilities available under a Unix Shell or a REXX command file.

In 1997, when Microsoft released the Option Pack v1.0, Windows Scripting Host (WSH) 1.0 was part of the product, and it was using the Windows Script 5.0. At that time, a new way to script under Windows was born. For the first time, WSH offered the administrator a way to script using VBScript or JScript from the command line. WSH 1.0 was available for Windows 95, 98, and NT. But like any first software version, WSH was quite limited, and scripters rapidly reached the limits of WSH 1.0. Nevertheless, this version provided scripters with the following features:

- Reading arguments from the command line.

- Providing information on the running script itself.

- Manipulating the environment variables.

- Accessing network information (e.g., the current user, the current domain).

- Creating, retrieving, and deleting network drive mappings.

- Running external programs.

- Manipulating desktop objects (i.e., creating shortcuts).

- Accessing the registry.

- Using registered COM object methods and properties, such as Messaging Application Programming Interface (MAPI), Active Directory Service Interfaces (ADSI), and Windows Management Instrumentation (WMI). Basically, all registered COM providers written for an automation language are usable from within WSH.

- Accessing the file system (via the **Scripting.FileSystemObject** object).

With the release of Windows 2000, version 2.0 of WSH became available. At the same time, Microsoft renamed Windows Scripting Host to Windows Script Host. This version addressed the limitations encountered in version 1.0. Mainly, WSH 2.0 offered scripters a new way to reuse script routines from any language supported by WSH (VBScript, JScript). At the same time, for WSH 2.0, Windows Script interfaces was also updated to version 5.1. WSH 2.0 provided all the features supported by version 1.0 and added new features, such as the following:

- The ability to include other VBScript or JScript functions in external files. This is performed by the use of XML in the WSH scripts.

- The ability to mix languages inside the same script. It is possible to reuse a function written in JavaScript in a script developed in VBScript. This function works in combination with the previous one and makes use of XML in the WSH script.

- Support for pausing a script.

- Support for standard input and standard output pipe redirection.

- The possibility to log an event in the Windows NT event log (or a WSH.log file under Windows 9x).

- Support for dragging and dropping files on a WSH script to start. The dropped filenames can be retrieved as an argument from the command line.

A few months later, Microsoft released version 5.5 of Windows Script Interfaces, which included enhancements for ECMA-262 version 3 Standard (ECMAScript) for JScript and an improvement of VBScript's regular expression support to match JScript. WSH was still at version 2.0, because nothing had changed in the WSH infrastructure.

In May 2000, the arrival of the I Love You virus changed the perception of scripting under Windows. Although most people in the Windows community welcomed a powerful scripting infrastructure, this facility also turned out to be a tremendous point of vulnerability. After releasing some Outlook patches to protect users against undesired startup of scripts attached, to received mails, Microsoft launched WSH 5.6 in September 2000. WSH jumped from version 2.0 to 5.6 simply because Microsoft decided to synchronize the WSH version with the Windows Script Interfaces version. One of the features addresses the I Love You phenomenon with a protection mechanism based on a digital signature. This version includes all the features of the previous versions plus the following additional enhancements:

- Command-line parameter improvements with a new infrastructure (based on XML) that makes reading command-line parameters a lot easier.

Figure 1.1
The various WSH versions.

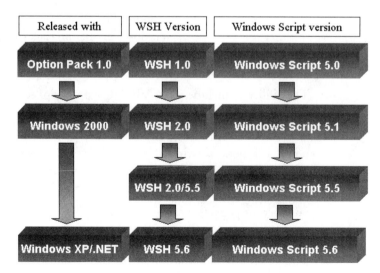

- The ability to run WSH scripts remotely on several remote computer systems.

- The ability to sign scripts and set policies to determine the system behavior with nonsigned scripts.

- The ability to start scripts in a command process that shares all the environment variables of the parent script, which allows the parent script to capture any output from the child process.

Now with this small historical recap in mind (see Figure 1.1), we can review the WSH implementation and all WSH features as they exist today under Windows XP and Windows.NET server.

1.3   What is Windows Script Host?

Briefly, WSH is an infrastructure designed to run scripts using Windows Script Interfaces. This is a language-independent host that allows scripts to run under Windows 9x, Windows NT, Windows 2000, Windows XP, and Windows.NET Server. WSH offers two forms of script host:

Command-line mode (Cscript.exe): This host will display the output as a regular batch file in a DOS command prompt (Cscript as command script). The default host can be forced from the command line: `Cscript.Exe //H:Cscript`

Window mode (WScript.exe): Instead of displaying messages in a DOS command prompt, this engine will create a message popup window to display each message (WScript as Window Script). The default host can be forced from the command line: `WScript.Exe //H:WScript`

You can execute scripts with either host; the results will be the same. However, running a script in window mode will require user intervention each time a message is displayed. When invoking a script from an interactive application, **WScript.exe** is a good choice. For a logon script, **Cscript.exe** is usually better. Note that by default, after the Windows installation, **WScript** is the default WSH host.

Windows Script Host supports both the Visual Basic and Java script languages, but the architecture permits extension of this support to any other language by developing new Windows Script interfaces (e.g., Perl, REXX). WSH is structured around the Windows Script interfaces. This means that WSH reuses scripting components already used by other exist-

Figure 1.2
The Microsoft scripting infrastructure.

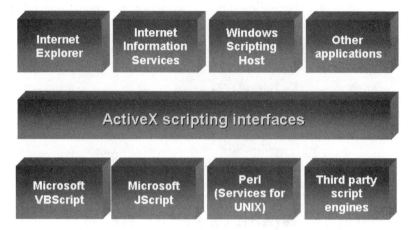

ing applications such as Internet Explorer or Internet Information Server (see Figure 1.2).

WSH accepts different forms of script languages and structure. Basically, WSH scripts are just simple text files with a particular extension. The extension plays a determinant role because it determines the language used by the script and how WSH must interpret the script content. Some scripts use a pure ASCII text with a coding language such as VBScript or Java-Script, but some others use XML to structure the script content. Let's examine some easy samples to get a rough idea.

- **.vbs** extension for VBScript. This is an ASCII file containing a script written in VBScript. For instance, the code below is a **Hello-World.vbs** script:

```
1: Dim strMessage
2: strMessage = "Hello world in VB Script!"
3: WScript.Echo strMessage
```

- **.js** extension for JavaScript. This is an ASCII file containing a script written in JavaScript. For instance, the code below is a **HelloWorld.js** script:

```
1: var strMessage;
2: strMessage = "Hello world in Java Script!";
3: WScript.Echo (strMessage);
```

- **.wsf** extension for Windows Script File. This ASCII file type can contain one or more scripts written with VBScript or JScript languages. The script uses XML tags to define the structure and separate script languages. For instance, the code below combines the previous **Hello-**

World.vbs and **HelloWorld.js** scripts into one **HelloWorld.wsf** by using WSH specific XML tags:

```
 1: <?xml version="1.0"?>
 2: <!--                              -->
 3: <!--  WScript Script File         -->
 4: <!--                              -->
 5: <package>
 6:   <job id="vbs">
 7:     <script language="VBScript">
 8:       Dim strMessage
 9:       strMessage = "Hello world!"
10:       WScript.Echo strMessage
11:     </script>
12:   </job>
13:   <job id="js">
14:     <script language="JScript">
15:       var strMessage;
16:       strMessage = "Hello world!";
17:       WScript.Echo (strMessage);
18:     </script>
19:   </job>
20: </package>
```

At first glance, this may look a bit ugly to read, but don't worry, we will come back to the XML tag signification later.

- **.wsc** extension for Windows Script Component. This is an ASCII file containing XML tags defining a scripted COM object. A Windows Script Component contains two sections: a descriptive section and a script section written in VBScript or JScript. The Windows Script Components must be registered in the system like any other COM object by using the **Regsvr32.exe** utility or with the help of a Windows Explorer context menu. We will discuss in depth this type of script. To give a quick view of what a Windows Script Component looks like, the script below performs exactly the same operation as **HelloWorld.vbs**; however, access to the string containing the "Hello World!" message is provided through a property of the Windows Script Component. The script below uses the Windows Script Component called **HelloWorld.wsc**:

```
1: Dim objHelloWorld
2: Set objHelloWorld = CreateObject("HelloWorld.WSC")
3: ' The message string is stored in the Windows Script Component
4: objHelloWorld.Message = "Hello World!"
5: ' The message string is read from the Windows Script Component
6: WScript.Echo objHelloWorld.Message
```

Here is the script HelloWorld.wsc:

```
 1: <?xml version="1.0"?>
 2: <!--                                  -->
 3: <!--  WScript Script Component -->
 4: <!--                                  -->
 5: <component>
 6:   <registration
 7:         description="HelloWorld"
 8:         progid="HelloWorld.WSC"
 9:         version="1.00"
10:         classid="{0d565d06-8cb4-49ba-8dba-48cc404c4e19}"
11:   >
12:   </registration>
13:   <public>
14:         <property name="Message">
15: <get/>
16:            <put/>
17:         </property>
18:   </public>
19:   <script language="VBScript">
20:     <![CDATA[
21:       Dim strMessage
22:       Function put_Message(newValue)
23:             strMessage = newValue
24:       End Function
25:
26:       Function get_Message()
27:             get_Message = strMessage
28:       End Function
29:     ]]>
30:   </script>
31: </component>
```

- **.vbe** extension for VBSscript Encrypted. This is an encrypted .vbs file containing a script written in VBScript.

- **.jse** extension for JavaScript Encrypted. This is an encrypted .js file containing a script written in JavaScript.

- **.wsh** extension for configuring the run-time parameters of a WSH script. For instance, it is possible to define a maximum execution time for the script.

This gives a quick overview of the various file types supported by WSH. Of course, there are many things to explain about these scripts. The purpose of this chapter is to provide, during the WSH exploration, greater detail about these features. WSH is the scripting environment for the WMI exploration in subsequent chapters. Therefore, it is important to understand the features of WSH.

1.4   **The run-time parameters**

Whatever the execution mode (Window or Console) of a script, it is possible to set options that determine the script behavior at run time. These options can be permanently saved in the current user profile. **Cscript.exe** and **WScript.exe** have almost the same command-line parameters. Here is a brief summary of these options:

//B   Forces batch-mode execution. This switch suppresses any output made during the script execution.

//D   Enables the Active Debugging. By default, the script stops to execute in case of error. By enabling the Active Debugging, if a fault occurs during the script execution, the script developer will automatically be prompted to debug the script.

//E: Selects the script engine. By default, the script extension (.vbs or .js for instance) determines the script engine to be used. If you want to run scripts contained in a file using another extension, the switch allows you to specify the script language engine to use. For instance, a script can be in a text file using the .txt extension. In such a case, it is possible to use the following command line:

Cscript //E:JsScript MyScript.Txt

By default, the VBScript and JScript engines are installed with WSH.

//H: Changes the default script host to Cscript or WScript.

//I   Forces interactive-mode execution. This switch is the opposite of **//B**.

//Job: Tells the script host which script code to execute in the Windows Script File.

//Logo   Displays the Microsoft logo once the script host has started.

//NoLogo   Disables display of the Microsoft logo once the script host has started.

//S   Saves current command-line options for the current user.

//T   Determines the maximum time a script is permitted to run.

//X   Executes the script in the debugger.

//U   Uses Unicode for redirected I/O from the console. This
               option is available only for the Cscript host.

Changing the options from the script host with the //S switch globally
changes the settings for the current user environment. It is also possible to
save some of these settings on a per-script basis by means of the .Wsh file.
The .Wsh file is an ASCII file containing sections and keywords like an .ini
file. If you have a script called **HelloWorld.vbs** and you want to define some
run-time options for that script, you can simply create a **HelloWorld.wsh**
file containing the following:

```
[ScriptFile]
Path=C:\HelloWorld.vbs
[Options]
Timeout=10
DisplayLogo=0
```

The .Wsh file does not contain more parameters than the ones shown in
this sample. The parameters available correspond exactly to the ones available from the user interface visible in Figure 1.3.

Figure 1.3
The user interface
WSH script
parameters.

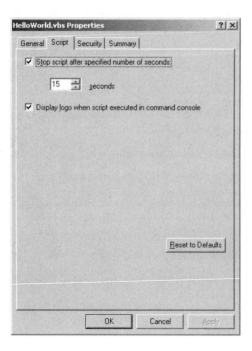

1.5   Windows Script Host Object Model

WSH is a COM component provider that creates an infrastructure to run scripts. The WSH COM components provide many functions designed to interface with the system. Basically, VBScript or JScript use the WSH infrastructure to obtain information about the running environment, start processes or scripts, create other COM object instances, and reuse other script modules or functions. The architecture is based on four main modules, along with an additional component.

- **WScript.exe or Cscript.exe:** Both implement the **WSH WScript** base object (with **WshArguments**, **WshNamed.** and **WshUnNamed** objects). These modules are the main components used by any WSH script. They provide all the basic functions used inside a WSH script. The **WScript** object is accessible only from the WSH run-time **WScript.exe** (Windows mode) or **Cscript.exe** (Console mode).

- **Wshom.ocx:** This is an ActiveX control offering other WSH objects (**WshShell**, **WshShortcut**, **WshURLShortcut**, **WshEnvironment**, **WshSpecialFolders**, **WshNetwork**, and **WshCollection**). Basically, this module provides access to the run-time environment of the script and allows you to perform actions in this environment, such as creating registry keys or values, establishing network connections, creating variables in the system or user environment, etc.

- **Wshcon.dll:** This implements the **WshController** and **WshRemote** objects. This module implements the necessary function to execute scripts remotely. This object is implemented as a DCOM object.

- **Wshext.dll:** This last component implements the scripting signer object (**WshScriptSigner**). This object implements the features, based on the CryptoAPI, to sign scripts digitally.

Now, let's examine the WSH Object Model organization. Initially, we will not examine the features provided by the objects. The purpose is to understand the WSH Object Model organization. It is very important to understand the logical position of all the objects and their relationships. Even if you don't know the exact purpose of the object, being able to position an object in a collection of objects is helpful because, as a script writer, you must first determine how to access an object before performing an action.

Figure 1.4 illustrates the WSH COM objects available and their relationships. Inside this object collection only four objects are directly instan-

Figure 1.4
*The WSH
components and
the object
hierarchy.*

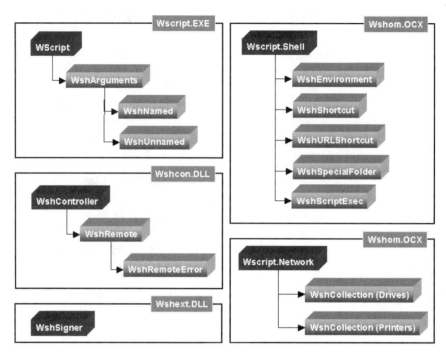

tiable (dark gray) because they have a ProgID defined in the Windows
System. All other objects, even if they are defined in the WSH Object
Model, must be accessed through one of the four directly instantiable
objects: **WScript.Shell**, **WScript.Network**, **WshController**, and **Wsh-
Signer.**

Note: The ProgID is an identifier of the COM object. To instantiate an
object in an application, the ProgID is used as a reference to the desired
COM object. ProgIDs are published in the registry HKCR\CLSID.

The **WScript** object is an exception because there is no ProgID available.
It is immediately available from the Windows Script Host run-time
WScript.exe (or Cscript.exe). So, there is no way to instantiate this object.
This is why the following script line refers directly to it and can invoke the
Echo method to display a sample text:

```
1: WScript.Echo "Hello World!"
```

By using some properties or methods exposed by the **WScript** object
(see Table 1.1), it is possible to access other objects implemented by the
WSH infrastructure.

Table 1.1   *The WScript Object*

Properties	.Application ()
	.Arguments ()
	.BuildVersion ()
	.FullName ()
	.Interactive ()
	.Name ()
	.Path ()
	.ScriptFullName ()
	.ScriptName ()
	.Stderr ()
	.Stdin ()
	.Stdout ()
	.Timeout ()
	.Version ()
Methods	.ConnectObject (objObjectName, strPrefix)
	.CreateObject (strProgID[,strPrefix])
	.DisconnectObject (objObjectName)
	.Echo ([Arg1] [,Arg2] [,Arg3] ...)
	.GetObject (strPathname [,strProgID], [strPrefix])
	.Quit ([intErrorCode])
	.Sleep (intTime)
Child objects	Set WshStdIN=WScript.StdIn
	Set WshStdOUT=WScript.StdOut
	Set WshStdERR=WScript.StdErr
	Set WshArguments=WScript.Arguments

The **WScript** object exposes three properties giving access to objects dedicated to the standard input/output streams usage (see Table 1.2).

For instance, this is the case for the **WshArguments** object. This object is not directly instantiable and the only way to access the **WshArguments** object is to refer to it via the **WScript** object. To access the **WshArguments** object, the *Arguments* property of the **WScript** object must be used:

```
1: Set WshArguments = WScript.Arguments
```

Table 1.2   *The Standard Input, Output, and Error Objects*

Set WshStdIN=WScript.StdIn	
Properties	.AtEndOfLine ()
	.AtEndOfStream ()
	.Line ()
	.Column ()
Methods	.Close
	.Read (characters)
	.Skip (characters)
	.SkipLine ()
	.ReadAll ()
	.ReadLine ()
Set WshStdOUT=WScript.StdOut	
Methods	.Close ()
	.WriteBlankLines (intLines)
	.Write (strText)
	.WriteLine (strText)
Set WshStdERR=WScript.StdErr	
Methods	.Close ()
	.WriteBlankLines (intLines)
	.Write (strText)
	.WriteLine (strText)

Table 1.3   *The WshArguments Object*

Set WshArguments=WScript.Arguments	
Properties	.Item (intIndex)
	.Length ()
	.Named ()
	.Unnamed ()
Methods	.Count ()
	.ShowUsage ()
Child objects	Set WshNamed=WshArguments.Named
	Set WshUnnamed=WshArguments.Unnamed

Table 1.4   *The WshNamed Object*

Set WshNamed=WshArguments.Named	
Properties	.Item (intIndex)
Methods	.Count ()
	.Exists (strArgName)

Once **WshArguments** instantiates, the object exposes its own set of properties and methods (see Table 1.3). The **WshArguments** exposes two subobjects called **WshNamed** and **WshUnNamed** (see Tables 1.4 and 1.5). These objects work in conjunction with XML tags to ease the reading of the command-line parameters. This means that the script using such objects will be a Windows Script File (.wsf) due to the XML requirements. We will come back to this later when we examine the XML tags.

Table 1.5   *The WshUnNamed Object*

Set WshUnNamed=WshArguments.UnNamed	
Properties	.Item (intIndex)
Methods	.Count ()
	.Exists (strArgName)

The **WScript.Shell** object is referenced by its ProgID. To instantiate this object, the script must use the related ProgID and the *CreateObject* method. For instance, to access the **WshShell** object, (see Table 1.6) the script will execute the following:

```
1: set WshShell = WScript.CreateObject ("WScript.Shell")
```

Again, once the **WshShell** object instantiates, it exposes some properties and methods from which some subobjects are available; these are described in Tables 1.7 to 1.11.

Whatever the shortcut type desired (.lnk or .url), only the set of parameters is different; the way to get access to the object is the same:

```
1: set WshShortCut=WshShell.CreateShortCut(...)
```

To access the **WshEnvironment** (Table 1.9), the *Environment* property of the **WshShell** object must be used:

```
1: Set WshEnvironment=WshShell.Environment(...)
```

Table 1.6   *The WshShell Object*

Set WshShell=CreateObject("Wscript.Shell")	
Properties	.CurrentDirectory ()
	.Environment (strType)
	.SpecialFolders (strSpecialFolderName)
Methods	.AppActivate (strTitle)
	.CreateShortCut (strPathName)
	.Exec (strCommand)
	.ExpandEnvironmentString (strString)
	.LogEvent (intType, strMessage [,strTarget])
	.Popup (strText,[nSecondsToWait],[strTitle],[nType])
	.RegDelete (strName)
	.RegRead (strName)
	.RegWrite (strName, anyValue [,strType])
	.Run(strCommand, [intWindowStyle], [boolWaitOnReturn])
	.SendKeys (strString)
Child objects	Set WshShortCut=WshShell.CreateShortCut (strPathName)
	Set WshURLShortCut=WshShell.CreateShortCut (strPathName)
	Set WshEnvironment=WshShell.Environment (strType)
	Set WshScriptExec=WShell.Exec (strCommand)
	Set WshSpecialFolders=WshShell.SpecialFolders (strSpecialFolderName)

Table 1.7   *The Wshhortcut Object*

Set WshShortCut=WshShell.CreateShortCut(…)	
Properties	.Arguments (strString)
	.Description (strString)
	.FullName (strString)
	.Hotkey (strHotKeyString)
	.IconLocation (strIconLocation)
	.TargetPath (strPathName)
	.WindowStyle (intWindowStyle)
	.WorkingDirectory (strWorkingDirectory)
Methods	.Save ()

Table 1.8   *The WshURLShortcut Object*

Set **WshURLShortCut=WshShell.CreateShortCut(...)**	
Properties	.FullName (strString)
	.TargetPath (strHttpURL)
Methods	.Save ()

Table 1.9   *The WshEnvironment Object*

Set **WshEnvironment=WshShell.Environment(...)**	
Properties	.Item (intIndex)
	.Lenght
Methods	.Count ()
	.Remove (strVarName)

Table 1.10   *The WshScriptExec Object*

Set **WshScriptExec=WshShell.Exec(...)**	
Properties	.ExitCode ()
	.ProcessID ()
	.Status ()
	.Stdin ()
	.Stdout ()
	.Stderr ()
Methods	.Terminate ()

Table 1.11   *The WshSpecialFolders Object*

Set **WshSpecialFolders=WshShell.SpecialFolders(...)**	
Properties	.Item (intIndex)
	.Length ()
Methods	.Count ()

Table 1.12   *The Special Folder Names*

AllUsersDesktop

AllUsersStartMenu

AllUsersPrograms

AllUsersStartup

Desktop

Favorites

Fonts

MyDocuments

NetHood

PrintHood

Programs

Recent

SendTo

StartMenu

Startup

Templates

To access the **WshScriptExec** (Table 1.10), the *Exec* method of the **WshShell** object must be used:

```
1: set WshScriptExec=WshShell.Exec(...)
```

To access the **WshSpecialFolders** (Table 1.11), the *SpecialFolders* property of the **WshShell** object must be used:

```
1: Set WshSpecialFolders=WshShell.SpecialFolders(...)
```

The *SpecialFolders* property helps to find the directory path of some particular Windows folders such as "Desktop" and "StartMenu." Refer to Table 1.12 for a complete list.

As the **WScript.Network** (Table 1.13) and **WshController** (Table 1.14) objects also have a ProgID, the same principle applies for their instantiation. For the **WshNetwork** object, we have

```
1: set WshNetwork = WScript.CreateObject ("WScript.Network")
```

For the **WshController** object, we have

```
1: set WshController = WScript.CreateObject ("WshController")
```

Table 1.13   *The WshNetwork Object*

Set **WshNetwork=CreateObject("Wscript.Network")**	
Properties	.ComputerName ()
	.UserDomain ()
	.UserName ()
Methods	.EnumNetworkDrives ()
	.MapNetworkDrive ()
	.RemoveNetworkDrive (strName, [bForce], [bUpdateProfile])
	.AddPrinterConnection (strLocalName, strRemoteName[,bUpdateProfile][,strUser][,strPassword])
	.AddWindowsPrinterConnection(strPrinterPath) *(Windows NT/2000/XP/.NET Server)*
	.AddWindowsPrinterConnection(strPrinterPath, strDriverName [,strPort]) *(Windows 95/98/Me)*
	.RemovePrinterConnection (strName, [bForce], [bUpdateProfile])
	.EnumPrinterConnection ()
	.SetDefaultPrinter (strPrinterName)
Child objects	Set WshCollection=WshNetwork.EnumNetworkDrives ()
	Set WshCollection=WshNetwork.EnumPrinterConnection ()

Once instantiated, these objects expose more methods and properties (see Tables 1.13 and 1.14).

There is one more ProgID available with WSH. It is the Scripting.Signer ProgID. Basically, it allows you to instantiate an object exposing methods to digitally sign and verify WSH scripts. It works on top of the Crypto API. We will revisit its features later.

With this logical organization, we know how to access the objects. For instance, if a script must access the command-line parameters, we know that the **WshArguments** object must be used; to use this object, the script must use the **WScript** object available from WSH at run time (Table 1.3). To give another example, if a script must create a shortcut on the Windows desktop, the **WshShortcut** object must be used (Table 1.8); to use this

Table 1.14   *The WshController Object*

Set **WshController=CreateObject("WshController")**	
Methods	.CreateScript(strCommandLine [,strMachineName])
Child objects	Set WshRemote=WshController.CreateScript(strCommandLine [.strMachineName])

object, the script must use the **WshShell** object, and the **WshShell** object must be instantiated with the WScript.Shell ProgID (Table 1.6). Here is a brief summary of the features provided by each object of the WSH Object Model:

WScript	Set and retrieve command-line arguments
	Determine the name of the script file
	Determine the host filename (**WScript.exe** or **Cscript.exe**)
	Determine the host version information
	Create, connect to, and disconnect from COM objects
	Sink events
	Stop a script's execution programmatically
	Output information to the default output device (for example, a dialog box or the command line)
WshArguments	Access the entire set of command-line arguments
WshNamed	Access the set of named command-line arguments
WshUnNamed	Access the set of unnamed command-line arguments
WshNetwork	Connect to and disconnect from network shares and network printers
	Map and unmap network shares
	Access information about the currently logged-on user
WshController	Create a remote script process using the controller method *CreateScript*
WshRemote	Remotely administer computer systems on a computer network
	Programmatically manipulate other programs/scripts (see Table 1.15)
WshRemoteError	Access the error information available when a remote script (a **WshRemote** object) terminates as a result of a script error

Table 1.15   *The WshRemote Object*

Set WshRemote=WshController.CreateScript(…)	
Properties	.Error ()
	.Status ()
Methods	.Execute ()
	.Terminate ()
Events	WshRemote_End
	WshRemote_Error
	WshRemote_Start
Child objects	Set WshRemoteError=WshController.Error ()
Set WshRemoteError=WshController.Error	
Properties	.Description ()
	.Line ()
	.Character ()
	.SourceText ()
	.Source ()
	.Number ()

WshShell	Manipulate the contents of the registry
	Send keystrokes in Windows applications
	Create a shortcut
	Access a system folder
	Manipulate environment variables (such as %WinDir%, %PATH%, or %PROMPT%)
WshShortcut	Programmatically create a shortcut
WshURLShortcut	Programmatically create a shortcut to an Internet resource
WshSpecialFolders	Access any of the Windows Special Folders
WshEnvironment	Access any of the environment variables (such as WINDIR, PATH, or PROMPT)

WshCollection   Contains a collection of network drive connec-
                             tions or printer conections (Table 1.16)

Table 1.16   *The WshCollection Object*

Set WshCollection=WshNetwork.EnumNetworkDrives	
Properties	.Item (intIndex)
	.Count ()
	.Length ()
Set WshCollection=WshNetwork.EnumPrinterConnection	
Properties	.Item (intIndex)
	.Count ()
	.Length ()

WshScriptExec   Determine status and error information about a
                             script run with *Exec* method

                             Access the stdIn, stdOut, and stdErr channels

WshScriptSigner   Digitally sign and verify digital signatures coded
                             in a script (see Table 1.17)

Table 1.17   *The WshSigner Object*

Set WshSigner=CreateObject("Scripting.Signer")	
Methods	.SignFile (strFileName, strCertificateName, strCertificateStoreName)
	.Sign (strFileExtension, Text, strCertificateName, strCertificateStoreName)
	.VerifyFile (strFileName, boolPromptUserUI)
	.Verify (strFileExtension, Text, boolPromptUserUI)

The object model is the most important thing to understand. Whether
the object model is the one from Windows Script Host (WSH), Active
Directory Service Interface (ADSI), or Windows Management Instrumentation (WMI), a perfect understanding of an object model allows the script
writer to locate objects easily. This conceptual approach is much more
important with WMI than WSH because WMI exposes more than 600
classes (that can be objects if they are instantiated) and 3,000 properties.

With such a huge amount of information, it is quite easy to get lost in the object collection. Having a good picture of the object model is a great help when it comes to navigating between objects.

Now that we know how to instantiate WSH objects and have an understanding of their relationships and purposes, we can start to look at the features provided by each object and some practical samples of their usage.

1.6   Features coming from the WSH COM components

Tables 1.1 through 1.17 provide a complete list of the properties and methods exposed by the WSH objects. All code samples presented in the following pages are part of a WSH sample called **WshScript.vbs**. As the extension indicates, this script is written in VBScript. It combines most of the basic features provided by the WSH Object Model. Each basic WSH function is encapsulated in a callable VBScript function.

Some functions presented below use global variables declared in the beginning of the script. Be sure to check the complete source code so that you know which variables are used internally in the functions. Only the most important parts of the scripts are presented. The purpose of the code fragments is to show how to use WSH to get specific information, not to show the complete coding. As a result, code has been removed in order to highlight the essential WSH operations. Missing lines are represented by an ellipsis (…).

Sample 1.1 contains the beginning of the **WshScript.vbs** script. Like any script, it starts with some constants (lines 11 to 33) and variables (lines 37 to 82) declarations. A class declaration is defined in lines 37 through 69. Without delving too much into the details of the VBScript language, this allows you to regroup various variables behind one logical entity. The logical entity is called a class. By pointing to this class name, the script will refer to a collection of variables. This eases coding when the variable collection must be passed to a function.

Sample 1.1   *The constants and variables declaration*

```
 6:Option Explicit
 7:
 8:' -----------------------------------------------------------------------
 9:' Internal contants used in the WSH Script
10:' -----------------------------------------------------------------------
11:Const cLocalDrive      = "Z:"
```

```
12:Const cRemoteShare        = "\\DP4000\SHARED"
13:Const cLocalPort          = "LPT3:"
14:Const cRemotePrinter      = "\\DP4000\LEXMARK"
15:
16:' ---------------------------------------------------------------------------
17:' Mouse click answer definitions
18:Const cOKClick            = 1
19:Const cCancelClick        = 2
..:
23:Const cYesClick           = 6
24:Const cNoClick            = 7
25:
26:' ---------------------------------------------------------------------------
27:' Window application styles used for Shortcut creation
28:Const SW_HIDE = 0
29:Const SW_SHOWNORMAL = 1
..:
32:Const SW_SHOWNOACTIVATE = 4
33:Const SW_MINIMIZE = 6
34:
35:' ---------------------------------------------------------------------------
36:' Define a VBScript class to hold all the Run-Time environment variables
37:Class RunTimeEnvironmentInfo
38:        Dim StartMenu
39:        Dim Desktop
40:        Dim Programs
41:        Dim SystemRoot
42:        Dim UserTemp
43:        Dim SystemTemp
44:        Dim System32
45:        Dim System
..:
64:        Dim EngineVersion
65:
66:        Dim NTVersion
67:        Dim NTBuild
68:        Dim NTServicePack
69:End Class
70:
71:' ---------------------------------------------------------------------------
72:' Public Variables declaration used in the WSH Script
73:Dim WshShell
74:Dim WshNetwork
75:
76:Dim objLogFileName
77:Dim strLogFileName
78:
79:Dim boolVerbose
80:Dim boolErrorPopup
81:
82:Dim classRunTimeEnvironmentInfo
```

1.6.1   Providing information on the script environment and the Windows system

Now that the variables and constants have been declared, we can examine the next part of the script, shown in Sample 1.2. The first operation is to instantiate the **WScript.Shell** (line 90) and the **WScript.Network** (line 92) objects. It is important to keep in mind that the only object available by default under WSH is the **WScript** object. All other objects must be instantiated via their ProgID. The basic objects (**WScript**, **WshShell**, and **WshNetwork**) provide access to the whole set of information available in the WSH run-time environment.

Sample 1.2   *The WSH object instantiation*

```
 86:' --------------------------------------------------------------------------
 87:' Create WSH base objects.
 88:
 89:' For the Shell operations -------------------------------------------------
 90:Set WshShell = WScript.CreateObject("WScript.Shell")
 91:' For the Network operations -----------------------------------------------
 92:Set WshNetwork = WScript.CreateObject("WScript.Network")
 93:
 94:' --------------------------------------------------------------------------
 95:WshShell.LogEvent 0, "WSH Script started."
 96:
 97:' --------------------------------------------------------------------------
 98:' Will be set to True if command line parameter "Verbose" specified.
 99:' Output is redirected to a file in %TEMP%\%USERNAME%.Log.
100:boolVerbose = False
101:
102:' Will be set to True if command line parameter 'ErrorPopup' specified.
103:' Any error is shown via a Popup window to the user.
104:' User interaction is mandatory to continue.
105:boolErrorPopup = False
106:
107:' --------------------------------------------------------------------------
108:' Get misc. information for script run-time environment to populate the class
109:Set classRunTimeEnvironmentInfo = new RunTimeEnvironmentInfo
110:GetRunTimeEnvInfo (classRunTimeEnvironmentInfo)
```

Once the WSH objects have been created, the script starts its execution by writing a record in the application event log (line 95). It uses the *LogEvent* method exposed by the **WshShell** object. The *LogEvent* method requires two parameters. The first parameter represents the message type. The second parameter can be any string text. Table 1.18 shows the various values and Figure 1.5 shows some sample results.

Table 1.18   *The WSH event log levels*

Type	Value
0	Success
1	Error
2	Warning
4	Infomation
8	Success Audit
16	Failure Audit

Note that the *LogEvent* method is able to write to the application event log only and not to other Windows event log files. Each time the script starts, a trace is created. The same type of action is performed at the end of the script. This feature is helpful when the script is executed in the background on remote computers.

Line 110 invokes a function called GetRunTimeEnvironmentInfo(). This function is shown in Sample 1.3. It collects a set of information concerning the run-time environment. Basically, it populates the Visual Basic class defined in the beginning of the script (Sample 1.1, lines 37 to 69, and

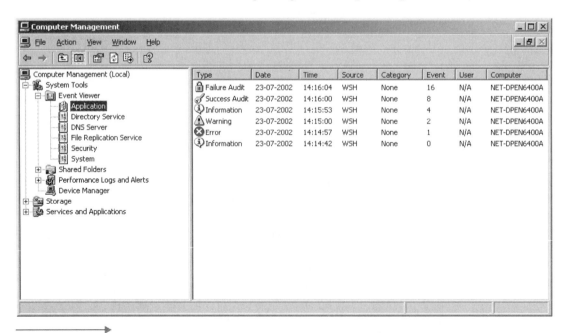

Figure 1.5   *The six message types created by the LogEvent method of the WshShell object.*

82; Sample 1.2, line 109) with information coming from the **WScript** object (lines 348 to 353), the **WshShell** object (lines 329 to 331), the **WshNetwork** object (lines 332 to 334), the variables located in the environment (lines 332 to 334 and lines 337 to 339), and the computer registry (lines 357 to 371). Once completed, the VB class contains a set of information that can be reused later in the script. For instance, this kind of information is very useful to have when executing a logon script.

Sample 1.3   *Retrieving the run-time environment information*

```
322:' ---------------------------------------------------------------------------
323:Private Function GetRunTimeEnvInfo (classRunTimeEnvironmentInfo)
324:
325:Dim varTemp
326:
327:      On Error Resume Next
328:
329:      classRunTimeEnvironmentInfo.StartMenu = WshShell.SpecialFolders("StartMenu") & "\"
330:      classRunTimeEnvironmentInfo.Desktop = WshShell.SpecialFolders("Desktop") & "\"
331:      classRunTimeEnvironmentInfo.Programs = WshShell.SpecialFolders("Programs") & "\"
332:      classRunTimeEnvironmentInfo.SystemRoot =
                      ReadEnvironmentVariable (Nothing, "Process", "SystemRoot") & "\"
333:      classRunTimeEnvironmentInfo.UserTemp =
                      ReadEnvironmentVariable (Nothing, "User", "Temp") & "\"
334:      classRunTimeEnvironmentInfo.SystemTemp =
                      ReadEnvironmentVariable (Nothing, "System", "Temp") & "\"
335:      classRunTimeEnvironmentInfo.System32 =
                      classRunTimeEnvironmentInfo.SystemRoot & "system32\"
336:      classRunTimeEnvironmentInfo.System =
                      classRunTimeEnvironmentInfo.SystemRoot & "system\"
337:      classRunTimeEnvironmentInfo.AllUsersStartMenu =
                      WshShell.SpecialFolders("AllUsersStartMenu") & "\"
338:      classRunTimeEnvironmentInfo.AllUsersDesktop =
                      WshShell.SpecialFolders("AllUsersDesktop") & "\"
339:      classRunTimeEnvironmentInfo.AllUsersPrograms =
                      WshShell.SpecialFolders("AllUsersPrograms") & "\"
340:
341:      ' Information about Network --------------------------------------------
342:      classRunTimeEnvironmentInfo.DomainName = WshNetwork.UserDomain
343:      classRunTimeEnvironmentInfo.UserName = WshNetwork.UserName
344:      classRunTimeEnvironmentInfo.LocalComputerName = WshNetwork.ComputerName
345:      classRunTimeEnvironmentInfo.LogonServerName =
                      Mid (ReadEnvironmentVariable (Nothing, "Process", "LogonServer"), 3)
...:
348:      classRunTimeEnvironmentInfo.ScriptName = WScript.ScriptName
349:      classRunTimeEnvironmentInfo.ScriptFullName = WScript.ScriptFullName
350:      classRunTimeEnvironmentInfo.ScriptingName = WScript.Name
351:      classRunTimeEnvironmentInfo.EngineFullName = WScript.FullName
352:      classRunTimeEnvironmentInfo.EnginePath = WScript.Path
353:      classRunTimeEnvironmentInfo.EngineVersion = WScript.Version
...:
357:      varTemp = ReadRegistry (Nothing, _
358:                         "HKLM\SOFTWARE\Microsoft\Windows NT\CurrentVersion", _
359:                         "CurrentVersion", _
360:                         "REG_SZ")
361:      classRunTimeEnvironmentInfo.NTVersion = varTemp (0)
```

```
362:          varTemp = ReadRegistry (Nothing, _
363:                            "HKLM\SOFTWARE\Microsoft\Windows NT\CurrentVersion", _
364:                            "CurrentBuildNumber", _
365:                            "REG_SZ")
366:          classRunTimeEnvironmentInfo.NTBuild = varTemp (0)
367:          varTemp = ReadRegistry (Nothing, _
368:                            "HKLM\SOFTWARE\Microsoft\Windows NT\CurrentVersion", _
369:                            "CSDVersion", _
370:                            "REG_SZ")
371:          classRunTimeEnvironmentInfo.NTServicePack = varTemp (0)
372:
373:End Function
```

1.6.2 Reading arguments from the command line

By default, the **WshScript.vbs** executes silently, which means that the script will perform some actions in the system without displaying any information on the screen. Even if some errors are detected, a message is not displayed to the operator. Moreover, a log file containing the activity of the script is not created by default. Because it could be nice to have a bit more information, the script accepts two optional parameters on the command line:

- **verbose** This parameter forces the script to display an activity message on the screen. Moreover a log file is created in %TEMP% with the %USERNAME%.LOG name.

- **errorpopup** If an error occurs, the operator receives a message popup on the screen showing the error. To continue the script execution, operator intervention is required.

To enable these features, it is necessary to mention one or both parameters on the command line as follows:

```
C:>wshScript.vbs verbose
```

or

```
C:>wshScript.vbs verbose errorpopup
```

or

```
C:>wshScript.vbs errorpopup
```

Sample 1.4 is an extract of the **WshScript.vbs**, which shows the logic implemented to check the parameter presence and perform the necessary actions. At line 125, the script invokes a function wrapping the logic to extract the parameters from the command line. Encapsulating this code in a function makes it easy to reuse (we will see later how to reuse functions with WSH). Once the parameters from the command line are extracted and saved in the array passed to the function, the script executes a loop (lines

126 to 138) to perform the appropriate action for each command-line parameter found.

Sample 1.4   *Reading command-line parameters*

```
120:' ---------------------------------------------------------------------------
121:' Command line argument reading.
...:
125:If (ReadCommandLineArgument (objLogFileName, strParameterList)) Then
126:   For intIndice = 0 to Ubound(strParameterList) - 1
127:       Select Case Ucase (strParameterList (intIndice))
128:           Case "VERBOSE"
129:               boolVerbose = True
130:               WshShell.LogEvent 0, "'Verbose' mode enabled."
131:           Case "ERRORPOPUP"
132:               boolErrorPopup = True
133:               WshShell.LogEvent 0, "'ErrorPopup' mode enabled."
134:           Case Else
135:               WshShell.LogEvent 1, "Invalid command line parameter detected: '" & _
136:                               strParameterList (intIndice) & "'."
137:       End Select
138:   Next
139:End If
```

How does the script read from the command line? This is performed by the ReadCommandLineArguments() function presented in Sample 1.5.

Sample 1.5   *The command-line parameters reading function*

```
801:' ---------------------------------------------------------------------------
802:Private Function ReadCommandLineArgument (objFileName, strParameterList)
...:
807:       On Error Resume Next
...:
811:       Set WshArguments = WScript.Arguments
812:
813:       If WshArguments.Count = 0 Then
814:          WriteToFile objFileName, "No command line arguments given"
815:       Else
816:          ReDim strParameterList (WshArguments.Count)
817:          For intIndice = 0 To WshArguments.Count - 1
...:
820:              strParameterList (intIndice) = WshArguments (intIndice)
821:          Next
822:       End If
823:
824:       ReadCommandLineArgument = WshArguments.Count
...:
828:End Function
```

This function uses the **WshArgument** object coming from the **WScript** object (line 811). First, the function tests the presence of any parameters (line 813) on the command line. If one or more parameters are present, the script starts to read the command line by executing a loop (lines 817 to

821) and populates the array strParameterList() (line 820). The array is one of the parameters passed to the ReadCommandLineArguments() function. You will notice that the other parameter is called objFileName. Every function coming from **WshScript.vbs** uses this parameter as its first parameter. This variable contains the file handle of the activity log created by the script. As we are in the early stages of the script, this variable does not contain any file handler yet. The activity log file handle is created once the command-line parameters are interpreted. This makes sense because to create the activity log file, the script must first check whether the keyword "verbose" has been given on the command line. Now, if this function contains the file handle as parameter, it is because the function can be reused in some other context where it may be necessary to log the command-line parsing. In such a case, the script logic must be changed to open the activity log before the line parsing. This is why the objFileName variable is passed to the ReadCommandLineArguments() function. Before exiting from the function, the code returns the number of parameters found on the command line (line 824).

This situation is quite easy because the script has to extract some words from the command line. Now, if the script should accept switches and parameters, such as /MyFirstSwitch:MyParameterA /MySecond-Switch:MyParameterB, this complicates the situation because the script must parse the string read from the command line. Some form of syntax parsing is required. Later samples show that there is an easier technique for reading command-line parameters by using a Windows Script File (.wsf). The Windows Script File uses XML to define the script structure. With the use of XML, it is possible to structure the command-line parameters and the help string associated with it. In some ways, XML extends the WSH capabilities. This eases considerably the command-line parameter reading. We will see how to perform command-line parameters reading when we examine the WSH XML features in Section 1.7.

1.6.3   Manipulating the environment variables

There are four types of environment variables: Process, User, System, and Volatile. Each environment type contains a specific set of variables. WSH offers methods to read, create, and delete environment variables. Each operation is encapsulated in a specific function. Note that regular Domain users do not have access to the System environment. Access to the System environment requires administrative privileges. Only the System and the User environments create permanent variables. Process variables are destroyed when the script stops, and Volatile variables are destroyed when the user logs off. Sample 1.6 invokes the miscellaneous functions manipulating the environment.

Sample 1.6   *Manipulating the environment variables*

```
163:' -------------------------------------------------------------------------
164:' Create three new environment variables
165:CreateEnvironmentVariable objLogFileName, "System", _
166:                                          "TIME", _
167:                                          FormatDateTime (Time, vbShortTime)
168:CreateEnvironmentVariable objLogFileName, "User", _
169:                                          "DATE", _
170:                                          FormatDateTime (Date, vbLongDate)
171:
172:' -------------------------------------------------------------------------
173:' Log environment variables content for System, User, Process
174:' and Volatile environment type.
175:' Warning! 'System' needs special permissions, regular users are denied
176:If boolVerbose Then
177:    GetAllEnvironmentVariables objLogFileName, "System"
178:    GetAllEnvironmentVariables objLogFileName, "User"
179:    GetAllEnvironmentVariables objLogFileName, "Process"
180:    GetAllEnvironmentVariables objLogFileName, "Volatile"
181:End If
```

The next three samples contain the code to read (Sample 1.7), create (Sample 1.8), and remove (Sample 1.9) environment variables. The initial operation is the instantiation of the **WshShell.Environment** object (lines 707, 736, and 764) to a specific environment type. The environment variable to be accessed determines the environment type to select. For instance, to read the %SystemRoot% variable, the script needs to access the Process environment. To read the %LogonServer% variable, the script must read the Volatile environment.

An example of reading an environment variable occurs when an environment variable's assignment contains another environment variable name. This is the case for the %Path% variable. The %SystemRoot% variable is part of the %Path% value. To resolve the content of the %Path% variable, the script must invoke the *ExpandEnvironmentString* method (line 713) of the **WshShell** object.

Sample 1.7   *Reading environment variables*

```
695:' -------------------------------------------------------------------------
696:Private Function ReadEnvironmentVariable (objFileName, strEnvironmentType, strVarName)
...:
700:        On Error Resume Next
...:
706:        ' Create a new variable via environment object.
707:        Set objEnvironment = WshShell.Environment (strEnvironmentType)
708:        If Err.Number Then
```

```
709:          ErrorHandler objFileName, "ReadEnvironmentVariable", Err, boolErrorPopup
710:          Exit Function
711:       End If
712:
713:       ReadEnvironmentVariable = WshShell.ExpandEnvironmentStrings
                                              (objEnvironment(strVarName))
714:       If Err.Number Then
715:          ErrorHandler objFileName, "ReadEnvironmentVariable", Err,
boolErrorPopup
716:          Exit Function
717:       End If
...:
721:End Function
```

Sample 1.8   *Creating environment variables*

```
723:' ---------------------------------------------------------------------------
724:Private Function CreateEnvironmentVariable(objFileName,strEnvironmentType,strVarName, varValue)
...:
728:       On Error Resume Next
...:
735:       ' Create a new variable via environment object.
736:       Set objEnvironment = WshShell.Environment (strEnvironmentType)
737:       If Err.Number Then
738:          CreateEnvironmentVariable = ErrorHandler (...
739:          Exit Function
740:       End If
741:
742:       objEnvironment (strVarName)=varValue
743:       If Err.Number Then
744:          CreateEnvironmentVariable = ErrorHandler (...
745:          Exit Function
746:       End If
...:
750:End Function
```

Sample 1.9   *Removing environment variables*

```
752:' ---------------------------------------------------------------------------
753:Private Function RemoveEnvironmentVariable (objFileName, strEnvironmentType, strVarName)
...:
757:       On Error Resume Next
...:
763:       ' Remove variable via environment object.
764:       Set objEnvironment = WshShell.Environment (strEnvironmentType)
765:       If Err.Number Then
766:          RemoveEnvironmentVariable  = ErrorHandler (...
767:          Exit Function
768:       End If
769:
770:       objEnvironment.Remove (strVarName)
...:
774:End Function
```

A nice way to read the environment variable is by using enumeration. To get a complete variable list, it is useless to know every variable name. **WshShell.Environment** can be used to enumerate the variables contained in a given environment. Sample 1.10, at lines 793 to 795, illustrates this feature.

Sample 1.10   *Reading all environment variables*

```
776:' -------------------------------------------------------------------------
777:Private Function GetAllEnvironmentVariables (objFileName, strEnvironmentType)
...:
782:        On Error Resume Next
...:
787:        Set objEnvironment = WshShell.Environment (strEnvironmentType)
788:        If Err.Number Then
789:           GetAllEnvironmentVariables = ErrorHandler (...
790:           Exit Function
791:        End If
792:
793:        For Each strVarName In objEnvironment
794:              WriteToFile objFileName, strVarName
795:        Next
...:
799:End Function
```

1.6.4   Using other registered COM objects

Now that the command line has been interpreted, the script logic can consider whether an activity log file must be created. This is determined by the boolVerbose Boolean variable. If the command line parameter "verbose" was set, this variable is equal to True (see Sample 1.4, line 129). To create the activity log file, the WSH script must use other objects that are not provided by the WSH Object Model. The purpose here is not to explore all object models available in Windows, but to show how from WSH it is possible to reference another object model to perform particular actions. Under Windows, there are many object models. Here is a short list (non-exhaustive):

- Active Directory Service Interface (ADSI)

- Message Application Programming Interface (MAPI)

- Collaboration Data Object (CDO)

- CDO for Exchange Management (CDOEXM)

- Windows Management Instrumentation (WMI)

- File System Object (FSO)

All these COM object models are publicly available from Windows. They can be instantiated from WSH by referencing their ProgID. Because WSH uses languages like VBScript or JavaSript, these COM object models must be written to support automation languages. The object models listed here support automation languages, but you should refer to the related documentation for more information.

Later samples show **WshScript.vbs** executing in the background. Having a trace logging function based on a command-line parameter makes it easier to locate any potential problems or errors during background execution. To do so, the script must create an activity log file by using the **File System** object, which is a COM object available in a Windows system, but not part of WSH. The script needs to instantiate the **File System** object by its publicly available ProgID **Scripting.FileSystemObject**.

Once created, **FileSystemObject** offers several methods to manipulate files. A full examination of **FileSystemObject** is beyond the scope of this book, but for more information about the object please refer to the Microsoft documentation at `http://msdn.microsoft.com/library/ en-us/script56/html/fsoorifilesystemobject.asp`.

As **WshScript.vbs** uses the **FileSystem** object to trace in a file all the operations performed during its execution, only three basic operations are used: file creation, writing data in the opened file, and closing the file.

Sample 1.11 invokes a function called CreateTextFile(). It uses one parameter that is the name of the file to be created (line 147). The file is built from the %TEMP% and the %USERNAME% variables initialized in the Visual Basic class. This is why the script refers to the class containing run-time information to get the script environment information (lines 145 and 146).

Sample 1.11   *Creating a text file for the activity log file*

```
141:If boolVerbose Then
142:    ' ------------------------------------------------------------------------
143:    ' Create the Text file for logging.
144:    ' Defines a .Log filename -------------------------------------------------
145:    strLogFileName = Ucase (classRunTimeEnvironmentInfo.UserTemp & _
146:                            classRunTimeEnvironmentInfo.UserName & ".log")
147:    Set objLogFileName = CreateTextFile (strLogFileName)
148:    WriteToFile objLogFileName, "** Log file '" & strLogFileName & "' created."
149:End If
...:
858:' ------------------------------------------------------------------------
859:Private Function CreateTextFile (strFileName)
...:
```

```
864:          On Error Resume Next
865:
866:          Set objFileSystem = WScript.CreateObject ("Scripting.FileSystemObject")
867:          If Err.Number Then
868:             CreateTextFile = ErrorHandler ("", "CreateTextFile", Err, True)
869:             Exit Function
870:          End If
871:
872:          Set objFileName = objFileSystem.CreateTextFile (strFileName, True)
873:          If Err.Number Then
874:             CreateTextFile = ErrorHandler ("", "CreateTextFile", Err, True)
875:             Exit Function
876:          End If
...:
881:          Set CreateTextFile = objFileName
882:
883:End Function
```

At line 866, in the CreateTextFile() function, the script instantiates the **FileSystem** object and invokes the *CreateTextFile* method to create the activity log file (line 872). Once finished, the function exits and assigns the activity log file handler as a returned parameter (line 881).

1.6.5   Creating, retrieving, and deleting drive connections

Network operations are completed using the **WshNetwork** object. With this object, a script can perform network drive or printer connections. Some basic network information can also be retrieved (such as the domain name, user name of the logged user, and the local machine name), as shown in Sample 1.3.

Sample 1.12   *Enumerating drive connections*

```
183:' -------------------------------------------------------------------------
184:' Enumerates Network Drive connections.
185:EnumerateDriveConnections objLogFileName
...:
187:EnumerateDriveConnections objLogFileName
...:
524:' -------------------------------------------------------------------------
525:Private Function EnumerateDriveConnections (objFileName)
...:
530:          On Error Resume Next
...:
534:          Set enumDrives = WshNetwork.EnumNetworkDrives
535:          If Err.Number Then
536:             EnumerateDriveConnections = ErrorHandler (...
537:             Exit Function
538:          End If
```

```
539:
540:          If enumDrives.Count = 0 Then
541:              WriteToFile objFileName, "No drive to list."
542:          Else
543:              WriteToFile objFileName, "Current network drive connections:"
544:              For intIndice = 0 To enumDrives.Count - 1 Step 2
545:                  WriteToFile objFileName, enumDrives (intIndice) & " -> " & _
546:                                          enumDrives (intIndice + 1)
547:              Next
548:          End If
549:
550:End Function
```

Sample 1.12 shows how to enumerate the current network drive connections. The drive connection enumeration uses a specific object for this purpose (line 534). Once the enumeration object has been created, a For ... Next loop retrieves all existing connections (lines 544 to 547). The existence of connections is tested by the *count* property available from the **Enumeration** object (line 540). The connections are available as an array from the **Enumeration** object. Even array elements contain the drive letter used for the connection; odd array elements contain the Universal Naming Convention (UNC) mapping used (lines 545, 546). The routine does not echo the result of the enumerations; it writes this result in the activity log file by invoking the WriteToFile function (line 545).

Sample 1.13   *Creating drive connections*

```
183:' -------------------------------------------------------------------------
184:' Enumerates Network Drive connections.
...:
186:ConnectNetworkDrive objLogFileName, cLocalDrive, cRemoteShare
...:
552:' -------------------------------------------------------------------------
553:Private Function ConnectNetworkDrive (objFileName, strDriveLetter, strShareName)
554:
555:          On Error Resume Next
...:
561:          WshNetwork.MapNetworkDrive strDriveLetter, strShareName
562:          If Err.Number Then
563:              ConnectNetworkDrive = ErrorHandler (...
564:              Exit Function
565:          End If
566:
567:End Function
```

The drive connection (Sample 1.13) and the drive disconnection (Sample 1.14) methods are pretty easy to use. The connection needs the drive letter and the UNC (line 561). The disconnection needs the drive letter only (line 590). To complete the disconnection process, a supplemental parameter (line 570, parameter boolConfirm) is added to the function input. This parameter specifies whether the user needs to confirm the drive disconnection (line 577 to 581). The user popup function is performed via the **WshShell** object *popup* method (line 577).

Sample 1.14   *Deleting drive connections*

```
183:' -------------------------------------------------------------------------
184:' Enumerates Network Drive connections.
...:
188:DisconnectNetworkDrive objLogFileName, cLocalDrive, False
...:
569:' -------------------------------------------------------------------------
570:Private Function DisconnectNetworkDrive (objFileName, strDriveLetter, boolConfirm)
...:
574:        On Error Resume Next
575:
576:        If boolConfirm Then
577:            intClick = WshShell.Popup ("Remove Network Drive connection '" & _
578:                                      UCase (strDriveLetter) & "' (Y/N) ?", _
579:                                      0, _
580:                                      "(WSHScript) Confirmation", _
581:                                      vbQuestion + vbYesNo)
582:            If intClick = cNoClick Then
583:                Exit Function
584:            End If
585:        End If
...:
590:        WshNetwork.RemoveNetworkDrive strDriveLetter
591:        If Err.Number Then
592:            DisconnectNetworkDrive = ErrorHandler (...
593:            Exit Function
594:        End If
595:
596:End Function
```

1.6.6   Creating, retrieving, and deleting printer connections

Network printer enumeration uses the same logic as network drive enumeration (see Sample 1.15). The only difference is that the invoked method refers to the network printers (line 608) instead of the network drives.

Sample 1.15   *Enumerating printer connections*

```
190:' -------------------------------------------------------------------------
191:' Network Printer connections.
192:EnumeratePrinterConnections objLogFileName
...:
194:EnumeratePrinterConnections objLogFileName
...:
197:EnumeratePrinterConnections objLogFileName
...:
```

```
199:EnumeratePrinterConnections objLogFileName
...:
598:' -------------------------------------------------------------------------
599:Private Function EnumeratePrinterConnections (objFileName)
...:
604:        On Error Resume Next
...:
608:        Set enumPrinters = WshNetwork.EnumPrinterConnections
609:        If Err.Number Then
610:            EnumeratePrinterConnections = ErrorHandler (...
611:            Exit Function
612:        End If
613:
614:        If enumPrinters.Count = 0 Then
615:            WriteToFile objFileName, "No printer to list."
616:        Else
617:            WriteToFile objFileName, "Current network printer connections:"
618:            For intIndice = 0 To enumPrinters.Count - 1 Step 2
619:                WriteToFile objFileName, enumPrinters (intIndice) & " -> " &
                                            enumPrinters (intIndice + 1)
620:            Next
621:        End If
622:
623:End Function
```

The creation of the printer connection offers two methods. One method is to create a printer connection in Windows mode (Sample 1.16); the other method is to create a printer connection in DOS mode (Sample 1.17).

Sample 1.16   *Creating printer connections in Windows mode*

```
190:' -------------------------------------------------------------------------
191:' Network Printer connections.
...:
198:ConnectWindowsNetworkPrinter objLogFileName, cRemotePrinter, True
...:
625:' -------------------------------------------------------------------------
626:Private Function ConnectWindowsNetworkPrinter (objFileName, strShareName,
627:
628:        On Error Resume Next
...:
632:        WshNetwork.AddWindowsPrinterConnection strShareName
633:        If Err.Number Then
634:            ConnectWindowsNetworkPrinter = ErrorHandler (..
635:            Exit Function
636:        End If
637:
638:        If boolDefault Then
...:
640:            WshNetwork.SetDefaultPrinter strShareName
641:            If Err.Number Then
642:                ConnectWindowsNetworkPrinter = ErrorHandler (...
643:                Exit Function
644:            End If
645:
646:        End If
647
648:End Function
```

Each method requires its own set of parameters (line 632). For a Windows printer connection, the UNC is enough. For a DOS printer connection, the parallel port with the UNC must be given (line 659).

Sample 1.17   *Creating printer connections in DOS mode*

```
190:' --------------------------------------------------------------------------
191:' Network Printer connections.
...:
193:ConnectNetworkPrinter objLogFileName, cLocalPort, cRemotePrinter
...:
650:' --------------------------------------------------------------------------
651:Private Function ConnectNetworkPrinter (objFileName, strLPT, strShareName)
652:
653:        On Error Resume Next
...:
659:        WshNetwork.AddPrinterConnection strLPT, strShareName
660:        If Err.Number Then
661:            ConnectNetworkPrinter = ErrorHandler (...
662:            Exit Function
663:        End If
664:
665:End Function
```

Deleting a printer connection (Sample 1.18) is the same as deleting a drive connection. For a drive, the parameter is the drive letter or a remote name. For a printer, the parameter is the printer port or the remote name (i.e., for a Windows printer connection) (line 687).

Sample 1.18   *Deleting printer connections*

```
190:' --------------------------------------------------------------------------
191:' Network Printer connections.
...:
195:DisconnectNetworkPrinter objLogFileName, cLocalPort, False
...:
667:' --------------------------------------------------------------------------
668:Private Function DisconnectNetworkPrinter (objFileName, strLPT, boolConfirm)
...:
672:        On Error Resume Next
673:
674:        If boolConfirm Then
675:            intClick = WshShell.Popup ("Remove Network Printer connection '" & _
676:                                       UCase (strLPT) & "' (Y/N) ?", _
677:                                       0, _
678:                                       "(WSHScript) Confirmation", _
679:                                       vbQuestion + vbYesNo)
680:            If intClick = cNoClick Then
681:                Exit Function
682:            End If
683:        End If
684:
685:        WriteToFile objFileName, "** Disconnect from Network Printer '" & UCase (strLPT) & "'"
686:
687:        WshNetwork.RemovePrinterConnection strLPT
```

```
688:        If Err.Number Then
689:            DisconnectNetworkPrinter = ErrorHandler (...
690:            Exit Function
691:        End If
692:
693:End Function
```

1.6.7   Creating shortcuts

WSH provides methods to create shortcuts in any folder available on the file system. Of course, shortcuts can be created in any special folders, such as the Desktop folder (see Table 1.12 for the SpecialFolders list). Shortcut creation is available directly from the **WshShell** object. The procedure is relatively explicit. All parameters available from a traditional GUI shortcut can be referenced through the **Shortcut** object in Sample 1.19.

Sample 1.19   *Creating shortcuts*

```
215:' --------------------------------------------------------------------------
216:' Create a Shortcut on the Desktop for this current user.
217:Dim objShortCut
218:
219:WriteToFile objLogFileName, "** Create a shortcut on the Desktop."
220:
221:Set objShortCut = WshShell.CreateShortCut(classRunTimeEnvironmentInfo.Desktop & _
222:                                    "\Windows NT Getting Started.Lnk")
223:objShortCut.Description = "Getting started with Windows NT Server"
224:objShortCut.Arguments = ""
225:objShortCut.HotKey = "ALT+CTRL+S"
226:objShortCut.IconLocation = classRunTimeEnvironmentInfo.System32 & "wizmgr.exe"
227:objShortCut.TargetPath = classRunTimeEnvironmentInfo.System32 & "wizmgr.exe"
228:objShortCut.WindowStyle = SW_SHOWNORMAL
229:objShortCut.WorkingDirectory = classRunTimeEnvironmentInfo.System32
230:objShortCut.Save
231:If Err.Number Then
232:    ErrorHandler objLogFileName, "MAIN - CreateShortCut", Err, boolErrorPopup
233:End If
```

1.6.8   Pausing a script

The ability to pause a script can be quite useful. The **WshScript.vbs** marks a pause of five seconds on two occasions: one after starting an external program and the other one before killing the started program (see Sample 1.20). The WSH method is available from the **WScript** object and uses only one parameter: the number of milliseconds to pause the script.

Sample 1.20 *Pausing a script*

```
281:' ------------------------------------------------------------------------
282:' Executing a pause of 5 sec.
283:WriteToFile objLogFileName, "** Pausing the script for 5 sec."
284:
285:WScript.Sleep (5000)
```

1.6.9 Accessing the registry

Access to the registry is available through the **WshShell** object. This object exposes methods to read, create, and delete registry keys or registry key values. If the user security context has the required permissions, any registry key can be accessed. The general rule for accessing the registry is to provide the following parameters:

- The key name

- The key value name

- The value for the given key value name

All methods to manipulate keys have the same behavior. If the passed parameter ends with a backslash (\), then the invoked method addresses a key path. If the passed parameter does not end with a backslash, then the invoked method addresses a key value name. Sample 1.21 shows how to proceed.

Sample 1.21 *Reading the registry*

```
250:' ------------------------------------------------------------------------
251:' Read the registry.
...:
254:varRegValue = ReadRegistry (objLogFileName, "HKCU\Software\CompaqTEST\Registry Access", _
255:                                            "ValueRegBinary", "REG_BINARY")
256:varRegValue = ReadRegistry (objLogFileName, "HKCU\Software\CompaqTEST\Registry Access", _
257:                                            "ValueRegDWord", "REG_DWORD")
258:varRegValue = ReadRegistry (objLogFileName, "HKCU\Software\CompaqTEST\Registry Access", _
259:                                            "ValueRegExpandSz", "REG_EXPAND_SZ")
260:varRegValue = ReadRegistry (objLogFileName, "HKCU\Software\CompaqTEST\Registry Access", _
261:                                            "ValueRegMultiSz", "REG_MULTI_SZ")
262:varRegValue = ReadRegistry (objLogFileName, "HKCU\Software\CompaqTEST\Registry Access", _
263:                                            "ValueRegSz", "REG_SZ")
...:
412:' ------------------------------------------------------------------------
413:Private Function ReadRegistry (objFileName, strKeyName, KeyValueName, strRegType)
...:
421:        On Error Resume Next
422:
```

```
423:        strRegKey = strKeyName & "\" & KeyValueName
...:
426:        varTempValue = WshShell.RegRead (strRegKey)
427:        If Err.Number Then
428:            ErrorHandler objFileName, "ReadRegistry", Err, boolErrorPopup
429:            Exit Function
430:        End If
431:
432:        Select Case strRegType
433:            Case "REG_BINARY"
434:                ReDim varRegKeyValue(Ubound(varTempValue))
435:                For intIndice = 0 to Ubound(varTempValue)
436:                    varRegKeyValue (intIndice)="&h" & Right("00" &
                                                 Hex(varTempValue(intIndice)), 2)
...:
439:                Next
440:            Case "REG_DWORD"
441:                ReDim varRegKeyValue(0)
442:                varRegKeyValue(0) = "&h" & Hex (varTempValue)
...:
445:            Case "REG_MULTI_SZ"
446:                ReDim varRegKeyValue(Ubound(varTempValue))
447:                For intIndice = 0 to Ubound(varTempValue)
448:                    varRegKeyValue (intIndice) = varTempValue(intIndice)
...:
451:                Next
452:
453:            Case "REG_EXPAND_SZ"
454:                ReDim varRegKeyValue(0)
455:                varRegKeyValue(0) = WshShell.ExpandEnvironmentStrings (varTempValue)
...:
458:            Case Else
459:                ReDim varRegKeyValue(0)
460:                varRegKeyValue(0) = varTempValue
...:
463:        End Select
464:
465:        ReadRegistry = varRegKeyValue
466:
467:End Function
```

The sample function concatenates the key path and the key value name (line 423). If the key value name is empty, then the parameter passed to the WSH registry method ends with a backslash and will address a key name. In this way, a single function can be used for both key names and key value names.

The registry contains values in various forms. Some registry values can be like a string (REG_SZ), a string containing a variable from the environment (REG_EXPAND_SZ), or a 16-bit value (REG_DWORD); others can be like an array of strings (REG_MULTI_SZ), and still others can be like an array of bytes (REG_BINARY). The first function to access the registry is the ReadRegistry() function (Sample 1.21). The function's behavior is dependent on the value type to be read. Some registry values are represented as single variable, whereas others are represented with an array of values. For this reason the ReadRegistry() function always returns an array of one or more elements. Whatever the nature of the value, the function always returns values as a string array. This will simplify the data handling on return of the function.

A REG_BINARY registry key value needs to be converted to a hexadecimal string. This is the purpose of line 436. Because a binary value can be an array of values, the script executes an enumeration (lines 435 to 439) to assign (and convert into a string) every single byte found in the registry value. When reading a REG_DWORD value, the script simply converts the value in a hexadecimal string (line 442). When reading a REG_EXPAND_SZ string, the script uses a method already seen when reading variables from the environment. By invoking the ExpandEnvironmentStrings from the **WshShell** object, the code resolves an environment variable to its value (line 455). The last case covers a single string registry value (REG_SZ) reading (line 460). In such a case, no conversion is necessary.

Writing to the registry is quite straightforward (Sample 1.22). The script does not have to deal with any data conversion because the **WshShell** *RegWrite* method handles this (line 496). An important point to note is that the *RegWrite* method does not support REG_MULTI_SZ registry value creation. Note also that the value written for a REG_BINARY or REG_DWORD must be between −2,147,483,648 and 2,147,483,647 (a 2^32 signed number).

Sample 1.22   *Writing to the registry*

```
235:' -------------------------------------------------------------------------
236:' Write the registry (Be sure that user has right to create it)
237:WriteRegistry objLogFileName, "HKCU\Software\CompaqTEST\Registry Access", _
238:                              "ValueRegBinary", "REG_BINARY", _
239:                              -2147483647
240:WriteRegistry objLogFileName, "HKCU\Software\CompaqTEST\Registry Access", _
241:                              "ValueRegDWord", "REG_DWORD", _
242:                              642522
243:WriteRegistry objLogFileName, "HKCU\Software\CompaqTEST\Registry Access", _
244:                              "ValueRegExpandSz", "REG_EXPAND_SZ", _
245:                              "This is an expanded '%SystemRoot%' string"
246:WriteRegistry objLogFileName, "HKCU\Software\CompaqTEST\Registry Access", _
247:                              "ValueRegSz", "REG_SZ", _
248:                              "This is another string"
...:
469:' -------------------------------------------------------------------------
470:Private Function WriteRegistry (objFileName,strKeyName,KeyValueName,strRegType, varRegKeyValue)
...:
474:        On Error Resume Next
475:
476:        strRegKey = strKeyName & "\" & KeyValueName
```

```
477:        Select Case strRegType
478:            Case "REG_BINARY"
...:
482:            Case "REG_DWORD"
...:
486:            Case "REG_MULTI_SZ"
487:                ' RegWrite from WSH does not support REG_MULTI_SZ
488:                Exit Function
489:
490:            Case Else
...:
494:        End Select
495:
496:        WshShell.RegWrite strRegKey, varRegKeyValue, strRegType
497:        If Err.Number Then
498:            WriteRegistry = ErrorHandler (...
499:            Exit Function
500:        End If
501:
502:End Function
```

Deleting from the registry is almost as simple as writing to the registry (see Sample 1.23). The **WshShell** object exposes the *RegDelete* method (line 514). To delete a registry tree it is important to keep in mind that child keys must be deleted. Note that WSH does not offer a way to enumerate registry keys. Later in this book we examine how registry keys can be enumerated with WMI. The **WshScript.vbs** shows a sample for the CompaqTEST subtree (lines 267 to 280).

Sample 1.23   *Deleting from the registry*

```
265:' -------------------------------------------------------------------------
266:' Delete the registry keys created.
267:DeleteRegistry objLogFileName, "HKCU\Software\CompaqTEST\Registry Access", _
268:                              "ValueRegBinary"
269:DeleteRegistry objLogFileName, "HKCU\Software\CompaqTEST\Registry Access", _
270:                              "ValueRegDWord"
271:DeleteRegistry objLogFileName, "HKCU\Software\CompaqTEST\Registry Access", _
272:                              "ValueRegExpandSz"
273:DeleteRegistry objLogFileName, "HKCU\Software\CompaqTEST\Registry Access", _
274:                              "ValueRegSz"
275:DeleteRegistry objLogFileName, "HKCU\Software\CompaqTEST\Registry Access", _
276:                              "ValueRegMultiSz"
277:DeleteRegistry objLogFileName, "HKCU\Software\CompaqTEST\Registry Access", _
278:                              ""
279:DeleteRegistry objLogFileName, "HKCU\Software\CompaqTEST", _
280:                              ""
...:
504:' -------------------------------------------------------------------------
505:Private Function DeleteRegistry (objFileName, strKeyName, KeyValueName)
...:
509:        On Error Resume Next
510:
511:        strRegKey = strKeyName & "\" & KeyValueName
...:
514:        WshShell.RegDelete strRegKey
```

```
515:        If Err.Number Then
516:            DeleteRegistry = ErrorHandler (...
517:            Exit Function
518:        End If
...:
522:End Function
```

1.6.10 Drag-and-drop support

Drag-and-drop support is implemented from WSH 2.0. This support enables the user to start a script by dragging and dropping a file on the desired script name. From the programming point of view, this is transparent because the dropped file name is presented to the script as an argument from the command line. So, to capture a dropped file name, the script uses the logic of the ReadCommandLineArgument() function shown previously. The **WshScript.vbs** is not designed for this feature (because the expected parameter is not a file name), but we will see in some subsequent samples how the drag-and-drop support can ease script startup.

1.6.11 Running external programs

The **WshShell** object exposes the *Run* method. This method launches an application from a WSH script. For instance, we can use this method in the following way:

```
WshShell.run "Notepad.Exe " & WScript.ScriptFullName, intWindowStyle,
True
```

This line code will launch **Notepad.Exe**, and Notepad will load the script itself because we specify the current script name on the command line. The WindowStyle parameter is an integer that indicates the appearance of the program's window. Note that not all programs make use of this information. Table 1.19 shows the possible values for the WindowStyle parameter.

The Boolean parameter is a "wait on run" parameter. If it is set to True, the script will pause until the process is stopped. If it is set to False (the default), the *Run* method returns immediately after starting the program. The *Run* method does not allow stopping the started process.

With WSH 5.6, the **WshShell** object provides another way to start an application by using the *Exec* method (see Sample 1.24). The big difference between the *Exec* method and the *Run* method is that the *Exec* method exposes a method to terminate the started process. Moreover, the *Exec* method works with the standard input and standard output streams.

Table 1.19   *The Popup Window Styles*

Window styles	
Values	*Description*
0	Hides the window and activates another window.
1	Activates and displays a window. If the window is minimized or maximized, the system restores it to its original size and position. An application should specify this flag when displaying the window for the first time.
2	Activates the window and displays it as a minimized window.
3	Activates the window and displays it as a maximized window.
4	Displays a window in its most recent size and position. The active window remains active.
5	Activates the window and displays it in its current size and position.
6	Minimizes the specified window and activates the next top-level window in the Z order.
7	Displays the window as a minimized window. The active window remains active.
8	Displays the window in its current state. The active window remains active.
9	Activates and displays the window. If the window is minimized or maximized, the system restores it to its original size and position. An application should specify this flag when restoring a minimized window.
10	Sets the show-state based on the state of the program that started the application.

If the started process is echoing its messages to the standard output, the script (the parent) can retrieve and manipulate the messages. This feature will be used in a sample showing how to use the standard input/output streams in Section 1.6.12.

Sample 1.24   *Starting an external program*

```
201:' -------------------------------------------------------------------------
202:' Running an external program
203:WriteToFile objLogFileName, "** Running external program. i.e. Notepad.Exe"
204:
205:Dim WshScriptExec
206:Set WshScriptExec = WshShell.Exec ("Notepad.Exe " & _
207:                                classRunTimeEnvironmentInfo.ScriptFullName)
```

Once the process starts, WSH retrieves the **WshScriptExec** object (line 206). In opposition to the *Run* method from the **WshShell** object, this object exposes a method to terminate the started process (Sample 1.25, line 291).

Sample 1.25   *Killing a started program*

```
287:' ------------------------------------------------------------------------
288:' Killing the launched external program
289:WriteToFile objLogFileName, "** Terminating external program. i.e. Notepad.Exe"
290:
291:WshScriptExec.Terminate
```

1.6.12   Standard input and standard output

Another nice feature from WSH is support for standard input and output pipes. This new feature lets you pipe input and output between scripts or any other application from the command line. For instance, if you type the following on the command line, the output of the DIR command is piped to the script:

```
DIR | Cscript.Exe StdInOut.vbs
```

Sample 1.26 demonstrates how the output of the DIR command can be written to the standard output. Of course, it is also possible to redirect the output to the standard error (WScript.StdErr) at line 13.

Sample 1.26   *Standard input and standard output usage*

```
 8:Option Explicit
 9:
10:Dim strInputString
11:Dim stdOut, stdIn
12:
13:Set stdOut = WScript.StdOut
14:Set stdIn  = WScript.StdIn
15:
16:Do While Not stdIn.AtEndOfStream
17:
18:    strInputString = stdIn.ReadLine
19:    stdOut.WriteLine "String piped: '" & strInputString & "'"
20:
21:Loop
```

In Sample 1.24, we discovered the **WshScriptExec** object comes from the execution of the *Exec* method exposed by the **WshShell** object. In the same way, we can reuse the *Exec* method to launch a process. For the sample, the process is the **WshScript.vbs** script. Sample 1.27, written in Java script, launches the VBScript WshScript.vbs as a child process (line 8).

Sample 1.27   *Standard input/output capture from a child script process*

```
 6:var WshShell = new ActiveXObject("WScript.Shell");
 7:
 8:var WshScriptExec = WshShell.Exec("%ComSpec% /C Wshscript.vbs verbose");
 9:
10:if (WshScriptExec.Status == 0)
11:    {
12:    WScript.Echo ("Job is started.");
13:    }
14:else
15:    {
16:    WScript.Echo ("Job is completed.");
17:    }
18:
19:WScript.Echo ("Process ID: " + WshScriptExec.ProcessID);
20:
21:do {
22:    var strOutput = WshScriptExec.StdOut.ReadLine();
23:    if (strOutput.indexOf ("ERROR") != -1)
24:        {
25:        WScript.Echo (strOutput);
26:        }
27:    }
28:while (!WshScriptExec.StdOut.AtEndOfStream);
29:
30:WScript.Echo ("Done.");
31:WScript.Sleep (5000);
```

Note on the command line that the verbose parameter is mentioned (line 8). It means that the **WshScript.vbs** will generate some output that can be intercepted by the standard input/output mechanism. This occurs at line 22. If the parent script detects the string ERROR in the output coming from **WshScript.vbs** (line 23), the message is echoed (line 25). Any other output is discarded. Therefore, Sample 1.27 acts as a parent process that filters the output of its child process.

1.7   Features coming from the use of XML in WSH

More than exposing an object collection with properties and methods to perform basic operations, WSH offers a lot of interesting features with the use of XML. Since WSH 2.0, the WSH engine is able to parse a set of defined XML tags. The collection of tags is used to structure a WSH script into many different parts. Each part has a role to play in the script. For instance, it is possible to define a set of routines to include in a script, or it is possible to parse the command line more easily. Last but not least, the most amazing WSH XML feature is probably the possibility to write scripts that behave like reusable COM components.

1.7.1   **Parsing the command line with XML**

As we have seen before, a script can start another script as a child process. In the previous sample the started script is hard-coded in the script code. It would be nice to have this as a parameter. Of course, we can reuse the function ReadCommandLineArgument() from the **WshScript.vbs**, but WSH offers a much better way to manipulate command-line arguments. By using an XML encapsulation of the previous **WshScriptExec.js** and with some changes to suit the requirements of the command-line parameters reading, it is possible to perform the same action as the ReadCommandLineArgument() function. In the next sample, the command-line parameter will be the process launched by the script. The process can be a script (if run with **Cscript.exe**) or any other executable application. To demonstrate the XML capabilities of the command line parsing, the sample accepts a new parameter: **/filter**. This switch is interpreted by the XML parsing feature and its associated object collection (**WshName** and **WshUnNamed**). It is possible to specify another string filter than the ERROR keyword as was used in the case before. Therefore, the logic of Sample 1.28 is almost the same as Sample 1.27.

Sample 1.28   *Parsing the command line with XML*

```
 1:<?xml version="1.0"?>
 .:
 8:<package>
 9:   <job>
..:
13:     <runtime>
14:       <named   name="filter" helpstring="the string to filter"
                                              required="false" type="string" />
15:       <unnamed name="process" helpstring="the process to execute"
                                              required="true" type="string" />
16:
17:       <example>Example: WshScriptExec.wsf /filter:MyString MyProcess.Exe</example>
18:
19:     </runtime>
20:
21:     <script language="JScript">
22:     <![CDATA[
23:       var strFilter;
24:       var WshArguments= WScript.Arguments;
25:
26:       if (WshArguments.Unnamed.Count == 0)
27:          {
```

```
28:             WshArguments.ShowUsage();
29:             WScript.Quit();
30:             }
31:
32:       if (WshArguments.Named.Count == 1)
33:             {
34:             var strFilter = WshArguments.Named("filter");
35:             }
36:       else
37:             {
38:             var strFilter = "ERROR"
39:             }
40:
41:       var WshShell = new ActiveXObject("Wscript.Shell");
42:
43:       var WshScriptExec = WshShell.Exec(WshArguments.Unnamed.Item(0));
44:
45:       if (WshScriptExec.Status == 0)
46:             {
47:             WScript.Echo ("Job is started.");
48:             }
49:       else
50:             {
51:             WScript.Echo ("Jos is completed.");
52:             }
53:
54:       WScript.Echo ("Process ID: " + WshScriptExec.ProcessID);
55:
56:       do {
57:             var strOutput = WshScriptExec.StdOut.ReadLine();
58:             if (strOutput.indexOf (strFilter) != -1)
59:                 {
60:                 WScript.Echo (strOutput);
61:                 }
62:             }
63:       while (!WshScriptExec.StdOut.AtEndOfStream);
64:
65:       WScript.Echo ("Done.");
66:       WScript.Sleep (5000);
67:
68:    ]]>
69:    </script>
70:  </job>
71:</package>
```

Let's examine the XML tags and their meaning.

<?xml version="1.0"?> statement: This is a declaration that specifies that the file should be parsed as XML. This declaration must be the first element in the file and cannot be preceded by any blank lines. The existence of this declaration puts the script component compiler into strict XML mode, where element types and attribute names are case- sensitive. Attribute values must be enclosed in single or double quotation marks, and all elements are parsed. If the declaration is not included, the compiler allows syntax that is less strict. You should include this declaration and follow XML conventions if your script component file will be edited in an editor that supports XML (such as XML Spy, for instance).

```
<?XML version="version" [standalone="DTDflag"] ?>
```

The version is a string in the form *n.n* specifying the XML level of the file. For WSH use the value 1.0. The DTDflag is optional. This is a Boolean value indicating whether the XML file includes a reference to an external Document Type Definition (DTD). Scripts using XML components do not include such a reference, so the value for this attribute is always yes, which is the default.

<package></package> section: This tag encloses multiple job definitions in a Windows Script Host file. This tag is optional when a Windows Script File contains only one job. The reason for having many jobs in one Windows Script File is to combine many different scripts using different languages in one single file.

<job></job> section: This tag allows multiple jobs to be defined in a single file.

```
<job [id=JobID]>
   job code
</job>
```

<?job?> section: This tag is a processing instruction that specifies attributes for error handling. Two parameters are valid for this tag. False is the default value for the parameters.

- Error. This parameter is a Boolean value. When set to true it allows error messages for syntax or run-time errors in the Windows Script File.
- Debug. This parameter is a Boolean value. When set to True it enables debugging. If debugging is not enabled, it is impossible to launch the script debugger to trace the execution of the Windows Script File.

```
<?job error="flag" debug="flag" ?>
```

<runtime></runtime> section: This is where the required or optional command-line arguments are defined. The tag groups together the set of run-time command-line arguments for a script. The *ShowUsage* method from the **WshArguments** object (line 28) uses the information tagged by the <runtime> element (lines 13 to 19) to display the run-time parameters for a script. Since the <runtime> element is enclosed within a set of job tags (lines 9 to 70), the defined run-time arguments apply to that job only. If the script takes more than one argument, each one must be enclosed within a set of named or unnamed tags (lines 14 and 15).

<named></named> section: The <named> element is enclosed within the run-time tags part of a job. An argument with the name *filter* would provide a **/filter** switch at the command line and an argument with the name *script* would provide a command line switch named **/script** in the **WshNamed** arguments collection (line 32). If the type is string, the argument is a string. The argument is passed to the script as **/filter:mystring**. If the type is Boolean, the argument is Boolean. The argument is passed to the script as **/named+** to turn it on, or **/named-** to turn it off. If the type is simple, the argument takes no additional value and is passed as just the name, **/named**.

```
<named
    name = namedname
    helpstring = helpstring
    type = "string|boolean|simple"
    required = boolean
/>
```

For instance, Sample 1.28 can be started with the following command line:

```
C:>WshScriptExec.wsf /filter:ERROR "%COMSPEC% /C WshScript.vbs
verbose"
```

where the named parameter is the filter and represented on the command line by **/filter** with the value ERROR.

<unnamed></unnamed> section: This tag marks a particular unnamed argument to the script part of a job. The <unnamed> element is enclosed within a set of run-time tags. An unnamed element's name appears only in the usage from the **WshArguments** object. Because it is an unnamed argument, it can be referenced by using the *item* property of the **UnNamed** object (line 43). If the type is string, the argument is a string. If the type is Boolean, the argument is Boolean. If the type is simple, the argument takes no additional value and is passed as just the name.

The required argument behaves as a Boolean variable if you set it with a Boolean value (supply True/False, on/off, 1/0). You can also set it with an integer that represents the number of required elements.

```
<unnamed
    name       = unnamedname
    helpstring = helpstring
    many       = boolean
    required   = boolean or integer
/>
```

For instance, the script Sample 1.28 can be started with the following command line:

```
C:>WshScriptExec.wsf /filter:ERROR "%COMSPEC% /C WshScript.vbs
verbose"
```

or with the following command line:

```
C:>WshScriptExec.wsf /filter:ERROR "Cscript.Exe WshScript.vbs
verbose"
```

where the unnamed parameter is the script startup command and is represented on the command line by the value "%COMSPEC% /C **WshScript.vbs** verbose" or "**Cscript.Exe** WshScript.vbs verbose." An important consideration with the *Exec* method is to pass a Win32 process. This is why the %COMSPEC% or the **Cscript.Exe** is given. You can't pass a script name alone; it must be a Win32 process.

If the /? switch is specified on the command line, the script produces the following output:

```
C:>"WshScriptExec.wsf" /?
Microsoft (R) Windows Script Host Version 5.6
Copyright (C) Microsoft Corporation 1996-2000. All rights reserved.
Usage: WshScriptExec.wsf [/filter:value] script
Options:
filter  : the string to filter
process : the script to execute
Example : WshScriptExec.wsf /filter:MyString MyProcess.Exe
```

We can clearly see that the XML tags participate in the creation of the help text.

<script></script> section: This section (lines 21 to 69) encapsulates the script code to be executed and defines the script language in order to invoke the right script engine.

```
<script language="language" [src="strFile"]>
    script here
</script>
```

<![CDATA[ ]]> section: This is the character data delimiter (Lines 22 and 68). This delimiter guarantees XML 1.0 compliance (line 1). VBScript and JScript use some characters (such as &) that will confuse the XML parser because the XML parser, expects version 1.0–compliant coding. The CDATA delimiter tells the XML parser to skip parsing operations on that piece of code.

As mentioned before, Sample 1.28, encapsulated between the <script></script> tags, is almost the same as the previous one (Sample 1.27) except for the following:

- Lines 26 to 39 add the support for command-line arguments checking. The lines 26 to 30 check the presence of the unnamed argument (which is a mandatory one as stated in the XML definition at line 15). If this parameter is not given, the script shows the help message by invoking the *ShowUsage* method of the **WshArguments** object.

- Lines 32 to 39 check the presence of the named argument called **/filter**. Because this parameter is optional, the script defines a default value for the filter at line 38.

The rest of the script uses the same logic as Sample 1.27.

1.7.2   Combining different scripts and languages in one file

In the first pages of this chapter, we briefly mentioned the possibility of combining different languages in one script by using a Windows Script File (.wsf). By simply creating different jobs in the same .wsf file, it is possible to have different scripts written in different languages. If we take a quick look at the script presented in the beginning of the chapter, we have the coding in Sample 1.29

Sample 1.29   *Two easy scripts in different languages combined in one Windows Script File*

```
 1: <?xml version="1.0"?>
 2: <!--                          -->
 3: <!--  WScript Script File -->
 4: <!--                          -->
 5: <package>
 6:   <job id="vbs">
 7:     <script language="VBScript">
 8:       Dim strMessage
 9:       strMessage = "Hello world!"
10:       WScript.Echo strMessage
11:     </script>
12:   </job>
13:   <job id="js">
14:     <script language="JScript">
```

```
15:          var strMessage;
16:          strMessage = "Hello world!";
17:          WScript.Echo (strMessage);
18:        </script>
19:     </job>
20:  </package>
```

As we can see, the XML part has exactly the same structure as Sample 1.28 except that we have two <job> sections: one section for a script written in VBScript (lines 6 to 12) and one second section for a script written in JavaScript (lines 13 to 19). This feature is quite interesting because it allows a script writer to combine many different scripts written in different languages in one unique file. How do we start a script from a specific section? Since each section has a name (lines 6 and 13), it is possible to refer to the section to be started from the command prompt. If you want to start the VBScript, with the section name VBS (line 6), you must type:

```
Cscript.Exe //Job:VBS MyScript.wsf
```

If you want to start the JavaScript, which the section name is JS (line 13), you must type:

```
Cscript.Exe //Job:JS MyScript.wsf
```

Of course, including two functions implementing the same process and written in different languages in a single Windows Script File does not make much sense. But including different script logics written in different languages inside the same Windows Script File with the ability to start them separately is really interesting. For instance, inside one Windows Script File, it is possible to group all the scripts needed for an administrative purpose or a logon process.

Unfortunately, this structure does not allow one script of one <job> section to be called by one script from another <job> section. But by adding a <script> statement, it is possible to reuse some code. Moreover, it is possible to call different languages from different script modules.

1.7.3   Working with reusable code

To illustrate this, let's take another script routine. For instance, we will use a script that performs a conversion of a standard string to a base64-coded string and vice versa. The base64 conversion routines are written as separate functions in VBScript. We will not go into the details of the base64 conversion algorithm, but for complete documentation, the source code is given in Samples 1.30 and 1.31.

Sample 1.30   *The base64 decoding routine*

```
 .:
 3:Const cBase64CodeBase = "ABCDEFGHIJKLMNOPQRSTUVWXYZabcdefghijklmnopqrstuvwxyz0123456789+/="
 .:
 7:' ------------------------------------------------------------------------------------------
 8:Function DecodeBase64 (base64String)
..:
17:        intBase64StringLen = Len(base64String)
18:
19:        If intBase64StringLen Mod 4 <> 0 Then
20:            WScript.Echo "Bad Base64 string."
21:            Exit Function
22:        End If
23:
24:        For intGroupIndice = 1 To intBase64StringLen Step 4
25:
26:            ' Each data group encodes up To 3 actual bytes.
27:            intCharIndex = 3
28:            intGroupValue = 0
29:
30:            For intCharIndice = 0 To 3
..:
36:                strCurrentChar = Mid(base64String, intGroupIndice + intCharIndice, 1)
37:
38:                If strCurrentChar = "=" Then
39:                    intCharIndex = intCharIndex - 1
40:                    intCurrentCharValue = 0
41:                Else
42:                    intCurrentCharValue = InStr(cBase64CodeBase, strCurrentChar) - 1
43:                End If
44:
45:                If intCurrentCharValue = -1 Then
46:                    WScript.Echo "Bad character In Base64 string."
47:                    Exit Function
48:                End If
49:
50:                intGroupValue = 64 * intGroupValue + intCurrentCharValue
51:            Next     52:
53:            ' Convert 3-byte integer into up To 3 characters
54:            For intCharIndice = 1 To intCharIndex
55:                Select Case intCharIndice
56:                    Case 1:
57:                        varTemp = intGroupValue \ 65536
58:                    Case 2:
59:                        varTemp = (intGroupValue And 65535) \ 256
60:                    Case 3:
61:                        varTemp = (intGroupValue And 255)
62:                End Select
63:
64:                strBase64StringDecoded = strBase64StringDecoded & Chr(varTemp)
65:            Next
66:        Next
67:
68:        DecodeBase64 = strBase64StringDecoded
69:
70:End Function
```

Sample 1.31 *The base64 coding routine*

```
72:' ----------------------------------------------------------------------------------
73:Function EncodeBase64 (strClearString)
..:
81:         intClearStringLen = Len (strClearString)
..:
86:         For intIndice = 1 To intClearStringLen Step 3
87:             bool4Th = vbFalse
88:             bool3rd = vbFalse
89:
90:             intTemp = Asc (Mid (strClearString, intIndice, 1))
91:
92:             intTemp = intTemp * 256
93:             If ((intIndice + 1) =< intClearStringLen) Then
94:                 intTemp = intTemp Or Asc (Mid (strClearString, intIndice + 1, 1))
95:                 bool3rd = vbTrue
96:             End If
97:
98:             intTemp = intTemp * 256
99:             If ((intIndice + 2) =< intClearStringLen) Then
100:                 intTemp = intTemp Or Asc (Mid (strClearString, intIndice + 2, 1))
101:                 bool4Th = vbTrue
102:             End If
103:
104:             If bool4Th Then
105:                 varTempQuadBlock = Mid (cBase64CodeBase, (intTemp And &h3F) + 1, 1)
106:             Else
107:                 varTempQuadBlock = Mid (cBase64CodeBase, 65, 1)
108:             End If
109:
110:             intTemp = Int (intTemp / 64)
111:             If bool3rd Then
112:                 varTempQuadBlock = Mid (cBase64CodeBase,
                                           (intTemp And &h3F) + 1, 1) & varTempQuadBlock
113:             Else
114:                 varTempQuadBlock = Mid (cBase64CodeBase, 65, 1) & varTempQuadBlock
115:             End If
116:
117:             intTemp = Int (intTemp / 64)
118:             varTempQuadBlock = Mid (cBase64CodeBase,
                                       (intTemp And &h3F) + 1, 1) & varTempQuadBlock
119:
120:             intTemp = Int (intTemp / 64)
121:             varTempQuadBlock = Mid (cBase64CodeBase,
                                       (intTemp And &h3F) + 1, 1) & varTempQuadBlock
122:
123:             strBase64String = strBase64String & varTempQuadBlock
124:         Next
125:
126:         EncodeBase64 = strBase64String
127:
128:End Function
```

The module that calls these functions is written in VBScript and JScript. We will illustrate how it is possible to reuse some code and how to call it from a different script language. Basically, there are two tactics for reuse-ing code:

1.   The first method consists of reusing the code as a function included in the main routine.

2.   The second method consists of reusing the code as a COM scripted component (Windows Script Component) invoked from the main routine.

1.7.3.1   Using script inclusions

In order to use the base64 conversion routines, we must use a Windows Script File (.wsf) and use the <script> XML tag to include the functions (Sample 1.32). Basically, the script structure is the same as in Sample 1.29. Previously, the script used two <job> sections to incorporate two scripts written in different languages: the first in VBScript and the second in JScript. Of course, the script logic enclosed between the <script></script> XML sections is adapted to the base64 functions usage. To include the base64 functions in the script code, the Windows Script File uses a <script> XML tag at line 12 for the VBScript caller and at line 36 for the JScript caller. This is the only thing to add to the XML tags to include another script code in the Windows Script File.

Sample 1.32   *Using the base64 conversion routine by inclusion*

```
 1:<?xml version="1.0"?>
 . :
 8:<package>
 9:
10:   <job id="vbs">
11:
12:      <script language="VBScript" src="..\Functions\Base64Function.vbs" />
13:
14:      <script language="VBScript">
15:      <![CDATA[
16:          Option Explicit
17:
18:          Dim strData
19:          Dim strEncoded
20:
21:          WScript.Echo "In VBScript:"
22:
23:          strData = "This is my test string!"
24:
```

```
25:          WScript.Echo "Original: '" & strData & "'"
26:          strEncoded = EncodeBase64 (strData)
27:          WScript.Echo "Encoded:  '" & strEncoded & "'"
28:          WScript.Echo "Decoded:  '" & DecodeBase64 (strEncoded) & "'"
29:
30:      ]]>
31:      </script>
32:  </job>
33:
34:  <job id="js">
35:
36:      <script language="VBScript" src="..\Functions\Base64Function.vbs" />
37:
38:      <script language="JScript">
39:      <![CDATA[
40:          var strData;
41:          var strEncoded;
42:
43:          WScript.Echo ("In JScript:");
44:
45:          strData = "This is my test string!";
46:
47:          WScript.Echo ("Original: '" + strData + "'");
48:          strEncoded = EncodeBase64 (strData);
49:          WScript.Echo ("Encoded:  '" + strEncoded + "'");
50:          WScript.Echo ("Decoded:  '" + DecodeBase64 (strEncoded) + "'");
51:
52:      ]]>
53:      </script>
54:
55:  </job>
56:</package>
```

Note that the <script></script> XML tag is enclosed in the <job> section. The language engine to be used is determined by the language parameter of the <script> XML tag.

The most interesting part is located in the <job=js> section where the main code is written in JavaScript (lines 38 to 53), but the invoked functions (lines 48 and 50) are written in VBScript and included at line 36.

Both versions produce the same output. More than making a simple reuse of the base64 conversion functions, the Windows Script File is also shared between different languages. This last sample illustrates perfectly the language combination inside one script file, the code reusability, and the language mixing. This is one of the most important and most desirable features provided by the WSH infrastructure.

Another sample especially designed to work with file inclusion is the **WshScript.wsf**. This script is exactly the same as the **WshScript.vbs**. The only change is that all function parts of the **WshScript.vbs** file are now removed and saved in a dedicated .vbs file. The **WshScript.wsf** executes the function inclusions with the <script> tag from lines 12 to 31 in Sample 1.33.

Sample 1.33   *The WshScript Windows Script File with the reusable functions*

```
1:<?xml version="1.0"?>
 .:
8:<package>
9:  <job id="WSHScript">
 .:
12:    <script language="VBScript" src="..\Functions\Include.vbs" />
13:    <script language="VBScript" src="..\Functions\GetRunTimeEnvInfoFunction.vbs" />
14:    <script language="VBScript" src="..\Functions\LogRunTimeEnvInfoFunction.vbs" />
15:    <script language="VBScript" src="..\Functions\ReadRegistryFunction.vbs" />
16:    <script language="VBScript" src="..\Functions\WriteRegistryFunction.vbs" />
17:    <script language="VBScript" src="..\Functions\DeleteRegistryFunction.vbs" />
18:    <script language="VBScript" src="..\Functions\EnumerateDriveConnectionsFunction.vbs" />
19:    <script language="VBScript" src="..\Functions\ConnectNetworkDriveFunction.vbs" />
20:    <script language="VBScript" src="..\Functions\DisconnectNetworkDriveFunction.vbs" />
21:    <script language="VBScript" src="..\Functions\EnumeratePrinterConnectionsFunction.vbs" /
22:    <script language="VBScript" src="..\Functions\ConnectWindowsNetworkPrinterFunction.vbs">
23:    <script language="VBScript" src="..\Functions\ConnectNetworkPrinterFunction.vbs" />
24:    <script language="VBScript" src="..\Functions\DisconnectNetworkPrinterFunction.vbs" />
25:    <script language="VBScript" src="..\Functions\ReadEnvVariableFunction.vbs" />
26:    <script language="VBScript" src="..\Functions\CreateEnvVariableFunction.vbs" />
27:    <script language="VBScript" src="..\Functions\RemoveEnvVariableFunction.vbs" />
28:    <script language="VBScript" src="..\Functions\GetAllEnvVariables.vbs" />
29:    <script language="VBScript" src="..\Functions\ReadCmdLineArgFunction.vbs" />
30:    <script language="VBScript" src="..\Functions\ErrorHandlerFunction.vbs" />
31:    <script language="VBScript" src="..\Functions\CreateTextFileFunction.vbs" />
32:
33:    <script language="VBScript">
34:    <![CDATA[
35:
36:        Option Explicit
37:
38:        ' ------------------------------------------------------------------
39:        ' Internal contants used in the WSH Script
40:        ' ------------------------------------------------------------------
41:        Const cLocalDrive      = "Z:"
42:        Const cRemoteShare     = "\\DP4000\SHARED"
43:        Const cLocalPort       = "LPT3:"
44:        Const cRemotePrinter   = "\\DP4000\LEXMARK"
```

1.7.3.2 *Using Windows Script Components*

Beside the script inclusion to reuse code and mix languages, Windows scripting technologies offers another technique by implementing Windows Script Components (formerly known as a Scriptlet). Like a Windows Script File, a Windows Script Component uses XML to define its structure. Of course, as the nature of the script is different, this implies the use of some new XML tags. The Windows Script Component makes a script file behave like a COM object. To publish a script as a COM object, the following information must be provided:

1.   The COM object is a binary file, so a well-known binary file must be doing the job for the script.

2.   To build a COM object, available interfaces and methods must be exposed.

3.   To register the COM object, a registration and CLSID are needed.

In previous samples, some references to existing COM objects are used (e.g., **WScript.Shell** or **Scripting.FileSystemObject**). Windows Script Components work in the same way. Each time a .wsc script is registered, a pointer in the registry to a COM compliant binary object called **SCROBJ.DLL** is created. This creates the definition of the WSC in the system. The .wsc file can be easily registered from the Windows Explorer as shown in Figure 1.6.

Figure 1.6
The registration of a Windows Script Component.

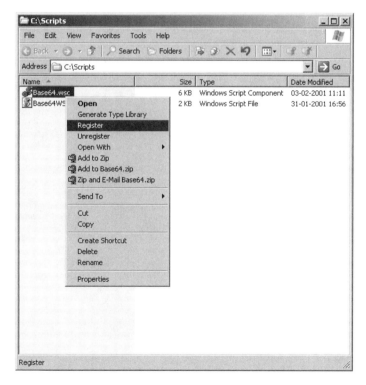

Once the registration has been completed, a registry entry is created for the file **Base64.WSC** as shown below:

```
Windows Registry Editor Version 5.00
[HKEY_CLASSES_ROOT\CLSID\{DD3DEC85-9DA6-4FC5-8E1F-6C6AA70539BD}]
@="Base64"
[HKEY_CLASSES_ROOT\CLSID\{DD3DEC85-9DA6-4FC5-8E1F-6C6AA70539BD}\
InprocServer32]
@="I:\\WINNT\\System32\\scrobj.dll"
"ThreadingModel"="Apartment"
[HKEY_CLASSES_ROOT\CLSID\{DD3DEC85-9DA6-4FC5-8E1F-6C6AA70539BD}\ProgID]
@="Base64.WSC.1.00"
[HKEY_CLASSES_ROOT\CLSID\{DD3DEC85-9DA6-4FC5-8E1F-6C6AA70539BD}\
ScriptletURL]
@="file://I:\\Scripts\\Base64.wsc"
[HKEY_CLASSES_ROOT\CLSID\{DD3DEC85-9DA6-4FC5-8E1F-6C6AA70539BD}\
VersionIndependentProgID]
@="Base64.WSC"
```

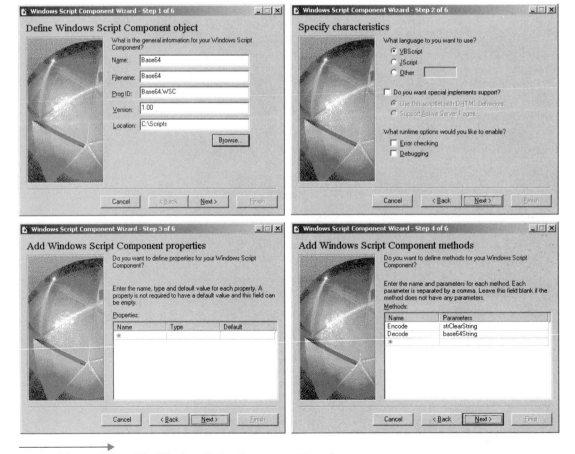

Figure 1.7   *The Windows Script Component Wizard.*

Of course, a CLSID must be provided to make the registration. To assist in this task, Microsoft provides a wizard called the Windows Script Component Wizard (Figure 1.7). This wizard helps to build a .wsc core file with all the requested data for a COM object definition:

- CLSID

- Properties definition with variables mapping

- Methods definition

A Windows Script Component is created through four important steps in the Windows Script Component Wizard. During step 1, the WSC Name and its associated ProgID are given. During step 2, the language used by the script is specified. Steps 3 and 4 are related to the definition of the properties and methods available from the script. The names entered during steps 3 and 4 are the references to properties and methods used from any automation client using the COM object.

The "dummy" Base64.wsc that the wizard generates is ready to receive the base64 functions. Of course, the generated file needs to be adapted in order to suit the input parameters used by the base64 functions. Before we examine those changes, look at Sample 1.34, which shows the "dummy" base64 Windows Script Components generated by the wizard. Note the CLSID in the registration section generated by the wizard (Line 8).

Sample 1.34   *The XML dummy file generated by the Wizard Script Component*

```
 1:<?xml version="1.0"?>
 2:<component>
 3:
 4:<registration
 5:    description="Base64"
 6:    progid="Base64.WSC"
 7:    version="1.00"
 8:    classid="{7df7e642-bcc1-4cd7-994c-fd7ab0913360}"
 9:>
10:</registration>
11:
12:<public>
13:    <method name="Encode">
14:    <parameter name="strClearString"/>
15:    </method>
16:
17:    <method name="Decode">
18:    <parameter name="base64String"/>
19:    </method>
20:</public>
21:
22:<script language="VBScript">
```

```
23:<![CDATA[
24:
25:Function Encode(strClearString)
26:    Encode = "Temporary Value"
27:End Function
28:
29:Function Decode(base64String)
30:    Decode = "Temporary Value"
31:End Function
32:
33:]]>
34:</script>
35:
36:</component>
```

The XML file that the wizard creates has the following sections:

<Components></Components> section: This section (lines 2 to 36) is equivalent to the <job></job> section shown in previous samples. This element encloses the entire source code. As with the <job> tag, an identifier attribute can be specified. This id attribute is mandatory only when several components are included in the same file.

<Registration></Registration> section: This section (lines 4 to 10) contains all the information necessary to perform a correct registration of the script as a COM object. All data entered during step 1 of the wizard is entered in this section. The only new element in this section is the CLSID generated by the wizard (line 8).

<Public></Public> section: This section (lines 12 to 20) defines the properties and methods available from the module. In step 3, the wizard prompts the user to enter property definitions. The current Windows Script Component design will not expose properties. This is why nothing was entered during that step. During step 4, two methods (with one parameter each) are defined. We retrieve these method definitions from lines 13 to 19 and lines 25 to 31. The <Public></Public> section may contain several <property></property> and <method></method> sections. The decision to have properties and methods is part of the Windows Script Component design. We will see later how to enhance and correlate the selected names with the variables originally used by the base64 functions.

<Script></Script> section: This section (lines 22 to 34) has the same role as in the previous Windows Script Files. It encapsulates the script code to be executed and defines the script language to invoke the right script engine.

<![CDATA[…]]> **section:** This section (lines 23 to 33) has the same role as in the previous Windows Script Files. This is the character data delimiter to guarantee XML 1.0 compliance (line 1). The base64 functions are inserted into the CDATA section.

Sample 1.35 shows the final base64 Windows Script Component. It shows how to interface the existing base64 functions with these COM interfaces and methods (lines 18 and 22).

Sample 1.35   *The base64 Windows Script Component*

```
 1:<?xml version="1.0"?>
 .:
 7:<component>
 8:
 9:  <registration
10:        description="Base64"
11:        progid="Base64.WSC"
12:        version="1.00"
13:        classid="{dd3dec85-9da6-4fc5-8e1f-6c6aa70539bd}"
14:  >
15:  </registration>
16:
17:  <public>
18:    <method name="Encode" internalname="EncodeBase64">
19:      <parameter name="strClearString" />
20:    </method>
21:
22:    <method name="Decode" internalname="DecodeBase64">
23:      <parameter name="base64String" />
24:    </method>
25:  </public>
26:
27:  <script language="VBScript">
28:  <![CDATA[
29:
30:  Option Explicit
31:
32:  Const cBase64CodeBase = "ABCDEFGHIJKLMNOPQRSTUVWXYZabcdefghijklmnopqrstuvwxyz0123456789+/="
..:
36:  ' -----------------------------------------------------------------------
37:  Function DecodeBase64 (base64String)
..:
46:          intBase64StringLen = Len(base64String)
47:
48:          If intBase64StringLen Mod 4 <> 0 Then
49:              Exit Function  50:          End If
..:
73:                  If intCurrentCharValue = -1 Then
74:                      Exit Function
75:                  End If
..:
95:          DecodeBase64 = strBase64StringDecoded
96:
97:  End Function
98:
```

```
 99:  ' ----------------------------------------------------------------------
100:  Function EncodeBase64 (strClearString)
...:
108:          intClearStringLen = Len (strClearString)
...:
113:          For intIndice = 1 To intClearStringLen Step 3
114:              bool4Th = vbFalse
 ..:
150:                  strBase64String = strBase64String & varTempQuadBlock
151:          Next
152:
153:          EncodeBase64 = strBase64String
154:
155:  End Function
156:
157:  ]]>
158:  </script>
159:
160:</component>
```

To use the base64 functions as Windows Script Components, some changes must be made to the "dummy" .wsc file. The changes are as follows:

- Line 18 and 22. The statement "InternalName" is added to map the exposed method to the function name used internally in the base64 functions. This will permit the use of the original function name and expose a friendlier name for the COM object methods.

  - <method name="Encode" internalname="EncodeBase64"> is mapped to the internal function name "EncodeBase64."
  - <method name="Decode" internalname="DecodeBase64"> is mapped to the internal function name "DecodeBase64."

- Lines 37 and 100. This is the location where the base64 functions are inserted. Only one change to the original code is made: In the original DecodeBase64() function, the WScript.Echo statement was used to echo a message when the base64-coded string was invalid. It is important to know that this VBScript runs in a different context than **WScript.exe** or **Cscript.exe** hosts. The code runs in the **SCROBJ.DLL** context. In this context, the WSH base object is not available, and any reference to the **WScript** object must be removed. We will see later how it is possible to fix the problem to echo a message from a Windows Script Component with the event sinking support.

Now, the base64 functions can be called from any type of client application. The key condition is to use a client application written in a language supporting automation (e.g., VB, Java, or Perl). The functions are now reusable. To complete the topic of the base64 COM scripted object,

Sample 1.36 shows how to use the object. This sample is a Windows Script File including a VBScript and a JavaScript invoking the Windows Script Component.

Sample 1.36   *Calling the base64 Windows Script Component from VBScript or JavaScript*

```
 1:<?xml version="1.0"?>
 .:
 8:<package>
 9:
10:  <job id="vbs">
11:    <script language="VBScript">
12:    <![CDATA[
..:
19:        WScript.Echo "In VBScript:"
20:
21:        strData = "This is my test string!"
22:
23:        Set objBase64 = WScript.CreateObject("Base64.WSC")
24:
25:        WScript.Echo "Original: '" & strData & "'"
26:        strEncoded = objBase64.Encode (strData)
27:        WScript.Echo "Encoded:  '" & strEncoded & "'"
28:        WScript.Echo "Decoded:  '" & objBase64.Decode (strEncoded) & "'"
29:
30:    ]]>
31:    </script>
32:  </job>
33:
34:  <job id="js">
35:    <script language="JScript">36:      <![CDATA[
..:
41:        WScript.Echo ("In JScript:");
42:
43:        strData = "This is my test string!";
44:
45:        objBase64 = new ActiveXObject("Base64.WSC");
46:
47:        WScript.Echo ("Original: '" + strData + "'");
48:        strEncoded = objBase64.Encode (strData);
49:        WScript.Echo ("Encoded:  '" + strEncoded + "'");
50:        WScript.Echo ("Decoded:  '" + objBase64.Decode (strEncoded) + "'");
51:
52:    ]]>
53:    </script>
54:
55:  </job>
56:</package>
```

Note the small change made in comparison to the initial Windows Script reusing the base64 functions by file inclusion with the <script> XML tag. In line 23 (or line 45 in JScript) a base64 object instance is created.

Lines 26 and 28 (or line 48 and 50) invoke the coding and decoding methods respectively.

1.7.3.2.1   Windows Script Components event support

Note that at lines 19 and 45 of the base64 decoding function (Sample 1.30) a check is made on the base64 string to ensure that the coded string is valid. In case of an invalid base64 string, the function echoes a message and returns an empty string as a result. This way of working is fine when using a function, but when using Windows Script File, it becomes an issue. Echoing a message uses the *Echo* method of the **WScript** object. As stated before, the **WScript** object is part of the WSH host, and there is no ProgID to create this object. Because the Windows Script works in the context of the **SCROBJ.DLL**, the **WScript** object is not available. To avoid a fault during the Windows Script Component execution, the *Echo* method must not be used.

In order to echo a message in case of an invalid base64 string, we can use the event support provided with Windows Script File. The event support is also referred to as *event sinking*. Event sinking is a technology that implements mechanisms to create events inside the Windows Script Components. The calling module can capture (sink) these events via a specific function reference during the object creation. This specific function will capture the events from the **Windows Script Component** object.

The previous base64 Windows Script Component can be used as is. Only a few lines need to be added to enable event support in the Windows Script Component and in the Windows Script File invoking the coding and decoding *base64* methods. This tactic is implemented in Samples 1.37 and 1.38.

Sample 1.37   *Base64 Windows Script Component triggering event*

```
 1:<?xml version="1.0"?>
 .:
 7:<component>
 8:
 9:   <registration
10:         description="Base64"
11:         progid="Base64.WSC"
12:         version="1.00"
13:         classid="{e3e75dbb-cd42-4aa5-aa11-f46f1e28012e}"
14:   >
15:   </registration>
16:
17:   <public>
18:         <method name="Encode" internalname="EncodeBase64">
19:           <parameter name="base64String" />
20:         </method>
```

```
 21:
 22:             <method name="Decode" internalname="DecodeBase64">
 23:               <parameter name="base64String" />
 24:             </method>
 25:
 26:             <event name="Debug">
 27:               <parameter name="Value" />
 28:             </event>
 29:   </public>
 30:
 31:   <script language="VBScript">
 32:   <![CDATA[
 33:
 34:   Option Explicit
 35:
 36:   Const cBase64CodeBase = "ABCDEFGHIJKLMNOPQRSTUVWXYZabcdefghijklmnopqrstuvwxyz0123456789+/="
 ..:
 40:   ' -------------------------------------------------------------------------
 41:   Function DecodeBase64 (base64String)
 ..:
 50:           intBase64StringLen = Len(base64String)
 51:
 52:           If intBase64StringLen Mod 4 <> 0 Then
 53:               FireEvent "Debug", "Bad Base64 string."
 54:               Exit Function
 55:           End If
 56:
 57:           For intGroupIndice = 1 To intBase64StringLen Step 4
 ..:
 78:                   If intCurrentCharValue = -1 Then
 79:                       FireEvent "Debug", "Bad character In Base64 string."
 80:                       Exit Function
 81:                   End If
 ..:
 86:                   ' Convert 3-byte integer into up To 3 characters
 87:                   For intCharIndice = 1 To intCharIndex
 88:                       Select Case intCharIndice
 89:                           Case 1:
 90:                                   varTemp = intGroupValue \ 65536
 91:                           Case 2:
 92:                                   varTemp = (intGroupValue And 65535) \ 256
 93:                           Case 3:
 94:                                   varTemp = (intGroupValue And 255)
 95:                       End Select
 96:
 97:                       FireEvent "Debug", Chr(varTemp)
...:
101:           Next
102:
103:           DecodeBase64 = strBase64StringDecoded
104:
105:   End Function
106:
107:   ' -------------------------------------------------------------------------
108:   Function EncodeBase64 (strClearString)
...:
116:           intClearStringLen = Len (strClearString)
117:
...:
```

```
121:          For intIndice = 1 To intClearStringLen Step 3
...:
158:              FireEvent "Debug", varTempQuadBlock
159:
160:                  strBase64String = strBase64String & varTempQuadBlock
161:          Next
162:
163:          EncodeBase64 = strBase64String
164:
165:   End Function
166:
167:   ]]>
168:   </script>
169:
170:</component>
```

Sample 1.38   *Base64 Windows Script File capturing events*

```
 1:<?xml version="1.0"?>
 .:
 8:<package>
 9:
10:   <job id="vbs">
11:    <script language="VBScript">
12:    <![CDATA[
13:        Option Explicit
..:
19:        Wscript.Echo "In VBScript:"
20:
21:        strData = "This is my test string!"
22:
23:        Set objBase64 = WScript.CreateObject("Base64.WSC", "Base64_")
24:
25:        Wscript.Echo "Original: '" & strData & "'"
26:        strEncoded = objBase64.Encode (strData)
27:        Wscript.Echo "Encoded:  '" & strEncoded & "'"
28:        Wscript.Echo "Decoded:  '" & objBase64.Decode (strEncoded) & "'"
29:
30:        ' -------------------------------------------------------------------
31:        ' Event Handler
32:        Sub Base64_Debug(Value)
33:            WScript.Echo "Debug: " & Value
34:        End Sub
35:
36:    ]]>
37:    </script>
38:   </job>
39:
40:   <job id="js">
41:    <script language="JScript">
42:    <![CDATA[
..:
47:        WScript.Echo ("In JScript:");
48:
49:        strData = "This is my test string!";
```

```
50:
51:         objBase64 = WScript.CreateObject("Base64.WSC", "Base64_");
52:
53:         WScript.Echo ("Original: '" + strData + "'");
54:         strEncoded = objBase64.Encode (strData);
55:         WScript.Echo ("Encoded:  '" + strEncoded + "'");
56:         WScript.Echo ("Decoded:  '" + objBase64.Decode (strEncoded) + "'");
57:
58:         // ------------------------------------------------------------------
59:         // Event Handler
60:         function Base64_Debug(Value)
61:             {
62:             WScript.Echo ("Debug: " + Value);
63:             }64:
65:     ]]>
66:     </script>
67:
68:  </job>
69:</package>
```

This modification is made in four steps:

1. In the <public></public> section of the Windows Script File, the following lines are added (Sample 1.37, lines 26 to 28):

    ```
    <event name="Debug">
            <parameter name="Value" />
    </event>
    ```

    This new element in the section defines the event handler function name and the variable name to be used as the parameter to the event handler function. The event handler function is added in the script invoking the Windows Script Component—in this case, the Windows Script File presented in Sample 1.38.

2. In the coding and decoding functions of the Windows Script Component (Sample 1.37), the following lines are added in several places (lines 53, 79, 97, and 158).

    ```
    FireEvent "Debug", ...
    ```

    To fire the event, the FireEvent() function is used. Two parameters are needed: the event name defined in the <event></event> section and the value assigned to the parameter named Value. In the example, two messages will be fired from the Windows Script Component: an event message in case of an invalid base64 input string (lines 53 and 79) and a message for each piece of information converted (line 97 for the decoding and line 158 for the coding).

3.   In the Windows Script File (Sample 1.38), the following line is modified from:

```
Set objBase64 = Wscript.CreateObject("Base64.WSC")
```

to

```
Set objBase64 = Wscript.CreateObject("Base64.WSC", "Base64_")
```

This concerns the VBScript statements; for the JScript statement, the line

```
objBase64 = new ActiveXObject("Base64.WSC");
```

is changed to

```
objBase64 = WScript.CreateObject("Base64.WSC", "Base64_");
```

With this **Base64** object instantiation, a reference between the event handler and the event name (defined in the Windows Script Component) is performed. This task is completed during the **Base64** object creation by adding a new parameter, which is the "main" label used for the event handler function—in this case, "Base64_."

In the initial JScript code, the instantiation of the **Base64** object was made with the standard JScript library function (new ActiveX). To support the WSC event sink, the **Base64** object must be instantiated with the *CreateObject* method of the **WScript** object from WSH. The *CreateObject* method lets you specify the additional parameter.

4.   In the Windows Script File (Sample 1.38), an event handler function is added in the VBScript version

```
' Event Handler
sub ADSearch_Debug(Value)
    WScript.Echo "Debug: " & Value
end sub
```

and in the JScript version:

```
// Event Handler
function Base64_Debug(Value)
        {
        WScript.Echo ("Debug: " + Value);
        }
```

This last change is the addition of the event-handler function. This is a standard function definition. The only restriction is that the function must match the previous definitions made for the event. The function must be named by combining the names given at steps 1 and 3 (Event name and main function name). The parameter of the function is referenced as given during step 1.

Executing the scripts with events will display the following output (in VBScript or JScript versions)

```
Microsoft (R) Windows Script Host Version 5.6
Copyright (C) Microsoft Corporation 1996-2000. All rights reserved.
In VBScript:
Original: 'This is my test string!'
Debug: VGhp
Debug: cyBp
Debug: cyBt
Debug: eSB0
Debug: ZXN0
Debug: IHN0
Debug: cmlu
Debug: ZyE=
Encoded:  'VGhpcyBpcyBteSB0ZXN0IHN0cmluZyE='
Debug: T
Debug: h
Debug: i
Debug: s
Debug:
Debug: i
Debug: s
Debug:
Debug: m
Debug: y
Debug:
Debug: t
Debug: e
Debug: s
Debug: t
Debug:
Debug: s
Debug: t
Debug: r
Debug: i
Debug: n
Debug: g
Debug: !
Decoded:  'This is my test string!'
```

As we can see, we have the normal display output of coded and decoded strings and in between, the coding and decoding base64 functions trigger an event for each piece of data converted. Each event displays a string starting with "Debug:" followed by the converted data.

1.7.4   Using a type library

As WSH offers the capability to use various objects available in a Windows
system, it can be useful to reference the constants defined in these objects.
Usually, type library information is available in .tlb, .olb, and .dll files.
Using type libraries implies including a reference to the library in the script.
Accessing the type library information can be done with a simple reference
or while creating the object instance. For this purpose, the WSH XML
schema implements two tags: <reference> and <objects>. Let's take the easy
sample of creating a file. This sample will be reused later while exploring the
remote script execution (see Sample 1.39).

Sample 1.39   *A simple script using constants to create a file*

```
 1:<?xml version="1.0"?>
 .:
 8:<package>
 9:  <job>
10:    <script language="JScript">
11:      var ForReading = 1, ForWriting = 2, ForAppending = 8;
12:      var TristateFalse = 0, TristateTrue = -1, TristateUseDefault = -2;
13:
14:      var strFileName = "c:\\RemoteScript.txt";
15:
16:      var objFileSystem = new ActiveXObject("Scripting.FileSystemObject");
17:
18:      var objfile = objFileSystem.OpenTextFile(strFileName, ForAppending, true, TristateFalse);
19:
20:      objfile.WriteLine(new Date);
21:
22:      objfile.Close();
23:
24:      WScript.Sleep (5000);
25:
26:    </script>
27:  </job>
28:</package>
```

<reference> tag:

As done during the LOG file creation of the **WshScript.vbs**, to create a file,
a reference to the **Scripting.FileSystemObject** must be made (line 16 in
Sample 1.39). The particularity of this file creation sample is that it creates
a file if the file does not exist; otherwise, the file is appended (line 18). To
perform this, the script must use a method other than the *CreateTextFile*
method. The *OpenTextFile* method is perfect, but it requires some constants
defined at lines 11 and 12.

As the script is a Windows Script File (.wsf), instead of defining variables
containing constants (lines 11 and 12), it is possible to reference these con-

stants directly by using the type library of the file system objects. This can be done as shown in Sample 1.40 with the <reference> XML tag.

Sample 1.40   *Referencing a type library from a Windows Script File*

```
 1:<?xml version="1.0"?>
 .:
 8:<package>
 9:  <job>
10:    <reference object="Scripting.FileSystemObject"/>
11:    <script language="JScript">
12:      var strFileName = "c:\\RemoteScript.txt";
13:
14:      var objFileSystem = new ActiveXObject("Scripting.FileSystemObject");
15:
16:      var objfile = objFileSystem.OpenTextFile(strFileName, ForAppending, true, TristateFalse);
17:
18:      objfile.WriteLine(new Date);
19:
20:      objfile.Close();
21:
22:      WScript.Sleep (5000);
23:
24:    </script>
25:  </job>
26:</package>
```

Now, this object is instantiated at line 14. Note that the variable containing the constants are not part of the script any more, simply because the constants used at line 18 are coming from the type library reference of line 10.

<object> tag:

As this script code uses the file system object why not combine the type library reference and the object instantiation? This is possible with the <object> XML tag as shown in Sample 1.41.

Sample 1.41   *Creating an object while referencing its type library*

```
 1:<?xml version="1.0"?>
 .:
 8:<package>
 9:  <job>
10:    <object progid="Scripting.FileSystemObject" id="objFileSystem" reference="true"/>
11:    <script language="JScript">
12:      var strFileName = "c:\\RemoteScript.txt";
13:
14:      var objfile = objFileSystem.OpenTextFile(strFileName, ForAppending, true, TristateFalse);
15:
16:      objfile.WriteLine(new Date);
17:
18:      objfile.Close();
```

```
19:
20:      WScript.Sleep (5000);
21:
22:    </script>
23:  </job>
24:</package>
```

This sample replaces the <reference> XML tag by the <object> XML tag at line 10. The basic principle is the same as the <reference> XML tag; the ProgID is used to reference the object. Of course, as the purpose is to instantiate an object used in the script, the id parameter contains the name of the variable used in the script to represent the object. The reference parameter mentions that the type library must be loaded. It is mandatory to define the reference parameter as True in the XML tag; otherwise, no reference to the type library is made. The rest of the script uses exactly the same logic, except that no object instantiation is performed by the JavaScript code itself. This makes sense because the XML tag performs the object instantiation.

Therefore, as shown in the script sample, it is possible to avoid the use of the CreateObject statement from VBScript and new ActiveX-

Figure 1.8
*Creating the type
library with the
Windows Explorer
context menu.*

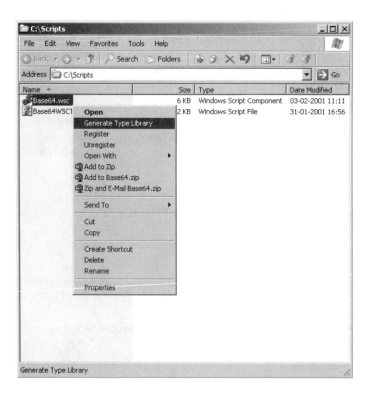

Object from JavaScript. Of course, if the script needs to work with event sinks coming from a Windows Script Component, the Wscript.CreateObject statement must be used instead. Now, with large object models defining collections of objects and constants, proceeding this way is very useful because it avoids redefining the required constants, as shown in the very first sample (**WshScript.vbs**) presented in this chapter. This is very useful when working with Windows Management Instrumentation.

1.7.5 Creating a type library

It is possible to generate a type library for a Windows Script Component. By doing so, your component will support the IntelliSense drop-down lists when you use it from a full-featured development tool like Visual Basic. There are two ways to perform this: with the Windows Explorer context menu (Figure 1.8) or with a script (see Sample 1.42).

Sample 1.42   *A script to create the type library*

```
 . :
 6:Set objTypeLibrary = WScript.CreateObject("Scriptlet.TypeLib")
 7:
 8:objTypeLibrary.AddURL "Base64.wsc"
 9:objTypeLibrary.Path = "Base64.tlb"
10:objTypeLibrary.Doc = "Base64 Type Library"
11:objTypeLibrary.Name = "Base64TLB"
12:objTypeLibrary.Write
```

1.7.6 Using a resource

A type library provides access to constants defined in an object model used by a script. Although it can be useful to create some constants or variables defining data used in a script, there are some kinds of data for which it is not easy to assign to constants or variables. WSH offers an XML tag that may help in such circumstances. Sample 1.41 requests the current system date (line 16) to save it in the created file. Now, we can imagine saving something other than a system date. For instance, the script could create HTML text. Why HTML text? Well, proposing to save a simple string does not show the real interest of the <resource> XML tag. However, HTML text is a bit more complex than a simple string, and this will illustrate perfectly the advantage of the <resource> tag.

Sample 1.43   *Using resources to create an HTML file*

```
 1:<?xml version="1.0"?>
 .:
 8:<package>
 9:  <job>
10:  <resource id="MyHTMLText">
11:    <![CDATA[
12:
13:    <!DOCTYPE HTML PUBLIC "-//W3C//DTD HTML 4.0 Transitional//EN">
14:    <HTML><HEAD>
15:    <META http-equiv=Content-Type content="text/html; charset=iso-8859-1">
16:    <META content="MSHTML 5.50.4916.2300" name=GENERATOR></HEAD>
17:    <BODY>
18:    <DIV> </DIV>
19:    <P><FONT face=Tahoma
20:    size=2>_____<BR><B></B></FONT><B><FONT
21:    face=Tahoma color=#0000ff size=2>Alain Lissoir</FONT></B><FONT face=Tahoma
22:    color=#000000 size=2> -</FONT><B><FONT face=Tahoma size=2> </FONT><FONT
23:    face=Tahoma color=#000000 size=2>Technology Consultant</FONT></B><FONT
24:    face=Tahoma size=2><BR></FONT><B><FONT
25:    face="Futura Bk" color=#0000ff size=2>HPCI Technology Leadership Group</FONT></B>
26:    </P>
27:    <P><B><I><FONT face=Impact color=#ff0000 size=5>Compaq</FONT><FONT face=Impact
28:    size=5></FONT> <FONT face=Tahoma color=#ff0000 size=2>Computer
29:    BVBA/SPRL,</FONT></I> <FONT face="Futura Bk" color=#0000ff size=2>now part of
30:    the new</FONT> <FONT face="Futura Bk" color=#0000ff
31:    size=4>HP</FONT></B><BR>
32:    <B><FONT face="Futura Bk" color=#0000ff size=2>email:
33:    alain.lissoir@hp.com</FONT></B><BR><BR>
34:    </BODY></HTML>
35:
36:    ]]>
37:  </resource>
38:
39:    <object progid="Scripting.FileSystemObject" id="objFileSystem" reference="true"/>
40:    <script language="JScript">
41:      var strFileName = "c:\\MyHTMLText.htm";
42:
43:      var objfile = objFileSystem.OpenTextFile(strFileName, ForAppending, true, TristateFalse);
44:
45:      objfile.WriteLine(getResource("MyHTMLText"));
46:
47:      objfile.Close();
48:
49:      WScript.Sleep (5000);
50:
51:    </script>
52:  </job>
53:</package>
```

Sample 1.43 does not contain big changes compared with Sample 1.41 except for the insertion of the HTML data. At first glance, the HTML data is a bit messy. This is intentional. The HTML blob is derived from the e-mail signature configured in my current Outlook 2000. This sample just includes (as is) the HTML text created by Outlook. By using the getResource() function (line 45), the script binds the HTML data delimited by the <resource> XML tag (lines 10 to 37) to the *WriteLine* method. Note the presence of the id parameter in the <resource> XML tag (line 10) to link the HTML data with the getResource() function (line 45). As HTML text may contain illegal characters, to guarantee XML 1.0 compliance, the HTML data is enclosed in a <![CDATA[]]> section (lines 11 to 36).

1.8   Controlling the WSH script execution

When the I LOVE YOU virus arrived, the world discovered the inconvenience of having a too-versatile scripting technology in the Windows platforms and related products. After the wide distribution of the virus through e-mail systems, which was unfortunately started by users receiving a nice "I LOVE YOU" e-mail, many administrators began to think about a good way to avoid such situations in the future. The Windows.NET Server WSH version includes several registry keys controlling WSH behavior. Either set of keys can be defined at the machine level (HKEY_LOCAL_MACHINE), or at the user level (HKEY_CURRENT_USER). They are located in

```
HKEY_CURRENT_USER\Software\Microsoft\Windows Script Host\Settings
```

For the machine settings, they are located in

```
HKEY_LOCAL_MACHINE\Software\Microsoft\Windows Script Host\Settings
```

Some of these registry keys are accessible through Windows policy definitions. Now let's examine the features available through the configuration of these registry keys.

1.8.1   Enabling/Disabling WSH

A registry key setting can enable or disable WSH. The name of the key is Enabled. It must be set to 1 (enabled) or 0 (disabled). By default, when WSH 5.6 is installed under Windows 2000 or before, the key is set to 1. Under Windows XP and Windows.NET Server, by default the key doesn't exist, which enables WSH (equivalent to Enabled=1). When WSH 5.6 is installed under Windows 2000 or before, the Enabled key is a REG_SZ key. If the key must be created under Windows XP or Windows.NET Server, it must be created as a REG_DWORD key (see Figure 1.9). If WSH is disabled and if a script is started, the following message is displayed:

```
Windows Script Host access is disabled on this machine. Contact your
administrator for details.
```

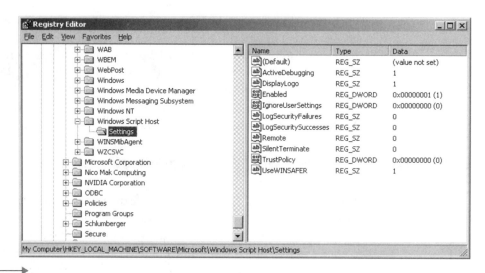

Figure 1.9   *The WSH registry keys as visible under Windows.NET Server.*

By default, the user settings have precedence on the machine settings, but this situation can be reversed. WSH implements another registry key called "IgnoreUserSettings." Under Windows 2000 and before, when WSH 5.6 is installed, this key is set to 0 in the machine settings by default. Under Windows XP and Windows.NET Server, this key does not exist by default, which sets the precedence to the user settings. Under Windows XP and Windows.NET Server, if the key must be created, it must be created as a REG_DWORD key (see Figure 1.9). For example, if you disable WSH at the user level (Disabled=0) and if you set the registry key "IgnoreUserSettings" to 1 at the machine level, it is possible to run a WSH script. In such a case, the machine settings have precedence over the user settings (provided that the machine settings allow WSH to run). Note that only the "IgnoreUserSettings" key at the machine level must be changed.

1.8.2   Tracing the WSH script startups

When a script is started, by default no trace is saved in the system event log. Again, WSH provides two REG_SZ registry keys to save a trace in the system event log. One key ("LogSecuritySuccesses") is used to trace the successful WSH script startups, and the other ("LogSecurityFailures") is used to trace the WSH script startup failures. By default, both keys are set to 0 (see Figure 1.9).

Let's take a sample. Imagine that we work at the user settings level and that there is no machine setting precedence to keep the situation clear. If, at

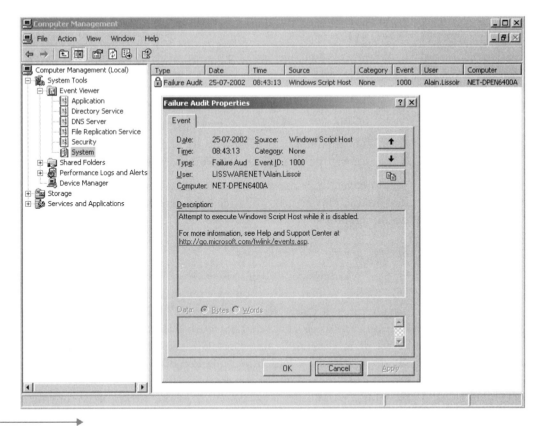

Figure 1.10   *The WSH Security Failure system event log trace.*

the user level, WSH is disabled and "LogSecurityFailures" is set to 1, if a user tries to start a script, a trace in the system event log will be saved as shown in Figure 1.10.

In the same way, to save a trace each time a WSH script is started, the "LogSecuritySuccesses" must be set to 1.

1.8.3   **Running scripts from trusted origins**

Even if the ability to disable WSH can be useful, the all-or-nothing aspect of this feature is not ideal. You may have situations where scripts must be run to perform some management tasks even though users are not allowed to run scripts. Basically, scripts performing management tasks are developed or distributed by administrators. This means that those scripts are produced and distributed by a trusted source. On the other hand, it is not desired that scripts coming from a source other than the administrators be executed. For instance, scripts coming via e-mail may come from anywhere (like the I LOVE YOU virus).

WSH offers the ability to digitally sign scripts. This has two practical advantages:

1.   The script signer can be identified by the presence of a digital signature.

2.   The digital signature protects the script from tampering while it is transferred through the network (via mail, file copy, etc.)

Moreover, from an operational point of view, WSH is able to run scripts that are digitally signed while rejecting scripts that do not contain a valid digital signature.

1.8.3.1   Script signing requirements

Under Windows, the technology that provides the code signing is Microsoft's Authenticode coupled with an infrastructure of trusted entities, usually called a Public Key Infrastructure (PKI). Authenticode is based on industry standards. It allows software publishers to include information about themselves and their code with their programs through the use of digital signatures. While Authenticode cannot guarantee that signed code is safe to run, it is the mechanism by which users are informed as to whether the software publisher is participating in the infrastructure of trusted entities (PKI). Thus, Authenticode serves the needs of both software publishers and users.

We will not focus on the details of the Authenticode and PKI here; however, in order to be able to sign scripts trusted by other parties, some requirements must be met. Let's examine these requirements.

1.8.3.2   Obtaining a digital signature for code signing

First of all, as a script writer you must obtain a certificate. A certificate is a set of data that completely identifies an entity (in such a case, you!). The authority issuing the certificate is called a certification authority (CA). The certificate is issued only after that authority has verified your identity. The data set includes your public cryptographic key. When you sign a script with your private key, the other parties can use your public key to verify your identity. Your public key can be retrieved from the certificate either contained in the script or possibly available elsewhere in a directory service.

To obtain a certificate from a CA, you must meet the criteria for either a commercial or an individual publishing certificate and submit these credentials to either a certification authority or a local registration authority.

If you want to get more information about the process to obtain a certificate for code signing, you can refer to the following URLs: http://www.verisign.com or http://www.thawte.com. For more information on Authenticode or other Microsoft Security technologies, please visit http://www.microsoft.com/security/default.asp. Keep in mind that this certification authority is not free. Based on the security practices in your company, make sure that you are not in conflict with the rules in place. Maybe your company is already using a PKI. Does your company already own an external CA for its employees?

If there is nothing available to sign your scripts, as a Windows administrator or developer you can obtain a certificate by using the Windows PKI. Of course, keep in mind that it is for testing purposes only! Installing your own PKI without respecting the practices related to the PKI implementation may get you into serious trouble. Moreover, using your own PKI will not make you trusted by other parties because your CA will be unknown.

Now, for testing purposes, you can install a Windows PKI in your lab and get your public/private key pair for code signing. If you run your signed scripts in the lab infrastructure, there is no problem recognizing the signature. As Windows comes with a certificate server, please refer to the Windows PKI documentation to perform its installation.

Once the Microsoft certificate server is in place, you must submit your certificate for code signing. This can be done through a Web interface pointing to http://www.MyCaServer.com/certsrv or from the MMC console by loading the Certificates snap-in. However, as the purpose is to digitally sign scripts, it is likely that the code-signing certificate template is not yet installed in your Microsoft PKI. This template is not available by default under Windows 2000 or Windows.NET Server; however, under Windows 2000, the so-called Administrator template has the code-signing feature enabled. You can install the code-signing certificate template by loading the Certificate Authority snap-in in the MMC console and select the Certificate Template to Issue option from the Certificate Template container, as shown in Figure 1.11.

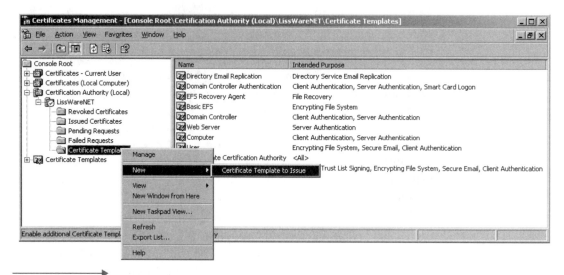

Figure 1.11   *Installing the code-signing certificate template.*

Next, select the code-signing certificate template in the template list, as shown in Figure 1.12.

To obtain a certificate for code signing from the certificate snap-in (installed for the current user), you must select the "Request New Certificate" option from the "Personal" container, as shown in Figure 1.13 .

Figure 1.12
The certificate
template list.

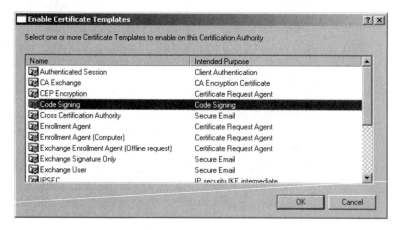

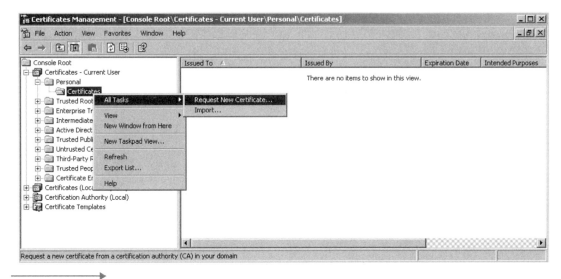

Figure 1.13   *Requesting a new certificate.*

Of course, as you are the person who needs the certificate for your test environment, make sure that you perform this task with your credentials. Next, select the code-signing certificate from the list. If you want to be warned each time a process accesses your certificate, select the "Advanced" option, as shown in Figure 1.14. This will enable you to select a specific option.

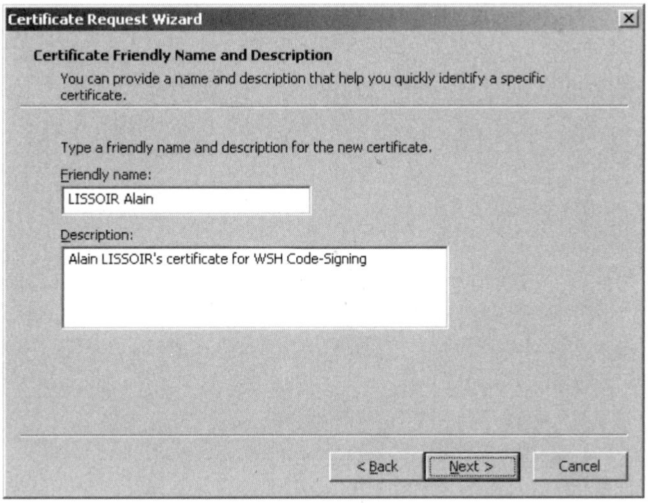

Figure 1.14
Define a friendly name for the code-signing certificate.

Figure 1.15
*Enabling the strong
private key
protection.*

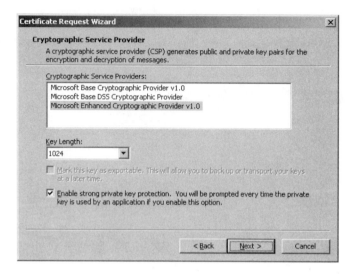

The next screen to appear is the screen displaying the cryptographic service providers (see Figure 1.15). On this screen, you can enable the strong private key protection. This option will prompt you each time an application accesses the private key.

For the last step, you must choose a friendly name for your certificate, as shown in Figure 1.16.

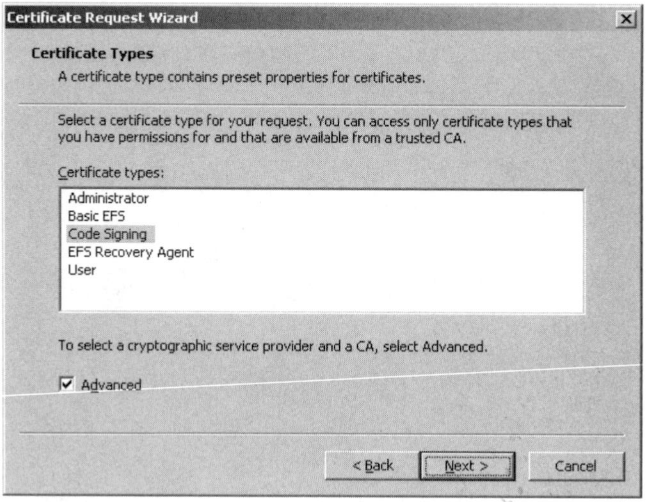

Figure 1.16
*Choosing the code-
signing certificate.*

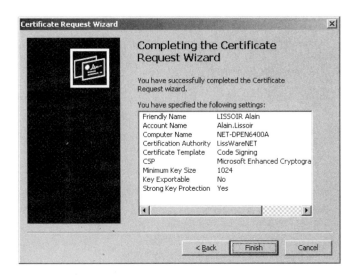

Figure 1.17
The code-signing certificate request summary.

Once completed, the wizard should show a summary similar to Figure 1.17.

Once completed, you can use the Certificates snap-in to examine the user certificate store and find your certificate, as shown in Figure 1.18.

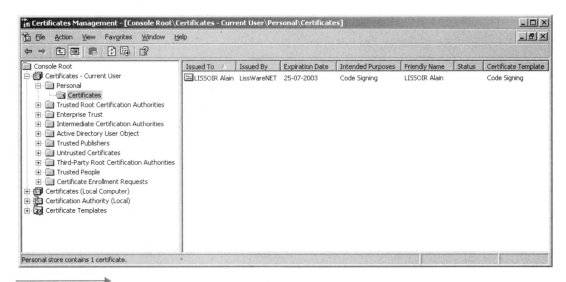

Figure 1.18   *Looking into the certificate store.*

Figure 1.19
*Looking the
certificate.*

Click on your certificate to get more detailed information, as shown in Figure 1.19.

Now, everything is in place to perform script code signing.

1.8.3.3   *Signing scripts*

Basically, there are different ways to digitally sign your scripts. Let's examine the easiest one. The first method is to use the Digital Signature Wizard.

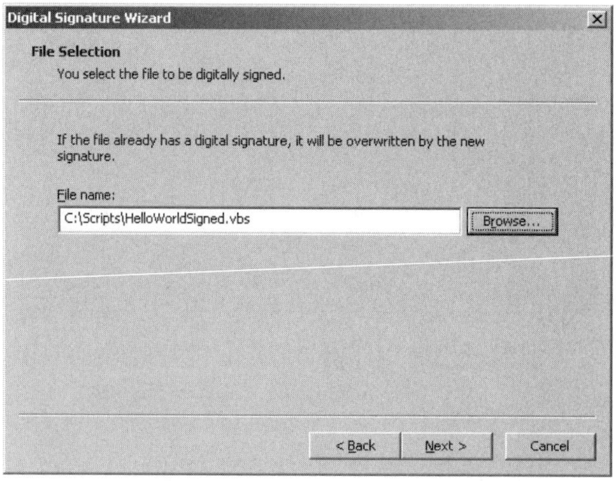

Figure 1.20
*Selecting the script
to sign.*

Figure 1.21
*The Digital
Signature Wizard.*

This wizard is provided with the Microsoft Authenticode tools located at http://msdn.microsoft.com/downloads/sample.asp?url=/MSDN-FILES/ 027/000/219/msdncompositedoc.xml. From the downloaded package, you will find a tool called **Signcode.exe**. Start it, and a screen similar to Figure 1.20 should appear.

The first step in the Wizard is to provide the script to be signed (see Figure 1.21).

Next, choose the typical procedure (see Figure 1.22). The advanced procedure allows you to select the location of the private key, the hash algorithm used for the digital signature and the list of certificates that you

Figure 1.22
*Selecting the typical
procedure.*

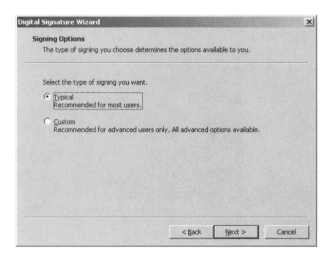

Figure 1.23
*Selecting the code-
signing certificate.*

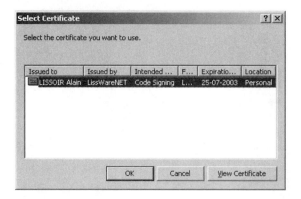

Figure 1.23
*Selecting the code-
signing certificate.*

would like to include in your signature. As we want to make things easy, we can use the typical procedure. But again, make sure that these choices are in phase with your company's security policies.

Next, select the certificate you would like to use for the signature (see Figure 1.23). Normally, you would select the one you created before. At this step, you have the option to view the certificate. If you have many certificates, you must choose the one providing the code-signing functionalities.

Next, you should provide a timestamp (see Figure 1.24). As a well-established security rule, digital certificates should expire. Usually, certificates expire one year after they are issued. However, it is likely that your scripts are intended to have a lifetime longer than one year. To avoid having to

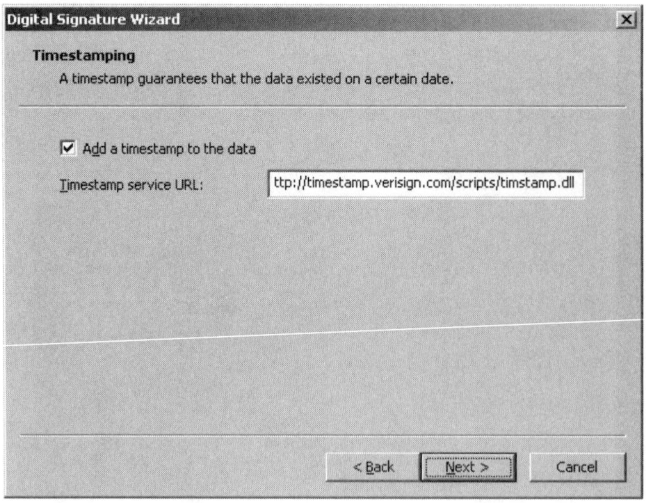

Figure 1.24
*Timestamping the
digital signature.*

resign software every time your certificate expires, you should timestamp your script with a timestamping service. Now, when you sign, a hash of your code will be sent to the timestamping service to be timestamped. So, when your script is executed, clients will be able to distinguish between the following:

- Code signed with an expired certificate. This code should NOT be trusted.

- Code signed with a certificate that was valid at the time the code was signed, but which has subsequently expired. This code SHOULD be trusted.

This means that you will not need to worry about resigning code when your digital ID expires if you make use of a timestamp. For instance, Verisign is offering a free timestamping service to all VeriSign Commercial and Individual Software Publishers. The wizard expects you to provide URL for the timestamping service. For instance, if we use the one from VeriSign, the URL will be http://timestamp.verisign.com/scripts/timstamp.dll. Note that it is not mandatory to timestamp your signature for testing purposes, and until the certificate has expired, this is not a problem.

Once all information has been entered in the wizard, you are ready to sign your script (see Figure 1.25). If you specified a timestamping service, make sure that your Internet connection is working; otherwise, you won't be able to sign your script.

Figure 1.25
The wizard completion will sign the script.

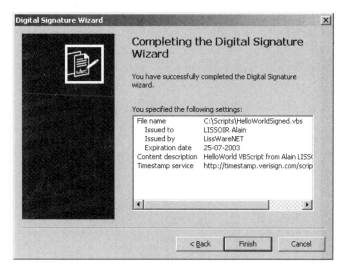

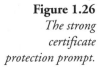

Figure 1.26
*The strong
certificate
protection prompt.*

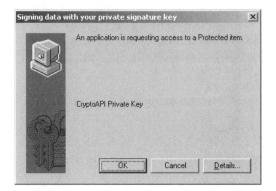

If strong certificate protection was enabled during the private key creation (see Figure 1.15), you are prompted to confirm the certificate access, as Figure 1.26 shows.

1.8.3.4 *Signature implementation*

Once the script has been signed, the digital signature is part of the script. As the script is an ASCII file, how is this signature implemented? Well, the signature is base64-coded and placed in some commented-out script lines. Based on the extension used by the script, the Digital Signature Wizard will add the signature accordingly. Samples 1.44 to 1.46 show how the signature is added to the script.

Sample 1.44   *The digital signature in a .vbs script*

```
 .:
 8:Dim strMessage
 9:
10:strMessage = "Hello world!"
11:
12:Wscript.Echo strMessage
13:
14:'' SIG '' Begin signature block
15:'' SIG '' MIIRKQYJKoZIhvcNAQcCoIIRGjCCERYCAQExCzAJBgUr
16:'' SIG '' DgMCGgUAMGcGCisGAQQBgjcCAQSgWTBXMDIGCisGAQQB
17:'' SIG '' gjcCAR4wJAIBAQQQTvApFpkntU2P5azhDxfrqwIBAAIB
 ..:
146:'' SIG '' YgZUxUsc/aDeL1SVAEv0o0/jemrJnVSW2vBnjB4OaGG1
147:'' SIG '' s1t8ocWlRUefHOdMIZ7Bssx+SOnf+PUv81Evl9+aZCxK
148:'' SIG '' tgqZ4DWO88c=
149:'' SIG '' End signature block
```

Sample 1.45 *The digital signature in a .js script*

```
 .:var strMessage;
  9:
 10:strMessage = "Hello world!";
 11:
 12:WScript.Echo (strMessage);
 13:
 14:// SIG // Begin signature block
 15:// SIG // MIIRLQYJKoZIhvcNAQcCoIIRHjCCERoCAQExCzAJBgUr
 16:// SIG // DgMCGgUAMGcGCisGAQQBgjcCAQSgWTBXMDIGCisGAQQB
 17:// SIG // gjcCAR4wJAIBAQQQEODJBs441BGiowAQS9NQkAIBAAIB
 ..:
146:// SIG // dYck2W5xcIycahTnWsAt+jDjPVpSIeOsotXfTcMl82QJ
147:// SIG // a9TgqM7DGOOzKpaOUHodDDGxs71RqrGMU8rQO4f+6fF4
148:// SIG // g/quZ43MghAZ7/Sc
149:// SIG // End signature block
```

Sample 1.46 *The digital signature in a .wsf script*

```
 1:<?xml version="1.0"?>
 ..:
 12:<package>
 13:    <job id="vbs">
 14:        <script language="VBScript">
 15:        <![CDATA[
 16:
 17:        Dim strMessage
 18:
 19:        strMessage = "Hello world in VB Script!"
 20:
 21:        Wscript.Echo strMessage
 22:
 23:        ]]>
 24:        </script>
 25:    </job>
 26:
 27:    <job id="js">
 28:        <script language="JScript">
 29:        <![CDATA[
 30:
 31:        var strMessage;
 32:
 33:        strMessage = "Hello world in Java Script!";
 34:
 35:        WScript.Echo (strMessage);
 36:
 37:        ]]>
 38:        </script>
 39:    </job>
 40:
```

```
 41:
 42:<signature>
 43:** SIG ** MIIRMwYJKoZIhvcNAQcCoIIRJDCCESACAQExCzAJBgUr
 44:** SIG ** DgMCGgUAMGcGCisGAQQBgjcCAQSgWTBXMDIGCisGAQQB
 45:** SIG ** gjcCAR4wJAIBAQQQcAVhGs441BGiowAQS9NQkAIBAAIB
 46:** SIG ** AAIBAAIBAAIBADAhMAkGBSsOAwIaBQAEFDsOK5gjOXoJ
 ..:
173:** SIG ** 9ScznWWRblFZZp8Bf3N047QaXBjWNh1gmkXDCeMKrknw
174:** SIG ** 1QrgVNlY9e5ZcXoi/3dIYHP5wowDRCeDd2ApGVmZ4mMS
175:** SIG ** 5fQNn88ofJZAKOEeuJHBPyZAoq4AMHU17ExR+FO+grmB
176:** SIG ** Ne/NSa1zxi7/zChl0hjBWngM
177:</signature>
178:</package>
```

Note the new section added by the wizard to
encapsulate the digital signature.

1.8.3.5   Using script to sign you scripts

WSH provides an extension, implemented by WshExt.dll, to digitally sign
scripts programmatically. In the WSH Object model, there is an object with
the ProgID **Scripting.Signer** exposing methods to digitally sign and verify
digital signatures. With the combination of this object and other WSH
facilities, such as XML parsing to read command-line parameters, it is possible to have a basic script performing the code signing (e.g., the Microsoft
Wizard). Basically, there are two required parameters: the script name and
the certificate name. This is the purpose of the next sample.

Sample 1.47 instantiates the **Scripting.Signer** object at line 26 and
retrieves the parameters from the command line with the help of the WSH
XML tags from lines 28 to 30. Next, the *SignFile* method of the script
signer object is invoked (line 32). There is no need for the script writer to
manage the signature placement in the script to be signed. The script signer
object handles this on behalf of the script extension.

Sample 1.47   *A command-line script performing script signing*

```
 1:<?xml version="1.0"?>
 .:
 8:<package>
 9:  <job>
10:    <runtime>
11:      <named name="file" helpstring="the file to sign"
                                 required="true" type="string"/>
12:      <named name="cert" helpstring="the name of the signing certificate"
                                 required="true" type="string"/>
13:      <named name="store" helpstring="the name of the certificate store"
                                 required="false" type="string"/>
14:    </runtime>
15:
16:    <script language="JScript">
```

```
17:      <![CDATA[
18:        var WshScriptingSigner, strFile, strCert, strStore;
19:
20:        if (!(WScript.Arguments.Named.Exists("cert") && WScript.Arguments.Named.Exists("file")))
21:           {
22:           WScript.Arguments.ShowUsage();
23:           WScript.Quit();
24:           }
25:
26:        WshScriptingSigner = new ActiveXObject("Scripting.Signer");
27:
28:        strFile  = WScript.Arguments.Named("file");
29:        strCert  = WScript.Arguments.Named("cert");
30:        strStore = WScript.Arguments.Named("store");
31:
32:        WshScriptingSigner.SignFile(strFile, strCert, strStore);
33:
34:     ]]>
35:     </script>
36:   </job>
37:</package>
```

This script can be used from the command line as follows:

```
C:>SignScript.wsf /file:MyScript.vbs /cert:"MyCertificateName"
```

You will notice that we don't specify the **/Store** parameter. As specified on line 13, this switch is not required to execute the script. Of course, it can be specified, but, by default, the script retrieves the certificate from the Personal Store. In this example, there is no need to sign a script with a key other than the one stored in the Personal Store of the user executing the signing script. This is why this parameter is optional. If you want to be explicit and specify the name of the Personal Store, you must use the keyword "My." The command line will be as follows:

```
C:>SignScript.wsf /file:MyScript.vbs /cert:"MyCertificateName" /
store:"My"
```

We have seen before that WSH has a drag-and-drop feature. This is the perfect application in which to use this feature. If we drag-and-drop a file on the **SignScript.wsf** file, the dropped filename will appear as a parameter of the command line. This is perfect. But what about the certificate name? If someone is dropping a file, how can the script retrieve the certificate name of the person? Well, here a trick must be used! In general, the certificate has the name of the user. As the script runs in the user context of the user dropping the file, it will be easy to get the user's name. The problem is that the certificate name is not built from the userID of the user, but from the name of the user. This is where we will use a small piece of ADSI code. Under Windows 2000 and later versions, ADSI exposes an object called **AdsSystemInfo**. This object exposes a property containing the *distinguishedName* of the currently logged user. Knowing this, the script will be

able to look in Active Directory to retrieve the name of the user. This functionality is realized in Sample 1.48.

Sample 1.48   *Digitally signing a script with WSH drag-and-drop support*

```
 1:<?xml version="1.0"?>
 . :
 8:<package>
 9:  <job>
10:    <runtime>
11:      <unnamed name="script" helpstring="the script to sign" required="true" type="string" />
12:    </runtime>
13:
14:    <script language="JScript">
15:    <![CDATA[
16:      var WshScriptingSigner, objSysInfo, objUser, strFile, strCert;
17:
18:      var WshArguments = WScript.Arguments;
19:
20:      if (WshArguments.Unnamed.Count == 0)
21:        {
22:        WshArguments.ShowUsage();
23:        WScript.Quit();
24:        }
25:
26:      WshScriptingSigner = new ActiveXObject("Scripting.Signer");
27:
28:      strFile  = WshArguments.Unnamed.Item(0);
29:
30:      objSysinfo = new ActiveXObject("ADSystemInfo");
31:      objUser = GetObject("GC://" + objSysinfo.UserName)
32:      strCert = objUser.Get("Name")
33:
34:      WshScriptingSigner.SignFile(strFile, strCert);
35:
36:    ]]>
37:    </script>
38:  </job>
39:</package>
```

The logic of this script is exactly the same as that of the previous one.
The differences reside in the parameters expected from the command line.
The script name is now an unnamed parameter (line 11), and the real user
name, which is also the certificate name, is retrieved with ADSI (lines 30 to
32). With these changes, any WSH script dropped on the signing script by
Windows Explorer will launch the signing script and perform a digital signing of the dropped WSH script.

1.8.3.6   *The trust policy*

Now that we can sign scripts, we must ensure that the WSH Host checks
the validity of the signature added to the script. By default, WSH does not
check any signature and will run scripts that do not have a signature or

scripts that do have a signature, even if it is invalid. This means that there is no security mechanism; signing your scripts in such a context is useless. Depending on the Windows version used, there are different mechanisms to enforce security. Under Windows.NET Server, the software restriction policies are used for this purpose (formerly known as WinSafer). With other platforms, such as Windows 2000 or Windows NT, some registry keys must be modified.

1.8.3.6.1   Under Windows 2000 and previous versions

To activate the security feature under Windows 2000 or Windows NT 4.0, a registry key value must be modified. This registry key value is located in the registry in the same place as other WSH registry keys. For user settings, this key is located in

```
HKEY_CURRENT_USER\Software\Microsoft\Windows Script Host\Settings
```

For the machine settings, this key is located in

```
HKEY_LOCAL_MACHINE\Software\Microsoft\Windows Script Host\Settings
```

The REG_SZ registry key value is called "TrustPolicy." By default, its value is equal to 0. The key can have a value of 1 or 2 based on the policy choice made. By setting the registry key to 1, the WSH Host verifies the presence of the digital signature and its validity. Every time a script starts, the user is prompted with a message. The message is determined by the state of the signature in the script; possible states are as follows:

- The started script does not contain a signature (Figure 1.27).

Figure 1.27
Message when the digital signature is not present in the startup script.

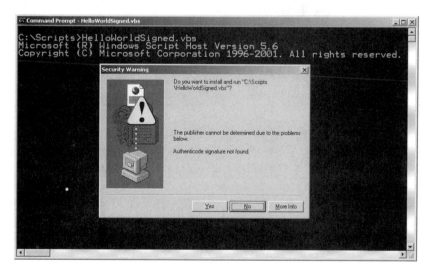

Figure 1.28
*Message when the
digital signature
does not match the
startup script
(tampered).*

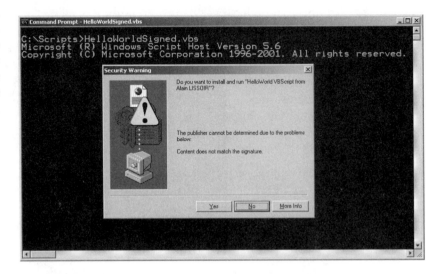

- The started script contains a signature but has been tampered with (Figure 1.28).

- The started script contains a signature, but the certificate chain process terminated in a root certificate, which is not trusted by the trust provider (Figure 1.29).

Figure 1.29
*Message when the
digital signature
contains a root
certificate not
trusted by the trust
provider.*

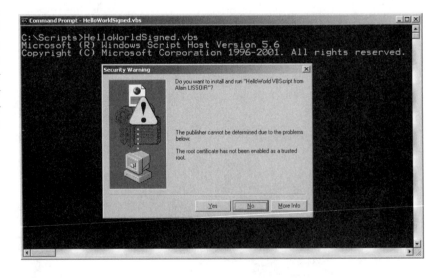

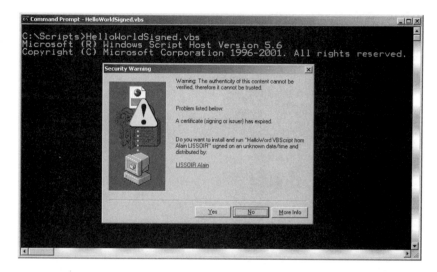

Figure 1.30
Message when the digital signature has expired.

- The started script has an expired signature (Figure 1.30). Note that if you timestamped the digital signature, this prompt should not occur (see "Signing Scripts" above and Figure 1.31).

Figure 1.31
Message when the digital signature has expired (with a valid timestamp).

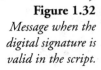

Figure 1.32
Message when the digital signature is valid in the script.

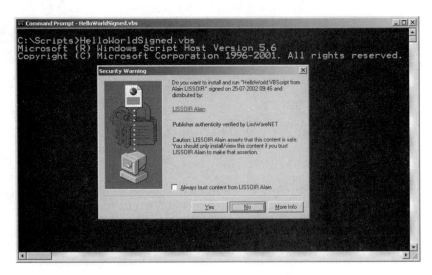

- The started script contains a valid signature (Figure 1.32).

At this time, the user has the choice either to refuse to execute the script or to accept it. If the user answers no, he or she receives the following message:

```
Execution of the Windows Script Host failed. (The subject is not trusted
for the specified action.)
```

Basically, the WSH script startup works in a similar way as occurs when a user is surfing on the Internet and gets a prompt because Internet Explorer is about to download an ActiveX control. It is up to the user to decide what to do. Now, if the registry key value is set to 2, the user is never prompted and only the scripts that have a valid digital signature are allowed to run. This is the most restrictive mode. If a user or a process attempts to start a nonsigned script, the following message appears:

```
Execution of the Windows Script Host failed. (No signature was present
in the subject.)
```

If the script has been tampered with, the user will get the following message:

```
Execution of the Windows Script Host failed. (The digital signature of
the object did not verify.)
```

As WSH comes with a set of registry keys to enable or disable some security features, it is possible to edit the registry keys of every system to define the WSH behavior. However, Microsoft makes available an administrative template (called **windowsscript.adm** and included in the Windows XP Resource Kit) that implements a local policy to configure WSH. Figure 1.33 shows the

Figure 1.33
*The WSH local
policy.*

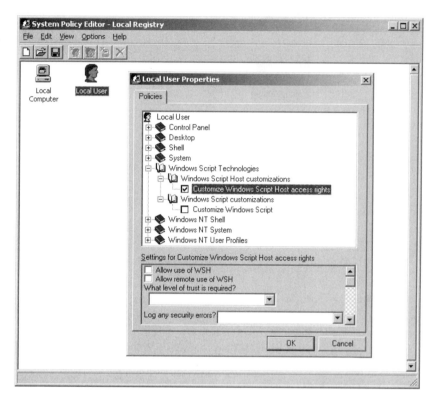

policy at the level of the local user. To activate that policy template, make sure it is copied in the %SystemRoot%\Inf folder and added to the template via the Options menu of the System Policy Editor.

1.8.3.6.2   Under Windows.NET Server

Windows XP and Windows.NET Server are designed to use the software restriction policies (SRPs) are available from the Group Policy MMC as shown in Figure 1.34. They are available only under Windows XP and Windows.NET Server.

To enable WSH to SRP, a REG_SZ registry key called "UseWinSAFER" must be set to 1. This key is located at

```
HKEY_LOCAL_MACHINE\Software\Microsoft\Windows Script Host\Settings
```

Note that it is possible to use the "TrustPolicy" mechanism under Windows XP and Windows.NET Server as well. In this case, the "UseWinSAFER" key must be set to 0 first. Next, as the "TrustPolicy" key is not available by default under Windows XP and Windows.NET Server, it must be created as a REG_DWORD key under the same registry hive as the

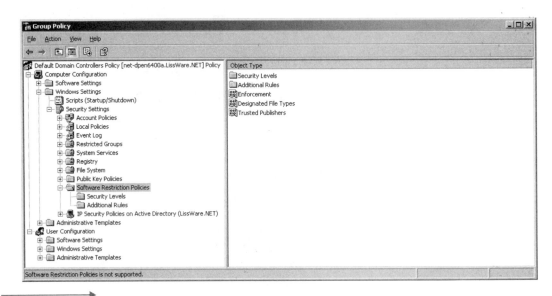

Figure 1.34   *The software restriction policies.*

"UseWinSAFER" key (see Figure 1.9). Once set, the "TrustPolicy" mechanism will behave as in Windows 2000. Therefore, setting the "UseWin-
SAFER" key to 1 disables the use of the "TrustPolicy" mechanism and
enables the "WinSAFER" mechanism.

WinSAFER allows code to be classified as either trusted or untrusted.
Trusted code can be executed; untrusted code cannot. SRPs are a powerful
mechanism. No code stored on your XP Professional or .NET Server system can hide from WinSAFER policies—no matter where that code comes
from and no matter who or what (i.e., a user, a machine, or a service) executes it. The code that SRPs apply to can be any piece of scripting code, an
executable, or a dynamic link library (DLL). You can use WinSAFER policies to prohibit an administrator from starting a script from a particular
server, restrict user access to Minesweeper, and prohibit the execution of
ActiveX controls that Microsoft hasn't signed.

From a management, distribution, and enforcement point of view, Win-
SAFER is tightly integrated with the Windows Group Policy Object (GPO)
technology Microsoft introduced in Windows 2000. To enforce SRPs,
administrators need to configure the corresponding GPO settings. Because
enforcement of the WinSAFER settings requires the appropriate GPO cli-
ent-side extension, you can't enforce them on earlier servers and clients.
They will simply ignore the WinSAFER policy settings

To define a software-restriction policy, you first need to set one of two default security levels: unrestricted (meaning an account can run any piece of code if it has the appropriate access rights) or disallowed (meaning an account can't run any code no matter what its access rights are).

The security levels are defined in the "Security Levels" GPO container that's located in the Windows Settings\Security Settings\Software Restriction Policies GPO containers (see Figure 1.34). If you're trying to define SRPs for a particular GPO for the first time, this container will not show up. Instead, Windows will display a warning message "No Software Restriction Policies Defined." To make the container visible, right-click the "Software Restriction Policies" container and select "Create New Policies."

After you set the default security level, you can create additional rules to refine and set exceptions to the default security level. A software restriction policy rule basically identifies a piece of software. If the default security level is set to unrestricted, all additional rules will identify code that is disallowed to execute. If the default security level is set to disallowed, the additional rules will identify code that is allowed to execute.

Pieces of software can be identified using one of the following four rules:

1.   A hash rule identifies code based on its hash thumbprint.

2.   A certificate rule identifies code based on the software signing certificate that was used to sign the code.

3.   A path rule uses the file system path to the folder where the code is stored for code identification.

4.   A zone rule identifies code using the Internet zone of the Web site from which the code was downloaded.

You create rules by right-clicking the "Additional Rules" container and selecting "New Certificate Rule..." or any of the other three rules. Note that for a certificate rule, the certificate to be used must be exported from the certificate store to base64-encoded X.509 format (or DER-encoded format).

For instance, if the SRP security level is set to unrestricted, which is the default when enabling SRP for the first time (see Figure 1.35), and if you want to block execution of all nonsigned scripts, four additional rules must be created: Three path rules must be created to disallow execution of scripts using extensions .vbs, .js, and .wsc and one certificate rule must be created to allow execution of signed scripts from a trusted source. In the example, scripts signed by "LISSOIR Alain" will be allowed to run; all other scripts will be blocked (see Figure 1.36).

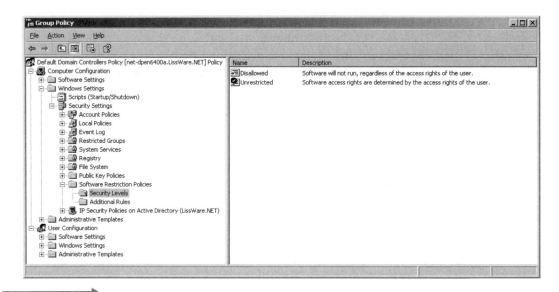

Figure 1.35   *The default SRP security level.*

If the script execution is rejected, the following message will be displayed:

```
CScript Error: Execution of the Windows Script Host failed. (Windows
cannot open this program because it has been prevented by a software
restriction policy. For more information, open Event Viewer or contact
your system administrator.
```

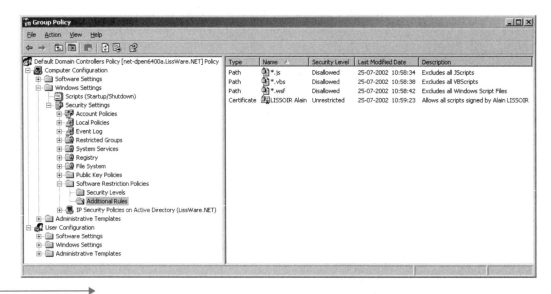

Figure 1.36   *Running scripts only when they are signed by a trusted source.*

As with any GPO setting, SRPs can be configured for users and machines at different levels of Active Directory hierarchy (domain, OU) and topology (sites). This means that you may end up with multiple SRP rules linked to the same piece of code or program. A rule of thumb to decide which rule will be applied is that "higher-quality" SRPs always take precedence over "lower-quality" SRPs. This means that a hash rule (which can match only a single program) will always have precedence over a path rule (which can match all programs contained in the same file system folder). This rule of thumb brings up the following order of precedence:

1. Hash rules

2. Certificate rules

3. Path rules

4. Zone rules

If two rules have the same quality level (for example, two path rules that point to the same program), the most restrictive one will apply. The example shown in Figure 1.36 illustrates the precedence of the certificate rule over the path rule.

1.8.4 Executing scripts remotely

Up to now, the different ways to start a process from a script start the process as a local child process. This means that the process starts in the same machine. Neither the *Exec* method nor the *Run* method of the **WshShell** object allows starting a process on another system. To perform this, WSH proposes another extension implemented by **WshCon.dll**. This extension exposes a method to start a script remotely. Warning: It is important to note that we are talking about starting a script remotely and not about starting a process remotely! It means that a script must be given as parameter and not as a Win32 program. This is another difference from the *Exec* or the *Run* method, which starts a Win32 process. Of course, if all the Windows systems starts scripts remotely, this may represent a serious security risk. This is why, by default, this option is not enabled. Again, a registry key setting will activate this feature. In the same registry hive as other registry key values (for both user and machine), a REG_SZ registry key value called "Remote" must be set to 1. By default, its value is 0 (see Figure 1.9), but under Windows XP and Windows.NET Server, this key is not created by default. Setting this key to 1 enables the remote script execution.

As the **WshCon.dll** implements the remote script functionality, it exposes a ProgID called "WshController" to instantiate the **WshController** object. The Sample 1.49 shows how to use this object.

Sample 1.49   *Executing scripts remotely*

```
 1:<?xml version="1.0"?>
 .:
 8:<package>
 9:  <job>
10:    <runtime>
11:      <named name="script" helpstring="the script to be run"
                                            required="true" type="string"/>
12:      <named name="machine" helpstring="the machine to run the script"
                                            required="true" type="string"/>
13:    </runtime>
14:
15:    <script language="VBScript">
16:    <![CDATA[
..:
28:    Set WshArguments = WScript.Arguments
29:
30:    If Not (WshArguments.Named.Exists ("script") And
                          WshArguments.Named.Exists ("machine")) Then
31:        WshArguments.ShowUsage
32:        WScript.Quit
33:    End If
34:
35:    Set WshController = WScript.CreateObject("WshController")
36:    Set WshRemote = WshController.CreateScript(WshArguments.Named("script"), _
37:                                        WshArguments.Named("machine"))
38:    WScript.ConnectObject WshRemote, "Remote_"
39:
40:    WshRemote.Execute()
41:
42:    Do
43:        Select Case WshRemote.Status
44:              Case cScriptNotStarted
45:                    WScript.Echo "Script not started!"
46:              Case cScriptRunning
47:                    WScript.Echo "Script running ..."
48:              Case cScriptFinished
49:                    WScript.Echo "Script Finished."
50:        End Select
..:
54:    Loop while (WshRemote.Status <> cScriptFinished)
55:
56:    WScript.Echo("Done.")
57:
58:    ' -----------------------------------------------------------
59:    Function Remote_Start()
60:
```

```
61:                WScript.Echo "Start."
62:
63:     End Function
64:
65:     ' -------------------------------------------------------------
66:     Function Remote_End()
67:
68:                WScript.Echo "End."
69:
70:     End Function
71:
72:     ' -------------------------------------------------------------
73:     Function Remote_Error()
..:
79:                Set WshRemoteError = WshRemote.Error
80:
81:                WScript.Echo "0x" & Hex (WshRemoteError.Number) & " - " &
                                       WshRemoteError.Description
82:                WScript.Echo "Caused by " & WshRemoteError.Source
83:                WScript.Echo "Line : " & WshRemoteError.Line
84:                WScript.Echo "Column: " & WshRemoteError.Character
85:                If Len (WshRemoteError.SourceText) Then
86:                    WScript.Echo "Source code is: " & vbCRLF
87:                    WScript.Echo Len (WshRemoteError.SourceText)
88:                End If
89:
90:                WScript.Quit (1)
91:
92:     End Function
93:     ]]>
94:     </script>
95:   </job>
96:</package>
```

Basically, to run a script remotely, two parameters are needed. The first parameter is the script to be run remotely, and the second parameter is the machine on which the script must be run. This is why the sample uses an XML structure to parse the command-line parameters (lines 10 to 13 and lines 28 to 33).

```
C:\>RemoteRUN.Wsf /Script:"WSHScript.vbs verbose"
                  /Machine:net-dpep6400a.Emea.LissWare.Net
```

Once the **WshController** object has been created (line 35), the sample script invokes the *CreateScript* method of the **WshController** object (line 36). This is the only method exposed by this object. By invoking this method, the script obtains access to an object called **WshRemote**. The **WshRemote** object allows you to administer computer systems on a network remotely. It represents an instance of a WSH script. As with any running script, a script instance is a process. The process can be run either on the local machine or on a remote machine. If no network path (computer name) is provided, it will run locally. Note that the remote computer name for the *CreateScript* method is an optional parameter, but for the script sample, as defined in the XML tags, this parameter is required. When a **WshRemote** object is created, the script is copied to the target computer system. Once there, the script does not begin executing immediately; it begins execution only when the **WshRemote** *Execute* method is invoked (line 40). To monitor the remote script execution, the **WshRemote** object offers three event types:

1.   The Start event (lines 59 to 63) when the *Execute* method is invoked (line 40)

2.   The End event (lines 66 to 70)

3.   The Error event (lines 73 to 92) when an error occurs in the remotely executed script

As events are implemented, such as event routines, these events must be linked to a function name. The way to link the events to the **WshRemote** object is to invoke the *ConnectObject* method of the **WScript** object (line 38). As with Sample 1.38, where we use the **WScript** *CreateObject* method to link the events to the instantiated object, here we connect the event routines to an object already instantiated. This is the reason why the *Connect-Object* method is used. From that point, everything is ready to monitor the remote script execution.

While the remote script executes, Sample 1.49 executes a loop to show its running status (lines 42 to 54). This loop is purely academic, but it helps to see what's happening during the remote script execution. It shows also how to detect the end of the script by looking at the status of the **Wsh-Remote** object (line 54).

The Error event (lines 73 to 92) contains an interesting object. The **WshRemote** object exposes an Error property to retrieve the **WshRemote-Error** object (line 79). This object exposes various properties (lines 81 to 88) related to an error that occurs during the remote script execution.

To use the WSH remote script functionality, you can start with a very simple script, such as the one used in Sample 1.41. This script creates a file containing the system date. If the script is executed remotely, the created file contains the date of the remote computer. The remote script execution does not allow retrieval of the standard output/input of the script remotely executed. Creating a file is one of the easiest ways to get a trace of its execution.

Another script that you can use is the **WshScript.vbs**. Remember that when this script is started with the verbose parameter, it creates a log file summarizing all the activity. By combining Sample 1.49 and the **Wsh-Script.vbs**, you will see how you can run a script remotely while accessing its file system, its registry keys, or its environment. This is one of the reasons for the activity trace logging (in a log file and in the application event log) of the **WshScript.vbs**. This makes the tracing of the remote execution very easy. You can use the following command line to remotely run **Wsh-Script.vbs**:

```
RemoteRUN.wsf /script:"WshScript.vbs verbose" /machine:MyRemoteMachine
```

After execution, edit the **WshScript.log** file and look at the username variable. You will notice that the **WshScript.vbs** is running under the credentials of users starting Sample 1.49. This point demonstrates that the user starting the remote execution must have access to the remote system with his or her credentials. As the remote execution is based on DCOM, if you want to enforce security, you must use the **Dcomcnfg.exe** program to review the defined security (Figure 1.37). The **WshRemote** object security settings use the default DCOM settings and may require some adaptations to suit

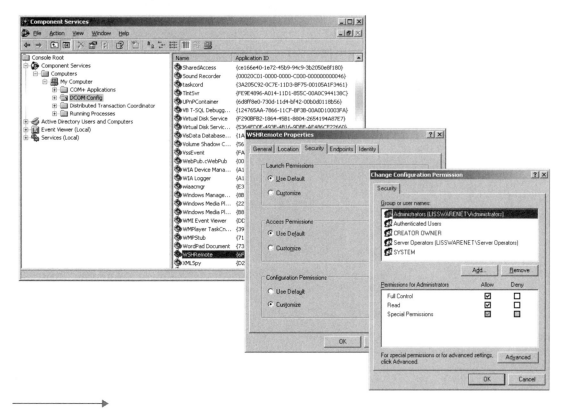

Figure 1.37   *The DCOM security settings can be changed with DCOMCNFG.EXE.*

some security requirements. Keep in mind that, by default, the Remote registry key is set to 0. This setting has precedence over any security change.

1.9   Encrypting WSH script code

When we talked about digitally signed script, we saw an interesting way to protect the script source code from tampering. Of course, even if the script content can't be changed, it is possible to read the source code. Some script writers will be interested in protecting their source from some people. With the introduction of Windows Script 5.0, Microsoft introduced a feature that lets script engines read encoded script, so any application that uses VBScript and JScript can use the encoding feature. Besides the decoding capabilities of Windows Script 5.0, Microsoft distributes a free tool able to encode the scripts. The tool is not dedicated to WSH; it also allows you to encode scripts included in ASP pages. This tool must be installed separately and is not included with Windows by default. The Script Encoder (**Screnc.exe**) is available at http://msdn.microsoft.com/scripting/VBScript/download/x86/sce10en.exe. The script encoder supports .vbs and .js files by default. It encodes script according to the language used. The file extension determines how to proceed. For instance, to encode the **DecodedScript.vbs**, the following command line must be used:

```
ScrEnc.Exe DecodedScript.vbs EncodedScript.vbe
```

The **DecodedScript.vbs** is shown in Sample 1.50. It is a very simple script but this is enough to demonstrate the script encoder capabilities.

Sample 1.50   *A simple script to encode*

```
Dim strMessage

strMessage = "This is my script to encode!"

Wscript.Echo strMessage
```

After encryption, the **EncodedScript.vbe** is shown in Sample 1.51.

Sample 1.51   *An encoded simple script*

```
#@~^2AEAAA==v,.nM/
bWx,FcT!,O~b^lrU,SkkdWbDP,~~P,P,P~P~~,P~P,~P,P~~,PP~~,P~P,~,P~,P,PP,P,~P,P~PE@#@&v,ZWs21$P
ZKh2ED+MP/
W.2KDCYbGx,O~!^W4Cs,?nD7r1+d,O,A+^ob;:,O~P,P~~,PP,~P,PP,~~P,P,Pv@#@&v,P~P,~P,P~~,PP~~,P~P,
~,P~,P,PP,P,~P,P~P,P~~,PP,~P,PP,~~P,P,P~P~~,P~P,~P,P~~,PP~~,B@#@&E~zxz,mK::-xDdPKD~;!+dObW
```

```
xklP,PP,~~P,P,P~P~~,P~P,~P-:Cr^)lsCbx VbdkWrM@$1W:al$
mK:~B@#@&@#@&EP.~~?1DkaO@#@&@#@&GkhPdOMHn/kCo-@#@&@#@&/Y.\-/dlTn,'~rK4k/
,kk~:HPdmMk2O,YW,nx1WN-ZE@#@&@#@&-dm.raY 214W,/O.t+/dCT+@#@&iGwAAA==^#~@
```

Besides a different script name (which is optional), the extension of the script has changed. The extension change is very important because it informs the Windows Script Components that the script is a VBScript encoded script. The .vbe corresponds to VBScript-encoded scripts and .jse corresponds to JScript encoded scripts. If the .vbe script is renamed with a .vbs extension, the Windows script will not be informed that the script is encoded and it will declare a VBScript compilation error. If the encoded script has the same name as the original script, make sure that the .vbe extension is specified to execute the encoded version of the script. The only reason to change the script name is to avoid confusion.

Now, how do you encode the Windows Script File? Since its release, the script encoder has not been updated to support Windows Script Files (.wsf). But there is a workaround. Imagine that we have the following Windows Script File shown in Sample 1.52.

Sample 1.52   *A Windows Script File to encode*

```
<?xml version="1.0"?>
<package>
    <job>
        <script language="VBScript">
        <![CDATA[
        Dim strMessage
        strMessage = "This is my script to encode!"
        Wscript.Echo strMessage
        ]]>
        </script>
    </job>
</package>
```

The script encoder will not accept the Windows Script File content because it is not aware of the XML tags used by WSH. Even if the **Screnc.exe** supports ASP pages and recognizes the ASP page tags, it does not support the WSH. Wsf files. Now, let's cut-and paste- the VBScript code in the CDATA section. We have:

```
Dim strMessage

strMessage = "This is my script in clear!"

Wscript.Echo strMessage
```

If this script is saved an a .vbs file, we can encrypt it. With Notepad, we cut-and-paste the encoded result in the CDATA section and we get results shown in Sample 1.53.

Sample 1.53 *An encoded Windows Script File*

```
<?xml version="1.0"?>
<package>
    <job id="vbs">
        <script language="VBScript.Encode">
        <![CDATA[
#@~^2AEAAA==v,.nM/
bWx,FcT!,O~b^1rU,SkkdWbDP,~~P,P,P~P~~,P~P,~P,P~~,PP~~,P~P,~,P~,P,PP,P,~P,P~PE@#@&v,ZWs21$PZKh2ED+MP/
W.2KDCYbGx,O~!^W4Cs,?nD7r1+d,O,A+^ob;:,O~P,P~~,PP,~P,PP,~~P,P,Pv@#@&v,P~P,~P,P~~,PP~~,P~P,~,P~,P,PP,P,~P
,P~P,P~~,PP,~P,PP,~~P,P,P~P~~,P~P,~P,P~~,PP~~,B@#@&E~zxz,mK::~xDdPKD~;!+dObWxk1P,PP,~~P,P,P~P~~,P~P,~P-:
Cr^)lsCbx VbdkWrM@$1W:al$ mK:~B@#@&@#@&EP.~~?1DkaO@#@&@#@&GkhPdOMHn/kCo~@#@&@#@&/Y.\~/d1Tn,'~rK4k/
,kk~:HPdmMk2O,YW,nx1WN~ZE@#@&@#@&~dm.raY 214W,/O.t+/dCT+@#@&iGwAAA==^#~@
        ]]>
        </script>
    </job>
</package>
```

You will notice that VBScript.Encode is the language definition. The encoding features of the script engines are enabled when you set the language name to VBScript.Encode or JScript.Encode. The .Encode suffix on the language name means that the same script engine is used, but its ability to interpret encoded scripts is turned on and its debugging features are turned off. This ensures that people don't load up the script debugger and take a look at your code. Besides the encryption mechanism, it is up to you to decide to digitally sign the encoded script. If you do so, your code protection will be perfect!

To complete the information about script encoding, the script encoder uses the scripting run-time module (**Scrrun.dll**) to perform all the encoding. All the script encoder does is provide a command-line mechanism for calling the **Scripting.Encoder** object that is implemented in the scripting run-time. This setup provides an extensible mechanism for using encoding in applications.

Sample 1.54 *A script to encode other .vbs and .js scripts by drag-and-drop*

```
 1:<?xml version="1.0"?>
 .:
 8:<package>
 9:  <job>
10:    <runtime>
11:      <unnamed name="script" helpstring="the script to encode" required="true" type="string" />
12:    </runtime>
13:
14:    <script language="JScript">
```

```
15:    <![CDATA[
..:
19:
20:       var WshArguments = WScript.Arguments;
21:
22:       if (WshArguments.Unnamed.Count == 0)
23:           {
24:           WshArguments.ShowUsage();
25:           WScript.Quit();
26:           }
27:
28:       strScript = WshArguments.Unnamed.Item(0);
29:       strScript = strScript.toUpperCase();
30:
31:       var objFileSystem = new ActiveXObject("Scripting.FileSystemObject");
32:
33:       // Read the script file content to encode.
34:       var objFile = objFileSystem.OpenTextFile(strScript, ForReading);
35:       var strData = objFile.ReadAll();
36:       objFile.Close();
37:
38:       WshScriptingEncoder = new ActiveXObject("Scripting.Encoder");
39:
40:       if ((intDot = strScript.indexOf (".VBS")) != -1)
41:           {
42:           WScript.Echo ("Coding VB Script ...");
43:           strCodedScriptName = strScript.substr (0, intDot) + ".vbe";
44:           strCoded = WshScriptingEncoder.EncodeScriptFile(".VBS", strData, 0, "");
45:           boolValidExtension = true;
46:           }
47:
48:       if ((intDot = strScript.indexOf (".JS")) != -1)
49:           {
50:           WScript.Echo ("Coding Java Script ...");
51:           strCodedScriptName = strScript.substr (0, intDot) + ".jse";
52:           strCoded = WshScriptingEncoder.EncodeScriptFile(".JS", strData, 0, "");
53:           boolValidExtension = true;
54:           }
55:
56:       if (boolValidExtension)
57:           {
58:           // Write the coded script file.
59:           objFile = objFileSystem.OpenTextFile(strCodedScriptName, ForWriting, true);
60:           objFile.Write(strCoded);
61:           objFile.Close();
62:
63:           WScript.Echo ("Done.");
64:           }
65:       else
66:           {
67:           WScript.Echo ("Unknown extension.");
68:           }
69:
70:       WScript.Sleep (5000);
71:
72:    ]]>
73:    </script>
74:  </job>
75:</package>
```

Sample 1.54 proceeds in the same way as the drag-and-drop sample to digitally sign scripts (see Sample 1.48). After the command parameters are reading (lines 10 to 12 and 20 to 26), some changes are made to suit the needs of the **Scripting.Encoder** object. This object exposes the *Encode-ScriptFile* method. This method requires the extension of the source script and the data content coming from that source script. This implies that Sample 1.54 must read the script name passed from the command line as a standard file (lines 34 to 36). Once the extension of the original script is known (line 40 for VBScript and line 48 for JScript), the sample extracts the original script name and concatenates the encoded corresponding extension (line 43 for VBScript and line 51 for JScript). Next, the script sample invokes the *EncodeScriptFile* method (line 44 for VBScript and line 52 for JScript). To complete the process, the script saves the encoded script on the file system (lines 59 to 61). Now, the encoded script is ready to be used.

1.10 Debugging WSH scripts

Under Windows 2000, to perform script debugging, the script debugger must be installed (see Figure 1.38).

Under Windows XP and Windows.NET Server, it is installed with the system. It is also available from the Microsoft Web site (see Section 1.12, "Useful Internet URLs").

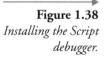

Figure 1.38
Installing the Script debugger.

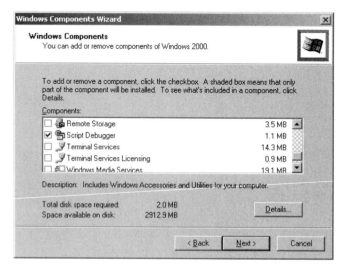

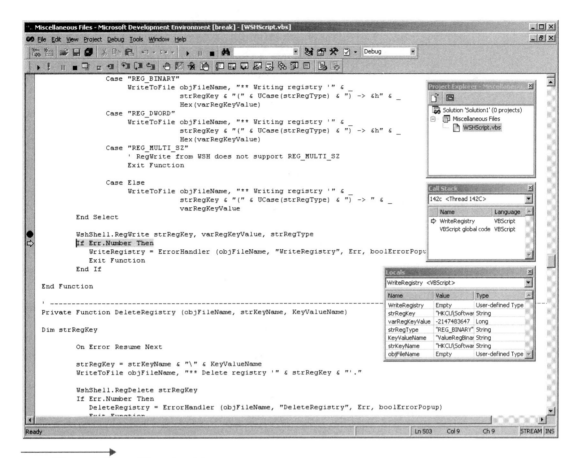

Figure 1.39   *The script debugger.*

Once the script debugger has been installed, you are ready to execute scripts step by step and place break-points to troubleshoot your code (see Figure 1.39).

To debug a .vbs or .js script file, no particular statement is required in the script. The only required action is to start the script with the //X switch to force the debugger to load and execute the script. Note that the //D switch activates the debugger too. The only difference with the //D switch is that the script is not executed in the debugger until a fault occurs. At that time the script user is prompted whether to load the debugger or not. Beside the .vbs or .js type, the .wsf file type requires a particular statement in the script to enable the debugging, as shown in the following sample at line 10.

```
  1:<?xml version="1.0"?>
  .:
  8:<package>
  9:  <job id="MyScript">
 10:    <?job error="True" debug="True" ?>
 ..:
 31:    <script language="JScript" src="..\Functions\..." />
 32:
 33:    <script language="VBScript">
 34:    <![CDATA[
 ..:
328:    ]]>
329:    </script>
330:  </job>
331:</package>
```

By default, all the parameters of the <?job?> XML tag are set to False (line 10). If set to True, the first parameter (error) determines the Windows Script File (.wsf) behavior in regards to syntax or run-time errors. The second parameter (debug) enables debugging. If debugging is not enabled, you will be unable to launch the script debugger for a Windows Script file.

As we have seen before, it is possible to encode .vbs and .js files. When running encoded scripts, the script engine activates its ability to interpret encoded scripts, but debugging features are disabled. This means that an encoded script is impossible to debug, which is basically the purpose.

A last note about the <?job error="true"debug="True"?> XLM tag. This line is included by default in all Windows Script Files, but for space reasons and to avoid obvious repetitions, all samples presented in this book omit this line.

1.11   Summary

In this chapter we reviewed most of the WSH features available today. The WSH Object Model offers many features for extending language capabilities. Beside the facilities to gather information about the script itself and access the run-time environment, WSH is also very powerful for accessing some system components, such as the registry. The current WSH version is powerful enough to scare any administrator, given how many things it is able to do. Besides the WSH facilities, the script infrastructure allows you to enforce some security mechanisms with registry settings or policies to determine how a system must behave with regard to script execution. In addition to script execution protection, WSH implements a script origin verification mechanism based on cryptography. The digital signature, included in a script, assures an administrator that only scripts coming from a trusted source can be run.

WSH is a good foundation on which to build administration scripts. Unfortunately, despite all these nice features, WSH still has some limitations. For instance, even if a script can manipulate the registry, WSH does not offer a way to manipulate the registry remotely. Of course, it is possible to launch a script in a remote system. Next, the remotely started script will access the local registry, but even if this represents a valid solution, an administrator may prefer to keep the WSH remote feature disabled for obvious security reasons. Another limitation with regard to the registry is the inability to create REG_MULTI_SZ registry keys. The *RegWrite* method exposed by the **WshShell** object does not support this type of key. Another limitation is the ability to write only event log records. WSH does not expose a method to read messages present in the event log.

Of course, after reviewing the complete WSH Object Model, we need not worry about the list of the WSH limitations. But this shows clearly that to manage an enterprise network with scripts, it is mandatory to fill some gaps with other complementary technologies. Active Directory Service Interface (ADSI) is a good example of a powerful combination with WSH. Even if you can retrieve the name of a user running a script with the **Wsh-Network** object, ADSI helps to retrieve much more information about the user from Active Directory. If you would like to obtain more information about ADSI, you can refer to the Compaq ActiveAnswers Web site listed in Section 1.12.

Besides the complementary functions offered by ADSI to access Active Directory (and all LDAP v3–compliant directories in general), Windows Management Instrumentation (WMI) is the perfect companion to develop WSH administration scripts. This is exactly what is discussed in the following chapters.

1.12   Useful Internet URLs

WSH 5.6:

http://msdn.microsoft.com/downloads/sample.asp?url=/MSDN-FILES/027/001/
733/msdncompositedoc.xml

WSH 5.6 Documentation:

http://msdn.microsoft.com/downloads/sample.asp?url=/MSDN-FILES/027/001/
728/msdncompositedoc.xml

Windows Script Component Wizard:

http://msdn.microsoft.com/downloads/sample.asp?url=/msdn-files/027/001/
788/msdncompositedoc.xml

Authenticode for Internet Explorer 5.0:

```
http://msdn.microsoft.com/downloads/sample.asp?url=/MSDN-FILES/027/000/
219/msdncompositedoc.xml
```

Script Encoder:

```
http://msdn.microsoft.com/downloads/sample.asp?url=/MSDN-FILES/027/001/
789/msdncompositedoc.xml
```

Microsoft Windows Script Debugger:

```
http://msdn.microsoft.com/downloads/sample.asp?url=/MSDN-FILES/027/001/
731/msdncompositedoc.xml
```

TechNET Script Center:

```
http://www.microsoft.com/technet/treeview/default.asp?url=/technet/
scriptcenter/Default.asp
```

Compaq Active Answers White Papers:

```
http://activeanswers.compaq.com/ActiveAnswers/Render/1,1027,2366-6-100-
225-1,00.htm
```

- Part 1—Understanding Microsoft WSH and ADSI in Windows 2000.

- Part 2—The powerful combination of WSH and ADSI under Windows 2000.

- Part 1—Introduction to the use of Exchange 2000 with Windows Script Host.

- Part 2—Managing Exchange with Scripts—Advanced Topics.

Under the *Available Information* selection box, select the *Technology* section, next, select *Windows 2000 and Exchange*.

2

Starting with WMI

2.1 Objective

After reviewing WSH, we can start the exploration of Windows Management Instrumentation (WMI). Of course, before scripting on top of WMI, we must learn what WMI is. This implies a theoretical approach to the technology. Like any technology, WMI is a kind of "computing environment" in which you must be able to navigate. It is important to understand how WMI is implemented under Windows and its key components. WMI refers to some standards defined by a committee called the Distributed Management Task Force (DMTF). We will see what this committee is and the initiatives behind it. Of course, the purpose of this chapter is not to delve into the discovery of the DMTF standards, but to provide the necessary background information to understand WMI. Throughout this chapter, we discover the WMI architecture and review its concepts and terms. We explore the WMI database and examine the definition of its elements and how they are related. As we progress through the chapter, we build an alerting system that helps to illustrate the various concepts as they are explained.

2.2 What is the DMTF?

To understand Windows Management Instrumentation, we must first look at the DMTF and its relation to Web-based Enterprise Management (WBEM) and WMI. The DMTF was founded in 1992 as the Desktop Management Task Force, and it focused on standards for managing desktop PCs. With the evolution of the industry, the management of several single entities at the enterprise level was challenging. To reflect this evolution, the DMTF kept its acronym, but the meaning was changed to the Distributed Management Task Force. Today, the DMTF's mission is to lead the development of management standards for distributed desktop, network, enterprise, and Internet environments. The DMTF is composed of several computer industry key players such as 3Com, Hewlett-Packard, Cisco, Microsoft, SUN, Intel, IBM/Tivoli Systems, Novell, and others. Beside these computer companies, there are also smaller software companies and universities (called academic members). All participants in the DMTF have made different contributions to the initiative based on their DMTF membership. The list of members participating in the DMTF initiative is quite impressive. For a complete list go to http://www.dmtf.org. It is important to note that the DMTF is a not-for-profit organization!

The DMTF started many unifying management initiatives while focusing on distributed management. Here is a brief overview of these initiatives:

- *Desktop Management Interface (DMI):* DMI is a standard framework for managing and tracking components in desktop PCs, notebooks, or servers. DMI is currently the only desktop standard in adoption for today's PCs. Version 2.0 of the DMI specification was released by the DMTF in April 1996. You can go to http://www.dmtf.org/standards/index.php for more information.

- *Web-based Enterprise Management (WBEM):* WBEM is a set of management and Internet standard technologies developed to unify the management of enterprise computing environments. The DMTF has developed a core set of standards that make up WBEM, which includes a data model, an encoding specification, and a transport mechanism. You can go to http://www.dmtf.org/standards/index.php for more information, but we revisit WBEM throughout the chapter as WMI implements the WBEM standards.

- *Common Information Model (CIM):* CIM is a common data model of an implementation-neutral schema to describe overall management information in a network/enterprise environment. CIM includes a specification and a schema. The specification defines the details for integration with other management models such as SNMP's MIBs or CMIP. The schema provides the data model descriptions. You can go to http://www.dmtf.org/standards/index.php for more information, but we revisit it throughout this chapter as WMI uses CIM extensively.

- *Directory Enabled Networks (DEN):* The DEN specification is designed to provide the building blocks for more intelligent networks by mapping users to network services and mapping business criteria to the delivery of network services. This enables applications and services to leverage the network infrastructure transparently on behalf of the user, empower end-to-end services, and support distributed network-wide service creation, provisioning, and management. DEN specifies a common data model with LDAP mappings from CIM to X.500. This provides a template for exchanging information and enables vendors to share a common definition of a device, application, or service, and allows for extensions. DEN also provides a level of interoperability with WBEM-based solutions. Both DEN and WBEM are built on the CIM specifications. You can go to http://www.dmtf.org/standards/index.php for more information.

- *Service Incident Standard (SIS) and Solution Exchange Standard (SES):* The DMTF has worked closely with the Customer Support Consortium in the joint development of standards for customer support and help-desk applications by providing common data models for incident and solution exchange. For more information, you can go to http://www.dmtf.org/standards/index.php and http://www.serviceinnovation.org.

- *Alert Standard Forum (ASF):* ASF is a standard for managing pre-OS environments. The term *system manageability* represents a wide range of technologies. This involves access to and control of remote systems. The term *remote systems* includes systems with OS-present (e.g., any computer system such as Unix systems, Windows systems, mainframes) and with OS-absent (e.g., printers, hubs). The DMTF defines DMI and CIM interfaces to serve clients' OS-present environments. The ASF specification defines remote control and alerting interfaces that best serve clients' OS-absent environments.

Why did the DMTF take these initiatives? We know a computer network is composed of many devices, computers, peripherals, and the like. These components are themselves manageable in various ways. Although computers from various manufacturers may differ, they all have some common characteristics. Every computer has network devices, hard disks, controllers, tapes, memory, and processors, regardless of the manufacturer. In the same way, operating systems also have common characteristics, such as the memory available to run applications, the processes running, disk space available, users configured in the system, print queues and print jobs, and network adapters status. All these things represent a collection of objects or entities that require particular care when some management tasks are executed. As one would expect, you do not manage a hard disk in the same way as you manage a user or a print job!

In the early stages of the computer industry, each time it was required to get access to a component (to retrieve some information such as its status, for instance), it was necessary to know how to play with that component because the manufacturer implemented a proprietary access method. So, the fact that the component was part of an IBM system or a HP system implied that the method used to retrieve the desired information was not the same. Moreover, the information representing the relevant data was likely to be coded in a format specific to the manufacturer. The access methods were based on a collection of functions often provided by the computer manufacturer (generally part of the BIOS). This manufacturer-specific implementation required an adapted knowledge of the considered computer to retrieve the information. Besides the hardware differences, the operating systems used by computers determined the method used to retrieve the desired information. All these differences increased the complexity and resulted in poor interoperability from a management perspective. The real world rarely uses one computer type with one operating system. Over the years, many initiatives were developed to collect management information—for example, Simple Network Management Protocol (SNMP), Desktop Management Information (DMI), and Common Management Information Protocol (CMIP). As a result, a solution was needed to deal with this mix of technologies and differences with one main objective: making the real world more manageable from a global perspective. This is exactly the purpose of the DMTF.

2.3   What is WBEM?

Since 1996, the goal has been to provide a standard that defines how these entities can be managed and provide system managers with a low cost solution for their management needs without having to learn all the details and specificities from various computer manufacturers and developers. One of the initiatives of the DMTF is Web-Based Enterprise Management (WBEM). WBEM is a set of management and Internet standard technologies developed to unify the management of enterprise computing environments. Unifying means not only having a common access to the manageable entities (HTTP), but also having a common way to represent these manageable entities with its characteristics (CIM and xmlCIM).

WBEM can be summarized as a set of standards that define abstraction layers that hide the complexity of accessing management information.

2.4 What is CIM?

The DMTF delivers to the industry a core set of standards that creates WBEM. As previously mentioned, one of the key elements is to have a common representation of the manageable entities of the real world. This implies the creation of a data model that everyone can use. All the components that must be managed in a computer network (i.e., computers, disks, printers, memory, CPU, processes) can be seen as objects. All these objects represent a set of information that could be described in a data model. To produce this data model, the WBEM initiative includes the CIM standard. CIM is a conceptual information model describing management information that is not bound to a particular implementation. For example, a disk from one computer manufacturer has a set of characteristics common to any disk provided by any other manufacturer. Even if they are not the same, all disks have a capacity, an access speed, and a certain number of sectors and tracks (or cylinders). Even if a computer component has some particularities, there is always a common set of characteristics that you will retrieve in every implementation. A disk is a disk, just as an adapter is an adapter regardless of whether it is from IBM or HP. All adapters use I/O addresses, and a bus connector type. It is possible to delve further and differentiate between adapters. We may have modem adapters, network adapters, video adapters, among others. Again, a video adapter from one manufacturer is different from a video adapter from another manufacturer, but they share a common set of characteristics, such as the refresh rate, resolution, and number of colors supported. By examining carefully each manageable component available in the computer industry, it is possible to create a model, such as the CIM data model, that describes their characteristics in a generic way. In a fully CIM-compliant world, it is possible to build applications using management data from a variety of sources and different management systems. The management data is collected, stored, and analyzed using a common format. The CIM standard has two parts: the CIM specification and the CIM Schema.

2.4.1 The CIM specification

The CIM specification defines a data model for the CIM standard. This describes the way the data model is encoded (i.e., how an object representing a disk is coded) by using Managed Object Format (MOF) files or Extended Markup Language (xmlCIM). A MOF file is an ASCII file that uses a specific syntax and language definition to code CIM definitions. We will revisit MOF files in Section 2.5. The xmlCIM encoding defines XML elements (XML tags) written in a Document Type Definition (DTD), which can be used to represent objects (i.e., disks, memory, adapters, and software components, such as files, volumes, processes) in an XML format. The transport mechanism over HTTP of the XML representation allows implementations of CIM to interoperate in an open and standardized manner. This means that System A of one constructor will be able to interoperate with System B of another constructor.

Note that under Microsoft Windows.NET Server and SUN OS 8.0 (both implement a version of WBEM), it is possible to represent CIM elements in XML. However, at the time of this writing, it is not possible to exchange CIM XML information over HTTP. In Chapter 5 we will see how to get an XML representation of a CIM object.

The CIM specification also provides naming and mapping techniques to other management models, such as Simple Network Management Protocol Management Information Base (SNMP MIB), Desktop Management Interface (DMI), and Common Management Information Protocol (CMIP).

The specification also defines a *metaschema*. The metaschema is the formal definition of the data model used. As CIM represents miscellaneous manageable components, such as disks, software, and processes, the data model needs some structure to represent these manageable objects. To implement a data model, some elements or building blocks must be used. These elements can help to define the nature of things. For example, a disk is a disk, and it is not an adapter or a process. In the CIM data model this is represented as a *class*. Each object has a specific nature and specific properties. For example, a disk has a capacity, speed, and geometry. On the other hand, a network adapter has a media type and a link speed. These characteristics are called *properties*, which represent another element of the CIM data model. A video card has a resolution property that can be modified by specific actions. In the CIM data model, these actions are known as *methods* and are exposed by the object itself. The metaschema CIM specification defines elements like classes, properties, and methods. Classes in CIM can be of different types (e.g., indications and associations). The same approach can be applied to the properties, as they can be of a type called *references*. The CIM specification is the definition of all the terms, methods and concepts used to produce the data model used by CIM. Like any specification, these documents are not always easy to read, but if you would like more information about the CIM specification you can go to http:// www.dmtf.org.

2.4.2   The CIM Schema

The CIM Schema is the key component that represents the data model. It contains the management schemas that represent the building blocks to manage computer systems and applications. The CIM Schema represents a collection of objects with different relationships. The CIM Object Model represents objects that are available in the real world. It has nothing to do with object-oriented programming, as object-oriented programming does not necessarily represent things from the real world. It is important to understand that an object that represents a manageable entity exists in the CIM object model. The CIM schema uses specific terminology to define its elements. A summary of these elements includes the following:

- **Classes** represent the nature of an object. For example, a computer system can use several disks with different characteristics, but all the disks will have a common representation defining their nature; in the case of this example, the class will be *disk*. However, for the computer, as the nature of a computer is different from the nature of a disk, we will have another class called *computer*. Therefore, a class is a template defining the nature of an object. Moreover, it is also a template defining a list of properties typical to the nature of the object it represents. For example, in the case of a *disk* class, the class will have properties such as *disk size* or *access time*.

- **Subclasses** are a subtype of a class (the latter is called a *superclass* or *parent class*). For example, a manageable component can be a medium of any type. Therefore, the CIM representation has a *media* class that represents media in general. As media exist in various forms such as disks, CD-ROMs, tape drives, and optical drives, the *media* super-class will have subclasses representing the disks, CD-ROM, tape drives, and optical drives. In this example, we will have the *disk*, *cdrom* and *tape* classes defined as subclasses of the *media* superclass. Because there is a notion of parent-child between the *media* super-class—and, for example, the *disk* class—there is a notion of inheritance between the classes. Actually, a subclass inherits the characteristics of its superclass. When a class is built from a superclass, we could also say the subclass is derived from the superclass. Therefore, a subclass is a template defining the nature of an object, but it defines the nature of the object more specifically.

- **Instances** represent objects or items of the real world. An instance is always created from the class representing the template for the real-world objects. For example, a disk instance represents a real disk where its template is defined by the *disk* class.

- **Properties** are the attributes of real-world objects. For example, an attribute can be the size of a disk, the process ID of a process, the name of installed software. The definition of the properties is made in the class definition. When an instance of a real-world object is created, the values representing the characteristics of that object are stored in the instance properties as defined by the corresponding class. Therefore, in the case of a disk, we have a *disk* class defining the template representing the disks with a set of properties common to all disks. Once an instance of a disk is created, the characteristics of a real-world disk are stored in the properties of the instance created from the *disk* class.

- **Relationships** are elements used in the CIM schema to associate different objects. For example, a disk volume cannot exist if it is not associated with a disk partition and a disk partition cannot exist without a disk. We will see further that there are different types of relationships.

Note that the concept of data modeling can be dedicated to other universes than the computing universe, but CIM represents manageable software and hardware items only. To present objects of a data model, a specific language is used: the Unified Modeling Language (UML). UML uses boxes and lines to represent objects and relationships. Let's take an easy example not related to the computing world, something that everybody knows, something that everybody has tasted at some stage—a cheeseburger! A cheeseburger is composed of various things: bread, beef, a gherkin, cheese, and ketchup. How do we represent a cheeseburger with UML? We must start at the highest generic level, which means that we will have a representation of the various types of ingredients as shown in Figure 2.1. These ingredients will be the superclasses.

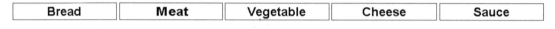

| Bread | Meat | Vegetable | Cheese | Sauce |

Figure 2.1   *The generic ingredients of the cheeseburger.*

We have generic classes representing the family of each ingredient; for example, *meat* represents the beef, and *vegetable* represents the gherkin. In UML, the classes are represented in a rectangle. Each class may have properties. Properties are represented in a second region of the rectangle (see Figure 2.2).

Bread	**Meat**	**Vegetable**	**Cheese**	**Sauce**
Name:String ProductDate:DateTime ValidDays:uint8	Name:String ProductDate:DateTime ValidDays:uint8	Name:String ProductDate:DateTime ValidDays:uint8	Name:String ProductDate:DateTime ValidDays:uint8	Name:String ProductDate:DateTime ValidDays:uint8

Figure 2.2   *The generic ingredients of the cheeseburger with its properties.*

To check the validity of the ingredients, the data model can provide a method to determine whether an aliment is still good to eat. A third section in the rectangle represents methods (see Figure 2.3).

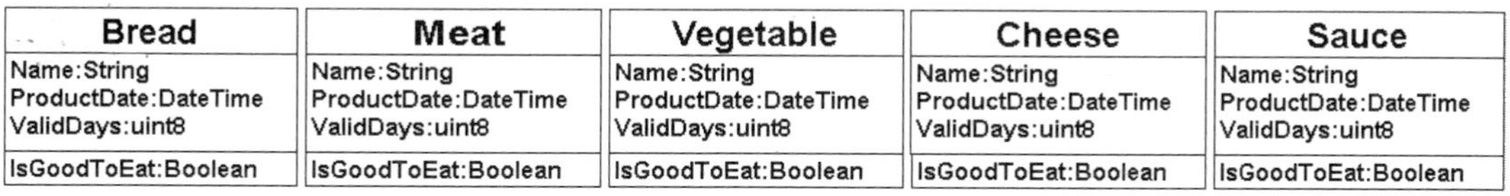

Bread	**Meat**	**Vegetable**	**Cheese**	**Sauce**
Name:String ProductDate:DateTime ValidDays:uint8	Name:String ProductDate:DateTime ValidDays:uint8	Name:String ProductDate:DateTime ValidDays:uint8	Name:String ProductDate:DateTime ValidDays:uint8	Name:String ProductDate:DateTime ValidDays:uint8
IsGoodToEat:Boolean	IsGoodToEat:Boolean	IsGoodToEat:Boolean	IsGoodToEat:Boolean	IsGoodToEat:Boolean

Figure 2.3   *The generic ingredients of the cheeseburger with its properties and method.*

There are many different types of meat such as *beef, pork,* or *lamb.* In this case, we have subclasses. The *meat* class is a superclass of the *beef,* the *pork,* and the *lamb* classes. In other words, the *beef,* the *pork,* and the *lamb* classes are subclasses of the *meat* class. We can also say that the *beef,* the *pork* and the *lamb* classes are derived from the *meat* class, which makes those classes inheritors of the properties of the *meat* class. UML uses a line to represent the relationship between the superclasses and the subclasses. An arrowhead points to the superclass to indicate that it is the parent class (see Figure 2.4).

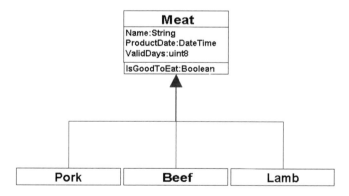

Figure 2.4   *The meat generic ingredient derivation.*

Of course, we have the same relationship for the vegetable (where we may have subclasses such as *salad, gherkin, onions, potatoes,* etc.), the sauces (where we may have subclasses such as *ketchup, mayonnaise, mustard,* etc.) For the *bread* and the *cheese* superclasses, we have a *toasted bun* and a *processed cheese slice* as subclasses, respectively. The UML representation for each of the subclasses is shown in Figure 2.5.

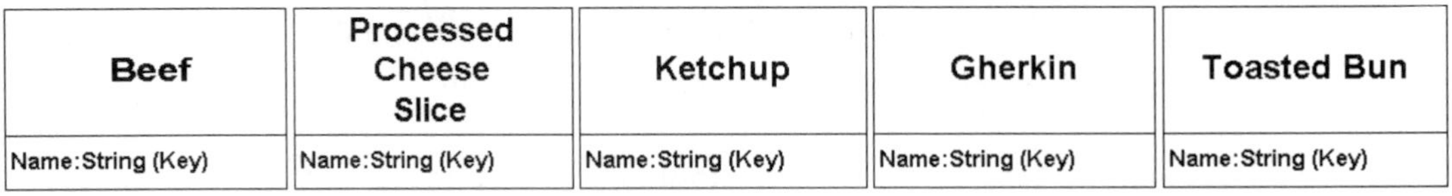

Beef	**Processed Cheese Slice**	**Ketchup**	**Gherkin**	**Toasted Bun**
Name:String (Key)	Name:String (Key)	Name:String (Key)	Name:String (Key)	Name:String (Key)

Figure 2.5   *The base ingredients of the cheeseburger.*

Note that one property is already defined in the subclasses. As mentioned, subclasses can inherit the properties from their superclasses and, at the same time, new properties can be added to the subclass. Figure 2.5 shows that an added property can have the same name as a property defined in the superclass. Therefore, in the CIM representation, a subclass can override a property defined in its superclass. These possibilities are defined by schema elements known as qualifiers.

To produce a cheeseburger, we must combine all these ingredients together; for this, we create some associations. Figure 2.6 shows the associations required for a cheeseburger. The associations illustrate that a cheeseburger is composed of beef, processed cheese slice, ketchup, gherkin, and toasted bun.

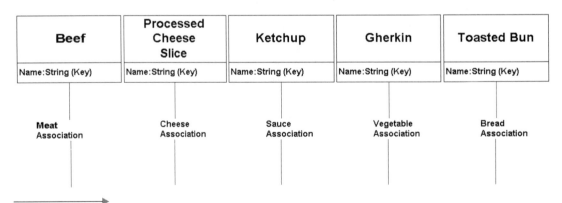

Figure 2.6   *The association of the base ingredients of the cheeseburger.*

Associations are represented by lines with the name of the association usually placed near the center of the line. In CIM, associations are classes and always have a role. Roles are defined in a set of properties known as references, which are valid only in the context of an association. For example, to produce a cheeseburger, we must have at least one toasted bun, one gherkin, an amount of ketchup, one processed cheese slice, and one or two slices of beef (although two slices of beef will produce a double cheeseburger, but let's say for simplicity that it is still a cheeseburger). Each item plays the role of ingredient within its own context; each item plays a particular ingredient role. With regard to the ingredients, we have five roles: *MeatAssociation*, *CheeseAssociation*, *SauceAssociation*, *VegetableAssociation*, and *BreadAssociation*.

Each role is part of an association. As soon as the ingredients classes are associated via the defined references, we have a cheeseburger. Figure 2.7 shows that each association has references. For example, the association *MeatAssociation* has the references *Burger* and *MeatIngredient*. The *cheeseburger* is a class, which has some associations with the various ingredients. Moreover, the *cheeseburger* may also have some properties such as its weight.

CIM also has the notion of an aggregation relationship in which one entity is made up of the aggregation of some number of other entities. An aggregation is just a variation on the concept of an association. For example,

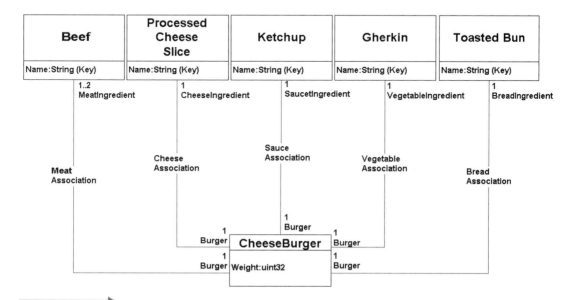

Figure 2.7   *The cheeseburger constitution with the association of the base ingredients.*

Figure 2.8
*The burger menu
constitution with
the product
aggregations.*

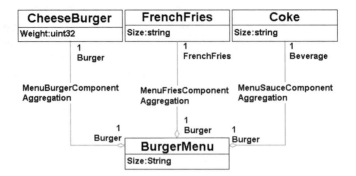

if we aggregate the cheeseburger with some french fries and a Coke, we get a burger menu (see Figure 2.8).

Aggregations are represented, like associations, by lines with the name of the aggregation placed near the center of the line. To distinguish an association from an aggregation, the aggregation terminates on one end with a lozenge.

This example shows the concept behind the CIM representation of real objects and how the abstraction is organized. The CIM data model starts always from the most general representation and tends to define things in a more precise way by using associations and inheritances between objects.

Microsoft delivers some tools to work with CIM. One of the tools used to explore the CIM repository is called **WMI CIM Studio**. It available as a separated download for Windows 2000, Windows XP, and Windows.NET Server from http://www.microsoft.com/downloads/release.asp?ReleaseID=40804. We will revisit this tool in more detail in Section 2.8.5.2. Figure 2.9 shows a sample screen shot of the **WMI CIM Studio**.

The tree view is expanded at the level of the *CIM_ManagedSystemElement* class (left pane). Below the *CIM_ManagedSystemElement* class we have a collection of classes, the *CIM_LogicalElement* class being the first. The *CIM_LogicalElement* subclass contains another set of classes, such as, *CIM_System*, *CIM_Service*, and *CIM_LogicalDevice* classes. When we arrive at the *CIM_LogicalDevice* class level, we can see that the class definition is becoming more and more precise because we started from a class called *CIM_ManagedSystemElement* to arrive at *CIM_LogicalDevice*. In the same way, below the *CIM_LogicalDevice*, we have a collection of classes representing the logical devices, such as the *CIM_MediaAccessDevice*, *CIM_CoolingDevice*, *CIM_Controller*, and *CIM_NetworkAdapter* classes. To complete the picture, if we look below the *CIM_MediaAccessDevice* class, we see classes such as *CIM_CDROMDrive*, *CIM_DiskDrive*, *CIM_TapeDrive*, and

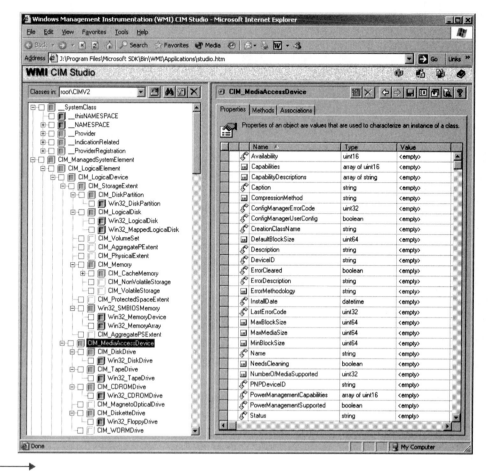

Figure 2.9 *WMI CIM Studio.*

CIM_DisketteDrive classes. The further we navigate down the tree, the definition of the CIM class tends to be more and more precise in defining its purpose

2.4.3 The CIM structure

A Core Model and a Common Model constitute the CIM schema. Since CIM starts from the most generic definition of the manageable objects in the computing world, it defines the Core Schema and the appropriate Common Schema area. After the CIM Core Schema come the Extension Schemas. The number of Extension Schemas depends on the CIM Schema version. Each new release of the schema added a new Extension Schema (see Figure 2.10).

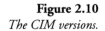

Figure 2.10
The CIM versions.

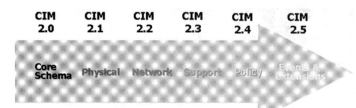

DMTF recently released version 2.7 of the CIM Schema. Regardless of the version, the structure always determines three levels of classes:

1. **Classes representing managed objects that apply to all areas of management.** These classes provide a basic vocabulary for analyzing and describing managed systems. They are part of the Core Model. The Core Model is not specific to any platform. In Figure 2.9, the *CIM_ManagedSystemElement* class is a class of the Core Schema. This class does not relate to any particular real managed object or domain.

2. **Classes representing managed objects that apply to specific management areas, but are independent of a particular implementation or technology.** These classes are part of what is called the Common Model, which is an extension of the Core Model. The management areas included in the Common Model are System, Application, Physical, Device, Network, Metric, Supports, and User. In Figure 2.9, *CIM_LogicalDevice* class and the subclass *CIM_MediaAccessDevice* are two sample classes of the Common Model.

3. **Classes representing managed objects that are technology-specific additions to the common model.** These classes typically apply to specific platforms such as UNIX or Windows. For example, in Figure 2.9, *Win32_CDROMDrive* and *Win32_FloppyDrive* are two Microsoft classes from the extended CIM Schema that represent a CD-ROM and a floppy drive, respectively.

Figure 2.11 shows the logical representation of the CIM structure, where we have the Core Schema in the center with the Common Models acting as an extension of the Core Schema. Besides these two CIM general representations, we have the technology-specific additions such as WMI.

Applied to the computing environment, and to be CIM compliant, a product has to implement its representation in the same way. This implies that the Microsoft implementation of the CIM Schema will follow this

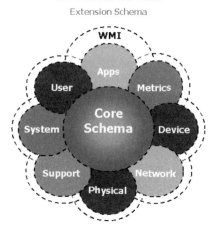

Figure 2.11   *The Core Schema and the Common Schema.*

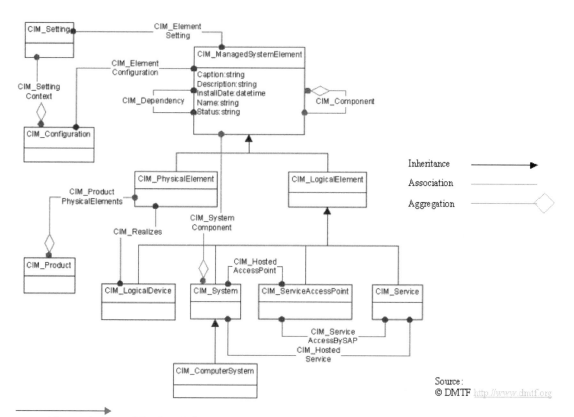

Figure 2.12   *The Core Schema UML representation.*

implementation as designed by the DMTF. A schema has a name and contains a collection of classes. The Core Schema contains a top-level set of classes applicable to all management domains. Figure 2.12 shows a partial UML representation of the CIM Core Schema. It is possible to download the complete UML representation of the CIM Core Schema and the CIM Common Schemas from http://www.dmtf.org. All schemas are greatly detailed and available in Visio or Adobe Acrobat file formats.

By observing Figure 2.12, you will notice that the UML representation shows clearly that the *CIM_LogicalElement* class has an inheritance with the *CIM_ManagedSystemElement* class. Next, the *CIM_LogicalElement* class is derived to produce the *CIM_System*, *CIM_LogicalDevice*, *CIM_Service* and *CIM_ServiceAccessPoint* classes. The UML representation matches the **WMI CIM Studio** view shown in Figure 2.9.

2.4.4   The CIM Schema elements

Now let's review the CIM Schema elements as they are named and used in CIM. While examining the different elements you can refer to Figure 2.13. This figure shows a logical representation of the relationship between the different terms we will examine in subsequent paragraphs. Keep in mind that the figure is just an abstract representation of the elements and does not show how the things are actually implemented or linked.

It is very important to have a clear idea of these terms and the things they represent, as they will be used in this book in many different situations. Failure to understand these terms will be a serious handicap when we dive deeper into WMI.

Figure 2.13
A theoretical representation of the CIM Schema element relationships.

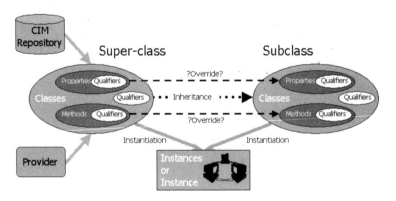

2.4.4.1 Namespace

A namespace is a portion of a schema. It is also a logical unit to group classes and instances inside the CIM repository. The notion of a namespace also defines the notion of scope and visibility for classes and instances. CIM supports namespace nesting to produce a kind of hierarchy. Even if namespaces can be arranged in a form of hierarchy, they don't play any role in class inheritances. Generally, managed objects of a particular environment are grouped beneath one namespace. Figure 2.14 shows the namespaces available in the

Figure 2.14
The CIM namespaces under Windows.NET Server as visible from the WMI MMC snap-in.

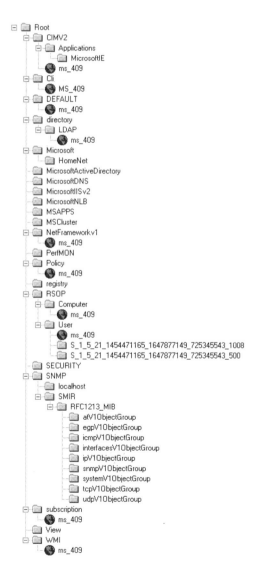

CIM repository under Windows.NET Server. For example, the **Root\ CIMv2** namespace contains most classes defined by Microsoft to represent the Windows world manageable entities (see Figure 2.14).

By default, all namespaces in the CIM repository contain language-neutral classes. However, some namespaces, such as the **Root\CIMv2** namespace, have a child namespace called **ms_409**, as shown in Figure 2.14. This namespace contains the U.S. version (code page 409) of the language-neutral classes contained in the **Root\CIMv2** namespace. In conclusion, besides the language-neutral classes, WMI allows storage of multiple localized versions of classes, where the ms_<CodePage> namespace contains the language-specific version of the classes (i.e., English, German, French). The language-specific class definitions are always stored in a child namespace beneath the namespace that contains the language-neutral class definition.

With **WMI CIM Studio**, it is possible to view the namespace instances. They are represented as instances of the *__Namespace* system class. When an instance of the *__Namespace* class is created, a new namespace is created. When an instance of the *__Namespace* class is deleted, a namespace is deleted. A list of existing namespaces under Windows.NET Server is available in Table 2.1.

Table 2.1   *The Windows.NET Server WMI Namespaces*

Root

Root/CIMV2

Root/CIMV2/Applications

Root/CIMV2/Applications/MicrosoftIE

Root/CIMV2/ms_409

Root/Cli

Root/Cli/MS_409

Root/DEFAULT

Root/DEFAULT/ms_409

Root/directory

Root/directory/LDAP

Root/directory/LDAP/ms_409

Root/Microsoft

Root/Microsoft/HomeNet

Root/MicrosoftActiveDirectory

Table 2.1   *The Windows.NET Server WMI Namespaces (continued)*

Root/MicrosoftDNS

Root/MicrosoftIISv2

Root/MicrosoftNLB

Root/MSAPPS

Root/MSCluster

Root/NetFrameworkv1

Root/NetFrameworkv1/ms_409

Root/PerfMON

Root/Policy

Root/Policy/ms_409

Root/registry

Root/RSOP

Root/RSOP/Computer

Root/RSOP/Computer/ms_409

Root/RSOP/User

Root/RSOP/User/ms_409

Root/SECURITY

Root/SNMP

Root/SNMP/localhost

Root/subscription

Root/subscription/ms_409

Root/View

Root/WMI

Root/WMI/ms_409

2.4.4.2   *Classes*

To recap, a class defines the basic unit of management and represents a template for a managed object. A class may have properties (characteristics) and methods (to perform some actions). Classes represent the nature of things, but just like things that exist, classes also have instances. An instance is the representation of a real-world managed object that belongs to a particular class and contains real data. For example, if a class defines a disk, we have one class type for the disk. In the real world, we may have many disks in one computer, which means that the *disk* class may have many instances.

Figure 2.15
*The CIM Object
Manager
positioning among
other WMI
components.*

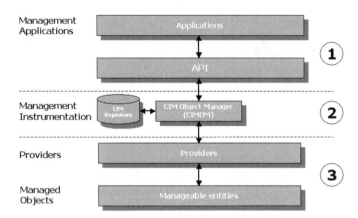

Under WBEM, classes can be static or dynamic. Static classes are stored in the CIM repository and retrieved on request by the CIM Object Manager (CIMOM). The CIMOM is a collection of application programming interfaces (API) that allow applications to interact with the CIM repository. The dynamic classes are generated by a WMI provider. A provider is a software component that communicates with the managed object to access its data. (See Figure 2.15.)

Besides the implementation type of the class (in the CIM repository for static classes and via a provider for dynamic classes), classes can also be qualified in different ways:

- **An abstract class is a class that does not have an instance of its own.** This class type can be derived to produce another class that may have an instance. An abstract class is a kind of template to produce other classes by inheritance. For example, the *CIM_ManagedSystemElement* class shown in Figure 2.9 is an abstract class.

- **System classes are a collection of predefined classes based on CIM and included in every namespace (a namespace is a portion of the schema).** In the Microsoft implementation, system classes are used to support the WMI activities such as provider registration, security, and event notification. System classes follow a naming convention that consists of a double-underscore followed by the class name. For example, the *__Systemclass* in Figure 2.9 is an abstract system class having some system subclasses such as *__provider* or *__NAMESPACE*.

- **A singleton class is a class that supports one instance of the managed object it represents.** For example, the Microsoft WMI class *Win32_WMISetting* is a singleton class as there is only one instance of the WMI Settings in a Windows system.

- **Classes can participate in associations.** In such a case, the produced associations (which can be another class) will have one or more references pointing to the classes participating in that association. For example, the *CIM_LogicalDiskBasedOnPartition* class in Figure 2.16 is an association class linking the *CIM_DiskPartition* and the *CIM_LogicalDisk* classes. We clearly realize the sense of such association because a disk partition cannot exist without a disk.

- **Classes can also be localized.** A class definition is (generally) a language-neutral class, but it may also exist in multiple language-specific classes (i.e., English, German, French). For example, the *Win32_Service* class, which is the class representing a Windows NT service, exists in a language-neutral form (in the **Root\CIMv2** namespace) and in an English U.S. (code page 409) form (in the

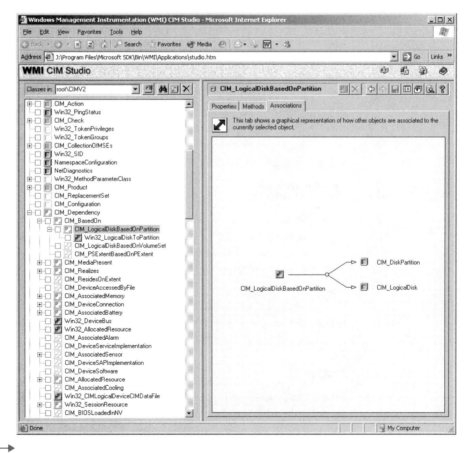

Figure 2.16   *The WMI CIM Studio tool.*

Root\CIMv2\ms_409 namespace). In such cases, a localized class will also be referred as an amended class. A localized class contains an amended qualifier in its definition. Briefly, a qualifier is an attribute of a class, property, or method definition. We will come back on the qualifiers in Section 2.4.4.10.

A class must belong to one schema, and its name must be unique within that particular schema. If some new management objects must be defined as new classes in CIM, a developer can use the CIMOM API or a MOF file to define its particularities. We will revisit MOF files in Section 2.5.

2.4.4.3   Superclasses and subclasses

In WBEM, subclasses can also be referred to as specialization classes. In the same way, a superclass, which is a parent class, can also be referred to as a generalization class. As we have seen before, the class definition always starts from the most general representation of the managed object. The organization of classes is like an upside-down tree with a base class at the root. The superclasses and the subclasses illustrate the notion of inheritance. It is important to note that multiple inheritances are not supported. This means that each class inherits from exactly one superclass. In the cheeseburger example, the *meat* class is a base class. The *beef* class and the *pork* class inherit only from the *meat* class. In the same way, in a computer system, we see in Figure 2.9 that the *CIM_LogicalDevice* class is a subclass of the *CIM_LogicalElement* class.

2.4.4.4   Domain and range

Properties and methods are declared within the scope of a class. The declaring class is referred to as the domain for the property or method. If you think about the ingredients used to produce a cheeseburger (see Figure 2.3), we have the properties, such as the *name* property, and a method, which is the *IsGoodToEat* method. The scope of the property and the method is limited to the class of the ingredient. In our example, the scope of the *name* property and the *IsGoodToEat* method is limited to the *cheese*, the *meat*, the *sauce*, the *vegetable,* and the *bread* classes.

2.4.4.5   Properties

Properties are values representing characteristics of a class. A property has a name and only one domain, which is the class that owns the property. In the case of the classes representing the cheeseburger ingredients, each ingredient has a name (with a value coded as a string), a production date (with a value coded as a datetime string), and a validity period (with a value coded as unsigned integer of 8 bits). As mentioned before, properties can also be inherited from superclasses by subclasses.

2.4.4.6 Methods

A method is an operation describing the behavior of an instance of a class. Not all classes have methods. A method has a name and only one domain, which is the class that owns the method. In the case of the classes representing the cheeseburger ingredients, each ingredient has a method called is *IsGoodToEat*. This method returns a Boolean value True or False to determine the freshness of the ingredient. Like properties, subclasses can inherit methods from superclasses.

2.4.4.7 Associations

An association is a class that contains two or more references. In the example of the cheeseburger, we have five references: *MeatIngredient*, *CheeseIngredient*, *SauceIngredient*, *VegetableIngredient*, and *BreadIngredient*. Each of these references points to the ingredients that are classes. References are properties of associations. An association represents a relationship between two or more objects. An association is a class type with a qualifier stating the nature of the class (an association qualifier). For instance, in Figure 2.16 (right pane), the *CIM_LogicalDiskBasedOnPartition* class is an association, as it associates the *CIM_DiskPartition* and *CIM_LogicalDisk* classes.

2.4.4.8 References

Talking about associations always implies the notion of references. A reference defines the role each object plays and represents the role name of a class in the context of an association. Therefore, the domain of a reference is an association. In the cheeseburger example, the reference between the cheeseburger and each ingredient determines the role of the ingredient, which constitutes the cheeseburger (see Figure 2.7). Associations can support multiple relationships for a given object, which implies that we may have many references. In computing words, a system can be related to many system components in many different ways. For instance, in Figure 2.16 (right pane of **WMI CIM Studio**), the references are illustrated by two arrows starting from *CIM_LogicalDiskBasedOnPartition* and pointing to the *CIM_DiskPartition* and *CIM_LogicalDisk* classes.

2.4.4.9 Indications

An indication is an object created as a result of the occurrence of an event. Indications are always subclasses and may contain properties or methods.

Since an indication is the result of an event, such a class type may have an association with one or more triggers. Triggers create the instance of the indications. In Chapter 6, we will examine what events are and how to work with them. For now, remember that an indication is nothing more than an instance coming from an event.

2.4.4.10 *Qualifiers*

A qualifier is used to characterize classes, properties, methods, and other elements of the CIM schema. When we talked about the associations, we saw that an association is a class of a particular type. To determine that a given class is an association class, a qualifier is used. Qualifiers are also used to determine whether a property of a class is required and to define the key of a class. Keys are properties that provide a unique value to distinguish instances of a class by using one or more properties as a unique identifier. In such a case, we refer to a key qualifier. Note that a singleton class (a class that has only one instance) does not need a key because it is already unique.

A qualifier has a name, a type, a value, a scope, and a flavor. Flavors describe rules that determine whether a qualifier can be propagated to a derived class or instance. It also determines whether a derived class or instance can override the qualifier's original value. In CIM, a qualifier may have a default value. The type of the default value must agree with the qualifier type (association qualifier, property qualifier, key qualifier, etc.). Figure 2.17 shows a logical representation of a qualifier with its miscellaneous possible values. Basically, qualifiers are sorted into four categories:

- **Metaqualifiers:** This qualifier type is used to define the actual usage of a class or property definition.

- **Standard qualifiers:** These qualifiers are CIM-compliant qualifiers. They are implemented by any compliant CIM product.

- **Optional qualifiers:** Optional qualifiers address situations that are uncommon to all CIM-compliant implementations. They are provided in the CIM specification to avoid random user-defined qualifiers.

- **WMI-specific qualifiers:** These qualifiers are especially added by Microsoft to support the WMI implementation. They are not part of the CIM specification and are purely Microsoft-related.

Qualifiers are visible in **WMI CIM Studio** by right-clicking on a class or an instance, or on a property or method of a class. Table 2.2 contains the lists of qualifiers available.

Figure 2.17
The qualifier types.

To avoid repetition of the Microsoft Platform SDK, as the list of qualifier is quite long, you can refer to WMI SDK to get the complete meaning of the available qualifiers.

Table 2.2   *Available Qualifiers*

Standard Qualifiers	Optional Qualifiers	MetaQualifiers	WMI Qualifiers
Abstract	Delete	Association	Amendment
Aggregate	Expensive	Indication	CIM_Key
Aggregation	IfDeleted		CIMType
Alias	Indexed		ClassContext
ArrayType	Invisible		Deprecated
Bitmap	Large		Display
Bitvalues	Not_Null		Dynamic
Description	Provider		DynProps
DisplayName	Syntax		ID
Gauge	SyntaxType		Implemented
In	TriggerType		InstanceContext
In, Out	UnknownValues		Locale
Key	UnsupportedValues		Optional
MappingStrings			Privileges
Max			PropertyContext

Table 2.2   *Available Qualifiers (continued)*

Standard Qualifiers	Optional Qualifiers	MetaQualifiers	WMI Qualifiers
MaxLen			Provider
MaxValue			Singleton
Min			Static
MinValue			SubType
ModelCorrespondence			UUID
Nonlocal			WritePrivileges
NonlocalType			
NullValue			
Out			
Override			
OverrideValue			
Propagated			
Read			
Required			
Revision			

2.4.4.11   Override

We have seen that classes are organized similarly to an upside-down tree. Each class has properties and methods. WBEM introduces the override relationship to indicate the substitution between a property or a method of a subclass and a property or a method inherited from a superclass. By using the override relationship, it is possible to overwrite a property or a method in a subclass from a superclass. This relation is made with the help of qualifiers and is illustrated in Figure 2.13 with the dashed line.

2.5   What is a MOF file?

A MOF file is an ASCII file using a specific syntax and language definition to code CIM definitions. MOF files are used to load the CIM repository with new definitions of managed objects without having to use the specific API to modify or extend the CIM Schema. In some ways, MOF files can be compared to the LDIF files used in the LDAP world. MOF files can be used to export or import a set of information to or from the CIM repository, just as LDIF files can be used to export or import a set of information from an LDAP directory. MOF files encode the definition of CIM objects as stated in the CIM specification. For example, you can implement the cheeseburger example in a MOF file. This produces the MOF file shown in Sample 2.1. With the knowledge we have of the cheeseburger data model we developed in UML notation, it will be quite easy to understand the MOF file content. Note that this MOF file creates a new namespace in the CIM repository. As the principle is the same for all ingredients, we skipped some lines representing ingredients in the reproduction of this MOF file.

Sample 2.1   *The cheeseburger MOF file*

```
 1:// File: Food.MOF
 2:
 3:// Changes focus to Root namespace
 4:#pragma namespace("\\\\.\\Root")
 5:
 6:// Create new namespace
 7:instance of __Namespace
 8:{
 9:     Name = "Food";
10:};
11:
12:// Changes focus to new namespace
13:#pragma namespace("\\\\.\\ROOT\\Food")
14:
15:// class: Bread
16:// Derived from:
17:[abstract: ToInstance ToSubclass]
18:class Bread
19:{
20:        [Description ("This is the bread name"): ToInstance ToSubclass,
            read: ToInstance ToSubclass]
21:        string Name;
22:        [Description ("This is the bread production date"): ToInstance ToSubclass,
            read: ToInstance ToSubclass]
23:        datetime ProductionDate;
24:        [Description ("This is the bread validity period"): ToInstance ToSubclass,
            read: ToInstance ToSubclass]
25:        datetime ValidDays;
26:        [Description ("Is the bread still good to eat?"): ToInstance ToSubclass]
27:        boolean IsGoodToEat();
28:};
29:
30:// class: ToastedBun
31:// Derived from: Bread
32:class ToastedBun : Bread
33:{
34:        [Key : ToInstance ToSubclass,
            Description ("This is the toasted bun name"): ToInstance ToSubclass]
35:        string Name;
36:};
37:
38:// class: Meat
39:// Derived from:
40:[abstract: ToInstance ToSubclass]
41:class Meat
42:{
```

```
43:         [Description ("This is the meat name"): ToSubclass,
             read: ToInstance ToSubclass]
44:         string Name;
45:         [Description ("This is the meat production date"): ToSubclass,
             read: ToInstance ToSubclass]
46:         datetime ProductionDate;
47:         [Description ("This is the meat validity period"): ToSubclass,
             read: ToInstance ToSubclass]
48:         datetime ValidDays;
49:         [Description ("Is the meat still good to eat?"): ToSubclass]
50:         boolean IsGoodToEat();
51:};
..:
61:// class: Beef
62:// Derived from: Meat
63:class Beef : Meat
64:{
65:         [Key : ToInstance ToSubclass,
             Description ("This is the beef name"): ToInstance ToSubclass]
66:         string Name;
67:};
..:
77:// class: Vegetable
78:// Derived from:
79:[abstract: ToInstance ToSubclass]
80:class Vegetable
81:{
82:         [Description ("This is the vegetable name"): ToSubclass,
             read: ToInstance ToSubclass]
83:         string Name;
84:         [Description ("This is the vegetable production date"): ToSubclass,
             read: ToInstance ToSubclass]
85:         datetime ProductionDate;
86:         [Description ("This is the vegetable validity period"): ToSubclass,
             read: ToInstance ToSubclass]
87:         datetime ValidDays;
88:         [Description ("Is the vegetable still good to eat?"): ToSubclass]
89:         boolean IsGoodToEat();
90:};
91:
92:// class: Salad
93:// Derived from: Vegetable
94:class Salad : Vegetable
95:{
96:         [Key : ToInstance ToSubclass,
             Description ("This is the salad name"): ToInstance ToSubclass]
97:         string Name;
98:};
99:
100:// class: Gherkin
101:// Derived from: Vegetable
102:class Gherkin : Vegetable
103:{
104:         [Key : ToInstance ToSubclass,
             Description ("This is the gherkin name"): ToInstance ToSubclass]
105:         string Name;
106:};
...:
116:// class: Potatoes
117:// Derived from: Vegetable
118:class Potatoes : Vegetable
```

```
119:{
120:        [Key : ToInstance ToSubclass,
             Description ("This is the potatoes name"): ToInstance ToSubclass]
121:        string Name;
122:};
123:
124:// class: FrenchFries
125:// Derived from: Potatoes
126:class FrenchFries : Potatoes
127:{
128:        [Description ("This is the french fries name"): ToInstance ToSubclass]
129:        string Name;
130:        [Description ("This is the french fries size"): ToInstance ToSubclass,
             ValueMap{"Small", "Medium", "Large"}: ToInstance ToSubclass,
             read: ToInstance ToSubclass]
131:        string Size;
132:};
133:
134:// class: Cheese
135:// Derived from:
136:[abstract: ToInstance ToSubclass]
137:class Cheese
138:{
139:        [Description ("This is the cheese name"): ToSubclass, read: ToInstance ToSubclass]
140:        string Name;
141:        [Description ("This is the cheese production date"): ToSubclass,
             read: ToInstance ToSubclass]
142:        datetime ProductionDate;
143:        [Description ("This is the cheese validity period"): ToSubclass,
             read: ToInstance ToSubclass]
144:        datetime ValidDays;
145:        [Description ("Is the cheese still good to eat?"): ToSubclass]
146:        boolean IsGoodToEat();
147:};
...:
165:// class: ProcessedCheeseSlice
166:// Derived from: Cheese
167:class ProcessedCheeseSlice : Cheese
168:{
169:        [Key : ToInstance ToSubclass,
             Description ("This is the processed cheese slice name"): ToInstance ToSubclass]
170:        string Name;
171:};
172:
173:// class: Sauce
174:// Derived from:
175:[abstract: ToInstance ToSubclass]
176:class Sauce
177:{
178:        [Description ("This is the sauce name"): ToSubclass,
             read: ToInstance ToSubclass]
179:        string Name;
180:        [Description ("This is the sauce production date"): ToSubclass,
             read: ToInstance ToSubclass]
181:        datetime ProductionDate;
182:        [Description ("This is the sauce validity period"): ToSubclass,
             read: ToInstance ToSubclass]
183:        datetime ValidDays;
184:        [Description ("Is the sauce still good to eat?"): ToSubclass]
185:        boolean IsGoodToEat();
186:};
```

```
187:
188:// class: Ketchup
189:// Derived from: Sauce
190:class Ketchup : Sauce
191:{
192:        [Key : ToInstance ToSubclass,
                Description ("This is the ketchup name"): ToInstance ToSubclass]
193:        string Name;
194:};
...:
212:// class: CheeseBurger
213:// Derived from:
214:[abstract: ToInstance ToSubclass]
215:class CheeseBurger
216:{
217:        uint32 Weight;
218:};
219:
220:// class: Beverage
221:// Derived from:
222:class Beverage
223:{
224:        [Key : ToInstance ToSubclass,
                Description ("This is the beverage name"): ToInstance ToSubclass]
225:        string Name;
226:};
227:
228:// class: Coke
229:// Derived from: Beverage
230:class Coke : Beverage
231:{
232:        [Description ("This is the Coke name"): ToInstance ToSubclass,
                read: ToInstance ToSubclass]
233:        string Name;
234:        [Description ("This is the Coke size"): ToInstance ToSubclass,
                ValueMap{"Small", "Medium", "Large"}: ToInstance ToSubclass,
                read: ToInstance ToSubclass]
235:        string Size;
236:};
237:
238:// class: MenuBurgerAggregation
239:// Derived from:
240:[association: ToInstance ToSubclass]
241:class MenuBurgerAggregation
242:{
243:        BurgerMenu ref Menu;
244:        CheeseBurger ref Burger;
245:};
246:
247:// class: Cheeseassociation
248:// Derived from:
249:[association: ToInstance ToSubclass]
250:class Cheeseassociation
251:{
252:        ProcessedCheeseSlice ref CheeseIngredient;
253:        CheeseBurger ref Burger;
254:};
255:
256:// class: Meatassociation
257:// Derived from:
```

```
258:[association: ToInstance ToSubclass]
259:class Meatassociation
260:{
261:        CheeseBurger ref Burger;
262:        Beef ref MeatIngredient;
263:};
264:
265:// class: Vegetableassociation
266:// Derived from:
267:[association: ToInstance ToSubclass]
268:class Vegetableassociation
269:{
270:        CheeseBurger ref Burger;
271:        Gherkin ref VegetableIngredient;
272:};
273:
274:// class: Sauceassociation
275:// Derived from:
276:[association: ToInstance ToSubclass]
277:class Sauceassociation
278:{
279:        CheeseBurger ref Burger;
280:        Ketchup ref SauceIngredient;
281:};
282:
283:// class: Breadassociation
284:// Derived from:
285:[association: ToInstance ToSubclass]
286:class Breadassociation
287:{
288:        ToastedBun ref BreadIngredient;
289:        CheeseBurger ref Burger;
290:};
291:
292:// class: BurgerMenu
293:// Derived from:
294:class BurgerMenu
295:{
296:};
297:
298:// class: MenuBeverageAggregation
299:// Derived from:
300:[association: ToInstance ToSubclass]
301:class MenuBeverageAggregation
302:{
303:        BurgerMenu ref Menu;
304:        Coke ref Beverage;
305:};
306:
307:// class: MenuFriesAggregation
308:// Derived from:
309:[association: ToInstance ToSubclass]
310:class MenuFriesAggregation
311:{
312:        BurgerMenu ref Menu;
313:        FrenchFries ref FrenchFries;
314:};
315:
316:// EOF Food.MOF
```

To load this MOF file in the CIM repository, it is necessary to use the MOF compiler, called **MOFCOMP.Exe**. We see how to use the MOF compiler that comes with WMI in Section 2.8.5.1. Basically, the command line to use in this particular case is as follows:

```
C:\>MOFCOMP.Exe Food.Mof
```

Once loaded in the CIM repository, this MOF file produces the output in Figure 2.18. We have set the **WMI CIM Studio** view on the cheeseburger class created with the different ingredients to show the result of the associations.

Microsoft provides a MOF editor on the DMTF Web site. You can download it for free from http://www.dmtf.org/standards/cimtools.php. The MOF editor eases the reading of MOF files, as the ASCII representation can be sometimes quite confusing to read.

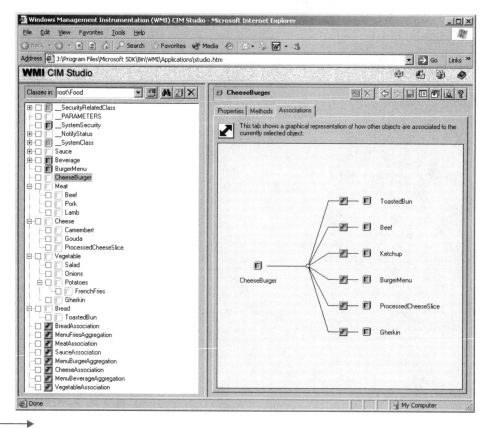

Figure 2.18   *The cheeseburger association class once created with a MOF file.*

Although it is important to have a basic understanding of the MOF file representation, a deep knowledge of MOF file creation is not required at all to script with WMI. However, if you are a WMI developer, it will be mandatory for you to dive into the MOF syntax details since a MOF file is required to register your WMI providers and their associated classes. Programming of WMI providers is beyond the scope of this book, but if you want to find out more about MOF files, we recommend that you take a look at the WMI SDK.

2.6   What is xmlCIM?

A MOF file defines a textual declaration format, but it is not a standard for CIM information interchange between systems. In order to be able to communicate management information between different systems, two aspects must be taken into consideration: The first consideration is to use a communication protocol common to any management platform; the second is to use a common representation of the managed information for the transport between platforms. The CIM specification defines HTTP as the common communication protocol. This makes sense because HTTP is available on every computer system in the industry. As a common representation, XML is used with a Document Type Definition (DTD). This also makes sense, because XML is understandable by any platform, and parsing components are widely available in the industry.

There are many different ways in which CIM operations can be represented within XML with the operations encapsulated in HTTP messages. For interoperability reasons between different implementations of CIM, there is an obvious requirement for standardization of both the XML representation of CIM and the HTTP encapsulation. For this reason xmlCIM defines the declarations of the CIM objects that can be transformed in XML and the CIM messages for encapsulation over HTTP. Under Windows.NET Server, it is possible to obtain the XML representation of the CIM objects, but it is not yet possible to communicate over HTTP. If you need more information about this subject, you can visit the DMTF Web site at http://www.dmtf.org/standards/published_documents.php.

2.7   The supported platforms

For Microsoft platforms, WMI is the Microsoft implementation of WBEM. It is installed by default under Windows.NET Server, Windows 2000, and Windows Millennium. It is possible to install WMI on platforms such as Windows 95, Windows 98, and Windows NT 4.0 (from SP4 or higher) as a separate download from the Microsoft download center at http://www.microsoft.com/downloads/search.asp. Since the release of Windows 2000, the Windows Driver Model also supports WMI, which means that a driver developer can expose some interesting information to WMI. This is supported only under Windows.NET Server, Windows XP, Windows 2000, Windows 98, and Windows Millennium. As mentioned before, WMI runs as a service under Windows NT, Windows 2000, and Windows.NET Server, whereas it runs as an application under Windows 98, Windows 95, and Windows Millennium. This is due to the structural differences between Windows NT and Windows 9x/Me. The WMI SDK is supported only on Windows.NET Server, Windows 2000, and Windows NT 4.0 (sP4 or higher).

In addition to the Microsoft WBEM implementation, HP has implemented WBEM on its HPUX and Tru64 UNIX platforms. The software component is called HP WBEM Services for HPUX (or Tru64). You can refer to http://www.hp.com/large/infrastructure/management/wbem for more information. HP also offers the HP WBEM Services for HP-UX SDK. This software component for HPUX platforms is the developer's kit for the HP WBEM Services for HP-UX product. This product is based on The Open Group (TOG) Pegasus Open Source Software (OSS) project (http://www.opengroup.org/pegasus).

SUN also announced its implementation of WBEM on the Solaris 8 Operating System. The official name is "Solaris™ WBEM Services and Sun™ WBEM SDK Support for XML and Java 2™ Technology." You can find the public announcement at http://www.sun.com/software/solaris/wbem/cover and additional details at http://www.sun.com/software/solaris/wbem/faq.html. The software kit is available for download at the same location. You can also contact SUN at wbem-support@sun.com for more information.

Novell also started the Zero Effort Network (ZEN) initiative. You can check the following URL for more information: http://www.novell.com/news/leadstories/98/jul22. Unfortunately, at the time of this writing, Novell does not yet implement the CIM database in its ZENworks for Desktops 3 Inventory Database (ZfD3). However, as part of the ZENworks for Networks, Novell also included some DMTF standards, such as DMI, for hardware inventory scanning in ZfD3 (see Section 2.2). ZfD3 is not compatible with WBEM, but desktop side clients could be compatible with both DMI and WBEM. Today, ZfD3 requires the DMI layer functionality in order to retrieve full hardware inventory correctly. See http://www.novell.com for more information.

Among the Novell, SUN, and Microsoft initiatives, there is also the WBEMsource initiative. The WBEMsource initiative is an umbrella organization providing coordination between open-source WBEM projects. Its goal is to achieve interoperability and portability. Individual development projects are completely autonomous projects that are voluntarily participating in the initiative. The mission of the WBEMsource initiative is to promote the widespread use of the DMTF's management technologies through the creation of an environment fostering open-source WBEM implementations. You can refer to http://www.opengroup.org/wbemsource for more information.

Although this book focuses on the Microsoft implementation of WBEM called WMI, it is quite clear that the WBEM implementation is not a Microsoft-only initiative.

2.8   The Microsoft CIM implementation: WMI

WMI is designed as a Schema extension of the CIM Core Schema and the CIM Common Model. WMI is implemented for the Windows platforms. WMI enables Windows systems, applications, networks, and other managed components to be represented using CIM as designed by the DMTF.

In addition to data modeling, WMI offers a set of services that includes query-based information retrieval and event notification. The Component Object Model (COM) programming interface allows access to the services and the management data while implementing an abstraction layer.

2.8.1   WMI architecture

WMI is implemented as a three-tiered architecture (see Figure 2.19). At the top of the architecture, we have the management applications. These applications interact with the WMI COM API. The WMI COM API has a collection of COM objects that are usable from various programming languages such as Visual Basic, C++, and scripting languages such as JScript or VBScript. Behind the WMI COM API, we find the Common Information Model Object Manager (CIMOM) component. CIMOM acts as a broker between the management applications (called the consumers), the CIM repository and the WMI providers.

Figure 2.19
The WMI architecture.

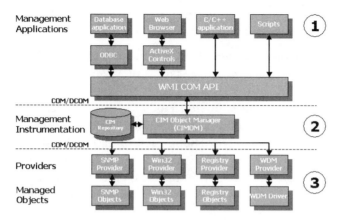

2.8.2 **Providers and consumers**

The WMI architecture introduces the notion of providers and consumers. Providers are the components accessing the management objects to gather the management data (layer 3 in Figure 2.19). On the other hand, a consumer is an application that uses the data collected by the providers (layer 1 in Figure 2.19). Basically, consumers will be applications such as HP Open-View Operations for Windows, Microsoft Operations Manager (MOM), or any other management application that consumes WMI information. The scripts developed in this book are also WMI Consumers. This layered architecture implies that the CIM repository has interfaces with an (upper) API for management applications (consumers) and an (lower) API for providers.

WMI providers are installed with the Windows system installation or with any installed application that provides its own WMI providers. This is why there is a distinction between the built-in WMI providers and application-specific WMI providers. For example, when Exchange 2000 is installed, it adds the necessary definitions (classes) related to the Exchange WMI providers to the CIM repository. The WMI architecture is extensible by simply creating new providers and adding the new classes to the CIM repository; as a result we have an unlimited list of available WMI providers. Table 2.3 shows a list of the most important WMI providers delivered with Windows.NET Server.

Application developers can add their own providers and extract the management data from their applications. By using classes, properties, and methods, developers can represent the management data in the CIM data model. To summarize, the provider is an abstraction layer for CIMOM, which hides the access complexity and interpretation of the management

Table 2.3   *Some Windows.NET Server WMI Providers*

Provider	Description
Directory Services Provider	Makes the classes and objects in the Microsoft® Active Directory™ available to WMI management applications
Event Log Provider	Provides access to data and notifications of events from the Microsoft® Windows_NT®/Microsoft® Windows®_2000 Event Log
Microsoft Windows Installer Provider	Provides access to information about applications that are installed using Windows Installer
Performance Counters Provider	Provides access to raw performance counter data
Performance Monitor Provider	Provides access to data from the Windows_NT/Windows_2000 Performance Monitor
Power Management Event Provider	Represents power management events resulting from power state changes
Registry Event Provider	Sends an event whenever a change occurs to a key, a value, or an entire tree in the registry
Registry Provider	Provides access to data from the registry
Security Provider	Provides access to security settings that control ownership, auditing, and access rights to the NTFS file system
SNMP Provider	Provides access to data and events from SNMP devices
View Provider	Creates new classes made of properties from different source classes, namespaces, or computers
WDM Provider	Provides access to data and events from device drivers that conform to the WMI interface
Win32 Provider	Provides access to data from the Win32 subsystem

data of a specific implementation. Once completed, consumers can access the class definitions related to the applications and retrieve the management data through CIMOM and the especially developed provider.

More than being a simple "pass-through" to access the management information, providers can be event driven. Simply said, an application can register with CIMOM to receive notifications about a particular event. In this case, CIMOM works in conjunction with the WMI providers to be notified about the expected events. Once the event occurs, the WMI provider notifies CIMOM. Next, CIMOM notifies the consumers that have made a registration for the event. This feature is a very important and useful function because it leaves an application or a script in a dormant state until the expected event occurs. WMI watches the event on behalf of the consumer. CIMOM is an abstraction layer for the consumers of the management information provided by the WMI providers. This abstraction layer allows the correlation of events coming from various WMI providers.

WMI providers are .dll files located in %SystemRoot%\system32\wbem. If you examine this directory, you will see a collection of .dll files. In addition to these DLLs, there is typically one file with the same name that uses a .mof extension. The MOF file is the file containing the necessary definitions to register the WMI provider and its related set of classes created in the CIM repository.

Beside the providers installed in a Windows system, WMI also provides some consumers. This means that consumers include not only the applications or scripts developed on top of WMI but also the components brought by WMI. Actually, WMI comes with a set of ready-to-use consumers that perform actions based on specific management events. You can associate a particular event monitored by a WMI provider and redirect this event to a built-in WMI consumer to perform a particular task. In this case, there is nothing to develop; only a registration of the expected event with the associated WMI consumer is required. Usually, the registration with CIMOM is made with the help of a MOF file provided with the consumer. Some of the WMI consumers provided with Windows.NET Server are listed in Table 2.4.

There is a clear distinction between two types of WMI consumers. There are permanent consumers and temporary consumers. Briefly, a permanent

Table 2.4   *Some Windows.NET Server WMI Consumer Providers*

Consumer	Description
SMTP Event Consumer	Sends an e-mail message using SMTP each time an event is delivered to it.
WMI Event Viewer	A permanent event consumer that allows users to sort and view the details of events received. As events are generated in WMI by Windows Management or by event providers, event objects are forwarded to any consumers registered for these types of events. You can register WMI Event Viewer for any event filters, so you can view only incoming events that match the filters.
Active Script Event Consumer	Executes a predefined script in an arbitrary scripting language whenever an event is delivered to it.
Command Line Event Consumer	Launches an arbitrary process in the local system context whenever an event is delivered to it.
Log File Event Consumer	Writes customized strings to a text log file whenever events are delivered to it.
NT EventLog Event Consumer	Logs a specific message to the Windows_NT event log whenever an event is delivered to it.

consumer receives event notifications regardless of whether it is running. The registration of the consumer is made in the CIM repository with a system class. As the registration is permanent in the CIM repository, WMI locates the consumer and starts it if necessary. A permanent consumer is written as a COM object. On the other hand, a temporary consumer is a component that makes a registration to receive notifications of events only when it is active. Once the component (an application or a script) is no longer running, notifications are no longer received. WMI temporary consumers will be used when we discuss scripting with WMI events in Chapter 6.

2.8.3 The CIM repository

The CIM repository is the database used by WMI to store the CIM data model. It is also called in the Microsoft documentation the WMI repository. In a Windows system, the CIM repository is located in \%SystemRoot%\System32\WBEM\Repository folder. No application directly accesses the CIM repository. Every access to the CIM repository goes through CIMOM. This is the only way that management applications can access the CIM repository (through the WMI COM API). The same rule applies for the WMI providers (by interacting with CIMOM).

By default, the CIM repository is saved in a .rec file every 30 minutes. Most of the default settings of WMI can be controlled with the computer management MMC as shown in Figure 2.20.

The CIM repository is initialized from various MOF files (located in %SystemRoot%\System32\wbem) at WMI installation time. If the CIM repository is damaged or deleted, when WMI is restarted the CIM repository is reinitialized from a collection of MOF files listed in a registry key named "Autorecover MOFs" and located in HKLM\SOFTWARE\ Microsoft\WBEM\CIMOM. Only the MOF files listed in this key are used to reinitialize the CIM repository. If any other installed applications extend the CIM repository for their own purposes, make sure that the MOF files used are also listed in this registry key. You can manually recompile the required MOF file later on with the MOF compiler (**MOFCOMP.Exe**).

Under Windows XP and Windows.NET Server, the CIM repository resides in the %SystemRoot%\system32\wbem\Repository\FS folder. This folders contains the following files:

- **Index.btr**: Binary-tree (btree) index file

- **Index.map:** Transaction control file

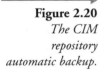

Figure 2.20
*The CIM
repository
automatic backup.*

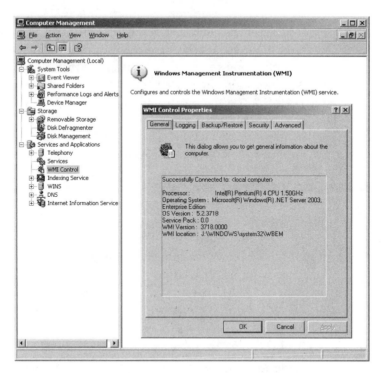

- **Objects.data:** CIM repository where managed resource definitions are stored

- **Objects.map:** Transaction control file

Under Windows 2000 and Windows NT 4.0 Service Pack 4, the CIM repository is located in the %SystemRoot%\system32\wbem\Respository folder. This folder contains **cim.rep** file, which implements the CIM database. Under Windows Millennium Edition (Me), Windows 98, and Windows 95, the **cim.rep** file is also the CIM database file. However, it is located in the %windir%\system\wbem\Respository folder.

2.8.4   The WMI query language

The WMI query language (WQL) is a subset of the ANSI SQL language with minor semantic changes to suit the WMI needs. WQL is a retrieval language only. It does not allow operations to modify, insert, or delete information. WQL is not part of the DMTF standard, but it has been proposed to be part of the standard. At the time of writing, WQL is under examination to be included in the DMTF standard. This language is mainly used to perform:

- **Data queries:** These queries are used to retrieve instances of classes. For example, to retrieve the instances of the *Win32_Service* class:

```
Select * From 'Win32_Service'
```

- **Event queries:** These queries are used by temporary consumers, permanent consumers, and event providers. Basically, event queries are used to filter events. For example, to receive a notification when a change is made to one *Win32_Service* instance (stopping or starting a service, for example):

```
Select * From __InstanceModificationEvent Within 10 Where
TargetInstance ISA 'Win32_Service'
```

- **Schema queries:** These queries are used to retrieve class definitions and information about schema associations. For example, to retrieve the class definition of the *Win32_Service* class:

```
SELECT * FROM meta_class Where __this ISA 'Win32_Service'
```

Or to retrieve the associations of the *Win32_Service* SNMP instance:

```
ASSOCIATORS OF {Win32_Service.Name='SNMP'}
```

When practicing exercises with the WMI Microsoft tools, we use two basic queries: one data query to retrieve the list of the Windows services and one event query to receive event notification changes performed to one or more Windows services. We revisit the possibilities offered by WQL in the following chapter.

2.8.5   The WMI Microsoft tools

As part of the WMI standard installation and the Platform SDK, Microsoft provides some tools to ease working with WMI. It is important to be familiar with these tools, because they will be helpful to discover, extend, and troubleshoot WMI.

2.8.5.1   *The MOF compiler: MOFCOMP.exe*

The MOF compiler parses a file containing MOF statements and adds the classes and class instances defined in the file to the CIM repository. **MOFCOMP.exe** is included in every WMI installation. Every definition existing in the CIM repository is initially defined in a MOF file. MOF files are located in %SystemRoot%\system32\wbem. During the WMI setup, they are loaded in the CIM repository.

Sample 2.1 showed a MOF file example (**Food.mof**) for the cheeseburger representation. The following example shows the MOF file (**SMTP-**

Cons.mof) used to register the permanent *SMTP* event consumer, SMTPCons.dll. This permanent consumer is a registered COM object DLL using the class ID C7A3A54B-0250-11d3-9CD1-00105A1F4801.

```
1:// Copyright (c) 1997-2001 Microsoft Corporation, All Rights Reserved
2:
3:[locale(1033)]
4:class SMTPEventConsumer : __EventConsumer
5:{
6:   [key] string Name;
7:   [not_null, write] string SMTPServer;
8:   [Template, write] string Subject;
9:   [Template, write] string FromLine;
10:  [Template, write] string ReplyToLine;
11:  [Template, write] string Message;
12:  [Template, write] string ToLine;
13:  [Template, write] string CcLine;
14:  [Template, write] string BccLine;
15:  [write] string HeaderFields[];
16:};
17:
18:Instance of __Win32provider as $SMTPCONS_P
19:{
20:  Name = "SMTPEventConsumer";
21:  Clsid = "{C7A3A54B-0250-11d3-9CD1-00105A1F4801}";
22:  HostingModel = "LocalSystemHost";
23:
24:};
25:
26:Instance of __EventConsumerproviderRegistration
27:{
28:  provider = $SMTPCONS_P;
29:  ConsumerclassNames = {"SMTPEventConsumer"};
30:};
..:
..:
..:
```

Briefly, we see that the first section defines the *SMTPConsumer* class derived from the *__EventConsumer* system class (line 4). This means that the *SMTPConsumer* class inherits from *__EventConsumer* system class. Next, the section contains the properties exposed by the consumer (lines 5 to 16). Notice that the first property of the consumer is its name (line 6) and is defined as a key. This means that the name property is used to uniquely identify the consumer. This implies that the name is a mandatory property to create an instance of the consumer. Next, there are two additional sections:

1.   One section references the consumer provider DLL file (lines 18 to 24), which is an instance of the *__Win32provider* system class used to register the WMI providers.

2.   The next section registers the component as a consumer provider in the CIM repository (lines 26 to 30). This section creates the link between the *SMTPConsumer* class definition (lines 5 to 43) and the provider itself (lines 18 to 24).

To load this MOF file in the CIM repository, the MOF compiler is used as follows from the command line:

```
C:\>MOFCOMP %SystemRoot%\System32\wbem\SMTPCons.MOF
```

We will not enter in the security considerations now (as this is deeply examined in the second volume dedicated to WMI, *Leveraging Windows Management Instrumentation Scripting*, ISBN 1555582990) but be aware that to register a permanent event consumer, you must be a member of the **Administrators** group.

By default every MOF file is loaded in the **Root\Default** namespace. Use the –N switch to overwrite the default. To get a complete list of the options available from **MOFCOMP.exe**, refer to Table 2.5.

Table 2.5   *MOFCOMP.exe Switches*

MOF Compiler Switches	
-autorecover	Adds the named MOF file to the list of files compiled during repository recovery. The list of autorecover MOF files is stored in the registry key named: HKEY_LOCAL_MACHINE\SOFTWARE\Microsoft\WBEM\CIMOM\Autorecover MOFs. The MOF files listed in this registry entry must reside on the local computer because MOF files that use the autorecover command cannot recover MOF files located on a remote computer.
-check	Requests that the compiler perform a syntax check only and print appropriate error messages. No other switch can be used with this switch. When this switch is used, no connection to WMI is established and no modifications to the CIM repository are made.
-N:<*namespacepath*>	Requests that the compiler load the MOF file into the namespace specified as "namespacepath." The default namespace (root\default) is used unless this switch is used or a #pragma namespace ("namespace path") statement appears in the MOF file. If both the -N namespace switch and #pragma namespace are used, #pragma namespace takes priority.
-class:createonly	Requests that the compiler not make any changes to existing classes. When this switch is used, the compilation terminates if a class specified in the MOF file already exists.
-class:forceupdate	Forces updates of classes when conflicting child classes exist. For example, suppose a class qualifier is defined in a child class and the base class tries to add the same qualifier. In -class:forceupdate mode, the MOF compiler resolves this conflict by deleting the conflicting qualifier in the child class. If the child class has instances, the forced update fails.

Table 2.5   *MOFCOMP.exe Switches (continued)*

MOF Compiler Switches	
-class:safeupdate	Allows updates of classes even if there are child classes, as long as the change does not cause conflicts with child classes. For example, this flag allows adding a new property to the base class that was not previously mentioned in child classes. If the child classes have instances, the update fails.
-class:updateonly	Requests that the compiler not create any new classes. When this switch is used, the compilation terminates if a class specified in the MOF file does not exist.
-instance:updateonly	Requests that the compiler not create any new instances. When this switch is used, the compilation terminates if an instance specified in the MOF file does not exist.
-instance:createonly	Requests that the compiler not make any changes to existing instances. When this switch is used, the compilation terminates if an instance specified in the MOF file already exists.
-B:*\<filename\>*	Requests that the compiler create a binary version of the MOF file with the name "filename" without making any modifications to the CIM repository.
-WMI	Requests that the compiler perform a WMI syntax check. The -B switch must be used with this switch. The -WMI switch is only used for building binary MOFs for use by WDM device drivers. This switch invokes a separate binary MOF file checker, which runs after the binary MOF file is created. To use this switch under Windows 2000, the Windows 2000 DDK must first be installed.
-P:\<Password\>	Specifies Password as the password for the computer's user to enter when logging on.
-U:\<UserName\>	Specifies UserName as the name of the user logging on.
-A:\<Authority\>	Specifies Authority as the authority (domain name) to use when logging on to WMI.
-MOF:*\<path\>*	Name of the language-neutral output. Used with the -AMENDEMENT switch to specify the name of the language-neutral MOF file that will be generated.
-MFL:*\<path\>*	Name of the language-specific output. Used with the -AMENDEMENT switch to specify the name of the language-specific MOF file that will be generated.
-AMENDMENT:\<Locale\>	Splits the MOF file into language-neutral and -specific versions. The MOF compiler creates a language neutral form of the MOF file that has all amended qualifiers removed. A localized version of the MOF file is also created with an MFL file extension. The Locale parameter specifies the name of the child namespace that contains the localized class definitions. The format of the Locale parameter is MS_*xxx* where *xxx* is the hexadecimal value of the Win32 LCID. For example, the locale for American English is MS_409. For more information, see WMI Localization.
\<MOFfile\>	Specifies MOFfile as the name of the file to parse.

2.8.5.2   WMI CIM Studio

WMI CIM Studio is an application included in the WMI Tools package. This package is available as a separate download for Windows 2000, Windows XP, and Windows.NET Server from http://www.microsoft.com/

downloads/release.asp?ReleaseID=40804. It uses a Web interface to display information, but it relies on the collection of ActiveX components installed on the system when it runs for the first time. **WMI CIM Studio** provides the ability to do the following:

- Connect to a chosen system and browse the CIM repository in any namespace available

- Search for classes by their names, descriptions, or property names

- Review the properties, methods, and associations related to a given class

- See the instances available for a given class of the examined system

- Perform queries in WQL language

- Generate a MOF file based on selected classes

- Compile a MOF file to load it in the CIM repository

Figures 2.9 and 2.16 show two screen-shot samples of the **WMI CIM Studio**. Each time a class is selected in **WMI CIM Studio**, the right pane shows its properties, methods, and associations. Take a few minutes to play with the **WMI CIM Studio,** as it will help you understand how the CIM repository is organized. Figure 2.21 shows the meaning of the various symbols used by the **WMI CIM Studio**.

In the previous section, we saw how to register the SMTP event consumer that comes with the WMI installation. You can find the *SMTP-EventConsumer* class with the **WMI CIM Studio** by performing a search on the namespace used for the registration. You will see that the definition made in the MOF file matches the view of the **WMI CIM Studio** as shown in Figure 2.22.

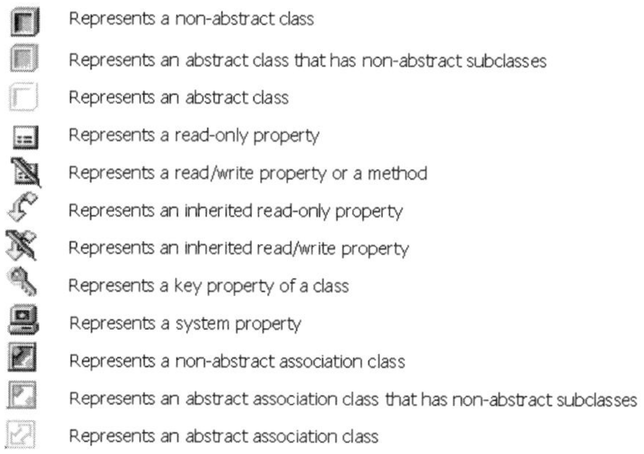

Figure 2.21
The WMI CIM Studio symbols.

▣	Represents a non-abstract class
▣	Represents an abstract class that has non-abstract subclasses
▢	Represents an abstract class
▤	Represents a read-only property
◩	Represents a read/write property or a method
◔	Represents an inherited read-only property
✗	Represents an inherited read/write property
◵	Represents a key property of a class
▣	Represents a system property
▨	Represents a non-abstract association class
▨	Represents an abstract association class that has non-abstract subclasses
▨	Represents an abstract association class

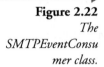

Figure 2.22
*The
SMTPEventConsu
mer class.*

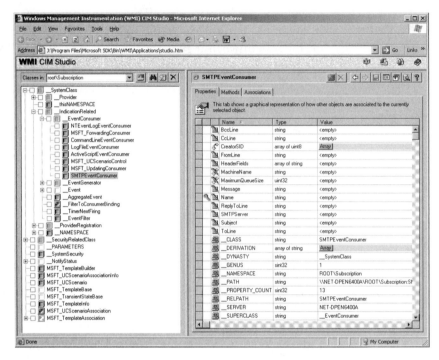

2.8.5.3 WMI Object Browser

The **WMI Object Browser** uses the same interface as **WMI CIM Studio**, but instead of browsing classes with related properties and methods, the **WMI Object Browser** browses instances only. Like **WMI CIM Studio**, the **WMI Object Browser** is also included in the WMI Tools package available for download from http://www.microsoft.com/downloads/ release.asp?ReleaseID=40804. By default, the **WMI Object Browser** starts from the computer object (see Figure 2.23) and retrieves all instances associated with the computer object. It retrieves associated instances using associations (and references) defined in the CIM repository. The *Win32_ComputerSystem* class has 19 associated classes. When using the **WMI Object Browser** to view the instances of the associated classes, it generates more than 10,000 instances associated with the *Win32_ComputerSystem* instance, which represents a lot of information available from a Windows system.

In addition to all instances displayed, you will find the *Win32_Service* class instances that represent every Windows Service available on the system along with their respective statuses. We use this class in a further exercise in Section 2.9.1 of this chapter.

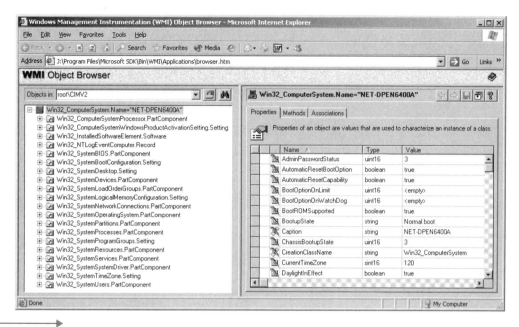

Figure 2.23   *The WMI Object Browser.*

2.8.5.4   **WMI event registration**

This tool is used to examine the permanent consumer registrations with their associated event filter and consumer instances in the CIM repository. It uses a Web interface to display the information such as **WMI CIM Studio** or the **WMI Object Browser**. It is also included in the WMI Tools package available for download from http://www.microsoft.com/downloads/release.asp?ReleaseID=40804. The tool is designed to add, view, or delete the event registration properties. It supports the consumer, filter, and timer events. This tool is also available from the Platform SDK. We use this tool in a practical exercise in Section 2.9.2 of this chapter.

2.8.5.5   **WMI Event Viewer**

The WMI Event Viewer is an application to be registered in the CIM repository as a permanent event consumer. Also included in the WMI Tools package available for download from http://www.microsoft.com/downloads/release.asp?ReleaseID=40804, it is an executable file called **WbemEventViewer.exe**. This application can be started from the command prompt, but as a permanent consumer, WMI launches this program if an event is registered for it. This means that the WMI event registration tool can be used to perform this event registration. Note that a MOF file can

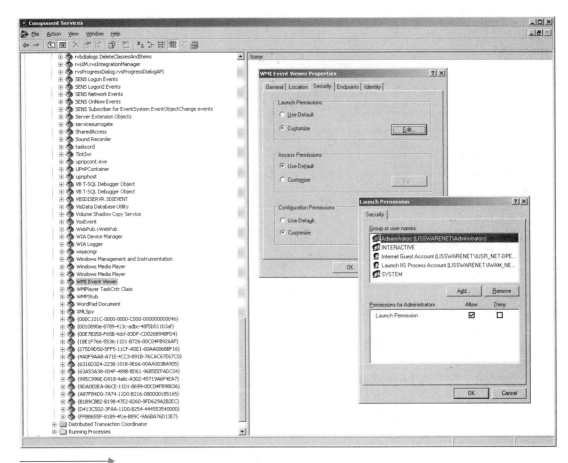

Figure 2.24   *The WMI Event Viewer DCOM security settings.*

also be used to perform this registration. Since a permanent consumer can
be launched remotely, this application is registered in a Windows system as
a COM/DCOM application and requires specific privileges to be started
remotely. You can examine the default security with the **DCOMCNFG.exe**
under Windows NT 4.0 and Windows 2000 or with the Component Services MMC snap-in under Windows XP and Windows.NET Server as visible in Figure 2.24.

As a permanent event consumer, the WMI Event Viewer must registered
in the CIM repository with a MOF called **Eviewer.mof** shown below:

```
1:// Copyright (c) 1997-1999 Microsoft Corporation
2:#pragma namespace("\\root\\cimv2")
3:
4:
5:// register me as a Physical Event Consumer provider.
```

```
 6:instance of __Win32provider as $P
 7:{
 8:Name = "EventViewerConsumer";
 9:Clsid = "{DD2DB150-8D3A-11d1-ADBF-00AA00B8E05A}";
10:};
11:
12:instance of __EventConsumerproviderRegistration
13:{
14:   provider = $P;
15:   ConsumerclassNames = {"EventViewerConsumer"};
16:};
17:
18:// this is my logical consumer class.
19:[Locale(0x049), UUID("{8502C596-5FBB-11D2-AAC1-006008C78BC7}")]
20:class EventViewerConsumer : __EventConsumer
21:{
22:[key]
23:string Name = "";
24:
25:[read,
26:ValueMap {"0", "1", "2"},
27:     Values {"Error", "Warning", "Information"}]
28:uint8 Severity = 0;               // 0-based.
29:
30:[read]
31:string Description = "";
32:};
```

The **Eviewer.mof** file is included in the WMI Tools package.

A few pages earlier, we saw the MOF file used to register the *SMTP* event consumer. To register the *WMI Event Viewer*, the MOF file uses the same structure. We have the following sections:

- **The Win32 provider section (lines 6 to 10)**: to reference the UUID of the COM/DCOM object implemented by the event consumer provider called **WbemEventViewer.exe**

- **The permanent event consumer provider section (lines 12 to 16)**: to associate the consumer class definition with the consumer provider references

- **The Event Viewer Consumer class definition (lines 20 to 32)**: to define the class representing the consumer provider with its name defined as a key (lines 22 and 23) and two optional parameters: severity with its possible values (lines 25 to 28) and description (lines 30 and 31)

It must be registered with the following command line:

```
C:\>mofcomp -N:ROOT\CIMv2 EViewer.Mof
Microsoft (R) 32-bit MOF Compiler Version 5.1.3590.0
Copyright (c) Microsoft Corp. 1997-2001. All rights reserved.
Parsing MOF file: EViewer.Mof
```

```
MOF file has been successfully parsed
Storing data in the repository...
Done!
```

In Section 2.9.2 of this chapter, we will see how to use the WMI Event Viewer with an associated event.

2.8.5.6   *WinMgmt.exe*

WinMgmt.exe is not a tool; it is the executable that implements the WMI service. Under Windows NT, Windows 2000 and Windows.NET Server, WMI runs as a service. However, under Windows XP and Windows.NET Server, don't expect to find a process called **WinMgmt.exe**, as it runs under the **SvcHost.exe** process. On computers running Windows 98, Windows 95, or Windows Millennium, WMI runs as an application. Under Windows NT, Windows 2000, Windows XP, or Windows.NET Server, it is also possible to run this executable as an application, in which case the executable runs in the current user context. For this, the WMI service must be stopped first. The executable supports some switches that can be useful when starting WMI as a service or as an application. Usually, when scripting with WMI there is no need to run the WMI service as an application. WMI provider developers who may want to debug their providers essentially need to run the WMI service as an application. For completeness, Table 2.6 contains a list of switches supported by **WinMgmt.exe**.

Table 2.6   *WmiMgmt.exe Switches*

/exe	Causes WinMgmt.exe to run as an application rather than as a Windows_NT/Windows_2000 service. You might use this switch only rarely because you will almost always want to run WMI as a service in Windows_NT/Windows_2000. When the /exe switch is used, WinMgmt.exe is run in the users security context. The primary use of the /exe switch in Windows_NT version 4.0 is to make it easier to debug providers. This switch is available on Windows_95, Windows_98, Windows_NT 4.0, and Windows_2000. Using this switch will place an icon in the task bar.
/kill	Terminates all WinMgmt.exe processes on the local system, including WMI processes started as a service by the Service Control Manager or invoked by using the /exe switch. This switch is available on Windows_95, Windows_98, Windows_NT 4.0, and Windows_2000 and later. To use this switch with Windows_NT, you must have administrative rights.
/regserver	Registers the Windows Management Service, adding entries to the operating system registry. The /regserver switch should be implemented by any .exe server. This switch is available on Windows_95, Windows_98, Windows_NT 4.0, and Windows_2000 and later.

Table 2.6   *WmiMgmt.exe Switches (continued)*

/unregserver	Removes registry entries added through the self-registration process and should rarely be used. This switch is available on Windows_95, Windows_98, Windows_NT 4.0, and Windows_2000 and later.
/backup *<filename>*	Causes WMI to back up the repository to the specified file name. The filename argument should contain the full path to the file location. This process requires a write lock on the repository so that write operations to the repository are suspended until the backup process is completed. This switch is available on Windows_95, Windows_98, Windows NT_4.0, and Windows_2000 and later.
/restore *<filename>*	Manually restores the WMI repository from the specified file. The filename argument should contain the full path to the file location. When restoring the repository, the process deletes the existing repository, writes the specified backup file to the automatic backup file, and then connects to WMI to perform the restoration. If exclusive access to the repository cannot be achieved, existing clients are disconnected from WMI. This switch is available on Windows_95, Windows_98, Windows_NT 4.0, and Windows_2000 and later.
/resyncperf *<winmgmt service process id>*	Invokes the AutoDiscovery/AutoPurge (ADAP) mechanism of WMI. For more information on ADAP, see Maintaining Performance Counter Classes. This switch is only available on Windows_2000 and later.
/clearadap	Removes all of the ADAP information from the registry, effectively resetting the state of each performance library. The ADAP utility stores state information about the system performance libraries in the registry. This switch is only available on Windows_2000 and later.

2.8.5.7   WBEMTEST.exe

WBEMTEST.exe is a WMI tester, which is delivered standard with WMI (see Figure 2.25). This tool allows an administrator or a developer to perform most of the tasks from a graphical interface that WMI provides at the API level. Although available under Windows NT, Windows 2000, Windows XP, and Windows.NET Server, this tool is not officially supported by Microsoft. Actually, the use of this tool is not obvious unless you are accustomed to the WMI COM API. It requires a good knowledge of the WMI concepts in relation to the implementation. As we script on top of WMI, we use the features available from the WMI API, which will help clarify **WBEMTEST.exe** usage. Basically, **WBEMTEST.exe** helps to perform the following tasks:

- Enumerate, open, create, and delete classes

- Enumerate, open, create, and delete instances of classes

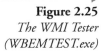

Figure 2.25
The WMI Tester
(WBEMTEST.exe)

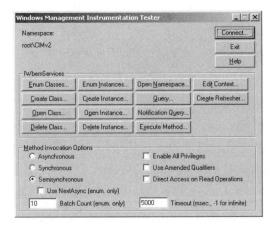

- Select a namespace

- Perform queries

- Perform queries in relation to events (notification queries)

- Execute methods associated with instances

- Execute every WMI operation asynchronously, synchronously, or semi-asynchronously (we examine this type of operation when we talk about the WMI scripting in Chapters 4, 5, and 6)

For example, if you want to obtain a list of the Windows services with **WBEMTEST.exe**, you can do the following:

1.   Connect to the **Root\CIMv2** namespace. If you are not running as an administrator, make sure that you provide the right credentials to access the namespace. By default, only the members of the Administrators group have full rights to the WMI namespaces.

2.   Select the "Enum Instances" button and enter the *Win32_Service* class name representing a Windows service and select "immediate only."

3.   Once done, you will see an output like that shown in Figure 2.26.

If you use the **WMI CIM Studio**, you can do the same thing. With CIM Studio, you can also see that the *Win32_Service* is a subclass of *Win32_BaseService*, and *Win32_BaseService* is a subclass of the *CIM_Service* class. With **WBEMTEST.exe**, if you perform the same operation as before with the *CIM_Service* class and choose the "Recursive" option, you retrieve all the instances of the class derived from the *CIM_Service* class. In this list, you retrieve the *Win32_Service* instances among other *Win32_SystemDriver*

Figure 2.26
*Viewing the
Windows Services
by enumerating the
Win32_Service
class instances with
WBEMTEST.exe.*

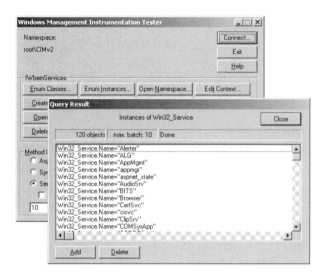

instances, since *Win32_Service* and *Win32_SystemDriver* are subclasses of the *CIM_Service* class.

To give another sample, it is also possible to retrieve the Windows service list by performing a query with **WBEMTEST.exe.** Proceed as follows:

1. Connect to the **Root\CIMv2** namespace. If you are not running as an administrator, make sure that you provide the right credentials to access the namespace.

2. Select the "Query" button and enter the following query string "Select * from Win32_Service" as shown in Figure 2.27.

3. The output of Figure 2.27 will be the same as Figure 2.26.

Figure 2.27
*Viewing the
Windows Services
by querying the
Win32_Service
class instances with
WBEMTEST.exe.*

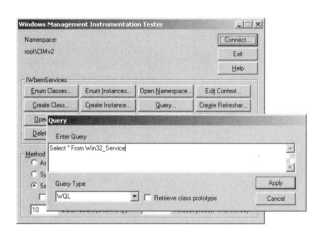

For a few more examples, try entering the queries shown in Section 2.8.4 used to explain the WMI query language. The data queries and schema queries must be executed via the "Query" button shown in Figure 2.25. The event query must be executed with the "Notification Query" button. This tool is very useful when working with WMI. As your knowledge about WMI increases, the understanding of **WBEMTEST.exe** becomes even clearer.

2.8.5.8   *The WMI command-line tool: WMIC*

WMIC is a command-line tool designed to ease WMI information retrieval from a system by using some simple keywords (aliases). **WMIC.exe** is available only under Windows XP Professional and Windows.NET Server. It is not included in other Windows platforms. By typing "WMIC /?" at the command line, you can obtain a complete list of the switches and reserved keywords available. Table 2.7 summarizes the global switches. By typing "WMIC switch-name /?", you can gather more information about the switch usage.

Table 2.8 summarizes the reserved keywords (called the WMIC aliases). By typing "WMIC alias /?", you can gather more information about the alias usage.

Table 2.9 shows some specific commands. By typing "WMIC (class | path | context) /?", you can gather more information about the alias usage.

Table 2.7   *WMIC Global Switches*

/NAMESPACE	Path for the namespace the alias operates against
/ROLE	Path for the role containing the alias definitions
/NODE	Servers the alias will operate against
/IMPLEVEL	Client impersonation level
/AUTHLEVEL	Client authentication level
/LOCALE	Language ID the client should use
/PRIVILEGES	Enables or disables all privileges
/TRACE	Outputs debugging information to stderr
/RECORD	Logs all input commands and output
/INTERACTIVE	Sets or resets the interactive mode
/USER	User to be used during the session
/PASSWORD	Password to be used for session login
/?[:<BRIEF|FULL>	Usage information

Table 2.8   *WMIC Aliases*

BASEBOARD	Provides access to the baseboard (also known as a motherboard or system board)
BIOS	Provides access to the attributes of the computer system's basic input/output services (BIOS) that are installed on the computer
BOOTCONFIG	Provides access to the boot configuration of a system
CDROM	Provides access to the CD-ROM drives on a computer system
COMPUTERSYSTEM	Provides access to the computer system operating in a user environment
CSPRODUCT	Corresponds to software and hardware products used on a computer system
DEVICEMEMORYADDRESS	Provides access to the device memory addresses on a system
DIRECTORY	Provides access to the directory entries on a computer system
DISKDRIVE	Describes a physical disk drive as seen by a computer
DMACHANNEL	Provides information on the direct memory access (DMA) channel on a computer system
DRIVERVXD	Provides access to the virtual device driver/s on a computer system
ENVIRONMENT	Provides access to the system environment settings on a computer system.
GROUP	Provides access to data about a group account
IRQRESOURCE	Provides access to the interrupt request line (IRQ) number on a computer system
LOADORDER	Provides access to the group of system services that define execution dependencies
LOGICALDISK	Provides access to the data source that resolves to an actual local storage device on a system
LOGICALMEMORY	Allows access to the configuration layout and examination of the availabe memory on a system
NETADAPTER	Provides access to the network adapters installed on a system
NETADAPTERCONFIG	Provides access to and allows changing the attributes and behaviors of a network adapter
NETCONNECTION	Provides access to the active network connection in an environment
NETLOGIN	Provides access to the network login information of a particular user on a system
NETPROTOCOL	Provides access to the protocols and their network characteristics on a computer system
NTEVENTLOG	Allows access to the NT eventlog file
ONBOARDDEVICE	Describes common adapter devices built into the motherboard (system board)
OS	Provides access to the operating system/s installed on a computer
PAGEFILE	Provides access to the files used for handling virtual memory file swapping on a system
PAGEFILESET	Provides access to the settings of a page file
PARTITION	Provides access to the capabilities and management capacity of a partitioned area of a physical disk on a system

Table 2.8   *WMIC Aliases (continued)*

PHYSICALMEMORY	Allows access to details about the computer system's physical memory
PORT	Provides access to the I/O ports on a computer system
PORTCONNECTOR	Provides access to the physical connection ports
PRINTER	Provides access to all printer devices connected to a computer system
PRINTERCONFIG	Allows review of the configuration for a printer device
PRINTJOB	Provides access to the print jobs generated by an application
PROCESS	Provides access to the sequence of events on a system
PRODUCT	Correlates tasks to a single installation package
RECOVEROS	Provides access to the types of information that will be gathered from memory when the operating system fails
REGISTRY	Provides access to the computer system registry
SCHEDULEDJOB	Provides access to the jobs scheduled using the schedule service
SERVER	Provides access to the server information
SERVICE	Provides access to the service applications on a computer system
SHARE	Allows access to the shared resources on a system
SOFTWAREELEMENT	Provides access to the elements of a software product installed on a system
SOFTWAREFEATURE	Provides access to and allows changing of the software product subsets of SoftwareElements
STARTUP	Allows access to the command that runs automatically when a user logs onto the computer system
SYSACCOUNT	Allows access to the system accounts
SYSDRIVER	Provides access to the system driver for a base service
SYSTEMENCLOSURE	Provides access to the properties associated with a physical system enclosure
SYSTEMSLOT	Provides access to the physical connection points including ports, slots and peripherals, and proprietary connections points
TAPEDRIVE	Describes a tape drive on a computer
TEMPERATURE	Allows access to the properties of a temperature sensor (electronic thermometer)
TIMEZONE	Provides access to the time-zone information for a system
UPS	Provides access to the capabilities and management capacity of an uninterruptible power supply (UPS)
USERACCOUNT	Provides access to information about a user account on a system
VOLTAGE	Allows access to the properties of a voltage sensor (electronic voltmeter)
WMISET	Provides access to and allows changes to be made to the operational parameters for the WMI service

Table 2.9   *WMIC Commands*

CLASS	Escapes to full WMI schema
PATH	Escapes to full WMI object paths
CONTEXT	Displays the state of all global switches
QUIT/EXIT	Exits the program

Basically, the WMIC interoperates with existing shells and utility commands. When starting WMIC for the first time, Windows installs it on the system and displays a command prompt:

```
wmic:root\cli>
```

From this prompt all aliases of Table 2.8 can be entered interactively. In the previous section, to retrieve the list of the Windows Services we used **WBEMTEST.exe.** This required use of the "Enum instances" button and the reference to the *Win32_Service* class (or a WQL data query like "Select * From Win32_Service" and the use of the "Query" button). With WMIC, it is possible to obtain the same type of information by using an alias (see Table 2.8), which greatly facilitates the command syntax. To locate, all *Win32_Service* instances with WMIC, you must use the *service* alias from the WMIC command prompt (interactive mode) or from the command line (noninteractive mode):

```
C:\>wmic service
AcceptPause AcceptStop Caption                                     CheckPoint CreationclassName →
FALSE       TRUE       Alerter                                     0          Win32_Service       →
FALSE       FALSE      Application Management                      0          Win32_Service       →
FALSE       TRUE       Windows Audio                               0          Win32_Service       →
FALSE       FALSE      Background Intelligent Transfer Service     0          Win32_Service       →
FALSE       TRUE       Computer Browser                            0          Win32_Service       →
TRUE        TRUE       Certificate Services                        0          Win32_Service       →
FALSE       FALSE      Indexing Service                            0          Win32_Service       →
FALSE       FALSE      ClipBook                                    0          Win32_Service       →
FALSE       FALSE      COM+ System Application                     0          Win32_Service       →
FALSE       TRUE       Cryptographic Services                      0          Win32_Service       →
FALSE       TRUE       Distributed File System                     0          Win32_Service       →
FALSE       TRUE       DHCP Client                                 0          Win32_Service       →
FALSE       FALSE      DHCP Server                                 0          Win32_Service       →
FALSE       FALSE      Logical Disk Manager Administrative Service 0          Win32_Service       →
FALSE       TRUE       Logical Disk Manager                        0          Win32_Service       →
TRUE        TRUE       DNS Server                                  0          Win32_Service       →
FALSE       TRUE       DNS Client                                  0          Win32_Service       →
FALSE       TRUE       Event Log                                   0          Win32_Service       →
FALSE       TRUE       COM+ Event System                           0          Win32_Service       →
FALSE       FALSE      Fast User Switching Compatibility Services  0          Win32_Service       →
FALSE       TRUE       Help and Support                            0          Win32_Service       →
...         ...        ...                                         ...        ...                 →
...         ...        ...                                         ...        ...                 →
...         ...        ...                                         ...        ...                 →
```

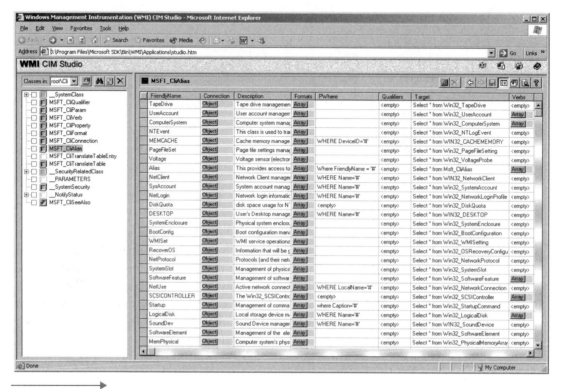

Figure 2.28   *WMIC alias instances.*

The above example all instances of the *Win32_Service* class are retrieved with the *service* alias. The aliases in Table 2.8 are nothing more than an abstraction of the syntax and the class name used to retrieve this information. Aliases are used to capture the features of a WMI class relevant to a specific task, such as disk or network administration. As shown in Figure 2.28, it is interesting to know that all WMIC aliases are stored in the CIM repository as instances of the *MSFT_CliAlias* class in the **Root\Cli namespace**. Therefore, by creating new instances of the *MSFT_CliAlias* class, it possible to extend the set of aliases available to WMIC.

In the previous example, WMIC accessed all instances of the *Win32_Service* class locally, but WMIC can access any WMI information on any WMI-enabled system. Therefore, WMIC is not required on the remote system, which makes it usable in a heterogeneous environment (e.g., Windows 2000, Windows XP, and Windows NT computers). With the **/Node** switch you can access a remote computer (see Table 2.7).

```
C:\>wmic /Node:"NET-DPEP6400.Emea.LissWare.NET" service
AcceptPause AcceptStop Caption                              CheckPoint CreationclassName →
FALSE       TRUE       Alerter                              0          Win32_Service        →
FALSE       FALSE      Application Management               0          Win32_Service        →
FALSE       TRUE       Windows Audio                        0          Win32_Service        →
FALSE       FALSE      Background Intelligent Transfer Service  0      Win32_Service        →
```

As another example, the **/Trace** switch enables the error tracing to returns error information for every executed command. The complete list of global switches is available in Table 2.7.

As we have seen, WMIC makes use of aliases, but it also uses verbs. Every alias has a series of supported verbs. For example, by typing

```
C:\>wmic service /?

SERVICE - Service application management.

HINT: BNF for Alias usage.
(<alias> [WMIObject] | <alias> [<path where>] | [<alias>] <path where>) [<verb clause>].

USAGE:

SERVICE ASSOC [<format specifier>]
SERVICE CALL <method name> [<actual param list>]
SERVICE CREATE <assign list>
SERVICE DELETE
SERVICE GET [<property list>] [<get switches>]
SERVICE LIST [<list format>] [<list switches>]
```

you can see the list of verbs related to the *service* alias. A verb represents an action that you can take for the specified alias. Basically, all verbs are the same for all aliases, but some of them are not supported by some aliases. For instance, if you compare the verbs of the *service* alias with the verbs available from the *bios* alias, you will see that the *call* verb is not available for the *bios* alias. For example, to gather information about the disk configuration of a remote system, we execute WMIC with the *logicaldisk* alias and the *get* verb to retrieve a limited set of properties from the class representing the logical disks (i.e., *Win32_LogicalDisk*):

```
C:\>wmic /Node:"net-dpen6400.lissware.net"
        logicaldisk get description,DeviceID,FileSystem,FreeSpace,Size,VolumeDirty,VolumeName
Description              DeviceID  FileSystem  FreeSpace    Size         VolumeDirty  VolumeName
3 1/2 Inch Floppy Drive  A:
Local Fixed Disk         C:        NTFS        821909504    843816448    FALSE        Boot
Local Fixed Disk         D:        NTFS        1094373376   3220406272   FALSE        APPS
Local Fixed Disk         E:        FAT         514031616    533848064    FALSE        DEV
Local Fixed Disk         F:        NTFS        763207680    1586962432   FALSE        SOURCES
Local Fixed Disk         G:        NTFS        172371968    3777789952   FALSE        DATA
Local Fixed Disk         H:        FAT         285442048    1416429568   FALSE        GAMES
Local Fixed Disk         I:        NTFS        2541527040   9932234752   FALSE        Windows 2000
Local Fixed Disk         J:        NTFS        1150111744   9932234752   FALSE        Windows.NET
CD-ROM Disc              L:
```

Next, as a logical disk can't exist without a disk partition, there is an association created in the CIM repository between logical disk instances and disk partitions. Therefore, with WMIC it is possible to view these associations. In this example, we examine the associations in place only by using the *assoc* verb and the where statement to specifically examine the C: logical disk:

```
C:\>wmic /node:"net-dpen6400.LissWare.NET" logicaldisk where deviceid="c:" assoc
__PATH
\\NET-DPEN6400A\ROOT\CIMV2:Win32_LogicalDisk.DeviceID="C:"                              →
\\NET-DPEN6400A\ROOT\CIMV2:Win32_Directory.Name="c:\\"                                  →
\\NET-DPEN6400A\ROOT\CIMV2:Win32_ComputerSystem.Name="NET-DPEN6400"                     →
\\NET-DPEN6400A\ROOT\CIMV2:Win32_QuotaSetting.VolumePath="C:\\"                         →
\\NET-DPEN6400A\ROOT\CIMV2:Win32_DiskPartition.DeviceID="Disk #0, Partition #0"         →
\\NET-DPEN6400A\ROOT\CIMV2:Win32_SystemAccount.Domain="NET-DPEN6400",Name="Administrators" →
```

As we can see, the C: logical disk is associated with the Disk#0, Partition #0" disk partition. Therefore, with WMIC we can gather information about the partition itself with the *partition* alias and the where statement to specifically examine the "Disk#0, Partition #0 disk partition:

```
C:\>wmic /node:"net-dpen6400.LissWare.NET" partition where
                DeviceID="Disk #0, Partition #0" get "bootpartition,description,deviceid,bootable"
Bootable   BootPartition  Description    DeviceID
TRUE       TRUE           MS-DOS V4 Huge Disk #0, Partition #0
```

With this WMIC command, we see that the C: logical drive located on the "Disk #0, Partition #0" is a bootable logical disk.

If you need to restart a service on a remote system, you can use the service alias combined with the *call* verb. For example, to restart the SNMP service, the WMIC command line to use is as follows:

```
C:\>wmic /node:"net-dpen6400.LissWare.NET" service where name='snmp' call stopservice
Executing (\\NET-DPEN6400\ROOT\CIMV2:Win32_Service.Name="SNMP")->stopservice()
Method execution successful.
Out Parameters:
instance of __PARAMETERS
{
        ReturnValue = 0;
};

C:\>wmic /node:"net-dpen6400.LissWare.NET" service where name='snmp' call startservice
Executing (\\NET-DPEN6400\ROOT\CIMV2:Win32_Service.Name="SNMP")->startservice()
Method execution successful.
Out Parameters:
instance of __PARAMETERS
{
        ReturnValue = 0;
};
```

An interesting feature of WMIC is the ability to request an output result in HTML. The only thing you need is a stylesheet (XSL file) to generate the HTML content. WMIC comes with more than 10 XSL files available from

%SystemRoot%\System32\WBEM. Each XSL files generates a specific output format. For instance, if we execute WMIC with the *service* alias and specify the **/Translate** switch to request the WMI information in XML and specify the **/Format** switch to define which XSL file to use for the transformation, we will generate the service list obtained in the beginning of this section in HTML:

```
C:\>wmic /Output:ServiceList.HTM service list /translate:basicxml /Format:htable.xsl
```

Htable.xsl is one of the stylesheets that comes with WMIC. The obtained result is shown in Figure 2.29.

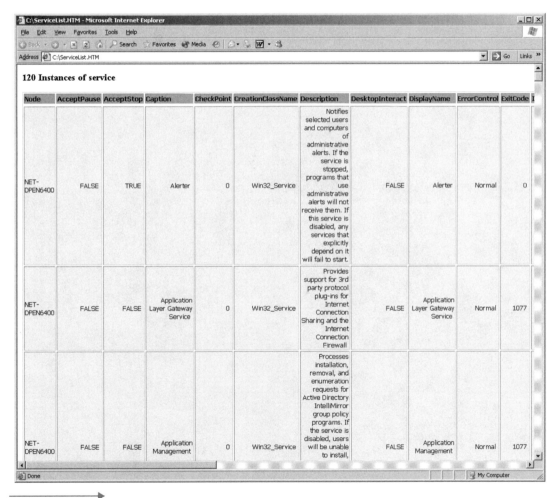

Figure 2.29   *An HTML file created WMIC to show the service list.*

To give another example, instead of generating a list of services, we can generate a simple form containing information about one service. Therefore, the WMIC command line will look like:

```
C:\>wmic /Output:ServiceSNMP.HTM service where
name='snmp' get /translate:basicxml /Format:hform.xsl
```

Hform.xsl is another stylesheet that comes with WMIC. The obtained result is shown in Figure 2.30.

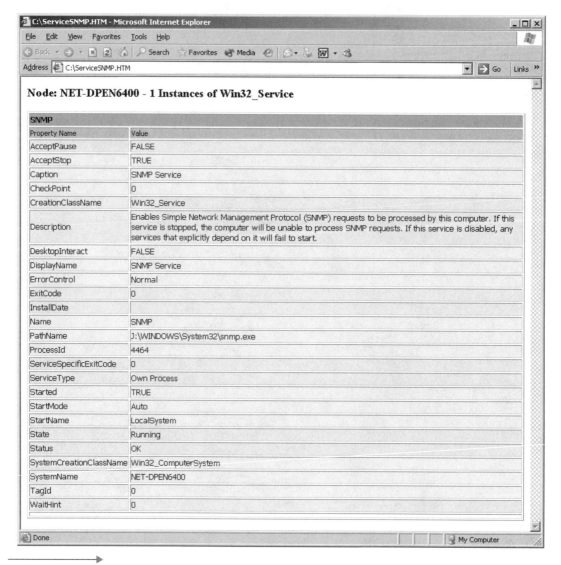

Figure 2.30   *An HTML file created WMIC to show service properties.*

Table 2.10   *Available WMIC Style Sheets*

WMIC Transformations	
csv.xsl	Generate a Comma Separated Value (CSV) file.
hform.xsl	Generate an HTML table with an item per form (See Figure 2.30).
htable.xsl	Generate an HTML table with an item per row (See Figure 2.29).
mof.xsl	Generate a MOF file.
rawxml.xsl	Generate a raw XML file.
texttable.xsl	Generate an ASCII table
textvaluelist.xsl	Generate an ASCII file containing the properties with their values.
xml.xsl	Generate an XML file.

Table 2.10 summarizes the various style sheets available.

We have now discovered some of the features available from WMIC. WMIC can be a good alternative to a WSH script development and is therefore a valuable tool to consider in some situations. It greatly facilitates access to the information provided by WMI without requiring specific WMI knowledge. It is an important addition to Windows XP and Windows.NET Server for the administrator not practicing WMI every day and for WMI beginners.

2.8.5.9   *WBEMDUMP.exe*

WBEMDUMP is a tool delivered with the Platform SDK. This command-line tool comes with its own Visual C++ project. Basically, the tool can show the CIM repository classes, instances, or both. It is possible to retrieve the same information as that retrieved with WMIC. However, **WBEMDUMP.Exe** requires more specific knowledge about WMI, as it doesn't abstract WMI as WMIC. However, it runs under Windows NT 4.0 and Windows 2000. It is also possible to execute methods exposed by classes or instances. Even if it is not a standard WMI tool delivered with the system installation, this tool can be quite useful for exploring the CIM repository. For example, to browse from the **Root** namespace across all namespaces and list all classes available without their properties, use the following command line:

```
C:\>WBEMDUMP /S /S2 /D Root
<ROOT>
  <ROOT\CIMV2>
    MSFT_WMI_NonCOMEventprovider
```

```
EventViewerConsumer
TriggerEventConsumer
SMTPEventConsumer
        Win32_PowerManagementEvent
        Win32_DeviceChangeEvent
                Win32_SystemConfigurationChangeEvent
                Win32_VolumeChangeEvent
        MSFT_WMI_GenericNonCOMEvent
        MSFT_NCProvEvent
                MSFT_NCProvNewQuery
                MSFT_NCProvAccessCheck
                MSFT_NCProvCancelQuery
                MSFT_NCProvClientConnected
        Win32_ComputerSystemEvent
                Win32_ComputerShutdownEvent
        MSFT_ForwardedMessageEvent
                MSFT_ForwardedEvent
        MSFT_WmiSelfEvent
                Msft_Wmiprovider_OperationEvent
                        Msft_Wmiprovider_ComServerLoadOperationEvent
                        Msft_Wmiprovider_InitializationOperationFailureEvent
                        Msft_Wmiprovider_LoadOperationEvent
                        Msft_Wmiprovider_OperationEvent_Pre
                                Msft_Wmiprovider_DeleteclassAsyncEvent_Pre
...
```

To get a complete list of the options available, run **WBEMDUMP.exe** as follows:

```
C:\>wbemdump /?
WBEMDUMP - Dumps the contents of the CIMOM database.

Syntax: wbemdump [switches] [Namespace [class|ObjectPath] ]
        wbemdump /Q [switches] Namespace QueryLanguage Query

Where:  'Namespace' is the namespace to dump (defaults to root\default)
        'class' is the name of a specific class to dump (defaults to none)
        'ObjectPath' is one instance (ex "SclassA.KeyProp=\"foobar\"")
        'QueryLanguage' is any WBEM supported query language (currently only
          "WQL" is supported).
        'Query' is a valid query for the specified language, enclosed in quotes
        'switches' is one of
          /S Recurse down the tree
          /S2 Recurse down Namespaces (implies /S)
          /E Show system classes and properties
          /E1 Like /E except don't show __SERVER or __PATH property
          /E2 Shows command lines for dumping instances (test mode)
          /D Don't show properties
          /G Do a GetObject on all enumerated instances
          /G2 Do a GetObject on all reference properties
          /G:<x> Like /G using x for flags (Amended=131072)
          /M Get class MOFS instead of data values
          /M2 Get Instance MOFS instead of data values
          /M3 Produce instance template
          /B:<num> CreateEnum flags (SemiSync=16; Forward=32)
          /W  Prompt to continue on warning errors
          /WY Print warnings and continue
          /W:1 Use IWbemclassObject::GetObjectText to show errors
          /H:<name>:<value> Specify context object value (test mode)
          /CQV:<name>[:value] Specify a class qualifier on which to filter
          /T Print times on enumerations
          /T2 Print times on enumerations using alternate timer
          /O:<file> File name for output (creates Unicode file)
```

```
          /C:<file> Command file containing multiple WBEMDUMP command lines
          /U:<UserID> UserID to connect with (default: NULL)
          /P:<Password> Password to connect with (default: NULL)
          /A:<Authority> Authority to connect with
          /I:<ImpLevel> Anonymous=1 Identify=2 Impersonate=3(dflt) Delegate=4
          /AL:<AuthenticationLevel> None=1 Conn=2 Call=3 Pkt=4 PktI=5 PktP=6
          /Locale:<localid> Locale to pass to ConnectServer
          /L:<LoopCnt> Number of times to enumerate instances (leak check)

Notes:  - You can redirect the output to a file using standard redirection.
        - If the /C switch is used, the namespace on the command line must
          be the same namespace that is used for each of the command lines.
          It is not possible to use different namespaces on the different lines
          in the command file.

EXAMPLES:

  WBEMDUMP /S /E root\default          - Dumps everything in root\default
  WBEMDUMP /S /E /M /M2 root\default   - Dump all class & instance mofs
  WBEMDUMP root\default foo            - Dumps all instances of the foo class
  WBEMDUMP root\default foo.name=\"bar\" - Dumps one instance of the foo class
  WBEMDUMP /S2 /M root    - Dumps mofs for all non-system classes in all NS's
  WBEMDUMP /Q root\default WQL "SELECT * FROM Environment WHERE Name=\"Path\""
```

You can refer to the platform SDK to get more information about this tool. We also use this tool when working with data queries and schema queries in Chapter 3. This will give us a chance to practice using the tool and its feature.

2.8.5.10   *Scriptomatic*

Scriptomatic is a very handy tool released by Microsoft in August 2002. It can be downloaded from http://www.microsoft.com/downloads/ release.asp?ReleaseID=41528. This tool is a hypertext application (HTA extension) loading all Win32 WMI classes available from the **Root\CIMv2** namespace. Based on the class selected on the user interface, it generates a VBScript able to list all instances of the class with their properties and values (see Figure 2.31).

In Chapter 4, we will examine the WMI scripting interfaces available and explain in detail the various aspects of WMI scripts similar to the one generated by Scriptomatic.

The main purpose of Scriptomatic is to generate a basic script. The script's intended purpose, in this first release, is to provide information about instances of Win32 classes. Nothing more! Therefore, Scriptomatic will not generate a fully customized script handling complete management business logic. However, for a beginner at WMI scripting, it can help a user to discover properties of the Win32 WMI classes and how to use the WMI API to enumerate properties and values. Therefore, although handy, Scriptomatic does not enable you to learn how to script on top of WMI and how to make use of the WMI class capabilities. Once you get used to the WMI

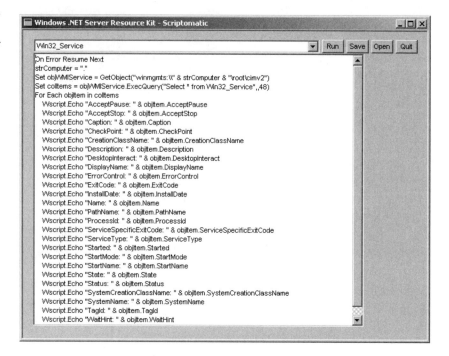

Figure 2.31
The Scriptomatic window.

scripting technique, you will see that the challenge does not reside in the scripting technique in itself but in knowledge of the WMI classes available and the features they provide.

When using Scriptomatic, keep in mind that the following limitations apply:

- **Scriptomatic is designed to work with only a subset of classes, the Win32 classes that return property values:** Only the classes that return instances, located in the **Root\CIMv2** namespace and having a name starting with Win32_ (i.e., Win32_Service) are supported by Scriptomatic.

- **Scriptomatic won't return values for all properties: Some classes return properties in the form of an array.** Scriptomatic does not return array properties in this first release. We will see throughout Chapter 4 how to examine array properties.

- **Scriptomatic won't interpret returned values for you:** Some properties return a value to reflect an instance status. We will see throughout Chapter 4 how to interpret values returned by properties.

- **Scriptomatic can only return property values; it can't be used to run methods:** Scriptomatic is a tool generating passive scripts returning information about classes. However, Scriptomatic does not generate scripts performing actions on instances of classes. Once more, we will see throughout Chapters 4 and 5 how to handle this from scripts.

- **Scriptomatic works only with WMI:** We will see in Chapter 5 that WMI also integrates with other technologies such as Active Directory Service Interfaces (ADSI). Scriptomatic focuses on WMI script creation only.

By learning the WMI scripting technique presented in the next chapters, we will see how to overcome the current limitations of Scriptomatic and how to understand WMI scripting techniques (Volume 1, *Understanding WMI Scripting*, ISBN 1555582664) and leverage WMI scripting (Volume 2, *Leveraging WMI Scripting*, ISBN 15555582990) to exploit the full power of WMI under Windows. However, as a start, it is a handy tool to play with. Don't wait to be an expert in WMI scripting; it can help you right now to work with some basic scripts.

2.9   Let's be more practical

Now that we have discovered the list of the WMI tools provided by Microsoft and the new vocabulary associated with the CIM repository and its WMI implementation, we are ready to take a closer look at this instrumentation and how it maps to the real world. As we said before, the CIM repository represents objects from the real world. Of course, after reviewing the terms commonly used in the WBEM world, this seems to be sometimes far from the real-world manageable entities. Some terms may still look a bit abstract and seem to be quite hard to apply to a real, manageable world. The purpose of the next two sections is to give a more practical view of these terms in relation to things that every Windows administrator knows. Most of the WMI or WBEM descriptions available today start with a highly descriptive theory, which is quite hard to assimilate. Although some theory is necessary, we examine the components that every Windows administrator is used to working with in a Windows system and see how WMI represents them.

In the first section we use the Windows service as sample. This exercise will directly map most of the WBEM and WMI terms discovered in a real-world manageable entity: a Windows service with its dependencies. In the second section, we create a usable application without programming by simply using some WMI features available out of the box. This exercise will explain the role of a WMI event consumer, the role of a MOF file, and the usefulness of the WMI query language (WQL). As you will see, when we use WQL statements, some small details will probably be not very clear in some places. Don't worry; we will revisit this topic in Chapter 3. For now, we are in the early stages of our WMI discovery. To get the full benefit of these two exercises, it is strongly recommended that you have a Windows 2000/Exchange 2000 Server system up and running to practice.

2.9.1 Understanding dependencies between classes

A very good example of dependencies is represented by the Windows services dependencies. To avoid some situations in which one Windows service can start before another, the Service Manager makes use of the following registry keys with their related meanings:

- **Group (REG_SZ) group name:** Specifies the name of the group of which the particular service is a member.

- **DependOnGroup (REG_MULTI_SZ) group name:** Specifies zero or more group names. If one or more groups are listed, at least one service from the named group must be loaded before this service is loaded.

- **DependOnService (REG_MULTI_SZ) service name:** Specifies zero or more services names. If a service is listed here, that named service must be loaded before this service is loaded.

A good example of a service having dependencies is the Microsoft Exchange System Attendant (named *MSExchangeSA* in the registry) shown in Figure 2.32.

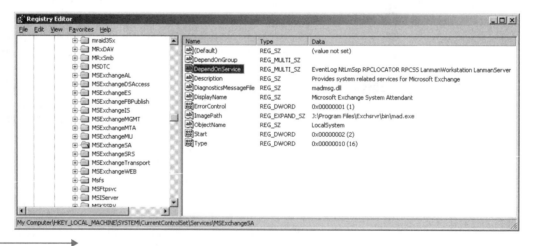

Figure 2.32   *The Microsoft Exchange 2000 System Attendant registry keys.*

This service depends on several other services, named *EventLog*, *NtLmSsp*, *RPCLOCATOR*, *RPCSS*, *LanmanWorkstation*, and *LanmanServer*. When using **WMI CIM Studio**, you can view the same information when starting from the *Win32_Service* class. Proceed as follows:

1.   Connect to the **Root\CIMv2** namespace.

2.   Expand the classes *CIM_ManagedSystemElement*, *CIM_Logical-Element*, *CIM_Service,* and *Win32_BaseService*.

3.   Select the *Win32_Service* class.

4.   Request to view instances of this service class by pressing the "view instances" button in the button bar located in the top right pane of **WMI CIM Studio**.

5.   **WMI CIM Studio** shows the list of Windows services available in your system. Browse the list until you find the *MSExchangeSA* service.

6.   Right click on it and select "Go to object." Now you have the properties of the *MSExchangeSA* service only.

7.   Select the "Associations" tab and you should get the Figure 2.33.

Besides the computer system where this service is running, we clearly see that **WMI CIM Studio** shows a list of Windows service instances. A portion of the services listed corresponds exactly to the list set in the registry in the *DependOnService* key. In the list of services, you will notice that **WMI CIM Studio** lists the *MSExchangeMTA* and *MSExchangeIS* even though they are not listed in the *DependOnService* registry key. These two services are also associated with the *MSExchangeSA,* but the relation is not the same as with the other services. *MSExchangeSA* relies, for example, on the *LanManWorkstation* and the *LanManServer* service. On the other hand, *MSExchangeMTA* and *MSExchangeIS* rely on the *MSExchangeSA* service. The association between these services is clearly there, but it works in the other direction. Later in this section we see how the dependency direction is set when we examine the association classes. Note that it is possible to see these associations with the **WMI Object Browser**. We do not use this tool here because the **WMI Object Browser** is not designed to review the class definitions; it is designed to examine the class instances only.

How does WMI make these links? By simply using the association mechanism defined in the CIM classes definitions. To understand this, we must go back to the *Win32_Service* class definition and, using the **WMI CIM Studio**, look at the associations made in the class definition. **WMI**

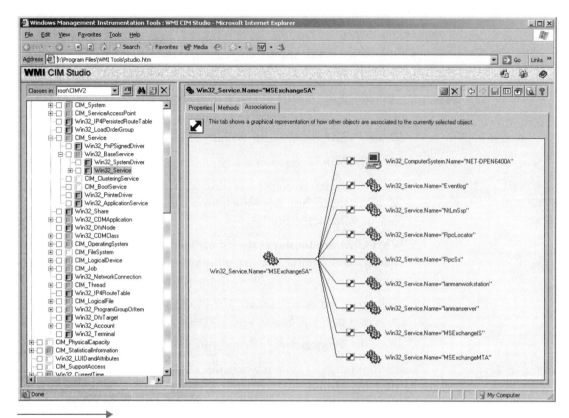

Figure 2.33   *Viewing the Microsoft Exchange 2000 System Attendant service dependencies with WMI CIM Studio.*

CIM Studio shows three dependencies from the *Win32_Service* class, as shown in Figure 2.34.

We see that the *Win32_Service* class is associated to *Win32_WMISetting*, *Win32_ServiceSpecification,* and *Win32_ComputerSystem* classes. The association is made with three association classes (represented in Figure 2.34

Figure 2.34
The associated classes and associations classes of the Win32_Service class.

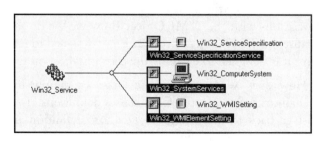

Figure 2.35
The associated classes and associations classes of the Win32_BaseService class.

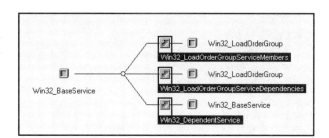

with a circled icon with its name in a black box), which are *Win32_WMI-ElementSetting,   Win32_ServiceSpecificationService,*   and   *Win32_System-Services* classes.

Now, if we examine the parent class (the class from which the *Win32_Service* is derived), we see that *Win32_BaseService* also has associations with specific classes (see Figure 2.35). These are *Win32_Load-OrderGroup* and *Win32_BaseService* classes. In the same way as before, these associations are made with some association classes that include: *Win32_LoadOrderGroupServiceMembers,   Win32_DependentService,* and *Win32_LoadOrderGroupServiceDependencies* classes. You will notice in Figure 2.35 that the *Win32_BaseService* class is associated with itself. This makes sense, since a service can rely on another service.

Because these associations are inheritable by the subclasses, the *Win32_Service* class also inherits these associations. Why are these associations inheritable? To give the answer, we must examine the association class qualifiers. Let's view the association class called *Win32_DependentService* by performing a search with **WMI CIM Studio** to locate the class. Once found, select the class and right-click the right pane showing the properties. Then select the Object qualifiers. You should obtain what is shown in Figure 2.36. This figure shows the list of qualifiers used to define the class type and behavior. In the list you will find the provider qualifier stating that the class is working with the Win32 provider (*CIMWin32*); you will also see a qualifier stating that the class is dynamic because any class instance is provided by the provider itself and not stored statically in the CIM repository. In that list, the association qualifier is presented at the top and set to True.

Figure 2.36 shows that the association qualifier is checked to replicate to instances and derived classes. This means that every instance of this association class or every class derived from this association class will also inherit these associations.

Figure 2.36
*The
Win32_Dependent
Service association
class qualifiers.*

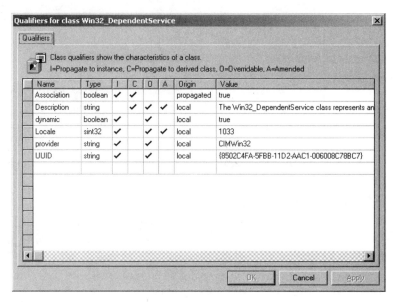

Qualifiers for class Win32_DependentService

Qualifiers

Class qualifiers show the characteristics of a class.
I=Propagate to instance, C=Propagate to derived class, O=Overridable, A=Amended

Name	Type	I	C	O	A	Origin	Value
Association	boolean	✔	✔			propagated	true
Description	string		✔	✔	✔	local	The Win32_DependentService class represents an
dynamic	boolean	✔		✔		local	true
Locale	sint32	✔		✔	✔	local	1033
provider	string	✔		✔		local	CIMWin32
UUID	string	✔		✔		local	{8502C4FA-5FBB-11D2-AAC1-006008C78BC7}

OK   Cancel   Apply

In summary, the *Win32_Service* class is associated by inheritance or directly with the following classes:

- *Win32_WMISettings* directly from *Win32_Service* class.

- *Win32_ServiceSpecification* directly from *Win32_Service* class.

- *Win32_ComputerSystem* directly from *Win32_Service* class.

- *Win32_LoadOrderGroup* by inheritance from *Win32_BaseService* class.

- *Win32_BaseService* by inheritance from *Win32_BaseService* class with the following association classes:

  - *Win32_WMIElementSetting* directly from *Win32_Service* class.
  - *Win32_ServiceSpecificationService* directly from *Win32_Service* class.
  - *Win32_SystemServices* directly from *Win32_Service* class.

- *Win32_LoadOrderGroupServiceMembers* by inheritance from *Win32_BaseService* class.

- *Win32_DependentService* by inheritance from *Win32_BaseService* class.

- *Win32_LoadOrderGroupServiceDependencies* by inheritance from *Win32_BaseService* class.

Figure 2.37
*Win32_Service
MSExchangeSA
instance associated
instances and
associations
instances.*

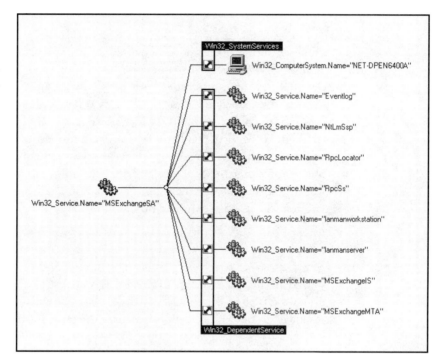

So, as in the beginning of this section, when we looked at the associated instances of the *MSExchangeSA* service instance, we found associated instances made from only two different classes (see Figure 2.37):

1. One *Win32_ComputerSystem* instance coming directly from the association of the *Win32_Service* class

2. Eight *Win32_Service* instances coming from the inheritance of *Win32_BaseService* class.

Why two class instances and not all the associated class instances? It is very simple: There is no other existing instance of the associated classes other than the two listed with the *MSExchangeSA* instance. In short, we can say that the *MSExchangeSA* relies only on some instances of the *Win32_Service* class and on one instance of the *Win32_ComputerSystem* class. Now, you can take another service such, as Windows Management Instrumentation (WinMgmt), and you will see that there are differences. The service dependency is different. You see that there is a new instance associated with it that comes from the *Win32_WMISetting* class. This class represents nothing more than the WMI settings configurable by an administrator via the MMC shown in Figure 2.20. In this case, it makes sense to have such a class instance associated with the **WinMgmt.exe** service instance.

Now, how does the association class work? If we consider the *Win32_DependentService* association class properties, you will see that the class defines three properties, two of which are used as a key to uniquely identify the associated classes. These two keys are *Antecedent* and *Dependent*. Both point to a *Win32_Service* class as stated by their type "ref:Win32_Service." As these two keys are properties using a "ref:" type in an association, they are also references. If you remember, we mentioned in this chapter that the properties of an association are the references. This is why when we talked earlier about associations, references, and domain, we said that the references have a domain limited to the association.

In Figure 2.38, the *Antecedent* reference points to a *Win32_Service* instance that must be started in order to start the *MSExchangeSA* service. The *Dependent* reference points to a *Win32_Service* instance that can be started if the *MSExchangeSA* service is started. The reference type determines the type of dependency that the class has with its associated class. As instances come from classes, it is exactly the same for the instances, which is why the *MSExchangeMTA* and *MSExchangeIS* are listed in the associated instance list in Figure 2.23. The *MSExchangeMTA* and *MSExchangeIS* depend on the *MSExchangeSA* to start. In the same window, if you move

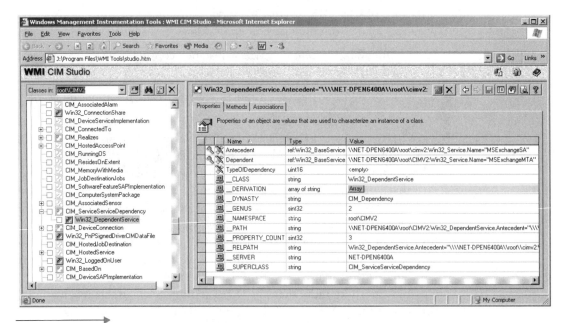

Figure 2.38   *The Win32_DependentService association class with its reference definitions.*

Figure 2.39
*The association
inversion based on
the relationships
between instances.*

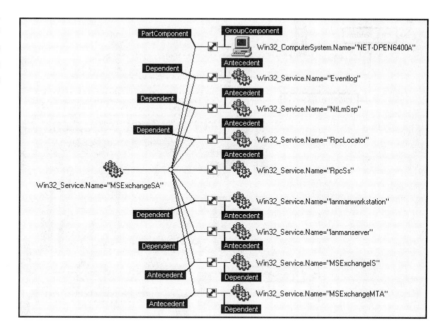

the mouse over the lines linking the association instances with the class instances, the reference name appears on top. Basically, you see a view of the names of references similar to that shown in Figure 2.39.

Note the inversion of the Antecedent and Dependent references, for example, if you compare the *MSExchangeMTA* service and the *LanMan-Server* service. The definitions of the references that point to the computer object where the *MSExchangeMTA* service resides come from the association class *Win32_SystemServices*. Even if the classes are different, the logic is exactly the same for all classes, class instances, and associations exposed by WMI.

Based on this discovery, it is easy to imagine that we can take advantage of these associations to retrieve the Windows service dependencies without reading the content of the registry key.

Figure 2.40
*Legend for Figure
2.41.*

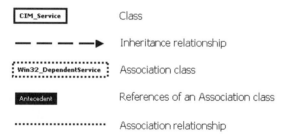

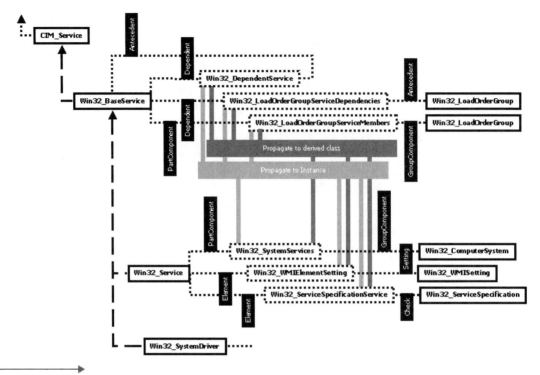

Figure 2.41   *A schematic representation of the various links between the service classes.*

To avoid any confusion, it is important to keep in mind that the associations that exist between the superclasses are inherited by the subclasses. Figures 2.40 and 2.41 show a logical representation of these relations. However, this representation is not a formal representation of these relationships since it is not an UML representation. The only purpose of this representation is to illustrate explicitly all logical links that exist between the various classes (superclasses and subclasses). The Windows services dependency of the *MSExchangeSA* service is a nice example that is reused throughout subsequent chapters.

2.9.2   An event consumer application without scripting

While talking about the providers and the consumers, we saw that WMI comes with its own set of ready-to-use event consumers. It is possible, with the help of a MOF file, to associate an event that comes from a particular provider with a permanent event consumer. We know that the *WMI Event Viewer* is a permanent event consumer. Based on this, it is possible to create a simple alerting system using the various WMI Microsoft components and tools. This can be achieved without writing a single line of code and by simply using the WMI architecture and its implementation. The alert system monitors any changes made to the Windows services and receives an alert when such a change occurs. If a startup state of one service is changed or if one service is started or stopped, WMI will trigger an event forwarded to the event consumer. Of course, this exercise introduces the notion of events that we examine later in Chapter 6, but let's take a shortcut to illustrate the concepts we have covered in this chapter.

When we used the **WBEMTEST.exe** tool, we used a query string to list the Windows Services. This query string was

```
Select * From Win32_Service
```

By adapting this query string to the event notification mechanism, we can formulate the following query:

```
Select * From __InstanceModificationEvent Within 10 Where
TargetInstance ISA 'Win32_Service'
```

Basically, both queries retrieve the same information, except that the latter retrieves the information only when a change occurs in an instance of the *Win32_Service* class. Simply said, each time a modification is made to a Windows Sservice, the query finds a match and returns all of the properties of the modified service. The **Within 10** statement informs WMI to perform a polling every 10 seconds to detect changes made. The presence of this parameter is determined by the nature of the WMI provider.

To link an event detected by a WMI provider to a WMI permanent event consumer, there are three important things to define:

1. **The event consumer instance:** When talking about the *WMI Event Viewer*, we saw a MOF file that defines the class representing the *WMI Event Viewer* template. Now, the idea is to create an instance of the permanent event consumer class in order to get a real permanent event consumer. A real permanent event consumer has a name and a set of parameters associated with it. This means that we will use the permanent event consumer class of the *WMI Event Viewer* as a template to create the real *WMI Event Viewer* object with a set of explicitly defined parameters. Don't forget that the *WMI Event Viewer* must be registered in the CIM repository; the following command line will perform the registration:

    ```
    C:\>mofcomp "%ProgramFiles%\WMI Tools\EViewer.mof"
    Microsoft (R) 32-bit MOF Compiler Version 5.1.3590.0
    Copyright (c) Microsoft Corp. 1997-2001. All rights reserved.
    Parsing MOF file: EViewer.Mof
    MOF file has been successfully parsed
    ```

```
Storing data in the repository...
Done!
```

2.   **The event filter:** Because the idea is to receive a notification for every change made to the Windows services, the event filter will filter the events that match the submitted query.

3.   **The link between the event filter and the permanent event consumer:** Its purpose is to link the event filter instance with the permanent event consumer instance. This element is typically the case of an association. So, every event that matches the filter is sent to the WMI Event Viewer.

There are several ways to achieve this. First, we can use a script to create the necessary definition in the CIM repository. Because we don't have the required WMI scripting background yet, let's skip this method and save it for later. A second method is to use the WMI Event Registration tool. Using this tool implies coding, through the user interface, of all the necessary parameters. Although possible, this is not the easiest way to perform this task. It is best to use the WMI Event Registration tool to modify an existing registration. The last method, and also the easiest, is to use a MOF file similar to that shown in Sample 2.2.

Sample 2.2   *A MOF file to associate the permanent WMI Event Viewer consumer and any change notification coming from the Win32_Service instances (EventViewerConsumerInstanceReg.mof)*

```
 1://  -----------------------------
 2://   Sample for EventViewerConsumer
 3://-----------------------------
 4:instance of __EventFilter as $ef
 5:{
 6:  Name = "FilterForWin32_Services";
 7:  Query = "SELECT * FROM __InstanceModificationEvent WITHIN 10 Where "
 8:          "TargetInstance ISA 'Win32_Service'";
 9:  QueryLanguage = "WQL";
10:};
11:
12:// create the consumer
13:instance of EventViewerConsumer as $eventvwrec
14:{
15:  Name = "EventViewerForSvc";
16:  Severity = 2;
17:  Description = "Event viewer consumer associated to any Win32_Service event";
18:};
19:
20:// bind the filter and the consumer
```

```
21:instance of __FilterToConsumerBinding
22:{
23:  Filter = $ef;
24:  Consumer = $eventvwrec;
25:};
```

As previously mentioned, the MOF file contains three sections. The first section defines the event filter (lines 4 to 10). Besides the name given to the event filter (line 6) we recognize the query acting as a filter (lines 7 and 8). The next section defines the instance of the permanent event consumer (lines 12 to 18). This instance is created from the *WMI Event Viewer* class. This is why line 13 contains a statement with the word *EventViewerConsumer*, as this is the class name of the permanent event consumer registered in the CIM repository (see the MOF file presented in Section 2.8.5.5). We also see that some properties are set, such as the name (mandatory as the name is a key of the class), severity, and a description property. Table 2.11 summarizes the parameters of the *WMI Event Viewer* event consumer.

Once the filter event instance and the permanent event consumer instance are defined, the MOF file associates these two instances together with the help of third instance made from the *_FilterToConsumerBinding* system class. This class is simply an association class linking the consumer instance with its filter instance. You will notice that the association is made by referencing an alias *$ef* (for the event filter at lines 4 and 23) and *$eventvwrec* (for the *Event Viewer* event consumer at lines 13 and 24). By compiling the MOF file, these three instances will be loaded in the CIM

Table 2.11   *The WMI Event Viewer Event Consumer Class*

Name	AccessType: Read
	Qualifier: Key
	String the unique identifier of the event consumer
Severity	AccessType: Read
	Qualifier: Template
	0 Error
	1 Warning
	2 Information
Description	AccessType: Read
	Qualifier: Template
	String describing the event

repository. This will also inform CIMOM about the action to perform. Let's compile the MOF file with the following command line:

```
C:\>mofcomp -n:Root\CIMv2 EventViewerConsumerInstanceReg.Mof
Microsoft (R) 32-bit MOF Compiler Version 5.1.3590.0
Copyright (c) Microsoft Corp. 1997-2001. All rights reserved.
Parsing MOF file: EventViewerConsumerInstanceReg.Mof
MOF file has been successfully parsed
Storing data in the repository...
Done!
```

Before loading Sample 2.2 in the CIM repository, the Eviewer.mof (see Section 2.8.5.5) must be loaded first. The Eviewer.mof registers the WMI Event Viewer COM components in the **Root\CIMv2** namespace of the CIM repository. Next, when registering Sample 2.2, it is important to specify the –N switch to force the selected namespace to **Root\CIMV2;** otherwise the default selected namespace will be **Root\Default**. In this case, the compilation will not work because the WMI event consumer class and the *Win32_Service* are not registered in the **Root\Default** namespace of the CIM repository. Both the *EventViewerConsumer* class and the *Win32_Service* class are registered by default in the **Root\CIMV2** namespace. WQL does not support cross-namespace queries or associations. You cannot query for instances of a specified class residing in all the namespaces on the target computer. Furthermore, you cannot associate two objects across a namespace boundary and retrieve or query for the associations. All items must reside beneath the same namespace. However, there is limited support for cross-namespace bindings in that all statically defined (repository-based) objects can reference each other across namespace boundaries. Once providers become involved, there is no such support and queries are always executed with reference to a particular namespace.

Once completed, you can use the WMI Event Registration tool to check the event filter instance and the WMI permanent event consumer instance, as shown in Figure 2.42.

If a modification must be made after the registration, it is always possible to modify the MOF file and perform a new compilation (in such a case, make sure that you don't change the instance names to address the existing instances). Alternatively, you can use the WMI Event Registration tool to perform the changes. If you take a look at these instances with the WMI Event Registration tool, you should start to understand why it is easier to create these three classes with a MOF file.

Do we need to do something else before getting notifications? No! Everything is ready! In a previous paragraph we saw that the WMI event

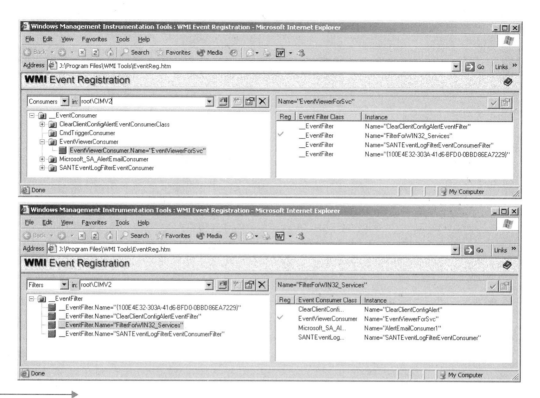

Figure 2.42   *Viewing the WMI Event Viewer instance and the Event Filter instance with the WMI Event Registration tool.*

provider application is a permanent event consumer; this implies that WMI will start the application if an event related to a *Win32_Service* instance occurs. Let's test this by selecting a Windows service that you can stop or start (i.e., take the SNMP service as it is not a key service to run Windows). If everything is fine, the WMI Event Viewer should start, and the screen shown in Figure 2.43 will appear.

Each time something changes in the *Win32_Service*, a similar event will be visible in the WMI Event Viewer. If you click twice on the event, you will see the properties of the event (see Figure 2.44).

Among the various properties, two are particularly interesting: the *PreviousInstance* and the *TargetInstance* properties. The *PreviousInstance* property represents the *Win32_Service* instance as it was before the change occurred. Therefore, if the action triggering the change notification was a service start, this implies that the service was stopped; the object embedded in this property will be in a stopped state. The *TargetInstance* property shows the instance in its current state. So, in the case of our example, the instance

Figure 2.43
*The WMI Event
Viewer receiving
the event.*

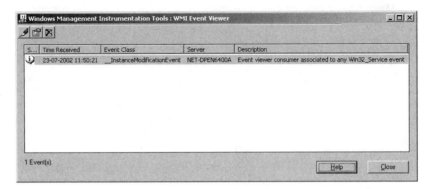

embedded in the *TargetInstance* property will be in a started state. Besides the state of the service, both instances show the properties of the Windows service.

It is nice to get a popup window with the *WMI Event Viewer*, but it would be nicer to receive an e-mail each time a change occurs. As previously shown, WMI provides a permanent *SMTP* event consumer. This means that we can use the same principle as the *WMI Event Viewer* consumer, but in this case, we must create an instance of the *SMTP* event consumer with the necessary SMTP parameters. When we previously discussed the **MOF-COMP.exe** tool, we showed the MOF file that defines the permanent *SMTP* event consumer in the CIM repository (see Section 2.8.5.1). This MOF file shows the required properties for the permanent *SMTP* event consumer. Note that the registration is made during the WMI installation

Figure 2.44
*The event
properties as visible
in the WMI Event
Viewer.*

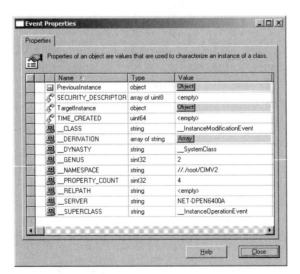

in the **Root\Subscription** namespace, but the *Win32_Service* class is available only in the **Root\CIMv2** namespace. Since we cannot work across two different namespaces, it is mandatory to register the permanent *SMTP* event consumer in the **Root\CIMv2** namespace by using the following command line:

```
C:\>mofcomp -N:Root\CIMv2 %SystemRoot%\System32\Wbem\SMTPCons.Mof
Microsoft (R) 32-bit MOF Compiler Version 5.1.3590.0
Copyright (c) Microsoft Corp. 1997-2001. All rights reserved.
Parsing MOF file: J:\WINDOWS\System32\Wbem\SMTPCons.Mof
MOF file has been successfully parsed
Storing data in the repository...
```

As the permanent *SMTP* event consumer class is now available in the **Root\CIMv2** namespace, it is now possible to associate a permanent *SMTP* event consumer instance with an event filter instance (as we made before for the *WMI Event Viewer* consumer). The MOF file performing this definition is shown in Sample 2.3.

Sample 2.3   *A MOF file to associate the permanent SMTP event consumer and any change notification coming from the Win32_Service instances (SMTPConsumerInstanceReg.mof)*

```
 1:// -------------------------------
 2://    Sample for SMTPEventConsumer
 3://-------------------------------
 4:instance of __EventFilter as $ef
 5:{
 6:  Name = "FilterForWin32_Services";
 7:  Query = "SELECT * FROM __InstanceModificationEvent WITHIN 10 Where "
 8:          "TargetInstance ISA 'Win32_Service'";
 9:  QueryLanguage = "WQL";
10:};
11:
12:// create the consumer
13:instance of SMTPEventConsumer as $smtpec
14:{
15:  Name = " SMTPForSvc";
16:  Subject = "Service %TargetInstance.DisplayName% is %TargetInstance.State%";
17:  Message = "Service %TargetInstance.DisplayName% (%TargetInstance.Name%) "
18:          "is %TargetInstance.State%.\n"
19:          "Startup mode is %TargetInstance.StartMode%.";
20:  FromLine = "WMISystem@LissWare.NET";
21:  ToLine = "Alain.Lissoir@LissWare.NET";
22:  SMTPServer = "smtp.LissWare.NET";
23:};
24:
25:// bind the filter and the consumer
26:instance of __FilterToConsumerBinding
27:{
28:  Filter = $ef;
29:  Consumer = $smtpec;
30:};
```

As we can see, the MOF file redefines the event filter. As this filter is the same as the one used with the *WMI Event Viewer*, it is not necessary to redefine it here. We can use the MOF file listed in Sample 2.4.

Sample 2.4 *A MOF file to associate the permanent SMTP event consumer and an existing event filter (SMTPConsumerInstanceReg2.mof)*

```
1:// ------------------------------
2://    Sample for SMTPEventConsumer
3://------------------------------
4:
5:// create the consumer
6:instance of SMTPEventConsumer as $smtpec
7:{
8:   Name = "SMTPForSvc";
9:   Subject = "Service %TargetInstance.DisplayName% is %TargetInstance.State%";
10:  Message = "Service %TargetInstance.DisplayName% (%TargetInstance.Name%) "
11:            "is %TargetInstance.State%.\n"
12:            "Startup mode is %TargetInstance.StartMode%.";
13:  FromLine = "WMISystem@LissWare.NET";
14:  ToLine = "Alain.Lissoir@LissWare.NET";
15:  SMTPServer = "smtp.LissWare.NET";
16:};
17:
18:// bind the filter and the consumer
19:instance of __FilterToConsumerBinding
20:{
21:  Filter = "FilterForWin32_Services";
22:  Consumer = $smtpec;
23:};
```

Only the definition of the event filter is missing. The association class (lines 19 to 23) references the existing event filter made for the *WMI Event Viewer* (line 21). In any case, the MOF definition for the permanent *SMTP* event consumer instance will not disconnect the *WMI Event Viewer* from the event filter, because the association class instance *__Filter-ToConsumerBinding* uses two keys to be differentiated from the association class instance made for the *WMI Event Viewer*. These two keys combine the name of the event filter (which is the same) and the name of the event consumer (which is different). As the combination of the two keys is not the same, the previous association instance is not overwritten as shown in Figure 2.45. Make sure that both consumers are registered as shown in the figure. The two keys are defined in the *__FilterToConsumerBinding* system class (visible with the **WMI CIM Studio**).

Besides the association aspect, the event consumer is different and requires specific parameters related to SMTP. The first thing needed is an SMTP server available in your network. This server is mandatory. Any of

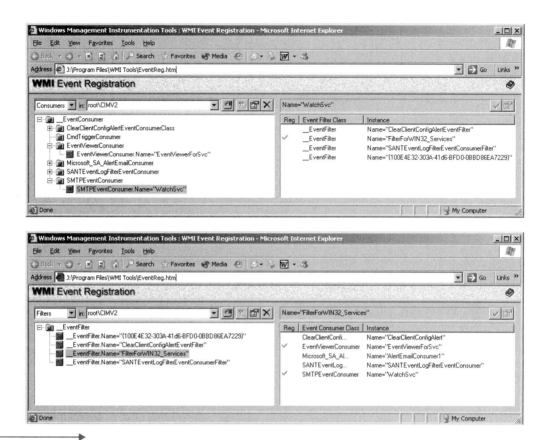

Figure 2.45   *The WMI event filter registration for two different permanent event consumers.*

the To, Cc, and Bcc parameters can be null, but they may not all be null. Next, the server name is set at line 15; the target recipient is set at line 14. The permanent *SMTP* event consumer does not support attachments in mail. Table 2.12 summarizes the available parameters for the permanent *SMTP* event consumer. In addition to these parameters, make sure that the SMTP server relaying the message is well configured. If the SMTP server requires an authentication mechanism, this will fail as the permanent *SMTP* event consumer does not provide parameters to perform an authentication mechanism. Make sure that the SMTP server allows anonymous access. Compile the MOF file as follows:

```
C:\>MOFCOMP -N:Root\CIMV2 SMTPConsumerInstanceReg.mof
```

or, if the filter instance already exists:

```
C:\>MOFCOMP -N:Root\CIMV2 SMTPConsumerInstanceReg2.mof
```

Table 2.12   *The SMTP Event Consumer Class*

Name	Access type: Read/write
	Qualifiers: Key
	String the unique identifier of the event consumer.
Subject	Access type: Read/write
	Qualifiers: Template
	Template string containing the subject of the e-mail message.
Message	Access type: Read/write
	Qualifiers: Template
	Template string containing the body of the e-mail message.
ToLine	Access type: Read/write
	Qualifiers: Template
	String containing a comma or semicolon-separated list of e-mail addresses where the message is to be sent.
FromLine	Access type: Read-only
	Qualifiers: Template
	From line of the e-mail message. If NULL, a From line is constructed of the form WinMgmt@MachineName.
ReplyToLine	Access type: Read-only
	Qualifiers: Template
	Reply-to line of the e-mail message. If NULL, no reply-to line is used.
SMTPServer	Access type: Read/write
	Qualifiers: Not null
	String that names the SMTP server through which the e-mail is to be sent. Permissible names are an IP address, or a DNS or NetBIOS name. This property cannot be NULL.
CcLine	Access type: Read/write
	Qualifiers: Template
	String containing a semicolon-separated list of addresses to which the message is sent as a carbon copy.
BccLine	Access type: Read/write
	Qualifiers: Template
	String containing a semicolon-separated list of addresses to which the message is sent as a blind carbon copy.
HeaderFields	Access type: Read-only
	String array of header fields that are inserted into the e-mail message without interpretation.

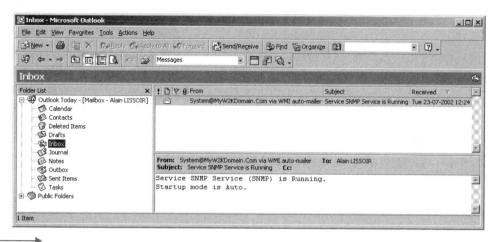

Figure 2.46   *The received mail from the permanent SMTP event consumer.*

Once completed, the only way to test the new CIM instance definition
for the *SMTP* event consumer is to perform a change on a Windows service
(by stopping or starting a service or modifying the startup mode of a service). When a change occurs the target recipient will receive an e-mail similar to that shown in Figure 2.46.

2.10   Summary

This chapter explained the basic foundation of WMI. Some of the WMI
features available were used to illustrate the possibilities offered by this management instrumentation without programming. A very important point is
that you should be trained with the WMI tools provided by Microsoft
because each time it is necessary to work with or gather information about
classes, instances, events, providers or consumers, these tools are extremely
useful. When we examine the scripting techniques on top of WMI, these
tools will also be a complementary aid to the development process.

Gathering knowledge about the CIM repository and its object model is
a long process. The most difficult part is to distinguish clearly the difference
between the CIM elements and how they interact with one another. Understanding the difference between a class and an instance is probably basic,
but it is also very important! Under CIM everything is defined in the form
of classes and instances; therefore, the WMI tools delivered by Microsoft
with the standard WMI installation or as a separate download from the
Web are particularly helpful. We encourage you to play with these tools and
examine how various elements are defined.

As the CIM repository is a specialized database modeling real-world manageable entities, with the help of the tools (e.g., WMIC, WBEMTEST, WBEMDUMP, and **WMI CIM Studio**) and the specialized WMI query language (WQL), it is possible to perform various queries to retrieve the information stored in the CIM repository. This language is an important key player when creating scripts that monitor real-world manageable entities. The next chapter delves into the WQL world.

2.11   Useful Internet URLs

Windows Management Instrumentation (WMI) CORE 1.5 (Windows 95/98/NT 4.0):

`http://www.microsoft.com/downloads/release.asp?releaseid=18490`

Windows Management Instrumentation (WMI) SDK 1.5 (Windows NT 4.0 and 2000):

`http://www.microsoft.com/downloads/release.asp?releaseid=19157`

Platform SDK:

`http://www.microsoft.com/msdownload/platformsdk/sdkupdate`

WMI Tools:

`http://www.microsoft.com/downloads/release.asp?ReleaseID=40804`

Scriptomatic:

`http://www.microsoft.com/downloads/release.asp?ReleaseID=41528`

The WMI Query Language

3.1 Objective

In the previous chapter, when we performed basic monitoring using the *SMTP* event consumer, we used a WQL query to define and filter the event. When we used the **WMI CIM Studio** to browse the content of the CIM repository, we did not use a WQL query to retrieve the information, even though **WMI CIM Studio** provides the ability to perform WQL queries to retrieve CIM information. In the same way, **WBEMTEST.exe** and **WBEMDump.exe** are also capable of performing WQL queries. Mastering WQL is very important because it can be used in different places. When working with the scripting interfaces and the WMI events, it is impossible to avoid its usage because a WQL query is the required primary input. This is why, in this chapter, we do not dive immediately into the scripting technique, and instead we focus on WQL. After completion of this chapter, we will be ready to start exploring the WMI scripting API.

Important notice: At this stage, it is really important to understand the relationship between the Windows services as described in Chapter 2 (Section 2.9.1). Don't hesitate to compare the result of WQL queries with what is available from **WMI CIM Studio**. It will be very important for you to practice the queries during this learning phase. It is easy to get lost and confused without practicing!

3.2 The WMI query language

As the purpose of the CIM repository is to create a data model that represents real-world manageable entities, it is important to have a powerful technique to retrieve the information stored in the repository. Besides the simple browsing or the exploration of WMI possibilities, WMI also comes with a specific query language, which is an alternate method to retrieve information from the CIM repository. The query language is a subset of the American National Standards Institute Structured Query Language (ANSI SQL) and is called WMI Query Language (WQL). However, it differs from the standard SQL in that it retrieves from classes rather than tables and returns WMI classes or instances rather than rows. This language is an important tool addition to WMI because it facilitates data retrieval and can be used in various ways from many different tools. To suit WMI's needs, WQL has some semantic changes when compared with SQL. Unlike SQL, WQL is a read-only language. This means that WQL does not allow operations to modify, insert, or delete information from the CIM repository. As briefly mentioned in the previous chapter, WQL is mainly used to perform the following:

- **Data queries**: to retrieve instances of classes and information about instance associations

- **Schema queries**: to retrieve class definitions and information about schema associations

- **Event queries**: to be used by temporary consumers or permanent consumers. Basically, these queries are used to filter WMI events

All WQL queries use reserved keywords. Table 3.1 lists the supported WQL keywords with the context in which they can be used.

Table 3.1   *WQL Keywords*

Keywords	Query Type			Description
	Data	Schema	Event	
__CLASS	*	*		References the class of the object in the query. This keyword is available in Windows 2000 and later.
AND	*(1)		*	Combines two Boolean expressions and returns TRUE when both of the expressions are TRUE.
ASSOCIATORS OF	*	*		Retrieves all instances that are associated with a source instance. Use this statement with schema queries and data queries.
BY			*	Indicates which properties to use when grouping. Use this clause with the GROUP clause.

(1) Not usable with the "Associators of" and the "References of" statements.

Table 3.1 *WQL Keywords (continued)*

Keywords	Query Type			Description
	Data	Schema	Event	
FALSE	*	*	*	Boolean operator that evaluates to 0.
FROM	*	*	*	Specifies the classes that contain the properties listed in a SELECT statement.
GROUP			*	Causes WMI to generate a single notification to represent a group of events. Use this clause with event queries.
HAVING			*	Filters the events that are received during the grouping interval specified in the WITHIN clause.
IS			*	Comparison operator used with NOT and NULL. The syntax for this statement is IS [NOT] NULL where NOT is optional.
ISA	*	*	*	Operator that applies a query to the subclasses of the specified class. For more information, see ISA Operator for Event Queries, ISA Operator for Data Queries, and ISA Operator for Schema Queries.
KEYSONLY	*			Used in REFERENCES OF and ASSOCIATORS OF queries so that the resulting instances are only populated with the keys of the instances, thereby reducing the overhead of the call. This keyword is available in Windows XP and later.
LIKE	*			Operator that determines whether a given character string matches a specified pattern
NOT	*		*	Comparison operator that can be used in any WQL SELECT query.
NULL	*		*	Indicates that an object has no explicitly assigned value. NULL is not equivalent to zero or blank.
OR	*(1)		*	Combines two conditions. When more than one logical operator is used in a statement, OR operators are evaluated after AND operators.
REFERENCES OF	*	*		Retrieves all association instances that refer to a particular source instance. Use this statement with schema and data queries. The REFERENCES OF statement is similar to the ASSOCIATORS OF statement. However, rather than retrieving endpoint instances, it retrieves the intervening association instances.

(1) Not usable with the "Associators of" and the "References of" statements.

Table 3.1   *WQL Keywords (continued)*

Keywords	Query Type			Description
	Data	Schema	Event	
SELECT	*	*	*	Specifies the properties that will be used in a query. For more information, see SELECT Statement for Data Queries, SELECT Statement for Event Queries, or SELECT Statement for Schema Queries.
TRUE	*		*	Boolean operator that evaluates to −1.
WHERE	*	*	*	Narrows the scope of a data, event, or schema query.
WITHIN			*	Specifies either a polling interval or a grouping interval. Use this clause with event queries.

(1) Not usable with the "Associators of" and the "References of" statements.

Besides the reserved keywords, WQL also uses operators. Some of the keywords can be considered as operators. Table 3.2 contains a list of the operators that can be used in a WQL query.

As we examine the different types of queries, we revisit each keyword and operator usage. For now, let's start with the first one: the data queries.

Table 3.2   *WQL Operators*

Operator	Definition
=	Equal to
<	Less than
>	Greater than
<=	Less than or equal to
>=	Greater than or equal to
!= or <>	Not equal to
IS	Test if a constant is NULL
IS NOT	Test if a constant is NOT NULL
ISA	For Data and Event queries, tests embedded objects for a class hierarchy. For Schema Queries, Newly-created and existing subclasses of the requested class are automatically included in the result set.

3.2.1 **Data queries**

In the previous chapter, we saw that instances contain information about real-world manageable entities. The data quey's purpose is to retrieve information from these real-world manageable entities. We saw that some classes are associated together, which implies that instances of these classes are also associated together. In other words, it is possible to retrieve the associations and the references related to an instance of a class.

3.2.1.1 *Retrieving instances of classes*

As the philosophy of this book is to learn by practice, let's take the same easy sample used in the previous chapter:

```
Select * From Win32_Service
```

The **SELECT** statement is one of three statements available to perform a data query. We revisit the other two later in this section. To perform this query, we can use any tool offering WQL query capabilities. Instead of using **WBEMTEST.exe** or **WMI CIM Studio** as before, we use **WBEMDump.exe**. As a reminder, **WBEMDump.exe** is an application sample that comes with the Platform SDK (see Chapter 2). To execute this sample query with **WBEMDump.exe**, use the following command line:

```
C:\>wbemdump /E /Q Root\CIMV2 WQL "Select * From Win32_Service"
```

The **/E** enables to display the system classes and the system properties. The **/Q** enables the WMI query features of **WBEMDump.exe**. Next, the query is executed in the **Root\CIMv2** namespace, and WQL is used to perform the query (currently, this is the only language supported by WMI). The last parameter is the WQL query itself. Once executed, the query output is similar to that shown in Sample 3.1. The output has been reduced to minimize the amount of data, as this query displays all information available from all *Win32_Service* instances. In the system properties, we can see the *__CLASS* property containing the name of the class. This information shows the class name of the instance.

Sample 3.1 *Using the SELECT statement to get all properties of all instances of a given class*

```
C:\>wbemdump /E /Q Root\CIMV2 WQL "Select * From Win32_Service"
(WQL) Select * From Win32_Service
       __CLASS (CIM_STRING/)  = "Win32_Service"
       ...
       __RELPATH (CIM_STRING/)  = "Win32_Service.Name="Alerter""
       ...
       __SUPERCLASS (CIM_STRING/)  = "Win32_BaseService"
       AcceptPause (CIM_BOOLEAN/boolean)  = FALSE
```

```
AcceptStop (CIM_BOOLEAN/boolean)  = TRUE
Caption (CIM_STRING/string)  = "Alerter"
CheckPoint (CIM_UINT32/uint32)  = 0 (0x0)
CreationClassName (CIM_STRING/string)  = "Win32_Service"
Description (CIM_STRING/string)  = "Alerter"
DesktopInteract (CIM_BOOLEAN/boolean)  = FALSE
Displayname (CIM_STRING/string)  = "Alerter"
ErrorControl (CIM_STRING/string)  = "Normal"
ExitCode (CIM_UINT32/uint32)  = 0 (0x0)
InstallDate (CIM_DATETIME/datetime)  = <null>
Name (CIM_STRING/string)*  = "Alerter"
PathName (CIM_STRING/string)  = "I:\WINNT\System32\services.exe"
ProcessId (CIM_UINT32/uint32)  = 228 (0xE4)
ServiceSpecificExitCode (CIM_UINT32/uint32)  = 0 (0x0)
ServiceType (CIM_STRING/string)  = "Share Process"
Started (CIM_BOOLEAN/boolean)  = TRUE
StartMode (CIM_STRING/string)  = "Auto"
StartName (CIM_STRING/string)  = "LocalSystem"
State (CIM_STRING/string)  = "Running"
Status (CIM_STRING/string)  = "OK"
SystemCreationClassName (CIM_STRING/string)  = "Win32_ComputerSystem"
SystemName (CIM_STRING/string)  = "NET-DPEN6400A"
TagId (CIM_UINT32/uint32)  = 0 (0x0)
WaitHint (CIM_UINT32/uint32)  = 0 (0x0)

__CLASS (CIM_STRING/)  = "Win32_Service"
...
__RELPATH (CIM_STRING/)  = "Win32_Service.Name="AppMgmt""
...
__SUPERCLASS (CIM_STRING/)  = "Win32_BaseService"
AcceptPause (CIM_BOOLEAN/boolean)  = FALSE
AcceptStop (CIM_BOOLEAN/boolean)  = FALSE
Caption (CIM_STRING/string)  = "Application Management"
CheckPoint (CIM_UINT32/uint32)  = 0 (0x0)
CreationClassName (CIM_STRING/string)  = "Win32_Service"
Description (CIM_STRING/string)  = "Application Management"
DesktopInteract (CIM_BOOLEAN/boolean)  = FALSE
Displayname (CIM_STRING/string)  = "Application Management"
ErrorControl (CIM_STRING/string)  = "Normal"
ExitCode (CIM_UINT32/uint32)  = 1077 (0x435)
InstallDate (CIM_DATETIME/datetime)  = <null>
Name (CIM_STRING/string)*  = "AppMgmt"
PathName (CIM_STRING/string)  = "I:\WINNT\system32\services.exe"
ProcessId (CIM_UINT32/uint32)  = 0 (0x0)
ServiceSpecificExitCode (CIM_UINT32/uint32)  = 0 (0x0)
ServiceType (CIM_STRING/string)  = "Share Process"
Started (CIM_BOOLEAN/boolean)  = FALSE
StartMode (CIM_STRING/string)  = "Manual"
StartName (CIM_STRING/string)  = "LocalSystem"
State (CIM_STRING/string)  = "Stopped"
...

__CLASS (CIM_STRING/)  = "Win32_Service"
...
__SUPERCLASS (CIM_STRING/)  = "Win32_BaseService"
...
Name (CIM_STRING/string)*  = "Browser"
...
```

```
        __CLASS (CIM_STRING/)  = "Win32_Service"
        ...
        __SUPERCLASS (CIM_STRING/)  = "Win32_BaseService"
        ...
        Name (CIM_STRING/string)*  = "CertSvc"
        ...


        __CLASS (CIM_STRING/)  = "Win32_Service"
        ...
        __SUPERCLASS (CIM_STRING/)  = "Win32_BaseService"
        ...
        Name (CIM_STRING/string)*  = "cisvc"
        ...
        ...
        ...
```

If you carefully observe the *Name* property, you will see that a star follows the property name. This indicates that this property is a key. As explained in Chapter 2, a key is an instance property used as a unique identifier. This query generates a lot of information. If we are interested only in some of the properties, such as the service *State* (running, stopped, etc.) with the name of all *Win32_Service* instances, the WQL query can be modified as shown in Sample 3.2.

Sample 3.2   *Using the SELECT statement to retrieve some properties of all instances*

```
C:\>wbemdump /E /Q Root\CIMV2 WQL "Select State, Displayname From Win32_Service"
(WQL) Select State, Displayname From Win32_Service
        __CLASS (CIM_STRING/)  = "Win32_Service"
        ...
        Displayname (CIM_STRING/string)  = "Alerter"
        State (CIM_STRING/string)  = "Running"

        __CLASS (CIM_STRING/)  = "Win32_Service"
        ...
        Displayname (CIM_STRING/string)  = "Application Management"
        State (CIM_STRING/string)  = "Stopped"

        __CLASS (CIM_STRING/)  = "Win32_Service"
        ...
        Displayname (CIM_STRING/string)  = "Computer Browser"
        State (CIM_STRING/string)  = "Running"

        __CLASS (CIM_STRING/)  = "Win32_Service"
        ...
        Displayname (CIM_STRING/string)  = "Certificate Services"
        State (CIM_STRING/string)  = "Running"

        __CLASS (CIM_STRING/)  = "Win32_Service"
        ...
        Displayname (CIM_STRING/string)  = "Indexing Service"
        State (CIM_STRING/string)  = "Stopped"
        ...
        ...
        ...
```

```
__CLASS (CIM_STRING/)  = "Win32_Service"
...
Displayname (CIM_STRING/string)  = "Windows Management Instrumentation Driver Extensions"
State (CIM_STRING/string)  = "Running"
```

The list of properties is limited to the two requested properties: *State* and *Displayname*. It is important to note that the **FROM** statement retrieves all instances of the *Win32_Service* class, including all instances derived from the *Win32_Service* class. As the *Win32_Service* class is not derived in the current CIM Schema, we get only the *Win32_Service* instances. Now, for the exercise, you can perform the same query, but instead of using the *Win32_Service* class, you can use the *Win32_Base-Service* class. You will see that you will retrieve all *Win32_Service* instances and all *Win32_SystemDriver* instances. The query will look like this:

```
Select * FROM Win32_BaseService
```

To limit the result of the query to one instance type, you can use the system property called *__CLASS* with the **WHERE** statement. In such a case, the query will look like this:

```
Select * FROM Win32_BaseService Where __CLASS="Win32_Service"
```

Due to the filtering effect of the **WHERE** statement, the query will return the exact same list shown in Sample 3.1, because we retrieve only the list of all *Win32_Service* instances available. Instead of retrieving the complete list of the *Win32_Service* instances, we can also reduce the scope to a specific *Win32_Service* instance by using the **WHERE** statement with a different filter. Note that the **WHERE** statement can be used in the three types of query: data, schema, and event. Samples 3.4 and 3.5 looks at the data query case.

Sample 3.3   *Using the WHERE statement to limit the scope to one instance*

```
C:\>wbemdump /Q Root\CIMV2 WQL "Select State, Displayname From Win32_Service Where Name='SNMP'"
(WQL) Select State, Displayname From Win32_Service Where Name='SNMP'
      __CLASS (CIM_STRING/)  = "Win32_Service"
      ...
      Displayname (CIM_STRING/string)  = "SNMP Service"
      State (CIM_STRING/string)  = "Stopped"
```

In data queries the **WHERE** statement refers to a property of the instance that must match the selection criteria. In Sample 3.3 the selection criteria specifies that the *Name* property must match the value "SNMP." Note that the match is case insensitive. We mentioned before that the *Name* property is a key of the *Win32_Service* class. Of course, it is possible to use another property than a key for the selection criteria. For instance, to get the list of all *Win32_Service* instances that are stopped, the query can be formulated as shown in Sample 3.4.

Sample 3.4   *Using the WHERE statement to limit the scope to some instances*

```
C:\>wbemdump /E /Q Root\CIMV2 WQL "Select Displayname From Win32_Service Where State='Stopped'"
(WQL) Select Displayname From Win32_Service Where State='Stopped'
        __CLASS (CIM_STRING/)  = "Win32_Service"
        ...
        Displayname (CIM_STRING/string)  = "Application Management"

        __CLASS (CIM_STRING/)  = "Win32_Service"
        ...
        Displayname (CIM_STRING/string)  = "Indexing Service"

        __CLASS (CIM_STRING/)  = "Win32_Service"
        ...
        Displayname (CIM_STRING/string)  = "ClipBook"

        __CLASS (CIM_STRING/)  = "Win32_Service"
        ...
        Displayname (CIM_STRING/string)  = "DHCP Server"

        __CLASS (CIM_STRING/)  = "Win32_Service"
        ...
        Displayname (CIM_STRING/string)  = "Logical Disk Manager Administrative Service"

        __CLASS (CIM_STRING/)  = "Win32_Service"
        ...
        Displayname (CIM_STRING/string)  = "Fax Service"

        __CLASS (CIM_STRING/)  = "Win32_Service"
        ...
        Displayname (CIM_STRING/string)  = "NetMeeting Remote Desktop Sharing"

        __CLASS (CIM_STRING/)  = "Win32_Service"
        ...
        Displayname (CIM_STRING/string)  = "Microsoft Exchange Event"

       __CLASS (CIM_STRING/)  = "Win32_Service"
        ...
        ...
        ...
        Displayname (CIM_STRING/string)  = "Visual Studio Analyzer RPC bridge"
```

In Sample 3.3, we get only one instance of the *Win32_Service* class. We can reuse this query and extend it to get two instances by using the logical **OR** operator, as shown in Sample 3.5.

Sample 3.5   *Using the WHERE statement to limit the scope to two instances with a logical operator in a WQL data query*

```
C:\>wbemdump /E /Q Root\CIMV2 WQL
    "Select State, Displayname From Win32_Service Where Name='SNMP' Or Name='Alerter'"

(WQL) Select State, Displayname From Win32_Service Where Name='SNMP' Or Name='Alerter'
        __CLASS (CIM_STRING/)  = "Win32_Service"
        ...
```

```
Displayname (CIM_STRING/string)  = "Alerter"
State (CIM_STRING/string)  = "Running"

__CLASS (CIM_STRING/)  = "Win32_Service"
...
Displayname (CIM_STRING/string)  = "SNMP Service"
State (CIM_STRING/string)  = "Stopped"
```

Our needs for data retrieval may force us to use other logical operators such as **AND** or **NOT**. For example, to retrieve all *Win32_Service* instances other than the Alerter or the SNMP Windows services, we can use the query of Sample 3.6.

Sample 3.6   *Using the NOT logical operator to exclude two instances from a data query*

```
C:\>wbemdump /E /Q Root\CIMV2 WQL
    "Select State, Displayname From Win32_Service Where NOT (Name='SNMP' Or Name='Alerter')"

(WQL) Select State, Displayname From Win32_Service Where NOT (Name='SNMP' Or Name='Alerter')
      __CLASS (CIM_STRING/)  = "Win32_Service"
      ...
      Displayname (CIM_STRING/string)  = "Application Management"
      State (CIM_STRING/string)  = "Stopped"

      __CLASS (CIM_STRING/)  = "Win32_Service"
      ...
      Displayname (CIM_STRING/string)  = "Computer Browser"
      State (CIM_STRING/string)  = "Running"

      __CLASS (CIM_STRING/)  = "Win32_Service"
      ...
      Displayname (CIM_STRING/string)  = "Certificate Services"
      State (CIM_STRING/string)  = "Running"

      __CLASS (CIM_STRING/)  = "Win32_Service"
      ...
      Displayname (CIM_STRING/string)  = "Indexing Service"
      State (CIM_STRING/string)  = "Stopped"

      __CLASS (CIM_STRING/)  = "Win32_Service"
      ...
      Displayname (CIM_STRING/string)  = "ClipBook"
      State (CIM_STRING/string)  = "Stopped"
      ...
      ...
      ...
      WaitHint (CIM_UINT32/uint32)  = 0 (0x0)
```

Notice that the result of the query does not list the Alerter Windows service as made in query Sample 3.2. The SNMP Windows service is not listed either, but, as the output is quite long, we skipped the rest of the display output. If you perform this exercise on your own, you will easily verify this. The query used the **NOT** logical operator for academic purposes. The same query can be made by changing the matching test and using the **AND** operator:

```
Select State, Displayname From Win32_Service Where (Name<>'SNMP' And Name<>'Alerter')
```

or

```
Select State, Displayname From Win32_Service Where (Name!='SNMP' And Name!='Alerter')
```

Note that two forms of the "not equal to" operator (!= or <>) can be used.

3.2.1.2   *Retrieving the associators of a class instance*

The second statement that can be used to perform data queries is the **Associators Of** statement. This statement can be used to retrieve the associations related to an instance of a class or to a class only. This means that the **Associators Of** statement can be used for data queries and schema queries. In the previous chapter, to understand the class dependencies, we used the Microsoft Exchange System Attendant (named MSExchangeSA in the system registry). To visualize its associations, we used the **WMI CIM Studio** graphical interface. Now, as we discover WQL, we can also use a WQL query to obtain the exact same information.

Sample 3.7 shows the command line to use with **WBEMDump.exe** and its display output. Note that for readability purposes, the output displays only the *Key* property of the *Win32_Service* class because the WQL query retrieves all the properties of the listed instances.

Sample 3.7   *Retrieving the associated instances of a given instance with the Associators Of WQL statement*

```
C:\>wbemdump /E /Q Root\CIMV2 WQL "Associators Of {Win32_Service='MSExchangeSA'}"
(WQL) Associators Of {Win32_Service='MSExchangeSA'}
        __CLASS (CIM_STRING/)  = "Win32_ComputerSystem"
        ...
        Name (CIM_STRING/string)*  = "NET-DPEN6400A"
        ...

        __CLASS (CIM_STRING/)  = "Win32_Service"
        ...
        Name (CIM_STRING/string)*  = "MSExchangeIS"
        ...

        __CLASS (CIM_STRING/)  = "Win32_Service"
        ...
        Name (CIM_STRING/string)*  = "MSExchangeMTA"
        ...

        __CLASS (CIM_STRING/)  = "Win32_Service"
        ...
```

```
Name (CIM_STRING/string)*  = "Eventlog"
...

__CLASS (CIM_STRING/)  = "Win32_Service"
...
Name (CIM_STRING/string)*  = "NtLmSsp"
...

__CLASS (CIM_STRING/)  = "Win32_Service"
...
Name (CIM_STRING/string)*  = "RpcLocator"
...

__CLASS (CIM_STRING/)  = "Win32_Service"
...
Name (CIM_STRING/string)*  = "RpcSs"
...

__CLASS (CIM_STRING/)  = "Win32_Service"
...
Name (CIM_STRING/string)*  = "lanmanworkstation"
...

__CLASS (CIM_STRING/)  = "Win32_Service"
...
Name (CIM_STRING/string)*  = "lanmanserver"
...
...
...
WaitHint (CIM_UINT32/uint32)  = 0 (0x0)
```

If you look to the service dependencies of the Microsoft Exchange System Attendant visible in Figure 3.1, you will see that the list returned by the WQL query is exactly the same as the one shown with **WMI CIM Studio**. All instances associated with the *Win32_Service* instance MSExchangeSA are listed in the WQL query result. Note that the property used to identify the *Win32_Service* MSExchangeSA instance is the *Name* property defined as a key. To be formal, the query can also be specified as follows:

```
C:\>wbemdump /E /Q Root\CIMV2 WQL "Associators Of {Win32_Service.Name='MSExchangeSA'}"
```

This syntax variation can be useful in a case where the instance to be identified has several keys. By explicitly specifying the key name, you select the key to use to perform the test on. For example, the *Win32_Account* class uses two keys: the *Name* and the *Domain* properties. Therefore; the query will be as follows:

```
C:\>wbemdump /E /Q Root\CIMV2 WQL
    "Associators Of {Win32_Account.Name='Alain.Lissoir',Domain='LisswareNET'}"
```

For items having only one key, this formal notation is unnecessary as the unique key is used by default to perform the test. Note that this notation is

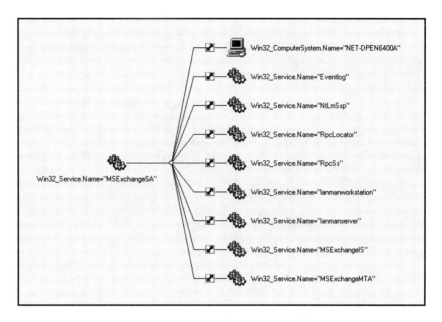

Figure 3.1
Viewing the Microsoft Exchange 2000 System Attendant service dependencies with WMI CIM Studio.

valid for data and schema queries. This notation is also applicable to the **References Of** statement that we will see in the next section.

The **Associators Of** statement can be used in combination with the **WHERE** statement. The formal syntax representation of the **Associators Of** statement is as follows:

```
ASSOCIATORS OF {ObjectPath} [WHERE ClassDefsOnly]
                           [WHERE KeysOnly]
                           [WHERE AssocClass = AssocClassName] [ClassDefsOnly]
                           [WHERE RequiredAssocQualifier = QualifierName] [ClassDefsOnly]
                           [WHERE RequiredQualifier = QualifierName] [ClassDefsOnly]
                           [WHERE ResultClass = ClassName] [ClassDefsOnly]
                           [WHERE ResultRole = PropertyName] [ClassDefsOnly]
                           [WHERE Role = PropertyName] [ClassDefsOnly]
```

As we can see, the **Associators Of** statement can be combined with some extra keywords to refine the selection criteria of the WQL query.

The next sample uses the **ClassDefsOnly** keyword and performs the exact same query as Sample 3.7, but the retrieved information is the class definition of the associated instances, instead of the instances themselves. It is important to note that the query is still a data query because it queries an instance (the MSExchangeSA *Win32_Service* instance) and retrieves the classes of the associated instances. Making the same query with the **Class-DefsOnly** keyword will give the result shown in Sample 3.8.

Sample 3.8   *Retrieving the associated instance class definitions of a given instance with the Associators Of WQL statement (Associators Of statement and ClassDefsOnly keyword)*

```
C:\>wbemdump /E /Q Root\CIMV2 WQL
    "Associators Of {Win32_Service='MSExchangeSA'} Where ClassDefsOnly"

(WQL) Associators Of {Win32_Service='MSExchangeSA'} Where ClassDefsOnly
       __CLASS (CIM_STRING/)  = "Win32_ComputerSystem"
       ...
       __SUPERCLASS (CIM_STRING/) = "CIM_UnitaryComputerSystem"
       AdminPasswordStatus (CIM_UINT16/uint16) = <null>
       AutomaticResetBootOption (CIM_BOOLEAN/boolean) = <null>
       AutomaticResetCapability (CIM_BOOLEAN/boolean) = <null>
       BootOptionOnLimit (CIM_UINT16/uint16) = <null>
       BootOptionOnWatchDog (CIM_UINT16/uint16) = <null>
       BootROMSupported (CIM_BOOLEAN/boolean) = <null>
       BootupState (CIM_STRING/string) = <null>
       Caption (CIM_STRING/string) = <null>
       ChassisBootupState (CIM_UINT16/uint16) = <null>
       CreationClassName (CIM_STRING/string) = <null>
       CurrentTimeZone (CIM_SINT16/sint16) = <null>
       ...
       Status (CIM_STRING/string) = <null>
       SupportContactDescription (CIM_STRING | CIM_FLAG_ARRAY/string) = <null>
       SystemStartupDelay (CIM_UINT16/uint16) = <null>
       SystemStartupOptions (CIM_STRING | CIM_FLAG_ARRAY/string) = <null>
       SystemStartupSetting (CIM_UINT8/uint8) = <null>
       SystemType (CIM_STRING/string) = <null>
       ThermalState (CIM_UINT16/uint16) = <null>
       TotalPhysicalMemory (CIM_UINT64/uint64) = <null>
       UserName (CIM_STRING/string) = <null>
       WakeUpType (CIM_UINT16/uint16) = <null>


       __CLASS (CIM_STRING/)  = "Win32_Service"       ...
       __SUPERCLASS (CIM_STRING/) = "Win32_BaseService"
       AcceptPause (CIM_BOOLEAN/boolean) = <null>
       AcceptStop (CIM_BOOLEAN/boolean) = <null>
       Caption (CIM_STRING/string) = <null>
       CheckPoint (CIM_UINT32/uint32) = <null>
       CreationClassName (CIM_STRING/string) = <null>
       Description (CIM_STRING/string) = <null>
       ...
       ServiceType (CIM_STRING/string) = <null>
       Started (CIM_BOOLEAN/boolean) = <null>
       StartMode (CIM_STRING/string) = <null>
       StartName (CIM_STRING/string) = <null>
       State (CIM_STRING/string) = <null>
       Status (CIM_STRING/string) = <null>
       SystemCreationClassName (CIM_STRING/string) = <null>
       SystemName (CIM_STRING/string) = <null>
       TagId (CIM_UINT32/uint32) = <null>
       WaitHint (CIM_UINT32/uint32) = <null>
```

As the query retrieves the class definitions of the associated instances and not the associated instances themselves, there are only two classes listed: the *Win32_ComputerSystem* class and the *Win32_Service* class (see Figure 3.2).

Figure 3.2
*Win32_Service
MSExchangeSA
instance associated
instances and
Associations
instances.*

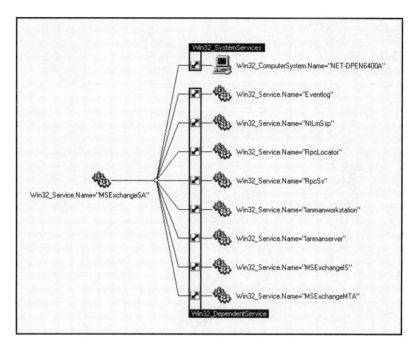

If you examine the output of the previous sample (see Sample 3.7), you will see that every instance retrieved uses one of these two classes. These associations are made via association classes called *Win32_SystemServices* and *Win32_DependentService* (see Figure 3.2).

Every time the **ClassDefsOnly** keyword is specified, the query retrieves the class definitions of the instances instead of the instances themselves. This keyword can be combined with the other valid keywords of the **Associators Of** statement.

Now, if we want to retrieve the *Win32_Service* associated instances (which means without the *Win32_ComputerSystem* instance), we can narrow the WQL query to retrieve the associated instance only when the Association instance is made from a *Win32_DependentService* class. This is achieved by using the **AssocClass** keyword, as shown in Sample 3.9.

Sample 3.9   *Retrieving the associated instances of a given instance that are using a particular association class name (Associators Of statement and AssocClass keyword)*

```
C:\>wbemdump /E /Q Root\CIMV2 WQL
    "Associators Of {Win32_Service='MSExchangeSA'} Where AssocClass=Win32_DependentService"

(WQL) Associators Of {Win32_Service='MSExchangeSA'} Where AssocClass=Win32_DependentService
```

```
__CLASS (CIM_STRING/)  = "Win32_Service"
...
Name (CIM_STRING/string)*  = "MSExchangeIS"
...

__CLASS (CIM_STRING/)  = "Win32_Service"
...
Name (CIM_STRING/string)*  = "MSExchangeMTA"
...

__CLASS (CIM_STRING/)  = "Win32_Service"
...
Name (CIM_STRING/string)*  = "Eventlog"

__CLASS (CIM_STRING/)  = "Win32_Service"
...
Name (CIM_STRING/string)*  = "NtLmSsp"
...

__CLASS (CIM_STRING/)  = "Win32_Service"
...
Name (CIM_STRING/string)*  = "RpcLocator"

__CLASS (CIM_STRING/)  = "Win32_Service"
...
Name (CIM_STRING/string)*  = "RpcSs"
...

__CLASS (CIM_STRING/)  = "Win32_Service"
...
Name (CIM_STRING/string)*  = "lanmanworkstation"
...

__CLASS (CIM_STRING/)  = "Win32_Service"
...
Name (CIM_STRING/string)*  = "lanmanserver"
...
...
...
WaitHint (CIM_UINT32/uint32)  = 0 (0x0)
```

We see in this query result that only the *Win32_Service* instances are listed because these instances are associated with the association instances made from the *Win32_DependentService* class. The associated instance *Win32_ComputerSystem* (shown in Sample 3.7) is not listed any more with this **Where** filter because this instance is associated with an association instance made from the *Win32_SystemServices* class (see Figure 3.2 for the visual representation of the associations in place).

In this last sample, we filter on the association class name; it is also possible to filter on the presence of a qualifier defined in the association instance. In the previous chapter, we examined the qualifiers of the *Win32_DependentService* association class. This association class had the following qualifiers defined: Association, Description, Dynamic, Locale, Provider, and UUID (see Figure 3.3).

Figure 3.3
*The
Win32_Dependent
Service Association
class qualifiers.*

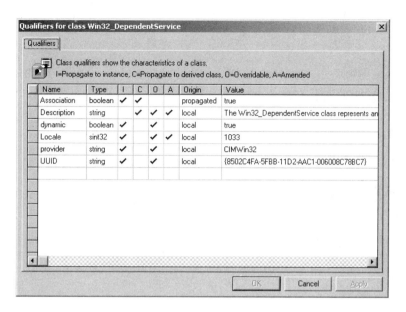

Therefore, if we want to get a list of instances using association instances that have a particular qualifier, the WQL query will use the **RequiredAssoc-Qualifier** keyword as shown in Sample 3.10.

Sample 3.10 *Retrieving the associated instances of a given instance where the Association class instances contain a specific qualifier (Associators Of statement and RequiredAssocQualifier keyword)*

```
C:\>wbemdump /E /Q Root\CIMV2 WQL
    "Associators Of {Win32_Service='MSExchangeSA'} Where RequiredAssocQualifier=Dynamic"

(WQL) Associators Of {Win32_Service='MSExchangeSA'} Where RequiredAssocQualifier=Dynamic
      __CLASS (CIM_STRING/) = "Win32_ComputerSystem"
      ...
      Name (CIM_STRING/string)* = "NET-DPEN6400A"
      ...

      __CLASS (CIM_STRING/) = "Win32_Service"
      ...
      Name (CIM_STRING/string)* = "MSExchangeIS"
      ...

      __CLASS (CIM_STRING/) = "Win32_Service"
      ...
      Name (CIM_STRING/string)* = "MSExchangeMTA"
      ...

      __CLASS (CIM_STRING/) = "Win32_Service"
      ...
      Name (CIM_STRING/string)* = "Eventlog"
      ...
```

```
    __CLASS (CIM_STRING/)  = "Win32_Service"
    ...
Name (CIM_STRING/string)* = "NtLmSsp"
    ...

    __CLASS (CIM_STRING/)  = "Win32_Service"
    ...
Name (CIM_STRING/string)* = "RpcLocator"
    ...

    __CLASS (CIM_STRING/)  = "Win32_Service"
    ...
Name (CIM_STRING/string)* = "RpcSs"
    ...

    __CLASS (CIM_STRING/)  = "Win32_Service"
    ...
Name (CIM_STRING/string)* = "lanmanworkstation"
    ...

    __CLASS (CIM_STRING/)  = "Win32_Service"
    ...
Name (CIM_STRING/string)* = "lanmanserver"
    ...
    ...
    ...
  WaitHint (CIM_UINT32/uint32)  = 0 (0x0)
```

Of course, in this case, we get the exact same result as Sample 3.7 because both the *Win32_SystemServices* and *Win32_DependentService* Association instances contain the Dynamic qualifier. As both association instances contain the same qualifiers, it is impossible to distinguish them with a query using this qualifier.

This last query filters on the presence of a qualifier in an association instance. So, instead of filtering on a qualifier defined in an association instance, as before, we filter on a qualifier present in the associated instance. The WQL query uses the RequiredQualifier keyword as shown in Sample 3.11.

Sample 3.11   *Retrieving the associated instances of a given instance where the associated instances contain a specific qualifier (Associators Of statement and RequiredQualifier keyword)*

```
C:\>wbemdump /E /Q Root\CIMV2 WQL
    "Associators Of {Win32_Service='MSExchangeSA'} Where RequiredQualifier=Dynamic"

(WQL) Associators Of {Win32_Service='MSExchangeSA'} Where RequiredQualifier=Dynamic
        __CLASS (CIM_STRING/)  = "Win32_ComputerSystem"
        ...
    Name (CIM_STRING/string)* = "NET-DPEN6400A"
        ...
```

```
      __CLASS (CIM_STRING/)  = "Win32_Service"
      ...
      Name (CIM_STRING/string)*  = "MSExchangeIS"
      ...

      __CLASS (CIM_STRING/)  = "Win32_Service"
      ...
      Name (CIM_STRING/string)*  = "MSExchangeMTA"
      ...

      __CLASS (CIM_STRING/)  = "Win32_Service"
      ...
      Name (CIM_STRING/string)*  = "Eventlog"
      ...

      __CLASS (CIM_STRING/)  = "Win32_Service"
      ...
      Name (CIM_STRING/string)*  = "NtLmSsp"
      ...

      __CLASS (CIM_STRING/)  = "Win32_Service"
      ...
      Name (CIM_STRING/string)*  = "RpcLocator"
      ...

      __CLASS (CIM_STRING/)  = "Win32_Service"
      ...
      Name (CIM_STRING/string)*  = "RpcSs"
      ...

      __CLASS (CIM_STRING/)  = "Win32_Service"
      ...
      Name (CIM_STRING/string)*  = "lanmanworkstation"
      ...

      __CLASS (CIM_STRING/)  = "Win32_Service"
      ...
      Name (CIM_STRING/string)*  = "lanmanserver"
      ...
      ...
      ...
      WaitHint (CIM_UINT32/uint32)  = 0 (0x0)
```

Again, because the *Win32_ComputerSystem* instance and the *Win32_Service* instances use the Dynamic qualifier, we get the same result as in Sample 3.7. Because the associated instances contain the same qualifiers, it is impossible to distinguish them with a query using this qualifier. However, if one of these two classes were defined as a singleton class (a class that has only one instance in a system), it would be possible to use the **RequiredQualifier** keyword to filter on the presence of the singleton qualifier.

It is possible to obtain the same result as in Sample 3.9 by using the **ResultClass** keyword instead of the **AssocClass** keyword. In this case, the test is performed on the class of the instances associated with the instance given in the WQL query. In Sample 3.9, the test was performed on the class of the association instances. This query with its result is shown in Sample 3.12 (see Figure 3.2 for the visual representation of the used classes).

Sample 3.12 *Retrieving the associated instances of a given instance where the associated instances match a specific class name (Asssociators Of statement and ResultClass keyword)*

```
C:\>wbemdump /E /Q Root\CIMV2 WQL
    "Associators Of {Win32_Service='MSExchangeSA'} Where ResultClass=Win32_Service"

(WQL) Associators Of {Win32_Service='MSExchangeSA'} Where ResultClass=Win32_Service
        __CLASS (CIM_STRING/)  = "Win32_Service"
        ...
        Name (CIM_STRING/string)*  = "MSExchangeIS"
        ...

        __CLASS (CIM_STRING/)  = "Win32_Service"
        ...
        Name (CIM_STRING/string)*  = "MSExchangeMTA"
        ...

        __CLASS (CIM_STRING/)  = "Win32_Service"
        ...
        Name (CIM_STRING/string)*  = "Eventlog"
        ...

        __CLASS (CIM_STRING/)  = "Win32_Service"
        ...
        Name (CIM_STRING/string)*  = "NtLmSsp"
        ...

        __CLASS (CIM_STRING/)  = "Win32_Service"
        ...
        Name (CIM_STRING/string)*  = "RpcLocator"
        ...

        __CLASS (CIM_STRING/)  = "Win32_Service"
        ...
        Name (CIM_STRING/string)*  = "RpcSs"
        ...

        __CLASS (CIM_STRING/)  = "Win32_Service"
        ...
        Name (CIM_STRING/string)*  = "lanmanworkstation"
        ...

        __CLASS (CIM_STRING/)  = "Win32_Service"
        ...
        Name (CIM_STRING/string)*  = "lanmanserver"
        ...
        ...
        ...
        WaitHint (CIM_UINT32/uint32)  = 0 (0x0)
```

In this sample, we see that the same results can be obtained even if the test uses different information. Instead of testing on the class of the association instances, the test is performed on the class of the Windows service instances.

In regard to the association class *Win32_DependentService*, we saw that associations are made in two ways: the Windows services that depend on the *Win32_Service* instance startup and the Windows services that must be started to start the *Win32_Service* instance. By using the **Associators Of** statement in combination with the **ResultRole** keyword, it is possible to find the list of instances that depend on each other based on the role defined in the associations. For instance, we saw that the MSExchangeMTA and MSExchangeIS services depend on the MSExchangeSA service. By using the **ResultRole** keyword, it is possible to retrieve the service list with a WQL query. The query with its result will be:

Sample 3.13   *Retrieving the associated instances of a given instance based on the associated instances role (Associators Of statement and ResultRole keyword)*

```
C:\>wbemdump /E /Q Root\CIMV2 WQL
    "Associators Of {Win32_Service='MSExchangeSA'} Where ResultRole=Dependent"

(WQL) Associators Of {Win32_Service='MSExchangeSA'} Where ResultRole=Dependent
      __CLASS (CIM_STRING/)   = "Win32_Service"
      ...
      Name (CIM_STRING/string)* = "MSExchangeIS"
      ...

      __CLASS (CIM_STRING/)   = "Win32_Service"
      ...
      Name (CIM_STRING/string)* = "MSExchangeMTA"
      ...
      ...
      ...
      WaitHint (CIM_UINT32/uint32)  = 0 (0x0)
```

Therefore, if we want to retrieve the *Win32_Service* instances that must be started in order to start the MSExchangeSA *Win32_Service* instance, we must use the following query:

Sample 3.14   *Retrieving the associated instances of a given instance based on the associated instances role (Associators Of statement and ResultRole keyword) (complementary query)*

```
C:\>wbemdump /E /Q Root\CIMV2 WQL
    "Associators Of {Win32_Service='MSExchangeSA'} Where ResultRole=Antecedent"

(WQL) Associators Of {Win32_Service='MSExchangeSA'} Where ResultRole=Antecedent
      __CLASS (CIM_STRING/)   = "Win32_Service"
      ...
      Name (CIM_STRING/string)* = "Eventlog"
      ...
```

```
__CLASS (CIM_STRING/)   = "Win32_Service"
...
Name (CIM_STRING/string)*  = "NtLmSsp"
...


__CLASS (CIM_STRING/)   = "Win32_Service"
...
Name (CIM_STRING/string)*  = "RpcLocator"
...


__CLASS (CIM_STRING/)   = "Win32_Service"
...
Name (CIM_STRING/string)*  = "RpcSs"
...


__CLASS (CIM_STRING/)   = "Win32_Service"
...
Name (CIM_STRING/string)*  = "lanmanworkstation"
...


__CLASS (CIM_STRING/)   = "Win32_Service"
...
Name (CIM_STRING/string)*  = "lanmanserver"
...
...
...
WaitHint (CIM_UINT32/uint32)  = 0 (0x0)
```

In the last two WQL queries (Sample 3.13 and 3.14), filtering is performed on the role played by the associated instances in relation to the given *Win32_Service* instance. In the same way, it is possible to filter the

Figure 3.4
The role of the association between the given instance and the associated instances.

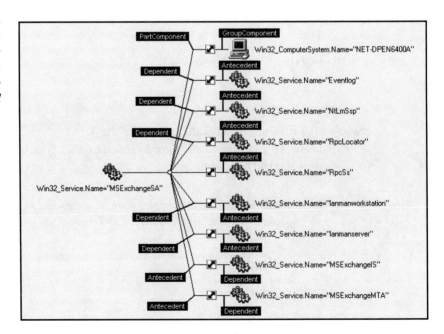

associated instances based on the role played by the given *Win32_Service* instance. This query is the complementary result of the two previous queries, as the MSExchangeSA is an antecedent Windows service for the MSExchangeIS and MSExchangeMTA Windows services, and MSExchangeIS and MSExchangeMTA are dependent Windows services of the MSExchangeSA Windows service (see Figure 3.4).

As a reminder, Section 2.9.1 explains what antecent and dependent Windows services are. To obtain the result of Sample 3.13 with the role played by the given instance, we must use the **Role** keyword as shown in Sample 3.15.

Sample 3.15 *Retrieving the associated instances of a given instance based on the given instance role (Associators Of statement and Role keyword)*

```
C:\>wbemdump /E /Q Root\CIMV2 WQL
    "Associators Of {Win32_Service='MSExchangeSA'} Where Role=Antecedent"

(WQL) Associators Of {Win32_Service='MSExchangeSA'} Where Role=Antecedent
        __CLASS (CIM_STRING/)  = "Win32_Service"
        ...
        Name (CIM_STRING/string)*  = "MSExchangeIS"
        ...

        __CLASS (CIM_STRING/)  = "Win32_Service"
        ...
        Name (CIM_STRING/string)*  = "MSExchangeMTA"
        ...
        ...
        ...
        WaitHint (CIM_UINT32/uint32)  = 0 (0x0)
```

The query shown in Sample 3.16 produces a complementary result for Sample 3.15 (same result as Sample 3.14).

Sample 3.16 *Retrieving the associated instances of a given instance based on the given instance role (Associators Of statement and Role keyword) (complementary query)*

```
C:\>wbemdump /E /Q Root\CIMV2 WQL
    "Associators Of {Win32_Service='MSExchangeSA'} Where Role=Dependent"

(WQL) Associators Of {Win32_Service='MSExchangeSA'} Where Role=Dependent
        __CLASS (CIM_STRING/)  = "Win32_Service"
        ...
        Name (CIM_STRING/string)*  = "Eventlog"
        ...

        __CLASS (CIM_STRING/)  = "Win32_Service"
        ...
        Name (CIM_STRING/string)*  = "NtLmSsp"
        ...
```

```
__CLASS (CIM_STRING/)  = "Win32_Service"
...
Name (CIM_STRING/string)* = "RpcLocator"
...

__CLASS (CIM_STRING/)  = "Win32_Service"
...
Name (CIM_STRING/string)* = "RpcSs"
...

__CLASS (CIM_STRING/)  = "Win32_Service"
...
Name (CIM_STRING/string)* = "lanmanworkstation"
...

__CLASS (CIM_STRING/)  = "Win32_Service"
...
Name (CIM_STRING/string)* = "lanmanserver"
...
...
...
WaitHint (CIM_UINT32/uint32)  = 0 (0x0)
```

It is important to note that an **Associators Of** statement that uses the **WHERE** statement cannot use the **AND** or the **OR** logical operator to separate keywords. However, any of the keywords can be combined in the same query to have an implicit **AND** logical operation. This important detail shows that it is crucial not to confuse WQL with SQL even if there are some similarities. For instance, you may have the following:

```
C:\>wbemdump /E /Q Root\CIMV2 WQL
   "Associators Of {Win32_Service} Where ResultClass=Win32_ServiceSpecification
                      RequiredQualifier=Dynamic SchemaOnly"
```

Furthermore, the equal sign is the only valid operator that can be used with the keywords in these queries.

As we have seen in this section, the last 12 samples deal with associations. When we talk about associations, this always implies the use of references. It is possible to perform data queries that take advantage of the defined references in the associations, which leads us to the next section.

3.2.1.3   Retrieving the references of a class instance

To define the association between a given *Win32_Service* instance and any other *Win32_Service* instances, two specific properties of the *Win32_DependentService* Association class are used: the *Dependent* property and the *Antecedent* property. As we saw in Section 2.9.1, these properties are called the references. It is possible to retrieve the references of an association instance by browsing with the **WMI CIM Studio,** but it is also possible to retrieve the references of an association instance with a WQL query. The statement used to perform this data query is the **References Of** statement. This is the third statement type able to perform a data query. Note that as with the **Associators Of** statement, the **References Of** statement can also be used for WQL schema queries. We revisit schema queries in Section 3.2.2.

In the previous sections, we retrieved the instances associated with the given *Win32_Service* instance. Even if the information retrieved is related to the associated instances, behind the scenes, the association instances play an important role. Here, we retrieve the association instances with their related properties (which are the references). Sample 3.17 performs this data query using the **References Of** statement.

Sample 3.17   *Retrieving the Association class instances of a given instance with the References Of WQL statement*

```
C:\>wbemdump /E /Q Root\CIMV2 WQL "References Of {Win32_Service='MSExchangeSA'}"
(WQL) References Of {Win32_Service='MSExchangeSA'}
        __CLASS (CIM_STRING/)  = "Win32_SystemServices"
        ...
        GroupComponent (CIM_REFERENCE/ref:Win32_ComputerSystem)* =
                    "\\MYSERVER\root\cimv2:Win32_ComputerSystem.Name="NET-DPEN6400A""
        PartComponent (CIM_REFERENCE/ref:Win32_Service)* =
                    "\\MYSERVER\root\cimv2:Win32_Service.Name="MSExchangeSA""

        __CLASS (CIM_STRING/)  = "Win32_DependentService"
        ...
        Antecedent (CIM_REFERENCE/ref:Win32_BaseService)* =
                    "\\MYSERVER\root\cimv2:Win32_Service.Name="MSExchangeSA""
        Dependent (CIM_REFERENCE/ref:Win32_BaseService)* =
                    "\\MYSERVER\root\cimv2:Win32_Service.Name="MSExchangeIS""
        TypeOfDependency (CIM_UINT16/uint16)  = <null>
        __CLASS (CIM_STRING/)  = "Win32_DependentService"
        ...
        Antecedent (CIM_REFERENCE/ref:Win32_BaseService)* =
                    "\\MYSERVER\root\cimv2:Win32_Service.Name="MSExchangeSA""
        Dependent (CIM_REFERENCE/ref:Win32_BaseService)* =
                    "\\MYSERVER\root\cimv2:Win32_Service.Name="MSExchangeMTA""
        TypeOfDependency (CIM_UINT16/uint16)  = <null>

        __CLASS (CIM_STRING/)  = "Win32_DependentService"
        ...
        Antecedent (CIM_REFERENCE/ref:Win32_BaseService)* =
                    "\\MYSERVER\root\cimv2:Win32_Service.Name="Eventlog""
        Dependent (CIM_REFERENCE/ref:Win32_BaseService)* =
                    "\\MYSERVER\root\cimv2:Win32_Service.Name="MSExchangeSA""
        TypeOfDependency (CIM_UINT16/uint16)  = <null>

        __CLASS (CIM_STRING/)  = "Win32_DependentService"
        ...
        Antecedent (CIM_REFERENCE/ref:Win32_BaseService)* =
                    "\\MYSERVER\root\cimv2:Win32_Service.Name="NtLmSsp""
        Dependent (CIM_REFERENCE/ref:Win32_BaseService)* =
                    "\\MYSERVER\root\cimv2:Win32_Service.Name="MSExchangeSA""
        TypeOfDependency (CIM_UINT16/uint16)  = <null>
```

```
__CLASS (CIM_STRING/)  = "Win32_DependentService"
...
  Antecedent (CIM_REFERENCE/ref:Win32_BaseService)*  =
              "\\MYSERVER\root\cimv2:Win32_Service.Name="RpcLocator""
      Dependent (CIM_REFERENCE/ref:Win32_BaseService)*  =
              "\\MYSERVER\root\cimv2:Win32_Service.Name="MSExchangeSA""
TypeOfDependency (CIM_UINT16/uint16)  = <null>
Dependent (CIM_REFERENCE/ref:Win32_BaseService)*  =
              "\\MYSERVER\root\cimv2:Win32_Service.Name="MSExchangeSA""
TypeOfDependency (CIM_UINT16/uint16)  = <null>


__CLASS (CIM_STRING/)  = "Win32_DependentService"
...
Antecedent (CIM_REFERENCE/ref:Win32_BaseService)*  =
              "\\MYSERVER\root\cimv2:Win32_Service.Name="RpcSs""
__CLASS (CIM_STRING/)  = "Win32_DependentService"
...
Antecedent (CIM_REFERENCE/ref:Win32_BaseService)*  =
              "\\MYSERVER\root\cimv2:Win32_Service.Name="lanmanworkstation""
Dependent (CIM_REFERENCE/ref:Win32_BaseService)*  =
              "\\MYSERVER\root\cimv2:Win32_Service.Name="MSExchangeSA""
TypeOfDependency (CIM_UINT16/uint16)  = <null>


__CLASS (CIM_STRING/)  = "Win32_DependentService"
...
Antecedent (CIM_REFERENCE/ref:Win32_BaseService)*  =
              "\\MYSERVER\root\cimv2:Win32_Service.Name="lanmanserver""
Dependent (CIM_REFERENCE/ref:Win32_BaseService)*  =
              "\\MYSERVER\root\cimv2:Win32_Service.Name="MSExchangeSA""
TypeOfDependency (CIM_UINT16/uint16)  = <null>
```

As we can see in the query result, we retrieve all association instances related to the given *Win32_Service* instance. In the property list of association instances, we find the references (see Figure 3.4):

- *GroupComponent* and *PartComponent* for the *Win32_SystemServices* Association instance

- *Antecedent* and *Dependent* for the *Win32_DependentService* association instance

These references point to the associated instances. Each reference contains the full WMI path of the associated instance. For any associated *Win32_Service* instances, based on the dependency type, the associated instances are assigned to the *Antecedent* or *Dependent* reference. Notice that since the references are the unique identifiers of the association instances, they are marked with a star to indicate that these properties are defined as Keys.

The formal syntax of the **References Of** statement is as follows:

```
REFERENCES OF {SourceObject} [WHERE ClassDefsOnly]
                             [WHERE KeysOnly]
                             [WHERE RequiredQualifier = QualifierName] [ClassDefsOnly]
                             [WHERE ResultClass = ClassName] [ClassDefsOnly]
                             [WHERE Role = PropertyName] [ClassDefsOnly]
```

The **References Of** statement is similar to the **Associators Of** statement since it can also be combined with some extra keywords to refine the selection criteria of the WQL query. Although we retrieve some of the keywords already seen for the **Associators Of** statement, the **References Of** statement retrieves the properties of the association instances.

When executing the query shown in Sample 3.17, we retrieve the association instances. With the **ClassDefsOnly** keyword, the query retrieves the association class definitions of these association instances instead of the association instances themselves. An example of this type of query is shown in Sample 3.18.

Sample 3.18 *Retrieving the Association instance class definitions of a given instance with the References Of WQL statement (References Of statement and ClassDefsOnly keyword)*

```
C:\>wbemdump /E /Q Root\CIMV2 WQL "References Of {Win32_Service='MSExchangeSA'} Where ClassDefsOnly"
WQL) References Of {Win32_Service='MSExchangeSA'} Where ClassDefsOnly
     __CLASS (CIM_STRING/)  = "Win32_SystemServices"
     ...        __SUPERCLASS (CIM_STRING/)  = "CIM_SystemComponent"
     GroupComponent (CIM_REFERENCE/ref:Win32_ComputerSystem)*  = <null>
     PartComponent (CIM_REFERENCE/ref:Win32_Service)*  = <null>

     __CLASS (CIM_STRING/)  = "Win32_DependentService"
     ...
     __SUPERCLASS (CIM_STRING/)  = "CIM_ServiceServiceDependency"
     Antecedent (CIM_REFERENCE/ref:Win32_BaseService)*  = <null>
     Dependent (CIM_REFERENCE/ref:Win32_BaseService)*  = <null>
     TypeOfDependency (CIM_UINT16/uint16)  = <null>
```

If you examine the output from Sample 3.17 you will notice that every association instance uses one of the association class definitions listed in the output result of Sample 3.18. The principle of using the **ClassDefsOnly** keyword with the **References Of** statement is exactly the same as we saw in the context of the **Associators Of** statement. Every time the **ClassDefsOnly** keyword is specified, the query retrieves the class definitions of the instances (instead of the instances themselves). This keyword can be combined with the other valid keywords of the **References Of** statement.

The **RequiredQualifier** keyword (used in Sample 3.19) has the exact same role as the one we saw for the **Associators Of** statement. The **RequiredQualifier** keyword verifies the presence of a specific qualifier in the examined instances. Here, however, it looks for the presence of the qualifier in the association instances and not in the associated instances. So the **RequiredQualifier** keyword is the same keyword as the one used previously (see Sample 3.11), but because we use the **References Of** statement (instead of the **Associators Of** statement), the examined instance is different. To summarize: when the **RequiredQualifier** keyword is used with the **Associa-**

tors Of statement it looks for a qualifier in the associated instances; when the **RequiredQualifier** keyword is used with the **References Of** statement it looks for a qualifier in the association instances. The **References Of** statement retrieves the association instances, and the **Associators Of** statement retrieves the associated instances. Let's take a look at Sample 3.19 below (see Figure 3.2 for the visual representation of the associations in place).

Sample 3.19   *Retrieving the Association class instances of a given instance when the Association class instances contain a particular qualifier (References Of statement and RequiredQualifier keyword)*

```
C:\>wbemdump /E /Q Root\CIMV2 WQL
    "References Of {Win32_Service='MSExchangeSA'} Where RequiredQualifier=Dynamic"
(WQL) References Of {Win32_Service='MSExchangeSA'} Where RequiredQualifier=Dynamic
        __CLASS (CIM_STRING/)  = "Win32_SystemServices"
        ...
        __SUPERCLASS (CIM_STRING/)  = "CIM_SystemComponent"
        GroupComponent (CIM_REFERENCE/ref:Win32_ComputerSystem)*  =
                "\\W2K-DPEN6400\root\cimv2:Win32_ComputerSystem.Name="W2K-DPEN6400""
        PartComponent (CIM_REFERENCE/ref:Win32_Service)*  =
                "\\W2K-DPEN6400\root\cimv2:Win32_Service.Name="MSExchangeSA""

        __CLASS (CIM_STRING/)  = "Win32_DependentService"
        ...
        __SUPERCLASS (CIM_STRING/)  = "CIM_ServiceServiceDependency"
        Antecedent (CIM_REFERENCE/ref:Win32_BaseService)*  =


                "\\W2K-DPEN6400\root\cimv2:Win32_Service.Name="MSExchangeSA""
        Dependent (CIM_REFERENCE/ref:Win32_BaseService)*  =
                "\\W2K-DPEN6400\root\cimv2:Win32_Service.Name="MSExchangeIS""
        TypeOfDependency (CIM_UINT16/uint16)  = <null>

        __CLASS (CIM_STRING/)  = "Win32_DependentService"
        ...
        __SUPERCLASS (CIM_STRING/)  = "CIM_ServiceServiceDependency"
        Antecedent (CIM_REFERENCE/ref:Win32_BaseService)*  =
                "\\W2K-DPEN6400\root\cimv2:Win32_Service.Name="MSExchangeSA""
        Dependent (CIM_REFERENCE/ref:Win32_BaseService)*  =
                "\\W2K-DPEN6400\root\cimv2:Win32_Service.Name="MSExchangeMTA""
        TypeOfDependency (CIM_UINT16/uint16)  = <null>

        __CLASS (CIM_STRING/)  = "Win32_DependentService"
        ...
        __SUPERCLASS (CIM_STRING/)  = "CIM_ServiceServiceDependency"
        Antecedent (CIM_REFERENCE/ref:Win32_BaseService)*  =
                "\\W2K-DPEN6400\root\cimv2:Win32_Service.Name="Eventlog""
        Dependent (CIM_REFERENCE/ref:Win32_BaseService)*  =
                "\\W2K-DPEN6400\root\cimv2:Win32_Service.Name="MSExchangeSA""
        TypeOfDependency (CIM_UINT16/uint16)  = <null>

        __CLASS (CIM_STRING/)  = "Win32_DependentService"
        ...
        __SUPERCLASS (CIM_STRING/)  = "CIM_ServiceServiceDependency"
        Antecedent (CIM_REFERENCE/ref:Win32_BaseService)*  =
                "\\W2K-DPEN6400\root\cimv2:Win32_Service.Name="NtLmSsp""
```

```
Dependent (CIM_REFERENCE/ref:Win32_BaseService)* =
        "\\W2K-DPEN6400\root\cimv2:Win32_Service.Name="MSExchangeSA""
      "TypeOfDependency (CIM_UINT16/uint16) = <null>


__CLASS (CIM_STRING/) = "Win32_DependentService"
...
__SUPERCLASS (CIM_STRING/) = "CIM_ServiceServiceDependency"
Antecedent (CIM_REFERENCE/ref:Win32_BaseService)* =
        "\\W2K-DPEN6400\root\cimv2:Win32_Service.Name="RpcLocator""
Dependent (CIM_REFERENCE/ref:Win32_BaseService)* =
        "\\W2K-DPEN6400\root\cimv2:Win32_Service.Name="MSExchangeSA""
      "TypeOfDependency (CIM_UINT16/uint16) = <null>


__CLASS (CIM_STRING/) = "Win32_DependentService"
...
__SUPERCLASS (CIM_STRING/) = "CIM_ServiceServiceDependency"
Antecedent (CIM_REFERENCE/ref:Win32_BaseService)* =
        "\\W2K-DPEN6400\root\cimv2:Win32_Service.Name="RpcSs""
Dependent (CIM_REFERENCE/ref:Win32_BaseService)* =
        "\\W2K-DPEN6400\root\cimv2:Win32_Service.Name="MSExchangeSA""
TypeOfDependency (CIM_UINT16/uint16) = <null>


__CLASS (CIM_STRING/) = "Win32_DependentService"
...
__SUPERCLASS (CIM_STRING/) = "CIM_ServiceServiceDependency"
Antecedent (CIM_REFERENCE/ref:Win32_BaseService)* =
        "\\W2K-DPEN6400\root\cimv2:Win32_Service.Name="lanmanworkstation""
Dependent (CIM_REFERENCE/ref:Win32_BaseService)* =
        "\\W2K-DPEN6400\root\cimv2:Win32_Service.Name="MSExchangeSA""
TypeOfDependency (CIM_UINT16/uint16) = <null>


__CLASS (CIM_STRING/) = "Win32_DependentService"
...
__SUPERCLASS (CIM_STRING/) = "CIM_ServiceServiceDependency"
Antecedent (CIM_REFERENCE/ref:Win32_BaseService)* =
        "\\W2K-DPEN6400\root\cimv2:Win32_Service.Name="lanmanserver""
Dependent (CIM_REFERENCE/ref:Win32_BaseService)* =
        "\\W2K-DPEN6400\root\cimv2:Win32_Service.Name="MSExchangeSA""
TypeOfDependency (CIM_UINT16/uint16) = <null>
```

Again, because both association instances of a *Win32_Service* instance contain the same qualifiers, the complete list of association instances related to the given *Win32_Service* instance is returned by the query. This means that we get the exact same output as Sample 3.17, which retrieved all the association instances. For example, if the *Win32_DependentService* association class had a different qualifier than the *Win32_SystemServices* association class, it would be possible to match a different qualifier name with the WQL query to retrieve results based on this criteria. But as these association instances use the same qualifiers, we retrieve all association instances.

When using the **References Of** statement in combination with the **ResultClass** keyword, it is possible to select the association instances to be retrieved by the WQL query based on the association class used by the association instances (see Sample 3.20). Again, see Figure 3.2 for the visualrepresentation of the associations in place.

Sample 3.20 *Retrieving the Association class instances of a given instance where the Association class instances match a given class name (References Of statement and ResultClass keyword)*

```
C:\>wbemdump /E /Q Root\CIMV2 WQL
    "References Of {Win32_Service='MSExchangeSA'} Where ResultClass=Win32_SystemServices"
(WQL) References Of {Win32_Service='MSExchangeSA'} Where ResultClass=Win32_SystemServices
    __CLASS (CIM_STRING/)  = "Win32_SystemServices"
    ...
    __SUPERCLASS (CIM_STRING/)  = "CIM_SystemComponent"
    GroupComponent (CIM_REFERENCE/ref:Win32_ComputerSystem)*  =
        "\\MYSERVER\root\cimv2:Win32_ComputerSystem.Name="NET-DPEN6400A""
    PartComponent (CIM_REFERENCE/ref:Win32_Service)*  =
        "\\MYSERVER\root\cimv2:Win32_Service.Name="MSExchangeSA""
```

Sample 3.21 uses the exact same query as Sample 3.20, but it uses the other association class name to retrieve the complementary result of the previous query.

Sample 3.21 *Retrieving the Association class instances of a given instance where the Association class instances match a given class name (References Of statement and ResultClass keyword) (complementary query)*

```
C:\>wbemdump /E /Q Root\CIMV2 WQL
    "References Of {Win32_Service='MSExchangeSA'} Where ResultClass=Win32_DependentService"
(WQL) References Of {Win32_Service='MSExchangeSA'} Where ResultClass=Win32_DependentService
    __CLASS (CIM_STRING/)  = "Win32_DependentService"
    ...
    __SUPERCLASS (CIM_STRING/)  = "CIM_ServiceServiceDependency"
    Antecedent (CIM_REFERENCE/ref:Win32_BaseService)*  =
        "\\W2K-DPEN6400\root\cimv2:Win32_Service.Name="MSExchangeSA""
    Dependent (CIM_REFERENCE/ref:Win32_BaseService)*  =
        "\\W2K-DPEN6400\root\cimv2:Win32_Service.Name="MSExchangeIS""
    TypeOfDependency (CIM_UINT16/uint16)  = <null>

    __CLASS (CIM_STRING/)  = "Win32_DependentService"
    ...
    __SUPERCLASS (CIM_STRING/)  = "CIM_ServiceServiceDependency"
    Antecedent (CIM_REFERENCE/ref:Win32_BaseService)*  =
        "\\W2K-DPEN6400\root\cimv2:Win32_Service.Name="MSExchangeSA""
    Dependent (CIM_REFERENCE/ref:Win32_BaseService)*  =
        "\\W2K-DPEN6400\root\cimv2:Win32_Service.Name="MSExchangeMTA""
    TypeOfDependency (CIM_UINT16/uint16)  = <null>

    __CLASS (CIM_STRING/)  = "Win32_DependentService"
    ...
    __SUPERCLASS (CIM_STRING/)  = "CIM_ServiceServiceDependency"
    Antecedent (CIM_REFERENCE/ref:Win32_BaseService)*  =
        "\\W2K-DPEN6400\root\cimv2:Win32_Service.Name="Eventlog""
    Dependent (CIM_REFERENCE/ref:Win32_BaseService)*  =
        "\\W2K-DPEN6400\root\cimv2:Win32_Service.Name="MSExchangeSA""
    TypeOfDependency (CIM_UINT16/uint16)  = <null>
```

```
        __CLASS (CIM_STRING/)  = "Win32_DependentService"
        ...
        __SUPERCLASS (CIM_STRING/)  = "CIM_ServiceServiceDependency"
        Antecedent (CIM_REFERENCE/ref:Win32_BaseService)*  =
                "\\W2K-DPEN6400\root\cimv2:Win32_Service.Name="NtLmSsp""
        Dependent (CIM_REFERENCE/ref:Win32_BaseService)*  =
                "\\W2K-DPEN6400\root\cimv2:Win32_Service.Name="MSExchangeSA""
        TypeOfDependency (CIM_UINT16/uint16)  = <null>
        __CLASS (CIM_STRING/)  = "Win32_DependentService"
        ...
        __SUPERCLASS (CIM_STRING/)  = "CIM_ServiceServiceDependency"
        Antecedent (CIM_REFERENCE/ref:Win32_BaseService)*  =
                "\\W2K-DPEN6400\root\cimv2:Win32_Service.Name="RpcLocator""
        Dependent (CIM_REFERENCE/ref:Win32_BaseService)*  =
                "\\W2K-DPEN6400\root\cimv2:Win32_Service.Name="MSExchangeSA""
        TypeOfDependency (CIM_UINT16/uint16)  = <null>

        __CLASS (CIM_STRING/)  = "Win32_DependentService"
        ...
        __SUPERCLASS (CIM_STRING/)  = "CIM_ServiceServiceDependency"
        Antecedent (CIM_REFERENCE/ref:Win32_BaseService)*  =
                "\\W2K-DPEN6400\root\cimv2:Win32_Service.Name="RpcSs""
        Dependent (CIM_REFERENCE/ref:Win32_BaseService)*  =
                "\\W2K-DPEN6400\root\cimv2:Win32_Service.Name="MSExchangeSA""
        TypeOfDependency (CIM_UINT16/uint16)  = <null>

        __CLASS (CIM_STRING/)  = "Win32_DependentService"
        ...
        __SUPERCLASS (CIM_STRING/)  = "CIM_ServiceServiceDependency"
        Antecedent (CIM_REFERENCE/ref:Win32_BaseService)*  =
                "\\W2K-DPEN6400\root\cimv2:Win32_Service.Name="lanmanworkstation""
        Dependent (CIM_REFERENCE/ref:Win32_BaseService)*  =
                "\\W2K-DPEN6400\root\cimv2:Win32_Service.Name="MSExchangeSA""
        TypeOfDependency (CIM_UINT16/uint16)  = <null>

        __CLASS (CIM_STRING/)  = "Win32_DependentService"
        ...
        __SUPERCLASS (CIM_STRING/)  = "CIM_ServiceServiceDependency"
        Antecedent (CIM_REFERENCE/ref:Win32_BaseService)*  =
                "\\W2K-DPEN6400\root\cimv2:Win32_Service.Name="lanmanserver""
        Dependent (CIM_REFERENCE/ref:Win32_BaseService)*  =
                "\\W2K-DPEN6400\root\cimv2:Win32_Service.Name="MSExchangeSA""
        TypeOfDependency (CIM_UINT16/uint16)  = <null
```

It is also possible to retrieve the association instances based on the role played by the given instance in the association. For this, the **Role** keyword must be used as shown in Sample 3.22.

Sample 3.22   *Retrieving the Association class instances of a given instance where the given instance plays a specific role name in the Association instance (References Of statement and Role keyword)*

```
C:\>wbemdump /E /Q Root\CIMV2 WQL
    "References Of {Win32_Service='MSExchangeSA'} Where Role=Antecedent"

(WQL) References Of {Win32_Service='MSExchangeSA'} Where Role=Antecedent
        __CLASS (CIM_STRING/)  = "Win32_DependentService"
        ...
```

```
__SUPERCLASS (CIM_STRING/)  = "CIM_ServiceServiceDependency"
Antecedent (CIM_REFERENCE/ref:Win32_BaseService)*  =
        "\\W2K-DPEN6400\root\cimv2:Win32_Service.Name="MSExchangeSA""
Dependent (CIM_REFERENCE/ref:Win32_BaseService)*  =
        "\\W2K-DPEN6400\root\cimv2:Win32_Service.Name="MSExchangeIS""
TypeOfDependency (CIM_UINT16/uint16)  = <null>


__CLASS (CIM_STRING/)  = "Win32_DependentService"
...
__SUPERCLASS (CIM_STRING/)  = "CIM_ServiceServiceDependency"
Antecedent (CIM_REFERENCE/ref:Win32_BaseService)*  =
        "\\W2K-DPEN6400\root\cimv2:Win32_Service.Name="MSExchangeSA""
Dependent (CIM_REFERENCE/ref:Win32_BaseService)*  =
        "\\W2K-DPEN6400\root\cimv2:Win32_Service.Name="MSExchangeMTA""
TypeOfDependency (CIM_UINT16/uint16)  = <null>
```

In Sample 3.22 we have two references in the association that are based on the role played by the *Win32_Service* instance. Sample 3.23 retrieves the complementary query result of Sample 3.22. Once more, see Figure 3.4 for the visual representation of the roles in place.

Sample 3.23   *Retrieving the Association class instances of a given instance where the given instance plays a specific role name in the Association instance (References Of statement and Role keyword) (complementary query)*

```
C:\>wbemdump /E /Q Root\CIMV2 WQL
    "References Of {Win32_Service='MSExchangeSA'} Where Role=Dependent"

(WQL) References Of {Win32_Service='MSExchangeSA'} Where Role=Dependent
    __CLASS (CIM_STRING/)  = "Win32_DependentService"
    ...
    __SUPERCLASS (CIM_STRING/)  = "CIM_ServiceServiceDependency"
    Antecedent (CIM_REFERENCE/ref:Win32_BaseService)*  =
            "\\W2K-DPEN6400\root\cimv2:Win32_Service.Name="Eventlog""
    Dependent (CIM_REFERENCE/ref:Win32_BaseService)*  =
            "\\W2K-DPEN6400\root\cimv2:Win32_Service.Name="MSExchangeSA""
    TypeOfDependency (CIM_UINT16/uint16)  = <null>

    __CLASS (CIM_STRING/)  = "Win32_DependentService"
    ...
    __SUPERCLASS (CIM_STRING/)  = "CIM_ServiceServiceDependency"
    Antecedent (CIM_REFERENCE/ref:Win32_BaseService)*  =
            "\\W2K-DPEN6400\root\cimv2:Win32_Service.Name="NtLmSsp""
    Dependent (CIM_REFERENCE/ref:Win32_BaseService)*  =
            "\\W2K-DPEN6400\root\cimv2:Win32_Service.Name="MSExchangeSA""
    TypeOfDependency (CIM_UINT16/uint16)  = <null>
    __CLASS (CIM_STRING/)  = "Win32_DependentService"
    ...
    __SUPERCLASS (CIM_STRING/)  = "CIM_ServiceServiceDependency"
    Antecedent (CIM_REFERENCE/ref:Win32_BaseService)*  =
            "\\W2K-DPEN6400\root\cimv2:Win32_Service.Name="RpcLocator""
```

```
Dependent (CIM_REFERENCE/ref:Win32_BaseService)*  =
        "\\W2K-DPEN6400\root\cimv2:Win32_Service.Name="MSExchangeSA""
TypeOfDependency (CIM_UINT16/uint16)  = <null>


__CLASS (CIM_STRING/)  = "Win32_DependentService"
...
__SUPERCLASS (CIM_STRING/)  = "CIM_ServiceServiceDependency"
Antecedent (CIM_REFERENCE/ref:Win32_BaseService)*  =
        "\\W2K-DPEN6400\root\cimv2:Win32_Service.Name="RpcSs""
Dependent (CIM_REFERENCE/ref:Win32_BaseService)*  =
        "\\W2K-DPEN6400\root\cimv2:Win32_Service.Name="MSExchangeSA""
TypeOfDependency (CIM_UINT16/uint16)  = <null>


__CLASS (CIM_STRING/)  = "Win32_DependentService"
...
__SUPERCLASS (CIM_STRING/)  = "CIM_ServiceServiceDependency"
Antecedent (CIM_REFERENCE/ref:Win32_BaseService)*  =
"\\W2K-DPEN6400\root\cimv2:Win32_Service.Name="lanmanworkstation""
Dependent (CIM_REFERENCE/ref:Win32_BaseService)*  =
        "\\W2K-DPEN6400\root\cimv2:Win32_Service.Name="MSExchangeSA""
TypeOfDependency (CIM_UINT16/uint16)  = <null>


__CLASS (CIM_STRING/)  = "Win32_DependentService"
...
__SUPERCLASS (CIM_STRING/)  = "CIM_ServiceServiceDependency"
Antecedent (CIM_REFERENCE/ref:Win32_BaseService)*  =
        "\\W2K-DPEN6400\root\cimv2:Win32_Service.Name="lanmanserver""
Dependent (CIM_REFERENCE/ref:Win32_BaseService)*  =
        "\\W2K-DPEN6400\root\cimv2:Win32_Service.Name="MSExchangeSA""
TypeOfDependency (CIM_UINT16/uint16)  = <null>
```

It is important to note that the **WHERE** statement that uses the **References Of** statement cannot use the **AND** or the **OR** logical operators to separate keywords. But, similar to the **Associators Of** statement, keywords can be combined in the same query. Furthermore, the equal sign is the only valid operator that can be used with the keywords in these queries.

Although quite abstract, this notion of associations and references between instances makes more sense when performing WQL queries. Since these data queries can be quite confusing at first glance, Table 3.3 summarizes the different WQL data-query types with the obtained results.

3.2.2   Schema queries

With the previous category of query, we focused on the real-world manageable entities themselves. Manageable entities are nothing more than instances of classes; therefore it can be interesting to perform queries on the classes themselves. Classes are the templates of real-world manageable enti-

Table 3.3 WQL Data Queries

Statements	Keywords				Obtained Results
Select *	PropertyName	From	{SourceClass}	—		All instances of the SourceClass and instances derived from the SourceClass.
	From	{SourceClass}	Where	PropertyName = Value	Any instances of the SourceClass matching the selection criteria.
Associators Of	—	{SourceObject}	—		Any instances associated with the SourceObject.
	—	{SourceObject}	Where	ClassDefsOnly	Forces to retrieve any instance class definitions (instead of the instances themselves) that are associated with the SourceObject.
	—	{SourceObject}	Where	AssocClass = AssocClassName	Any instances where the Association instances have a class name matching AssocClassName and that are associated with the SourceObject.
	—	{SourceObject}	Where	RequiredAssocQualifier = QualiferName	Any instances where the Association instances are using the QualiferName and that are associated with the SourceObject.
	—	{SourceObject}	Where	RequiredQualifier = QualiferName	Any instances containing the QualiferName and that are associated with the SourceObject.
	—	{SourceObject}	Where	ResultClass = ClassName	Any instances having a class name matching the ClassName and that are associated with the SourceObject.
	—	{SourceObject}	Where	ResultRole = PropertyName	Any instances where the role of the instances in the association matches the PropertyName and that are associated with the SourceObject.
	—	{SourceObject}	Where	Role = PropertyName	Any instances where the role of the SourceObject matches the PropertyName and that are associated with the SourceObject.

Table 3.3   *WQL Data Queries (continued)*

Statements	Keywords			Obtained Results
References Of	{SourceObject}	–	–	Any Association instances doing an Association with the *SourceObject*.
	{SourceObject}	Where	ClassDefsOnly	Any Association instance class definitions doing an Association with the *SourceObject*.
	{SourceObject}	Where	RequiredQualifier = *QualifierName*	Any Association instances containing the *QualifierName* and been an Association instance for the *SourceObject*.
	{SourceObject}	Where	ResultClass = *ClassName*	Any Association instances matching the *ClassName* and been an Association instance for the *SourceObject*.
	{SourceObject}	Where	Role = *PropertyName*	Any Association instances where the *SourceObject* plays a role matching the *PropertyName*.

ties. When we examine the class definitions, we are actually examining the CIM repository schema, which leads us to the topic of schema queries.

3.2.2.1   *Retrieving a class*

In the previous section we retrieved instances of the *Win32_Service* class by using the following query:

```
Select * From Win32_Service
```

With such a WQL query, the retrieved information always relates to instances. The data queries examined so far have not retrieved the schema definition of the queried instance. In order to retrieve the schema definition of the queried instance, we need to use a schema query. Schema queries retrieve the CIM schema definition of a class. For example, to retrieve the schema definition of the *Win32_Service* class with a schema query, we must use a WQL query as shown in Sample 3.24.

Sample 3.24   *Retrieving the class definition of a given class with the SELECT statement*

```
C:\>wbemdump /E /Q Root\CIMV2 WQL "SELECT * FROM meta_class WHERE __this ISA 'Win32_Service'"
(WQL) SELECT * FROM meta_class WHERE __this ISA 'Win32_Service'
        __CLASS (CIM_STRING/)  = "Win32_Service"
        ...
        __SUPERCLASS (CIM_STRING/)  = "Win32_BaseService"
        AcceptPause (CIM_BOOLEAN/boolean)  = <null>
        AcceptStop (CIM_BOOLEAN/boolean)  = <null>
        Caption (CIM_STRING/string)  = <null>
        CheckPoint (CIM_UINT32/uint32)  = <null>
        CreationClassName (CIM_STRING/string)  = <null>
        Description (CIM_STRING/string)  = <null>
        DesktopInteract (CIM_BOOLEAN/boolean)  = <null>
        Displayname (CIM_STRING/string)  = <null>
        ErrorControl (CIM_STRING/string)  = <null>
        ExitCode (CIM_UINT32/uint32)  = <null>
        InstallDate (CIM_DATETIME/datetime)  = <null>
        Name (CIM_STRING/string)*  = <null>
        PathName (CIM_STRING/string)  = <null>
        ProcessId (CIM_UINT32/uint32)  = <null>
        ServiceSpecificExitCode (CIM_UINT32/uint32)  = <null>
        ServiceType (CIM_STRING/string)  = <null>
        Started (CIM_BOOLEAN/boolean)  = <null>
        StartMode (CIM_STRING/string)  = <null>
        StartName (CIM_STRING/string)  = <null>
        State (CIM_STRING/string)  = <null>
        Status (CIM_STRING/string)  = <null>
        SystemCreationClassName (CIM_STRING/string)  = <null>
        SystemName (CIM_STRING/string)  = <null>
        TagId (CIM_UINT32/uint32)  = <null>
        WaitHint (CIM_UINT32/uint32)  = <null>
```

The result of the query produces a list of classes made from the *Win32_Service* class specified. With the "*," all the properties of the class definition are listed. In a schema query, when using the **SELECT** statement, there is no other option than using the "*" to retrieve the properties. A schema query does not support the selection of some properties as a data query.

In this query, we have three new keywords: the **ISA** keyword, the **meta_class** keyword, and the **__THIS** keyword. Let's talk about the **ISA** keyword first. In the context of a schema query, the **ISA** keyword retrieves all the class definitions using the class type given in the query and all the subclasses derived from the class type given. In the context of Sample 3.24, since the *Win32_Service* has no subclass, this is the only class retrieved.

Another new keyword is the **meta_class** keyword. This keyword performs the magic of retrieving the class definitions instead of the class instance data. If you execute the previous query without specifying a **WHERE** statement, the query will retrieve the class definition of all classes present in the given namespace. Once again, the **WHERE** statement narrows the scope of the query. Removing the **WHERE** statement and performing the query with the **meta_class** statement enlarges the scope of the classes retrieved. The query will resemble the following:

```
SELECT * FROM meta_class
```

The produced output is too large to show in this book, but we recommend you perform this query to see the classes available in the CIM repository (in a given namespace like **Root\CIMv2** as used in previous samples). You will retrieve all the classes you are able to browse when using the **WMI CIM Studio**.

The last new keyword we need to talk about is the **__THIS** keyword. This keyword is used only in schema queries and identifies the target class for a schema query. In the case of the previous samples, the **__THIS** keyword identifies a target class that must be a *Win32_Service* class (see Sample 3.24).

Previously, we saw that the *Win32_Service* is a subclass of the *Win32_BaseService* class. We also know that the *Win32_BaseService* has two subclasses: *Win32_Service* and *Win32_SystemDrive*. If we repeat the same query but instead of using the *Win32_Service* class we use the *Win32_BaseService* class, we receive the results shown in Sample 3.25.

Sample 3.25   *Retrieving the class definition with the subclasses of a given class with the SELECT statement*

```
C:\>wbemdump /E /Q Root\CIMV2 WQL "SELECT * FROM meta_class WHERE __this ISA 'Win32_BaseService'"
(WQL) SELECT * FROM meta_class WHERE __this ISA 'Win32_BaseService'
        __CLASS (CIM_STRING/)  = "Win32_BaseService"
        ...
        __SUPERCLASS (CIM_STRING/)  = "CIM_Service"
        AcceptPause (CIM_BOOLEAN/boolean)  = <null>
        AcceptStop (CIM_BOOLEAN/boolean)  = <null>
        Caption (CIM_STRING/string)  = <null>
        CreationClassName (CIM_STRING/string)  = <null>
        Description (CIM_STRING/string)  = <null>
        DesktopInteract (CIM_BOOLEAN/boolean)  = <null>
        Displayname (CIM_STRING/string)  = <null>
        ErrorControl (CIM_STRING/string)  = <null>
        ExitCode (CIM_UINT32/uint32)  = <null>
        InstallDate (CIM_DATETIME/datetime)  = <null>
        Name (CIM_STRING/string)*  = <null>
        PathName (CIM_STRING/string)  = <null>
        ServiceSpecificExitCode (CIM_UINT32/uint32)  = <null>
        ServiceType (CIM_STRING/string)  = <null>
        Started (CIM_BOOLEAN/boolean)  = <null>
        StartMode (CIM_STRING/string)  = <null>
        StartName (CIM_STRING/string)  = <null>
        State (CIM_STRING/string)  = <null>
        Status (CIM_STRING/string)  = <null>
        SystemCreationClassName (CIM_STRING/string)  = <null>
        SystemName (CIM_STRING/string)  = <null>
        TagId (CIM_UINT32/uint32)  = <null>

         __CLASS (CIM_STRING/)  = "Win32_SystemDriver"
        ...
        __SUPERCLASS (CIM_STRING/)  = "Win32_BaseService"
        AcceptPause (CIM_BOOLEAN/boolean)  = <null>
        AcceptStop (CIM_BOOLEAN/boolean)  = <null>
        Caption (CIM_STRING/string)  = <null>
        CreationClassName (CIM_STRING/string)  = <null>
        Description (CIM_STRING/string)  = <null>
        DesktopInteract (CIM_BOOLEAN/boolean)  = <null>
        Displayname (CIM_STRING/string)  = <null>
        ErrorControl (CIM_STRING/string)  = <null>
        ExitCode (CIM_UINT32/uint32)  = <null>
        InstallDate (CIM_DATETIME/datetime)  = <null>
        Name (CIM_STRING/string)*  = <null>
        PathName (CIM_STRING/string)  = <null>
        ServiceSpecificExitCode (CIM_UINT32/uint32)  = <null>
        ServiceType (CIM_STRING/string)  = <null>
        Started (CIM_BOOLEAN/boolean)  = <null>
        StartMode (CIM_STRING/string)  = <null>
        StartName (CIM_STRING/string)  = <null>
        State (CIM_STRING/string)  = <null>
        Status (CIM_STRING/string)  = <null>
        SystemCreationClassName (CIM_STRING/string)  = <null>
        SystemName (CIM_STRING/string)  = <null>
        TagId (CIM_UINT32/uint32)  = <null>
```

```
__CLASS (CIM_STRING/)  = "Win32_Service"
...
__SUPERCLASS (CIM_STRING/)  = "Win32_BaseService"
AcceptPause (CIM_BOOLEAN/boolean)  = <null>
AcceptStop (CIM_BOOLEAN/boolean)  = <null>
Caption (CIM_STRING/string)  = <null>
CheckPoint (CIM_UINT32/uint32)  = <null>
CreationClassName (CIM_STRING/string)  = <null>
Description (CIM_STRING/string)  = <null>
DesktopInteract (CIM_BOOLEAN/boolean)  = <null>
Displayname (CIM_STRING/string)  = <null>
ErrorControl (CIM_STRING/string)  = <null>
ExitCode (CIM_UINT32/uint32)  = <null>
InstallDate (CIM_DATETIME/datetime)  = <null>
Name (CIM_STRING/string)*  = <null>
PathName (CIM_STRING/string)  = <null>
ProcessId (CIM_UINT32/uint32)  = <null>
ServiceSpecificExitCode (CIM_UINT32/uint32)  = <null>
ServiceType (CIM_STRING/string)  = <null>
Started (CIM_BOOLEAN/boolean)  = <null>
StartMode (CIM_STRING/string)  = <null>
StartName (CIM_STRING/string)  = <null>
State (CIM_STRING/string)  = <null>
Status (CIM_STRING/string)  = <null>
SystemCreationClassName (CIM_STRING/string)  = <null>
SystemName (CIM_STRING/string)  = <null>
TagId (CIM_UINT32/uint32)  = <null>
 WaitHint (CIM_UINT32/uint32)  = <null>
```

In this case, the **ISA** keyword allows us to retrieve the class definition of the *Win32_BaseService* class with its two subclasses: *Win32_Service* and *Win32_SystemDriver*.

3.2.2.2   *Retrieving the associators of a class*

Schema associations determine how instance associations behave. The **Associators Of** and **References Of** statements are applicable to schema queries; however, instead of returning associated instances or association instances, the schema query returns associated class definitions (with the **Associators Of** statement) or association class definitions (with the **References Of** statement). In this context, there are two differences in the schema queries when compared with data queries:

- The source object given in a data query (which is an instance) must be a class rather than an instance.

- The **ClassDefsOnly** keyword is no longer valid and the keyword **SchemaOnly** must be used instead.

The formal notation for the **Associators Of** statement is as follows:

```
ASSOCIATORS OF {SourceClass} [WHERE SchemaOnly]
                    [WHERE AssocClass = AssocClassName] [SchemaOnly]
                    [WHERE RequiredAssocQualifier = QualifierName] [SchemaOnly]
```

```
                    [WHERE RequiredQualifier = QualifierName] [SchemaOnly]
                    [WHERE ResultClass = ClassName] [SchemaOnly]
                    [WHERE ResultRole = PropertyName] [SchemaOnly]
                    [WHERE Role = PropertyName] [SchemaOnly]
```

The formal notation for the **References Of** statement is as follows:

```
REFERENCES OF {SourceClass} [WHERE SchemaOnly]
                    [WHERE ResultClass = ClassName] [SchemaOnly]
                    [WHERE Role = PropertyName] [SchemaOnly]
                    [WHERE RequiredQualifier = QualifierName] [SchemaOnly]
```

Sample 3.26   *Retrieving the associated class definitions with the Associators Of statement (Associators Of statement and SchemaOnly keyword)*

```
C:\>wbemdump /E /Q Root\CIMV2 WQL "Associators Of {Win32_Service} Where SchemaOnly"
(WQL) Associators Of {Win32_Service} Where SchemaOnly
        __CLASS (CIM_STRING/)  = "Win32_ComputerSystem"
        ...
        __SUPERCLASS (CIM_STRING/)  = "CIM_UnitaryComputerSystem"
        AdminPasswordStatus (CIM_UINT16/uint16)  = <null>
        AutomaticResetBootOption (CIM_BOOLEAN/boolean)  = <null>
        AutomaticResetCapability (CIM_BOOLEAN/boolean)  = <null>
        BootOptionOnLimit (CIM_UINT16/uint16)  = <null>
        BootOptionOnWatchDog (CIM_UINT16/uint16)  = <null>
        BootROMSupported (CIM_BOOLEAN/boolean)  = <null>
        BootupState (CIM_STRING/string)  = <null>
        Caption (CIM_STRING/string)  = <null>
        ChassisBootupState (CIM_UINT16/uint16)  = <null>
        CreationClassName (CIM_STRING/string)  = <null>
        CurrentTimeZone (CIM_SINT16/sint16)  = <null>
        DaylightInEffect (CIM_BOOLEAN/boolean)  = <null>
        Description (CIM_STRING/string)  = <null>
        ...
        PrimaryOwnerName (CIM_STRING/string)  = <null>
        ResetCapability (CIM_UINT16/uint16)  = <null>
        ResetCount (CIM_SINT16/sint16)  = <null>
        ResetLimit (CIM_SINT16/sint16)  = <null>
        Roles (CIM_STRING | CIM_FLAG_ARRAY/string)  = <null>
        Status (CIM_STRING/string)  = <null>
        SupportContactDescription (CIM_STRING | CIM_FLAG_ARRAY/string)  = <null>
        SystemStartupDelay (CIM_UINT16/uint16)  = <null>
        SystemStartupOptions (CIM_STRING | CIM_FLAG_ARRAY/string)  = <null>
        SystemStartupSetting (CIM_UINT8/uint8)  = <null>
        SystemType (CIM_STRING/string)  = <null>
        ThermalState (CIM_UINT16/uint16)  = <null>
        TotalPhysicalMemory (CIM_UINT64/uint64)  = <null>
        UserName (CIM_STRING/string)  = <null>
        WakeUpType (CIM_UINT16/uint16)  = <null>

        __CLASS (CIM_STRING/)  = "Win32_WMISetting"
        ...
        __SUPERCLASS (CIM_STRING/)  = "CIM_Setting"
        ASPScriptDefaultNamespace (CIM_STRING/string)  = \\root\cimv2
        ASPScriptEnabled (CIM_BOOLEAN/boolean)  = <null>
        AutorecoverMofs (CIM_STRING | CIM_FLAG_ARRAY/string)  = <null>
        AutoStartWin9X (CIM_UINT32/uint32)  = <null>
        BackupInterval (CIM_UINT32/uint32)  = <null>
```

```
        BackupLastTime (CIM_DATETIME/datetime)  = <null>
            BuildVersion (CIM_STRING/string)  = <null>
...
    MaxLogFileSize (CIM_UINT32/uint32)  = <null>
    MaxWaitOnClientObjects (CIM_UINT32/uint32)  = <null>
    MaxWaitOnEvents (CIM_UINT32/uint32)  = <null>
    MofSelfInstallDirectory (CIM_STRING/string)  = <null>
    SettingID (CIM_STRING/string)  = <null>

    __CLASS (CIM_STRING/)  = "Win32_ServiceSpecification"
    ...
    __SUPERCLASS (CIM_STRING/)  = "CIM_Check"
    Caption (CIM_STRING/string)  = <null>
    CheckID (CIM_STRING/string)*  = <null>
    CheckMode (CIM_BOOLEAN/boolean)  = <null>
    Dependencies (CIM_STRING/string)  = <null>
    Description (CIM_STRING/string)  = <null>
    Displayname (CIM_STRING/string)  = <null>
    ErrorControl (CIM_SINT32/sint32)  = <null>
    ID (CIM_STRING/string)  = <null>
    LoadOrderGroup (CIM_STRING/string)  = <null>
    Name (CIM_STRING/string)  = <null>
    Password (CIM_STRING/string)  = <null>
    ServiceType (CIM_SINT32/sint32)  = <null>
    SoftwareElementID (CIM_STRING/string)  = <null>
    SoftwareElementState (CIM_UINT16/uint16)  = <null>
    StartName (CIM_STRING/string)  = <null>
    StartType (CIM_SINT32/sint32)  = <null>
    TargetOperatingSystem (CIM_UINT16/uint16)  = <null>
     Version (CIM_STRING/string)  = <null>
```

In Sample 3.26 output, we see that the class definitions retrieved are directly associated to the *Win32_Service* class: *Win32_ComputerSystem, Win32_WMISetting,* and *Win32_ServiceSpecification.* Now, if you want to retrieve only the classes that are associated with the *Win32_Service* class with a particular association class, you must use the **AssocClass** keyword. The query and its results are shown in Sample 3.27.

Sample 3.27   *Retrieving the associated class definitions with the Associators Of statement (Associators Of statement and AssocClass keyword)*

```
C:\>wbemdump /E /Q Root\CIMV2 WQL
    "Associators Of {Win32_Service} Where AssocClass=Win32_WMIElementSetting SchemaOnly"
(WQL) Associators Of {Win32_Service} Where AssocClass=Win32_WMIElementSetting SchemaOnly
    __CLASS (CIM_STRING/)  = "Win32_WMISetting"
    ...
    __SUPERCLASS (CIM_STRING/)  = "CIM_Setting"
    ASPScriptDefaultNamespace (CIM_STRING/string)  = \\root\cimv2
    ASPScriptEnabled (CIM_BOOLEAN/boolean)  = <null>
    AutorecoverMofs (CIM_STRING | CIM_FLAG_ARRAY/string)  = <null>
    AutoStartWin9X (CIM_UINT32/uint32)  = <null>
    BackupInterval (CIM_UINT32/uint32)  = <null>
    BackupLastTime (CIM_DATETIME/datetime)  = <null>
    BuildVersion (CIM_STRING/string)  = <null>
    Caption (CIM_STRING/string)  = <null>
    DatabaseDirectory (CIM_STRING/string)  = <null>
```

```
DatabaseMaxSize (CIM_UINT32/uint32)  = <null>
Description (CIM_STRING/string)  = <null>
EnableAnonWin9xConnections (CIM_BOOLEAN/boolean)  = <null>
EnableEvents (CIM_BOOLEAN/boolean)  = <null>
EnableStartupHeapPreallocation (CIM_BOOLEAN/boolean)  = <null>
HighThresholdOnClientObjects (CIM_UINT32/uint32)  = <null>
HighThresholdOnEvents (CIM_UINT32/uint32)  = <null>
InstallationDirectory (CIM_STRING/string)  = <null>
LastStartupHeapPreallocation (CIM_UINT32/uint32)  = <null>
LoggingDirectory (CIM_STRING/string)  = <null>
LoggingLevel (CIM_UINT32/uint32)  = <null>
LowThresholdOnClientObjects (CIM_UINT32/uint32)  = <null>
LowThresholdOnEvents (CIM_UINT32/uint32)  = <null>
MaxLogFileSize (CIM_UINT32/uint32)  = <null>
MaxWaitOnClientObjects (CIM_UINT32/uint32)  = <null>
MaxWaitOnEvents (CIM_UINT32/uint32)  = <null>
MofSelfInstallDirectory (CIM_STRING/string)  = <null>
SettingID (CIM_STRING/string)  = <null>
```

Note the presence of the **SchemaOnly** keyword. In the context of a schema query that uses the **Associators Of** or the **References Of** statements, the **SchemaOnly** keyword must be specified, otherwise, nothing is returned from the query.

For other keywords that can be used with the **Associators Of** statement, the logic is the same as that for the data queries; therefore, the same rules apply. You can then refer to the data queries section to see the use of these keywords.

3.2.2.3   *Retrieving the references of a class*

By using the **References Of** statement in the context of a schema query, we retrieve the association class definitions.

Sample 3.28   *Retrieving the Association class definitions with the References Of statement (References Of statement and SchemaOnly keyword)*

```
I:\>wbemdump /E /Q Root\CIMV2 WQL "References Of {Win32_Service} Where SchemaOnly"
(WQL) References Of {Win32_Service} Where SchemaOnly
     __CLASS (CIM_STRING/)  = "Win32_SystemServices"
     ...
     GroupComponent (CIM_REFERENCE/ref:Win32_ComputerSystem)*  = <null>
     PartComponent (CIM_REFERENCE/ref:Win32_Service)*  = <null>

     __CLASS (CIM_STRING/)  = "Win32_WMIElementSetting"
     ...
     Element (CIM_REFERENCE/ref:Win32_Service)*  = <null>
     Setting (CIM_REFERENCE/ref:Win32_WMISetting)*  = <null>

     __CLASS (CIM_STRING/)  = "Win32_ServiceSpecificationService"
     ...
     Check (CIM_REFERENCE/ref:Win32_ServiceSpecification)*  = <null>
     Element (CIM_REFERENCE/ref:Win32_Service)*  = <null>
```

With this query, we retrieve the association classes directly referring to the *Win32_Service*, *Win32_SystemServices*, *Win32_WMIElementSetting*, and *Win32_ServiceSpecificationService* classes with their related references, which are *GroupComponent* and *PartComponent*, *Element* and *Setting*, and *Check* and *Element*, respectively.

Keywords of the **Associators Of** and **References Of** statements for schema queries have the same purpose as the keywords of the **Associators Of** and **References Of** statement for data queries. The difference is that they address the classes of the CIM repository instead of the instances created from the classes of the CIM repository. This is the only difference; for the rest, the logic is the same as before. Table 3.4 summarizes the different WQL schema query types with the obtained results.

If you reexamine the data queries and compare some results obtained with the schema queries, the relation between the obtained instances and the obtained classes is not necessarily obvious. You may be confused because associated class definitions retrieved from schema queries are not the same as those retrieved from data queries. The result of performing the data query shown in Sample 3.8 to retrieve the associated instance class definitions of a *Win32_Service* instance lists the following classes:

- *Win32_ComputerSystem*

- *Win32_Service*

The result of performing a schema query of the *Win32_Service* class in Sample 3.26 lists the following classes:

- *Win32_ComputerSystem*

- *Win32_WMISetting*

- *Win32_ServiceSpecification*

The classes listed differ between the data query and the schema query (see Figure 3.5).

Once again, in Chapter 2, when using the **WMI CIM Studio** to understand the dependencies between classes, we used the *Win32_Service* class as an example and saw how the relationships between the different classes were made. We saw that the *Win32_Service* MSExchangeSA instance has no associated instance of the *Win32_WMISetting* and *Win32_ServiceSpecification*. We also saw that the associated instances of some *Win32_Service* instances came from two things: the associations made at the *Win32_BaseService* class (a superclass of the *Win32_Service* class) and the inheritance of the *Win32_DependentService* association class to the subclass. It is for this

Table 3.4   *WQL Schema Queries*

Statement	Keywords						Obtained Result
Select *	From	meta_class	—	—	ISA	—	All classes.
	From	meta_class	_This	Where	—	*SourceClass*	Any classes made from the *SourceClass*.
Associators Of	—	{*SourceClass*}	—	—	—	—	Nothing is returned
	—	{*SourceClass*}	Where	—	—	SchemaOnly	Any classes where the Association classes associated with the *SourceClass*.
	—	{*SourceClass*}	Where	—	—	AssocClass = *AssocClassName* SchemaOnly	Any classes where the Association classes have a class name matching *AssocClassName* and that are associated with the *SourceClass*.
	—	{*SourceClass*}	Where	—	—	RequiredAssocQualifier = *QualifierName* SchemaOnly	Any classes where the Association classes are using the *QualifierName* and that are associated with the *SourceClass*.
	—	{*SourceClass*}	Where	—	—	RequiredQualifier = *QualifierName* SchemaOnly	Any classes containing the *QualifierName* and that are associated with the *SourceClass*.
	—	{*SourceClass*}	Where	—	—	ResultClass = *ClassName* SchemaOnly	Any classes having a class name matching the *ClassName* and that are associated with the *SourceClass*.
	—	{*SourceClass*}	Where	—	—	ResultRole = *PropertyName* SchemaOnly	Any classes where the role of the classes matches the *PropertyName* and that are associated with the *SourceClass*.
	—	{*SourceClass*}	Where	—	—	Role = *PropertyName* SchemaOnly	Any classes where the role of the *SourceClass* matches the *PropertyName* and that are associated with the *SourceClass*.

Table 3.4   *WQL Schema Queries (continued)*

Statement	Keywords				Obtained Result
References Of	{*SourceClass*}	—	—	—	Nothing is returned
	{*SourceClass*}	Where	—	SchemaOnly	Any Association classes been an Association class for the *SourceClass*.
	{*SourceClass*}	Where	—	RequiredQualifier = *QualifierName* SchemaOnly	Any Association classes containing the *QualifierName* and been an Association class for the *SourceClass*.
	{*SourceClass*}	Where	—	ResultClass = *ClassName* SchemaOnly	Any Association classes matching the *ClassName* and been an Association class for the *SourceClass*.
	{*SourceClass*}	Where	—	Role = *PropertyName* SchemaOnly	Any Association classes where the *SourceClass* plays a role matching the *PropertyName*.

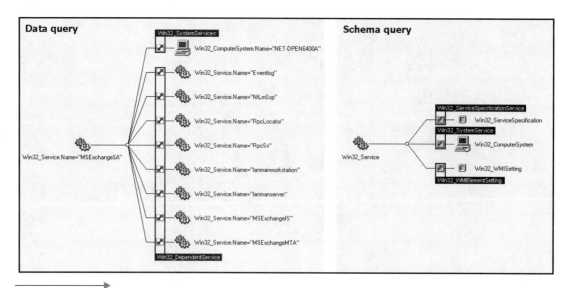

Figure 3.5   *The association differences between a WQL data query and a WQL schema query.*

reason the classes listed differ depending on whether we are examining the schema or the actual instances. It is sometimes quite difficult to see the relationships between classes and instances. Don't hesitate to examine the CIM Schema thoroughly to get a clear understanding of the relationships between classes, between instances, and between classes and instances.

3.2.3   **Event queries**

Event queries are used to filter events that WMI can return to an application. As we saw in Chapter 2, applications requesting WMI events are called *event consumers*. We briefly described two types of consumers: permanent consumers and temporary consumers. When we practiced the exercise with the permanent *SMTP* event consumer, we used an event query in a MOF file to create the event filter. The *SMTP* event consumer is a permanent consumer because it is registered in the CIM repository as a permanent consumer and is implemented in the form of a .dll. When we script on top of WMI, the scripts that make use of an event query are typically temporary consumers. Whatever the type of consumer we have, the subscription to an event is always performed with a WQL event query. Of course, there are many types of events that an application can receive from WMI. To exploit the capabilities of the WMI events fully, it is necessary to examine these events more closely. Chapter 6 covers WMI event scripting. However, this section provides enough information for you to understand how

WQL event queries work and how we can formulate them for later use in an application or a script.

The best tool to use for event queries without scripting is **WBEM-TEST.exe**. As previously mentioned, with an event query an application performs a kind of subscription for a particular event. This means that the application must be active or activated to receive the event notification. **WBEMDump.exe** and **WMI CIM Studio** are not designed for that type of query. This is an important difference between the data queries or the schema queries compared with the event queries. When executing a data query or a schema query, the query produces an immediate result based on the selection criteria. In the context of an event query, the application does not necessarily receive an immediate answer from the submitted query. This is an important difference because to receive a result from an event query, an event matching the submitted query must occur. This forces the application to wait for an undetermined period to get a result. If no event occurs, the application will wait forever if the logic has been written to do so.

To familiarize ourselves with WQL event queries, we will use (for now) only one event type called the _InstanceModificationEvent_. The _InstanceModificationEvent_ is a system class used to report an instance modification event, which is an event generated when an instance of a class changes in the examined namespace. For example, as we worked with the _Win32_Service_ instances, the event reported can be due to the modification of the default startup mode of a Windows service. Changing a Windows service from manual to automatic will be enough to trigger an event if the _Win32_Service_ instances of the **Root\CIMv2** namespace match the submitted event query. With the _SMTP_ event consumer, the query we used to filter the event was:

```
SELECT * FROM __InstanceModificationEvent WITHIN 10 Where TargetInstance ISA 'Win32_Service'
```

There are many things to say about such a query. First, we recognize the **SELECT** and the **FROM** statements we used in data queries and schema queries. With the **FROM** statement, instead of performing the query on a class (such as a schema query) or on an instance (such as a data query), the query is made on the instance modification event represented by the _InstanceModificationEvent_ system class. Let's examine this query in detail.

3.2.3.1   *Polling for events*

A new keyword specific to event queries is the **WITHIN** keyword. This keyword, placed before the **WHERE** statement, is not always mandatory in an event query. Its presence is required if the provider delivering information about the monitored instance is not implemented as an event provider.

Some providers implement a specific interface to inform WMI that an event matching the submitted event query occurred. In such a case, the event provider performs the monitoring and provides an immediate notification in case of modification. When performing event queries on some other instances, there is no event provider developed to monitor the instance modifications. This forces WMI to poll the instances for the provider. It must be clear that the event consumer never performs the poll. Polling is always handled by an event provider or by WMI itself.

If there is no event provider available, at a regular time interval WMI will query the instances (in the CIM repository or via a provider exposing dynamic instances) to determine whether a modification occurred. This means that the notification will be available from WMI at a regular time interval and not when the event occurs. In other words, this interval is the maximum amount of time that can pass before an event notification is delivered. The time specified with the **WITHIN** keyword represents the polling interval in seconds. In the query sample we use, the provider exposing the *Win32_Service* instances has no event provider interface implemented and imposes the use of the **WITHIN** statement. The polling interval can be fractional to deal with values smaller than one second. However, the interval should represent a number of seconds, rather than an extremely small value, because specifying a too-small value can cause WMI to reject the statement as invalid due to the resource-intensive nature of the polling. As a best practice, it is recommended to use an interval greater than five minutes (300 seconds). While doing exercises in this chapter and for academic purposes only, we use a value of two seconds to get faster results.

When using the **WITHIN** statement in such a context, only the instances that have changed during the polling interval will be detected. For example, if the SNMP service is in a running *state* at T (T for time), when we are at $T + 1$ (the beginning of a new polling interval), it makes sense that if nothing has changed, there will be no notification. Now, if the SNMP service is stopped and started again during the polling interval (between T and $T + 1$), the result will be the same, because the service *state* is not different at $T + 1$ compared with its *state* at T. Of course, there was an intermediate change as the service was stopped and restarted, but this intermediate change was made during the polling interval. Because the service was back to its original *state* before $T + 1$, no change is detected. Therefore, a notification is created only when the *state* of the instance at T is different at $T + 1$. Any intermediate modification (that conducts to the same situation as the original one) will not be detected. To ensure that intermediate changes are detected, the polling interval must be shorter or an event provider must be available (which does not force you to use **WITHIN** statement and, thereby, triggers an immediate notification).

3.2.3.2 *Limiting the scope*

The **WHERE** statement has the same purpose in an event query as it has in the context of a data query or a schema query. Although it is used to narrow the scope of the query, its use has some particularities related to the context of an event query. As we saw when working with the *SMTP* event consumer, the *__InstanceModificationEvent* returns two objects embedded in the instance properties—*PreviousInstance* and *TargetInstance*. The *PreviousInstance* property contains a copy of the instance before modification. The *TargetInstance* property contains the new version of the modified instance. The filtering of an event could be executed on the instance contained in the *PreviousInstance* or the *TargetInstance* properties. The usage of the **PreviousInstance** and **TargetInstance** keywords is similar to the usage of the **__THIS** keyword of the schema query. How? In the sense that the **__THIS** keyword identifies the target class for a schema query, and the **PreviousInstance** and **TargetInstance** keywords identify the instance before or after modification for an event query. Both *PreviousInstance* and *TargetInstance* properties are retrieved because the **SELECT** statement uses the "*" filter.

```
SELECT * FROM __InstanceModificationEvent WITHIN 2 Where TargetInstance ISA 'Win32_Service'
```

It is possible to formulate the query to retrieve only the *TargetInstance* of the *__InstanceModificationEvent* instance:

```
SELECT TargetInstance FROM __InstanceModificationEvent WITHIN 2
                                    Where TargetInstance ISA 'Win32_Service'
```

The **ISA** operator is a WQL-specific operator that can also be used in event queries. When **ISA** is included in the **WHERE** statement of an event query, it requests notification of events for all classes within a class hierarchy rather than a specific event class. Therefore, its use in an event query is very similar to its use in a schema query. Let's try this WQL event query by using the **WBEMTEST.exe** tool "Notification Query" window. Make sure that you use asynchronous notification to get the best performance. Again, later we see the different notification types available.

Once the query has been coded in **WBEMTEST.exe** GUI and applied as shown in Figure 3.6, any modification of a Windows service instance will generate an event. For example, start the SNMP service to see what happens.

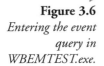

Figure 3.6
Entering the event query in WBEMTEST.exe.

Once the SNMP service starts, the query result window, which appears as soon as you submit the query, contains an instance of the *__InstanceModificationEvent* (see Figure 3.7). By clicking twice on this event, it is possible to examine the *__InstanceModificationEvent* instance (see Figure 3.8). The **WBEMTEST.exe** tool displays two embedded objects in the *PreviousInstance* and *TargetInstance* properties.

By double-clicking each of these objects, you can see the properties of the instances contained in the *PreviousInstance* (Figure 3.9) and the *Target-Instance* properties (Figure 3.10) when starting the SNMP service.

3.2.3.3   Limiting the scope with data selection

Just as with data queries, it is possible to combine some logical operators to add some selection criteria. The event query we used reacts to any *Win32_Service* instance modification. If we want to receive event notification only when the "SNMP" service is stopped, the query is as follows:

```
SELECT * FROM __InstanceModificationEvent WITHIN 2 Where
                              TargetInstance ISA 'Win32_Service' And
                              TargetInstance.Name='SNMP' And
                              TargetInstance.State='Stopped'
```

Figure 3.7
The WBEMTEST.exe query result window for event queries.

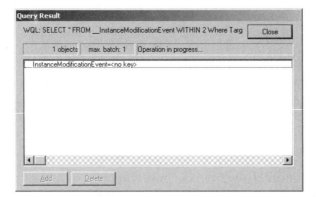

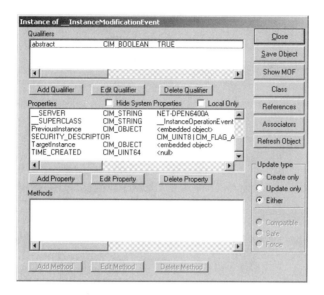

Figure 3.8
*Examining the
event query result
with
WBEMTEST.exe.*

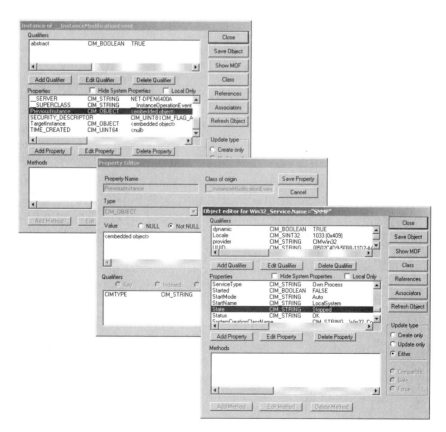

Figure 3.9
*Viewing the
PreviousInstance
result with
WBEMTEST.exe.*

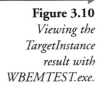

Figure 3.10
*Viewing the
TargetInstance
result with
WBEMTEST.exe.*

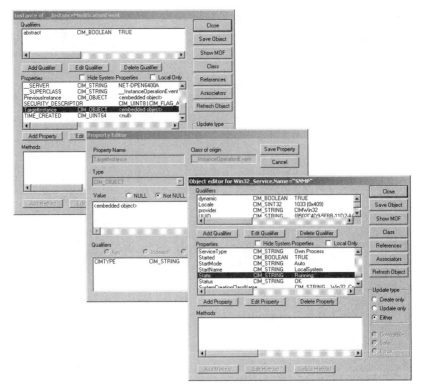

3.2.3.4   Limiting the scope by grouping events

The last query narrows the scope based on a matching data set related to the object instance. Using the data instance is not the only method for narrowing an event query scope. With event queries, it is also possible to narrow the scope in time. For this the **WITHIN** and the **HAVING** statements can be used. In this context, the **WITHIN** statement is used differently (see the **WITHIN** statement for the polling interval in Section 3.2.3.1) and in combination with the **GROUP** statement. These statements are used to protect event consumers from being flooded with notifications that occur too frequently. Consumers that do not require notification each time an event occurs can use these statements.

The **GROUP** statement causes WMI to generate a single notification to represent a group of events. Previously, the obtained result was an instance of the *__InstanceModificationEvent* for each event. With the **GROUP** statement, the obtained result is an instance of the *__AggregateEvent* for a group of events. We will not delve into the details of such a system class instance in this chapter, because we will focus on the events in the WMI events scripting in Chapter 6. However, we can say that the _AggregateEvent_ instance contains an object that is representative of the events that occurred in the group. This statement concentrates on a group of events, and since event notifications occur over an undefined period of time, grouping events implies the definition of an interval. This period of time is known as the _grouping interval_ and is defined in seconds with the **WITHIN** statement. This is why the **WITHIN** statement is always used in combination with the **GROUP** statement. Let's take a sample:

```
Select * FROM __InstanceModificationEvent WITHIN 2 WHERE TargetInstance ISA 'Win32_Service' And
                                        TargetInstance.State = 'Stopped'
                            GROUP WITHIN 60
```

It is important to note that the **WITHIN** statement is referenced twice in this WQL query. The first **WITHIN** statement sets the polling frequency to two seconds, because there is no event provider for the _Win32_Service_ instances. You will notice that we use a shorter interval period to make sure that we detect any service change to the "stopped" _state_ fast enough. Now, let's talk about the second **WITHIN** statement by examining the following query first:

```
Select * FROM __InstanceModificationEvent WITHIN 2 WHERE TargetInstance ISA 'Win32_Service' And
                                        TargetInstance.State = 'Stopped'
```

With this query, if we start and stop the SNMP service three times, we will generate several events. If we stop the service to get a "stopped" _state_ when the polling interval terminates and on the condition that the service _state_ was "started" at the beginning of the same polling interval, we generate the same event three times. By adding the **GROUP WITHIN 60** statement, we will receive only one event grouping all the changes of the same nature performed during a period of 60 seconds. Therefore, even if the detection of the "stopped" _state_ of the service was made three times, the grouping interval of 60 seconds will create one notification of the _AggregateEvent_ instance instead of three notifications of the _InstanceModificationEvent_ instance. Figure 3.11 shows the _AggregateEvent_ instance received, and Figure 3.12 shows the content of the _AggregateEvent_ instance.

The last window in Figure 3.12 shows that we obtain an _InstanceModificationEvent_ instance embedded in the _AggregateEvent_ instance. From the _InstanceModificationEvent_ instance, we see the _PreviousInstance_ and _TargetInstance_ properties. From this point, we are examining an object similar to the one obtained in Figure 3.10. Like the _InstanceModificationEvent_ instance, the _AggregateEvent_ exposes two

Figure 3.11
*The
WBEMTEST.exe
query result
window for
aggregated event
queries.*

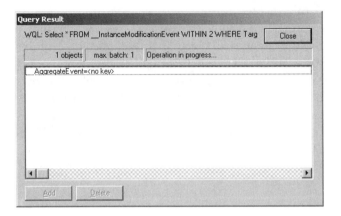

Figure 3.12
*Examining the
aggregated event
query result with
WBEMTEST.exe.*

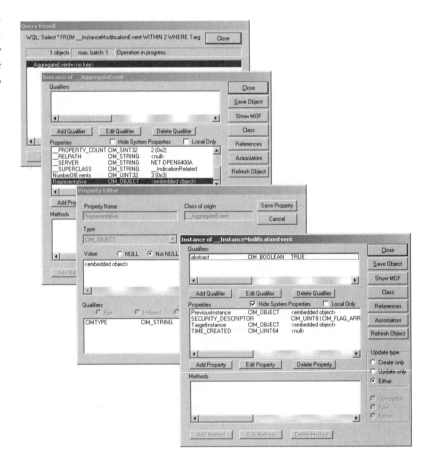

specific properties called *NumberOfEvents* and *Representative*. Like the *PreviousInstance* and the *TargetInstance* properties, the *Representative* property contains an embedded object. The *NumberOfEvents* property contains the number of times the event occurred for the *__AggregateEvent* instance.

3.2.3.5 *Limiting the scope with a minimum of occurrences in a group*

This is where the **HAVING** statement is used. The previous event query triggers one notification if any *Win32_Service* instance is stopped one or more times during a period of 60 seconds. For example, it would be interesting to get an event notification only if five occurrences of the same event occur during the same period of time. Any other similar event generated less than five times in the same grouping interval will not trigger a notification. In this case, the WQL event query is as follows:

```
Select * FROM __InstanceModificationEvent WITHIN 2 WHERE TargetInstance ISA 'Win32_Service' And
                                 TargetInstance.State = 'Stopped'
                          GROUP WITHIN 60 HAVING NumberOfEvents>=5
```

This means that if a *Win32_Service* instance is detected as "stopped," with a polling interval of two seconds at least five times during a 60-second period, a notification event will be sent in the form of an *__AggregateEvent* instance containing a representative instance of the modified instances. This form of query particularly suits the event log monitoring to track specific message creations. Moreover, the WMI provider that gives access to the event log is also implemented as an event provider, which eases the notification of new event log message creations, given that the **WITHIN** statement for the polling technique is no longer necessary.

3.2.3.6 *Criteria to group events*

In the previous queries, because we changed only the SNMP service state, it was easy to get in the *__AggregateEvent* instance a representative *__InstanceModificationEvent* instance of the SNMP service, as it was always the same service. But what happens if we stop the SNMPTRAP service during the same period? Let's try this with the following query:

```
Select * FROM __InstanceModificationEvent WITHIN 2 WHERE TargetInstance ISA 'Win32_Service' And
                                 TargetInstance.State = 'Stopped'
                          GROUP WITHIN 60
```

Notice that we removed the **HAVING** statement to eliminate the required number of changes for the "stopped" *state* during the grouping interval. Next, as we have two Windows services to stop (SNMP and SNMPTRAP), we will use a very small command file to ease our work:

```
@ECHO OFF
IF .%1.==.. GOTO END
IF .%1.==.0. GOTO END

SET /A I=%1
SET /A C=0

:LOOP
SET /A C=%C%+1
ECHO ------------- Loop number %C% -------------

CALL :STOPSVC SNMP
CALL :STOPSVC SNMPTRAP

IF NOT .%C%.==.%I%. GOTO LOOP
GOTO END

:STOPSVC
NET START %1
NET STOP %1
GOTO :EOF


GOTO :EOF
:END
```

This command file takes a number as a parameter. This number represents the number of times that the SNMP and SNMPTRAP services must be stopped. For this, the command file executes a loop until the given number is reached. This command file is a pretty easy one and will be a great help for simulating the expected behavior of the WQL event query. So, if we execute this command file with the parameter "2," we will stop the SNMP and SNMPTRAP services twice. The command file output will be

```
C:\>Stop 2
------------- Loop number 1 -------------
The SNMP Service service is starting.
The SNMP Service service was started successfully.

The SNMP Service service is stopping...
The SNMP Service service was stopped successfully.

The SNMP Trap Service service is starting.
The SNMP Trap Service service was started successfully.

The SNMP Trap Service service is stopping.
The SNMP Trap Service service was stopped successfully.

------------- Loop number 2 -------------
The SNMP Service service is starting.
The SNMP Service service was started successfully.
```

```
The SNMP Service service is stopping..
The SNMP Service service was stopped successfully.

The SNMP Trap Service service is starting.
The SNMP Trap Service service was started successfully.

The SNMP Trap Service service is stopping.
The SNMP Trap Service service was stopped successfully.
```

Now, if we look in the **WBEMTEST.exe** result query window (see Figure 3.13), we see that we get one __*AggregateEvent*__ instance.

As we stopped two different services, what does the __*AggregateEvent*__ instance contain? First, the *NumberOfEvents* property contains the value

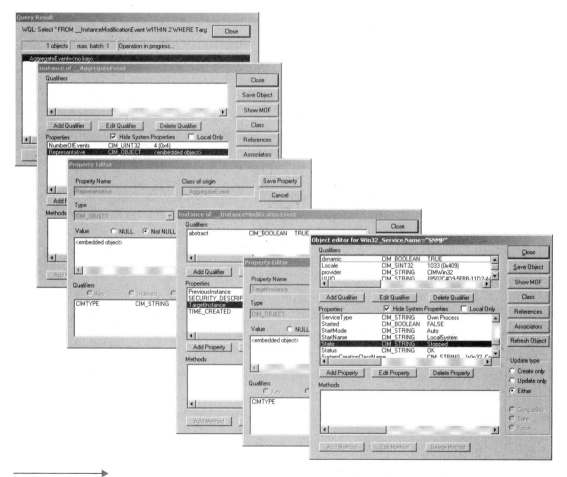

Figure 3.13   *Examining the aggregated event query result with WBEMTEST.exe when two different services are stopped.*

4—exactly the number of Windows services stopped (twice for the two services). Now, if we look at the *Representative* property, we find an instance representing the SNMP service. What about the SNMPTRAP service? Well, this modified instance is simply not represented. Now, with the command file, we stop the SNMP service first, and the SNMPTRAP service next. If we invert the order, the *Representative* property will contain the SNMPTRAP service and not the SNMP service. In any case, we always lose one modified instance. This is where the **BY** statement is useful. The BY statement allows the grouping of events by criteria. Let's modify the previous query as follows:

```
Select * FROM __InstanceModificationEvent WITHIN 2 WHERE TargetInstance ISA 'Win32_Service' And
                                                        TargetInstance.State = 'Stopped'
                                          GROUP WITHIN 60
                                          BY TargetInstance.Name
```

If we submit this query and restart the command file with the same value, we execute the same modification on the two Windows service instances, but the obtained result is different (see Figure 3.14).

Here we are! Now, we get two *__AggregateEvent* instances. Because the **BY** statement groups each event on the *Name* property of the object embedded in the *__InstanceModificationEvent* instance, we get two different event instances for each stopped service. If we stop a third service during the grouping interval, we will get three *__AggregateEvent* instances.

We can add the *NumberOfEvents* filter used before and, with the help of the command file, we can try the following query:

```
Select * FROM __InstanceModificationEvent WITHIN 2 WHERE TargetInstance ISA 'Win32_Service' And
                                                        TargetInstance.State = 'Stopped'
                                          GROUP WITHIN 120
                                          BY TargetInstance.Name HAVING NumberOfEvents>=3
```

Notice that we extended the grouping interval to make sure that we can stop the Windows services at least three times. This query will produce a number of notification events equal to the number of Windows services stopped at least three times in a period of 120 seconds.

The formal syntax representation of an event query is as follows:

```
SELECT * FROM EventClass [WITHIN polling_interval] WHERE property operator value
       [GROUP WITHIN grouping_interval] [BY property_list]
       [HAVING NumberOfEvents operator integer]
```

When using the **GROUP** statement, the **WHERE**, **BY**, and **HAVING** statements are optional. From a semantic point of view, the **WHERE** statement is also optional, but must be specified from an operational point of view to get a match on an event class representing the modified instance.

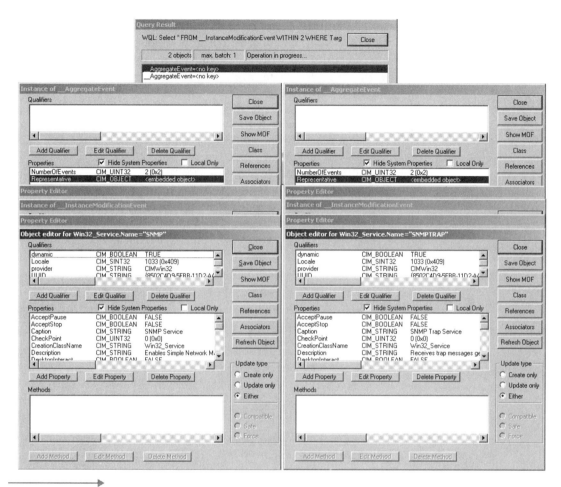

Figure 3.14   *The effect of the BY statement on the aggregated event query results when two different services are stopped.*

3.3   Extended WQL

The Extended WMI Query Language is provided with the installation of Microsoft Systems Management Server (SMS). Since we do not talk about SMS in this book, we just mention the existence of Extended WQL to clarify its positioning with regard to WQL. Extended WQL supports a superset of WQL. Extended WQL is like WQL in that it is a retrieval-only language used to create queries. It cannot be used to create, modify, or delete classes or instances. Extended WQL, as with WQL, is based on the ANSI SQL standard, but includes a much broader range of operations than WQL, especially oriented for the use of SMS. Extended WQL comes with SMS Service Pack 2, is fully case insensitive, and supports the standard WQL comparison operators, plus the **LIKE** and **IN** operators. For those of you working with SMS, please refer to the SMS documentation for more information about Extended WQL.

3.4   Summary

Throughout this chapter, we reviewed the possibilities of WQL. As WQL is one of the key elements required to work with WMI, it is a valuable study for the discoveries we make in the subsequent chapters. In most cases, WQL is a primary input to execute WMI tasks. The difficulty in learning WQL is that we have to work with some WMI elements that are still unknown at this stage, but are examined later in the book. However, because WMI is a mix of various features interacting with each other, it is necessary to start from somewhere. When we dive deeper into the elements constituting WMI, the interactions between various elements will become clearer.

Usually, when a script writer starts to develop on top of a COM abstraction layer, the key element is to master the object model used, such as Active Directory Service Interfaces (ADSI), Collaborative Data Objects (CDO), or CDO for Exchange Management (CDOEXM). With WMI, the learning phase starts at the level of the CIM repository with WQL. Learning the CIM Object Model is necessary in order to understand the kind of information available from a WMI system. Learning WQL is essential to be able to formulate inputs to gather data from the CIM repository. When working with WMI event scripting, WQL is the primary input to formulate event queries. Of course, being able to script with the WMI events and learning the scripting interfaces exposed by WMI is another learning process, which is independent of the CIM repository and the knowledge of WQL. At this stage, we are ready to start the discussion of the WMI scripting interfaces, which leads us to the next chapter.

Scripting with WMI

4.1   **Objective**

In previous chapters, we examined the WMI architecture, WMI-related tools, and WQL. We now have the necessary knowledge to start the discussion of WMI scripting. Scripting on top of WMI implies the use of WMI COM objects. A script uses two types of objects: the objects obtained from the various class definitions located in the CIM repository (instances) and the objects exposed by the WMI scripting API (COM objects). As previously mentioned, in order to script on top of a COM abstraction layer, it is important to know how to navigate in the object model. To script on top of WMI, it is important to master both object models: the CIM repository object model and the WMI COM API object model. In Chapter 2, we focused on the tools that help understand and discover the CIM repository. In this chapter and the next, we focus on the WMI scripting API and show how this API can help to instantiate objects from the CIM repository and retrieve information about the CIM classes. We also find out how to work with real-world managed objects via this API by using CIM representations. The WMI scripting API is a collection of COM objects usable from most programming languages (such as Visual Basic or C++) and scripting languages (such as VBScript or JScript). In order to use the WMI COM objects they must first be instantiated. In addition, the CIM repository classes must also be instantiated as objects in order to reference the manageable entities of the real world. We are now in front of two instantiation types: the instantiation of the WMI scripting COM objects and the instantiation of the manageable entities. Both object types must be located in the system or in the CIM repository based on their nature (from the WMI scripting COM object collection or from the CIM repository definitions). In this chapter, we discover the techniques for using WMI scripting objects with real-world manageable entities and examine the functionalities offered by these objects.

4.2 The WMI object path

To address manageable entities from the real world as defined in the CIM repository, it is necessary to locate their definitions (classes) in the CIM repository. The object path uniquely identifies the definitions made in the CIM repository. This path is used to locate three things:

1.   A WMI namespace on a server

2.   The classes defined in a particular namespace

3.   The instances of a class in particular namespace.

The WMI object path can be compared with the concept of the universal resource locator (URL) used for the Internet. Both are hierarchical and use a number of elements in their structures, although the real representation does not look the same. The number of elements is determined by the nature of the object to locate. We can clearly distinguish three types of WMI object path:

1.   **The namespace object path:** This path is used to locate a particular namespace in the CIM repository on a server. It uses two elements: the server name and the CIM repository namespace name. For example, the following string is a valid namespace object path:

     ```
     \\NET-DPEN6400A\Root\CIMv2
     ```

     where the server is NET-DPEN6400A and the namespace is **Root\CIMv2**. The generic representation of a namespace object path is

     ```
     \\Server\Namespace
     ```

     or

     ```
     //Server/Namespace
     ```

     or

     ```
     \\.\Namespace
     ```

     if the local server is referenced.

2.   **The class object path:** This path is used to locate a particular class in a namespace on a server. It uses three elements: the server

name, the namespace, and the class name. For example, the following string is a valid class object path:

```
\\NET-DPEN6400A\Root\CIMv2\Win32_Service
```

where the server is NET-DPEN6400A, the namespace **Root\ CIMv2**, and the class is *Win32_Service*. The generic representation of a class object path is:

```
\\Server\Namespace\ClassName
```

and follows the same variation as before.

3.   **The instance object path:** This path is used to locate an instance of a particular class in a namespace on a server. It uses four elements: the server name, the namespace, and the instance name identified with the key property as defined by the class template. For example, the following string is a valid instance object path:

```
\\NET-DPEN6400A\Root\CIMv2\Win32_Service.Name="SNMP"
```

where the server is NET-DPEN6400A, the namespace **Root\ CIMv2**, and the instance is the SNMP service of the *Win32_Service* class referenced by its key property, *name*. The generic representation of an instance object path is

```
\\Server\Namespace\ClassName.KeyName="KeyValue"
```

4.3   The WMI moniker

A moniker is a string (also called a display name) that provides a location and an identity to an object that must be instantiated in a script. This term comes from the COM object programming and represents another programmatic identifier (called ProgID) that maps to a class identifier (called CLSID). This CLSID points to a COM object implemented as a .dll containing the desired object. To define the location and the identity of an object, the moniker uses a syntax that is specific to any implementation. The WMI moniker is a string that combines some WMI-specific information with a WMI object path. That string is used to access information exposed by WMI. The specific information of a WMI moniker contains:

- A namespace (WinMgmts: for WMI)

- Some optional localization data

- Some optional security settings used for the object instantiation

The string "WinMgmts:" is not case sensitive and is dedicated to refer to WMI monikers. This will make the system point to the WBEMDISP.Dll located in %SystemRoot\System32\WBEM directory that is the .dll containing the WMI scripting COM API. Let's take a sample. In the previous paragraph, we saw an instance object path for the SNMP service. The moniker used to instantiate this *Win32_Service* instance in a script is

```
WinMgmts:\\NET-DPEN6400A\Root\CIMv2:Win32_Service.Name="SNMP"
```

To access this object instance in a script, the code can be written in VBScript as follows:

```
Set objWMIInstance = GetObject("WinMgmts:\\NET-DPEN6400A\Root\CIMv2:Win32_Service.name=""SNMP""")
```

You will notice the double quotes to respect the VBScript syntax. To ease reading this in VBScript, it can be changed to

```
Set objWMIInstance = GetObject("WinMgmts:\\NET-DPEN6400A\Root\CIMv2:Win32_Service.name='SNMP'")
```

In JScript, the backslashes and the quotes must be escaped (with a supplemental backslash [\]); therefore, the line will be

```
var objWMIInstance = GetObject("winmgmts:\\\\NET-DPEN6400A\\Root\\CIMv2:Win32_Service.name=\"SNMP\"");
```

Or, to suppress the escape sequence of the backslashes and the quotes to make the line more readable, it will be

```
var objWMIInstance = GetObject("winmgmts://NET-DPEN6400A/Root/CIMv2:Win32_Service.name='SNMP'");
```

or

```
var objWMIInstance = GetObject('winmgmts://NET-DPEN6400A/Root/CIMv2:Win32_Service.name="SNMP"');
```

4.3.1 Getting the SWbemObject with the moniker

Many things can be said about the previous moniker samples. The first thing to note is the nature of the object obtained and the fact that it is stored in the **objWMIInstance** variable. As this moniker points to an instance object path, it makes sense that we obtain an object instance. This object corresponds to the **SWbemObject** object as defined in the WMI scripting object model. We revisit this object later in Section 4.4.2. This object exposes properties and methods associated with the SNMP service provided by the *Win32_Service* class defined in the CIM repository. The list of properties and methods provided by the *Win32_Service* class is shown in Table 4.1.

Table 4.1   *The Win32_Service Properties and Methods*

Properties	AcceptPause	**Boolean**
		Read-only
		Indicates whether the service can be paused.
	AcceptStop	**Boolean**
		Read-only
		Indicates whether the service can be stopped.
	Caption	**string**
		Read-only
		Short description (one-line string) of the object.
	CheckPoint	**uint32**
		Read-only
		Value that the service increments periodically to report its progress during a lengthy start, stop, pause, or continue operation. For example, the service should increment this value as it completes each step of its initialization when it is starting up. The user interface program that invoked the operation on the service uses this value to track the progress of the service during a lengthy operation. This value is not valid and should be zero when the service does not have a start, stop, pause, or continue operation pending.
	CreationClassName	**string**
		Read-only
		Name of the first concrete class to appear in the inheritance chain used in the creation of an instance. When used with the other key properties of the class, the property allows all instances of this class and its subclasses to be uniquely identified.
	Description	**string**
		Read-only
		Description of the object.

Table 4.1   *The Win32_Service Properties and Methods (continued)*

Properties (contd.)	DesktopInteract	**Boolean**
		Read-only
		Indicates whether the service can create or communicate with windows on the desktop.
	DisplayName	**string**
		Read-only
		Display name of the service. This string has a maximum length of 256 characters. The name is case-preserved in the Service Control Manager; however, **DisplayName** comparisons are always case-insensitive. Constraints: Accepts the same value as the **Name** property.
	ErrorControl	**string**
		Read-only
		Severity of the error if this service fails to start during startup. The value indicates the action taken by the startup program if failure occurs. All errors are logged by the computer system.
	ExitCode	**uint32**
		Read-only
		Win32 error code defining any problems encountered in starting or stopping the service. This property is set to ERROR_SERVICE_SPECIFIC_ERROR (1066) when the error is unique to the service represented by this class, and information about the error is available in the **ServiceSpecificExitCode** property. The service sets this value to NO_ERROR when running, and again upon normal termination.
	InstallDate	**datetime**
		Read-only
		Indicates when the object was installed. A lack of a value does not indicate that the object is not installed.
	Name	**string**
		Read-only
		Uniquely identifies the service and provides an indication of the functionality that is managed. This functionality is described in more detail in the object's **Description** property.

Table 4.1   *The Win32_Service Properties and Methods (continued)*

Properties (cont'd.)		
	PathName	**string**
		Read-only
		Fully qualified path to the service binary file that implements the service.
	ProcessId	**uint32**
		Read-only
		Process identifier of the service.
	ServiceSpecificExitCode	**uint32**
		Read-only
		Service-specific error code for errors that occur while the service is either starting or stopping. The exit codes are defined by the service represented by this class. This value is only set when the ExitCode property value is ERROR_SERVICE_SPECIFIC_ERROR, 1066.
	ServiceType	**string**
		Read-only
		Type of service provided to calling processes.
	Started	**Boolean**
		Read-only
		Indicates whether the service has been started.
	StartMode	**string**
		Read-only
		Start mode of the Win32 base service.

Table 4.1   *The Win32_Service Properties and Methods (continued)*

Properties (cont'd.)	StartName	**string** Read-only
		Account name under which the service runs. Depending on the service type, the account name may be in the form of DomainName\Username. The service process will be logged using one of these two forms when it runs. If the account belongs to the built-in domain, .\Username can be specified. If NULL is specified, the service will be logged on as the LocalSystem account. For kernel or system level drivers, StartName contains the driver object name (that is, \FileSystem\Rdr or \Driver\Xns) which the input and output (I/O) system uses to load the device driver. Additionally, if NULL is specified, the driver runs with a default object name created by the I/O system based on the service name.
	State	**string** Read-only
		Current state of the base service.
	Status	**string** Read-only
		Current status of the object. Various operational and nonoperational statuses can be defined. Operational statuses include OK, Degraded, and Pred Fail (an element, such as a SMART-enabled hard drive, may be functioning properly but predicting a failure in the near future). Nonoperational statuses include Error,Starting, Stopping, and Service. The latter, Service, could apply during mirror-resilvering of a disk, reload of a user permissions list, or other administrative work. Not all such work is on-line, yet the managed element is neither OK nor in one of the other states.
	SystemCreationClassName	**string** Read-only
		Type name of the system that hosts this service.
	SystemName	**string** Read-only
		Name of the system that hosts this service.

Table 4.1   *The Win32_Service Properties and Methods (continued)*

Properties (cont'd.)	TagId	**uint32**
		Read-only
		Unique tag value for this service in the group. A value of 0 indicates that the service has not been assigned a tag. A tag can be used for ordering service startup within a load order group by specifying a tag order vector in the registry located at: HKEY_LOCAL_MACHINE\System\CurrentControlSet\Control\ GroupOrderList. Tags are only evaluated for kernel driver and file system driver start-type services that have boot or system start modes.
	WaitHint	**uint32**
		Read-only
		Estimated time required (in milliseconds) for a pending start, stop, pause, or continue operation. After the specified amount of time has elapsed, the service makes its next call to the **SetServiceStatus** method with either an incremented **CheckPoint** value or a change in **CurrentState**. If the amount of time specified by **WaitHint** passes, and **CheckPoint** has not been incremented, or **CurrentState** has not changed, the service control manager or service control program assumes that an error has occurred.
Methods	StartService	Class method that attempts to place the service into its startup state
	StopService	Class method that places the service in the stopped state
	PauseService	Class method that attempts to place the service in the paused state
	ResumeService	Class method that attempts to place the service in the resumed state
	InterrogateService	Class method that requests that the service update its state to the service manager
	UserControlService	Class method that attempts to send a user-defined control code to a service
	Create	Class method that creates a new service
	Change	Class method that modifies a service
	ChangeStartMode	Class method that modifies the start mode of a service
	Delete	Class method that deletes an existing service

If the script runs on the local server, the server name can be skipped in the moniker. In this case, the line is

```
Set objWMIInstance = GetObject("WinMgmts:\\.\Root\CIMv2:Win32_Service.name='SNMP'")
```

or

```
Set objWMIInstance = GetObject("WinMgmts:\Root\CIMv2:Win32_Service.name='SNMP'")
```

or

```
Set objWMIInstance = GetObject("WinMgmts:Root\CIMv2:Win32_Service.name='SNMP'")
```

Next, the scripting API uses the **Root\CIMv2** namespace by default. This setting is modifiable via the Computer Management MMC by editing the advanced properties of the WMI Control snap-in located in the Services and Applications.

As the **Root\CIMv2** namespace is the same as the default namespace, the line can be coded as follows:

```
Set objWMIInstance = GetObject("WinMgmts::Win32_Service.name='SNMP'")
```

or

```
Set objWMIInstance = GetObject("WinMgmts:Win32_Service.name='SNMP'")
```

Because the *name* property is defined as the only key in the *Win32_Service* class, the line can be coded as follows:

```
Set objWMIInstance = GetObject("WinMgmts:Win32_Service='SNMP'")
```

In all variations, the returned object is an instance of the SNMP service, and the COM nature of the **objWMIInstance** variable comes from the COM scriptable object called **SWbemObject**. Now, if the equality test of the line is removed as follows:

```
Set objWMIInstance = GetObject("WinMgmts:Win32_Service")
```

the returned object is not a real-world manageable object instance any more but an instance of the *Win32_Service* class. What is the difference? The difference is very small from a coding point of view, but very important! In the previous case, the instance returned pointed to the SNMP service itself, because the object path was a WMI instance object path. In the second case, the returned instance points to the class definition of the *Win32_Service* itself because the object path is a WMI class object path. Let's make a small test by using the following lines of code:

```
Set objWMIInstance = GetObject("WinMgmts:Win32_Service='SNMP'")
WScript.Echo objWMIInstance.Name
```

If this script runs, it echoes the name of the service: SNMP. Now, if the following piece of code is used instead:

```
Set objWMIInstance = GetObject("WinMgmts:Win32_Service")
WScript.Echo objWMIInstance.Name
```

it echoes a null. Why? Simply because the value associated with the name property for the *Win32_Service* class is empty. This can be easily checked using the **WMI CIM Studio** by examining the class definition of the *Win32_Service*. You will see that the value associated with the *name* key property is empty in the right pane containing the column names, column types, and column values. To complete the test, you can eventually set a value in this row and run the prior lines of code to see the change. In this case, you will see the value you typed in the class definition for the *name* key property (to clear the typed value, you must right-click on the value and select "set to <empty>"). This small test practically demonstrates the difference between a class instance and a real-world manageable object instance. In both cases, the script creates an instance but one represents the CIM class from the CIM repository and the other represents the real-world manageable entity represented by the CIM class and located with the object path contained in the moniker.

4.3.2   Getting the SWbemServices with the moniker

Using the same sample line of code:

```
Set objWMIInstance = GetObject("WinMgmts:Root\CIMv2:Win32_Service.name='SNMP'")
```

if we change the WMI object path to

```
Set objWMIServices = GetObject("WinMgmts:Root\CIMv2")
```

the code will open a namespace because the given path is a namespace object path. The obtained object is a COM scriptable object called **SWbemServices**. In this case the moniker is not changing from a real-world manageable object to an object representing a class from the CIM repository; it is changing the nature of the returned COM object. This implies that the object exposes other properties and methods. However, it is still possible, by using some of its methods, to retrieve a WMI instance representing a class from the CIM repository or a real-world manageable object. We revisit this object in Section 4.4.1. We also see that the WMI scripting API offers objects that can be used as an alternative to the moniker. But again, this will be covered later. Let's get back to the moniker. There are still a few things to say about this particular string.

As we can see, the way the moniker is coded influences the object type instantiated in the script. Besides the object instantiation at the script level, the composition of the moniker is directly related to the CIM repository. This is another reason why it is very important to understand and gather knowledge about the CIM repository object model.

4.3.3   The security settings of the moniker

Another feature of the moniker with the WMI object path is that it may contain security settings. These security settings correspond to the DCOM security settings visible with the **DCOMCNFG.exe** tool under Windows NT 4.0 and Windows 2000 or with the Component Services MMC snap-in under Windows XP and Windows.NET Server. There are three types of DCOM security settings:

1.   **Authentication level:** As DCOM is used behind the scene, it is also possible to specify the DCOM authentication level to use. The authentication level can have seven different levels: *Default* (uses the default Windows authentication setting), *None, Connect, Call, Pkt, PktIntegrity,* and *PktPrivacy.* To specify the authentication level in the moniker, the moniker must be changed to

```
WinMgmts:{AuthenticationLevel=default}!Root\CIMv2:Win32_Service.name='SNMP'
```

Refer to Table 4.2 for the list of authentication levels and their related meanings.

2.   **Impersonation level:** As WMI uses DCOM, it is possible that WMI must authenticate on behalf of the user to some other COM objects located in local and remote systems. In this case, the WMI providers may refuse to perform certain operations, or they may return an incomplete set of information because the impersonation level is not sufficient. By default, WMI allows DCOM objects to use the credentials of the user. But some situations may require that DCOM objects use anonymous authentication or query the credentials of the user. The impersonation level determines how WMI must behave in regard to the user credentials. The impersonation level can have four different types: *Anonymous, Identify, Impersonate* (the default), and *Delegate.* To specify the impersonation level in the moniker, the previous string

```
WinMgmts:Root\CIMv2:Win32_Service.name='SNMP'
```

must be changed to

```
WinMgmts:{impersonationLevel=impersonate}!Root\CIMv2:Win32_Service.name='SNMP'
```

Table 4.2   *The WMI authentication levels*

Moniker Name	Scripting API Contants	Value	Description
Default	wbemAuthenticationLevelDefault	0	WMI uses the default Windows Authentication setting
None	wbemAuthenticationLevelNone	1	Uses no authentication
Connect	WbemAuthenticationLevelConnect	2	Authenticates the credentials of the client only when the client establishes a relationship with the server
Call	WbemAuthenticationLevelCall	3	Authenticates only at the beginning of each call when the server receives the request
Pkt	WbemAuthenticationLevelPkt	4	Authenticates that all data received is from the expected client
PktIntegrity	WbemAuthenticationLevelPktIntegrity	5	Authenticates and verifies that none of the data transferred between client and server has been modified
PktPrivacy	WbemAuthenticationLevelPktPrivacy	6	Authenticates all previous impersonation levels and encrypts the argument value of each remote procedure call

By default, the impersonation level under Windows NT 4.0, Windows 2000, Windows XP, and Windows.NET Server is set in the registry to *Impersonate* (see Figure 4.1). Earlier versions of WMI for Windows NT 4.0 installed with WMI 1.1 used an

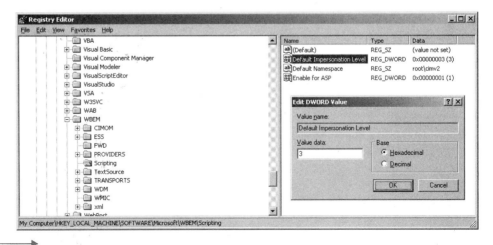

Figure 4.1   *The default impersonation level.*

impersonation level set to *Identify*. This implies that this setting is not required any more in the moniker. The default impersonation level is sufficient to perform most WMI operations.

However, it is a good practice to specify the impersonation level from the script to avoid any side effects due to the default value modification. Refer to Table 4.3 for the list of impersonation levels and their related meanings.

3.   **Privileges:** To perform some WMI operations, it is sometimes required to provide some privileges. For instance, with WMI, it is possible to shut down a system or read the content of the NT Security Event Log. Without mentioning any privileges, these operations will fail. To specify privileges in the moniker, the moniker must be changed to

```
WinMgmts:{impersonationLevel=impersonate,(RemoteShutdown)}!Root\CIMv2:Win32_Service.name='SNMP'
```

Alternatively, it is possible to reset privileges. In this case, use the following moniker:

```
WinMgmts:{impersonationLevel=impersonate,(!RemoteShutdown)}!Root\CIMv2:Win32_Service.name='SNMP'
```

The "!" provides the negation of the privilege. Of course, the moniker can also include the privilege only:

```
WinMgmts:{(RemoteShutdown)}!Root\CIMv2:Win32_Service.name='SNMP'
```

Table 4.3   *The WMI Impersonation Levels*

Moniker Name	Scripting API Contants	Value	Description
Anonymous	wbemImpersonationLevelAnonymous	1	Hides the credentials of the caller. Calls to WMI may fail with this impersonation level.
Identify	wbemImpersonationLevelIdentify	2	Allows objects to query the credentials of the caller. Calls to WMI may fail with this impersonation level.
Impersonate	wbemImpersonationLevelImpersonate	3	Allows objects to use the credentials of the caller. This is the recommended impersonation level for WMI Scripting API calls.
Delegate	wbemImpersonationLevelDelegate	4	Allows objects to permit other objects to use the credentials of the caller. This impersonation, which will work with WMI Scripting API calls but may constitute an unnecessary security risk, is supported only under Windows_2000.

If several privileges must be set, the moniker will look as follows:

```
WinMgmts:{(RemoteShutdown, Security)}!Root\CIMv2:Win32_Service.name='SNMP'
```

Refer to Table 4.4 for the list of privilege levels and their related meanings.

When working with privileges, it is important to consider the Windows platform used. Under Windows 2000 and Windows.NET Server, privileges can be set or revoked at any time. Under Windows NT 4.0, the privileges must be set at connection time with the WMI system or when using the moniker string. Under Windows 95, Windows 98, and Windows Millennium, privileges can be set, but they do not have any effect.

The authentication type can also be specified with the authority parameter. In this case, the moniker not only specifies the authentication protocol to use (NTLM or Kerberos), it also mentions the authority. For a Kerberos authentication, the moniker is

```
WinMgmts:{authority=kerberos:MyDomain\RemoteServer}!\\RemoteServer\Root\CIMv2:Win32_Service.name='SNMP'
```

For NTLM, the moniker is

```
WinMgmts:{authority=ntlmdomain:MyDomain}!\\RemoteServer\Root\CIMv2:Win32_Service.name='SNMP'
```

The authority parameter can be used only with remote WMI connections. If it is used to connect locally, the operation will fail. This is the reason for the *RemoteServer* name addition in the WMI object path.

Even if it is possible to simplify the moniker string by assuming some system defaults, it is recommended to specify the defaults to avoid any surprises when running scripts with other systems. For instance, the minimal moniker string with the namespace, the impersonation level, and the authentication level to obtain a class instance is

```
WinMgmts:{impersonationLevel=impersonate,AuthenticationLevel=default}!Root\CIMv2:Win32_Service
```

4.3.4   The localization string of the moniker

The last element of information included in a moniker is the localization string. In Chapter 2, we saw that some namespaces have a child namespace containing a language-specific version of the classes. When opening a language-specific class, WMI combines the language-neutral definition with the language-specific definition to provide the localized version of the class. To obtain the localized version of an object, information must be added to

Table 4.4   *The WMI Privileges*

Moniker Name	Privilege String	Scripting API Contants	Value	Description
CreateToken	SeCreateTokenPrivilege	wbemPrivilegeCreateToken	1	Required to create a primary token.
PrimaryToken	SeAssignPrimaryTokenPrivilege	wbemPrivilegePrimaryToken	2	Required to assign the primary token of a process.
LockMemory	SeLockMemoryPrivilege	wbemPrivilegeLockMemory	3	Required to lock physical pages in memory.
IncreaseQuota	SeIncreaseQuotaPrivilege	wbemPrivilegeIncreaseQuota	4	Required to increase the quota assigned to a process.
MachineAccount	SeMachineAccountPrivilege	wbemPrivilegeMachineAccount	5	Required to create a machine account.
Tcb	SeTcbPrivilege	wbemPrivilegeTcb	6	Identifies its holder as part of the trusted computer base. Some trusted, protected subsystems are granted this privilege.
Security	SeSecurityPrivilege	wbemPrivilegeSecurity	7	Required to perform a number of security-related functions, such as controlling and viewing audit messages. This privilege identifies its holder as a security operator.
TakeOwnership	SeTakeOwnershipPrivilege	wbemPrivilegeTakeOwnership	8	Required to take ownership of an object without being granted discretionary access. This privilege allows the owner value to be set only to those values that the holder may legitimately assign as the owner of an object.
LoadDriver	SeLoadDriverPrivilege	wbemPrivilegeLoadDriver	9	Required to load or unload a device driver.
SystemProfile	SeSystemProfilePrivilege	wbemPrivilegeSystemProfile	10	Required to gather profiling information for the entire system.
Systemtime	SeSystemtimePrivilege	wbemPrivilegeSystemtime	11	Required to modify the system time.
ProfileSingleProcess	SeProfileSingleProcessPrivilege	wbemPrivilegeProfileSingleProcess	12	Required to gather profiling information for a single process.

Table 4.4 *The WMI Privileges (continued)*

Moniker Name	Privilege Sstring	Scripting API Contants	Value	Description
IncreaseBasePriority	SeIncreaseBasePriorityPrivilege	wbemPrivilegeIncreaseBasePriority	13	Required to increase the base priority of a process.
CreatePagefile	SeCreatePagefilePrivilege	wbemPrivilegeCreatePagefile	14	Required to create a paging file.
CreatePermanent	SeCreatePermanentPrivilege	wbemPrivilegeCreatePermanent	15	Required to create a permanent object.
Backup	SeBackupPrivilege	wbemPrivilegeBackup	16	Required to perform backup operations.
Restore	SeRestorePrivilege	wbemPrivilegeRestore	17	Required to perform restore operations. This privilege enables you to set any valid user or group SID as the owner of an object.
Shutdown	SeShutdownPrivilege	wbemPrivilegeShutdown	18	Required to shut down a local system.
Debug	SeDebugPrivilege	wbemPrivilegeDebug	19	Required to debug a process.
Audit	SeAuditPrivilege	wbemPrivilegeAudit	20	Required to generate audit-log entries.
SystemEnvironment	SeSystemEnvironmentPrivilege	wbemPrivilegeSystemEnvironment	21	Required to modify the nonvolatile RAM of systems that use this type of memory to store configuration information.
ChangeNotify	SeChangeNotifyPrivilege	wbemPrivilegeChangeNotify	22	causes the system to skip all traversal access checks. It is enabled by default for all users.
RemoteShutdown	SeRemoteShutdownPrivilege	wbemPrivilegeRemoteShutdown	23	Required to shut down a system using a network request.
Undock	SeUndockPrivilege	wbemPrivilegeUndock	24	Required to remove computer from docking station.
SyncAgent	SeSyncAgentPrivilege	wbemPrivilegeSyncAgent	25	Required to synchronize directory service data.
EnableDelegation	SeEnableDelegationPrivilege	wbemPrivilegeEnableDelegation	26	Required to enable computer and user accounts to be trusted for delegation.

the moniker to specify that the localized version of the class must be used. In this case, the moniker becomes

```
WinMgmts:[locale=ms_409]!Root\CIMv2:Win32_Service='SNMP'
```

where the **ms_409** specifies the U.S. language localized version.

4.3.5   A first script sample using the WMI moniker

Sample 4.1 shows a VBScript sample listing the properties of a *Win32_Service* instance called "SNMP." The moniker has been adapted to put the miscellaneous parameters in VBScript constants (lines 18 to 28). From lines 30 to 55, the script displays the properties of the WMI object instance set at line 25 with the moniker.

Sample 4.1   *A VBScript listing the Win32_Service instance properties*

```
 1:<?xml version="1.0"?>
 .:
 8:<package>
 9:  <job>
..:
13:    <script language="VBscript">
14:    <![CDATA[
..:
18:    Const cComputerName = "LocalHost"
19:    Const cWMINameSpace = "root/cimv2"
20:    Const cWMIClass     = "Win32_Service"
21:    Const cWMIInstance  = "SNMP"
..:
25:    Set objWMIInstance = GetObject("winmgmts:{impersonationLevel=impersonate}!//" & _
26:                                    cComputerName & "/" & _
27:                                    cWMINameSpace & ":" & _
28:                                    cWMIClass & ".Name='" & cWMIInstance & "'")
29:
30:    WScript.Echo objWMIInstance.Name & " (" & objWMIInstance.Description & ")"
31:    WScript.Echo "    AcceptPause=" & objWMIInstance.AcceptPause
32:    WScript.Echo "    AcceptStop=" & objWMIInstance.AcceptStop
33:    WScript.Echo "    Caption=" & objWMIInstance.Caption
34:    WScript.Echo "    CheckPoint=" & objWMIInstance.CheckPoint
35:    WScript.Echo "    CreationClassName=" & objWMIInstance.CreationClassName
36:    WScript.Echo "    Description=" & objWMIInstance.Description
37:    WScript.Echo "    DesktopInteract=" & objWMIInstance.DesktopInteract
38:    WScript.Echo "    DisplayName=" & objWMIInstance.DisplayName
39:    WScript.Echo "    ErrorControl=" & objWMIInstance.ErrorControl
40:    WScript.Echo "    ExitCode=" & objWMIInstance.ExitCode
41:    WScript.Echo "    InstallDate=" & objWMIInstance.InstallDate
42:    WScript.Echo "    Name=" & objWMIInstance.Name
43:    WScript.Echo "    PathName=" & objWMIInstance.PathName
44:    WScript.Echo "    ProcessId=" & objWMIInstance.ProcessId
45:    WScript.Echo "    ServiceSpecificExitCode=" & objWMIInstance.ServiceSpecificExitCode
46:    WScript.Echo "    ServiceType=" & objWMIInstance.ServiceType
47:    WScript.Echo "    Started=" & objWMIInstance.Started
48:    WScript.Echo "    StartMode=" & objWMIInstance.StartMode
```

```
49:      WScript.Echo "    StartName=" & objWMIInstance.StartName
50:      WScript.Echo "    State=" & objWMIInstance.State
51:      WScript.Echo "    Status=" & objWMIInstance.Status
52:      WScript.Echo "    SystemCreationClassName=" & objWMIInstance.SystemCreationClassName
53:      WScript.Echo "    SystemName=" & objWMIInstance.SystemName
54:      WScript.Echo "    TagId=" & objWMIInstance.TagId
55:      WScript.Echo "    WaitHint=" & objWMIInstance.WaitHint
..:
59:      ]]>
60:      </script>
61:   </job>
62:</packages>
```

As we have seen in this section, the moniker offers many combinations. These combinations are summarized in generic notation as follows:

```
"WinMgmts:" securitySetting ["[" localeSetting "]"] ["!" objectPath]
Or,
"WinMgmts:" "[" localeSetting "]" ["!" objectPath]
Or,
"WinMgmts:" [objectPath]

Where: localeSetting : "locale" "=" localeID
|
Where: localeID      : a value of the form "ms_xxxx" where xxxx is a hex LCID value (e.g. "ms_409")
|
Where: objectPath    : a valid WMI Object Path
|
Where: securitySetting is equal to:
   |
   |  "{" authAndImpersonSettings [ "," privilegeOverrides] "}"
   |  Or,
   |  "{" privilegeOverrides "}"
   |
   Where: authAndImpersonSettings is equal to:
   |  |
   |  |  authenticationLevel
   |  |  Or,
   |  |  impersonationLevel
   |  |  Or,
   |  |  authority
   |  |  Or,
   |  |  authenticationLevel "," impersonationLevel [ "," authority]
   |  |  Or,
   |  |  authenticationLevel "," authority [ "," impersonationLevel]
   |  |  Or,
   |  |  impersonationLevel "," authenticationLevel [ "," authority]
   |  |  Or,
   |  |  impersonationLevel "," authority [ "," authenticationLevel]
   |  |  Or,
   |  |  authority "," impersonationLevel [ "," authenticationLevel]
   |  |  Or,
   |  |  authority "," authenticationLevel [ "," impersonationLevel]
   |  |
   |  Where: authority : "authority" "=" authorityValue
   |  |  |
   |  |  +-- Where: authorityValue : "kerberos:mydomain\RemoteServer" | "ntlmdomain:mydomain".
   |  |
   |  Where: authenticationLevel : "authenticationLevel" "=" authenticationValue
```

```
|   |   |
|   |   +-- Where: authenticationValue : "default" |
|   |                                    "none" |
|   |                                    "connect" |
|   |                                    "call" |
|   |                                    "pkt" |
|   |                                    "pktIntegrity" |
|   |                                    "pktPrivacy"
|   |
|   Where: impersonationLevel : "impersonationLevel" "=" impersonationValue
|       |
|       +-- Where: impersonationValue : "anonymous" |
|                                       "identify" |
|                                       "impersonate" |
|                                       "delegate"
|
Where: privilegeOverrides : "(" privileges ")"
    |
    +-- Where: privileges : privilege [ "," privilege [ "," privilege ]]*
            |
            +-- Where: privilege : ["!"] privilegeName
                |
                +-- Where: privilegeName is equal to:

                    "CreateToken"           | "PrimaryToken"    | "LockMemory" |
                    "IncreaseQuota"         | "MachineAccount"  | "Tcb" |
                    "Security"              | "TakeOwnership"   | "LoadDriver" |
                    "SystemProfile"         | "SystemTime"      | "ProfileSingleProcess" |
                    "IncreaseBasePriority"  | "CreatePagefile"  | "CreatePermanent" |
                    "Backup"                | "Restore"         | "Shutdown" |
                    "Debug"                 | "Audit"           | "SystemEnvironment" |
                    "ChangeNotify"          | "RemoteShutdown"  | "Udock" |
                    "SyncAgent"             | "EnableDelegation"
```

4.4   **Exploring the WMI scripting API**

In the previous paragraph, based on the moniker type provided, we saw that it is possible to obtain two different WMI objects:

1.   **SWbemObject** with the moniker

     ```
     winmgmts://NET-DPEN6400A/Root/CIMv2:Win32_Service.name="SNMP"'
     ```

     or

     ```
     winmgmts://NET-DPEN6400A/Root/CIMv2:Win32_Service
     ```

2.   **SWbemServices** with the moniker

     ```
     winmgmts://NET-DPEN6400A/Root/CIMv2
     ```

These two objects are part of the WMI scripting API. The WMI scripting API is a collection of COM objects enabling a script writer to read or write information and perform various operations with WMI and the real-world manageable entities that the CIM repository represents. The WMI scripting object model exposes two different natures of objects that can be categorized as follows:

1.   Single objects

2.   Collections of objects

The nature of the object desired determines the way the object is instantiated. There are two different ways to instantiate objects with WMI:

1.   Using a language statement to create an object with the COM ProgID. Based on the script language used, the script code will use a **CreateObject** for VBScript, a **new ActiveXObject** for JScript, or an XML <Object> tag in an ASP page or a Windows Script File.

2.   Using the WMI moniker with the **GetObject** statement for VBScript or JScript.

The different object natures with their associated instantiation methods are summarized in Figure 4.2 as represented by the Microsoft SDK.

Symbols are used to differentiate the objects. In the following sections, we examine the WMI scripting API object model tree and explain the relationship between the various objects. The symbols will help to locate objects and determine how they can be instantiated. By using different small pieces of script, we will navigate and explore the WMI object model step by step.

Figure 4.2
Symbols used to represent the WMI object model.

 Represent a collection of objects

 Represent a collection of objects that can be created with a moniker with **GetObject**

 Represent an object

 Represent an object that can be created with a moniker with **GetObject**

 Represent an object collection that can be created using progID with **CreateObject***

 Represent an object that can be created using progID with **CreateObject***

*with *CreateObject, new ActiveObject* or the HTML *<OBJECT>* tag.

4.4.1   **Establishing the WMI connection**

To be connected to a real-world manageable entity, we must connect to the object representing that entity in the WMI object model. This represents the first step of the WMI object model discovery. The first part of the object model is represented in Figure 4.3. A circled number labels each object on the figure. This will ease the reference to and the positioning of the object in the model in the text that follows.

Any object class, object instance, or setting that can be instantiated with the moniker can also be instantiated with the scripting API. Every element that constitutes a moniker can also be represented with a WMI COM object part of the WMI scripting API. Let's start from the beginning by using a sample. When using the moniker:

```
winmgmts://NET-DPEN6400A/Root/CIMv2
```

we already have two things: a namespace and the server to connect to. By using the WMI scripting API and decomposing the moniker elements, it is

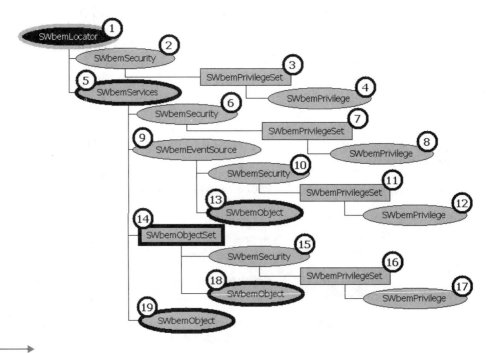

Figure 4.3   *The WMI object model (1/3).*

possible to perform the same operation. In other words, a script using this moniker

```
Set objWMIServices = GetObject ("winmgmts://NET-DPEN6400A/Root/CIMv2")
```

is equal to the following script:

```
 . :
 7:Set objWMILocator = CreateObject("WbemScripting.SWbemLocator")
 . . :
14:Set objWMIServices = objWMILocator.ConnectServer("NET-DPEN6400A", "Root\CIMv2", "", "")
```

The main difference is that there is no longer a moniker string, but the **objWMIServices** is obtained with the WMI scripting API by creating an **SWbemLocator** object (line 7) and using its *ConnectServer* method (line 14). The result of the method gives an **SWbemServices** object (line 14). The **SWbemLocator** is the first object to be created and is represented by the number 1 in Figure 4.3.

One interesting aspect of the **SWbemLocator** object is the possibility to specify other credentials and a localization string (i.e., ms_409) in the parameters of its *ConnectServer* methods. If your script must specify credentials to establish the connection, there is no alternative to using the **SWbemLocator** object because this is not supported by the WMI moniker.

The **SWbemLocator** object properties and methods are given in Table 4.5. In the table we see that a security property is available. This property can be used to set the same security settings as those set when using the moniker. For instance, in the moniker samples we saw in Section 4.3, we set

Table 4.5 *The SWbemLocator Object*

SWbemLocator			
Properties	Security_		Used to read or change the security settings.
Methods	ConnectServer	[strServer = ""], [strNameSpace = ""], [strUser = ""], [strPassword = ""], [strLocale = ""], [strAuthority = ""], [intSecurityFlags = 0], [objjwbemNamedValueSet = null]	Connects to WMI on the specified computer.

three different things: the impersonation level, the authentication method, and some privileges. In this case the moniker is as follows:

```
WinMgmts:{impersonationLevel=impersonate, AuthenticationLevel=default,
                            (RemoteShutdown, Security)}!\\NET-DPEN6400A\Root\CIMv2
```

How do we set the security settings used in the moniker via the scripting API? By referencing the *security_* property of the **SWbemLocator** object, it is possible to retrieve the **SWbemSecurity** object. In this case, the script creates the object represented by the number 2 in Figure 4.3. The code is as follows:

```
 .:
 7:Set objWMILocator = CreateObject("WbemScripting.SWbemLocator")
 8:Set objWMISecurity = objWMILocator.Security_
 ..:
14:Set objWMIServices = objWMILocator.ConnectServer("NET-DPEN6400A", "Root\CIMv2", "", "")
```

The **SWbemSecurity** object (line 8) exposes three properties (see Table 4.6) that correspond to the three security settings available from DCOM: authentication level, impersonation level, and the privileges.

Each of these settings can receive an assignment with a WMI constant from Table 4.2 for the authentication setting, Table 4.3 for the impersonation setting, and Table 4.4 for the privilege settings, respectively. The code is as follows:

```
 1:Const wbemImpersonationLevelImpersonate = 3
 2:Const wbemAuthenticationLevelDefault = 0
 3:
 4:Const wbemPrivilegeSecurity = 7
 5:Const wbemPrivilegeRemoteShutdown = 23
 6:
 7:Set objWMILocator = CreateObject("WbemScripting.SWbemLocator")
 8:Set objWMISecurity = objWMILocator.Security_
 9:objWMISecurity.AuthenticationLevel = wbemAuthenticationLevelDefault
10:objWMISecurity.ImpersonationLevel = wbemImpersonationLevelImpersonate
11:Set objWMIPrivilegeSet = objWMISecurity.Privileges
 ..:
14:Set objWMIServices = objWMILocator.ConnectServer("NET-DPEN6400A", "Root\CIMv2", "", "")
```

Table 4.6   *The SWbemSecurity Object*

SWbemSecurity		
Properties	AuthenticationLevel	Numeric value that defines the DCOM Authentication level assigned to this object. This setting determines how you protect information sent from WMI.
	ImpersonationLevel	Numeric value that defines the DCOM Impersonation level assigned to this object. This setting determines if processes owned by WMI can detect or use your security credentials when making calls to other processes.
	Privileges	An SWbemPrivilegeSet object that defines the Windows_NT/ Windows_2000 Privileges for this object.

Table 4.7   *The SWbemPrivilegeSet Object*

SWbemPrivilegeSet		
Properties	Count	The number of items in the collection.
Methods	Add intPrivilege, [boolIsEnabled = True]	Adds an SWbemPrivilege object to the SWbemPrivilegeSet collection using a WbemPrivilegeEnum constant.
	AddAsString strPrivilege, [boolIsEnabled = True]	Adds an SWbemPrivilege object to the SWbemPrivilegeSet collection using a Windows_NT/Windows_2000 privilege string.
	Item intPrivilege	Retrieves an SWbemPrivilege object from the collection. This is the default method of this object.
	DeleteAll ()	Deletes all the privileges from the collection.
	Remove intPrivilege	Removes an SWbemPrivilege object from the collection.

As we can see, the privileges property from the **SWbemSecurity** object does not take a constant as parameter, but retrieves another object (line 11). The obtained object is called **SWbemPrivilegeSet** and exposes one property and several methods to set the privileges (see Table 4.7). In the next sample, lines 12 and 13 add two privileges to the **SWbemPrivilegeSet** collection. The **SWbemPrivilegeSet** object in the WMI object model is represented by the number 3 in Figure 4.3. So, the script becomes

```
 1:Const wbemImpersonationLevelImpersonate = 3
 2:Const wbemAuthenticationLevelDefault = 0
 3:
 4:Const wbemPrivilegeSecurity = 7
 5:Const wbemPrivilegeRemoteShutdown = 23
 6:
 7:Set objWMILocator = CreateObject("WbemScripting.SWbemLocator")
 8:Set objWMISecurity = objWMILocator.Security_
 9:objWMISecurity.AuthenticationLevel = wbemAuthenticationLevelDefault
10:objWMISecurity.ImpersonationLevel = wbemImpersonationLevelImpersonate
11:Set objWMIPrivilegeSet = objWMISecurity.Privileges
12:objWMIPrivilegeSet.Add wbemPrivilegeRemoteShutdown, True
13:objWMIPrivilegeSet.Add wbemPrivilegeSecurity, True
14:Set objWMIServices = objWMILocator.ConnectServer("NET-DPEN6400A", "Root\CIMv2", "", "")
```

Each privilege addition represents an **SWbemPrivilege** object in the collection contained in **SWbemPrivilegeSet** object. The **SWbemPrivilege** object is represented by the number 4 in Figure 4.3. We can see that **SWbemPrivilege** is a child object of **SWbemPrivilegeSet**, which is in turn a child object of the **SWbemSecurity** object. The final script, which uses the features of WSH to access the WMI Type Library and instantiate objects, is shown in Sample 4.2.

Sample 4.2   *Obtaining an SWbemServices object with the WMI scripting API and the WMI privilege constants set at the SWbemLocator object level*

```
 1:<?xml version="1.0"?>
 . :
 8:<package>
 9:  <job>
..:
13:    <object progid="WbemScripting.SWbemLocator" id="objWMILocator" reference="true"/>
14:
15:    <script language="VBscript">
16:    <![CDATA[
..:
20:    Const cComputerName = "LocalHost"
21:    Const cWMINameSpace = "root/cimv2"
..:
27:    Set objWMISecurity = objWMILocator.Security_
28:    objWMISecurity.AuthenticationLevel = wbemAuthenticationLevelDefault
29:    objWMISecurity.ImpersonationLevel = wbemImpersonationLevelImpersonate
30:    Set objWMIPrivilegeSet = objWMISecurity.Privileges
31:    objWMIPrivilegeSet.Add wbemPrivilegeRemoteShutdown, True
32:    objWMIPrivilegeSet.Add wbemPrivilegeSecurity, True
33:    Set objWMIServices = objWMILocator.ConnectServer("NET-DPEN6400A", "Root\CIMv2", "", "")
..:
39:    ]]>
40:    </script>
41:  </job>
42:</package>
```

In Sample 4.3, as an alternative to using constants for privileges (lines 31 and 32), the **SWbemSecurity** object also accepts privileges as an explicit string (see Table 4.4) by using the *AddAsString* method of the **SwbemPrivilegeSet** object.

Sample 4.3   *Obtaining an SWbemServices object with the WMI scripting API and the WMI privilege strings set at the SWbemLocator object level*

```
 1:<?xml version="1.0"?>
 . :
 8:<package>
 9:  <job>
..:
13:    <object progid="WbemScripting.SWbemLocator" id="objWMILocator" reference="true"/>
14:
15:    <script language="VBscript">
16:    <![CDATA[
..:
20:    Const cComputerName = "LocalHost"
21:    Const cWMINameSpace = "root/cimv2"
..:
27:    Set objWMISecurity = objWMILocator.Security_
28:    objWMISecurity.AuthenticationLevel = wbemAuthenticationLevelDefault
29:    objWMISecurity.ImpersonationLevel = wbemImpersonationLevelImpersonate
30:    Set objWMIPrivilegeSet = objWMISecurity.Privileges
31:    objWMIPrivilegeSet.AddAsString "SeRemoteShutdownPrivilege", True
```

```
32:      objWMIPrivilegeSet.AddAsString "SeSecurityPrivilege", True
33:      Set objWMIServices = objWMILocator.ConnectServer(cComputerName, cWMINameSpace, "", "")
..:
39:      ]]>
40:      </script>
41:   </job>
42:</package>
```

The last two samples use the WMI scripting API and are equivalent to the following moniker sample shown in Sample 4.4.

Sample 4.4   *Obtaining an SWbemServices object with the WMI moniker*

```
 1:<?xml version="1.0"?>
 .:
 8:<package>
 9:   <job>
..:
13:      <script language="VBscript">
14:      <![CDATA[
..:
18:      Const cComputerName = "LocalHost"
19:      Const cWMINameSpace = "root/cimv2"
..:
23:      Set objWMIServices = GetObject("WinMgmts:{impersonationLevel=impersonate, " & _
24:                            "AuthenticationLevel=default, " & _
25:                            "(RemoteShutdown, Security)}!\\" & _
26:                            cComputerName & "\" & cWMINameSpace)
27:      Set objWMIServices = Nothing
28:      ]]>
29:      </script>
30:   </job>
31:</package>
```

As we can see the moniker version is much more compact, which is the biggest advantage of the moniker. One single line equals almost seven lines using the WMI scripting API. When using a moniker, the script starts directly at the level of the **SWbemServices** object (number 5 in Figure 4.3); when using the WMI scripting API, it requires the script to create the **SWBemLocator** object (number 1 in Figure 4.3) and **SWbemServices** (number 5 in Figure 4.3) with the associated security objects (numbers 2, 3, and 4 in Figure 4.3). Of course, if the script requires credentials to run in a different security context than the current user security context, the script must use the **SWbemLocator** object and the subsequent logic as shown in Sample 4.2 ("Obtaining an SWbemServices object with the WMI scripting API and the WMI privilege constants set at the SWbemLocator object level").

Although both samples produce the same **SWbemServices** object, there is an important difference between Sample 4.3 ("Obtaining an SWbemServices object with the WMI scripting API and the WMI privilege strings set at the SWbemLocator object level") and Sample 4.4 ("Obtaining an SWbemServices object with the WMI moniker"). The difference resides in where the security is set. Sample 4.3 sets the security at the level of the **SWbemLocator** object (lines 27 to 32) and Sample 4.4 sets the security at the level of the **SWbemServices** objects. With the WMI scripting API, the security settings can be set at different object levels. The impersonation level, the authentication level, and the privileges can be set on the **SWbemServices**, **SWbemObject**, **SWbemObjectSet**, **SWbemObjectPath**, and **SWbemLocator** objects by setting their properties to the desired values.

A script can take advantage of this possibility, but there are some restrictions when running under Windows NT regarding privileges. Under Windows NT, it is mandatory to set the privileges at connection time because privilege changes can be made only on the process security token. As the process security token is created at connection time, all the security settings are set in Sample 4.3 at the level of the **SWbemLocator** object and in Sample 4.4 at the level of the moniker creating the **SWbemServices** object. Because the connection is created with the security settings when these two objects are created, the two samples are compatible with Windows NT. Under Windows 2000, Windows XP, and Windows.NET Server, privileges can be set or removed at any time. For example, Sample 4.3 can be changed to set the privileges after establishing the connection (see Sample 4.5).

Sample 4.5   *Obtaining an SWbemServices object with the WMI scripting API and the WMI privilege strings set at the SWbemServices object level*

```
 1:<?xml version="1.0"?>
 .:
 8:<package>
 9:  <job>
..:
13:     <object progid="WbemScripting.SWbemLocator" id="objWMILocator" reference="true"/>
14:
15:     <script language="VBscript">
16:     <![CDATA[
..:
20:     Const cComputerName = "LocalHost"
21:     Const cWMINameSpace = "root/cimv2"
..:
25:     objWMILocator.Security_.AuthenticationLevel = wbemAuthenticationLevelDefault
26:     objWMILocator.Security_.ImpersonationLevel = wbemImpersonationLevelImpersonate
27:     Set objWMIServices = objWMILocator.ConnectServer(cComputerName, cWMINameSpace, "", "")
28:     objWMIServices.Security_.Privileges.AddAsString "SeRemoteShutdownPrivilege", True
29:     objWMIServices.Security_.Privileges.AddAsString "SeSecurityPrivilege", True
..:
33:     ]]>
34:     </script>
35:  </job>
36:</package>
```

In this sample, the privileges are set at the level of the **SWbemServices** object (lines 28 and 29) once the connection has been created (line 27). Valid under Windows 2000, Windows XP, or Windows.NET Server, this will not set the expected privileges under Windows NT because the privileges are set after establishing the connection (line 27).

The ability to set the security settings at the level of the **SWbemServices** object is represented by the numbers 6, 7, and 8 in the object model shown in Figure 4.3. You will also notice that it is possible to combine the object assignments in one line instead of creating an intermediate security object to assign authentication level (line 25), impersonation level (line 26), or privileges (lines 28 and 29). Once completed, the **SWbemServices** object obtained is the same as in previous samples (if running under Windows 2000, Windows XP, or Windows.NET Server).

4.4.2   Retrieving WMI objects

At this stage of the script, the WMI namespace is opened (i.e., **Root\ CIMv2**). The **SWbemServices** object provides access to the namespace regardless of how the object was retrieved (moniker or scripting API). From this point, it is possible to instantiate a WMI class representing a real-world manageable object. An **SWbemObject** object in the script can represent this real-world manageable object. In the WMI object model (Figure 4.3) numbers 13, 18, and 19 locate the **SWbemObject** object. As we can see, different WMI scripting objects can produce the **SWbemObject** object based on the initial WMI object (the parent object), methods, and parameters used. The WMI scripting objects that can be used to create an **SWbemObject** are the **SWbemServices** object (number 5), the **SWbemObjectSet** object (number 14), or the **SWbemEventSource** object (number 9). Whatever the technique used to retrieve the **SWbemObject** object, at this stage of the discovery the retrieved **SWbemObject** object is always the same. If we look at the last script samples (Samples 4.2 to 4.5), we are at the level of the **SWbemServices** object and use its exposed methods to create an **SWbem-Object** object.

As a first step, we examine how an **SWbemObject** object can be retrieved synchronously. "Synchronously" means that the code retrieving the **SWbemObject** waits for the retrieval operation to complete. In the next chapter we see that it is possible to retrieve an **SWbemObject** asynchronously, which means that the retrieval process is executed in parallel and the script does not wait for the operation to complete. Synchronously or asynchronously, the object method retrieval produces an **SWbemObject** object or an **SWbemObjectSet** object from **SWbemServices** object (number 5).

The **SWbemEventSource** object also produces an **SWbemObject** object, but only in the context of a WMI event. The WMI events scripting technique is examined in Chapter 6 of this book.

Now, what type of WMI objects can we obtain? The nature of the retrieved object can be a single class (in which case it is a single **SWbem-Object** object as represented by number 19 in Figure 4.3), a class collection (in which case it is a **SWbemObjectSet** collection object as represented by number 14 in Figure 4.3), an instance (again an **SWbemObject** object), or an instance collection (again an **SWbemObjectSet** object). In addition to retrieving classes or instances from a WMI class (i.e., *Win32_Service*), it is also possible to retrieve a collection of classes or instances that are associated, referenced, or inherited from the specified class name or instance name. To retrieve a WMI object, an **SWbemService** object method can be used. It is also possible to use a WQL query entered in a specific **SWbem-Service** object method.

The properties and methods of the **SWbemServices** object are shown in Table 4.8. The content of this table will be examined in the rest of this section.

To retrieve an **SWbemObject** object, many methods exposed by **SWbemServices** can be used, but the easiest one to start with is the *Get* method. The next line of code is:

```
Set objWMIInstance = objWMIServices.Get ("Win32_Service")
```

This line will retrieve the class instance of *Win32_Service* from the CIM repository. If the line is changed as follows:

```
Set objWMIInstance = objWMIServices.Get ("Win32_Service='SNMP'")
```

the script line retrieves an instance of the SNMP service. Note that you can combine the moniker creating the **SWbemService** with its associated method. If Sample 4.4 ("Obtaining an SWbemServices object with the WMI moniker") is modified, the line creating the moniker can be changed to

```
Set objWMIInstance = GetObject("WinMgmts:{impersonationLevel=impersonate, " & _
                               "AuthenticationLevel=default, " & _
                               "(RemoteShutdown, Security)}!\\" & _
                               cComputerName & "\" & cWMINameSpace).Get _
                               (cWMIClass & "='" & cWMIInstance & "'")
```

In such a case, the object returned by the combined use of the moniker and the **SWbemServices** *Get* method is also an instance of the SNMP service. Both ways are valid and return exactly the same object. The moniker creates an **SWbemServices** object, and, on the same line, the *Get* method is invoked. So, before diving deeper into the exploration of the **SWbemServices**

Table 4.8   *The SWbemServices Object*

SWbemServices (with SWbemServicesEx)

Properties	*Security_*	Used to read or change the security settings.

Methods	AssociatorsOf strObjectPath,
	   [strAssocClass = ""],
	   [strResultClass = ""],
	   [strResultRole = ""],
	   [strRole = ""],
	   [boolClassesOnly = FALSE],
	   [boolSchemaOnly = FALSE],
	   [strRequiredAssocQualifier = ""],
	   [strRequiredQualifier = ""],
	   [intFlags = wbemFlagReturnImmediately],
	   [objwbemNamedValueSet = null]
		Returns a collection of objects (classes or instances) that are associated with a specified object. This method performs the same function that the ASSOCIATORS OF WQL query performs.

	AssociatorsOfAsync objWbemSink,
	   strObjectPath,
	   [strAssocClass = ""],
	   [strResultClass = ""],
	   [strResultRole = ""],
	   [strRole = ""],
	   [boolClassesOnly = FALSE],
	   [boolSchemaOnly = FALSE],
	   [strRequiredAssocQualifier = ""],
	   [strRequiredQualifier = ""],
	   [intFlags = wbemFlagDontSendStatus],
	   [objWbemNamedValueSet = null],
	   [objWbemAsyncContext = null]
		Asynchronously returns a collection of objects (classes or instances) that are associated with a specified object. This method performs the same function that the ASSOCIATORS OF WQL query performs.

	Delete strObjectPath,
	   [intFlags = 0],
	   [objWbemNamedValueSet = null]
		Deletes an instance or class.

Table 4.8   *The SWbemServices Object (continued)*

SWbemServices (with SWbemServicesEx)

Methods (cont'd.)	DeleteAsync [objWbemSink = null], strObjectPath, [intFlags = 0], [objWbemNamedValueSet = null], [objWbemAsyncContext = null]	Asynchronously deletes an instance or class.
	ExecMethod strObjectPath, strMethodName, [objWbemInParams = null], [intFlags = 0], [objWbemNamedValueSet = null]	Executes an object method.
	ExecMethodAsync objWbemSink, strObjectPath, strMethodName, [objWbemInParams = null], [intFlags = 0], [objWbemNamedValueSet = null], [objWbemAsyncContext = null]	Asynchronously executes an object method.
	ExecNotificationQuery strQuery, [strQueryLanguage = "WQL"], [intFlags = (wbemFlagForwardOnly + wbemFlagReturnImmediately)], [objWbemNamedValueSet = null]	Executes a query to receive events.
	ExecNotificationQueryAsync objWbemSink, strQuery, [strQueryLanguage = "WQL"], [intFlags = 0], [objwbemNamedValueSet = null], [objWbemAsyncContext = null]	Asynchronously executes a query to receive events.
	ExecQuery strQuery, [strQueryLanguage = "WQL"], [intFlags = wbemFlagReturnImmediately], [objWbemNamedValueSet = null]	Executes a query to retrieve a collection of objects (classes or instances).

Table 4.8   *The SWbemServices Object (continued)*

SWbemServices (with SWbemServicesEx)

Methods *(cont'd.)*		
ExecQueryAsync [objWbemSink], strQuery, [strQueryLanguage = "WQL"], [intFlags], [objwbemNamedValueSet = null], [objWbemAsyncContext = null]	Asynchronously executes a query to retrieve a collection of objects (classes or instances).
Get [strObjectPath = ""], [intFlags = 0], [objWbemNamedValueSet = null]	Retrieves a class or instance.
GetAsync objWbemSink = null, [strObjectPath = ""], [intFlags = 0], [objwbemNamedValueSet = null], [objWbemAsyncContext = null]	Asynchronously retrieves a class or instance.
InstancesOf strClass, [intFlags = wbemFlagReturnImmediately], [objWbemNamedValueSet = null]	Returns a collection of instances of a specified class.
InstancesOfAsync objWbemSink, strClass, [intFlags], [objWbemNamedValueSet = null], [objWbemAsyncContext = null]	Asynchronously returns a collection of instances of a specified class.
Put objWbemObject, [intFlags = 0], [objWbemNamedValueSet = null]	Saves the object to the namespace bound to the SWbemServicesEx object.
PutAsync objWbemSink, ojBWbemObject, [intFlags = 0], [objWbemNamedValueSet = null], [objWbemAsyncContext = null]	Saves the object to the namespace bound to the SWbemServicesEx object asynchronously.

Table 4.8   *The SWbemServices Object (continued)*

SWbemServices (with SWbemServicesEx)

Methods (*cont'd.*)	ReferencesTo strObjectPath, 　　　　[strResultClass = ""], 　　　　[strRole = ""], 　　　　[boolClassesOnly = FALSE], 　　　　[boolSchemaOnly = FALSE], 　　　　[strRequiredQualifier = ""], 　　　　[intFlags = wbemFlagReturnImmediately], 　　　　[objWbemNamedValueSet = null]	Returns a collection of objects (classes or instances) that refer to a single object. This method performs the same function that the REFERENCES OF WQL query performs.
	ReferencesToAsync objWbemSink, 　　　　strObjectPath, 　　　　[strResultClass = ""], 　　　　[strRole = ""], 　　　　[boolClassesOnly = FALSE], 　　　　[boolSchemaOnly = FALSE], 　　　　[strRequiredQualifier = ""], 　　　　[intFlags], 　　　　[objWbemNamedValueSet = null], 　　　　[objWbemAsyncContext = null]	Asynchronously returns a collection of objects (classes or instances) that refer to a single object. This method performs the same function that the REFERENCES OF WQL query performs.
	SubclassesOf [strSuperclass = ""], 　　　　[intFlags = wbemFlagReturnImmediately+wbemQueryFlagDeep], 　　　　[objWbemNamedValueSet = null]	Returns a collection of subclasses of a specified class.
	SubclassesOfAsync objWbemSink, 　　　　[strSuperclass = ""], 　　　　[intFlags = wbemQueryFlagDeep], 　　　　[objwbemNamedValueSet = null], 　　　　[objWbemAsyncContext]	Asynchronously returns a collection of subclasses of a specified class.

methods, keep in mind that the **SWbemServices** object creation can be achieved with the moniker and that you can combine any of the methods exposed by the **SWbemServices** object.

The same rule applies for the **SWbemObject** object. This may seem very detailed, but sometimes it can be easier to code such a combination than to use the explicit WMI scripting API objects to create the **SWbemServices** object, as in Sample 4.3 ("Obtaining an SWbemServices object with the WMI scripting API and the WMI privilege strings set at the SWbemLocator object level") and Sample 4.5 ("Obtaining an SWbemServices object with the WMI scripting API and the WMI privilege strings set at the SWbemServices object level"). From this point of view, WMI scripting is very versatile and offers many ways to code a script to access information.

If instead of using the line:

```
Set objWMIInstance = objWMIServices.Get ("Win32_Service='SNMP'")
```

the script uses the line:

```
Set objWMIInstances = objWMIServices.InstancesOf ("Win32_Service")
```

Then, the script retrieves a collection of instances from the *Win32_Service* class represented by the **SWbemObjectSet** (number 14 in Figure 4.3). So, instead of retrieving one instance as the SNMP service (an **SWbemObject** located by number 19 in Figure 4.3), the *InstancesOf* method returns a list of all *Win32_Service* instances available in a Windows system. Sample 4.1 ("A VBScript listing the Win32_Service instance properties"), shown at the beginning of this chapter, lists the properties of the SNMP service. Now, because the returned object is a collection, a small adaptation with a For Each loop lists the properties of all Windows services. Sample 4.6 shows the script logic.

Sample 4.6   *Retrieving all instances of the Win32_Service class with their properties*

```
 1:<?xml version="1.0"?>
 .:
 8:<package>
 9:  <job>
..:
13:    <object progid="WbemScripting.SWbemLocator" id="objWMILocator" reference="true"/>
14:
15:    <script language="VBscript">
16:    <![CDATA[
..:
20:    Const cComputerName = "LocalHost"
21:    Const cWMINameSpace = "root/cimv2"
22:    Const cWMIClass = "Win32_Service"
..:
27:    objWMILocator.Security_.AuthenticationLevel = wbemAuthenticationLevelDefault
```

```
28:     objWMILocator.Security_.ImpersonationLevel = wbemImpersonationLevelImpersonate
29:     Set objWMIServices = objWMILocator.ConnectServer(cComputerName, cWMINameSpace, "", "")
30:     Set objWMIInstances = objWMIServices.InstancesOf (cWMIClass)
31:
32:     For Each objWMIInstance in objWMIInstances
33:         WScript.Echo objWMIInstance.Name & " (" & objWMIInstance.Description & ")"
34:         WScript.Echo "    AcceptPause=" & objWMIInstance.AcceptPause
35:         WScript.Echo "    AcceptStop=" & objWMIInstance.AcceptStop
36:         WScript.Echo "    Caption=" & objWMIInstance.Caption
..:
54:         WScript.Echo "    Status=" & objWMIInstance.Status
..:
59:     Next
..:
64:     ]]>
65:     </script>
66:   </job>
67:</package>
```

The *InstancesOf* method retrieves the collection. Note that using another **SWbemServices** method with a WQL query produces the same effect. So, line 30 can be changed to

```
Set objWMIInstances = objWMIServices.ExecQuery ("Select * From " & cWMIClass)
```

Previously, the script retrieved an instance of the SNMP service with the *Get* method of the **SWbemServices** object. The line using the *Get* method can also be replaced by a query returning one instance. So, the query becomes

```
Set objWMIInstances = objWMIServices.ExecQuery ("Select * From Win32_Service Where Name='SNMP'")
```

Even if there is only one instance of the SNMP service in the system, the query always returns an **SWbemObject** object collection. As usual, this collection is represented by an **SWbemObjectSet** object (number 14 in Figure 4.3). In this case, to display the properties of the SNMP service, the same tactic as used in Sample 4.6 with the For Each loop must be used. The **SWbemObjectSet** properties and methods are shown in Table 4.9. Notice that the **SWbemObjectSet** also has a security property to set the security

Table 4.9   *The SWbemObjectSet Object*

SWbemObjectSet		
Properties	Count	The number of items in the collection.
	Security	Used to read or change the security settings.
Methods	Item strObjectPath	Retrieves an SWbemObject object from the collection. This is the default method of the object.

settings. This possibility is shown in the WMI object model represented in Figure 4.3 by numbers 15, 16, and 17.

In addition to the property values retrieval of the *Win32_Service* real-world manageable object (represented by the **SWbemObject**), Table 4.1 also shows some methods associated with the *Win32_Service* class.

For an example of how to use one of the methods available from the *Win32_Service* class, imagine a script stopping a service when the service is running and starting the service when the service is stopped. This logic is implemented in Sample 4.7.

Sample 4.7   *Using one method of a Win32_Service instance directly*

```
 1:<?xml version="1.0"?>
 .:
 8:<package>
 9:   <job>
..:
13:      <object progid="WbemScripting.SWbemLocator" id="objWMILocator" reference="true"/>
14:
15:      <script language="VBscript">
16:      <![CDATA[
..:
20:      Const cComputerName = "LocalHost"
21:      Const cWMINameSpace = "root/cimv2"
22:      Const cWMIClass = "Win32_Service"
23:      Const cWMIInstance = "SNMP"
..:
29:      objWMILocator.Security_.AuthenticationLevel = wbemAuthenticationLevelDefault
30:      objWMILocator.Security_.ImpersonationLevel = wbemImpersonationLevelImpersonate
31:      Set objWMIServices = objWMILocator.ConnectServer(cComputerName, cWMINameSpace, "", "")
32:      Set objWMIInstance = objWMIServices.Get (cWMIClass & "='" & cWMIInstance & "'")
33:
34:      WScript.Echo vbCRLF & "'" & objWMIInstance.DisplayName & "' is currently " & _
35:                    objWMIInstance.State & "."
36:
37:      If objWMIInstance.State = "Stopped" Then
38:         intRC = objWMIInstance.StartService
39:         strMessage = "'" & objWMIInstance.DisplayName & "' is now Running."
40:      End If
41:      If objWMIInstance.State = "Running" Then
42:         intRC = objWMIInstance.StopService
43:         strMessage = "'" & objWMIInstance.DisplayName & "' is now Stopped ."
44:      End If
45:
46:      If intRC = 0 Then
47:         Wscript.Echo strMessage
48:      Else
49:         Wscript.Echo "Synchronous method execution failed."
50:      End If
..:
55:      ]]>
56:      </script>
57:   </job>
58:</package>
```

At lines 37 and 41, the script tests the status of the service. If the service is stopped, the script starts the service (line 38) and prepares a corresponding message (line 39). If the service is started, the script stops the service (line 42) and prepares the corresponding message (line 43). In both cases, the script tests the return code of the method execution and displays the output message accordingly (lines 46 to 50). As the method name is directly coded in the script code (lines 38 and 42), this technique refers to the direct method execution. In Section 4.4.4.4, we see another way to execute methods called indirect method execution.

4.4.3   Retrieving WMI class relationships

In Chapter 2 we saw that a class can be associated to other classes. In this case, CIM talks about association and implies the creation of references. We also saw that a class can be derived to create one or more subclasses. In such a case, there is an inheritance between classes. With the **SWbemServices** object methods, it is possible to retrieve the relations that a class has with other classes.

4.4.3.1   *The subclasses*

To retrieve the subclasses of a given class, the line invoking the **SWbemServices** method must be changed to

```
Set objWMIInstances = objWMIServices.SubClassesOf ("CIM_Service", wbemQueryFlagShallow)
```

The *CIM_Service* class is used here because the *Win32_Service* has no subclasses. In fact, the *Win32_Service* is not a direct subclass of the *CIM_Service*. *Win32_Service* is a direct subclass of *Win32_BaseService* class, and *Win32_BaseService* is a direct subclass of *CIM_Service* class. You can use the **WMI CIM Studio** tool to see this class implementation.

By default, the *SubClassesOf* method returns all the classes that are subclasses of the base class given, regardless of whether subclasses inherit directly or indirectly from the base class. To retrieve the list of classes that inherit directly from the base class only, a constant must be provided (**wbemQueryFlagShallow**) to modify the default behavior of the *SubClassesOf* method. Because the inheritance relationship between the classes in the CIM repository is arborescent, it is possible to retrieve the tree of the classes by using a recursive algorithm, as shown in Sample 4.8.

Sample 4.8   *Retrieving the class inheritance tree with the SWbemServices object*

```
 1:<?xml version="1.0"?>
 .:
 8:<package>
 9:  <job>
..:
13:     <object progid="WbemScripting.SWbemLocator" id="objWMILocator" reference="true"/>
14:
15:     <script language="VBscript">
16:     <![CDATA[
..:
20:     Const cComputerName = "LocalHost"
21:     Const cWMINameSpace = "root/cimv2"
22:     Const cWMIClass = "CIM_ManagedSystemElement"
..:
27:     objWMILocator.Security_.AuthenticationLevel = wbemAuthenticationLevelDefault
28:     objWMILocator.Security_.ImpersonationLevel = wbemImpersonationLevelImpersonate
29:     Set objWMIServices = objWMILocator.ConnectServer(cComputerName, cWMINameSpace, "", "")
30:
31:     DisplaySubClasses objWMIServices, cWMIClass
..:
35:     ' --------------------------------------------------------------------------------
36:     Function DisplaySubClasses (ByVal objWMIServices, ByVal strWMIClass)
..:
42:         Set objWMIInstances = objWMIServices.SubClassesOf (strWMIClass, wbemQueryFlagShallow)
43:
44:         WScript.Echo Space (intIndice) & strWMIClass
45:
46:         For Each objWMIInstance in objWMIInstances
47:             DisplaySubClasses objWMIServices, objWMIInstance.Path_.RelPath
48:         Next
..:
54:     End Function
55:
56:     ]]>
57:     </script>
58:  </job>
59:</package>
```

Because the script retrieves the inheritances, the code starts from the higher class available in the CIM Core Schema: *CIM_ManagedSystemElement* (see Chapter 2) defined in line 22. The script creates the **SWbemServices** object (lines 27 to 29) and calls the DisplaySubClasses() function used recursively (lines 31 and 47). In this function, the script invokes the *SubClassesOf* method exposed by the **SWbemServices** object. This retrieves an **SWbem-Object** collection contained in an **SWbemObjectSet** (line 42). If the class has some subclasses, the collection is enumerated with the For Each loop (lines 46 to 48). For each item in the collection, the function calls itself to display the related subclasses (line 44 and 47). The function that retrieves the name of the subclass uses two objects in a single line (line 47). Because each item in the collection represents an instance of the class in the **SWbemObject** object, the **SWbemObject** object exposes a property called *Path_*. This property produces a new object called **SWbemObjectPath**. This last object exposes another property called *Relpath* containing the name of the class. Later, we examine the properties and methods exposed by the **SWbemObject**. Running the script produces the following output:

```
CIM_ManagedSystemElement
  CIM_LogicalElement
  CIM_SystemResource
   CIM_IRQ
    Win32_IRQResource
   CIM_MemoryMappedIO
    Win32_SystemMemoryResource
     Win32_DeviceMemoryAddress
     Win32_PortResource
   CIM_DMA
    Win32_DMAChannel
   Win32_Environment
  CIM_System
   CIM_ComputerSystem
    CIM_UnitaryComputerSystem
     Win32_ComputerSystem
   CIM_ApplicationSystem
  CIM_Service
   CIM_ClusteringService
   CIM_BootService
   Win32_BaseService
    Win32_SystemDriver
    Win32_Service
   Win32_ApplicationService
   ...
   ...
   ...
```

This script will be the basic foundation of a script browsing the CIM repository.

4.4.3.2   The associations and the references

To retrieve the associations and the references related to the *Win32_Service*, the *AssociatorsOf* and *ReferencesTo* methods must be used. Sample 4.9 retrieves the associations from the *Win32_Service* class.

Sample 4.9   *Retrieving the class associations from the SWbemServices object for a CIM class*

```
1:<?xml version="1.0"?>
 .:
8:<package>
9:  <job>
 ..:
```

```
13:     <object progid="WbemScripting.SWbemLocator" id="objWMILocator" reference="true"/>
14:
15:     <script language="VBscript">
16:     <![CDATA[
..:
20:     Const cComputerName = "LocalHost"
21:     Const cWMINameSpace = "root/cimv2"
22:     Const cWMIClass = "Win32_Service"
..:
27:     objWMILocator.Security_.AuthenticationLevel = wbemAuthenticationLevelDefault
28:     objWMILocator.Security_.ImpersonationLevel = wbemImpersonationLevelImpersonate
29:     Set objWMIServices = objWMILocator.ConnectServer(cComputerName, cWMINameSpace, "", "")
30:     Set objWMIInstances = objWMIServices.AssociatorsOf (cWMIClass,,,,,,True)
31:
32:     For Each objWMIInstance in objWMIInstances
33:         WScript.Echo objWMIInstance.Path_ & " (" & objWMIInstance.Path_.RelPath & ")"
34:     Next
35:
36:     ]]>
37:     </script>
38:   </job>
39:</package>
```

By default, the *AssociatorsOf* method expects to have an object instance and not a class instance. Because the purpose of the script is to explore the CIM schema, a specific parameter must be given. This parameter corresponds to the True value given in the parameters of the *AssociatorsOf* method (line 30). This forces the examination of the classes instead of the instances of the classes. As a result, the CIM Schema is examined and produces the following output:

```
C:\>AssociatorsOfObjectClassWithAPI.wsf
Microsoft (R) Windows Script Host Version 5.6
Copyright (C) Microsoft Corporation 1996-2000. All rights reserved.

\\NET-DPEN6400A\ROOT\CIMV2:Win32_WMISetting (Win32_WMISetting)
\\NET-DPEN6400A\ROOT\CIMV2:Win32_ServiceSpecification (Win32_ServiceSpecification)
\\NET-DPEN6400A\ROOT\CIMV2:Win32_ComputerSystem (Win32_ComputerSystem)
```

As we can see, three classes are associated with the *Win32_Service* class: the *Win32_WMISetting*, the *Win32_ServiceSpecification*, and the *Win32_ComputerSystem*. Modifying line 30 of the previous code to use the *ReferencesTo* method to retrieve the references included in the *Win32_Service* class produces the code shown in Sample 4.10.

Sample 4.10   *Retrieving the class references from the SWbemServices object for a CIM class*

```
1:<?xml version="1.0"?>
.:
8:<package>
9:  <job>
..:
13:     <object progid="WbemScripting.SWbemLocator" id="objWMILocator" reference="true"/>
14:
```

```
15:     <script language="VBscript">
16:     <![CDATA[
..:
20:     Const cComputerName = "LocalHost"
21:     Const cWMINameSpace = "root/cimv2"
22:     Const cWMIClass = "Win32_Service"
..:
27:     objWMILocator.Security_.AuthenticationLevel = wbemAuthenticationLevelDefault
28:     objWMILocator.Security_.ImpersonationLevel = wbemImpersonationLevelImpersonate
29:     Set objWMIServices = objWMILocator.ConnectServer(cComputerName, cWMINameSpace, "", "")
30:     Set objWMIInstances = objWMIServices.ReferencesTo (cWMIClass,,,,True)
31:
32:     For Each objWMIInstance in objWMIInstances
33:         WScript.Echo objWMIInstance.Path_ & " (" & objWMIInstance.Path_.RelPath & ")"
34:     Next
35:
36:     ]]>
37:     </script>
38:   </job>
39:</package>
```

In this case the output will be

```
C:\>ReferencesOfObjectClassWithAPI.wsf
Microsoft (R) Windows Script Host Version 5.6
Copyright (C) Microsoft Corporation 1996-2000. All rights reserved.

\\NET-DPEN6400A\ROOT\CIMV2:Win32_WMIElementSetting (Win32_WMIElementSetting)
\\NET-DPEN6400A\ROOT\CIMV2:Win32_ServiceSpecificationService (Win32_ServiceSpecificationService)
\\NET-DPEN6400A\ROOT\CIMV2:Win32_SystemServices (Win32_SystemServices)
```

If you check the output for Sample 4.9 ("Retrieving the class associations from the SWbemServices object for a CIM class") and Sample 4.10 ("Retrieving the class references from the SWbemServices object for a CIM class") with the **WMI CIM Studio** tool, you will see that you retrieve the same information type when looking at the association pane of the *Win32_Service* class. The scripts retrieve the same associations and references defined with the *Win32_Service* class as seen in Section 2.9.1. If you remember, in that section, we used **WMI CIM Studio** to examine the dependencies of the MSExchangeSA service. If we modify Sample 4.9 to retrieve the associations of the *Win32_Service* MSExchangeSA instance, we obtain the MSExchangeSA Windows service dependencies. So, line 30

```
Set objWMIInstances = objWMIServices.AssociatorsOf (cWMIClass,,,,,,True)
```

becomes

```
Set objWMIInstances = objWMIServices.AssociatorsOf ("Win32_Service='MSExchangeSA'")
```

Sample 4.11 shows the same script as Sample 4.9 with different parameters for the *AssociatorsOf* method.

Sample 4.11   *Retrieving the class Associations from the SWbemServices object for a CIM class instance*

```
 1:<?xml version="1.0"?>
 .:
 8:<package>
 9:  <job>
..:
13:    <object progid="WbemScripting.SWbemLocator" id="objWMILocator" reference="true"/>
14:
15:    <script language="VBscript">
16:    <![CDATA[
..:
20:    Const cComputerName = "LocalHost"
21:    Const cWMINameSpace = "root/cimv2"
22:    Const cWMIClass = "Win32_Service"
23:    Const cWMIInstance = "MSExchangeSA"
..:
28:    objWMILocator.Security_.AuthenticationLevel = wbemAuthenticationLevelDefault
29:    objWMILocator.Security_.ImpersonationLevel = wbemImpersonationLevelImpersonate
30:    Set objWMIServices = objWMILocator.ConnectServer(cComputerName, cWMINameSpace, "", "")
31:    Set objWMIInstances = objWMIServices.AssociatorsOf (cWMIClass & "='" & cWMIInstance & "'")
32:
33:    For Each objWMIInstance in objWMIInstances
34:        WScript.Echo objWMIInstance.Path_ & " (" & objWMIInstance.Path_.RelPath & ")"
35:    Next
..:
40:    ]]>
41:    </script>
42:  </job>
43:</package>
```

In this case, the output will be

```
C:\>AssociatorsOfObjectInstanceWithAPI.wsfà
Microsoft (R) Windows Script Host Version 5.6
Copyright (C) Microsoft Corporation 1996-2000. All rights reserved.

\\NET-DPEN6400A\root\cimv2:Win32_ComputerSystem.Name="NET-DPEN6400A"
Win32_ComputerSystem.Name="NET-DPEN6400A")
\\NET-DPEN6400A\root\cimv2:Win32_Service.Name="MSExchangeIS" (Win32_Service.Name="MSExchangeIS")
\\NET-DPEN6400A\root\cimv2:Win32_Service.Name="MSExchangeMTA" (Win32_Service.Name="MSExchangeMTA")
\\NET-DPEN6400A\root\cimv2:Win32_Service.Name="Eventlog" (Win32_Service.Name="Eventlog")
\\NET-DPEN6400A\root\cimv2:Win32_Service.Name="NtLmSsp" (Win32_Service.Name="NtLmSsp")
\\NET-DPEN6400A\root\cimv2:Win32_Service.Name="RpcLocator" (Win32_Service.Name="RpcLocator")
\\NET-DPEN6400A\root\cimv2:Win32_Service.Name="RpcSs" (Win32_Service.Name="RpcSs")
\\NET-DPEN6400A\root\cimv2:Win32_Service.Name="lanmanworkstation"
(Win32_Service.Name="lanmanworkstation")
\\NET-DPEN6400A\root\cimv2:Win32_Service.Name="lanmanserver" (Win32_Service.Name="lanmanserver")
```

By referring to Section 2.9.1 or by using the **WMI CIM Studio**, you will see that the dependency list is exactly the same as the output produced by the script. Now, to determine the direction of the dependency, the script must use the *ReferencesOf* method. If we proceed in the same way, we replace line 30 of Sample 4.10 ("Retrieving the class references from the SWbemServices object for a CIM class") with

```
Set objWMIInstances = objWMIServices.ReferencesTo ("Win32_Service='MSExchangeSA'")
```

In this case, the output will be

```
C:\>ReferencesOfObjectInstanceWithQuery.wsf
Microsoft (R) Windows Script Host Version 5.6
Copyright (C) Microsoft Corporation 1996-2000. All rights reserved.

\\NET-DPEN6400A\root\cimv2:Win32_SystemServices
.GroupComponent="\\\\NET-DPEN6400A\\root\\cimv2:Win32_ComputerSystem.Name=\"NET-DPEN6400A\""
,PartComponent="\\\\NET-DPEN6400A\\root\\cimv2:Win32_Service.Name=\"MSExchangeSA\""
(Win32_SystemServices
.GroupComponent="\\\\NET-DPEN6400A\\root\\cimv2:Win32_ComputerSystem.Name=\"NET-DPEN6400A\""
,PartComponent="\\\\NET-DPEN6400A\\root\\cimv2:Win32_Service.Name=\"MSExchangeSA\"")

\\NET-DPEN6400A\root\cimv2:Win32_DependentService
.Antecedent="\\\\NET-DPEN6400A\\root\\cimv2:Win32_Service.Name=\"MSExchangeSA\""
,Dependent="\\\\NET-DPEN6400A\\root\\cimv2:Win32_Service.Name=\"MSExchangeIS\"" (Win32_DependentService
.Antecedent="\\\\NET-DPEN6400A\\root\\cimv2:Win32_Service.Name=\"MSExchangeSA\""
,Dependent="\\\\NET-DPEN6400A\\root\\cimv2:Win32_Service.Name=\"MSExchangeIS\"")

\\NET-DPEN6400A\root\cimv2:Win32_DependentService
.Antecedent="\\\\NET-DPEN6400A\\root\\cimv2:Win32_Service.Name=\"MSExchangeSA\""
,Dependent="\\\\NET-DPEN6400A\\root\\cimv2:Win32_Service.Name=\"MSExchangeMTA\"" (Win32_DependentService
.Antecedent="\\\\NET-DPEN6400A\\root\\cimv2:Win32_Service.Name=\"MSExchangeSA\""
,Dependent="\\\\NET-DPEN6400A\\root\\cimv2:Win32_Service.Name=\"MSExchangeMTA\"")

\\NET-DPEN6400A\root\cimv2:Win32_DependentService
.Antecedent="\\\\NET-DPEN6400A\\root\\cimv2:Win32_Service.Name=\"Eventlog\""
,Dependent="\\\\NET-DPEN6400A\\root\\cimv2:Win32_Service.Name=\"MSExchangeSA\"" (Win32_DependentService
.Antecedent="\\\\NET-DPEN6400A\\root\\cimv2:Win32_Service.Name=\"Eventlog\""
,Dependent="\\\\NET-DPEN6400A\\root\\cimv2:Win32_Service.Name=\"MSExchangeSA\"")

\\NET-DPEN6400A\root\cimv2:Win32_DependentService
.Antecedent="\\\\NET-DPEN6400A\\root\\cimv2:Win32_Service.Name=\"NtLmSsp\""
,Dependent="\\\\NET-DPEN6400A\\root\\cimv2:Win32_Service.Name=\"MSExchangeSA\"" (Win32_DependentService
.Antecedent="\\\\NET-DPEN6400A\\root\\cimv2:Win32_Service.Name=\"NtLmSsp\""
,Dependent="\\\\NET-DPEN6400A\\root\\cimv2:Win32_Service.Name=\"MSExchangeSA\"")

\\NET-DPEN6400A\root\cimv2:Win32_DependentService
.Antecedent="\\\\NET-DPEN6400A\\root\\cimv2:Win32_Service.Name=\"RpcLocator\""
,Dependent="\\\\NET-DPEN6400A\\root\\cimv2:Win32_Service.Name=\"MSExchangeSA\"" (Win32_DependentService
.Antecedent="\\\\NET-DPEN6400A\\root\\cimv2:Win32_Service.Name=\"RpcLocator\""
,Dependent="\\\\NET-DPEN6400A\\root\\cimv2:Win32_Service.Name=\"MSExchangeSA\"")

\\NET-DPEN6400A\root\cimv2:Win32_DependentService
.Antecedent="\\\\NET-DPEN6400A\\root\\cimv2:Win32_Service.Name=\"RpcSs\""
,Dependent="\\\\NET-DPEN6400A\\root\\cimv2:Win32_Service.Name=\"MSExchangeSA\"" (Win32_DependentService
.Antecedent="\\\\NET-DPEN6400A\\root\\cimv2:Win32_Service.Name=\"RpcSs\""
,Dependent="\\\\NET-DPEN6400A\\root\\cimv2:Win32_Service.Name=\"MSExchangeSA\"")

\\NET-DPEN6400A\root\cimv2:Win32_DependentService
.Antecedent="\\\\NET-DPEN6400A\\root\\cimv2:Win32_Service.Name=\"lanmanworkstation\""
,Dependent="\\\\NET-DPEN6400A\\root\\cimv2:Win32_Service.Name=\"MSExchangeSA\"" (Win32_DependentService
.Antecedent="\\\\NET-DPEN6400A\\root\\cimv2:Win32_Service.Name=\"lanmanworkstation\""
,Dependent="\\\\NET-DPEN6400A\\root\\cimv2:Win32_Service.Name=\"MSExchangeSA\"")
```

```
\\NET-DPEN6400A\root\cimv2:Win32_DependentService
.Antecedent="\\\\NET-DPEN6400A\\root\\cimv2:Win32_Service.Name=\"lanmanserver\""
,Dependent="\\\\NET-DPEN6400A\\root\\cimv2:Win32_Service.Name=\"MSExchangeSA\"" (Win32_DependentService
.Antecedent="\\\\NET-DPEN6400A\\root\\cimv2:Win32_Service.Name=\"lanmanserver\""
,Dependent="\\\\NET-DPEN6400A\\root\\cimv2:Win32_Service.Name=\"MSExchangeSA\"")
```

To improve readability, a blank line separates each reference. So, for one *Win32_Service* reference, we have

```
\\NET-DPEN6400A\root\cimv2:Win32_DependentService
.Antecedent="\\\\NET-DPEN6400A\\root\\cimv2:Win32_Service.Name=\"MSExchangeSA\""
,Dependent="\\\\NET-DPEN6400A\\root\\cimv2:Win32_Service.Name=\"MSExchangeIS\"" (Win32_DependentService
.Antecedent="\\\\NET-DPEN6400A\\root\\cimv2:Win32_Service.Name=\"MSExchangeSA\""
,Dependent="\\\\NET-DPEN6400A\\root\\cimv2:Win32_Service.Name=\"MSExchangeIS\"")
```

In Section 2.9.1, we saw that the *Win32_DependentService* association class has two defined keys: *Antecedent* and *Dependent* (shown in bold in the sample output line). If we decompose this line, we have

```
\\NET-DPEN6400A\root\cimv2:Win32_DependentService
.Antecedent="\\\\NET-DPEN6400A\\root\\cimv2:Win32_Service.Name=\"MSExchangeSA\""
,Dependent="\\\\NET-DPEN6400A\\root\\cimv2:Win32_Service.Name=\"MSExchangeIS\""

(Win32_DependentService
.Antecedent="\\\\NET-DPEN6400A\\root\\cimv2:Win32_Service.Name=\"MSExchangeSA\""
,Dependent="\\\\NET-DPEN6400A\\root\\cimv2:Win32_Service.Name=\"MSExchangeIS\"")
```

where the name of the association class instance is composed by the name of the keys defined in the *Win32_DependentService* class.

As we saw when learning WQL (Chapter 3), it is possible to retrieve the list of associations and references by using a WQL query. In this case, the line for the associations will be

```
Set objWMIInstances = objWMIServices.ExecQuery ("ASSOCIATORS OF {Win32_Service='MSExchangeSA'}")
```

For the references, the line will be

```
Set objWMIInstances = objWMIServices.ExecQuery ("REFERENCES OF {Win32_Service='MSExchangeSA'}")
```

The output is exactly the same. It is just another way to get the same information.

4.4.4 Retrieving the WMI object CIM information

Besides the relationships that a class definition may have in the CIM repository, there is another set of information that is important to know when writing scripts with the CIM classes. This information concerns the following:

- The nature of the class
- The properties exposed by the class

- The nature of the properties exposed by the class
- The methods exposed by the class
- The nature of the methods exposed by the class.
- The method properties exposed by the class
- The nature of the method properties exposed by the class

The following sections continue to explore the WMI scripting API object model and explain how this information can be retrieved by script from the CIM repository.

4.4.4.1   The CIM class qualifiers

As we saw in Chapter 2, a class can have various forms, such as static, dynamic, system, abstract, and association. This is determined with a qualifier. Every element defined in the CIM repository has qualifiers determining its nature and its behavior. To retrieve the class qualifier, we must examine the properties and methods exposed by the **SWbemObject** object in Table 4.10.

The portion of the WMI object model that represents **SWbemObject** is shown in Figure 4.4.

Figure 4.4
The WMI object model (2/3).

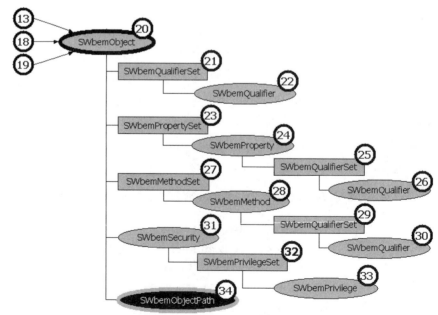

Table 4.10 *The SWbemObject Object*

SWbemObject (with SWbemObjectEx)

Properties	Derivation_	Contains an array of strings describing the derivation hierarchy for the class.
	Methods_	An SWbemMethodSet object that is the collection of methods for this object.
	Path_	Contains an SWbemObjectPath object that represents the object path of the current class or instance.
	Properties_	An SWbemPropertySet object that is the collection of properties for this object.
	Qualifiers_	An SWbemQualifierSet object that is the collection of qualifiers for this object.
	Security_	Contains an SWbemSecurity object used to read or change the security settings.
	SystemProperties_	An SWbemPropertySet object containing the collection of system properties that apply to the SWbemObjectEx represents.
Methods	Associators_ [strAssocClass = ""], [strResultClass = ""], [strResultRole = ""], [strRole = ""], [boolClassesOnly = FALSE], [boolSchemaOnly = FALSE], [strRequiredAssocQualifier = ""], [strRequiredQualifier = ""], [intFlags = wbemFlagReturnImmediately], [objwbemNamedValueSet = null]	Retrieves the associators of the object.

Table 4.10   *The SWbemObject Object (continued)*

SWbemObject (with SWbemObjectEx)

Methods (*cont'd.*)	AssociatorsAsync_ objWbemSink,
	  [strAssocClass = ""],
	  [strResultClass = ""],
	  [strResultRole = ""],
	  [strRole = ""],
	  [boolClassesOnly = FALSE],
	  [boolSchemaOnly = FALSE],
	  [strRequiredAssocQualifier = ""],
	  [strRequiredQualifier = ""],
	  [intFlags],
	  [objwbemNamedValueSet = null],
	  [objWbemAsyncContext]
		Asynchronously retrieves the associators of the object.

	Clone_ ( )	Makes a copy of the current object.
	CompareTo_ objwbemObject, [intFlags = wbemComparisonFlagIncludeAll]	Tests two objects for equality.
	Delete_ [intFlags = 0], [objwbemNamedValueSet = null]	Deletes the object from WMI.

	DeleteAsync_ objWbemSink,
	  [intFlags = 0],
	  [objwbemNamedValueSet = null],
	  [objWbemAsyncContext]
		Asynchronously deletes the object from WMI.

	ExecMethod_ strMethodName,
	  [objwbemInParams = null],
	  [intFlags = 0],
	  [objwbemNamedValueSet = null]
		Executes a method exported by a method provider.

Table 4.10 *The SWbemObject Object (continued)*

SWbemObject (with SWbemObjectEx)

Methods (cont'd.)	ExecMethodAsync_ objWbemSink, strMethodName, [objwbemInParams = null], [intFlags = 0], [objwbemNamedValueSet = null], [objWbemAsyncContext]	Asynchronously executes a method exported by a method provider.
	GetObjectText_ [intFlags = 0]	Retrieves the textual representation of the object (MOF syntax).
	Instances_ [intFlags = wbemFlagReturnImmediately], [objwbemNamedValueSet = null]	Returns a collection of instances of the object (which must be a WMI class).
	InstancesAsync_ [objWbemSink], [intFlags], [objwbemNamedValueSet = null], [objWbemAsyncContext]	Asynchronously returns a collection of instances of the object (which must be a WMI class).
	Put_ [intFlags = wbemChangeFlagCreateOrUpdate], [objwbemNamedValueSet = null]	Creates or updates the object in WMI.
	PutAsync_ objWbemSink, [intFlags = wbemChangeFlagCreateOrUpdate], [objWbemNamedValueSet = null], [objWbemAsyncContext]	Asynchronously creates or updates the object in WMI.
	References_ [strResultClass = ""], [strRole = ""], [boolClassesOnly = FALSE], [boolSchemaOnly = FALSE], [strRequiredQualifier = ""], [intFlags = wbemFlagReturnImmediately], [objwbemNamedValueSet = null]	Returns references to the object.

Table 4.10   *The SWbemObject Object (continued)*

SWbemObject (with SWbemObjectEx)

Methods *(cont'd.)*	ReferencesAsync_ objWbemSink,
	    [strResultClass = ""],
	    [strRole = ""],
	    [boolClassesOnly = FALSE],
	    [boolSchemaOnly = FALSE],
	    [strRequiredQualifier = ""],
	    [intFlags],
	    [objwbemNamedValueSet = null],
	    S[objWbemAsyncContext]
		Asynchronously returns references to the object.

	SpawnDerivedClass_ [intFlags = 0]	Creates a new derived class from the current object (which must be a WMI class).
	SpawnInstance_ [intFlags = 0]	Creates a new instance from the current object.
	Subclasses_ [intFlags = wbemFlagReturnImmediately+wbemQueryFlagDeep], [objwbemNamedValueSet = null]	Returns a collection of subclasses of the object (which must be a WMI class).

	SubclassesAsync_ objWbemSink,
	    [intFlags = wbemQueryFlagDeep],
	    [objWbemNamedValueSet = null],
	    [objWbemAsyncContext]
		Asynchronously returns a collection of subclasses of the object (which must be a WMI class).

	GetText_ intTextFormat,
	    [intFlags = 0],
	    [objWbemNamedValueSet]
		Returns a text file showing the contents of an object in XML.

	Refresh_ [intFlags = 0], [objWbemNamedValueSet = null]	Refreshes data in an object.

Table 4.11 *The SWbemQualifierSet Object*

SWbemQualifierSet

Properties	Count	Number of items in the collection.
Methods	Add strName, varVal, [boolPropagatesToSubclasses = TRUE], [boolPropagatesToInstances = TRUE], [boolOverridable = TRUE], [intFlags = 0]	
	Item strName, [intFlags = 0]	Adds an SWbemQualifier object to the SWbem-QualifierSet collection.
	Remove strName, [intFlags = 0]	Retrieves an SWbemQualifier object from the collection. This is the default method of this object.
	Add strName, varVal, [boolPropagatesToSubclasses = TRUE], [boolPropagatesToInstances = TRUE], [boolOverridable = TRUE], [intFlags = 0]	Removes an SWbemQualifier object from the collection.

The **SWbemObject** object exposes a *Qualifier_* property to retrieve an **SWbemQualifierSet** object (located as number 21 in Figure 4.4). As we saw in Chapter 2, we may have several qualifiers for a CIM element. The list of qualifiers associated with a CIM element is retrieved in the form of a collection and can be enumerated to retrieve every item part of the collection. Table 4.11 shows the list of properties and methods exposed by the **SWbemQualifierSet** object.

Each item in the **SWbemQualifierSet** object will be an **SWbemQualifier** object (located in Figure 4.4 as number 22). Table 4.12 shows the list of properties exposed by the **SWbemQualifier** object.

Table 4.12 *The SWbemQualifier Object*

SWbemQualifier

Properties	IsAmended	Boolean value that indicates if this qualifier has been localized using a merge operation
	IsLocal	Boolean value that indicates if this is a local qualifier.
	IsOverridable	Boolean value that indicates if this qualifier can be overridden when propagated.

Table 4.12   *The SWbemQualifier Object (continued)*

SWbemQualifier

Properties (cont'd.)	Name	Name of this qualifier.
	PropagatesToInstance	Boolean value that indicates if this qualifier can be propagated to an instance.
	PropagatesToSubclass	Boolean value that indicates if this qualifier can be propagated to a subclass.
	Value	Actual value of this qualifier. This is the default property of this object.

If we use a piece of sample script to retrieve an instance of the *Win32_Service* class as defined in the CIM repository and make use of the *Qualifier_* property associated with the retrieved **SWbemObject**, as shown in Sample 4.12, it is possible to retrieve the list of the class qualifiers with their properties.

Sample 4.12   *Retrieving the class qualifiers from the SWbemObject object for a CIM class*

```
1:<?xml version="1.0"?>
 .:
8:<package>
9:  <job>
..:
13:    <object progid="WbemScripting.SWbemLocator" id="objWMILocator" reference="true"/>
14:
15:    <script language="VBscript">
16:    <![CDATA[
..:
20:    Const cComputerName = "LocalHost"
21:    Const cWMINameSpace = "root/cimv2"
22:    Const cWMIClass = "Win32_Service"
..:
29:    objWMILocator.Security_.AuthenticationLevel = wbemAuthenticationLevelDefault
30:    objWMILocator.Security_.ImpersonationLevel = wbemImpersonationLevelImpersonate
31:    Set objWMIServices = objWMILocator.ConnectServer(cComputerName, cWMINameSpace, "", "")
32:
33:    Set objWMIInstance = objWMIServices.Get (cWMIClass, wbemFlagUseAmendedQualifiers)
34:
35:    Wscript.Echo String (60, 45)
36:    Wscript.Echo "Class Qualifiers:"
37:
38:    WScript.Echo "  " & objWMIInstance.Path_.RelPath
39:
40:    intIndent = 4
41:
42:    Set objWMIQualifiers = objWMIInstance.Qualifiers_
43:    For Each objWMIQualifier In objWMIQualifiers
44:        WScript.Echo Space (intIndent) & "Name: " & objWMIQualifier.Name
45:        If IsArray (objWMIQualifier.Value) Then
46:            For Each varElement In objWMIQualifier.Value
```

```
47:                    WScript.Echo Space (intIndent) & _
48:                         "  Value:                   " & varElement
49:           Next
50:        Else
51:           WScript.Echo Space (intIndent) & _
52:                      "  Value:                 " & objWMIQualifier.Value
53:        End if
54:        WScript.Echo Space (intIndent) & _
55:                      "  Amended:               " & objWMIQualifier.IsAmended
56:        WScript.Echo Space (intIndent) & _
57:                      "  Local:                 " & objWMIQualifier.IsLocal
58:        WScript.Echo Space (intIndent) & _
59:                      "  Overridable:           " & objWMIQualifier.IsOverridable
60:        WScript.Echo Space (intIndent) & _
61:                      "  Propagates to instance: " & objWMIQualifier.PropagatesToInstance
62:        WScript.Echo Space (intIndent) & _
63:                      "  Propagates to subclass: " & objWMIQualifier.PropagatesToSubclass
64:     Next
..:
69:     ]]>
70:     </script>
71:   </job>
72:</package>
```

The script structure from line 20 to line 33 is the same as before. However, to retrieve the instance of the CIM class in the **SWbemObject** (line
33), a particular flag is used with *Get* method. Because qualifiers are localized (or amended), if we want to retrieve all qualifiers available, it is important to specify the wbemFlagUseAmendedQualifiers constant to ensure that
the script retrieves the localized data. This is an important parameter
because, for example, the *Description* qualifier is a localized qualifier and
contains a descriptive text about the CIM element (class, property,
method). As mentioned before, when opening a language-specific class,
WMI combines the language-neutral definition with the language-specific
definition to provide the localized version of the class. The wbemFlagUseA-
mendedQualifiers constant is part of the wbemFlagEnum constants enumeration (Table 4.13). The constants of this collection can be used from
the *ExecQuery* method, the *ExecQueryAsync* method, the *SubclassesOf*
method, and the *InstancesOf* method of the **SWbemServices** object.

Table 4.13   *The wbemFlagEnum Constants*

WbemFlagEnum

Properties	Value	Description
wbemFlagReturnImmediately	16	Causes the call to return immediately.
wbemFlagReturnWhenComplete	0	Causes this call to block until the call has completed.
wbemFlagBidirectional	0	Causes WMI to retain pointers to objects of the enumeration until the client releases the enumerator.

Table 4.13   *The wbemFlagEnum Constants (continued)*

WbemFlagEnum

Properties	Value	Description
wbemFlagForwardOnly	32	Causes a forward-only enumerator to be returned. Use this flag in combination with wbemFlagReturnImmediately to request semi-synchronous access. For more information, see Making a Semi-synchronous Call. Forward-only enumerators are generally much faster and use less memory than conventional enumerators, but they do not allow calls to Clone or Reset.
wbemFlagNoErrorObject	64	Causes asynchronous calls to not return an error object in the event of an error.
wbemFlagReturnErrorObject	0	Causes asynchronous calls to return an error object in the event of an error.
wbemFlagSendStatus	128	Causes asynchronous calls to send status updates to the **OnProgress** event handler for your object sink.
wbemFlagDontSendStatus	0	Prevents asynchronous calls from sending status updates to the **OnProgress** event handler for your object sink.
wbemFlagUseAmendedQualifiers	131072	Causes asynchronous calls to send status updates to the OnProgress event handler for your object sink.

Next, the *Qualifier_* property is used to get an **SWbemQualifierSet** object (Sample 4.12, line 42). A For Each loop is executed to enumerate every qualifier contained in the collection (lines 43 to 64). In the loop, every property exposed by the **SWbemQualifier** object (see Table 4.12) is displayed. Special care is taken to make sure that the value contained in the qualifier is not an array (lines 45). In such a case, the value is processed accordingly (lines 46 to 49). For the *Win32_Service* class, the script retrieves five qualifiers (description, dynamic, locale, provider and UUID) displayed as follows:

```
1:C:\>QualifierForObjectClassWithAPI.wsf
2:Microsoft (R) Windows Script Host Version 5.6
3:Copyright (C) Microsoft Corporation 1996-2001. All rights reserved.
4:
5:------------------------------------------------------------
6:Class Qualifiers:
7:  Win32_Service
8:    Name: Description
9:      Value:          The Win32_Service class represents a service on a Win32 computer
                        system. A service application conforms to the interface rules of
                        the Service Control Manager (SCM) and can be started by a user
                        automatically at system boot through the Services control panel
                        utility, or by an application that uses the service functions
                        included in the Win32 API. Services can execute even when no user
                        is logged on to the system.
```

```
10:       Amended:                True
11:       Local:                  True
12:       Overridable:            True
13:       Propagates to instance: False
14:       Propagates to subclass: True
15:    Name: dynamic
16:       Value:                  True
17:       Amended:                False
18:       Local:                  True
19:       Overridable:            True
20:       Propagates to instance: True
21:       Propagates to subclass: False
22:    Name: Locale
23:       Value:                  1033
24:       Amended:                True
25:       Local:                  True
26:       Overridable:            True
27:       Propagates to instance: False
28:       Propagates to subclass: False
29:    Name: provider
30:       Value:                  CIMWin32
31:       Amended:                False
32:       Local:                  True
33:       Overridable:            True
34:       Propagates to instance: True
35:       Propagates to subclass: False
36:    Name: UUID
37:       Value:                  {8502C4D9-5FBB-11D2-AAC1-006008C78BC7}
38:       Amended:                False
39:       Local:                  True
40:       Overridable:            True
41:       Propagates to instance: True
42:       Propagates to subclass: False
```

For instance, this information tells us that the *Win32_Service* class is a dynamic class (lines 15 and 16) implemented by the *CIMWin32* provider (lines 29 and 30). We know that the class contains localized information (lines 11, 18, 25, 32, and 39). We can also see that every qualifier is differently propagated to instances and subclasses (lines 13 and 14, 20 and 21, 27 and 28, 34 and 35, 41 and 42).

4.4.4.2   *The CIM class properties*

Because we can retrieve information about the class qualifiers, we can also retrieve the list of properties exposed by a WMI class. In previous samples, it was necessary to display a property of the *Win32_Service* instance; the code contained the property in line. For instance, to get the name of the service instance retrieved, as in Sample 4.1 ("A VBScript listing the Win32_Service instance properties") and Sample 4.6 ("Retrieving all instances of the Win32_Service class with their properties"), the line was as follows:

```
WScript.Echo "   DisplayName=" & objWMIInstance.Name
```

Table 4.14   *The SWbemProperty Object*

Properties	CIMType	Type of this property.
	IsArray	Boolean value that indicates if this property has an array type.
	IsLocal	Boolean value that indicates if this is a local property.
	Name	Name of this property.
	Origin	Contains the originating class of this property.
	Qualifiers_	An SWbemQualifierSet object, which is the collection of qualifiers for this property.
	Value	Actual value of this property. This is the default automation property of this object.

This coding technique is referred to as *direct property access*. This way of coding is perfectly fine, given the condition that the **SWbemObject** object retrieved has a property called *name*. While the code considers a class exposing this property, there is no problem. If the class is different, it is likely that some properties are different, and the script code must be modified accordingly. It depends on the context of the developed script, but it could be interesting to develop code that is generic enough to retrieve the property list from an object class and for each property found to retrieve the associated value. This way of working is referred to as *indirect property access*.

The **SWbemObject** object exposes a property called *Properties_* (see Table 4.10), which produces an **SWbemPropertySet** object (located as number 23 in Figure 4.4). This object represents a collection of properties supported by the **SWbemObject** object. Each property is contained in an **SWbemProperty** object (located as number 24 in Figure 4.4). The **SWbemPropertySet** and the **SWbemProperty** objects properties and methods are available in Tables 4.14 and 4.15.

Table 4.15   *The SWbemPropertySet Object*

Properties	Count	The number of items in the collection.
Methods	Add strName, intCIMType, [boolIsArray = FALSE], [intFlags = 0]	Adds an SWbemProperty object to the SWbemPropertySet collection.
	Item strName, [intFlags = 0]	Retrieves an SWbemProperty from the collection. This is the default method of this object.
	Remove strName, [iFlags = 0]	Removes an SWbemProperty object from the collection.

Sample 4.13 illustrates the properties retrieval technique. The basic structure of the script is the same as prior scripts, except that the way to retrieve the *Win32_Service* properties differs. Note that the script retrieves an instance of the *Win32_Service* class (line 33), which makes it possible for the script to display the values of every retrieved property from that instance.

Sample 4.13   *Retrieving the property collection of a WMI instance*

```
 1:<?xml version="1.0"?>
 .:
 8:<package>
 9:  <job>
..:
13:     <object progid="WbemScripting.SWbemLocator" id="objWMILocator" reference="true"/>
14:
15:     <script language="VBscript">
16:     <![CDATA[
..:
20:     Const cComputerName = "LocalHost"
21:     Const cWMINameSpace = "root/cimv2"
22:     Const cWMIClass = "Win32_Service"
23:     Const cWMIInstance = "SNMP"
..:
30:     objWMILocator.Security_.AuthenticationLevel = wbemAuthenticationLevelDefault
31:     objWMILocator.Security_.ImpersonationLevel = wbemImpersonationLevelImpersonate
32:     Set objWMIServices = objWMILocator.ConnectServer(cComputerName, cWMINameSpace, "", "")
33:     Set objWMIInstance = objWMIServices.Get (cWMIClass & "='" & cWMIInstance & "'")
34:
35:     WScript.Echo objWMIInstance.Name & " (" & objWMIInstance.Description & ")"
36:
37:     Set objWMIPropertySet = objWMIInstance.Properties_
38:     For Each objWMIProperty In objWMIPropertySet
39:         If objWMIProperty.IsArray Then
40:            For Each varElement In objWMIProperty.Value
41:                WScript.Echo "  " & objWMIProperty.Name & " (" & varElement & ")"
42:            Next
43:         Else
44:            WScript.Echo "  " & objWMIProperty.Name & " (" & objWMIProperty.Value & ")"
45:         End If
46:     Next
..:
52:     ]]>
53:     </script>
54:  </job>
55:</package>
```

At line 37, the script refers to the **SWbemObject** *Properties_* property to get the property collection in an **SWbemPropertySet** object. Since this object represents a property collection, the For Each loop (lines 38 to 46) examines each property. To display the value of the property, the script refers to the *IsArray* property of the **SWbemProperty** object (line 39). If it is an array, the script makes another For Each loop to display the array values.

In both cases, the script shows the name of the property and its associated value or values (lines 41 and 44).

The *Win32_Service* has properties that are read only! There is no possibility for a script to change anything. Some classes also have properties that are read/write. For instance, this is the case for the *Win32_Registry* class, which exposes one read/write property called *ProposedSize*. Table 4.16 lists the properties available from the *Win32_Registry* class (there is no method exposed). Since we can read the class properties directly and indirectly, the purpose here is to show how to modify a property directly and indirectly.

The goal of the next script is to increase the registry database size limit of 10 MB. So, the script reads the current registry size and saves the new value back to the system. This logic is implemented in Sample 4.14.

Sample 4.14   *Setting one read/write property of a Win32_Registry class instance directly*

```
 1:<?xml version="1.0"?>
 .:
 8:<package>
 9:  <job>
 ..:
13:    <object progid="WbemScripting.SWbemLocator" id="objWMILocator" reference="true"/>
14:
15:    <script language="VBscript">
16:    <![CDATA[
..:
20:    Const cComputerName = "LocalHost"
21:    Const cWMINameSpace = "root/cimv2"
22:    Const cWMIClass = "Win32_Registry"
23:    Const cWMIInstance = "Microsoft Windows 2000 Server|C:\WINNT|\Device\Harddisk0\Partition1"
..:
28:    objWMILocator.Security_.AuthenticationLevel = wbemAuthenticationLevelDefault
29:    objWMILocator.Security_.ImpersonationLevel = wbemImpersonationLevelImpersonate
30:    Set objWMIServices = objWMILocator.ConnectServer(cComputerName, cWMINameSpace, "", "")
31:    Set objWMIInstance = objWMIServices.Get (cWMIClass & "='" & cWMIInstance & "'")
32:
33:    WScript.Echo objWMIInstance.Name & " (" & objWMIInstance.Description & ")"
34:
35:    Wscript.Echo "Current registry size is: " & objWMIInstance.ProposedSize  & " MB."
36:
37:    objWMIInstance.ProposedSize = objWMIInstance.ProposedSize + 10
38:    objWMIInstance.Put_ (wbemChangeFlagUpdateOnly Or wbemFlagReturnWhenComplete)
39:
40:    Wscript.Echo "Current registry size is now: " & objWMIInstance.ProposedSize  & " MB."
..:
45:    ]]>
46:    </script>
47:  </job>
48:</package>
```

As before, the first part of the script is always the same. The particularity starts at line 37, where the line performs the addition of 10 MB to the

Table 4.16   *The Win32_Registry Properties*

Properties	Caption	string
		Read-only
		Short description (one-line string) of the object.
	CurrentSize	**uint32**
		Read-only
		Qualifiers: Units(Megabytes)
		Current physical size of the Win32 registry.
	Description	**string**
		Read-only
		Description of the object.
	InstallDate	**datetime**
		Read-only
		When the object was installed. A lack of a value does not indicate that the object is not installed.
	MaximumSize	**uint32**
		Read-only
		Qualifiers: Units(Megabytes)
		Maximum size of the Win32 registry. If the system is successful in using the ProposedSize property, MaximumSize should contain the same value.
	Name	**string**
		Read-only
		Qualifiers: Key
		Name of the Win32 Registry. Maximum length is 256 characters.
	ProposedSize	**uint32**
		Read/Write
		Qualifiers: Units(Megabytes)
		Proposed size of the Win32 registry. It is the only registry setting that can be modified, and its proposal is attempted the next time the system boots.
	Status	**string**
		Read-only
		Current status of the object. Various operational and non-operational statuses can be defined. Operational statuses include: "OK", "Degraded", and "Pred Fail" (an element, such as a SMART-enabled hard drive, may be functioning properly but predicting a failure in the near future). Non-operational statuses include: "Error", "Starting", "Stopping", and "Service". The latter, "Service", could apply during mirror-resilvering of a disk, reload of a user permissions list, or other administrative work. Not all such work is on-line, yet the managed element is neither "OK" nor in one of the other states.

current registry size. The current registry size is read directly (as the property exposing the registry size is coded in the script code) and set directly to the new value on the same line (line 37). Setting the registry size property *ProposedSize* to the new value is not enough to commit the change. For this, another **SWbemObject** object method must be used. The *Put_* method flushes the modification back to the system (line 38). Some flags are passed to this method to ensure that the instance is updated and that thefunction returns once the execution is complete, at which time the registry size modification is saved.

Sample 4.15 indirectly sets the same property of the *Win32_Registry* class.

Sample 4.15   *Setting one read/write property of a Win32_Registry class instance indirectly*

```
 1:<?xml version="1.0"?>
 .:
 8:<package>
 9:  <job>
..:
13:    <object progid="WbemScripting.SWbemLocator" id="objWMILocator" reference="true"/>
14:
15:    <script language="VBscript">
16:    <![CDATA[
..:
20:    Const cComputerName = "LocalHost"
21:    Const cWMINameSpace = "root/cimv2"
22:    Const cWMIClass = "Win32_Registry"
23:    Const cWMIInstance = "Microsoft Windows 2000 Server|C:\WINNT|\Device\Harddisk0\Partition1"
..:
29:    objWMILocator.Security_.AuthenticationLevel = wbemAuthenticationLevelDefault
30:    objWMILocator.Security_.ImpersonationLevel = wbemImpersonationLevelImpersonate
31:    Set objWMIServices = objWMILocator.ConnectServer(cComputerName, cWMINameSpace, "", "")
32:    Set objWMIInstance = objWMIServices.Get (cWMIClass & "='" & cWMIInstance & "'")
33:
34:    WScript.Echo objWMIInstance.Name & " (" & objWMIInstance.Description & ")"
35:
36:    Set objWMIPropertySet = objWMIInstance.Properties_
37:
38:    Wscript.Echo "Current registry size is: " & objWMIPropertySet.Item("ProposedSize") & " MB."
39:
40:    objWMIPropertySet.Item("ProposedSize") = objWMIPropertySet.Item("ProposedSize") + 10
41:    objWMIInstance.Put_ (wbemChangeFlagUpdateOnly Or wbemFlagReturnWhenComplete)
42:
43:    Wscript.Echo "Current registry size is now: " & objWMIPropertySet.Item("ProposedSize") & " MB."
..:
50:    ]]>
51:    </script>
52:  </job>
53:</package>
```

First, the script retrieves an **SWbemPropertySet** object (line 36). With this object and the *Item* method, it is possible to reference the property *Pro-*

posedSize by passing its name as a parameter of the method (line 38). The rest of the process is exactly the same as before. The current registry size is read indirectly (as the property exposing the registry size is passed as a parameter of the *Item* method) and set indirectly on the same line (line 40). The update is executed at line 41.

Clearly, the big difference between the direct method and the indirect method is that the indirect method allows the creation of a generic code because the name of the referenced property is part of a parameter. This possibility is valuable when creating a generic script to retrieve CIM class information.

4.4.4.3   *The CIM class property qualifiers*

The technique for retrieving the qualifiers of the properties part of a CIM class is almost the same as retrieving the qualifiers for a CIM class (see Sample 4.12 ("Retrieving the class qualifiers from the SWbemObject object for a CIM class"). The difference resides in the level of the object model where the **SWbemQualifierSet** object is retrieved. For a class, the **SWbemQualifierSet** object was retrieved from an **SWbemObject** object; for a property, the **SWbemQualifierSet** object will be retrieved from an **SWbemProperty** object. The **SWbemQualifierSet** and **SWbemQualifier** objects linked to the **SWbemProperty** object are represented in the object model in Figure 4.4 by numbers 25 and 26. The script retrieving the property qualifiers is presented in Sample 4.16.

Sample 4.16   *Retrieving the property qualifiers of a WMI class*

```
 1:<?xml version="1.0"?>
 .:
 8:<package>
 9:  <job>
..:
13:    <script language="VBScript" src="..\Functions\DisplayQualifiersFunction.vbs" />
14:
15:    <object progid="WbemScripting.SWbemLocator" id="objWMILocator" reference="true"/>
16:
17:    <script language="VBscript">
18:    <![CDATA[
..:
22:    Const cComputerName = "LocalHost"
23:    Const cWMINameSpace = "root/cimv2"
24:    Const cWMIClass = "Win32_Service"
..:
30:    objWMILocator.Security_.AuthenticationLevel = wbemAuthenticationLevelDefault
31:    objWMILocator.Security_.ImpersonationLevel = wbemImpersonationLevelImpersonate
32:    Set objWMIServices = objWMILocator.ConnectServer(cComputerName, cWMINameSpace, "", "")
33:
34:    Set objWMIInstance = objWMIServices.Get (cWMIClass, wbemFlagUseAmendedQualifiers)
35:
```

```
36:    Wscript.Echo String (60, 45)
37:    Wscript.Echo "Class Qualifiers:"
38:
39:    WScript.Echo "  " & objWMIInstance.Path_.RelPath
40:    DisplayQualifiers objWMIInstance.Qualifiers_, 0
41:
42:    Wscript.Echo String (60, 45)
43:    Wscript.Echo "Property Qualifiers:"
44:
45:    Set objWMIPropertySet = objWMIInstance.Properties_
46:    For Each objWMIProperty In objWMIPropertySet
47:        WScript.Echo "  " & objWMIProperty.Name
48:        DisplayQualifiers objWMIProperty.Qualifiers_, 0
49:    Next
..:
54:    ]]>
55:    </script>
56:  </job>
57:</package>
```

The script retrieves the class qualifiers (lines 36 to 40) and the property qualifiers (lines 42 to 49). Because the tactic to display the qualifiers is the same whether it is a class qualifier or a property qualifier, the process to enumerate the qualifier properties is encapsulated in a subfunction stored in an external file (line 13). To retrieve the property qualifiers, the script must first retrieve the property list (line 45). Next, it enumerates the property list of the class (lines 46 to 49). The function displaying the qualifier properties is as follows:

```
 .:
 .:
 6:' --------------------------------------------------------
 7:Function DisplayQualifiers (objWMIQualifiers, intIndent)
..:
12:    intIndent = intindent + 4
13:
14:    For Each objWMIQualifier In objWMIQualifiers
15:        WScript.Echo Space (intIndent) & "Name: " & objWMIQualifier.Name
16:        If IsArray (objWMIQualifier.Value) Then
17:            For Each varElement In objWMIQualifier.Value
18:                WScript.Echo Space (intIndent) & _
19:                           " Value:                " & varElement
20:            Next
21:        Else
22:            WScript.Echo Space (intIndent) & _
23:                       " Value:                " & objWMIQualifier.Value
24:        End if
25:        WScript.Echo Space (intIndent) & _
26:                   " Amended:              " & objWMIQualifier.IsAmended
27:        WScript.Echo Space (intIndent) & _
28:                   " Local:                " & objWMIQualifier.IsLocal
29:        WScript.Echo Space (intIndent) & _
30:                   " Overridable:          " & objWMIQualifier.IsOverridable
31:        WScript.Echo Space (intIndent) & _
32:                   " Propagates to instance: " & objWMIQualifier.PropagatesToInstance
```

```
33:         WScript.Echo Space (intIndent) & _
34:                     " Propagates to subclass: " & objWMIQualifier.PropagatesToSubclass
35:     Next
36:
37:End Function
```

You can see that the logic is the same as in Sample 4.12 ("Retrieving the class qualifiers from the SWbemObject object for a CIM class") for the class qualifiers retrieval. The only addition concerns an input parameter to indent the qualifier output. This feature is used in subsequent samples when we examine the method qualifiers with the method parameter qualifiers. An extract of the output of the *State* property part of the *Win32_Service* class is

```
State
  Name: CIMTYPE
    Value:                  string
    Amended:                False
    Local:                  False
    Overridable:            True
    Propagates to instance: True
    Propagates to subclass: True
  Name: Description
    Value:                  The State property indicates the current state of the base service.
    Amended:                True
    Local:                  True
    Overridable:            True
    Propagates to instance: False
    Propagates to subclass: True
  Name: MappingStrings
    Value:                  Win32API|Service Structures|SERVICE_STATUS|dwCurrentState
    Amended:                False
    Local:                  False
    Overridable:            True
    Propagates to instance: False
    Propagates to subclass: True
  Name: read
    Value:                  True
    Amended:                False
    Local:                  False
    Overridable:            True
    Propagates to instance: False
    Propagates to subclass: True
  Name: ValueMap
    Value:                  Stopped
    Value:                  Start Pending
    Value:                  Stop Pending
    Value:                  Running
    Value:                  Continue Pending
    Value:                  Pause Pending
    Value:                  Paused
    Value:                  Unknown
    Amended:                False
    Local:                  False
    Overridable:            True
    Propagates to instance: False
    Propagates to subclass: True
```

Table 4.17   *The SWbemMethodSet Object*

Properties	Count	The number of items in the collection.
Methods	Item strName, [iFlags = 0]	Retrieves an SWbemMethod object from the collection. This is the default automation method of this object.

4.4.4.4   The CIM class methods

To retrieve the methods available from an **SWbemObject** object, the technique is the same as shown previously for the properties. The **SWbemObject** object exposes a property, *Methods_*, that provides an **SWbemMethodSet** object that contains the collection of methods available. Each item in the **SWbemMethodSet** object contains an **SWbemMethod** object. Both **SWbemMethodSet** and **SWbemMethod** object properties and methods are, respectively, available in Tables 4.17 and 4.18 and are located in the WMI scripting object model in Figure 4.4 as numbers 27 and 28.

By adapting Sample 4.13 ("Retrieving the property collection of a WMI instance") to suit the needs of the methods retrieval, we have Sample 4.17.

Sample 4.17   *Retrieving the method collection of a WMI class*

```
 1:<?xml version="1.0"?>
 .:
 8:<package>
 9:   <job>
..:
13:      <object progid="WbemScripting.SWbemLocator" id="objWMILocator" reference="true"/>
14:
15:      <script language="VBscript">
16:      <![CDATA[
..:
20:      Const cComputerName = "LocalHost"
21:      Const cWMINameSpace = "root/cimv2"
22:      Const cWMIClass = "Win32_Service"
23:      Const cWMIInstance = "SNMP"
..:
30:      objWMILocator.Security_.AuthenticationLevel = wbemAuthenticationLevelDefault
31:      objWMILocator.Security_.ImpersonationLevel = wbemImpersonationLevelImpersonate
32:      Set objWMIServices = objWMILocator.ConnectServer(cComputerName, cWMINameSpace, "", "")
33:      Set objWMIInstance = objWMIServices.Get (cWMIClass & "='" & cWMIInstance & "'")
34:
35:      WScript.Echo objWMIInstance.Name & " (" & objWMIInstance.Description & ")"
36:
37:      Set objWMIMethodSet = objWMIInstance.Methods_
38:      For Each objWMIMethod In objWMIMethodSet
39:          WScript.Echo "   " & objWMIMethod.Name
40:      Next
..:
46:      ]]>
47:      </script>
48:   </job>
49:</package>
```

Table 4.18   *The SWbemMethod Object*

Properties	InParameters	An SWbemObject object whose properties define the input parameters for this method.
	Name	Name of the method.
	Origin	Originating class of the method.
	OutParameters	An SWbemObject object whose properties define the out parameters and return type of this method.
	Qualifiers_	An SWbemQualifierSet object that contains the qualifiers for this method.

Again, the script structure is the same as before. The only change resides in lines 37 to 40 where the **SWbemMethodSet** object is created (line 37) and enumerated as a collection to retrieve each **SWbemMethod** object (line 39) with its associated *name* property.

When talking about the method execution in Sample 4.7 ("Using one method of a Win32_Service instance directly"), the script uses a technique referred to as direct-method execution because the method name was hard coded in the script code. For instance, in the case of the *Win32_Service StartService* and *StopService* methods, the lines used were

```
intRC = objWMIInstance.StartService
```

and

```
intRC = objWMIInstance.StopService
```

The WMI scripting API allows the execution of methods indirectly. This means that it is possible to refer to an indirect way to execute a method. This technique uses the *ExecMethod* of the **SWbemServices** object (see Table 4.8) or the *ExecMethod_* of the **SWbemObject** object (see Table 4.10). The same script as Sample 4.7 can be adapted to invoke the *StartService* and *StopService* methods indirectly. Sample 4.18 shows how to proceed.

Sample 4.18   *Using one method of a Win32_Service instance indirectly*

```
 1:<?xml version="1.0"?>
 .:
 8:<package>
 9:  <job>
..:
13:     <object progid="WbemScripting.SWbemLocator" id="objWMILocator" reference="true"/>
14:
15:     <script language="VBscript">
16:     <![CDATA[
..:
20:     Const cComputerName = "LocalHost"
21:     Const cWMINameSpace = "root/cimv2"
```

```
22:     Const cWMIClass = "Win32_Service"
23:     Const cWMIInstance = "SNMP"
..:
29:     objWMILocator.Security_.AuthenticationLevel = wbemAuthenticationLevelDefault
30:     objWMILocator.Security_.ImpersonationLevel = wbemImpersonationLevelImpersonate
31:     Set objWMIServices = objWMILocator.ConnectServer(cComputerName, cWMINameSpace, "", "")
32:     Set objWMIInstance = objWMIServices.Get (cWMIClass & "='" & cWMIInstance & "'")
33:
34:     WScript.Echo vbCRLF & "'" & objWMIInstance.DisplayName & "' is currently " & _
35:                 objWMIInstance.State & "."
36:
37:     If objWMIInstance.State = "Stopped" Then
38:        Set objWMIOutParameters = objWMIInstance.ExecMethod_("StartService")
39:        intRC = objWMIOutParameters.ReturnValue
40:        strMessage = "'" & objWMIInstance.DisplayName & "' is now Running."
41:     End If
42:     If objWMIInstance.State = "Running" Then
43:        Set objWMIOutParameters = objWMIInstance.ExecMethod_("StopService")
44:        intRC = objWMIOutParameters.ReturnValue
45:        strMessage = "'" & objWMIInstance.DisplayName & "' is now Stopped ."
46:     End If
47:
48:     If intRC = 0 Then
49:        Wscript.Echo strMessage
50:     Else
51:        Wscript.Echo "Synchronous method execution failed."
52:     End If
..:
58:     ]]>
59:     </script>
60:  </job>
61:</package>
```

Sample 4.18 (indirect method) uses the same structure as Sample 4.7 (direct method). The particularity resides in the method invocation (lines 38 and 43). As AAWE can see, in both cases the method name is a parameter of the *ExecMethod_* method exposed by the **SWbemObject** object. The method name is no longer encoded in the script code. The second particularity concerns the returned result of the method execution. With the direct method, it is possible to retrieve the result directly in a variable; now with the indirect method execution, the return code is returned in an **SWbemObject** object (lines 38 and 43) whose properties define the output parameters and the return value of the executed method (lines 39 and 44).

The *StartService* and *StopService* methods do not require any input parameters, but how do we deal with methods invoked indirectly that require input parameters? To explain this, let's take another script sample, swapping the service startup mode. To change the startup mode of a *Win32_Service*, the *ChangeStartMode* method must be executed with one parameter. When the startup mode is automatic, the script will change it to manual and vice versa. Sample 4.19 implements this logic.

Sample 4.19   *Using one method of a Win32_Service instance indirectly with one parameter*

```
 1:<?xml version="1.0"?>
 .:
 8:<package>
 9:  <job>
..:
13:    <object progid="WbemScripting.SWbemLocator" id="objWMILocator" reference="true"/>
14:
15:    <script language="VBscript">
16:    <![CDATA[
..:
20:    Const cComputerName = "LocalHost"
21:    Const cWMINameSpace = "root/cimv2"
22:    Const cWMIClass = "Win32_Service"
23:    Const cWMIInstance = "SNMP"
..:
31:    objWMILocator.Security_.AuthenticationLevel = wbemAuthenticationLevelDefault
32:    objWMILocator.Security_.ImpersonationLevel = wbemImpersonationLevelImpersonate
33:    Set objWMIServices = objWMILocator.ConnectServer(cComputerName, cWMINameSpace, "", "")
34:    Set objWMIInstance = objWMIServices.Get (cWMIClass & "='" & cWMIInstance & "'")
35:
36:    WScript.Echo vbCRLF & "'" & objWMIInstance.DisplayName & "' startup is currently " & _
37:                      objWMIInstance.StartMode & "."
38:
39:    Set objWMIMethod = objWMIInstance.Methods_("ChangeStartMode")
40:    Set objWMIInParameters = objWMIMethod.InParameters
41:
42:    If objWMIInstance.StartMode = "Manual" Then
43:       objWMIInParameters.Properties_.Item("StartMode") = "Automatic"
44:       Set objWMIOutParameters = objWMIInstance.ExecMethod_("ChangeStartMode", _
45:                                                   objWMIInParameters)
46:       intRC = objWMIOutParameters.ReturnValue
47:       strMessage = "'" & objWMIInstance.DisplayName & "' startup mode is now Automatic."
48:    End If
49:    If objWMIInstance.StartMode = "Auto" Then
50:       objWMIInParameters.Properties_.Item("StartMode") = "Manual"
51:       Set objWMIOutParameters = objWMIInstance.ExecMethod_("ChangeStartMode", _
52:                                                   objWMIInParameters)
53:       intRC = objWMIOutParameters.ReturnValue
54:       strMessage = "'" & objWMIInstance.DisplayName & "' startup mode is now Manual."
55:    End If
56:
57:    If intRC = 0 Then
58:       Wscript.Echo strMessage
59:    Else
60:       Wscript.Echo "Synchronous method execution failed."
61:    End If
..:
69:    ]]>
70:    </script>
71:  </job>
72:</package>
```

As with previous samples, the script structure is the same. Because the invoked method has one parameter, the script must instantiate an object used to store the method parameter. This object is an **SWbemObject** object whose properties define the input parameters of the executed method (lines 39 and 40). In the sample case, the input parameter is "StartMode" (line 43) since the examined method is *ChangeStartMode* (line 39). To set the parameter required by the method (lines 43 and 50), the **SWbemObject** object containing the input parameter refers to the *Properties_* property (see Table 4.10) to obtain an **SWbemObjectPropertySet** object (see Table 4.14), which, in turn, refers the *Item* method to set the property value. The last step executes the method (lines 44 and 51). This step is almost the same as in Sample 4.18 ("Using one method of a Win32_Service instance indirectly") except that the **SWbemObject** object containing the input parameters is passed as a parameter of the *ExecMethod_* exposed by **SWbemObject** representing the Windows service instance (lines 45 and 52).

Note that the **SWbemMethod** object created to retrieve the **SWbemObject** object containing the input parameter is created in two steps (lines 39 and 40). It is possible to create this object in one line without creating an explicit **SWbemMethod** object. In this case lines 39 and 40 can be replaced by

```
Set objWMIInParameters = objWMIInstance.Methods_("ChangeStartMode").InParameters
```

The effect is exactly the same. The reason for this initial coding is to ease the readability of the code and to show that an intermediate WMI scripting API object is used, in this case the **SWbemMethod** object.

To invoke methods, the previous scripts referred to the methods (directly or indirectly) from **SWbemObject** representing the WMI class instance. It is also possible to invoke a WMI class method from the **SWbemServices** object by invoking its *ExecMethod* method (see Table 4.8). In this case, the instance name of the real-world manageable entity is passed as a parameter. Sample 4.20 shows this technique.

Sample 4.20   *Using one method of a Win32_Service instance from the SWbemServices object*

```
 1:<?xml version="1.0"?>
 .:
 8:<package>
 9:   <job>
..:
13:      <object progid="WbemScripting.SWbemLocator" id="objWMILocator" reference="true"/>
14:
15:      <script language="VBscript">
16:      <![CDATA[
..:
20:      Const cComputerName = "LocalHost"
21:      Const cWMINameSpace = "root/cimv2"
22:      Const cWMIClass = "Win32_Service"
```

```
23:     Const cWMIInstance = "SNMP"
..:
28:     Set objWMIServices = objWMILocator.ConnectServer(cComputerName, cWMINameSpace, "", "")
29:
30:     Set objWMIOutParameters = objWMIServices.ExecMethod _
31:                               (cWMIClass & "='" & cWMIInstance & "'", "StopService")
32:
33:     If objWMIOutParameters.ReturnValue = 0 Then
34:        Wscript.Echo "Synchronous method execution successful."
35:     Else
36:        Wscript.Echo "Synchronous method execution failed."
37:     End If
..:
42:     ]]>
43:     </script>
44:   </job>
45:</package>
```

As we can see in lines 30 and 31, the instance name and the method name are passed as parameters of the *ExecMethod* exposed by the **SWbemServices** object. Of course, there is no way to retrieve the status of the Windows service from an **SWbemServices** object to determine whether the script must stop or start the service. If this is required, an object representing the instance of the service must be created to read its status. Sample 4.21 performs the exact same operation, but uses a moniker and invokes the *ExecMethod* method directly from the **GetObject** statement.

Sample 4.21 *Using one method of a Win32_Service instance from an SWbemServices object created with a moniker*

```
1:<?xml version="1.0"?>
.:
8:<package>
9:   <job>
..:
13:     <object progid="WbemScripting.SWbemLocator" id="objWMILocator" reference="true"/>
14:
15:     <script language="VBscript">
16:     <![CDATA[
..:
20:     Const cComputerName = "LocalHost"
21:     Const cWMINameSpace = "root/cimv2"
22:     Const cWMIClass = "Win32_Service"
23:     Const cWMIInstance = "SNMP"
..:
28:     Set objWMIOutParameters = GetObject("WinMgmts:{impersonationLevel=impersonate, " & _
29:                                 "AuthenticationLevel=default, " & _
30:                                 "(RemoteShutdown, Security)}!\\" & _
31:                                 cComputerName & "\" & cWMINameSpace).ExecMethod _
32:                                 (cWMIClass & "='" & cWMIInstance & "'", "StopService")
33:
34:     If objWMIOutParameters.ReturnValue = 0 Then
35:        Wscript.Echo "Synchronous method execution successful."
36:     Else
37:        Wscript.Echo "Synchronous method execution failed."
```

```
38:     End If
..:
42:     ]]>
43:     </script>
44:  </job>
45:</package>
```

As we can see, line 28 immediately returns an **SWbemObject** object containing the return code of the invoked method. A connection a to particular WMI namespace on a remote computer is made only in one single executed line with the moniker (lines 28 to 32). The required impersonation and authentication levels with some privileges are set to create an **SWbemServices** object (lines 28 to 31). Next, a *Win32_Service* class instance is referenced and one method exposed by the *Win32_Service* class is executed from the selected instance (line 32).

4.4.4.5   *The CIM class method qualifiers*

Retrieving the method qualifiers is no different than the tactic used to retrieve the property qualifiers. Again, the principle is exactly the same. First, the script must retrieve the collection of methods exposed by a CIM class (stored in **SWbemMethodSet** object) and perform a loop to enumerate every method in the collection. Each method is stored in an **SWbemMethod** object. The object containing the collection of qualifiers defining the methods is, as usual, an **SWbemQualifierSet** object. This object contains every defined qualifier in an **SWbemQualifier** object. As we look to the method qualifiers, the **SWbemQualifierSet** object must be retrieved with the *Qualifier_* property exposed by the **SWbemMethod** object (see Table 4.18). The **SWbemQualifierSet** and **SWbemQualifier** objects are represented by numbers 29 and 30 in the WMI object model shown in Figure 4.4. Sample 4.22 shows this logic.

Sample 4.22   *Retrieving the method qualifiers of a WMI class*

```
1:<?xml version="1.0"?>
 .:
8:<package>
9:   <job>
..:
13:     <script language="VBScript" src="..\Functions\DisplayQualifiersFunction.vbs" />
14:
15:     <object progid="WbemScripting.SWbemLocator" id="objWMILocator" reference="true"/>
16:
17:     <script language="VBscript">
18:     <![CDATA[
..:
22:     Const cComputerName = "LocalHost"
23:     Const cWMINameSpace = "root/cimv2"
24:     Const cWMIClass = "Win32_Service"
..:
```

```
30:      objWMILocator.Security_.AuthenticationLevel = wbemAuthenticationLevelDefault
31:      objWMILocator.Security_.ImpersonationLevel = wbemImpersonationLevelImpersonate
32:      Set objWMIServices = objWMILocator.ConnectServer(cComputerName, cWMINameSpace, "", "")
33:
34:      Set objWMIInstance = objWMIServices.Get (cWMIClass, wbemFlagUseAmendedQualifiers)
35:
36:      Wscript.Echo String (60, 45)
37:      Wscript.Echo "Class Qualifiers:"
38:
39:      WScript.Echo "  " & objWMIInstance.Path_.RelPath
40:      DisplayQualifiers objWMIInstance.Qualifiers_, 0
41:
42:      Wscript.Echo String (60, 45)
43:      Wscript.Echo "Method Qualifiers:"
44:
45:      Set objWMIMethodSet = objWMIInstance.Methods_
46:      For Each objWMIMethod In objWMIMethodSet
47:         WScript.Echo "  " & objWMIMethod.Name
48:         DisplayQualifiers objWMIMethod.Qualifiers_, 0
49:      Next
..:
54:      ]]>
55:      </script>
56:   </job>
57:</package>
```

After retrieving the class instance (line 34), the script shows the class qualifiers with the help of a function enumerating and showing the properties of every qualifier (see Sample 4.16 ["Retrieving the property qualifiers of a WMI class"]). Once completed, the script retrieves the list of methods exposed by the class (lines 45 to 49). For every method, the script invokes the function to display the qualifier information (line 48). Here is a sample output for the *StartService* and *StopService* methods.

```
Method Qualifiers:
  StartService
    Name: Description
      Value:                    The StartService method attempts to place the service into its startup
                                state. It returns one of the following integer values:
                                0 - The request was accepted.
                                1 - The request is not supported.
                                2 - The user did not have the necessary access.
                                3 - The service cannot be stopped because other services that are
                                    running are dependent on it.
                                4 - The requested control code is not valid, or it is unacceptable to
                                    the service.
                                5 - The requested control code cannot be sent to the service because
                                    the state of the service (Win32_BaseService:State) is equal to 0,
                                    1, or 2.
                                6 - The service has not been started.
                                7 - The service did not respond to the start request in a timely
                                    fashion.
                                8 - Unknown failure when starting the service.
                                9 - The directory path to the service executable was not found.
                                10 - The service is already running.
                                11 - The database to add a new service is locked.
                                12 - A dependency for which this service relies on has been removed
```

```
                                      from the system.
                        13 - The service failed to find the service needed from a dependent
                             service.
                        14 - The service has been disabled from the system.
                        15 - The service does not have the correct authentication to run on
                             the system.
                        16 - This service is being removed from the system.
                        17 - There is no execution thread for the service.
                        18 - There are circular dependencies when starting the service.
                        19 - There is a service running under the same name.
                        20 - There are invalid characters in the name of the service.
                        21 - Invalid parameters have been passed to the service.
                        22 - The account which this service is to run under is either invalid
                             or lacks the permissions to run the service.
                        23 - The service exists in the database of services available from the
                             system.
                        24 - The service is currently paused in the system.
    Amended:            True
    Local:              True
    Overridable:        True
    Propagates to instance: False
    Propagates to subclass: True
Name: MappingStrings
    Value:              Win32API|Service Functions|StartService
    Amended:            False
    Local:              False
    Overridable:        True
    Propagates to instance: False
    Propagates to subclass: True
Name: Override
    Value:              StartService
    Amended:            False
    Local:              False
    Overridable:        True
    Propagates to instance: False
    Propagates to subclass: True
Name: Values
    Value:              Success
    Value:              Not Supported
    Value:              Access Denied
    Value:              Dependent Services Running
    Value:              Invalid Service Control
    Value:              Service Cannot Accept Control
    Value:              Service Not Active
    Value:              Service Request Timeout
    Value:              Unknown Failure
    Value:              Path Not Found
    Value:              Service Already Running
    Value:              Service Database Locked
    Value:              Service Dependency Deleted
    Value:              Service Dependency Failure
    Value:              Service Disabled
    Value:              Service Logon Failed
    Value:              Service Marked For Deletion
    Value:              Service No Thread
    Value:              Status Circular Dependency
    Value:              Status Duplicate Name
    Value:              Status Invalid Name
    Value:              Status Invalid Parameter
    Value:              Status Invalid Service Account
```

```
       Value:                     Status Service Exists
       Value:                     Service Already Paused
       Amended:                   True
       Local:                     True
       Overridable:               True
       Propagates to instance: False
       Propagates to subclass: True
  StopService
    Name: Description
       Value:                     The StopService method places the service in the stopped state. It
                                  returns an integer value of 0 if the service was successfully stopped,
                                  1 if the request is not supported, and any other number to indicate an
                                  error.
       Amended:                   True
       Local:                     True
       Overridable:               True
       Propagates to instance: False
       Propagates to subclass: True
    Name: MappingStrings
       Value:                     Win32API|Service Functions|ControlService|dwControl|SERVICE_CONTROL_STOP
       Amended:                   False
       Local:                     False
       Overridable:               True
       Propagates to instance: False
       Propagates to subclass: True
    Name: Override
       Value:                     StopService
       Amended:                   False
       Local:                     False
       Overridable:               True
       Propagates to instance: False
       Propagates to subclass: True
```

4.4.4.6   The CIM class method parameters

A CIM class may expose some properties and methods, but a method may also have some input and output parameters. By using the WMI scripting API, it is possible to retrieve the parameters associated to a method. Sample 4.23 executes this task.

Sample 4.23   *Retrieving the method properties with their qualifiers of a WMI class*

```
 1:<?xml version="1.0"?>
 .:
 8:<package>
 9:   <job>
..:
13:     <script language="VBScript" src="..\Functions\DisplayQualifiersFunction.vbs" />
14:
15:     <object progid="WbemScripting.SWbemLocator" id="objWMILocator" reference="true"/>
16:
17:     <script language="VBscript">
18:     <![CDATA[
..:
22:     Const cComputerName = "LocalHost"
23:     Const cWMINameSpace = "root/cimv2"
24:     Const cWMIClass = "Win32_Service"
```

```
. . :
32:    On Error Resume Next
33:
34:    objWMILocator.Security_.AuthenticationLevel = wbemAuthenticationLevelDefault
35:    objWMILocator.Security_.ImpersonationLevel = wbemImpersonationLevelImpersonate
36:    Set objWMIServices = objWMILocator.ConnectServer(cComputerName, cWMINameSpace, "", "")
37:
38:    Set objWMIInstance = objWMIServices.Get (cWMIClass, wbemFlagUseAmendedQualifiers)
39:
40:    Wscript.Echo String (60, 45)
41:    Wscript.Echo "Class Qualifiers:"
42:
43:    WScript.Echo "  " & objWMIInstance.Path_.RelPath
44:    DisplayQualifiers objWMIInstance.Qualifiers_, 0
45:
46:    Wscript.Echo String (60, 45)
47:    Wscript.Echo "Method Qualifiers:"
48:
49:    Set objWMIMethodSet = objWMIInstance.Methods_
50:    For Each objWMIMethod In objWMIMethodSet
51:        WScript.Echo "  " & objWMIMethod.Name
52:        DisplayQualifiers objWMIMethod.Qualifiers_, 0
53:
54:        Set objWMIObject = objWMIMethod.InParameters
55:        WScript.Echo "  " & objWMIObject.Path_.RelPath
56:        DisplayQualifiers objWMIObject.Qualifiers_, 2
57:
58:        Set objWMIPropertySet = objWMIObject.Properties_
59:        If Err.Number = 0 Then
60:          For Each objWMIProperty In objWMIPropertySet
61:              WScript.Echo "    " & objWMIProperty.Name
62:              DisplayQualifiers objWMIProperty.Qualifiers_, 4
63:          Next
64:        Else
65:            Err.Clear
66:        End If
. . :
71:        Set objWMIObject = objWMIMethod.OutParameters
72:        WScript.Echo "  " & objWMIObject.Path_.RelPath
73:        DisplayQualifiers objWMIObject.Qualifiers_, 2
74:
75:        Set objWMIPropertySet = objWMIObject.Properties_
76:        If Err.Number = 0 Then
77:          For Each objWMIProperty In objWMIPropertySet
78:              WScript.Echo "    " & objWMIProperty.Name
79:              DisplayQualifiers objWMIProperty.Qualifiers_, 4
80:          Next
81:        Else
82:            Err.Clear
83:        End If
. . :
88:    Next
. . :
93:    ]]>
94:    </script>
95:  </job>
96:</package>
```

Basically, the script is the same as Sample 4.22 ("Retrieving the method qualifiers of a WMI class"). It first retrieves the CIM class with its qualifiers (line 44). Next, it retrieves the method collection available (line 49). While enumerating the method collection in a "For Each" loop (lines 50 to 88), the script displays the qualifiers associated with each method (line 52) and retrieves the associated parameters:

- With the *InParameters* property of the **SWbemMethod** object (see Table 4.18) for the input parameters (line 54)

- With the *OutParameters* property of the **SWbemMethod** object (see Table 4.18) for the output parameters (line 71)

Each of these properties returns an **SWbemObject** object whose properties define the input parameters or the output parameters of the executed method. If we look at the WMI object model presented in Figure 4.4, this implies that these two used properties of the **SWbemMethod** object (located as number 28 on the Figure 4.4) produce a new **SWbemObject** object that will be located as number 20 in the same figure. As this **SWbemObject** object represents the method parameters, it is possible to retrieve the qualifiers of such object. For this, the script uses the object number 21 of the WMI object model to retrieve the qualifier collection. This is performed on line 56 for the input parameters and line 73 for the output parameters.

As with any **SWbemObject** object, it is possible to retrieve a collection of properties and methods with their associated qualifiers (see Table 4.10). Of course, it is not sure that every method defined for a CIM class will have input parameters. Input or output parameters can be retrieved with the *Properties_* property exposed by the **SWbemObject** object. In such a case an **SWbemPropertySet** object containing a collection of **SWbemProperty** objects is returned. This is achieved on line 58 for the input parameters and line 75 for the output parameters. If some input or output parameters exist, then the returned **SWbemPropertySet** object can be enumerated. In this case, the script uses objects 23 and 24 in the WMI object model (see Figure 4.4).

4.4.4.7   *The CIM class method parameter qualifiers*

Because input or output parameters also have some characteristics, such as syntax, some qualifiers are also defined. When enumerating the input parameters (lines 60 to 63) and the output parameters (lines 77 to 80), the script invokes the function displaying the associated qualifiers (lines 62 and 79). At this stage of the script, we are using objects 25 and 26 in the WMI object model (see Figure 4.4) as a method parameter is represented by an

SWbemProperty object. Finally, once run, the script will output a lot of information. Below, a partial set of the retrieved information is visible for the *ChangeStartMode* method of the *Win32_Service* class with all input and output parameters and all associated qualifiers:

```
ChangeStartMode
  Name: Description
    Value:                   The ChangeStartMode method modifies the StartMode of a service. It
                             returns an integer value of 0 if the service was successfully modified,
                             1 if the request is not supported, and any other number to indicate an
                             error.
    Amended:                 True
    Local:                   True
    Overridable:             True
    Propagates to instance:  False
    Propagates to subclass:  True
  Name: MappingStrings
    Value:                   Service Functions|ChangeServiceConfig|dwStartType
    Amended:                 False
    Local:                   False
    Overridable:             True
    Propagates to instance:  False
    Propagates to subclass:  True
__PARAMETERS
  Name: abstract
    Value:                   True
    Amended:                 False
    Local:                   True
    Overridable:             True
    Propagates to instance:  False
    Propagates to subclass:  False
  StartMode
    Name: CIMTYPE
      Value:                 string
      Amended:               False
      Local:                 True
      Overridable:           True
      Propagates to instance: True
      Propagates to subclass: True
    Name: ID
      Value:                 0
      Amended:               False
      Local:                 True
      Overridable:           False
      Propagates to instance: True
      Propagates to subclass: False
    Name: In
      Value:                 True
      Amended:               False
      Local:                 True
      Overridable:           True
      Propagates to instance: False
      Propagates to subclass: False
    Name: MappingStrings
      Value:                 Win32API|Service Structures|QUERY_SERVICE_CONFIG|dwStartType
      Amended:               False
      Local:                 True
      Overridable:           True
```

```
            Propagates to instance: False
            Propagates to subclass: True
         Name: ValueMap
            Value:                  Boot
            Value:                  System
            Value:                  Automatic
            Value:                  Manual
            Value:                  Disabled
            Amended:                False
            Local:                  True
            Overridable:            True
            Propagates to instance: False
            Propagates to subclass: True
__PARAMETERS
      Name: abstract
         Value:                  True
         Amended:                False
         Local:                  True
         Overridable:            True
         Propagates to instance: False
         Propagates to subclass: False
      ReturnValue
         Name: CIMTYPE
            Value:                  uint32
            Amended:                False
            Local:                  True
            Overridable:            True
            Propagates to instance: True
            Propagates to subclass: True
         Name: out
            Value:                  True
            Amended:                False
            Local:                  True
            Overridable:            True
            Propagates to instance: False
            Propagates to subclass: False
```

If you run the script, you will notice that a lot of information scrolls on the screen. At the end of the chapter, based on the structure developed here and with the previous scripts, we will create a script that loads the CIM class information into an Excel sheet. This makes the retrieved information easy to review. But for now, there is another important topic to look at: the WMI object path retrieved from the WMI scripting API.

4.4.5   Retrieving WMI object information with its WMI path

At the beginning of this chapter, we saw that the WMI object path is an important parameter for locating objects in the CIM repository. Added to this, the WMI moniker completes the set of information required to establish the connection to a real-world manageable entity. The WMI scripting API offers various ways to navigate through the CIM classes. From one class it is possible to retrieve many classes based on their relationships with each

Figure 4.5
The WMI object
model (3/3).

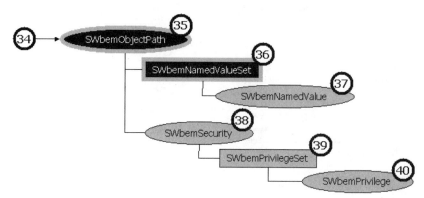

other. As classes have a relation, the instances of the classes also have the same kind of relation. At a certain time, after moving from one class to another, or from one instance to another, it would be interesting to retrieve the WMI object path of the examined class or instance. For this **SWbem-Object** exposes a property called *Path_*. This property retrieves a new object called **SWbemObjectPath**. This object is represented in Figure 4.4 with the number 34.

Since this object contains some other objects, the WMI object model organization for the **SWbemObjectPath** object is represented in Figure 4.5.

Let's take a look at Sample 4.24. The script retrieves the WMI object path information.

Sample 4.24   *Retrieving the WMI object path properties of a WMI class*

```
 1:<?xml version="1.0"?>
 .:
 8:<package>
 9:   <job>
..:
13:      <object progid="WbemScripting.SWbemLocator" id="objWMILocator" reference="true"/>
14:
15:      <script language="VBscript">
16:      <![CDATA[
..:
20:      Const cComputerName = "LocalHost"
21:      Const cWMINameSpace = "root/cimv2"
22:      Const cWMIClass = "Win32_Service"
..:
30:      objWMILocator.Security_.AuthenticationLevel = wbemAuthenticationLevelDefault
31:      objWMILocator.Security_.ImpersonationLevel = wbemImpersonationLevelImpersonate
32:      Set objWMIPrivilegeSet = objWMILocator.Security_.Privileges
33:      objWMIPrivilegeSet.AddAsString "SeRemoteShutdownPrivilege", True
34:      objWMIPrivilegeSet.AddAsString "SeSecurityPrivilege", True
35:      Set objWMIServices = objWMILocator.ConnectServer(cComputerName, cWMINameSpace, "", "")
36:
```

```
37:     Set objWMIInstance = objWMIServices.Get (cWMIClass)
38:
39:     Set objWMIPath = objWMIInstance.Path_
40:
41:     WScript.Echo "Authority: " & objWMIPath.Authority
42:     WScript.Echo "Class: " & objWMIPath.Class
43:     WScript.Echo "DisplayName: " & objWMIPath.DisplayName
44:     WScript.Echo "IsClass: " & objWMIPath.IsClass
45:     WScript.Echo "IsSingleton: " & objWMIPath.IsSingleton
46:
47:     Set objWMINamedValueSet = objWMIPath.Keys
48:     WScript.Echo "Keys#: " & objWMINamedValueSet.Count
49:     For Each objWMINamedValue In objWMINamedValueSet
50:         WScript.Echo "    " & objWMINamedValue.Name & ": " & objWMINamedValue.Value
51:     Next
52:
53:     WScript.Echo "Locale: " & objWMIPath.Locale
54:     WScript.Echo "Namespace: " & objWMIPath.Namespace
55:     WScript.Echo "ParentNamespace: " & objWMIPath.ParentNamespace
56:     WScript.Echo "Path: " & objWMIPath.Path
57:     WScript.Echo "Relpath: " & objWMIPath.Relpath
58:
59:     WScript.Echo "Security_ (AuthenticationLevel): " & _
60:                     objWMIPath.Security_.AuthenticationLevel
61:     WScript.Echo "Security_ (ImpersonationLevel): " & _
62:                     objWMIPath.Security_.ImpersonationLevel
63:
64:     Set objWMIPrivilegeSet = objWMIPath.Security_.Privileges
65:     For Each objWMIPrivilege In objWMIPrivilegeSet
66:         WScript.Echo "    " & objWMIPrivilege.Name & ": " & _
67:                         objWMIPrivilege.Identifier & " (" & _
68:                         objWMIPrivilege.IsEnabled & ")."
69:         WScript.Echo "    ->" & objWMIPrivilege.DisplayName
70:     Next
71:
72:     WScript.Echo "Server: " & objWMIPath.Server
..:
81:     ]]>
82:     </script>
83:   </job>
84:</package>
```

Initially, the script establishes a connection to a WMI object (lines 30 to 35). This connection is established with some privileged settings (lines 33 and 34). These privileges are set for academic purposes, as they are not required for the operation to be performed. Once done, the script retrieves the **SWbemObjectPath** object (line 39). Next, the script displays the values of every property (lines 41 to 57) exposed by the **SWbemObjectPath** object in Table 4.19. Note that some properties return objects. This is the case for the *Keys* property (line 47). This property returns an **SWbemNamedValue-Set** object, which is a collection of **SWbemNamedValue** objects. These two objects are located as numbers 36 and 37, respectively, in the object model shown in Figure 4.5. The methods and the properties exposed are available in Tables 4.20 and 4.21.

Table 4.19   *The SWbemObjectPath Object*

Properties		
	Authority	String that defines the Authority component of the object path.
	Class	Name of the class that is part of the object path.
	DisplayName	String that contains the path in a form that can be used as a moniker display name. See Object Creation and Monikers.
	IsClass	Boolean value that indicates if this path represents a class. This is analogous to the __Genus property in the COM API.
	IsSingleton	Boolean value that indicates if this path represents a singleton instance.
	Keys	An SWbemNamedValueSet object that contains the key value bindings.
	Locale	String containing the locale for this object path.
	Namespace	Name of the namespace that is part of the object path. This is the same as the __Namespace property in the COM API.
	ParentNamespace	Name of the parent of the namespace that is part of the object path.
	Path	Contains the absolute path. This is the same as the __Path system property in the COM API. This is the default property of this object.
	Relpath	Contains the relative path. This is the same as the __Relpath system property in the COM API.
	Security_	Used to read or change the security settings.
	Server	Name of the server. This is the same as the __Server system property in the COM API.
Methods	SetAsClass ()	Forces the path to address a WMI class.
	SetAsSingleton ()	Forces the path to address a singleton WMI instance.

Table 4.20   *The SWbemNamedValueSet Object*

Properties		
	Count	The number of items in the collection.
Methods	Add strName, varVal, [iFlags = 0]	Adds an SWbemNamedValue object to the collection.
	Clone ()	Makes a copy of this SWbemNamedValueSet collection.
	DeleteAll ()	Removes all items from the collection, making the SWbemNamedValueSet object empty.
	Item strName, [iFlags = 0]	Retrieves an SWbemNamedValue object from the collection. This is the default method of the object.
	Remove strName, [iFlags = 0]	Removes an SWbemNamedValue object from the collection.

Table 4.21		*The SWbemNamedValue Object*
Properties	Name	Name of the SWbemNamedValue item.
	Value	Value of the SWbemNamedValue item. This is the default property of this object.

The second object returned is an **SWbemSecurity** object (lines 59 to 64). This object is exactly the same as the one we saw associated to the **SWbemLocator** object in the beginning of this chapter. In Figure 4.5, the **SWbemSecurity** object and its child objects are represented with numbers 38 to 40. When the script is executed with a connection to a class defined in the CIM repository, the output is as follows:

```
 1:   Authority:
 2:   Class: Win32_Service
 3:   DisplayName: WINMGMTS:{authenticationLevel=pktPrivacy,impersonationLevel=impersonate,
 4:                          (Security,RemoteShutdown)}!\\W2K-DPEN6400\ROOT\CIMV2:Win32_Service
 5:   IsClass: True
 6:   IsSingleton: False
 7:   Keys#: 0
 8:   Locale:
 9:   Namespace: ROOT\CIMV2
10:   ParentNamespace: ROOT
11:   Path: \\W2K-DPEN6400\ROOT\CIMV2:Win32_Service
12:   Relpath: Win32_Service
13:   Security_ (AuthenticationLevel): 6
14:   Security_ (ImpersonationLevel): 3
15:     SeSecurityPrivilege: 7 (True).
16:     ->Manage auditing and security log
17:     SeRemoteShutdownPrivilege: 23 (True).
18:     ->Force shutdown from a remote system
19:   Server: W2K-DPEN6400
```

In this output, notice that the *DisplayName* (lines 3 and 4) is nothing more than the WMI moniker to access the class definition. As we access a class, we also see that the *IsClass* property is set to True (line 5). During the connection, the script sets some security settings and privileges with the **SWbemLocator** object in order to have something to display when examining the **SWbemSecurity** object linked with the **SWbemObjectPath** (lines 13 to 18). Notice also that the script is able to retrieve more informative text about the privilege itself (line 15 and 18). In the first line of the display output, you can see that the *Authority* property doesn't return anything. This is normal, as no authority has been set to establish the WMI connection. Another interesting thing is the *Relpath* property. This property simply returns the relative path of the class, which is nothing more than the name of the class (line 12). As we examine a class definition, there is no real-world manageable object instantiated. This is why there is no key listed (line 7). If we change a few lines (lines 22 and 36) in the object connection to connect to a real-world manageable object, the script connection part becomes as follows:

```
..:
..:
20:    Const cComputerName = "LocalHost"
21:    Const cWMINameSpace = "root/cimv2"
22:    Const cWMIClass = "Win32_Service"
23:    Const cWMIInstance = "SNMP"
..:
31:    objWMILocator.Security_.AuthenticationLevel = wbemAuthenticationLevelDefault
32:    objWMILocator.Security_.ImpersonationLevel = wbemImpersonationLevelImpersonate
33:    Set objWMIPrivilegeSet = objWMILocator.Security_.Privileges
34:    objWMIPrivilegeSet.AddAsString "SeRemoteShutdownPrivilege", True
35:    objWMIPrivilegeSet.AddAsString "SeSecurityPrivilege", True
36:    Set objWMIServices = objWMILocator.ConnectServer(cComputerName, cWMINameSpace, "", "")
37:
38:    Set objWMIInstance = objWMIServices.Get (cWMIClass & "='" & cWMIInstance & "'")
..:
..:
```

This script is basically the same as Sample 4.24 except that a WMI instance is retrieved. In this case, the output is:

```
 1:Authority:
 2:Class: Win32_Service
 3:DisplayName: WINMGMTS:{authenticationLevel=pktPrivacy,impersonationLevel=impersonate,
              (Security,RemoteShutdown)}!\\W2K-DPEN6400\root\cimv2:Win32_Service.Name="SNMP"
 4:IsClass: False
 5:IsSingleton: False
 6:Keys#: 1
 7:  Name: SNMP
 8:Locale:
 9:Namespace: root\cimv2
10:ParentNamespace: root
11:Path: \\W2K-DPEN6400\root\cimv2:Win32_Service.Name="SNMP"
12:Relpath: Win32_Service.Name="SNMP"
13:Security_ (AuthenticationLevel): 6
14:Security_ (ImpersonationLevel): 3
15:  SeSecurityPrivilege: 7 (True).
16:  ->Manage auditing and security log
17:  SeRemoteShutdownPrivilege: 23 (True).
18:  ->Force shutdown from a remote system
19:Server: W2K-DPEN6400
```

The output is the same as before, except that we can notice three major differences:

1.   Now that the script addresses a real-world instance (the SNMP *Win32_Service*), the *IsClass* property is set to False (line 4).

2.   There is a key value (line 7).

3.   The *DisplayName, Path,* and *Relpath* properties include the name of the referred instance.

4.4.6   **Working with partial instances**

Throughout the samples, each time a script retrieves an object instances all properties available from this object instance are returned. With WMI, it is possible to retrieve only the properties that are needed. In many cases, it is more expensive to retrieve all the properties of an instance than to retrieve just a few properties. WMI providers that support partial-instance operations can be much faster and use fewer computer resources because they only need to set or retrieve specific properties.

4.4.6.1   *Reading partial instances*

Some of the classes in the **Root\CIMv2** namespace that use the *CIMWin32* provider support partial-instance operations. It is important to note that WMI does not support partial-instance operations on instances that reside in the CIM repository and are not associated with a provider. Partial-instance operations are supported only when a provider supplies the instance. It is not a requirement for a provider to support partial-instance operations. In such a case, a provider may do the following:

- Provide more properties than the client requested

- Support partial-instance operations for some classes but not others

- Support partial-instance retrieval but not partial-instance update, or vice versa

Requesting a partial-instance operation is done by setting specific values in an **SWBemNamedValueSet** object. This **SWBemNamedValueSet** object is passed when retrieving the instance. The specific values set in **SWBem-NamedValueSet** are summarized in Table 4.22.

Sample 4.25 shows how to proceed for partial instance retrieval.

Sample 4.25   *Retrieving one partial instance of the Win32_Service class*

```
 1:<?xml version="1.0"?>
 .:
 8:<package>
 9:  <job>
..:
13:     <object progid="WbemScripting.SWbemLocator" id="objWMILocator" reference="true"/>
14:     <object progid="WbemScripting.SWbemNamedValueSet" id="objWMINamedValueSet" />
15:
16:     <script language="VBscript">
17:     <![CDATA[
..:
21:     Const cComputerName = "LocalHost"
22:     Const cWMINameSpace = "root/cimv2"
23:     Const cWMIClass = "Win32_Service"
```

```
24:     Const cWMIInstance = "SNMP"
..:
31:     objWMILocator.Security_.AuthenticationLevel = wbemAuthenticationLevelDefault
32:     objWMILocator.Security_.ImpersonationLevel = wbemImpersonationLevelImpersonate
33:     Set objWMIServices = objWMILocator.ConnectServer(cComputerName, cWMINameSpace, "", "")
34:
35:     objWMINamedValueSet.Add "__GET_EXTENSIONS", True
36:     objWMINamedValueSet.Add "__GET_EXT_CLIENT_REQUEST", True
37:     objWMINamedValueSet.Add "__GET_EXT_PROPERTIES", Array ("Name", "State")
38:
39:     Set objWMIInstance = objWMIServices.Get (cWMIClass & "='" & cWMIInstance & "'", _
40:                                               , _
41:                                               objWMINamedValueSet)
42:
43:     Set objWMIPropertySet = objWMIInstance.Properties_
44:     For Each objWMIProperty In objWMIPropertySet
45:         If Not IsNull (objWMIProperty.Value) Then
46:             If objWMIProperty.IsArray Then
47:                 For Each varElement In objWMIProperty.Value
48:                     WScript.Echo "   " & objWMIProperty.Name & " (" & varElement & ")"
49:                 Next
50:             Else
51:                 WScript.Echo "   " & objWMIProperty.Name & " (" & objWMIProperty.Value & ")"
52:             End If
53:         End If
54:     Next
..:
60:     ]]>
61:     </script>
62:   </job>
63:</package>
```

If you compare Sample 4.25 with Sample 4.13 ("Retrieving the property collection of a WMI instance"), you will notice a few changes. The first modification is the instantiation of the **SWBemNamedValueSet** object (line 14). The second important modification is the content initialization of the **SWBemNamedValue** object contained in the **SWBemNamedValueSet** (lines 35 to 37). These values are used as an input for the WMI provider to inform how a partial-instance operation must be processed. Line 35 specifies that a partial-instance operation must be performed, line 36 informs WMI that information stored in the **SWBemNamedValueSet** is on request from the WMI client, and line 37 lists the properties to be retrieved. If we execute the script, only 14 properties will be retrieved. Curiously, we listed only two properties to retrieve. Providers that support partial-instance retrieval may return more properties than the client requests while not returning the complete instance. This relies on the WMI provider implementation. Sample 4.25 illustrates this behavior. If Sample 4.25 is executed without a partial-instance reading, it retrieves 24 properties. However, with the partial-instance feature, only 13 properties are retrieved, even if only two properties are specified in the **SWbemNamedValueSet** object. This

Table 4.22   *Partial Instance Keyword Commands*

Instance Retrieval Named Values

__GET_EXTENSIONS	Boolean value set to TRUE. Used to signal that partial-instance retrieval operations are being used. If any of the other values are used, this one must be set.
__GET_EXT_PROPERTIES	Array of strings listing the properties to be retrieved. Cannot be simultaneously specified with __GET_EXT_KEYS_ONLY.
__GET_EXT_KEYS_ONLY	Boolean value set to TRUE. Indicates that only key(s) should be provided in the returned object. Cannot be simultaneously specified with __GET_EXT_PROPERTIES.
__GET_EXT_CLIENT_REQUEST	Boolean value set to TRUE. Indicates that the caller was the one who wrote the value into the context object and that it was not propagated from another dependent operation.

Instance Update Named Values

__PUT_EXTENSIONS	Boolean value set to TRUE. A value indicating that one or more of the other context values has been specified.
__PUT_EXT_STRICT_NULLS	Boolean value set to TRUE. Indicates that the client has intentionally set properties to Null and expects the write operation to succeed. If the provider cannot set the values to NULL, an error should be reported.
__PUT_EXT_PROPERTIES	Array of strings that contains a list of property names to be updated. May be used alone or in combination with __PUT_EXT_PROPERTIES. The values are, of course, in the instance being written.
__PUT_EXT_ATOMIC	Boolean value set to TRUE. Indicates that all updates must succeed simultaneously (atomic semantics) or the provider must revert back. There can be no partial success. May be used alone or in combination with other flags.
__PUT_EXT_CLIENT_REQUEST	Boolean value set to TRUE. Set by the client during the initial request. Used to prevent reentrancy errors.

demonstrates the partial-instance retrieval feature and the limitation imposed by the WMI provider.

Now, if line 37

```
37:     objWMINamedValueSet.Add "__GET_EXT_PROPERTIES", Array ("Name", "State")
```

is modified as follows

```
37:     objWMINamedValueSet.Add "__GET_EXT_KEYS_ONLY", True
```

the script retrieves only the *Key* properties of the instance. You must use one *NamedValue* or the other. These two *NamedValues* cannot be combined in the same **SWbemNamedValueSet**. Only four methods from the **SWBem-Services** object that retrieve a single instance support the partial-instance retrieval. These methods are:

1.   *Get*

2.   *GetAsync*

3.   *InstancesOf*

4.   *InstancesOfAsync*

4.4.6.2   *Updating partial instances*

Occasionally, you may want to update only part of an instance. For example, some instances have a large number of properties, or the system you are writing to does not update an instance entirely. Updating a large number of instances may reduce system performance. Therefore, it is possible to update only a part of an instance, and thus reduce the amount of information sent to WMI. However, WMI does not directly support partial-instance operations, nor do most providers. Therefore, if you write an application that uses partial-instance operations, be prepared for your calls to fail with either the **wbemErrProviderNotCapable** or **wbemErrNotSupported** error codes. Currently, the classes and the WMI provider we have worked with until now do not support the partial-instance update. However, this functionality will be ubiquitous when you work with the *SNMP* and *Active Directory* WMI providers.

In scripting, this operation is necessary only to aid performance when updating one or two writeable properties in a very large number of objects over an enterprise. Otherwise the normal invocations of the *Put_* or *PutAsync_* methods, while seeming to write the entire object, are actually only updating the properties that the provider has write-enabled. To perform a partial-instance update, the coding is exactly the same as the partial-instance retrieval. The difference resides in the keyword (see Table 4.22) used in the **SWbemNamedValueSet** object. For instance, the code snippet below illustrates the coding technique:

```
1:    objWMINamedValueSet.Add "__PUT_EXTENSIONS", True
2:    objWMINamedValueSet.Add "__PUT_EXT_CLIENT_REQUEST", True
3:    objWMINamedValueSet.Add "__PUT_EXT_PROPERTIES", Array ("Property1, Property2")
4:
5:    objWMIInstance.Put_ wbemChangeFlagUpdateOnly Or wbemFlagReturnWhenComplete, _
6:                        objWMINamedValueSet
```

Note the presence of the wbemChangeFlagUpdateOnly flag when invoking the *Put_* method of the **SWbemObject** object. If it is not specified, the method invocation will fail.

4.4.7   **Retrieving WMI object system properties**

When discovering Sample 4.13 ("Retrieving the property collection of a WMI instance"), we used an **SWbemPropertySet** collection object initialized with the *Properties_* property of the **SWbemObject**. Although this method retrieves the properties of an **SWbemObject** instance, it does not retrieve the system properties of the object. Under Windows XP and Windows.NET Server, the **SWbemObject** object exposes a property called *SystemProperties_* (see Table 4.10), returning an **SWbemPropertySet** object, which contains a collection of **SWbemProperty** objects representing system properties. This *SystemProperties_* property usage is illustrated in Sample 4.26.

Sample 4.26   *Retrieving the system properties of an SWbemObject*

```
 1:<?xml version="1.0"?>
 .:
 8:<package>
 9:  <job>
..:
13:    <object progid="WbemScripting.SWbemLocator" id="objWMILocator" reference="true"/>
14:
15:    <script language="VBscript">
16:    <![CDATA[
..:
20:    Const cComputerName = "LocalHost"
21:    Const cWMINameSpace = "root/cimv2"
22:    Const cWMIClass = "Win32_Service"
23:    Const cWMIInstance = "SNMP"
..:
30:    objWMILocator.Security_.AuthenticationLevel = wbemAuthenticationLevelDefault
31:    objWMILocator.Security_.ImpersonationLevel = wbemImpersonationLevelImpersonate
32:    Set objWMIServices = objWMILocator.ConnectServer(cComputerName, cWMINameSpace, "", "")
33:    Set objWMIInstance = objWMIServices.Get (cWMIClass & "='" & cWMIInstance & "'")
34:
35:    Set objWMIPropertySet = objWMIInstance.SystemProperties_
36:    For Each objWMIProperty In objWMIPropertySet
37:        If objWMIProperty.IsArray Then
38:            For Each varElement In objWMIProperty.Value
39:                WScript.Echo "  " & objWMIProperty.Name & " (" & varElement & ")"
40:            Next
41:        Else
42:            WScript.Echo "  " & objWMIProperty.Name & " (" & objWMIProperty.Value & ")"
43:        End If
44:    Next
..:
50:    ]]>
51:    </script>
52:  </job>
53:</package>
```

The *SystemProperties_* property reference at line 35 retrieves the list of system properties. Except for this small change, the script is exactly the same as that in Sample 4.13 ("Retrieving the property collection of a WMI instance"). The output of Sample 4.26 is as follows:

```
C:\>"GetSingleInstanceWithAPI (System Properties).wsf"
Microsoft (R) Windows Script Host Version 5.6
Copyright (C) Microsoft Corporation 1996-2001. All rights reserved.

    __PATH (\\PPC284346\root\cimv2:Win32_Service.Name="SNMP")
    __NAMESPACE (root\cimv2)
    __SERVER (PPC284346)
    __DERIVATION (Win32_BaseService)
    __DERIVATION (CIM_Service)
    __DERIVATION (CIM_LogicalElement)
    __DERIVATION (CIM_ManagedSystemElement)
    __PROPERTY_COUNT (25)
    __RELPATH (Win32_Service.Name="SNMP")
    __DYNASTY (CIM_ManagedSystemElement)
    __SUPERCLASS (Win32_BaseService)
    __CLASS (Win32_Service)
    __GENUS (2)
```

In this sample output, we see that the derivation hierarchy of the class is available. Although it is possible to use this method to retrieve the parent classes of the examined class (Sample 4.26 examines the *Win32_Service* class), the **SWbemObject** object exposes a more specialized property called *Derivation_*. Sample 4.27 shows how to use this property.

Sample 4.27   *Retrieving the parent classes (superclasses) of an SWbemObject*

```
 1:<?xml version="1.0"?>
 .:
 8:<package>
 9:  <job>
..:
13:    <object progid="WbemScripting.SWbemLocator" id="objWMILocator" reference="true"/>
14:
15:    <script language="VBscript">
16:    <![CDATA[
..:
20:    Const cComputerName = "LocalHost"
21:    Const cWMINameSpace = "root/cimv2"
22:    Const cWMIClass = "Win32_Service"
23:    Const cWMIInstance = "SNMP"
..:
30:    objWMILocator.Security_.AuthenticationLevel = wbemAuthenticationLevelDefault
31:    objWMILocator.Security_.ImpersonationLevel = wbemImpersonationLevelImpersonate
32:    Set objWMIServices = objWMILocator.ConnectServer(cComputerName, cWMINameSpace, "", "")
33:    Set objWMIInstance = objWMIServices.Get (cWMIClass & "='" & cWMIInstance & "'")
34:
35:    arrayParentClasses = objWMIInstance.Derivation_
36:    For Each varElement In arrayParentClasses
37:        WScript.Echo "  " & varElement
38:    Next
..:
```

```
43:    ]]>
44:    </script>
45:  </job>
46:</package>
```

The main difference of the *Derivation_* property is that it returns an array that contains the list of parent classes instead of a collection stored in an **SWbemPropertySet** object. The first element in the array defines the superclass and the last element defines the dynasty class (the top class of the hierarchy). A sample output for the *Win32_Service* class follows:

```
C:\>"GetSingleInstanceWithAPI (Derivation Property).wsf"
Microsoft (R) Windows Script Host Version 5.6
Copyright (C) Microsoft Corporation 1996-2001. All rights reserved.

   Win32_BaseService
   CIM_Service
   CIM_LogicalElement
   CIM_ManagedSystemElement
```

4.5   Browsing the namespaces in the CIM repository

Throughout this chapter, we have worked in the **Root\CIMv2** namespace. Although it is an important namespace because it contains most of the WMI Win32 class representing Windows manageable entities, there are other namespaces that contain quite useful information. As previously mentioned, instead of listing all namespaces and classes in tables, it is much more interesting to have a script to retrieve such information. This protects against any new non-documented WMI extensions, because a script can retrieve this information from the CIM repository for you. Note, as already mentioned, using a WQL query to retrieve all namespaces available is not possible because WQL does not support cross-namespace queries.

Since the classes are contained in namespaces, let's retrieve the namespaces first. In Chapter 2, we listed in Table 2.1 the namespaces available in the CIM repository. Sample 4.28 shows how to retrieve the namespaces available in the CIM repository.

Sample 4.28   *Browsing all namespaces defined in the CIM repository*

```
 1:<?xml version="1.0"?>
 .:
 8:<package>
 9:  <job>
..:
13:    <object progid="WbemScripting.SWbemLocator" id="objWMILocator" reference="true"/>
14:
```

```
15:     <script language="VBscript">
16:     <![CDATA[
..:
20:     Const cComputerName = "LocalHost"
21:     Const cWMINameSpace = "Root"
22:     Const cWMINamespaceClass = "__NAMESPACE"
23:
24:     DisplayNameSpaces cWMINameSpace
25:
26:     ' -----------------------------------------------------------------------
27:     Function DisplayNameSpaces (ByVal strWMINameSpace)
..:
32:         objWMILocator.Security_.AuthenticationLevel = wbemAuthenticationLevelDefault
33:         objWMILocator.Security_.ImpersonationLevel = wbemImpersonationLevelImpersonate
34:         Set objWMIServices = objWMILocator.ConnectServer(cComputerName, strWMINameSpace, "", "")
35:
36:         Set objWMINSInstances = objWMIServices.InstancesOf (cWMINamespaceClass,
wbemQueryFlagShallow)
37:
38:         For Each objWMINSInstance in objWMINSInstances
39:             WScript.Echo strWMINameSpace & "/" & objWMINSInstance.Name
40:             DisplayNameSpaces strWMINameSpace & "/" & objWMINSInstance.Name
41:         Next
..:
47:     End Function
48:
49:     ]]>
50:     </script>
51:   </job>
52:</package>
```

This script is a quite easy script as it uses just a few of the WMI scripting API objects mentioned in this chapter. Basically, the script starts to browse from the root namespace (line 21) by invoking a recursive function called DisplayNameSpaces() (line 24). This function performs a connection to the CIM repository with the **SWbemLocator** object (line 34). Once connected, the script requests the instances of the *__NAMESPACE* system class with the *InstancesOf* method of the **SWbemServices** object (line 36). As this method retrieves a collection, the script enumerates in a For Each loop the namespace collection. For instance, the script output when executed on a Windows.NET Server system is:

```
C:\>BrowseNameSpaceWithAPI.wsf
Microsoft (R) Windows Script Host Version 5.6
Copyright (C) Microsoft Corporation 1996-2000. All rights reserved.

Root/CIMV2
Root/CIMV2/ms_409
Root/Cli
Root/DEFAULT
Root/DEFAULT/ms_409
Root/directory
Root/directory/LDAP
Root/directory/LDAP/ms_409
```

```
            Root/Microsoft
            Root/Microsoft/HomeNet
            Root/MicrosoftActiveDirectory
            Root/MicrosoftADStatus
            Root/MicrosoftCluster
            Root/MicrosoftDNS
            Root/MicrosoftIISv2
            Root/MicrosoftIISv2/ms_409
            Root/MicrosoftNLB
            Root/MSAPPS
            Root/Policy
            Root/Policy/ms_409
            Root/RSOP
            Root/RSOP/Computer
            Root/RSOP/Computer/ms_409
            Root/RSOP/User
            Root/RSOP/User/ms_409
            Root/RSOP/User/S_1_5_21_2025429265_507921405_1202660629_1112
            Root/RSOP/User/S_1_5_21_2025429265_507921405_1202660629_1113
            Root/RSOP/User/S_1_5_21_2025429265_507921405_1202660629_500
            Root/Security
            Root/Security/SCE
            Root/snmp
            Root/snmp/localhost
            Root/subscription
            Root/subscription/ms_409
            Root/WMI
            Root/WMI/ms_409
```

If we reuse Sample 4.28 with some minor modifications based on our WMI object model knowledge, we can create a script that browses the WMI name spaces and locates instances of a given class. This is the purpose of Sample 4.29.

Sample 4.29   *Browsing the namespaces to find instances of a given class*

```
 1:<?xml version="1.0"?>
 .:
 8:<package>
 9:  <job>
..:
13:    <runtime>
14:      <unnamed name="Class" helpstring="the WMI Class instances to retrieve across all namespaces."
                            required="true" type="string" />
15:      <named name="Machine" helpstring="determine the WMI system to connect to. (default=LocalHost)"
                            required="false" type="string"/>
16:      <named name="User" helpstring="determine the UserID to perform the remote connection.
                            (default=none)" required="false" type="string"/>
17:      <named name="Password" helpstring="determine the password to perform the remote connection.
                            (default=none)" required="false" type="string"/>
18:    </runtime>
19:
20:    <script language="VBScript" src="..\Functions\DisplayInstanceProperties.vbs" />
21:    <script language="VBScript" src="..\Functions\TinyErrorHandler.vbs" />
```

```
22:
23:    <object progid="WbemScripting.SWbemLocator" id="objWMILocator" reference="true"/>
24:
25:    <script language="VBscript">
26:    <![CDATA[
..:
30:    Const cComputerName = "LocalHost"
31:    Const cWMINameSpace = "Root"
32:    Const cWMINamespaceClass = "__NAMESPACE"
33:    Const cWMIClass = "__EventProviderRegistration"
..:
39:    ' -----------------------------------------------------------------------------
40:    ' Parse the command line parameters
41:    If WScript.Arguments.Unnamed.Count = 0 Then
42:       strWMIClass = InputBox ("Enter the WMI Class to examine: ", _
43:                               "WMI Class:", _
44:                               cWMIClass)
45:
46:       If Len (strWMIClass) = 0 Then
47:          WScript.Arguments.ShowUsage ()
48:          WScript.Quit
49:       End If
50:    Else
51:       strWMIClass = WScript.Arguments.Unnamed.Item(0)
52:    End If
53:       strWMIClass = Ucase (strWMIClass)
54:
55:    strUserID = WScript.Arguments.Named("User")
56:    If Len(strUserID) = 0 Then strUserID = ""
57:
58:    strPassword = WScript.Arguments.Named("strPassword")
59:    If Len(strPassword) = 0 Then strPassword = ""
60:
61:    strComputerName = WScript.Arguments.Named("Machine")
62:    If Len(strComputerName) = 0 Then strComputerName = cComputerName
63:
64:    DisplayNameSpaces cWMINameSpace, strWMIClass, strUserID, strPassword, strComputerName
65:
66:    ' -----------------------------------------------------------------------------
67:    Function DisplayNameSpaces (ByVal strWMINameSpace, _
68:                                ByVal strWMIClass, _
69:                                ByVal strUserID, _54:
70:                                ByVal strPassword, _
71:                                ByVal strComputerName)
..:
81:       objWMILocator.Security_.AuthenticationLevel = wbemAuthenticationLevelDefault
82:       objWMILocator.Security_.ImpersonationLevel = wbemImpersonationLevelImpersonate
83:       Set objWMIServices = objWMILocator.ConnectServer(strComputerName, strWMINameSpace,
                                                           strUserID, strPassword)
84:       If Err.Number Then ErrorHandler (Err)
85:
86:       Set objWMIInstances = objWMIServices.InstancesOf (strWMIClass, wbemQueryFlagShallow)
87:       If Err.Number Then
88:          Err.Clear
89:       Else
90:          WScript.Echo strWMINameSpace
91:          For Each objWMIInstance in objWMIInstances
92:             DisplayProperties objWMIInstance, 2
93:          Next
94:          Set objWMIInstances = Nothing
```

```
 95:        End If
 96:
 97:        Set objWMINSInstances = objWMIServices.InstancesOf (cWMINamespaceClass, wbemQueryFlagShallow)
 98:        For Each objWMINSInstance in objWMINSInstances
 99:            DisplayNameSpaces strWMINameSpace & "/" & objWMINSInstance.Name, _
100:                              strWMIClass, strUserID, strPassword, strComputerName
101:        Next
...:
106:    End Function
107:
108:    ]]>
109:    </script>
110:  </job>
111:</package>
```

The script uses the same structure as Sample 4.28. The addition concerns the retrieval of the instances of a given class. By default, the script retrieves the instances of the __*EventProviderRegistration* system class across all namespaces. Any other class can be provided, as the script accepts another class name from its command line parameters. For this, the script uses the WSH XML command line parsing features (lines 41 to 62) explained in Chapter 1. Next, the script calls the same recursive function (line 64) as Sample 4.28. In the recursive function, the script connects to the examined namespace (line 83) and instantiates the given class at line 86. If no error occurs, the script enumerates the instances (lines 91 to 93) and lists their related properties (lines 92). The DisplayProperties() function, displaying the instance properties, encapsulates the same logic used throughout this chapter to explore the **SWBemPropertySet** object. This is nothing new from a WMI scripting API point of view; it is just a different organization used to retrieve information (see Sample 4.30 below). Note that the routine adds information about the syntax used by the property (line 33, 38, 45, 53, 61, 66, and 74) and converts any Date/Time value to a readable format by using a new WMI object called **SWBemDateTime** (line 50). We will revisit this object in the next chapter. The routine is shown in Sample 4.30.

Sample 4.30   *A generic routine to display the SWbemPropertySet object*

```
 .:
 .:
 .:
 6:' --------------------------------------------------------------------------------------
 7:Function DisplayProperties (objWMIInstance, intIndent)
..:
14:    Set objWMIPropertySet = objWMIInstance.Properties_
15:    For Each objWMIProperty In objWMIPropertySet
16:
17:        boolCIMKey = objWMIProperty.Qualifiers_.Item("key").Value
18:        If Err.Number Then
19:            Err.Clear
```

```
20:            boolCIMKey = False
21:        End If
22:        If boolCIMKey Then
23:            strCIMKey = "*"
24:        Else
25:            strCIMKey = ""
26:        End If
27:
28:        If Not IsNull (objWMIProperty.Value) Then
29:            If objWMIProperty.CIMType = wbemCimtypeObject Then
30:                If objWMIProperty.IsArray Then
31:                    For Each varElement In objWMIProperty.Value
32:                        WScript.Echo Space (intIndent) & strCIMKey & objWMIProperty.Name & _
33:                                    " (" & GetCIMSyntaxText (objWMIProperty.CIMType) & ")"
34:                        DisplayProperties varElement, intIndent + 2
35:                    Next
36:                Else
37:                    WScript.Echo Space (intIndent) & strCIMKey & objWMIProperty.Name & _
38:                                " (" & GetCIMSyntaxText (objWMIProperty.CIMType) & ")"
39:                    DisplayProperties objWMIProperty.Value, intIndent + 2
40:                End If
41:            Else
42:                If objWMIProperty.IsArray Then
43:                    For Each varElement In objWMIProperty.Value
44:                        WScript.Echo Space (intIndent) & strCIMKey & objWMIProperty.Name & _
45:                                    " (" & GetCIMSyntaxText (objWMIProperty.CIMType) & ") = " & _
46:                                        varElement
47:                    Next
48:                Else
49:                    If objWMIProperty.Name = "TIME_CREATED" Then
50:                        objWMIDateTime.SetFileTime (objWMIProperty.Value)
51:
52:                        WScript.Echo Space (intIndent) & strCIMKey & objWMIProperty.Name & _
53:                                    " (" & GetCIMSyntaxText (objWMIProperty.CIMType) & ") = " & _
54:                                        objWMIDateTime.GetVarDate (True) & _
55:                                        " (" & objWMIDateTime.Value & ")
56:                    Else
57:                        If objWMIProperty.CIMType = wbemCimtypeDatetime Then
58:                            objWMIDateTime.Value = objWMIProperty.Value
59:
60:                            WScript.Echo Space (intIndent) & strCIMKey & objWMIProperty.Name & _
61:                                        " (" & GetCIMSyntaxText (objWMIProperty.CIMType) & ") = " & _
62:                                            objWMIDateTime.GetVarDate (True) & _
63:                                            " (" & objWMIProperty.Value & ")"
64:                        Else
65:                            WScript.Echo Space (intIndent) & strCIMKey & objWMIProperty.Name & _
66:                                        " (" & GetCIMSyntaxText (objWMIProperty.CIMType) & ") = " & _
67:                                            objWMIProperty.Value
68:                        End If
69:                    End If
70:                End If
71:            End If
72:        Else
73:            WScript.Echo Space (intIndent) & strCIMKey & objWMIProperty.Name & _
74:                        " (" & GetCIMSyntaxText (objWMIProperty.CIMType) & ") = (null)"
75:        End If
76:    Next
..:
79:End Function
80:
```

```
 81:' -------------------------------------------------------------------------------
 82:Function GetCIMSyntaxText (intCIMType)
 83:
 84:    Select Case intCIMType
 85:           ' Signed 16-bit integer
 86:           Case 2
 87:               GetCIMSyntaxText = "wbemCimtypeSint16"
 88:           ' Signed 32-bit integer
 89:           Case 3
 90:               GetCIMSyntaxText = "wbemCimtypeSint32"
 91:           ' 32-bit real number
 92:           Case 4
 93:               GetCIMSyntaxText = "wbemCimtypeReal32"
 94:           ' 64-bit real number
 95:           Case 5
 96:               GetCIMSyntaxText = "wbemCimtypeReal64"
 97:           ' String
 98:           Case 8
 99:               GetCIMSyntaxText = "wbemCimtypeString"
100:           ' Boolean value
101:           Case 11
102:               GetCIMSyntaxText = "wbemCimtypeBoolean"
...:
124:           ' Date/time value
125:           Case 101
126:               GetCIMSyntaxText = "wbemCimtypeDatetime"
127:           ' Reference to a CIM object.
128:           Case 102
129:               GetCIMSyntaxText = "wbemCimtypeReference"
130:           ' 16-bit character
131:           Case 103
132:               GetCIMSyntaxText = "wbemCimtypeChar16"
133:    End Select
134:
135:End Function
```

There are two particularities in this routine. First, if the property syntax is an object (**wbemCimtypeObject**), then the routine is executed recursively to examine the properties of the object (lines 34 and 39). This ensures that an object is encapsulated in a property (as will be the case when we capture WMI events from scripts in Chapter 6) to display the object's properties content. Second, if the property name is *TIME_CREATED* or if its syntax is a time (**wbemCimtypeDatetime**), the property value is stored in **SWbemDateTime** object. An **SWbemDateTime** object is a helper object designed to convert the DMTF time format into some more readable forms.

The following output shows the results obtained when executing Sample 4.30, if we are searching for all instances of the *Win32_WMISetting* class. Notice that the property information mentions the CIM syntax.

```
C:\>BrowseNameSpaceForInstancesWithAPI.wsf Win32_WMISetting
Microsoft (R) Windows Script Host Version 5.6
Copyright (C) Microsoft Corporation 1996-2000. All rights reserved.
```

```
Root/CIMV2
  ASPScriptDefaultNamespace (wbemCimtypeString) = root\cimv2
  ASPScriptEnabled (wbemCimtypeBoolean) = (null)
  AutorecoverMofs (wbemCimtypeString) = J:\WINDOWS\system32\WBEM\cimwin32.mof
  AutorecoverMofs (wbemCimtypeString) = J:\WINDOWS\system32\WBEM\cimwin32.mfl
  AutorecoverMofs (wbemCimtypeString) = J:\WINDOWS\system32\WBEM\system.mof
  AutorecoverMofs (wbemCimtypeString) = J:\WINDOWS\system32\WBEM\wmipcima.mof
  AutorecoverMofs (wbemCimtypeString) = J:\WINDOWS\system32\WBEM\wmipcima.mfl
  AutorecoverMofs (wbemCimtypeString) = J:\WINDOWS\system32\WBEM\regevent.mof
  . . . . . . . . . . . . . . . . .
  . . . . . . . . . . . . . . . . .
  AutorecoverMofs (wbemCimtypeString) = J:\WINDOWS\system32\wbem\ADStatus\TrustMon.mof
  AutorecoverMofs (wbemCimtypeString) = J:\WINDOWS\System32\replprov.mof
  AutorecoverMofs (wbemCimtypeString) = J:\WINDOWS\system32\WBEM\MOF\good\msioff9.mof
  AutorecoverMofs (wbemCimtypeString) = J:\Program Files\Microsoft Platform SDK\Bin\WMI\Ev
  AutoStartWin9X (wbemCimtypeUint32) = (null)
  BackupInterval (wbemCimtypeUint32) = 30
  BackupLastTime (wbemCimtypeDatetime) = 13-05-2001 15:24:28
  BuildVersion (wbemCimtypeString) = 2462.0000
  Caption (wbemCimtypeString) = (null)
  DatabaseDirectory (wbemCimtypeString) = J:\WINDOWS\system32\WBEM\Repository
  DatabaseMaxSize (wbemCimtypeUint32) = (null)
  Description (wbemCimtypeString) = (null)
  EnableAnonWin9xConnections (wbemCimtypeBoolean) = (null)
  EnableEvents (wbemCimtypeBoolean) = True
  EnableStartupHeapPreallocation (wbemCimtypeBoolean) = False
  HighThresholdOnClientObjects (wbemCimtypeUint32) = 20000000
  HighThresholdOnEvents (wbemCimtypeUint32) = 20000000
  InstallationDirectory (wbemCimtypeString) = J:\WINDOWS\system32\WBEM
  LastStartupHeapPreallocation (wbemCimtypeUint32) = (null)
  LoggingDirectory (wbemCimtypeString) = J:\WINDOWS\system32\WBEM\Logs\
  LoggingLevel (wbemCimtypeUint32) = 1
  LowThresholdOnClientObjects (wbemCimtypeUint32) = 10000000
  LowThresholdOnEvents (wbemCimtypeUint32) = 10000000
  MaxLogFileSize (wbemCimtypeUint32) = 65536
  MaxWaitOnClientObjects (wbemCimtypeUint32) = 60000
  MaxWaitOnEvents (wbemCimtypeUint32) = 2000
  MofSelfInstallDirectory (wbemCimtypeString) = J:\WINDOWS\system32\WBEM\MOF
  SettingID (wbemCimtypeString) = (null)
```

Another variation of the script is shown in Sample 4.31. It uses basically the same logic as Sample 4.29 ("Browsing the namespaces to find instances of a given class"), but instead of retrieving the class instances, it retrieves the class definition across namespaces. The code is similar to that shown in Sample 4.29, but instead of using the *InstancesOf* method of the **SWbem-Services** object, it uses the *Get* method of the **SWbemServices** object (line 85) with logic modified accordingly.

Sample 4.31   *Browsing the namespaces to find class definitions*

```
. . :
. . :
. . :
82:          objWMILocator.Security_.AuthenticationLevel = wbemAuthenticationLevelDefault
83:          objWMILocator.Security_.ImpersonationLevel = wbemImpersonationLevelImpersonate
```

```
 84:          Set objWMIServices = objWMILocator.ConnectServer(strComputerName, strWMINameSpace,
                                                               strUserID, strPassword)
 85:          If Err.Number Then ErrorHandler (Err)
 86:
 87:          Set objWMIInstance = objWMIServices.Get (strWMIClass)
 88:          If Err.Number Then
 89:             Err.Clear
 90:          Else
 91:             WScript.Echo strWMINameSpace
 92:             DisplayProperties objWMIInstance, 2
 93:             Set objWMIInstance = Nothing
 94:          End If
 95:
 96:          Set objWMINSInstances = objWMIServices.InstancesOf (cWMINamespaceClass, wbemQueryFlagShallow)
 97:          For Each objWMINSInstance in objWMINSInstances
 98:             DisplayNameSpaces strWMINameSpace & "/" & objWMINSInstance.Name, _
 99:                               strWMIClass, strUserID, strPassword, strComputerName
100:          Next
101:          Set objWMINSInstances = Nothing
102:
103:          Set objWMIServices = Nothing
...:
...:
...
```

The following output shows the results obtained when executing Sample 4.31 if we are searching for the *Win32_WMISetting* class. Notice that the property value is empty, as we retrieve the class definition and not its instance.

```
C:\>BrowseNameSpaceForClassWithAPI.wsf Win32_WMISetting
Microsoft (R) Windows Script Host Version 5.6
Copyright (C) Microsoft Corporation 1996-2001. All rights reserved.

Root/CIMV2
  ASPScriptDefaultNamespace (wbemCimtypeString) = \\root\cimv2
  ASPScriptEnabled (wbemCimtypeBoolean) = (null)
  AutorecoverMofs (wbemCimtypeString) = (null)
  AutoStartWin9X (wbemCimtypeUint32) = (null)
  BackupInterval (wbemCimtypeUint32) = (null)
  BackupLastTime (wbemCimtypeDatetime) = (null)
  BuildVersion (wbemCimtypeString) = (null)
  Caption (wbemCimtypeString) = (null)
  DatabaseDirectory (wbemCimtypeString) = (null)
  DatabaseMaxSize (wbemCimtypeUint32) = (null)
  Description (wbemCimtypeString) = (null)
  EnableAnonWin9xConnections (wbemCimtypeBoolean) = (null)
  EnableEvents (wbemCimtypeBoolean) = (null)
  EnableStartupHeapPreallocation (wbemCimtypeBoolean) = (null)
  HighThresholdOnClientObjects (wbemCimtypeUint32) = (null)
  HighThresholdOnEvents (wbemCimtypeUint32) = (null)
  InstallationDirectory (wbemCimtypeString) = (null)
  LastStartupHeapPreallocation (wbemCimtypeUint32) = (null)
  LoggingDirectory (wbemCimtypeString) = (null)
  LoggingLevel (wbemCimtypeUint32) = (null)
  LowThresholdOnClientObjects (wbemCimtypeUint32) = (null)
  LowThresholdOnEvents (wbemCimtypeUint32) = (null)
  MaxLogFileSize (wbemCimtypeUint32) = (null)
```

```
  MaxWaitOnClientObjects (wbemCimtypeUint32) = (null)
  MaxWaitOnEvents (wbemCimtypeUint32) = (null)
  MofSelfInstallDirectory (wbemCimtypeString) = (null)
  SettingID (wbemCimtypeString) = (null)
Root/CIMV2/ms_409
  ASPScriptDefaultNamespace (wbemCimtypeString) = (null)
  ASPScriptEnabled (wbemCimtypeBoolean) = (null)
  AutorecoverMofs (wbemCimtypeString) = (null)
  AutoStartWin9X (wbemCimtypeUint32) = (null)
  BackupInterval (wbemCimtypeUint32) = (null)
  BackupLastTime (wbemCimtypeDatetime) = (null)
  BuildVersion (wbemCimtypeString) = (null)
  Caption (wbemCimtypeString) = (null)
  DatabaseDirectory (wbemCimtypeString) = (null)
  DatabaseMaxSize (wbemCimtypeUint32) = (null)
  Description (wbemCimtypeString) = (null)
  EnableAnonWin9xConnections (wbemCimtypeBoolean) = (null)
  EnableEvents (wbemCimtypeBoolean) = (null)
  EnableStartupHeapPreallocation (wbemCimtypeBoolean) = (null)
  HighThresholdOnClientObjects (wbemCimtypeUint32) = (null)
  HighThresholdOnEvents (wbemCimtypeUint32) = (null)
  InstallationDirectory (wbemCimtypeString) = (null)
  LastStartupHeapPreallocation (wbemCimtypeUint32) = (null)
  LoggingDirectory (wbemCimtypeString) = (null)
  LoggingLevel (wbemCimtypeUint32) = (null)
  LowThresholdOnClientObjects (wbemCimtypeUint32) = (null)
  LowThresholdOnEvents (wbemCimtypeUint32) = (null)
  MaxLogFileSize (wbemCimtypeUint32) = (null)
  MaxWaitOnClientObjects (wbemCimtypeUint32) = (null)
  MaxWaitOnEvents (wbemCimtypeUint32) = (null)
  MofSelfInstallDirectory (wbemCimtypeString) = (null)
  SettingID (wbemCimtypeString) = (null)
```

4.6   A script to explore the CIM repository

As we explore WMI we discover many tables describing the methods and the properties exposed by the different objects that constitute the WMI scripting API. Besides the WMI scripting API features list, there are also the CIM class definitions. The only CIM class definition really used (up to now) is the *Win32_Service* class shown in Table 4.1. WMI offers more than 600 CIM classes. As the number of CIM classes is quite huge, it is impossible to list all the properties and methods exposed by these classes.

Based on the materials covered in this chapter, it is much more valuable to think about a script retrieving the interesting information about any CIM classes. Because everything resides in the CIM repository, it is possible to produce readable output of that content. This is the purpose of the next sample, which summarizes the miscellaneous WMI scripting APIs we have discovered.

What do we mean by "readable output"? Since there is a lot of information to display, a good place to load this information is in an Excel sheet.

This facilitates the review of the information once the script has been executed. Which information is to loaded in the Excel sheet? The script retrieves all information related to the CIM class definitions. This implies the following:

- The CIM class with its related qualifiers

- The CIM class properties with their related qualifiers

- The CIM class methods with their related qualifiers

- The CIM class method parameters with their related qualifiers

- The CIM classes derived from a CIM class

Of course, retrieving all the information in a single run is probably too much in some cases. A nice thing would be to specify a script input parameter that defines the level of information to be retrieved. This filters the retrieved information. Doing so, the script user would be able to select the quantity of information to load into the Excel sheet.

The script performing this task is displayed in Sample 4.32. Before examining the script code, let's see how the script can be used and the type of result it will produce. This will help to understand the code. First, the script makes extensive use of the WSH features for a Windows Script File (see Chapter 1) to read the command-line parameters. Here is the Help output of the script input parameters:

```
C:\>LoadCIMinXL.Wsf /?
Microsoft (R) Windows Script Host Version 5.6
Copyright (C) Microsoft Corporation 1996-2000. All rights reserved.

Usage: LoadCIMinXL Class [/Machine:value][/NameSpace:value][/Level:value][/Sub[+|-]][/Origin[+|-]]

Options:

Class      : the WMI Class to explore.
Machine    : determine the WMI system to connect to. (default=LocalHost)
User       : determine the UserID to perform the remote connection. (default=none)
Password   : determine the password to perform the remote connection. (default=none)
NameSpace  : determine the WMI namespace to connect to. (default=Root\CIMv2
Level      : determine the depth of the CIM repository exploration. (default=5)
               1: Load the class name(s) only.
               2: Load the class name(s) with the class properties.
               3: Load the class name(s) with the class properties and methods.
               4: Load the class name(s) with the class properties, methods
                  and method input parameters.
               5: Load the class name(s) with the class properties, methods
                  and method input/output parameters.
               6: Load the class name(s) with the class properties, methods,
                  method input/output parameters and qualifiers.
Sub        : Explore subclasses. (Default=False)
Origin     : Show properties and methods if examined class is the origin. (Default=False)
```

Because the purpose of the script is to examine a CIM class definition, the script requests an existing class name as a mandatory parameter. This is the purpose of the **/Class** parameter. It is now possible to specify another machine than the one on which the script is running. This optional parameter is a switch called **/Machine**. If you perform a connection to another system, the script proposes to specify a UserID and a password with the switches **/User** and **/Password**. By default, the script uses the current security context. The script examines the **Root\CIMv2** namespace, but it is possible to specify another WMI namespace by using the **/Namespace** switch. Next, it is possible to determine the amount of information to be retrieved with the **/Level** switch. Each level corresponds to a certain quantity of information to be retrieved from the CIM repository. Let's examine the different levels and what they retrieve:

- **Level 1:** This level retrieves only the class name from the CIM repository. This level is of interest only when the **/Sub** switch is enabled. In this case, if the class is derived, the script will load all the subclasses in an indented way. This shows the parent-child relationship between classes.

- **Level 2:** This level retrieves the information provided in level 1 plus the properties exposed by the CIM class. Note that the combination of the **/Sub** switch produces the output of the properties for the given class and the classes derived from that class.

- **Level 3:** This level retrieves the information provided by previous levels plus the methods exposed by the CIM class. If the **/Sub** switch is provided, the method of the derived class is also retrieved.

- **Level 4:** This level retrieves the information provided by previous levels plus the input parameters of the retrieved methods. The script behaves in the same way as before if the **/Sub** switch is given.

- **Level 5:** This level is the same as level 4, except that the script will also retrieve the output parameters returned by the methods associated with the CIM classes. The script behaves in the same way as before if the **/Sub** switch is given. This level is the default level used by the script if no level is specified.

- **Level 6:** This level retrieves the biggest set of information from the CIM repository. It retrieves all information given by previous levels plus all WMI qualifiers related to every property, method, and method parameter.

There is another switch we have not yet mentioned. This is the **/Origin** switch. Usually, the script retrieves the information from a CIM class even if

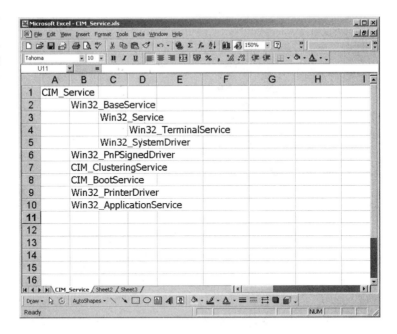

Figure 4.6
*The CIM_Service
class and its child
classes loaded in an
Excel sheet.*

the considered CIM class has a property or a method inherited from a parent class. By specifying the **/Origin** switch, the script will retrieve the information associated with a class only if that information is directly defined in that class. In other words, if the property or the method is inherited from a parent class, the script will not display that information. This switch has a real interest if it is used in combination with the **/Sub** switch. During the examination of the parent class and any derived classes, the output shows where the properties and the methods are defined. Note that with level 6, the output contains information showing the origin of the related property or method (which class defines that property or method).

Let's examine an output sample with the following command line:

```
C:\>LoadCIMinXL.Wsf CIM_Service /Sub+ /Level:1
```

Figure 4.6 contains the output.

Of course, using Excel to load such information is not really interesting. But now, let's examine the output obtained by examining the *Win32_Service* class with the following command line:

```
C:\>LoadCIMinXL.Wsf Win32_Service /Machine:MyLocalMachine /Namespace:ROOT\CIMv2 /Level:5
```

This is the same as issuing the same command without parameters, since the previous command-line sample uses the defaults used by the script:

```
C:\>LoadCIMinXL.Wsf Win32_Service
```

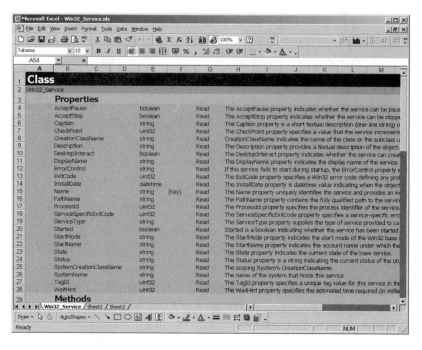

Figures 4.7 and 4.8 contain the output.

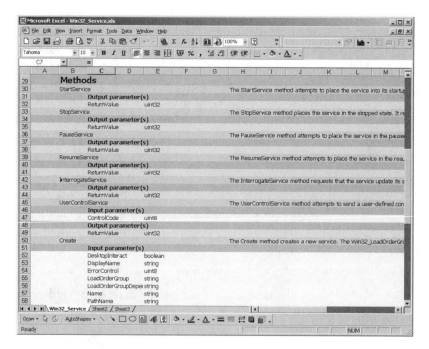

The script makes extensive use of colors to clarify the distinction between the CIM class properties, the CIM class methods, and the CIM class method input and output parameters.

By using the following command line:

```
C:\>LoadCIMinXL.Wsf Win32_Service /Level:6
```

the script will retrieve the maximum information available. In this case, every qualifier available for every CIM class property, CIM class method, and CIM class method input and output parameter will be loaded in to the Excel sheet. Sample output is shown in Figure 4.9.

For instance, with the qualifiers displayed, it is easy to determine whether a CIM class is an association class or a singleton class. For the properties, the qualifiers inform you whether a CIM class property is read-only or read/write. The qualifier also determines whether the CIM class property is a key. Since the amount of information can be very large, Figure 4.9 can't

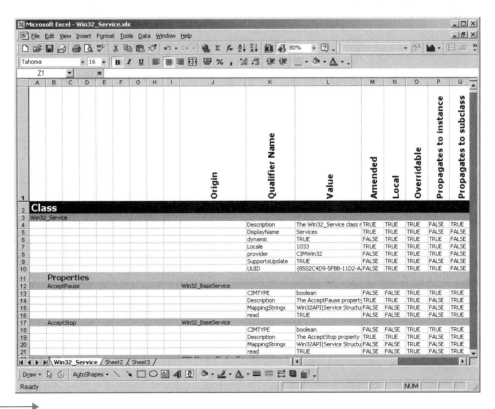

Figure 4.9   *The Win32_Service class with its properties, methods, and all existing qualifiers in an Excel sheet.*

display the complete output, but we recommend that you play with the script to discover its possibilities. Once you get used to it, you will realize the real possibilities offered by the script (as a real tool) to retrieve live information about a CIM class definition. This script will be helpful for all subsequent programming that can be performed on any class available from the CIM repository.

Now that we know what we can perform with the script, let's examine how the script is coded. It is only a brief examination as all of the materials used in this script have been discussed throughout this chapter. The script code is presented in Sample 4.32.

Since the data read from the CIM repository is loaded into an Excel sheet, the script performs a lot of Excel sheet formatting operations. Based on the nature of the information loaded (directly in relation with the **/Level** switch defined), the script formats the cell with a particular font size and background color. To get a complete understanding of Microsoft Excel object programming, you can refer to the Microsoft Office Programming SDK. If you don't have access to such a reference, you will see by reading the script that most of the statements are easy to understand.

Sample 4.32   *A Windows Script File self-documenting the CIM repository classes in an Excel sheet*

```
 1:<?xml version="1.0"?>
 .:
 8:<package>
 9:  <job>
..:
13:    <runtime>
..:
31:    </runtime>
32:
33:    <script language="VBScript" src="..\Functions\TinyErrorHandler.vbs" />
34:
35:    <object progid="WbemScripting.SWbemLocator" id="objWMILocator" reference="true"/>
36:    <object progid="EXCEL.application" id="objXL"/>
37:    <object progid="WScript.Shell" id="WshSHell"/>
38:
39:    <script language="VBscript">
40:    <![CDATA[
..:
44:    Const cLevelClassOnly = 1
45:    Const cLevelClassWithProps = 2
46:    Const cLevelClassWithPropsAndMethods = 3
47:    Const cLevelClassWithPropsAndMethodsWithInParams = 4
48:    Const cLevelClassWithPropsAndMethodsWithInOutParams = 5
49:    Const cLevelClassWithPropsQAndMethodsQWithParamsQ = 6
..:
63:    Const cComputerName = "LocalHost"
64:    Const cWMINameSpace = "Root/CIMv2"
```

```
 ..:
 81:    ' ----------------------------------------------------------------------------
 82:    ' Parse the command line parameters
 83:    If WScript.Arguments.Unnamed.Count = 0 Then
 84:        strWMIClass = InputBox ("Enter the WMI Class to examine: ", _
 85:                                "WMI Class:", _
 86:                                "Win32_Service")
 87:
 88:        If Len (strWMIClass) = 0 Then
 89:           WScript.Arguments.ShowUsage()
 90:           WScript.Quit
 91:        End If
 92:    Else
 93:        strWMIClass = WScript.Arguments.Unnamed.Item(0)
 94:    End If
 95:    ' strWMIClass = Ucase (strWMIClass)
 96:
 97:    strUserID = WScript.Arguments.Named("User")
 98:    If Len(strUserID) = 0 Then strUserID = ""
 99:
100:    strPassword = WScript.Arjuments.Named(Password:)
101:    If Len(strPassword) = 0 Then strPassword = ""
102:
103:    strComputerName = WScript.Arguments.Named("Machine")
104:    If Len(strComputerName) = 0 Then strComputerName = cComputerName
105:
106:    strWMINameSpace = WScript.Arguments.Named("NameSpace")
107:    If Len(strWMINameSpace) = 0 Then strWMINameSpace = cWMINameSpace
108:    strWMINameSpace = UCase (strWMINameSpace)
109:
110:    intExplorationDepth = Cint (WScript.Arguments.Named("Level"))
111:    If intExplorationDepth = 0 Then
112:        intExplorationDepth = cLevelClassWithPropsAndMethodsWithInOutParams
113:    End If
114:
115:    boolSubClass = WScript.Arguments.Named("Sub")
116:    boolOrigin = Not WScript.Arguments.Named("Origin")
117:
118:    ' ----------------------------------------------------------------------------
119:    ' Prepare an Excel worksheet
120:    ' Make it visible, don't hide it because for the save, the user will be prompted!
121:    objXL.Visible = True
122:
123:    ' Open Excel and start an empty workbook
124:    objXL.Workbooks.Add
125:
126:    ' Put the cursor on the A1 cell
127:    objXL.ActiveSheet.range("A1").Activate
128:    objXL.ActiveSheet.Name = Mid (strWMIClass, 1, 31)
129:
130:    objXL.Columns("A:Z").Font.Name = "Tahoma"
131:    objXL.Columns("A:Z").IndentLevel = 0
132:    objXL.Columns("A:Z").VerticalAlignment = 2
133:
134:    If intExplorationDepth > cLevelClassWithPropsAndMethodsWithInOutParams Then
135:
136:        ' Format the XL Sheet
137:        objXL.Columns("A:I").ColumnWidth = 5
138:        objXL.Columns("J").ColumnWidth = 22
```

```
139:        objXL.Columns("K").ColumnWidth = 16
140:        objXL.Columns("L").ColumnWidth = 22
141:        objXL.Columns("M:Z").ColumnWidth = 7
142:        objXL.Rows("1").Orientation = 90
143:        objXL.Rows("1").VerticalAlignment = 3
144:        objXL.Rows("1").HorizontalAlignment = 3
145:
146:        objXL.Range("A" & objXL.ActiveCell.Row & ":Z" & objXL.ActiveCell.Row).Font.Bold = True
147:        objXL.Range("A" & objXL.ActiveCell.Row & ":Z" & objXL.ActiveCell.Row).Font.Size = 16
148:
149:        intX = cOriginPosition
150:        ' Origin
151:        objXL.Activecell.Offset(0, intX).Value = "Origin"
152:
153:        intX = cQualifierPosition
154:        ' Name
155:        objXL.Activecell.Offset(0, intX).Value = "Qualifier Name"
156:        ' Value
157:        objXL.Activecell.Offset(0, intX + 1).Value = "Value"
158:        ' Amended
159:        objXL.Activecell.Offset(0, intX + 2).Value = "Amended"
160:        ' Local
161:        objXL.Activecell.Offset(0, intX + 3).Value = "Local"
162:        ' Overridable
163:        objXL.Activecell.Offset(0, intX + 4).Value = "Overridable"
164:        ' Propagates to instance
165:        objXL.Activecell.Offset(0, intX + 5).Value = "Propagates to instance"
166:        ' Propagates to subclass
167:        objXL.Activecell.Offset(0, intX + 6).Value = "Propagates to subclass"
168:
169:        intX = 0
170:        objXL.Activecell.Offset(1, 0).Activate
171:    End If
172:
173:    ' ----------------------------------------------------------------------------
174:    ' Connect to WMI
175:    objWMILocator.Security_.AuthenticationLevel = wbemAuthenticationLevelDefault
176:    objWMILocator.Security_.ImpersonationLevel = wbemImpersonationLevelImpersonate
177:    Set objWMIServices = objWMILocator.ConnectServer(strComputerName, _
178:                                                     strWMINameSpace, _
179:                                                     strUserID, _
180:                                                     strPassword)
181:    If Err.Number Then ErrorHandler (Err)
182:
183:    DisplayClasses intX, objWMIServices, strWMIClass
...:
187:    ' ----------------------------------------------------------------------------
188:    objXL.ActiveSheet.range("A1").Activate
189:
190:    ' Save & Close the Workbook. If file exists, user will be prompted.
192:         (WshShell.CurrentDirectory & "\" & objXL.ActiveSheet.Name)
193:    objXL.Workbooks.close
194:    objXL.Quit
195:
196:    ' ----------------------------------------------------------------------------
197:    Function DisplayClasses (ByVal intX, ByVal objWMIServices, ByVal strWMIClass)
...:
209:        Set objWMIInstance = objWMIServices.Get (strWMIClass, wbemFlagUseAmendedQualifiers)
210:        If Err.Number Then ErrorHandler (Err)
211:
```

```
191:    objXL.Workbooks.Application.ActiveWorkbook.SaveAs _
212:        If intExplorationDepth > cLevelClassOnly Then
213:            ' Format the XL sheet
214:            objXL.Range(...).Font.Bold = True
215:            objXL.Range(...).Font.Size = 18

216:            objXL.Range(...).Font.ColorIndex = White1
217:            objXL.Range(...).Interior.ColorIndex = Black
218:
219:            ' List the classes
220:            ' Class
221:            objXL.Activecell.Offset(0, 0).Value = "Class"
222:            objXL.Activecell.Offset(1, 0).Activate
223:        End If
224:
225:        WScript.Echo Space (intX) & strWMIClass
226:        objXL.Activecell.Offset(0, intX).Value = strWMIClass
227:
228:        If intExplorationDepth > cLevelClassOnly Then
229:            ' Format the XL sheet
230:            objXL.Range(...).Interior.ColorIndex = Aqua1
231:        End If
232:
233:        If intExplorationDepth > cLevelClassWithPropsAndMethodsWithInOutParams Then
234:            DisplayQualifiers (objWMIInstance.Qualifiers_)
235:        End If
236:
237:        objXL.Activecell.Offset(1, 0).Activate
238:
239:        If intExplorationDepth > cLevelClassOnly Then
240:            Set objWMIPropertySet = objWMIInstance.Properties_
241:            If objWMIPropertySet.Count Then
242:                intX = intX + 1
243:
244:                ' Format the XL Sheet
245:                objXL.Range(...).Font.Bold = True
246:                objXL.Range(...).Font.Size = 14
247:                objXL.Range(...).Interior.ColorIndex = Silver
248:
249:                ' List the properties of the Class
250:                ' Properties
251:                objXL.Activecell.Offset(0, intX).Value = "Properties"
252:                objXL.Activecell.Offset(1, 0).Activate
253:
254:                For Each objWMIProperty In objWMIPropertySet
255:
256:                    If (objWMIProperty.Origin = strWMIClass) Or boolOrigin Then
257:                        objXL.Activecell.Offset(0, intX).Value = objWMIProperty.Name
258:                        objXL.Range(...).Interior.ColorIndex = Aqua2
259:                        If intExplorationDepth < cLevelClassWithPropsQAndMethodsQWithParamsQ Then
260:                            objXL.Activecell.Offset(0, intX + 3).Value =
                                               objWMIProperty.Qualifiers_.Item("CIMTYPE").Value
261:
262:                        boolCIMKey = objWMIProperty.Qualifiers_.Item("key").Value
263:                        If Err.Number Then
264:                            Err.Clear
265:                            boolCIMKey = False
266:                        End If
267:                        If boolCIMKey Then
268:                            objXL.Activecell.Offset(0, intX + 4).Value = "(Key)"
```

```
269:                    End If
270:
271:                    boolCIMRead = objWMIProperty.Qualifiers_.Item("read").Value
272:                    If Err.Number Then
273:                        Err.Clear
274:                        boolCIMRead = False
275:                    End If .
276:
277:                    boolCIMWrite = objWMIProperty.Qualifiers_.Item("write").Value
278:                    If Err.Number Then
279:                        Err.Clear
280:                        boolCIMWrite = False
281:                    End If
282:
283:                    If boolCIMRead ANd boolCIMWrite Then
284:                        objXL.Activecell.Offset(0, intX + 5).Value = "Read/Write"
285:                    Else
286:                        If boolCIMRead Then
287:                            objXL.Activecell.Offset(0, intX + 5).Value = "Read"
288:                        End If
289:                        If boolCIMWrite Then
290:                            objXL.Activecell.Offset(0, intX + 5).Value = "Write"
291:                        End If
292:                    End If
293:
294:                    strDescription = objWMIProperty.Qualifiers_.Item("Description").Value
295:                    If Err.Number Then
296:                        Err.clear
297:                    Else
298:                        objXL.Activecell.Offset(0, intX + 6).Value = strDescription
299:                        objXL.Activecell.Offset(0, intX + 6).WrapText = False
300:                    End If
301:
302:                End If
303:                If intExplorationDepth >
                    cLevelClassWithPropsAndMethodsWithInOutParams Then
304:                    objXL.Activecell.Offset(0, cOriginPosition).Value =
                                    objWMIProperty.Origin
305:                    DisplayQualifiers (objWMIProperty.Qualifiers_)
306:                End If
307:
308:                objXL.Activecell.Offset(1, 0).Activate
309:            End If
310:        Next
311:    End If
312:    Set objWMIPropertySet = Nothing
313:
314:    If intExplorationDepth > cLevelClassWithProps Then
315:        Set objWMIMethodSet = objWMIInstance.Methods_
316:        If objWMIMethodSet.Count Then
317:            ' Format the XL Sheet
318:            objXL.Range(...).Font.Bold = True
319:            objXL.Range(...).Font.Size = 14
320:            objXL.Range(...).Interior.ColorIndex = Silver
321:
322:            ' List the methods of the Class
323:            ' Properties
324:            objXL.Activecell.Offset(0, intX).Value = "Methods"
325:            objXL.Activecell.Offset(1, 0).Activate
```

```
326:
327:                     For Each objWMIMethod In objWMIMethodSet
328:                         If (objWMIMethod.Origin = strWMIClass) Or boolOrigin Then
329:                             objXL.Activecell.Offset(0, intX).Value = objWMIMethod.Name
330:                             objXL.Range(...).Interior.ColorIndex = White2
331:                             If intExplorationDepth >
                                     cLevelClassWithPropsAndMethodsWithInOutParams Then
332:                                 objXL.Activecell.Offset(0, cOriginPosition).Value =
                                                     objWMIMethod.Origin
333:                                 DisplayQualifiers (objWMIMethod.Qualifiers_)
334:                             Else
335:                                 strDescription = objWMIMethod.Qualifiers_.Item("Description").Value
336:                                 If Err.Number Then
337:                                     Err.clear
338:                                 Else
339:                                     objXL.Activecell.Offset(0, intX + 6).Value = strDescription
340:                                     objXL.Activecell.Offset(0, intX + 6).WrapText = False
341:                                 End If
342:                             End If
343:                             objXL.Activecell.Offset(1, 0).Activate
344:
345:                             If intExplorationDepth > cLevelClassWithPropsAndMethods Then
346:                                 Set objWMIObject = objWMIMethod.InParameters
347:                                 Set objWMIPropertySet = objWMIObject.Properties_
348:                                 If Err.Number = 0 Then
349:                                     intX = intX + 1
350:
351:                                     ' Format the XL Sheet
352:                                     objXL.Range(...).Font.Bold = True
353:                                     objXL.Range(...).Font.Size = 10
354:                                     objXL.Range(...).Interior.ColorIndex = Silver
355:
356:                                     ' List the methods of the Class
357:                                     ' Parameters
358:                                     objXL.Activecell.Offset(0, intX).Value = "Input parameter(s)"
359:                                     If intExplorationDepth >
                                             cLevelClassWithPropsAndMethodsWithInOutParams Then
360:                                         DisplayQualifiers (objWMIObject.Qualifiers_)
361:                                     End If
362:                                     objXL.Activecell.Offset(1, 0).Activate
363:
364:                                     For Each objWMIProperty In objWMIPropertySet
365:
366:                                         If (objWMIProperty.Origin = strWMIClass) Or boolOrigin Then
367:                                             objXL.Activecell.Offset(0, intX).Value =
                                                             objWMIProperty.Name
368:                                             objXL.Range(...).Interior.ColorIndex = White3
369:                                             If intExplorationDepth =
                                                     cLevelClassWithPropsAndMethodsWithInParams Or _
370:                                                 intExplorationDepth =
                                                     cLevelClassWithPropsAndMethodsWithInOutParams Then
371:                                                 objXL.Activecell.Offset(0, intX + 2).Value =
                                                     objWMIProperty.Qualifiers_.Item("CIMTYPE").Value
372:                                                 strDescription =
                                                     objWMIProperty.Qualifiers_.Item("Description").Value
373:                                                 If Err.Number Then
374:                                                     Err.clear
375:                                                 Else
376:                                                     objXL.Activecell.Offset(0, intX + 5).Value =
                                                             strDescription
```

```
377:                            objXL.Activecell.Offset(0, intX + 5).WrapText =
                                  False
378:                        End If
379:                      End If
380:                      If intExplorationDepth >
                            cLevelClassWithPropsAndMethodsWithInOutParams Then
381:                          objXL.Activecell.Offset(0, cOriginPosition).Value =
                                objWMIProperty.Origin
382:                          DisplayQualifiers (objWMIProperty.Qualifiers_)
383:                        End If
384:                        objXL.Activecell.Offset(1, 0).Activate
385:                    End If

387:              Next
388:              intX = intX - 1
389:            Else
390:              Err.Clear
391:            End If
392:            Set objWMIPropertySet = Nothing
393:            Set objWMIObject = Nothing
394:          End If

396:          If intExplorationDepth >
                cLevelClassWithPropsAndMethodsWithInParams Then
397:            Set objWMIObject = objWMIMethod.OutParameters
398:            Set objWMIPropertySet = objWMIObject.Properties_
399:            If Err.Number = 0 Then
400:              intX = intX + 1

402:              ' Format the XL Sheet
403:              objXL.Range(...).Font.Bold = True
404:              objXL.Range(...).Font.Size = 10
405:              objXL.Range(...).Interior.ColorIndex = Silver

407:              ' List the methods of the Class
408:              ' Parameters
409:              objXL.Activecell.Offset(0, intX).Value = "Output parameter(s)"
410:              If intExplorationDepth >
                    cLevelClassWithPropsAndMethodsWithInOutParams Then
411:                DisplayQualifiers (objWMIObject.Qualifiers_)
412:              End If
413:              objXL.Activecell.Offset(1, 0).Activate

415:              For Each objWMIProperty In objWMIPropertySet

417:                If (objWMIProperty.Origin = strWMIClass) Or boolOrigin Then
418:                    objXL.Activecell.Offset(0, intX).Value =
                                    objWMIProperty.Name
419:                    objXL.Range(...).Interior.ColorIndex = Yellow
420:                    If intExplorationDepth =
                        cLevelClassWithPropsAndMethodsWithInOutParams Then
421:                      objXL.Activecell.Offset(0, intX + 2).Value =
                            objWMIProperty.Qualifiers_.Item("CIMTYPE").Value
422:                      strDescription =
                          objWMIProperty.Qualifiers_.Item("Description").Value
423:                      If Err.Number Then
424:                        Err.clear
425:                      Else
426:                        objXL.Activecell.Offset(0, intX + 5).Value =
                              strDescription
```

```
427:                                        objXL.Activecell.Offset(0, intX + 5).WrapText =
                                                       False
428:                                    End If
429:                                End If
430:                                If intExplorationDepth >
                                        cLevelClassWithPropsAndMethodsWithInOutParams Then
431:                                    objXL.Activecell.Offset(0, cOriginPosition).Value =
                                                      objWMIProperty.Origin
432:                                    DisplayQualifiers (objWMIProperty.Qualifiers_)
433:                                End If
434:                                objXL.Activecell.Offset(1, 0).Activate
435:                            End If
436:
437:                        Next
438:                        intX = intX - 1
439:                    Else
440:                        Err.Clear
441:                    End If
442:                    Set objWMIPropertySet = Nothing
443:                    Set objWMIObject = Nothing
444:                End If
445:            End If
446:
447:        Next
448:      End If
449:      Set objWMIMethodSet = Nothing
450:    End If451:
452:    Set objWMIInstance = Nothing
453:
454:    intX = intX - 1
455: End If
456:
457: If boolSubClass Then
458:    Set objWMISubClasses = objWMIServices.SubClassesOf (strWMIClass, _
459:                                         wbemQueryFlagShallow)
460:    For Each objWMISubClass in objWMISubClasses
461:        DisplayClasses intX + 1, objWMIServices, objWMISubClass.Path_.RelPath
462:    Next
463:    Set objWMISubClasses = Nothing
464: End If
465:
466: End Function
467:
468: ' ----------------------------------------------------------------------------
469: Function DisplayQualifiers (objWMIQualifiers)
...:
478:    intX = cQualifierPosition
479:
480:    For Each objWMIQualifier In objWMIQualifiers
481:        objXL.Activecell.Offset(1, 0).Activate
482:        objXL.Activecell.Offset(0, intX).Value = objWMIQualifier.Name
483:        If IsArray (objWMIQualifier.Value) Then
484:            For Each varElement In objWMIQualifier.Value
485:                If Len (objXL.Activecell.Offset(0, intX + 1).Value) = 0 Then
486:                    objXL.Activecell.Offset(0, intX + 1).Value = varElement
487:                Else
488:                    objXL.Activecell.Offset(0, intX + 1).Value =
                                objXL.Activecell.Offset(0, intX + 1).Value & _
489:                                                Chr(10) & _
490:                                                varElement
```

```
491:                    End If
492:                    If Ucase (objWMIQualifier.Name) = "DESCRIPTION" Then
493:                        objXL.Activecell.Offset(0, intX + 1).WrapText = False
494:                    End If
495:                Next
496:            Else
497:                objXL.Activecell.Offset(0, intX + 1).Value = objWMIQualifier.Value
498:                If Ucase (objWMIQualifier.Name) = "DESCRIPTION" Then
499:                    objXL.Activecell.Offset(0, intX + 1).WrapText = False
500:                End If
501:            End if
502:
503:            ' Amended
504:            objXL.Activecell.Offset(0, intX + 2).Value = objWMIQualifier.IsAmended
505:            ' Local
506:            objXL.Activecell.Offset(0, intX + 3).Value = objWMIQualifier.IsLocal
507:            ' Overridable
508:            objXL.Activecell.Offset(0, intX + 4).Value = objWMIQualifier.IsOverridable
509:            ' Propagates to instance
510:            objXL.Activecell.Offset(0, intX + 5).Value = objWMIQualifier.PropagatesToInstance
511:            ' Propagates to subclass
512:            objXL.Activecell.Offset(0, intX + 6).Value = objWMIQualifier.PropagatesToSubclass
513:        Next
514:
515:    End Function
516:
517:    ]]>
518:    </script>
519:  </job>
520:</package>
```

Basically, the script contains three distinct sections:

1.   **The initialization part (lines 40 to 183).** This section contains the variables and constants declaration (line 44 to 81), the command-line parameters reading with the defaults (lines 83 to 116), the Excel sheet creation and formatting (lines 120 to 171), and the WMI connection with the WMI scripting API (lines 175 to 181).

2.   **The section loading the information in the Excel sheet.** This part of the script is contained in a subfunction called at line 183. Basically, this subfunction (lines 197 to 466) implements the same structure as the function created in Sample 4.8 ("Retrieving the class inheritance tree with the SWbemServices object") to examine the subclasses recursively (lines 458 to 463). Before examining the subclasses, the script also looks at the following:

     ■   The class qualifiers (line 234)

     ■   The class properties (lines 240 to 312)

     ■   The class property qualifiers (line 305)

     ■   The class methods (lines 315 to 449)

- The class method qualifiers (line 333)

- The class method input parameters (lines 346 to 393)

- The class method input parameter qualifiers (line 360)

- The class method output parameters (lines 397 to 443)

- The class method output parameter qualifiers (line 411)

Even if this part of the script looks more complex simply because of the presence of the Excel statements formatting and loading data in the Excel sheet, by looking carefully at the pure WMI code logic you will notice that the logic is exactly the same as that discovered in the previous scripts. This script combines everything together.

3. **The section containing the function displaying the qualifiers (lines 469 to 515).** Basically, this function is the same as the one used before, but instead of outputting to a DOS command-prompt screen, the data is loaded in to the created Excel sheet.

4.7 Summary

This chapter is the first to discuss WMI scripting. We thoroughly recommend that you practice this technology to achieve a better active knowledge of the WMI scripting API.

As we have seen, it is possible to instantiate CIM classes or real-world manageable entities (mapped on defined CIM classes) by using a moniker or a series of WMI scripting APIs. Moreover, the security can be set at different object levels of the WMI scripting API. Besides these two aspects, it is also possible to combine the WMI scripting API with WQL queries.

However, we didn't examine all the WMI scripting API capabilities. Throughout the various samples we mainly discovered how the object model is organized. There are many more things to discover. For instance, we must still discover how asynchronous WMI operations can be performed, how WMI integrates with ADSI, and how a WMI instance can be represented in XML. These techniques are explained in the following chapter.

Mastering the scripting possibilities of the WMI COM API is key to developing management scripts for a production environment. This is why we focus on the WMI COM object capabilities before discussing the application of this technology to the real world.

5

Advanced WMI Scripting Techniques

5.1 Objective

In the previous chapter, we examined the WMI scripting object model with its basic operations to retrieve real-world manageable object information. Although, we perform the exact same task in this chapter, we explore some advanced scripting techniques with the same set of WMI scriptable objects. In the previous chapter, we used a specific set of methods that implemented synchronous scripting techniques, which resulted in a WMI operation (i.e., retrieving instance information) executing in-line with the code execution. In this chapter, we see how to use the WMI asynchronous operations by examining another set of methods available from the same WMI object collection. The asynchronous scripting techniques allow the execution of one more subroutine in parallel, which increases the execution performance. WMI extends ADSI by adding new properties and methods to facilitate the instantiation of some WMI scriptable objects. Moreover, WMI also exposes some helper objects to manipulate the DMTF date format or to retrieve instance information in XML. Let's see how these advanced features work.

5.2 Working with CIM instances asynchronously

The **SWbemServices** and **SWbemObject** objects expose various methods to perform different tasks (see Tables 4.8 and 4.10). Some of these methods are executed in line with the script code and force the script to pause until the method is executed (synchronous execution). Depending on the action to be performed, some methods may take some time to execute (i.e., stopping the Exchange Information Store service of an Exchange server hosting a mailbox store of 25 GB or more). To increase script execution performance and responsiveness, the WMI scripting API exposes a second set of identical methods but, at invocation time, these methods do not wait for the end of the WMI method execution; they are executed asynchronously. This allows execution of the script to continue while the invoked method is performed. When monitoring a system, it is likely that a process watching different manageable entities must perform several actions at the same time. A process that stops while executing one operation may cause trouble if an action with higher priority must be taken at the same time.

Table 5.1   *The Synchronous Methods Versus the Asynchronous Methods*

SWbemServices *Methods*

Synchronous	*Asynchronous*	
AssociatorsOf	AssociatorsOfAsync	Returns a collection of objects (classes or instances) that are associated with a specified object. This method performs the same function that the ASSOCIATORS OF WQL query performs.
Delete	DeleteAsync	Deletes an instance or class.
ExecMethod	ExecMethodAsync	Executes an object method.
ExecNotificationQuery	ExecNotificationQueryAsync	Executes a query to receive events.
ExecQuery	ExecQueryAsync	Executes a query to retrieve a collection of objects (classes or instances).
Get	GetAsync	Retrieves a class or instance.
InstancesOf	InstancesOfAsync	Returns a collection of instances of a specified class.
ReferencesTo	ReferencesToAsync	Returns a collection of objects (classes or instances) that refer to a single object. This method performs the same function that the REFERENCES OF WQL query performs.
SubclassesOf	SubclassesOfAsync	Returns a collection of subclasses of a specified class.

SWbemObject *Methods*

Synchronous	*Asynchronous*	
Associators_	AssociatorsAsync_	Retrieves the associators of the object.
Delete_	DeleteAsync_	Deletes the object from WMI.
ExecMethod_	ExecMethodAsync_	Executes a method exported by a method provider.
Instances_	InstancesAsync_	Returns a collection of instances of the object (which must be a WMI class).
Put_	PutAsync_	Creates or updates the object in WMI.
References_	ReferencesAsync_	Returns references to the object.
Subclasses_	SubclassesAsync_	Returns a collection of subclasses of the object (which must be a WMI class).

Moving from the WMI synchronous scripting technique to the WMI asynchronous scripting technique moves us closer to the WMI event scripting we discover in the next chapter. The asynchronous scripting provides a good foundation to work with the WMI event scripting because it allows a simultaneous event management. Table 5.1 shows the list of asynchronous methods available from **SWbemServices** and **SWbemObject** objects with their synchronous equivalent methods.

5.2.1   Retrieving a CIM instance

Basically, all operations that can be performed with a synchronous method can be performed with an asynchronous method. In the previous chapter, we saw that the *Get* method of the **SWbemServices** object was able to retrieve a class or an instance based on the WMI path used. We can perform the same operation with the *GetAsync* method. In this case the *GetAsync* method does not return an object. However, if the method invocation is successful, a sink routine receives an **SWbemObject** equivalent to the one obtained with the *Get* method.

Here we introduce a new term in the WMI scripting vocabulary: a sink routine. When working with the WMI asynchronous scripting technique, the script structure is a bit different. Although the WMI connection processed with the **SWbemLocator** object (or with a moniker) and the creation of the **SWbemServices** object are the same, the way the object instance is retrieved is different. Basically, every asynchronous method corresponds to a subroutine that must be part of the script invoking the method. When invoking an asynchronous method, an **SWbemSink** object must be created. This object is passed as a parameter to reference the subroutines that receive the created instance. WMI asynchronous scripting supports four subroutines (called *sink routines*):

1.   *OnCompleted* is triggered when an asynchronous operation is completed.

2.   *OnObjectPut* is triggered after an asynchronous put operation.

3.   *OnObjectReady* is triggered when an object provided by an asynchronous call is available.

4.   *OnProgress* is triggered to provide the status of an asynchronous operation. It is important to note that the WMI provider must support the status update to use this sink routine.

Let's look at an example instead of going through long theoretical explanations. Sample 5.1 retrieves the *Win32_Service* SNMP instance asynchronously. It performs the exact same task as Sample 4.1 ("A VBScript listing the Win32_Service instance properties"). Sample 4.1 retrieves the *Win32_Service* SNMP instance synchronously, whereas Sample 5.1, retrieves the same information asynchronously.

Sample 5.1   *A Windows Script File listing the Win32_Service instance properties asynchronously*

```
 1:<?xml version="1.0"?>
 .:
 8:<package>
 9:  <job>
..:
13:     <object progid="WbemScripting.SWbemLocator" id="objWMILocator" reference="true"/>
14:
15:     <script language="VBscript">
16:     <![CDATA[
..:
24:     ' -------------------------------------------------------------------------------------
25:     Const cComputerName = "LocalHost"
26:     Const cWMINameSpace = "root/cimv2"
27:     Const cWMIClass   = "Win32_Service"
28:     Const cWMIInstance = "SNMP"
..:
33:     Set objWMISink = WScript.CreateObject ("WbemScripting.SWbemSink", "SINK_")
34:
35:     objWMILocator.Security_.AuthenticationLevel = wbemAuthenticationLevelDefault
36:     objWMILocator.Security_.ImpersonationLevel = wbemImpersonationLevelImpersonate
37:     Set objWMIServices = objWMILocator.ConnectServer(cComputerName, cWMINameSpace, "", "")
38:
39:     objWMIServices.GetAsync objWMISink, cWMIClass & "='" & cWMIInstance & "'"
40:
41:     WScript.Echo "Continuing script execution ..."
42:     PauseScript "Click on 'Ok' to terminate the script ..."
43:
44:     objWMISink.Cancel
..:
51:     ' -------------------------------------------------------------------------------------
52:     Sub SINK_OnCompleted (intHResult, objWMILastError, objWMIAsyncContext)
53:
54:         Wscript.Echo
55:         Wscript.Echo "BEGIN - OnCompleted."
56:
57:         If intHResult = 0 Then
58:             WScript.Echo "WMI Scripting API Asynchronous call successful."
59:         Else
60:             WScript.Echo "WMI Scripting API Asynchronous call failed."
61:         End If
62:
63:         Wscript.Echo "END   - OnCompleted."
64:
65:     End Sub
66:
67:     ' -------------------------------------------------------------------------------------
68:     Sub SINK_OnObjectPut (objWMIPath, objWMIAsyncContext)
69:
70:         Wscript.Echo
```

```
 71:          Wscript.Echo "BEGIN - OnObjectPut."
 72:          Wscript.Echo "END   - OnObjectPut."
 73:
 74:      End Sub
 75:
 76:      ' ------------------------------------------------------------------------------
 77:      Sub SINK_OnObjectReady (objWMIInstance, objWMIAsyncContext)
 78:
 79:          Wscript.Echo
 80:          Wscript.Echo "BEGIN - OnObjectReady."
 81:          WScript.Echo objWMIInstance.Name & " (" & objWMIInstance.Description & ")"
 82:          WScript.Echo "    AcceptPause=" & objWMIInstance.AcceptPause
 83:          WScript.Echo "    AcceptStop=" & objWMIInstance.AcceptStop
 84:          WScript.Echo "    Caption=" & objWMIInstance.Caption
..:
 98:          WScript.Echo "    Started=" & objWMIInstance.Started
 99:          WScript.Echo "    StartMode=" & objWMIInstance.StartMode
100:          WScript.Echo "    StartName=" & objWMIInstance.StartName
101:          WScript.Echo "    State=" & objWMIInstance.State
102:          WScript.Echo "    Status=" & objWMIInstance.Status
103:          WScript.Echo "    SystemCreationClassName=" & objWMIInstance.SystemCreationClassName
104:          WScript.Echo "    SystemName=" & objWMIInstance.SystemName
105:          WScript.Echo "    TagId=" & objWMIInstance.TagId
106:          WScript.Echo "    WaitHint=" & objWMIInstance.WaitHint
107:          Wscript.Echo "END   - OnObjectReady."
108:
109:      End Sub
110:
111:      ' ------------------------------------------------------------------------------
112:      Sub SINK_OnProgress (intUpperBound, intCurrent, strMessage, objWMIAsyncContext)
113:
114:          Wscript.Echo
115:          Wscript.Echo "BEGIN - OnProgress."
116:          Wscript.Echo "END   - OnProgress."
117:
118:      End Sub
119:
120:      ' ------------------------------------------------------------------------------
121:      Function PauseScript (strMessage)
122:
123:      Dim WshShell
124:
125:          Set WshShell = Wscript.CreateObject("Wscript.Shell")
126:          WshShell.Popup strMessage, 0, "Pausing Script ...", cExclamationMarkIcon + cOkButton
127:          Wscript.DisconnectObject (WshShell)
128:          Set WshShell = Nothing
129:
130:      End Function
131:
132:      ]]>
133:      </script>
134:   </job>
135:</package>
```

Once the **SWbemServices** object is created (line 37), the *GetAsync* method can be invoked (line 39). The particularity of the invocation resides in the parameter containing an **SWbemSink** object. Accessing information asynchronously implies a call to a subroutine for the desired operation. It means that the invoked asynchronous method must know where the call must be executed. We saw that we have four possible sink routines with WMI asynchronous operations, each of which corresponds to a particular event. As we saw in Chapter 1, when working with the Windows Script Components event support, a reference between the event handler and the event name is performed. With WMI, the logic is exactly the same. However, the mechanism is implemented with an **SWbemSink** object created at line 33. It links the sink routines targeted to receive asynchronous calls with the execution of the asynchronous **SWbemServices** method. Since the script specifies a "SINK_" name in an **SWbemSink** object (line 33) for the sink routines concerning the *GetAsync* method execution, the script may have four sink routines named as follows:

1.   SINK_OnCompleted () at line 52.

2.   SINK_OnObjectPut () at line 68.

3.   SINK_OnObjectReady () at line 77.

4.   SINK_OnProgress () at line 112.

Of course, because the script executes a *GetAsync* method, the SINK_OnObjectPut() function is never called, as it does not relate to this operation type.

The other parameter of the *GetAsync* method is a traditional instance name to select the WMI instance to work with (line 39). Once the asynchronous method is invoked, the script must pause or proceed with some other tasks. As it is only a small sample designed to show how things works, the script pauses by calling the PauseScript() subfunction (line 42). The PauseScript() function invokes the *Popup* method of the **Wshshell** object from WSH to display a message (lines 121 to 130). Even if the script is stopped by the popup message, you will see that by executing the script the properties of the instantiated SNMP *Win32_Service* are displayed on the screen (see Figure 5.1).

The output shown in Figure 5.1 is generated by the SINK_OnObjectReady() function that receives the instance from the *GetAsync* method. When the method is executed, it produces an **SWbemObject** available from the parameters provided by the sink routine itself (line 77). In comparison with the synchronous *Get* method of the **SWbemServices** object, the **SWbemObject** is produced on return of the call of the *Get* method. Now, with the asynchronous execution of the *GetAsync* method, the produced **SWbemObject** is available from the sink routine called SINK_OnObjectReady(). Except for the location where this object is available, this is

Figure 5.1   *The GetAsync method execution output.*

exactly the same object as before. This is why the routine displays all the properties available from the object instance (lines 81 to 106) as made in Sample 4.1. Once the *GetAsync* method is complete, the SINK_OnCompleted() executes. The execution of the SINK_OnCompleted() uses the **intHResult** parameter to determine whether the asynchronous method execution has been successful.

This last sample retrieves one instance of a *Win32_Service*. What happens if the script retrieves a collection of instances of the *Win32_Service* class? The same mechanisms take place, but every instance available from the asynchronous method generates a SINK_OnObjectReady() function call. To retrieve all instances of the *Win32_Service* class, line 39 can be changed to

```
39:     objWMIServices.InstancesOfAsync objWMISink, cWMIClass
```

or to

```
39:     objWMIServices.ExecQueryAsync objWMISink, "Select * From " & cWMIClass
```

Note the interesting aspect of such logic. With the synchronous scripting technique, when an **SWbemServices** method returns an object collection, it is necessary to enumerate the returned **SWbemObjectSet** object collection with a For Each loop. Now, as the method is asynchronous, there is no need to perform an enumeration, because the sink routine is called for every instance available. At the end of the asynchronous method execution, the SINK_OnCompleted() sink routine is called.

5.2.2   Retrieving CIM information

Because the WMI object retrieved in the sink routine is a traditional **SWbemObject**, all the properties and methods exposed by the COM object itself (see Table 4.10) and by its CIM class definition are available. The complete object model (see Figures 4.3 – 4.5) can be browsed as before to discover the properties, methods, and all related qualifiers. This means that the function SINK_OnObjectReady() in Sample 5.1 can be changed with the code developed in the previous chapter:

- Sample 4.13 "Retrieving the property collection of a WMI instance"

- Sample 4.16 "Retrieving the property qualifiers of a WMI class"

- Sample 4.17 "Retrieving the method collection of a WMI class"

- Sample 4.22 "Retrieving the method qualifiers of a WMI class"

- Sample 4.23 "Retrieving the method properties with their qualifiers of a WMI class"

Sample 5.2 reuses the DisplayQualifiers() function. The same set of information is retrieved as before, except that now the information is retrieved in the core of the SINK_OnObjectReady() function.

Sample 5.2   *Retrieving the properties, methods, and all associated qualifiers of a WMI class asynchronously*

```
 1:<?xml version="1.0"?>
 .:
 8:<package>
 9:   <job>
..:
13:     <script language="VBScript" src="..\Functions\DisplayQualifiersFunction.vbs" />
14:
15:     <object progid="WbemScripting.SWbemLocator" id="objWMILocator" reference="true"/>
16:
17:     <script language="VBscript">
18:     <![CDATA[
..:
26:     ' -------------------------------------------------------------------------------
27:     Const cComputerName = "LocalHost"
```

```
 28:      Const cWMINameSpace = "root/cimv2"
 29:      Const cWMIClass     = "Win32_Service"
 30:      Const cWMIInstance = "SNMP"
 ..:
 37:      Set objWMISink = WScript.CreateObject ("WbemScripting.SWbemSink", "SINK_")
 38:
 39:      objWMILocator.Security_.AuthenticationLevel = wbemAuthenticationLevelDefault
 40:      objWMILocator.Security_.ImpersonationLevel = wbemImpersonationLevelImpersonate
 41:      Set objWMIServices = objWMILocator.ConnectServer(cComputerName, cWMINameSpace, "", "")
 42:
 43:      objWMIServices.GetAsync objWMISink, cWMIClass & "='" & cWMIInstance & "'"
 44:
 45:      WScript.Echo "Continuing script execution ..."
 46:      PauseScript "Click on 'Ok' to terminate the script ..."
 47:
 48:      objWMISink.Cancel
 ..:
 55:      ' -------------------------------------------------------------------------------
 56:      Sub SINK_OnCompleted (intHResult, objWMILastError, objWMIAsyncContext)
 ..:
 71:      End Sub
 72:
 73:      ' -------------------------------------------------------------------------------
 74:      Sub SINK_OnObjectPut (objWMIPath, objWMIAsyncContext)
 ..:
 82:      End Sub
 83:
 84:      ' -------------------------------------------------------------------------------
 85:      Sub SINK_OnObjectReady (objWMIInstance, objWMIAsyncContext)
 ..:
 93:          Wscript.Echo
 94:          Wscript.Echo "BEGIN - OnObjectReady."
 95:
 96:          Wscript.Echo String (60, 45)
 97:          Wscript.Echo "Class Qualifiers:"
 98:
 99:          WScript.Echo "  " & objWMIInstance.Path_.RelPath
100:          DisplayQualifiers objWMIInstance.Qualifiers_, 0
101:
102:          Wscript.Echo String (60, 45)
103:          Wscript.Echo "Property Qualifiers:"
104:
105:          Set objWMIPropertySet = objWMIInstance.Properties_
106:          For Each objWMIProperty In objWMIPropertySet
107:              WScript.Echo "  " & objWMIProperty.Name
108:              DisplayQualifiers objWMIProperty.Qualifiers_, 0
109:          Next
110:          Set objWMIPropertySet = Nothing
111:
112:          Wscript.Echo String (60, 45)
113:          Wscript.Echo "Method Qualifiers:"
114:
115:          Set objWMIMethodSet = objWMIInstance.Methods_
116:          For Each objWMIMethod In objWMIMethodSet
117:              WScript.Echo "  " & objWMIMethod.Name
118:              DisplayQualifiers objWMIMethod.Qualifiers_, 0
119:
120:              Set objWMIObject = objWMIMethod.InParameters
121:              WScript.Echo "  " & objWMIObject.Path_.RelPath
122:              DisplayQualifiers objWMIObject.Qualifiers_, 2
```

```
123:
124:            Set objWMIPropertySet = objWMIObject.Properties_
125:            If Err.Number = 0 Then
126:               For Each objWMIProperty In objWMIPropertySet
127:                   WScript.Echo "    " & objWMIProperty.Name
128:                   DisplayQualifiers objWMIProperty.Qualifiers_, 4
129:               Next
130:            Else
131:               Err.Clear
132:            End If
133:            Set objWMIPropertySet = Nothing
134:
135:            Set objWMIObject = Nothing
136:
137:            Set objWMIObject = objWMIMethod.OutParameters
138:            WScript.Echo "  " & objWMIObject.Path_.RelPath
139:            DisplayQualifiers objWMIObject.Qualifiers_, 2
140:
141:            Set objWMIPropertySet = objWMIObject.Properties_
142:            If Err.Number = 0 Then
143:               For Each objWMIProperty In objWMIPropertySet
144:                   WScript.Echo "    " & objWMIProperty.Name
145:                   DisplayQualifiers objWMIProperty.Qualifiers_, 4
146:               Next
147:            Else
148:               Err.Clear
149:            End If
150:            Set objWMIPropertySet = Nothing
151:
152:            Set objWMIObject = Nothing
153:
154:         Next
155:         Set objWMIMethodSet = Nothing
156:
157:         Wscript.Echo "END   - OnObjectReady."
158:
159:      End Sub
160:
161:      ' -------------------------------------------------------------------------
162:      Sub SINK_OnProgress (intUpperBound, intCurrent, strMessage, objWMIAsyncContext)
...:
170:      End Sub
171:
172:      ' -------------------------------------------------------------------------
173:      Function PauseScript (strMessage)
...:
182:      End Function
183:
184:      ]]>
185:      </script>
186:   </job>
187:</package>
```

5.2.3   Modifying a CIM instance property

Up to now, the asynchronous script uses the SINK_OnObjectReady() and the SINK_OnCompleted() sink routines. The SINK_OnObjectPut() has not yet been used. Moreover, the asynchronous method invocation was always made from an **SWbemServices** object. In the previous chapter, Sample 4.14 ("Setting one read/write property of a Win32_Registry class instance directly") sets one read/write property of the *Win32_Registry* class instance. In this sample, the *Put_* method of an **SWbemObject** is used to commit the change. To perform the same operation asynchronously, the *PutAsync_* method must be used (see Table 4.10). Of course, to modify an object instance, the script must create the instance representing the manageable entity by using the *Get* method of an **SWbemServices** object. If the operation is also made asynchronously, the *GetAsync* method must be used (see Table 4.8). So, in such a situation, we face two asynchronous method invocations: one to get the object instance and one to commit the changes made to the object instance. Let's see how this works in Sample 5.3.

Sample 5.3 *Setting asynchronously one read/write property of a Win32_Registry class instance*

```
 1:<?xml version="1.0"?>
 .:
 8:<package>
 9:  <job>
 ..:
13:     <object progid="WbemScripting.SWbemLocator" id="objWMILocator" reference="true"/>
14:
15:     <script language="VBscript">
16:     <![CDATA[
..:
24:     ' --------------------------------------------------------------------------------
25:     Const cComputerName = "LocalHost"
26:     Const cWMINameSpace = "root/cimv2"
27:     Const cWMIClass = "Win32_Registry"
28:     Const cWMIInstance = "Microsoft Windows 2000 Server|C:\WINNT|\Device\Harddisk0\Partition1"
..:
33:     Set objWMISink = WScript.CreateObject ("WbemScripting.SWbemSink", "SINK_")
34:
35:     objWMILocator.Security_.AuthenticationLevel = wbemAuthenticationLevelDefault
36:     objWMILocator.Security_.ImpersonationLevel = wbemImpersonationLevelImpersonate
37:     Set objWMIServices = objWMILocator.ConnectServer(cComputerName, cWMINameSpace, "", "")
38:
39:     objWMIServices.GetAsync objWMISink, cWMIClass & "='" & cWMIInstance & "'"
40:
41:     WScript.Echo "Continuing script execution ..."
42:     PauseScript "Click on 'Ok' to terminate the script ..."
43:
44:     objWMISink.Cancel
..:
50:     ' --------------------------------------------------------------------------------
51:     Sub SINK_OnCompleted (intHResult, objWMILastError, objWMIAsyncContext)
..:
64:     End Sub
65:
66:     ' --------------------------------------------------------------------------------
67:     Sub SINK_OnObjectPut (objWMIPath, objWMIAsyncContext)
```

```
68:
69:          Wscript.Echo
70:          Wscript.Echo "BEGIN - OnObjectPut."
71:          Wscript.Echo "END   - OnObjectPut."
72:
73:      End Sub
74:
75:      ' -----------------------------------------------------------------------
76:      Sub SINK_OnObjectReady (objWMIInstance, objWMIAsyncContext)
77:
78:          Wscript.Echo
79:          Wscript.Echo "BEGIN - OnObjectReady."
80:
81:          WScript.Echo objWMIInstance.Name & " (" & objWMIInstance.Description & ")"
82:
83:          Wscript.Echo "Current registry size is: " & objWMIInstance.ProposedSize  & " MB."
84:
85:          objWMIInstance.ProposedSize = objWMIInstance.ProposedSize + 10
86:          objWMIInstance.PutAsync_ objWMISink, wbemChangeFlagUpdateOnly Or wbemFlagReturnWhenComplete
87:
88:          Wscript.Echo "Current registry size is now: " & objWMIInstance.ProposedSize  & " MB."
89:
90:          Wscript.Echo "END   - OnObjectReady."
91:
92:      End Sub
93:
94:      ' -----------------------------------------------------------------------
95:      Sub SINK_OnProgress (intUpperBound, intCurrent, strMessage, objWMIAsyncContext)
...:
101:     End Sub
102:
103:     ' -----------------------------------------------------------------------
104:     Function PauseScript (strMessage)
...:
113:     End Function
114:
115:     ]]>
116:     </script>
117:  </job>
118:</package>
```

As in previous samples, the script starts with the WMI connection (lines 35 to 37). The **SWbemSink** object is also created (line 33) with references to the sink routines starting with the name "SINK_". Next, the script executes the *GetAsync* method from the **SWbemServices** object (line 39) with the **SWbemSink** object just created. Once the asynchronous call is invoked, the script pauses (line 42).

When WMI retrieves the instance of the *Win32_Registry* class, the SINK_OnObjectReady() sink routine is called. Here, we recognize a code portion used in Sample 4.14 ("Setting one read/write property of a Win32_Registry class instance directly") to modify the current registry size limit and increase that limit by 10 MB (lines 81 to 88). There is no change in the logic. The only modification resides in the way the change is committed back to the instance. Sample 4.14 uses the synchronous *Put_* method of the **SWbemObject**, whereas Sample 5.3 uses the *PutAsync_* method of the **SWbemObject** (line 86).

The particularity of the *PutAsync_* asynchronous method invocation is that the **SWbemSink** object is the same as the one used for the *GetAsync* asynchronous method invocation. This means that the same set of sink routines are used for both asynchronous operations. Since these two asynchronous operations are different, the *GetAsync* method calls the SINK_OnObjectReady() sink routine, and the *PutAsync_* method calls the SINK_OnObjectPut() sink routine. Figure 5.2 shows the sequence of the sink routine execution.

Because we have two asynchronous calls in the script, Figure 5.2 shows that the SINK_OnCompleted() sink routine is called two times. Here, we face a tricky problem. As the same piece of code is executed for both asynchronous methods, how do we determine whether the SINK_OnCompleted() call is for the *GetAsync* method execution or for the *PutAsync_*

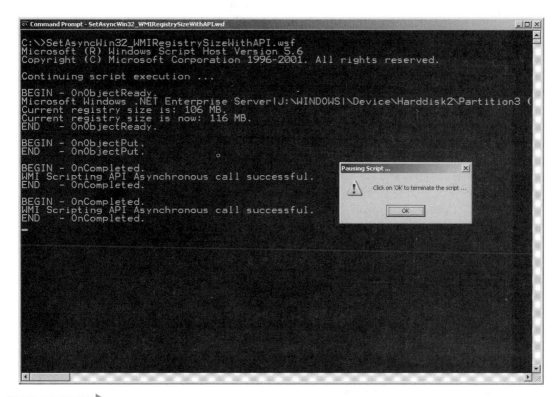

Figure 5.2   *Asynchronously setting one read/write property of a Win32_Registry class instance directly.*

method execution? Currently, the way the script is written there is no way to determine that from the sink routine. This is where the notion of context for an asynchronous call is helpful. Of course, there is another possibility. When invoking the *PutAsync_* method, it was possible to use another **SWbemSink** object that references another set of sink routines (with the name "SINK2_" for instance). Although this method is valid, it does not make use of the notion of context as provided by the WMI scripting API. The context is a parameter provided by every WMI sink routine at the condition that it is defined when invoking the asynchronous method. The context is an **SWbemNamedValueSet** object contained in the variable called **objWMIAsyncContext** passed as a parameter of the sink routine (see lines 51, 67, 76, and 95). In the previous chapter, in Figure 4.5 (number 36), we see that the **SWbemNamedValueSet** object is a collection that can be created using its progID with the **CreateObject** statement or any other equivalent technique (see Figure 4.2).

The question is: How do we define a context when invoking the asynchronous method? Sample 5.4 shows the same code as Sample 5.3, except that some additions were made (in boldface) to include this notion of context.

Sample 5.4   *Setting asynchronously with a context one read/write property of a Win32_Registry class instance*

```
 1:<?xml version="1.0"?>
 .:
 8:<package>
 9:  <job>
..:
13:    <object progid="WbemScripting.SWbemLocator" id="objWMILocator" reference="true"/>
14:    <object progid="WbemScripting.SWbemNamedValueSet" id="objWMISinkContext" reference="true"/>
15:
16:    <script language="VBscript">
17:    <![CDATA[
..:
25:    ' -------------------------------------------------------------------------------
26:    Const cComputerName = "LocalHost"
27:    Const cWMINameSpace = "root/cimv2"
28:    Const cWMIClass = "Win32_Registry"
29:    Const cWMIInstance = "Microsoft Windows 2000 Server|C:\WINNT|\Device\Harddisk0\Partition1"
..:
34:    Set objWMISink = WScript.CreateObject ("WbemScripting.SWbemSink", "SINK_")
35:
36:    objWMILocator.Security_.AuthenticationLevel = wbemAuthenticationLevelDefault
37:    objWMILocator.Security_.ImpersonationLevel = wbemImpersonationLevelImpersonate
38:    Set objWMIServices = objWMILocator.ConnectServer(cComputerName, cWMINameSpace, "", "")
39:
40:    objWMISinkContext.Add "WMIMethod", "GetAsync"
41:    objWMIServices.GetAsync objWMISink, _
42:                            cWMIClass & "='" & cWMIInstance & "'", _
43:                                    , _
44:                                    , _
```

```
 45:                          objWMISinkContext
 46:
 47:    WScript.Echo "Continuing script execution ..."
 48:    PauseScript "Click on 'Ok' to terminate the script ..."
 49:
 50:    objWMISink.Cancel
 ..:
 56:    ' -------------------------------------------------------------------------------
 57:    Sub SINK_OnCompleted (intHResult, objWMILastError, objWMIAsyncContext)
 ..:
 64:        Set objContextItem = objWMIAsyncContext.Item ("WMIMethod")
 65:
 66:        If intHResult = 0 Then
 67:            WScript.Echo "'" & objContextItem.Value & _
 68:                         "' WMI Scripting API Asynchronous call successful."
 69:        Else
 70:            WScript.Echo "'" & objContextItem.Value & _
 71:                         "' WMI Scripting API Asynchronous call failed."
 72:        End If
 ..:
 76:    End Sub
 77:
 78:    ' -------------------------------------------------------------------------------
 79:    Sub SINK_OnObjectPut (objWMIPath, objWMIAsyncContext)
 ..:
 85:    End Sub
 86:
 87:    ' -------------------------------------------------------------------------------
 88:    Sub SINK_OnObjectReady (objWMIInstance, objWMIAsyncContext)
 ..:
 92:        Wscript.Echo
 93:        Wscript.Echo "BEGIN - OnObjectReady."
 94:
 95:        Set objWMISinkContext = CreateObject ("WbemScripting.SWbemNamedValueSet")
 96:
 97:        WScript.Echo objWMIInstance.Name & " (" & objWMIInstance.Description & ")"
 98:
 99:        Wscript.Echo "Current registry size is: " & objWMIInstance.ProposedSize  & " MB."
100:
101:        objWMIInstance.ProposedSize = objWMIInstance.ProposedSize + 10
102:
103:        objWMISinkContext.Add "WMIMethod", "PutAsync"
104:        objWMIInstance.PutAsync_ objWMISink, _
105:                         wbemChangeFlagUpdateOnly Or wbemFlagReturnWhenComplete, _
106:                         , _
107:                         objWMISinkContext
108:
109:        Wscript.Echo "Current registry size is now: " & objWMIInstance.ProposedSize  & " MB."
110:
111:        Set objWMISinkContext = Nothing
112:
113:        Wscript.Echo "END   - OnObjectReady."
114:
115:    End Sub
116:
117:    ' ------------------------------------------------------------------------
118:    Sub SINK_OnProgress (intUpperBound, intCurrent, strMessage, objWMIAsyncContext)
...:
124:    End Sub
125:
```

```
126:      ' -------------------------------------------------------------------------------
127:      Function PauseScript (strMessage)
...:
136:      End Function
137:
138:      ]]>
139:      </script>
140:  </job>
141:</package>
```

The first change is the creation of an **SWbemNamedObjectSet** object (line 14). This object is used as a parameter when invoking the *GetAsync* method (lines 41 to 45). At line 40, the **SWbemNamedObjectSet** object is initialized. Since this object is a collection, the script uses the *Add* method to add an item to the collection. The first parameter is the name of the value to be put in the collection; the second parameter is the value itself. Once the *GetAsync* asynchronous method is completed, the SINK_On-Completed() sink routine is called. The sink routine provides the context information that comes from the **SWbemNamedObjectSet** collection. The first step is to retrieve the value initially provided. For this, the script retrieves the value by referencing the value name in the item list (line 64). Once the name of the value has been retrieved, it is possible for the sink routine to display the value (lines 67 and 70). Since the value is set to the name of the asynchronous method (line 40), the output will display the name of the asynchronous method.

The SINK_OnObjectReady() sink routine performs the same process to create context information. But this time, it is for the *PutAsync_* asynchronous method. Here, a new **SWbemNamedValueSet** object is created (line 95), initialized with the name of the asynchronous method to be executed (line 103) and passed as a parameter when the asynchronous method is invoked (lines 104 to 107). Note that the name of the value is the same as before (WMIMethod), the SINK_OnCompleted() sink routine searches for a WMIMethod value name (line 64), and the value name provided in the context must remain the same. It is possible to use a different value name, but then the SINK_OnCompleted() sink routine has to check two value names, which complicates the logic to determine the context. Why create a new **SWbemNamedValueSet** object in the SINK_OnObjectReady() sink routine? If the script didn't create a new object, the existing object created in the core of the script (line 14) would be used, because it is a global variable; instead of creating a new context object, the script adds one value name to the existing values in the collection. Doing so causes one **SWbemNamed-ValueSet** object to contain both contexts' information. Again, it is more difficult to differentiate the context during the SINK_OnCompleted() sink routine execution. The display output of Sample 5.4 is shown in Figure 5.3.

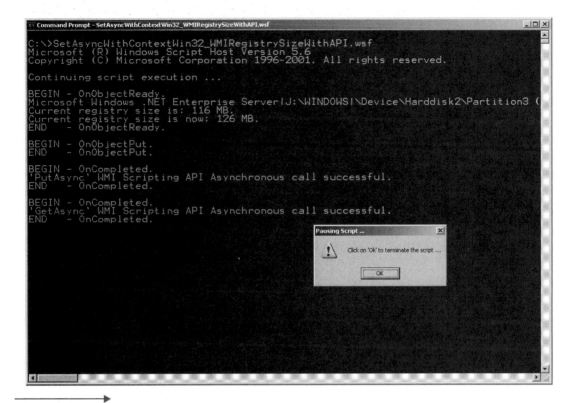

Figure 5.3   *Asynchronously setting one read/write property of a Win32_Registry class instance*
directly with a context.

5.2.4   Executing CIM instances methods

We have seen how to retrieve and modify the WMI instance properties
asynchronously. Since some of the WMI classes expose methods to manage
real world entities, it is also possible to execute CIM class methods asynchronously.

5.2.4.1   Executing CIM instances methods without context

Sample 4.18 ("Using one method of a Win32_Service instance indirectly")
executes the *StartService* and *StopService* method of the *Win32_Service* class
indirectly. If the service stops, the script starts the service and vice versa.
Both methods execute synchronously. An important point to note about
the method invocation (see Sample 4.18) is that the invocation is indirect.
Therefore, the method to be executed is passed as a parameter to a WMI
Scripting API object method and is not hard coded in the script code itself.

The indirect execution of the method is the base foundation on which to execute methods asynchronously. To implement the functionality of Sample 4.18 asynchronously, the script uses the *ExecMethodAsync_* of an **SWbem-Object**. The logic used is implemented in Sample 5.5.

Sample 5.5   *Using one method of a Win32_Service instance asynchronously*

```
 1:<?xml version="1.0"?>
 .:
 8:<package>
 9: <job>
..:
13:    <object progid="WbemScripting.SWbemLocator" id="objWMILocator" reference="true"/>
14:
15:    <script language="VBscript">
16:    <![CDATA[
..:
24:    ' ----------------------------------------------------------------------
25:    Const cComputerName = "LocalHost"
26:    Const cWMINameSpace = "root/cimv2"
27:    Const cWMIClass = "Win32_Service"
28:    Const cWMIInstance = "SNMP"
..:
34:    Set objWMISink = WScript.CreateObject ("WbemScripting.SWbemSink", "SINK_")
35:
36:    objWMILocator.Security_.AuthenticationLevel = wbemAuthenticationLevelDefault
37:    objWMILocator.Security_.ImpersonationLevel = wbemImpersonationLevelImpersonate
38:    Set objWMIServices = objWMILocator.ConnectServer(cComputerName, cWMINameSpace, "", "")
39:
40:    Set objWMIInstance = objWMIServices.Get(cWMIClass & "='" & cWMIInstance & "'")
41:
42:    WScript.Echo vbCRLF & "'" & objWMIInstance.DisplayName & "' is currently " & _
43:                LCase (objWMIInstance.State) & "."
44:
45:    If objWMIInstance.State = "Running" Then
46:       objWMIInstance.ExecMethodAsync_ objWMISink, "StopService"
47:    End If
48:    If objWMIInstance.State = "Stopped" Then
49:       objWMIInstance.ExecMethodAsync_ objWMISink, "StartService"
50:    End If
51:
52:    WScript.Echo "Continuing script execution ..."
53:    PauseScript "Click on 'Ok' to terminate the script ..."
54:
55:    objWMISink.Cancel
..:
63:    ' ----------------------------------------------------------------------
64:    Sub SINK_OnCompleted (intHResult, objWMILastError, objWMIAsyncContext)
65:
66:        Wscript.Echo
67:        Wscript.Echo "BEGIN - OnCompleted."
68:
69:        If intHResult = 0 Then
70:            WScript.Echo "WMI Scripting API Asynchronous call successful."
71:        Else
72:            WScript.Echo "WMI Scripting API Asynchronous call failed."
73:        End If
```

```
 74:
 75:          Wscript.Echo "END   - OnCompleted."
 76:
 77:      End Sub
 78:
 79:      ' ------------------------------------------------------------------------
 80:      Sub SINK_OnObjectPut (objWMIPath, objWMIAsyncContext)
 ..:
 86:      End Sub
 87:
 88:      ' ------------------------------------------------------------------------
 89:      Sub SINK_OnObjectReady (objWMIInstance, objWMIAsyncContext)
 90:
 91:          Wscript.Echo
 92:          Wscript.Echo "BEGIN - OnObjectReady."
 93:
 94:          If objWMIInstance.ReturnValue = 0 Then
 96:          Else
 97:              Wscript.Echo "Asynchronous method execution failed."
 98:          End If
 99:
100:          Wscript.Echo "END   - OnObjectReady."
101:
102:      End Sub
103:
104:      ' ------------------------------------------------------------------------
105:      Sub SINK_OnProgress (intUpperBound, intCurrent, strMessage, objWMIAsyncContext)
...:
111:      End Sub
112:
113:      ' ------------------------------------------------------------------------
114:      Function PauseScript (strMessage)
...:
123:      End Function
124:
125:      ]]>
126:    </script>
127:  </job>
128:</package>
```

The logic used to invoke an asynchronous process is the same as before. A WMI connection must be established (lines 36 to 38), and an **SWbem-Sink** object referencing the sink routines must be created (line 34). Note that the object instance of the SNMP *Win32_Service* is instantiated synchronously (line 40). Although it was possible to create the instance asynchronously, to avoid any confusion with the asynchronous method execution in the sink routine, it was decided to make the instantiation synchronously. This makes the script easier to understand, given that this is the first time that we are examining an asynchronous method execution. Next, the script tests the state of the service to determine whether the service must be stopped or started. This is where the asynchronous method invocation is performed (lines 45 to 47 and 48 to 50).

The particularity of an asynchronous method execution is the place where the result of the method execution is retrieved. Before, when using the *GetAsync* method, the instantiated **SWbemObject** was available in the SINK_OnObjectReady() sink routine. Now, with the *ExecMethodAsync_* method, the return code of the method invocation is also available in the SINK_OnObjectReady() sink routine. If you remember, in Sample 4.18 ("Using one method of a Win32_Service instance indirectly"), the returned result of the indirect method execution was available in an **SWbemObject** whose properties return the result of the executed method. It is the same when executing the method asynchronously except that the **SWbemObject** containing the result of the method execution is obtained in the SINK_OnObjectReady() sink routine. This is why the script tests the *ReturnValue* property (line 94) returned from the **SWbemObject** provided as a parameter of the SINK_OnObjectReady() sink routine.

To avoid any confusion in the sink routine, the object instantiation is synchronous (line 40), but the SINK_OnObjectReady() sink routine does not know whether the result of the asynchronous method execution is for the *StartService* or the *StopService*. So, by sharing the same set of sink routines, determining the context of the sink routine call remains ambiguous, especially for those actions that must be performed when the service is stopped. Of course, it depends on the purpose of the script and the type of operation to be performed in the sink routine. Let's see how we can clear up these ambiguities.

5.2.4.2   *Executing CIM instances methods with context*

If the previous Sample 5.5 was creating the SNMP *Win32_Service* instance with the *GetAsync* method (instead of the *Get* method) and used the same **SWbemSink** object for executing the method asynchronously, then the SINK_OnObjectReady() was called twice: once for the instantiation of the *Win32_Service* and once for execution of the method. Again, we see the real importance of the sink routine context, because the **SWbemObject** retrieved is the *Win32_Service* instance during the first sink routine and the result of the *StartService* or *StopService* method execution during the second sink routine. As previously shown, all sink functions use a parameter represented by the variable **objWMIAsyncContext**, which is an **SWbemNamed-ValueSet** object (number 36 in Figure 4.5).

Sample 5.6 performs the same logic as Sample 5.5 except that the notion of context has been added to differentiate the instance creation (which is asynchronous now) from the asynchronous method execution.

Sample 5.6   *Using one method of a Win32_Service instance asynchronously with*
context

```
 1:<?xml version="1.0"?>
 .:
 8:<package>
 9:  <job>
..:
13:     <object progid="WbemScripting.SWbemLocator" id="objWMILocator" reference="true"/>
14:     <object progid="WbemScripting.SWbemNamedValueSet" id="objWMIMethodSinkContext" reference="true"/>
15:     <object progid="WbemScripting.SWbemNamedValueSet" id="objWMIInstanceSinkContext" reference="true"/>
16:
17:     <script language="VBscript">
18:     <![CDATA[
..:
26:     ' -----------------------------------------------------------------------------------
27:     Const cComputerName = "LocalHost"
28:     Const cWMINameSpace = "root/cimv2"
29:     Const cWMIClass = "Win32_Service"
30:     Const cWMIInstance = "SNMP"
..:
35:     Set objWMISink = WScript.CreateObject ("WbemScripting.SWbemSink", "SINK_")
36:
37:     objWMILocator.Security_.AuthenticationLevel = wbemAuthenticationLevelDefault
38:     objWMILocator.Security_.ImpersonationLevel = wbemImpersonationLevelImpersonate
39:     Set objWMIServices = objWMILocator.ConnectServer(cComputerName, cWMINameSpace, "", "")
40:
41:     objWMIInstanceSinkContext.Add "WMIMethod", "GetAsync"
42:     objWMIServices.GetAsync objWMISink, _
43:                             cWMIClass & "='" & cWMIInstance & "'", _
44:                                  , _
45:                                  , _
46:                             objWMIInstanceSinkContext
47:
48:     WScript.Echo "Continuing script execution ..."
49:     PauseScript "Click on 'Ok' to terminate the script ..."
50:
51:     objWMISink.Cancel
..:
58:     ' -----------------------------------------------------------------------------------
59:     Sub SINK_OnCompleted (intHResult, objWMILastError, objWMIAsyncContext)
..:
63:         Wscript.Echo
64:         Wscript.Echo "BEGIN - OnCompleted."
65:
66:         Set objContextItem = objWMIAsyncContext.Item ("WMIMethod")
67:
68:         If intHResult = 0 Then
69:             WScript.Echo "'" & objContextItem.Value & _
70:                             "' WMI Scripting API Asynchronous call successful."
71:         Else
72:             WScript.Echo "'" & objContextItem.Value & _
73:                             "' WMI Scripting API Asynchronous call failed."
74:         End If
..:
78:         Wscript.Echo "END   - OnCompleted."
79:
80:     End Sub
```

```
81:
82:     ' -------------------------------------------------------------------------------
83:     Sub SINK_OnObjectPut (objWMIPath, objWMIAsyncContext)
..:
89:     End Sub
90:
91:     ' -------------------------------------------------------------------------------
92:     Sub SINK_OnObjectReady (objWMIInstance, objWMIAsyncContext)
..:
96:         Wscript.Echo
97:         Wscript.Echo "BEGIN - OnObjectReady."
98:
99:         Set objContextItem = objWMIAsyncContext.Item ("WMIMethod")
100:
101:        Select Case objContextItem.Value
102:               Case "GetAsync"
103:                   WScript.Echo "'" & objWMIInstance.DisplayName & "' is currently " & _
104:                                   LCase (objWMIInstance.State) & "."
105:
106:                   If objWMIInstance.State = "Running" Then
107:                       objWMIMethodSinkContext.Add "WMIMethod", "ExecMethodAsync"
108:                       objWMIMethodSinkContext.Add "CIMMethod", "StopService"
109:                       objWMIInstance.ExecMethodAsync_ objWMISink, _
110:                                                       "StopService", _
111:                                                       , _
112:                                                       , _
113:                                                       , _
114:                                                       objWMIMethodSinkContext
115:                   End If
116:                   If objWMIInstance.State = "Stopped" Then
117:                       objWMIMethodSinkContext.Add "WMIMethod", "ExecMethodAsync"
118:                       objWMIMethodSinkContext.Add "CIMMethod", "StartService"
119:                       objWMIInstance.ExecMethodAsync_ objWMISink, _
120:                                                       "StartService", _
121:                                                       , _
122:                                                       , _
123:                                                       , _
124:                                                       objWMIMethodSinkContext
125:                   End If
126:               Case "ExecMethodAsync"
127:                   Set objContextItem = objWMIAsyncContext.Item ("CIMMethod")
128:                   If objWMIInstance.ReturnValue = 0 Then
129:                       Wscript.Echo "'" & objContextItem.Value & _
130:                                       "' method execution successful."
131:                   Else
132:                       Wscript.Echo "'" & objContextItem.Value & _
133:                                       "' method execution failed."
134:                   End If
135:        End Select
...:
139:        Wscript.Echo "END   - OnObjectReady."
140:
141:     End Sub
142:
143:     ' -------------------------------------------------------------------------------
144:     Sub SINK_OnProgress (intUpperBound, intCurrent, strMessage, objWMIAsyncContext)
...:
150:     End Sub
151:
152:     ' -------------------------------------------------------------------------------
```

```
153:     Function PauseScript (strMessage)
...:
164:     ]]>
165:     </script>
166:  </job>
167:</package>
```

Sample 5.6 uses two **SWbemNamedObjectSet** objects, one for each context. The first is initialized (lines 15 and 41) for the *GetAsync* asynchronous method execution of the **SWbemServices** object (lines 42 to 46). This context uses a named variable called "WMIMethod" with a value equal to the method name *GetAsync*. When the *GetAsync* method is executed, this context is tested (lines 101, 102 and 126 of the **Select Case** statement) in the SINK_OnObjectReady() sink routine to determine if the current context relates to the instance creation (*GetAsync*) or the method execution (*ExecMethodAsync_*).

When the instance creation is completed, the SINK_OnCompleted() sink routine is called (lines 59 to 80). As the context is defined, the routine retrieves the named value WMIMethod (line 66) to display its value (lines 69 or 72) based on the result of the asynchronous call (line 68).

During the execution of the SINK_OnObjectReady() sink routine the script tests the state of the *Win32_Service* (lines 106 and 116) to determine whether the service must be stopped or started. In both cases, the script prepares the context of the *ExecMethodAsync_* asynchronous method. For this, the script uses the second **SWbemNamedValueSet** object created (line 14). Before the asynchronous method invocation, the script initializes two **SWbemNamedValue** objects. One contains the name of the WMI scripting API object method invoked—*ExecMethodAsync_* (lines 107 and 117)—and the other contains the *Win32_Service* method executed (line 108 or 118). Once the **SWbemNamedValueSet** object initializes, the *ExecMethodAsync_* is invoked (lines 109 and 119).

Once the asynchronous method executes, the SINK_OnObjectReady() sink routine is called again but this time in a different context. As the SINK_OnObjectReady() sink routine starts by retrieving the WMIMethod named value (line 99), it determines that the context is now related to the *ExecMethodAsync_* execution. In this case, the script branches to the statement at line 127. This statement retrieves the second named value called "CIMMethod." This named value contains the name of the CIM method executed asynchronously and defined during a preceding SINK_OnObjectReady() sink routine call (lines 108 or 118). As usual, the asynchronous method execution finishes with a call to the SINK_OnCompleted() sink routine. As before, the named value WMIMethod is retrieved, and

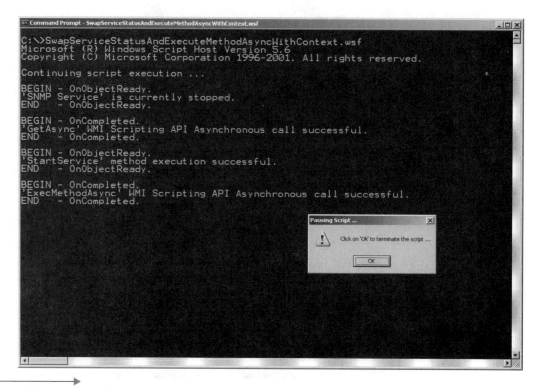

Figure 5.4　*The GetAsync method and ExecMethodAsync_ method execution output with context.*

now the context of this sink routine call relates to the *ExecMethodAsync_* method. The display output of the script is visible on Figure 5.4.

5.2.4.3　Executing CIM instances methods with context and parameters

Sample 5.6 is a full asynchronous and contextual script, but it does not use any parameters when invoking the *StartService* or *StopService* methods. When Sample 4.19 ("Using one method of a Win32_Service instance indirectly with one parameter") changes the startup mode of a *Win32_Service* instance, it uses the startup mode of the service as a parameter. This sample executes the method indirectly and uses a specific tactic to pass the method parameter. By combining the examined Sample 5.6 with Sample 4.19, it is possible to perform the same operation asynchronously with a full context determination. Only one routine in Sample 5.6 must be adapted to suit the need of the required input parameter. This routine is the SINK_OnObjectReady() sink routine shown in Sample 5.7. The rest of the script is exactly the same as Sample 5.6.

Sample 5.7   *Using one method with parameter of a Win32_Service instance asynchronously with context*

```
 1:<?xml version="1.0"?>
 .:
 8:<package>
 9:  <job>
..:
..:
..:
91:     ' -------------------------------------------------------------------------------------
92:     Sub SINK_OnObjectReady (objWMIInstance, objWMIAsyncContext)
..:
98:         Wscript.Echo
99:         Wscript.Echo "BEGIN - OnObjectReady."
100:
101:        Set objContextItem = objWMIAsyncContext.Item ("WMIMethod")
102:
103:        Select Case objContextItem.Value
104:              Case "GetAsync"
105:                   WScript.Echo "'" & objWMIInstance.DisplayName & _
106:                                "' startup is currently " & _
107:                                objWMIInstance.StartMode & "."
108:
109:                   Set objWMIMethod = objWMIInstance.Methods_("ChangeStartMode")
110:                   Set objWMIInParameters = objWMIMethod.InParameters
111:
112:                   If objWMIInstance.StartMode = "Manual" Then
113:                      objWMIMethodSinkContext.Add "WMIMethod", "ExecMethodAsync"
114:                      objWMIMethodSinkContext.Add "CIMMethod", "ChangeStartMode (Automatic)"
115:                      objWMIInParameters.Properties_.Item("StartMode") = "Automatic"
116:                      objWMIInstance.ExecMethodAsync_ objWMISink, _
117:                                                      "ChangeStartMode", _
118:                                                      objWMIInParameters, _
119:                                                      ' _
120:                                                      ' _
121:                                                      objWMIMethodSinkContext
122:                   End If
123:                   If objWMIInstance.StartMode = "Auto" Then
124:                      objWMIMethodSinkContext.Add "WMIMethod", "ExecMethodAsync"
125:                      objWMIMethodSinkContext.Add "CIMMethod", "ChangeStartMode (Manual)"
126:                      objWMIInParameters.Properties_.Item("StartMode") = "Manual"
127:                      objWMIInstance.ExecMethodAsync_ objWMISink, _
128:                                                      "ChangeStartMode", _
129:                                                      objWMIInParameters, _
130:                                                      ' _
131:                                                      ' _
132:                                                      objWMIMethodSinkContext
133:                   End If
134:
135:                   Set objWMIInParameters = Nothing
136:                   Set objWMIMethod = Nothing
137:
138:              Case "ExecMethodAsync"
139:                   Set objContextItem = objWMIAsyncContext.Item ("CIMMethod")
140:                   If objWMIInstance.ReturnValue = 0 Then
141:                      Wscript.Echo "'" & objContextItem.Value & _
142:                                   "' method execution successful."
```

```
143:                    Else
144:                        Wscript.Echo "'" & objContextItem.Value & _
145:                                     "' method execution failed."
146:                    End If
147:        End Select
...:
151:        Wscript.Echo "END   - OnObjectReady."
152:
153:    End Sub
...:
...:
...:
176:    ]]>
177:    </script>
178:  </job>
179:</package>
```

From the point of view of context definitions and usages, the script uses the same logic as Sample 5.6. The new detail is the creation of the **SWbem-Object** object targeted to carry the input parameter of the asynchronously executed method (line 110). In this sink routine, we recognize the indirect method execution with one parameter assignment as used in Sample 4.19. Depending on the current startup mode of the *Win32_Service* (line 112 and 123), the required parameter for the asynchronous method is set at line 115 or 126. Basically, Sample 5.7 is the same as Sample 4.19, but the task is executed asynchronously.

5.3   Error handling with WMI scripting

Up to now, all script samples shown in this book contain very little error management. This choice was made to ease the reading and understanding of the script principles. Although this approach is valid for an academic purpose, developing a script for a production environment is done quite differently. Whatever the programming language used, managing errors in a code is always a tricky problem because the software must include a lot of exceptions and error management that represent a supplemental logic added to the core logic. Working with WMI is no exception; a specific error-management technique must be included in the application. When scripting with WMI, there are different error types. We can classify these errors into two categories: run-time errors and WMI operational errors.

Let's take a look at the first category, the run-time errors. These errors stop the script execution when they occur. To avoid such a situation, in VBScript these errors must be processed with the **On Error Resume Next** statement combined with a test of the *Err.number* value. When *Err.number* is not equal to zero, it means that an error has occurred. With the **Err** object from VBScript, it is also possible to retrieve error messages by using the expression *Err.Description*. With JScript, error handling must be processed with the **Try ... catch ... finally** statement. We will first use a VBScript sample and next, at the end of this section, we will review the same script logic written with JScript to complete the picture. A WMI script handles the following run-time errors:

- **Script language errors.** These errors are typically present during the development phase. Once corrected, these types of errors should no longer be present. Consequently, the script logic does not have to handle this situation.

- **Win32 errors that have a number starting with 0x8007xxxx.** These errors are not directly related to WMI. If error management is missing in the script (maybe because it is under development), with this error category it is possible to retrieve the associated message with the **NET.exe** command-line utility. For this, you must take the last four digits and convert them to a decimal value. Next, you must execute the **NET.exe** tool. For example, if you get an error code of 0x800706BA, you would take the last four digits, 0x06BA; convert the value to a decimal value: 1722; and execute the following command line:

```
C:>Net HelpMsg 1722
The RPC server is unavailable.
```

- **WMI errors that have a number starting with 0x8004xxxx.** These errors are purely WMI run-time errors. The errors are part of the **wbemErrorEnum** constants list. This list of WMI run-time errors is shown in Table 5.2.

- **Any other errors related to any other object model, such as WSH, CDOEX, CDOEXM, and ADSI, if the script makes use of these objects.** In this case, please refer to the related object model documentation for any specific error codes.

Errors of the second category, consisting of WMI operational errors, are due to mistakes or problems when performing WMI operations. These errors are not run-time errors but are values returned by WMI method execution. In this case, we must distinguish the following:

- **Errors caused by the execution of methods exposed by the WMI scripting API objects.** Depending on the method execution context (synchronous or asynchronous), the error will be retrieved differently. If the method is executed synchronously, the error will be retrieved as a run-time error (i.e., in the VBScript **Err** object). However, by using the **SWbemLastError** object from WMI, more information can be

Table 5.2   *The wbemErrorEnum Values*

wbemNoErr		0x00000000	
wbemErrFailed	WBEM_E_FAILED	0x80041001	The call failed.
wbemErrNotFound	WBEM_E_NOT_FOUND	0x80041002	The object could not be found.
wbemErrAccessDenied	WBEM_E_ACCESS_DENIED	0x80041003	The current user does not have permission to perform the action.
wbemErrProviderFailure	WBEM_E_PROVIDER_FAILURE	0x80041004	The provider has failed at some time other than during initialization.
wbemErrTypeMismatch	WBEM_E_TYPE_MISMATCH	0x80041005	A type mismatch occurred.
wbemErrOutOfMemory	WBEM_E_OUT_OF_MEMORY	0x80041006	There was not enough memory for the operation.
wbemErrInvalidContext	WBEM_E_INVALID_CONTEXT	0x80041007	The IWbemContext object is not valid.
wbemErrInvalidParameter	WBEM_E_INVALID_PARAMETER	0x80041008	One of the parameters to the call is not correct.
wbemErrNotAvailable	WBEM_E_NOT_AVAILABLE	0x80041009	The resource
wbemErrCriticalError	WBEM_E_CRITICAL_ERROR	0x8004100a	An internal
wbemErrInvalidStream	WBEM_E_INVALID_STREAM	0x8004100b	One or more network packets were corrupted during a remote session.
wbemErrNotSupported	WBEM_E_NOT_SUPPORTED	0x8004100c	The feature or operation is not supported.
wbemErrInvalidSuperclass	WBEM_E_INVALID_SUPERCLASS	0x8004100d	The superclass specified is not valid.
wbemErrInvalidNamespace	WBEM_E_INVALID_NAMESPACE	0x8004100e	The namespace specified could not be found.
wbemErrInvalidObject	WBEM_E_INVALID_OBJECT	0x8004100f	The specified instance is not valid.
wbemErrInvalidClass	WBEM_E_INVALID_CLASS	0x80041010	The specified class is not valid.
wbemErrProviderNotFound	WBEM_E_PROVIDER_NOT_FOUND	0x80041011	A provider referenced in the schema does not have a corresponding registration.
wbemErrInvalidProviderRegistration	WBEM_E_INVALID_PROVIDER_REGISTRATION	0x80041012	A provider referenced in the schema has an incorrect or incomplete registration. This error may be caused by any of the following A missing pragma namespace command in the MOF file used to register the provider
wbemErrProviderLoadFailure		0x80041013	

Table 5.2   *The wbemErrorEnum Values (continued)*

wbemErrInitializationFailure	WBEM_E_INITIALIZATION_FAILURE	0x80041014	A component
wbemErrTransportFailure	WBEM_E_TRANSPORT_FAILURE	0x80041015	A networking error that prevents normal operation has occurred.
wbemErrInvalidOperation	WBEM_E_INVALID_OPERATION	0x80041016	The requested operation is not valid. This error usually applies to invalid attempts to delete classes or properties.
wbemErrInvalidQuery	WBEM_E_INVALID_QUERY	0x80041017	The query was not syntactically valid.
wbemErrInvalidQueryType	WBEM_E_INVALID_QUERY_TYPE	0x80041018	The requested query language is not supported.
wbemErrAlreadyExists	WBEM_E_ALREADY_EXISTS	0x80041019	In a put operation
wbemErrOverrideNotAllowed	WBEM_E_OVERRIDE_NOT_ALLOWED	0x8004101a	It is not possible to perform the add operation on this qualifier because the owning object does not permit overrides.
wbemErrPropagatedQualifier	WBEM_E_PROPAGATED_QUALIFIER	0x8004101b	The user attempted to delete a qualifier that was not owned. The qualifier was inherited from a parent class.
wbemErrPropagatedProperty	WBEM_E_PROPAGATED_PROPERTY	0x8004101c	The user attempted to delete a property that was not owned. The property was inherited from a parent class.
wbemErrUnexpected	WBEM_E_UNEXPECTED	0x8004101d	The client made an unexpected and illegal sequence of calls
wbemErrIllegalOperation	WBEM_E_ILLEGAL_OPERATION	0x8004101e	The user requested an illegal operation
wbemErrCannotBeKey	WBEM_E_CANNOT_BE_KEY	0x8004101f	There was an illegal attempt to specify a key qualifier on a property that cannot be a key. The keys are specified in the class definition for an object
wbemErrIncompleteClass	WBEM_E_INCOMPLETE_CLASS	0x80041020	The current object is not a valid class definition. Either it is incomplete
wbemErrInvalidSyntax	WBEM_E_INVALID_SYNTAX	0x80041021	Reserved for future use.
wbemErrNondecoratedObject	WBEM_E_NONDECORATED_OBJECT	0x80041022	Reserved for future use.
wbemErrReadOnly	WBEM_E_READ_ONLY	0x80041023	The property that you are attempting to modify is read-only.

Table 5.2   *The wbemErrorEnum Values (continued)*

wbemErrProviderNotCapable	WBEM_E_PROVIDER_NOT_CAPABLE	0x80041024	The provider cannot perform the requested operation. This would include a query that is too complex
wbemErrClassHasChildren	WBEM_E_CLASS_HAS_CHILDREN	0x80041025	An attempt was made to make a change that would invalidate a subclass.
wbemErrClassHasInstances	WBEM_E_CLASS_HAS_INSTANCES	0x80041026	An attempt has been made to delete or modify a class that has instances.
wbemErrQueryNotImplemented	WBEM_E_QUERY_NOT_IMPLEMENTED	0x80041027	Reserved for future use.
wbemErrIllegalNull	WBEM_E_ILLEGAL_NULL	0x80041028	A value of Nothing was specified for a property that may not be Nothing
wbemErrInvalidQualifierType	WBEM_E_INVALID_QUALIFIER_TYPE	0x80041029	The variant value for a qualifier was provided that is not of a legal qualifier type.
wbemErrInvalidPropertyType	WBEM_E_INVALID_PROPERTY_TYPE	0x8004102a	The CIM type specified for a property is not valid.
wbemErrValueOutOfRange	WBEM_E_VALUE_OUT_OF_RANGE	0x8004102b	The request was made with an out-of-range value
wbemErrCannotBeSingleton	WBEM_E_CANNOT_BE_SINGLETON	0x8004102c	An illegal attempt was made to make a class singleton
wbemErrInvalidCimType	WBEM_E_INVALID_CIM_TYPE	0x8004102d	The CIM type specified is not valid.
wbemErrInvalidMethod	WBEM_E_INVALID_METHOD	0x8004102e	The requested method is not available.
wbemErrInvalidMethodParameters	WBEM_E_INVALID_METHOD_PARAMETERS	0x8004102f	The parameters provided for the method are not valid.
wbemErrSystemProperty	WBEM_E_SYSTEM_PROPERTY	0x80041030	There was an attempt to get qualifiers on a system property.
wbemErrInvalidProperty	WBEM_E_INVALID_PROPERTY	0x80041031	The property type is not recognized.
wbemErrCallCancelled	WBEM_E_CALL_CANCELLED	0x80041032	An asynchronous process has been canceled internally or by the user. Note that due to the timing and nature of the asynchronous operation the operation may not have been truly canceled.
wbemErrShuttingDown	WBEM_E_SHUTTING_DOWN	0x80041033	The user has requested an operation while WMI is in the process of shutting down.

Table 5.2   *The wbemErrorEnum Values (continued)*

wbemErrPropagatedMethod	WBEM_E_PROPAGATED_METHOD	0x80041034	An attempt was made to reuse an existing method name from a superclass
wbemErrUnsupportedParameter	WBEM_E_UNSUPPORTED_PARAMETER	0x80041035	One or more parameter values
wbemErrMissingParameter	WBEM_E_MISSING_PARAMETER_ID	0x80041036	A parameter was missing from the method call.
wbemErrInvalidParameterId	WBEM_E_INVALID_PARAMETER_ID	0x80041037	A method parameter has an invalid ID qualifier.
wbemErrNonConsecutiveParameterIds	WBEM_E_NONCONSECUTIVE_PARAMETER_IDS	0x80041038	One or more of the method parameters have ID qualifiers that are out of sequence.
wbemErrParameterIdOnRetval	WBEM_E_PARAMETER_ID_ON_RETVAL	0x80041039	The return value for a method has an ID qualifier.
wbemErrInvalidObjectPath	WBEM_E_INVALID_OBJECT_PATH	0x8004103a	The specified object path was invalid.
wbemErrOutOfDiskSpace	WBEM_E_OUT_OF_DISK_SPACE	0x8004103b	There is not enough free disk space to continue the operation.
wbemErrBufferTooSmall	WBEM_E_BUFFER_TOO_SMALL	0x8004103c	The supplied buffer was too small to hold all the objects in the enumerator or to read a string property.
wbemErrUnsupportedPutExtension	WBEM_E_UNSUPPORTED_PUT_EXTENSION	0x8004103d	The provider does not support the requested put operation.
wbemErrUnknownObjectType	WBEM_E_UNKNOWN_OBJECT_TYPE	0x8004103e	An object with an incorrect type or version was encountered during marshaling.
wbemErrUnknownPacketType	WBEM_E_UNKNOWN_PACKET_TYPE	0x8004103f	A packet with an incorrect type or version was encountered during marshaling.
wbemErrMarshalVersionMismatch	WBEM_E_MARSHAL_VERSION_MISMATCH	0x80041040	The packet has an unsupported version.
wbemErrMarshalInvalidSignature	WBEM_E_MARSHAL_INVALID_SIGNATURE	0x80041041	The packet appears to be corrupted.
wbemErrInvalidQualifier	WBEM_E_INVALID_QUALIFIER	0x80041042	An attempt has been made to mismatch qualifiers
wbemErrInvalidDuplicateParameter	WBEM_E_INVALID_DUPLICATE_PARAMETER	0x80041043	A duplicate parameter has been declared in a CIM method.
wbemErrTooMuchData	WBEM_E_TOO_MUCH_DATA	0x80041044	Reserved for future use.
wbemErrServerTooBusy	WBEM_E_SERVER_TOO_BUSY	0x80041045	A call to IWbemObjectSink::Indicate has failed. The provider may choose to refire the event.

Table 5.2   *The wbemErrorEnum Values (continued)*

wbemErrInvalidFlavor	WBEM_E_INVALID_FLAVOR	0x80041046	The specified flavor was invalid.
wbemErrCircularReference	WBEM_E_CIRCULAR_REFERENCE	0x80041047	An attempt has been made to create a reference that is circular (for example
wbemErrUnsupportedClassUpdate	WBEM_E_UNSUPPORTED_CLASS_UPDATE	0x80041048	The specified class is not supported.
wbemErrCannotChangeKeyInheritance	WBEM_E_CANNOT_CHANGE_KEY_INHERITANCE	0x80041049	An attempt was made to change a key when instances or subclasses are already using the key.
wbemErrCannotChangeIndexInheritance	WBEM_E_CANNOT_CHANGE_INDEX_INHERITANCE	0x80041050	An attempt was made to change an index when instances or subclasses are already using the index.
wbemErrTooManyProperties	WBEM_E_TOO_MANY_PROPERTIES	0x80041051	An attempt was made to create more properties than the current version of the class supports.
wbemErrUpdateTypeMismatch	WBEM_E_UPDATE_TYPE_MISMATCH	0x80041052	A property was redefined with a conflicting type in a derived class.
wbemErrUpdateOverrideNotAllowed	WBEM_E_UPDATE_OVERRIDE_NOT_ALLOWED	0x80041053	An attempt was made in a derived class to override a non-overrideable qualifier.
wbemErrUpdatePropagatedMethod	WBEM_E_UPDATE_PROPAGATED_METHOD	0x80041054	A method was redeclared with a conflicting signature in a derived class.
wbemErrMethodNotImplemented	WBEM_E_METHOD_NOT_IMPLEMENTED	0x80041055	An attempt was made to execute a method not marked with [implemented] in any relevant class.
wbemErrMethodDisabled	WBEM_E_METHOD_DISABLED	0x80041056	An attempt was made to execute a method marked with [disabled].
wbemErrRefresherBusy	WBEM_E_REFRESHER_BUSY	0x80041057	The refresher is busy with another operation.
wbemErrUnparsableQuery	WBEM_E_UNPARSABLE_QUERY	0x80041058	The filtering query is syntactically invalid.
wbemErrNotEventClass	WBEM_E_NOT_EVENT_CLASS	0x80041059	The FROM clause of a filtering query refere class that is not an event class (not derived from _Event).
wbemErrMissingGroupWithin	WBEM_E_MISSING_GROUP_WITHIN	0x8004105a	A GROUP BY clause was used without the corresponding GROUP WITHIN clause.
wbemErrMissingAggregationList	WBEM_E_MISSING_AGGREGATION_LIST	0x8004105b	A GROUP BY clause was used. Aggregation on all properties is not supported.

Table 5.2   *The wbemErrorEnum Values (continued)*

Name	Constant	Value	Description
wbemErrPropertyNotAnObject	WBEM_E_PROPERTY_NOT_AN_OBJECT	0x8004105c	Dot notation was used on a property that is not an embedded object.
wbemErrAggregatingByObject	WBEM_E_AGGREGATING_BY_OBJECT	0x8004105d	A GROUP BY clause references a property that is an embedded object without using dot notation.
wbemErrUninterpretableProviderQuery	WBEM_E_UNINTERPRETABLE_PROVIDER_QUERY	0x8004105f	An event provider registration query (__EventProviderRegistration) did not specify the classes for which events were provided.
wbemErrBackupRestoreWinmgtRunning	WBEM_E_BACKUP_RESTORE_WINMGMT_RUNNING	0x80041060	An request was made to back up or restore the repository while WinMgmt.exe was using it.
wbemErrQueueOverflow	WBEM_E_QUEUE_OVERFLOW	0x80041061	The asynchronous delivery queue overflowed due to the event consumer being too slow.
wbemErrPrivilegeNotHeld	WBEM_E_PRIVILEGE_NOT_HELD	0x80041062	The operation failed because the client did not have the necessary security privilege.
wbemErrInvalidOperator	WBEM_E_INVALID_OPERATOR	0x80041063	The operator is not valid for this property type.
wbemErrLocalCredentials	WBEM_E_LOCAL_CREDENTIALS	0x80041064	The user specified a username/password/authority on a local connection. The user must use a blank username/password and rely on default security.
wbemErrCannotBeAbstract	WBEM_E_CANNOT_BE_ABSTRACT	0x80041065	The class was made abstract when its superclass is not abstract.
wbemErrAmendedObject	WBEM_E_AMENDED_OBJECT	0x80041066	An amended object was PUT without the WBEM_FLAG_USE_AMENDED_QUALIFIE RS flag being specified.
wbemErrClientTooSlow	WBEM_E_CLIENT_TOO_SLOW		The client was not retrieving objects quickly enough from an enumeration.
wbemErrRegistrationTooBroad	WBEMESS_E_REGISTRATION_TOO_BROAD	0x80042001	The provider registration overlaps with the system event domain.
wbemErrRegistrationTooPrecise	WBEMESS_E_REGISTRATION_TOO_PRECISE	0x80042002	A WITHIN clause was not used in this query.
wbemErrTimedout	WBEM_E_RETRY_LATER	0x80043001	Reserved for future use.
wbemErrResetToDefault	WBEM_E_RESOURCE_CONTENTION	0x80043002	Reserved for future use.

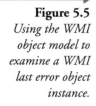

Figure 5.5
Using the WMI object model to examine a WMI last error object instance.

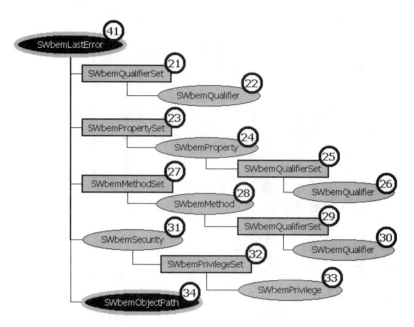

retrieved. If the method is executed asynchronously, the error will be retrieved from the **SWbemLastError** object available in the SINK_OnCompleted() sink routine. The **SWbemLastError** is an **SWbemObject** in its structure and contains information about the error. The **SWbemLastError** object available from Figure 5.5 is represented by the number 41 in the object model. You can compare it with the **SWbemObject** object available from Figure 4.4, represented by the number 20. As an **SWbemLastError** object has the same object model as an **SWbemObject**, all methods and properties exposed by this object are the same.

■ **Errors from the execution of a method exposed by a CIM class definition.** In this case, the return code is specific to the CIM class definition method execution and may vary from one CIM class to another. For instance, Table 5.3 contains the error codes returned when executing a method of a *Win32_Service* class instance.

If you execute the **LoadCIMinXL.wsf** script developed in the previous chapter (Sample 4.32, "A Windows Script File self-documenting the CIM repository classes in an Excel sheet"), the description qualifier related to each CIM class method contains a description of the return codes.

We can start with an easy sample. If we reuse Sample 4.1 and retrieve an instance of a *Win32_Service*, we can include some error checking when cre-

Table 5.3   *The Win32_Service Return Codes*

Methods	ReturnCode	
0x0	0	The request was accepted.
0x1	1	The request is not supported.
0x2	2	The user did not have the necessary access.
0x3	3	The service cannot be stopped because other services that are running are dependent on it.
0x4	4	The requested control code is not valid, or it is unacceptable to the service.
0x5	5	The requested control code cannot be sent to the service because the state of the service (Win32_BaseService State property) is equal to 0, 1, or 2.
0x6	6	The service has not been started.
0x7	7	The service did not respond to the start request in a timely fashion.
0x8	8	Unknown failure when starting the service.
0x9	9	The directory path to the service executable file was not found.
0xA	10	The service is already running.
0xB	11	The database to add a new service is locked.
0xC	12	A dependency for which this service relies on has been removed from the system.
0xD	13	The service failed to find the service needed from a dependent service.
0xE	14	The service has been disabled from the system.
0xF	15	The service does not have the correct authentication to run on the system.
0x10	16	This service is being removed from the system.
0x11	17	There is no execution thread for the service.
0x12	18	There are circular dependencies when starting the service.
0x13	19	There is a service running under the same name.
0x14	20	There are invalid characters in the name of the service.
0x15	21	Invalid parameters have been passed to the service.
0x16	22	The account which this service is to run under is either invalid or lacks the permissions to run the service.
0x17	23	The service exists in the database of services available from the system.
0x18	24	The service is currently paused in the system.

ating the instance. This logic is implemented in Sample 5.8 (lines 36 to 43). Notice the traditional VBScript error management at line 36. After the display of the VBScript run-time errors (line 37), the script creates an **SWbemLastError** object to retrieve more information about the WMI error (lines 38 to 41).

Sample 5.8   *Trapping error when creating a single instance*

```
 1:<?xml version="1.0"?>
 .:
 8:<package>
 9:  <job>
..:
13:     <object progid="WbemScripting.SWbemLocator" id="objWMILocator" reference="true"/>
14:
15:     <script language="VBscript">
16:     <![CDATA[
..:
20:     Const cComputerName = "LocalHost"
21:     Const cWMINameSpace = "root/cimv2"
22:     Const cWMIClass = "Win32_Service"
23:     Const cWMIInstance = "UNKNOWNSVC"
24:
25:     On Error Resume Next
..:
31:     objWMILocator.Security_.AuthenticationLevel = wbemAuthenticationLevelDefault
32:     objWMILocator.Security_.ImpersonationLevel = wbemImpersonationLevelImpersonate
33:     Set objWMIServices = objWMILocator.ConnectServer(cComputerName, cWMINameSpace, "", "")
34:     Set objWMIInstance = objWMIServices.Get (cWMIClass & "='" & cWMIInstance & "'")
35:
36:     If Err.Number Then
37:        WScript.Echo "0x" & Hex(Err.Number) & " - " & Err.Description
38:        Set objWMILastError = CreateObject("wbemscripting.swbemlasterror")
39:        WScript.Echo "Operation: " & objWMILastError.Operation
40:        WScript.Echo "ParameterInfo: " & objWMILastError.ParameterInfo
41:        WScript.Echo "ProviderName: " & objWMILastError.ProviderName
42:        WScript.Quit (1)
43:     End If
44:
45:     WScript.Echo objWMIInstance.Name & " (" & objWMIInstance.Description & ")"
46:     WScript.Echo "   AcceptPause=" & objWMIInstance.AcceptPause
47:     WScript.Echo "   AcceptStop=" & objWMIInstance.AcceptStop
..:
69:     WScript.Echo "   TagId=" & objWMIInstance.TagId
70:     WScript.Echo "   WaitHint=" & objWMIInstance.WaitHint
..:
75:     ]]>
76:     </script>
77:  </job>
78:</package>
```

Sample 5.8 references an invalid *Win32_Service* instance (line 23); as a result, the script fails during the instance retrieval (line 34). The obtained output is as follows:

```
C:\>"GetSingleInstanceWithAPI (Error).wsf"
Microsoft (R) Windows Script Host Version 5.6
Copyright (C) Microsoft Corporation 1996-2000. All rights reserved.

0x80041002 - Not found
Operation: GetObject
ParameterInfo: Win32_Service.Name="UNKNOWNSVC"
ProviderName: CIMWin32
```

Let's look at a more complex script sample that we are familiar with: Sample 5.7, which asynchronously changes the startup mode of a *Win32_Service* instance to Automatic if it was set on Manual and vice versa. This script is a nice application for an error management case because it uses many aspects of WMI, such as the following:

- The WMI connection operation

- The asynchronous *Win32_Service* instance retrieval

- The WMI method invocation to execute asynchronously the CIM class method *ChangeStartMode*

- The assignment of a parameter for the asynchronous CIM class method execution

- Some sink routine contexts

Let's see what the script looks like when we include some error management code. The modifications made to Sample 5.7 are in boldface and shown in Sample 5.9.

Sample 5.9 *Using one method with parameters of a Win32_Service instance asynchronously with context and error management from VBScript*

```
 1:<?xml version="1.0"?>
 .:
 8:<package>
 9:  <job>
 .:
13:     <script language="VBScript" src="..\Functions\TinyErrorHandler.vbs" />
14:
15:     <object progid="WbemScripting.SWbemLocator" id="objWMILocator" reference="true"/>
16:     <object progid="WbemScripting.SWbemNamedValueSet" id="objWMIMethodSinkContext" reference="true"/>
17:     <object progid="WbemScripting.SWbemNamedValueSet" id="objWMIInstanceSinkContext" reference="true"/>
18:
19:     <script language="VBscript">
20:     <![CDATA[
 .:
28:     ' -------------------------------------------------------------------------------
29:     Const cComputerName = "LocalHost"
30:     Const cWMINameSpace = "root/cimv2"
31:     Const cWMIClass = "Win32_Service"
32:     Const cWMIInstance = "SNMP"
 .:
37:     On Error Resume Next
38:
39:     Set objWMISink = WScript.CreateObject ("WbemScripting.SWbemSink", "SINK_")
40:
41:     objWMILocator.Security_.AuthenticationLevel = wbemAuthenticationLevelDefault
42:     objWMILocator.Security_.ImpersonationLevel = wbemImpersonationLevelImpersonate
43:     Set objWMIServices = objWMILocator.ConnectServer(cComputerName, cWMINameSpace, "", "")
44:     ' In case of WMI Connection problem
45:     If Err.Number Then ErrorHandler (Err)
46:
```

```
47:        objWMIInstanceSinkContext.Add "WMIMethod", "GetAsync"
48:        objWMIServices.GetAsync objWMISink, _
49:                            cWMIClass & "='" & cWMIInstance & "'", _
50:                            , _
51:                            , _
52:                            objWMIInstanceSinkContext
53:
54:        WScript.Echo "Continuing script execution ..."
55:        PauseScript "Click on 'Ok' to terminate the script ..."
56:
57:        objWMISink.Cancel
..:
63:
64:        ' ----------------------------------------------------------------------------
65:        Sub SINK_OnCompleted (intHResult, objWMILastError, objWMIAsyncContext)
..:
70:            On Error Resume Next
71:
72:            Wscript.Echo
73:            Wscript.Echo "BEGIN - OnCompleted."
74:
75:            Set objContextItem = objWMIAsyncContext.Item ("WMIMethod")
76:            ' In case of wrong context reference
77:            If Err.Number Then ErrorHandler (Err)
78:
79:            If intHResult = 0 Then
80:                WScript.Echo "'" & objContextItem.Value & _
81:                            "' WMI Scripting API Asynchronous call successful " & _
82:                            "(0x" & Hex(intHResult) & ")."
83:            Else
84:                WScript.Echo "------------------------------------------------------------"
85:
86:                WScript.Echo "'" & objContextItem.Value & _
87:                            "' WMI Scripting API Asynchronous call failed " & _
88:                            "(0x" & Hex(intHResult) & ")."
89:
90:                WScript.Echo vbCRLF & "SWbemLastError content:"
91:                Set objWMIPropertySet = objWMILastError.Properties_
92:                For Each objWMIProperty In objWMIPropertySet
93:                    WScript.Echo "  " & objWMIProperty.Name & "=" & objWMIProperty.Value
94:                Next
95:                Set objWMIPropertySet = Nothing
96:                WScript.Echo "------------------------------------------------------------"
97:            End If
98:
99:            Set objContextItem = Nothing
100:
101:            Wscript.Echo "END   - OnCompleted."
102:
103:        End Sub
...:
116:        ' ----------------------------------------------------------------------------
117:        Sub SINK_OnObjectReady (objWMIInstance, objWMIAsyncContext)
...:
123:            On Error Resume Next
124:
125:            Wscript.Echo
126:            Wscript.Echo "BEGIN - OnObjectReady."
127:
128:            Set objContextItem = objWMIAsyncContext.Item ("WMIMethod")
```

```
129:        ' In case of wrong context reference
130:        If Err.Number Then ErrorHandler (Err)
131:
132:        Select Case objContextItem.Value
133:            Case "GetAsync"
134:                WScript.Echo "'" & objWMIInstance.DisplayName & _
135:                             "' startup is currently '" & _
136:                             objWMIInstance.StartMode & "'."
137:
138:                Set objWMIMethod = objWMIInstance.Methods_("ChangeStartMode")
139:                ' In case of wrong method reference
140:                If Err.Number Then ErrorHandler (Err)
141:
142:                Set objWMIInParameters = objWMIMethod.InParameters
143:
144:                If objWMIInstance.StartMode = "Manual" Then
145:                    objWMIMethodSinkContext.Add "WMIMethod", "ExecMethodAsync"
146:                    objWMIMethodSinkContext.Add "CIMMethod", "ChangeStartMode (Automatic)"
147:                    objWMIInParameters.Properties_.Item("StartMode") = "Automatic"
148:                    ' In case of wrong parameter reference
149:                    If Err.Number Then ErrorHandler (Err)
150:
151:                    objWMIInstance.ExecMethodAsync_ objWMISink, _
152:                                        "ChangeStartMode", _
153:                                        objWMIInParameters, _
154:                                        ' _
155:                                        ' _
156:                                        objWMIMethodSinkContext
157:                End If
158:                If objWMIInstance.StartMode = "Auto" Then
159:                    objWMIMethodSinkContext.Add "WMIMethod", "ExecMethodAsync"
160:                    objWMIMethodSinkContext.Add "CIMMethod", "ChangeStartMode (Manual)"
161:                    objWMIInParameters.Properties_.Item("StartMode") = "Manual"
162:                    ' In case of wrong parameter reference
163:                    If Err.Number Then ErrorHandler (Err)
164:
165:                    objWMIInstance.ExecMethodAsync_ objWMISink, _
166:                                        "ChangeStartMode", _
167:                                        objWMIInParameters, _
168:                                        ' _
169:                                        ' _
170:                                        objWMIMethodSinkContext
171:                End If
...:
176:            Case "ExecMethodAsync"
177:                Set objContextItem = objWMIAsyncContext.Item ("CIMMethod")
178:                ' In case of wrong context reference
179:                If Err.Number Then ErrorHandler (Err)
180:
181:                If objWMIInstance.ReturnValue = 0 Then
182:                    Wscript.Echo "'" & objContextItem.Value & _
183:                             "' method execution successful " & _
184:                             "(0x" & Hex(objWMIInstance.ReturnValue) & ")."
185:                Else
186:                    Wscript.Echo "'" & objContextItem.Value & _
187:                             "' method execution failed " & _
188:                             "(0x" & Hex(objWMIInstance.ReturnValue) & ")."
189:                End If
190:        End Select
...
```

```
194:        Wscript.Echo "END    - OnObjectReady."
195:
196:    End Sub
...:
223:    ]]>
224:    </script>
225:  </job>
226:</package>
```

At line 13, the script starts by including a small function used as an error handler. This function is very basic, because its only purpose is to display the *Err.number* and the *Err.Description* before stopping the script execution. The function's code is as follows:

```
 1:' VB Script to handle errors occuring during a script execution.
 2:' This is a very simple error handling. No error recovery is made.
 3:' Only the error code number and the associated message is displayed.
 ..:
10:Option Explicit
11:
12:' ------------------------------------------------------------------
13:Function ErrorHandler (Err)
14:
15:        WScript.Echo "-----------------------------------------------"
16:        Wscript.Echo "Error: 0x" & Hex(Err.Number) & vbCRLF
17:        Wscript.Echo Err.Description
18:        WScript.Echo "-----------------------------------------------"
19:
20:        Wscript.Quit (1)
21:
22:End Function
```

When Sample 5.9 executes, several errors may occur. We may have some of the following cases:

- **A WMI connection error may occur when using the SWbemLocator object to create the SWbemServices object (line 43).** For instance, an error may occur because the system given in the constant at line 29 is not available. Another case could be a set of invalid credentials passed to the **SWbemLocator** *ConnectServer* method. In this case, line 45 of Sample 5.9 traps the error and calls the error handler function. This is typically a run-time error. For an unavailable server, the script output is

```
C:\>"SwapServiceStartupAndExecuteMethodAsyncWithContext (Error).wsf"
Microsoft (R) Windows Script Host Version 5.6
Copyright (C) Microsoft Corporation 1996-2000. All rights reserved.


-----------------------------------------------------------
Error: 0x800706BA

The RPC server is unavailable.
-----------------------------------------------------------
```

For a set of invalid credentials, the script output will be:

```
C:\>"SwapServiceStartupAndExecuteMethodAsyncWithContext (Error).wsf"
Microsoft (R) Windows Script Host Version 5.6
Copyright (C) Microsoft Corporation 1996-2000. All rights reserved.


------------------------------------------------------------
Error: 0x80070005

Access is denied.
------------------------------------------------------------
```

- **When creating the SWbemServices object, the referenced CIM class does not exist (line 31).** In this case, the asynchronous method *GetAsync* is executed (line 48), but because the class doesn't exist, no instance is retrieved. Because the WMI **SWbemServices** method uses an asynchronous method, the error is returned in the SINK_OnCompleted() sink routine in the context of the *GetAsync* method execution (line 75). In this case, *intHresult* is not equal to zero (line 79), which means that the **SWbemLastError** object is initialized from the sink routine parameters. Note that the *intHresult* value is displayed with the message (lines 86 to 88). In this case, the script shows the content of the **SWbemLastError** object. Because the **SWbemLastError** object is an **SWbemObject** object, the script enumerates the list of the properties available with their respective values (lines 90 to 95). This type of error is a WMI operational error. In this case, the script output is

```
C:\>"SwapServiceStartupAndExecuteMethodAsyncWithContext (Error).wsf"
Microsoft (R) Windows Script Host Version 5.6
Copyright (C) Microsoft Corporation 1996-2000. All rights reserved.

Continuing script execution ...

BEGIN - OnCompleted.
------------------------------------------------------------
'GetAsync' WMI Scripting API Asynchronous call failed (0x80041010).

SWbemLastError content:
  Description=
  Operation=GetObject
  ParameterInfo=Win32_RequestedClassName='SNMP'
  ProviderName=WinMgmt
  StatusCode=
------------------------------------------------------------
END   - OnCompleted.
```

- **When creating the SWbemServices object, the requested instance does not exist (line 32).** In this case, the asynchronous method *GetAsync* is executed, but because the referenced instance does not exist, no instance is retrieved. Since the problem occurs during the *GetA-sync* asynchronous method execution, the logic is the same as in the previous case. The error is retrieved during the execution of the SINK_OnCompleted() sink routine. This is a WMI operational error. In this case, the script output is

```
C:\>"SwapServiceStartupAndExecuteMethodAsyncWithContext (Error).wsf"
Microsoft (R) Windows Script Host Version 5.6
Copyright (C) Microsoft Corporation 1996-2000. All rights reserved.

Continuing script execution ...

BEGIN - OnCompleted.
-------------------------------------------------------------
'GetAsync' WMI Scripting API Asynchronous call failed (0x80041002).

SWbemLastError content:
  Description=
  Operation=GetObject
  ParameterInfo=Win32_Service.Name="RequestedInstanceName"
  ProviderName=CIMWin32
  StatusCode=
-------------------------------------------------------------
END    - OnCompleted.
```

- **When retrieving a sink routine context, the expected context is not found.** This can typically be the case if a sink routine looks for a context, but the **SWbemNamedValueSet** collection does not contain the expected context. This error may occur on lines 75, 128, and 177 of Sample 5.9. The code looks for a WMIContext or a CIMContext **SWbemNamedValue** (lines 75, 128, or 177). If another **SWbem-NamedValue** is requested (e.g., due to a mistyping of the **SWbem-NamedValue** name), this produces the following run-time error output and stops the script execution:

```
C:\>"SwapServiceStartupAndExecuteMethodAsyncWithContext (Error).wsf"
Microsoft (R) Windows Script Host Version 5.6
Copyright (C) Microsoft Corporation 1996-2000. All rights reserved.

Continuing script execution ...

BEGIN - OnObjectReady.
-------------------------------------------------------------
Error: 0x80041002

Not found
-------------------------------------------------------------
```

- **When referencing a CIM method to get the list of its parameters in an SWbemObject object, the expected CIM method is not found.**

This error may occur at line 138 of Sample 5.9 and is probably due to a mistyping of the method name. Basically, even if the error context is a bit different (it is related to a method name reference and not a WMI context name), the run-time error produced is the same as the previous one. In this case the output will be as follows:

```
C:\>"SwapServiceStartupAndExecuteMethodAsyncWithContext (Error).wsf"
Microsoft (R) Windows Script Host Version 5.6
Copyright (C) Microsoft Corporation 1996-2000. All rights reserved.

Continuing script execution ...

BEGIN - OnObjectReady.
'SNMP Service' startup is currently 'Auto'.
------------------------------------------------------------
Error: 0x80041002

Not found
------------------------------------------------------------
```

- **When referencing a CIM method parameter, the referenced parameter is not found.** Again, this is the same type of run-time error as in the previous case, but it is related to a method parameter name and not to the method name itself. This error may occur at lines 147 and 161 of Sample 5.9.

```
C:\>"SwapServiceStartupAndExecuteMethodAsyncWithContext (Error).wsf"
Microsoft (R) Windows Script Host Version 5.6
Copyright (C) Microsoft Corporation 1996-2000. All rights reserved.

Continuing script execution ...

BEGIN - OnObjectReady.
'SNMP Service' startup is currently 'Manual'.
------------------------------------------------------------
Error: 0x80041002

Not found
------------------------------------------------------------
```

- **The assigned CIM method parameter is invalid.** As the CIM method is executed asynchronously with the *ExecMethodAsync* method of the **SWbemObject** representing the SNMP *Win32_Service* instance, the error is retrieved in the SINK_OnObjectReady() sink routine, which is called when the *ExecMethodAsync* is executed. As shown previously, when examining the asynchronous event contexts, the *ExecMethodAsync* is invoked at lines 151 and 165, and, with the help of the context, the returned result of this method invocation is verified at line 181. Depending on the execution result, an appropriate message is displayed with the result value (lines 182 to 184, 186, and 188). This fault does not cause a run-time error; it is a WMI operational error because the CIM method parameter is wrong. The returned code is related to the CIM class method invoked. In this case, the result is one of the values presented in Table 5.3 for the *Win32_Service*. The error occurs during the SINK_OnCompleted() sink routine execution, but in the context of the *ExecMethodAsync* method invocation. The display output is as follows:

```
C:\>"SwapServiceStartupAndExecuteMethodAsyncWithContext (Error).wsf"
Microsoft (R) Windows Script Host Version 5.6
Copyright (C) Microsoft Corporation 1996-2000. All rights reserved.

Continuing script execution ...

BEGIN - OnObjectReady.
'SNMP Service' startup is currently 'Manual'.
END   - OnObjectReady.

BEGIN - OnCompleted.
'GetAsync' WMI Scripting API Asynchronous call successful (0x0).
END   - OnCompleted.

BEGIN - OnObjectReady.
'ChangeStartMode (Automatic)' method execution failed (0x15).
END   - OnObjectReady.

BEGIN - OnCompleted.
'ExecMethodAsync' WMI Scripting API Asynchronous call successful
(0x0).
END   - OnCompleted.
```

- **The executed CIM method name is invalid.** This error may occur at lines 152 and 166. Here the *ExecMethodAsync* invokes a CIM class method that does not exist for the instantiated CIM class. This results in a failure in the execution of the *ExecMethodAsync* method of the **SWbemObject** object. It is important to differentiate this error from the previous one. In the previous case, the *ExecMethodAsync* method invocation is successful, but the execution of the *ChangeStartMode* method fails due to an invalid parameter. In this case, the *ExecMethodAsync* method can't execute the CIM class method because it is not a valid method name. Both are WMI operational errors, but one is at the level of the WMI scripting API object method (this case), and the other is at the level of CIM class method execution (previous case). The display output is as follows:

```
C:\>"SwapServiceStartupAndExecuteMethodAsyncWithContext (Error).wsf"
Microsoft (R) Windows Script Host Version 5.6
Copyright (C) Microsoft Corporation 1996-2000. All rights reserved.

Continuing script execution ...

BEGIN - OnObjectReady.
'SNMP Service' startup is currently 'Manual'.
END   - OnObjectReady.

BEGIN - OnCompleted.
'GetAsync' WMI Scripting API Asynchronous call successful (0x0).
END   - OnCompleted.

BEGIN - OnCompleted.
-----------------------------------------------------------
'ExecMethodAsync' WMI Scripting API Asynchronous call failed
(0x80041055).

SWbemLastError content:
  Description=
  Operation=ExecMethod
  ParameterInfo=Win32_Service.Name="SNMP"
  ProviderName=WinMgmt
  StatusCode=
-----------------------------------------------------------
END   - OnCompleted.
```

- **The CIM method execution failed.** Even if all parameters required to execute the *ChangeStartMode* method are correct, it is possible that the CIM class method execution could fail because of external reasons. In this case, the script falls into the same scenario as an invalid method parameter input. So, the WMI scripting API object method *ExecAsyncMethod* works, but the CIM class method execution fails. The script receives a return code of the CIM class method execution during the SINK_OnCompleted() sink routine execution, in the context of the *ExecMethodAsync* method invocation.

Sample 5.9, shows how to handle errors from VBScript. Although the languages are different, the logic to manage the errors from JScript is the same. Only the statements are different. Sample 5.10 shows the same script as Sample 5.9 but written in JScript. Notice the inclusion of the VBScript error handler function previously used (line 13). Sample 5.10 takes advantage of the mixed language possibilities offered by WSH from a Windows Script File. The script is provided for reference. All comments made for the VBScript version remain valid for the JScript version.

Sample 5.10   *Using one method with parameters of a Win32_Service instance asynchronously with context and error management from JScript*

```
 1:<?xml version="1.0"?>
 .:
 8:<package>
 9:  <job>
..:
13:    <script language="VBScript" src="..\Functions\TinyErrorHandler.vbs" />
14:
15:    <object progid="WbemScripting.SWbemLocator" id="objWMILocator" reference="true"/>
16:    <object progid="WbemScripting.SWbemNamedValueSet" id="objWMIMethodSinkContext" reference="true"/>
17:    <object progid="WbemScripting.SWbemNamedValueSet" id="objWMIInstanceSinkContext" reference="true"/>
18:
19:    <script language="Jscript">
20:    <![CDATA[
21:
22:    // -----------------------------------------------------------------------------
23:    var cComputerName = "W2K-DPEN6400"
24:    var cWMINameSpace = "root/cimv2"
25:    var cWMIClass = "Win32_Service"
26:    var cWMIInstance = "SNMP"
..:
31:    objWMISink = Wscript.CreateObject ("WbemScripting.SWbemSink", "SINK_");
32:
33:    objWMILocator.Security_.AuthenticationLevel = wbemAuthenticationLevelDefault;
34:    objWMILocator.Security_.ImpersonationLevel = wbemImpersonationLevelImpersonate;
35:    try
36:      {
37:      objWMIServices = objWMILocator.ConnectServer(cComputerName, cWMINameSpace, "", "");
38:      }
39:    // In case of WMI Connection problem
40:    catch (Err)
41:      {
42:      ErrorHandler (Err)
43:      }
44:
45:    objWMIInstanceSinkContext.Add ("WMIMethod", "GetAsync");
46:    objWMIServices.GetAsync (objWMISink, cWMIClass + "='" + cWMIInstance + "'",
47:                             null,
48:                             null,
49:                             objWMIInstanceSinkContext);
50:
51:    Wscript.Echo ("Continuing script execution ...");
52:    PauseScript ("Click on 'Ok' to terminate the script ...");
53:
54:    objWMISink.Cancel;
55:
56:    // -----------------------------------------------------------------------------
57:    function SINK_OnCompleted (intHResult, objWMILastError, objWMIAsyncContext)
58:        {
..:
64:        Wscript.Echo ();
65:        Wscript.Echo ("BEGIN - OnCompleted.");
66:
67:        try
68:          {
69:          objContextItem = objWMIAsyncContext.Item ("WMIMethod");
```

```
 70:          }
 71:          // In case of wrong context reference
 72:          catch (Err)
 73:            {
 74:            ErrorHandler (Err)
 75:            }
 76:
 77:          if (intHResult == 0)
 78:            {
 79:            Wscript.Echo ("'" + objContextItem.Value +
 80:                          "' WMI Scripting API Asynchronous call successful " +
 81:                          "(" + intHResult + ").");
 82:            }
 83:          else
 84:            {
 85:            Wscript.Echo ("---------------------------------------------------------");
 86:
 87:            Wscript.Echo ("'" + objContextItem.Value +
 88:                          "' WMI Scripting API Asynchronous call failed " +
 89:                          "(" + intHResult + ").");
 90:
 91:            Wscript.Echo ();
 92:            Wscript.Echo ("SWbemLastError content:");
 93:            objWMIPropertySet = objWMILastError.Properties_;
 94:
 95:            enumWMIPropertySet = new Enumerator (objWMIPropertySet);
 96:            for (;! enumWMIPropertySet.atEnd(); enumWMIPropertySet.moveNext())
 97:                {
 98:                varItem = enumWMIPropertySet.item()
 99:                Wscript.Echo ("   " + varItem.name + "=" + enumWMIPropertySet.item());
100:                }
101:
102:            Wscript.Echo ("---------------------------------------------------------");
103:            }
104:
105:          Wscript.Echo ("END   - OnCompleted.");
106:
107:          }
108:
109:      // -----------------------------------------------------------------------------------
110:      function SINK_OnObjectPut (objWMIPath, objWMIAsyncContext)
...:
119:      // -----------------------------------------------------------------------------------
120:      function SINK_OnObjectReady (objWMIInstance, objWMIAsyncContext)
121:          {
...:
127:          Wscript.Echo ();
128:          Wscript.Echo ("BEGIN - OnObjectReady.");
129:
130:          try
131:            {
132:            objContextItem = objWMIAsyncContext.Item ("WMIMethod")
133:            }
134:          // In case of wrong context reference
135:          catch (Err)
136:            {
137:            ErrorHandler (Err)
138:            }
139:
140:          switch (objContextItem.Value)
```

```
141:                 {
142:             case "GetAsync":
143:                 Wscript.Echo ("'" + objWMIInstance.DisplayName +
144:                               "' startup is currently '" +
145:                                objWMIInstance.StartMode + "'.");
146:
147:                 try
148:                   {
149:                   objWMIMethod = objWMIInstance.Methods_("ChangeStartMode");
150:                   }
151:                 // In case of wrong method reference
152:                 catch (Err)
153:                   {
154:                   ErrorHandler (Err)
155:                   }
156:
157:                 objWMIInParameters = objWMIMethod.InParameters;
158:
159:                 if (objWMIInstance.StartMode == "Manual")
160:                   {
161:                   objWMIMethodSinkContext.Add ("WMIMethod", "ExecMethodAsync");
162:                   objWMIMethodSinkContext.Add ("CIMMethod", "ChangeStartMode Automatic)");
163:
164:                   try
165:                     {
166:                     objWMIInParameters.Properties_.Item("StartMode") = "Automatic";
167:                     }
168:                   // In case of wrong parameter reference
169:                   catch (Err)
170:                     {
171:                     ErrorHandler (Err)
172:                     }
173:
174:                   objWMIInstance.ExecMethodAsync_ (objWMISink,
175:                                                    "ChangeStartMode",
176:                                                    objWMIInParameters,
177:                                                    null,
178:                                                    null,
179:                                                    objWMIMethodSinkContext);
180:                   }
181:                 if (objWMIInstance.StartMode == "Auto")
182:                   {
183:                   objWMIMethodSinkContext.Add ("WMIMethod", "ExecMethodAsync");
184:                   objWMIMethodSinkContext.Add ("CIMMethod", "ChangeStartMode (Manual)");
185:
186:                   try
187:                     {
188:                     objWMIInParameters.Properties_.Item("StartMode") = "Manual";
189:                     }
190:                   // In case of wrong parameter reference
191:                   catch (Err)
192:                     {
193:                     ErrorHandler (Err)
194:                     }
195:
196:                   objWMIInstance.ExecMethodAsync_ (objWMISink,
197:                                                    "ChangeStartMode",
198:                                                    objWMIInParameters,
199:                                                    null,
200:                                                    null,
```

```
201:                                                       objWMIMethodSinkContext);
202:                          }
203:                    break;
204:
205:             case "ExecMethodAsync":
206:                    try
207:                      {
208:                      objContextItem = objWMIAsyncContext.Item ("CIMMethod");
209:                      }
210:                    // In case of wrong context reference
211:                    catch (Err)
212:                      {
213:                      ErrorHandler (Err)
214:                      }
215:
216:                    if (objWMIInstance.ReturnValue == 0)
217:                       {
218:                       Wscript.Echo ("'" + objContextItem.Value +
219:                                  "' method execution successful " +
220:                                  "(" + objWMIInstance.ReturnValue + ").");
221:                       }
222:                    else
223:                       {
224:                       Wscript.Echo ("'" + objContextItem.Value +
225:                                  "' method execution failed " +
226:                                  "(" + objWMIInstance.ReturnValue + ").");
227:                       }
228:                    break;
229:             }
230:
231:      Wscript.Echo ("END   - OnObjectReady.");
232:
233:        }
235:    // --------------------------------------------------------------------------------
236:    function SINK_OnProgress (intUpperBound, intCurrent, strMessage, objWMIAsyncContext)
...:
245:    // --------------------------------------------------------------------------------
246:    function PauseScript (strMessage)
...:
254:    ]]>
255:    </script>
256:  </job>
257:</package>
```

By examining the possible error types of Sample 5.9, we clearly see that we have the following:

- Traditional run-time errors that can be addressed with the **On Error Resume Next** statement combined with the *Err.Number* statement from VBScript or with the **try … catch … finally** statement from JScript.

- WMI scripting API errors that produce an **SWbemLastError** object available in the SINK_OnCompleted() sink routine if the call is asynchronous. Otherwise, these errors are produced as run-time errors.

- CIM class method execution errors that return specific return codes related to the CIM class method invoked (i.e., *Win32_Service* in Table 5.3).

We see that error handling makes reading the script code more difficult. Although it is a mandatory coding for a production script, these statements are not required during the learning phase. For this reason, subsequent scripts presented in the book, where possible, do not contain error management statements. But keep in mind that as a script developer, you must add the required tests in your production code to make sure that the written logic is reliable and behaves as expected.

5.4   WMI DateTime Helper

5.4.1   Under Windows XP and Windows.NET Server

WMI DateTime Helper is an object present in the WMI object model and added under Windows XP and Windows.NET Server to simplify date/time conversions. For instance, in the previous chapter, Table 4.16 contains the properties of the *Win32_Registry* class. In the property list, we have the *InstallDate* property. The *InstallDate* property contains a date and a time represented as follows:

```
yyyymmddHHMMSS.mmmmmmsUUU
```

This format is explained in Table 5.4.

This format is used in all date and time representations made in the CIM repository. Although this date and time representation is a simple string that can be parsed with the standard VBscript and JScript run-time

---

Table 5.4   *The DMTF Data and Time Format*

yyyy	Four-digit year (0000 through 9999). Your implementation can restrict the supported range. For example, an implementation can support only the years 1980 through 2099.
mm	Two-digit month (01 through 12).
dd	Two-digit day of the month (01 through 31). This value must be appropriate for the month. For example, February 31 is invalid. However, your implementation does not have to check for valid data.
HH	Two-digit hour of the day using the 24-hour clock (00 through 23).
MM	Two-digit minute in the hour (00 through 59).
SS	Two-digit number of seconds in the minute (00 through 59).

Table 5.4   *The DMTF Data and Time Format (continued)*

mmmmmm	Six-digit number of microseconds in the second (000000 through 999999). You implementation does not have to support evaluation using this field. However, this field must always be present to preserve the fixed-length nature of the string.
s	Plus sign (+) or minus sign (−) to indicate a positive or negative offset from Universal Time Coordinates (UTC).
UUU	Three-digit offset indicating the number of minutes that the originating time zone deviates from UTC. For WMI, it is encouraged, but not required, to convert times to GMT with a UTC offset of zero.

library functions, implementing a WMI object to abstract the string representation facilitates its manipulation and conversion to other formats. The WMI object abstracting the DateTime representation is called the **SWBemDateTime** object. Note that this object is available only under Windows XP and Windows.NET Server. Table 5.5 lists its properties and methods.

Table 5.5   *The SWBemDateTime Object*

Properties	Year	Year component
		Must be in range 0000-9999
	YearSpecified	Whether Year is significant
	Month	Month component
		Must be in range 01-12
	MonthSpecified	Whether Month is significant
	Day	Day component
		Must be in range 01-31 if IsInterval is FALSE, and 0-99999999 otherwise
	DaySpecified	Whether Day is significant
	Hours	Hour component
		Must be in range 0-23
	HoursSpecified	Whether Hour is significant
	Minutes	Minutes Component
		Must be in range 0-59
	MinutesSpecified	Whether Minute is significant
	Seconds	Seconds component
		Must be in range 0-59
	SecondsSpecified	Whether Seconds is significant

Table 5.5   *The SWBemDateTime Object (continued)*

Properties (cont'd.)	Microseconds	Microseconds component
		Must be in range 0 to 999999
	MicrosecondsSpecified	Whether Microseconds is significant
	UTC	UTC offset
		Signed number in the range -720,720
	UTCSpecified	Whether UTC is significant
	IsInterval	If TRUE, value represents an interval value. Otherwise it represents a Datetime value.
	Value	The raw DMTF-format string value representation of the date time.
Methods	SetVarDate()	The variant date value to be used to set this object.
		If TRUE the supplied vDate is interpreted as a local time and is converted internally to the correct UTC format. Otherwise vDate is converted directly into a UTC value with offset 0.
	GetVarDate()	If TRUE then the return value expresses a local time (for the client). Otherwise the return value is to be regarded as a UTC time.
	SetFileTime()	The FILETIME value used to set this object.
		If TRUE the supplied strFileTime is interpreted as a local time and is converted internally to the correct UTC format. Otherwise strFile-TIme is converted directly into a UTC value with offset 0.
	GetFileTime()	If TRUE then the return value expresses a local time (for the client). Otherwise the return value is to be regarded as a UTC time.

To illustrate the use of the **SWBemDateTime** object, Sample 5.11 shows how the DMTF DateTime format of the *Win32_Registry* instance can be converted to other formats.

Sample 5.11   *Converting a DateTime DMTF format to scripting run-time supported formats*

```
 1:<?xml version="1.0"?>
 .:
 8:<package>
 9:  <job>
..:
13:     <object progid="WbemScripting.SWbemLocator" id="objWMILocator" reference="true"/>
14:     <object progid="WbemScripting.SWbemDateTime" id="objWMIDateTime" />
15:
16:     <script language="VBscript">
17:     <![CDATA[
..:
21:     Const cComputerName = "LocalHost"
22:     Const cWMINameSpace = "root/cimv2"
23:     Const cWMIClass = "Win32_Registry"
24:     Const cWMIInstance = "Microsoft Windows Whistler Server|C:\WINNT|\Device\Harddisk0\Partition1"
```

```
..:
30:     objWMILocator.Security_.AuthenticationLevel = wbemAuthenticationLevelDefault
31:     objWMILocator.Security_.ImpersonationLevel = wbemImpersonationLevelImpersonate
32:     Set objWMIServices = objWMILocator.ConnectServer(cComputerName, cWMINameSpace, "", "")
33:     Set objWMIInstance = objWMIServices.Get (cWMIClass & "='" & cWMIInstance & "'")
34:
35:     WScript.Echo objWMIInstance.Name & "=" & objWMIInstance.Name
36:     WScript.Echo "   Caption=" & objWMIInstance.Caption
37:     WScript.Echo "   CurrentSize=" & objWMIInstance.CurrentSize
38:     WScript.Echo "   Caption=" & objWMIInstance.Caption
39:     WScript.Echo "   Description=" & objWMIInstance.Description
40:
41:     objWMIDateTime.Value = objWMIInstance.InstallDate
42:     WScript.Echo "   InstallDate (Value)=" & objWMIDateTime.Value
43:     WScript.Echo "   InstallDate (varDate UTC Time)=" & objWMIDateTime.GetVarDate (False)
44:     WScript.Echo "   InstallDate (varDate Local Time)=" & objWMIDateTime.GetVarDate (True)
45:     WScript.Echo "   InstallDate (FileTime UTC Time)=" & objWMIDateTime.GetFileTime (False)
46:     WScript.Echo "   InstallDate (FileTime Local Time)=" & objWMIDateTime.GetFileTime (True)
47:     WScript.Echo "   InstallDate (Year)=" & objWMIDateTime.Year
48:     WScript.Echo "   InstallDate (Month)=" & objWMIDateTime.Month
49:     WScript.Echo "   InstallDate (Day)=" & objWMIDateTime.Day
50:     WScript.Echo "   InstallDate (Hours)=" & objWMIDateTime.Hours
51:     WScript.Echo "   InstallDate (Minutes)=" & objWMIDateTime.Minutes
52:     WScript.Echo "   InstallDate (Seconds)=" & objWMIDateTime.Seconds
53:     WScript.Echo "   InstallDate (MicroSeconds)=" & objWMIDateTime.MicroSeconds
54:     WScript.Echo "   InstallDate (UTC)=" & objWMIDateTime.UTC
55:     WScript.Echo "   InstallDate (IsInterval)=" & objWMIDateTime.IsInterval
56:
57:     WScript.Echo "   MaximumSize=" & objWMIInstance.MaximumSize
58:     WScript.Echo "   ProposedSize=" & objWMIInstance.ProposedSize
59:     WScript.Echo "   Status=" & objWMIInstance.Status
..:
64:     ]]>
65:     </script>
66:   </job>
67:</package>
```

The script instantiates the **SWBemDateTime** object at line 14. Next, it retrieves the instance of the *Win32_Registry* class (lines 21 to 33) and lists the associated properties. The particularity resides at line 41, where the *InstallDate* property is assigned to the **SWBemDateTime** object *Value* property. Once loaded in the **SWBemDateTime** object, the script displays all the properties available from this object. The result is a display of the DMTF DateTime in various forms shown as follows:

```
C:\>ShowWin32_RegistryDateTime.wsf
Microsoft (R) Windows Script Host Version 5.6
Copyright (C) Microsoft Corporation 1996-2000. All rights reserved.

Microsoft Windows Whistler Server|C:\WINNT|\Device\Harddisk0\Partition1
    Caption=Registry
    CurrentSize=2
    Caption=Registry
    Description=Registry
    InstallDate (Value)=20010503021847.000000+120
```

```
InstallDate (varDate UTC Time)=03-05-2001 02:18:47
InstallDate (varDate Local Time)=03-05-2001 04:18:47
InstallDate (FileTime UTC Time)=126333299270000000
InstallDate (FileTime Local Time)=126333371270000000
InstallDate (Year)=2001
InstallDate (Month)=5
InstallDate (Day)=3
InstallDate (Hours)=2
InstallDate (Minutes)=18
InstallDate (Seconds)=47
InstallDate (MicroSeconds)=0
InstallDate (UTC)=120
InstallDate (IsInterval)=False
MaximumSize=51
ProposedSize=51
Status=OK
```

Of course, the **SWBemDateTime** object can be used with any properties containing a DMTF DateTime format. It is not dedicated to the
Win32_Registry class. Because it allows the DMTF date/time to be represented in a more readable way, it was already used in the previous chapter at
Sample 4.30 ("A generic routine to display the SWbemPropertySet object")
to display the **SWbemPropertySet** object content. In the next chapter, we
use this object again when we work with Absolute Timer events which are
events scheduled to occur at a precise date and time.

5.4.2   What about Windows 2000 and before?

If your system runs under Windows 2000 or any previous platforms, the
SWBemDateTime object is not available from the WMI COM object
model. As most scripts included in this book are written for Windows XP
or Windows.NET Server and make use of the **SWBemDateTime** object,
this represents a compatibility problem. It is possible to work around this
limitation without impacting the existing scripts with the use of the Windows Script Components (WSC) discussed in Chapter 1. As a reminder, a
WSC is nothing but a COM implementation where the COM logic is
coded in a script. If we write a WSC that emulates the behavior of the
SWBemDateTime object, it will be possible to run any scripts making use
of this object under Windows 2000 by simply modifying one single line.
For instance, with Sample 5.11, we can replace line 14

```
14:     <object progid="WbemScripting.SWbemDateTime" id="objWMIDateTime" />
```

with:

```
14:     <object progid="SWbemDateTime.WSC" id="objWMIDateTime" />
```

If the **SWwbemDateTime.wsc** exposes the same properties and methods as the native **SWBemDateTime** object, this will guarantee the same level of method and properties invocations. However, consider the **SWBemDateTime.wsc** example given as a framework as it implements only some of the functionalities offered by the native **SWBemDateTime** object. Currently, This WSC component supports all **SWBemDateTime** object features with the following restrictions:

- It cannot set and get a *FileTime*.

- The *SetVarDate* method always interprets the given time as a local time.

- There is no interval management capability.

- There is no support for wildcards in the DMTF Date/Time format.

Despite these restrictions, the **SWBemDateTime.wsc** offers a level of functionality sufficient to run on Windows 2000 the scripts using the **SWBemDateTime** object of Windows XP or Windows.NET Server. The **SWBemDateTime.wsc** code is available in Sample 5.12.

Sample 5.12   *The SWbemDateTime Windows Script Component*

```
 1:<?xml version="1.0"?>
 .:
 8:<component>
 9:
10:  <registration
11:         description="SWbemDateTime"
12:         progid="SWbemDateTime.WSC"
13:         version="1.00"
14:         classid="{46818027-a0d8-4729-9750-74640dd14dc8}"
15:  >
16:  </registration>
17:
18:  <!--
..:
48:  <public>
49:    <method name="SetVarDate" internalname="SetVarDate">
50:      <parameter name="strVarDate" />
51:    </method>
52:
53:    <method name="GetVarDate" internalname="GetVarDate">
54:      <parameter name="boolIsLocal" />
55:    </method>
..:
65:    <property name="Day" internalname="strDay">
66:      <get/>
67:      <put/>
68:    </property>
69:
```

```
 70:    <property name="DaySpecified" internalname="boolDaySpecified">
 71:      <get/>
 72:    </property>
 73:
 74:    <property name="Month" internalname="strMonth">
 75:      <get/>
 76:      <put/>
 77:    </property>
 78:
 79:    <property name="MonthSpecified" internalname="boolMonthSpecified">
 80:      <get/>
 81:    </property>
 82:
 83:    <property name="Year" internalname="strYear">
 84:      <get/>
 85:      <put/>
 86:    </property>
...:
146:  </public>
147:
148:  <script language="VBScript">
149:  <![CDATA[
...:
194:  ' ------------------------------------------------------------------------------------
195:  Function SetVarDate(strVarDate)
...:
200:          If Len (strVarDate) Then
201:              strDay = Right ("00" & Day (strVarDate),
202:              strMonth = Right ("00" & Month (strVarDate), 2)
203:              strYear = Right ("0000" & Year (strVarDate), 4)
204:              strHours = Right ("00" & Hour (strVarDate), 2)
205:              strMinutes = Right ("00" & Minute (strVarDate), 2)
206:              strSeconds = Right ("00" & Second (strVarDate), 2)
207:              strMicroseconds = "000000"
208:
209:              Set objWMIServices = GetObject ("Winmgmts:Root\CIMv2")
210:              Set objWMIInstances = objWMIServices.InstancesOf ("Win32_ComputerSystem")
211:              For Each objWMIInstance In objWMIInstances
212:                  strUTC = Right ("000" & objWMIInstance.CurrentTimeZone, 3)
213:              Next
214:              Set objWMIInstances = Nothing
215:
216:              If strUTC > 0 Then
217:                  strUTC = "+" & strUTC
218:              End If
219:
220:              strValue = strYear & _
221:                          strMonth & _
222:                          strDay & _
223:                          strHours & _
224:                          strMinutes & _
225:                          strSeconds & "." & _
226:                          strMicroSeconds & _
227:                          strUTC
228:          Else
229:              MsgBox "SetVarDate(): Invalid DateTime value", _
230:                      cExclamationMarkIcon, _
231:                      "SWBemDateTime.WSC"
232:          End If
```

```
233:
234:  End Function
...:
...:
...:
673:
674:  ]]>
675:  </script>
676:
677:</component>
```

Sample 5.12 contains only a portion of the complete code because it shows only the code of the *SetVarDate* method. Basically, the logic is always the same as the code consists of the manipulation of a string to extract and concatenate date and time items (day, month, year, hours, minutes, seconds). From line 1 to 146, we recognize the WSC component declaration as we saw in Chapter 1. From line 194, the various functions implementing the desired properties and methods are available. From line 195 to 234, Sample 5.12 shows the *SetVarDate* method logic. The *SetVarDate* method uses WMI to determine the time zone of the system with a class not yet used until now: the *Win32_ComputerSystem*. Basically, the instance of this class exposes the *CurrentTimeZone* property, which gives the time zone of the computer.

5.5   WMI extension for ADSI

Although we do not focus on Active Directory System Interfaces (ADSI) in this book, there is a very interesting particularity related to the combination of ADSI and WMI. ADSI comes with a collection of objects exposing their own properties and methods. As the ADSI implementation allows the object model to be extended, it means that new objects can be added to the model and also existing objects can expose some new properties and methods. This is exactly where the WMI extension comes into the game. With the WMI extension for ADSI, it is possible to manage systems represented by ADSI computer objects retrieved from Active Directory. For instance, when an application performs an LDAP query in Active Directory to retrieve all computers matching a specific name and performs an LDAP bind operation on the retrieved computer, the extension enables the software to obtain an **SWbemServices** object, a WMI object path, or a *Win32_ComputerSystem* instance directly from the ADSI **Computer** object. Table 5.6 contains the properties and methods directly available from the ADSI interface that represent a **Computer** object.

Table 5.6   *The ADSI IADsComputer Interface Properties*

ComputerID	Access: read
	The globally unique identifier assigned to each machine.
Department	Access: read/write
	The department (such as OU or organizational unit) within a company that this computer belongs to.
Description	Access: read/write
	The description of this computer.
Division	Access: read/write
	The division (such as organization) within a company that this computer belongs to.
Location	Access: read/write
	The physical location of the machine where this machine is typically located.
MemorySize	Access: read/write
	The size of random access memory (RAM) in megabytes (MB).
Model	Access: read/write
	The make/model of this machine.
NetAddresses	Access: read/write
	An array of NetAddress fields that represent the addresses by which this computer can be reached. NetAddress is a provider-specific **BSTR** composed of two substrings separated by a colon (":"). The left-hand substring indicates the address type, and the right-hand substring is a string representation of an address of that type. For example, TCP/IP addresses are of the form "IP:100.201.301.45. IPX type addresses are of the form "IPX:10.123456.80".
OperatingSystem	Access: read/write
	The name of the operating system used on this machine.
OperatingSystemVersion	Access: read/write
	The operating system version number.
Owner	Access: read/write
	The name of the person who typically uses this machine and has a license to run the installed software.
PrimaryUser	Access: read/write
	The name of the contact person, in case something needs to be changed on this machine.
Processor	Access: read/write
	The type of processor.
ProcessorCount	Access: read/write
	The number of processors.

Table 5.6   *The ADSI IADsComputer Interface Properties (continued)*

Role	Access: read/write
	The role of this machine, for example, workstation, server, domain controller.
Site	Access: read/write
	The globally unique identifier identifying the site this machine was installed in. A site represents a physical region of good connectivity in a network.
StorageCapacity	Access: read/write
	The disk space in megabytes.

Note: At writing time, this extension is available from WMI under Windows NT 4.0, Windows 2000, and Windows XP. However, the security push started at Microsoft early in 2002 has made the future of this extension uncertain. Microsoft removed the extension from Windows.NET Server and does not plan, at writing time, to make it available as a separate download from its Web site. This choice is driven by security reasons because this feature can be quite powerful in some circumstances and is rarely used. As we will see further, Sample 5.16 ("Using the WMI ADSI extension to reboot computers retrieved from an LDAP query") illustrates how easy to use, but powerful, this WMI extension for ADSI can be. We will revisit the Microsoft security push initiative and its impact on WMI in the second book dedicated to WMI, *Leveraging Windows Management Instrumentation (WMI) Scripting* (ISBN 1555582990).

When WMI is installed and ADSI is already present (which is the case for Windows 2000, Windows XP), WMI adds two methods and one property to the ADSI **Computer** object. Table 5.7 contains these new extensions.

Table 5.7   *The WMI ADSI Extension Property and Methods*

Properties	WMIObjectPath	A string value that contains a moniker. The moniker identifies the object path for the WMI computer object.
Methods	GetWMIObject	Returns the WMI computer object identified by the ADSI computer object.
	GetWMIServices	Returns the WMI services object that you can use to perform other WMI actions, such as executing methods or invoking queries.

5.5.1   The *WMIObjectPath* extension

Using the *WMIObjectPath* property, it is possible to retrieve the corresponding WMI moniker of an ADSI **Computer** object. This facilitates the instantiation of the *Win32_ComputerSystem* class by referencing the corresponding moniker. Sample 5.13 shows how to proceed.

Sample 5.13   *Retrieving the corresponding WMI moniker of an ADSI Computer object*

```
 1:<?xml version="1.0"?>
 .:
 8:<package>
 9:  <job>
..:
13:     <script language="VBscript">
14:     <![CDATA[
..:
18:     ' -----------------------------------------------------------------------------
19:     Const cComputerADsPath = "cn=NET-DPEN6400A,ou=Domain Controllers,dc=LissWare,dc=net"
..:
26:     Set objComputer = GetObject("LDAP://" & cComputerADsPath)
27:
28:     WScript.Echo objComputer.WMIObjectPath
29:     Set objWMIInstance = GetObject (objComputer.WMIObjectPath)
30:     Set objWMIPropertySet = objWMIInstance.Properties_
31:
32:     For Each objWMIProperty In objWMIPropertySet
33:         If IsArray (objWMIProperty.Value) Then
34:            For Each varElement In objWMIProperty.Value
35:                   WScript.Echo "  " & objWMIProperty.Name & " (" & varElement & ")"
36:            Next
37:         Else
38:            WScript.Echo "  " & objWMIProperty.Name & " (" & objWMIProperty.Value & ")"
39:         End If
40:     Next
..:
45:     ]]>
46:     </script>
47:   </job>
48:</package>
```

At line 19, the script defines the *distinguishedName* of the ADSI **Computer** object in a constant. As the script is for purely academic purposes, we proceed this way for convenience, but keep in mind that it can be any ADSI **Computer** object from Active Directory (i.e., issued by an LDAP query, as we will see in a subsequent example). Next, line 26 performs the LDAP bind operation to connect to the **Computer** object stored in Active Directory. At line 28, the script uses the WMI ADSI property extension to echo the corresponding WMI moniker. At line 29, the script uses the moniker to obtain the *Win32_ComputerSystem* instance and enumerates its properties (lines 30 to 40). The output is as follows:

```
 1:   C:\>WMIObjectPath.wsf
 2:   Microsoft (R) Windows Script Host Version 5.6
 3:   Copyright (C) Microsoft Corporation 1996-2001. All rights reserved.
 4:
 5:   WINMGMTS:{impersonationLevel=impersonate}!
                  //NET-DPEN6400A/root/cimv2:Win32_ComputerSystem.Name="NET-DPEN6400A"
 6:      AdminPasswordStatus (3)
 7:      AutomaticResetBootOption (True)
 8:      AutomaticResetCapability (True)
 9:      BootOptionOnLimit ()
10:      BootOptionOnWatchDog ()
11:      BootROMSupported (True)
12:      BootupState (Normal boot)
13:      Caption (NET-DPEN6400A)
14:      ChassisBootupState (3)
15:      CreationClassName (Win32_ComputerSystem)
16:      CurrentTimeZone (120)
17:      DaylightInEffect (True)
18:      Description (AT/AT COMPATIBLE)
19:      Domain (LissWare.Net)
20:      DomainRole (5)
21:      EnableDaylightSavingsTime (True)
22:      FrontPanelResetStatus (3)
23:      InfraredSupported (False)
24:      InitialLoadInfo ()
25:      InstallDate ()
26:      KeyboardPasswordStatus (3)
27:      LastLoadInfo ()
28:      Manufacturer (Compaq)
29:      Model (Deskpro EN Series)
30:      Name (NET-DPEN6400A)
31:      NameFormat ()
32:      NetworkServerModeEnabled (True)
33:      NumberOfProcessors (1)
34:      OEMLogoBitmap ()
35:      OEMStringArray (CDT v. 1.0)
..:
..:
..:
```

5.5.2   The *GetWMIObject* extension

As with the *GetWMIObject* method, it is possible to directly retrieve the corresponding *Win32_ComputerSystem* instance of the examined **Computer** object without creating an **SWbemServices** object and without referring to the WMI moniker. For example, Sample 5.14 lists all the WMI properties of the same **Computer** object by retrieving the *Win32_ComputerSystem* instance directly from the ADSI **Computer** object.

Sample 5.14   *Retrieving the WMI properties of a Win32_ComputerSystem instance from an ADSI Computer object*

```
1:<?xml version="1.0"?>
 .:
8:<package>
9:  <job>
..:
```

```
13:    <script language="VBscript">
14:    <![CDATA[
..:
18:    ' ---------------------------------------------------------------------------------
19:    Const cComputerADsPath = "cn=NET-DPEN6400A,ou=Domain Controllers,dc=LissWare,dc=net"
..:
26:    Set objComputer = GetObject("LDAP://" & cComputerADsPath)
27:
28:    Set objWMIInstance = objComputer.GetWMIObject
29:    Set objWMIPropertySet = objWMIInstance.Properties_
30:
31:    For Each objWMIProperty In objWMIPropertySet
32:        If IsArray (objWMIProperty.Value) Then
33:            For Each varElement In objWMIProperty.Value
34:                WScript.Echo "   " & objWMIProperty.Name & " (" & varElement & ")"
35:            Next
36:        Else
37:            WScript.Echo "   " & objWMIProperty.Name & " (" & objWMIProperty.Value & ")"
38:        End If
39:    Next
..:
44:    ]]>
45:    </script>
46:   </job>
47:</package>
```

The script logic is exactly the same as Sample 5.13, but with the *Get-WMIObject* method at line 28, the script retrieves the **SWbemObject** representing the *Win32_ComputerSystem* instance directly from the ADSI **Computer** object.

5.5.3   The *GetWMIServices* extension

The last method brought by WMI to ADSI is the *GetWMIServices* method. In the two previous samples, to retrieve the *Win32_ComputerSystem* class instance we used the WMI moniker or we retrieved the instance directly from the ADSI **Computer** object. With the *GetWMIServices* method, it is possible to retrieve the **SWbemServices** object directly from the ADSI **computer** object. As soon as the script has this object created, it is possible to retrieve any manageable instances available from the **Root\CIMv2** namespace of this computer (i.e., the *Win32_Service* instances). See Sample 5.15.

Sample 5.15   *Retrieving the Win32_Service instances from an ADSI Computer object*

```
1:<?xml version="1.0"?>
.:
8:<package>
9:  <job>
..:
13:    <script language="VBscript">
14:    <![CDATA[
```

```
..:
18:      ' ---------------------------------------------------------------------------------
19:      Const cComputerADsPath = "cn=W2K-DPEN6400,ou=Domain Controllers,dc=MyW2KDomain,dc=com"
20:
21:      ' ---------------------------------------------------------------------------------
22:      Const cWMIClass  = "Win32_Service"
..:
28:      Set objComputer = GetObject("LDAP://" & cComputerADsPath)
29:
30:      Set objWMIServices = objComputer.GetWMIServices
31:      Set objWMIInstances = objWMIServices.InstancesOf(cWMIClass)
32:
33:      For Each objWMIInstance in objWMIInstances
34:          WScript.Echo "'" & objWMIInstance.DisplayName & "' is currently " & _
35:                       LCase (objWMIInstance.State) & "."
36:      Next
..:
41:      ]]>
42:      </script>
43:   </job>
44:</package>
```

Again, the logic is exactly the same as the two previous samples, but now the **SWbemServices** object is created (line 30) with the usage of the *GetWMIServices* method associated with the ADSI **Computer** object. Once the **SWbemServices** object available, it represents a connection to the **Root\CIMv2** namespace of the real computer represented by the ADSI **Computer** object.

With the created **SWbemServices** object, the script instantiates a collection (line 31) containing the *Win32_Service* instances available from this computer. Once created, the script enumerates the Windows services available in the collection (lines 33 to 36).

The use of the *GetWMIServices* or *GetWMIObject* methods implies that the default security context of the script allows the connection to the computer name that comes from ADSI. As the ADSI **Computer** object comes from Active Directory, it can be any computer in the forest, and it is likely that some of the computer names are remote.

In the previous samples, it is important to note that these two methods use the default security context (the security context of the user running the script) to obtain the WMI objects:

- An **SWbemServices** for the *GetWMIServices* method

- An **SWbemObject** for the *GetWMIObject* method

If the ADSI bind operation is executed with the **IADsOpenDSObject** interface, it is likely that different credentials are used, in which case the ADSI connection is executed under a different security context than the default security context. In this example, it is fair to think that the **SWbem-**

Services and **SWbemObject** objects obtained from the WMI ADSI extension are also created under the same security context as the ADSI security context. Unfortunately, this is not the case, and the default security context is used despite the credentials provided for the ADSI bind operation. This limitation must be taken into consideration when writing a script that uses the WMI ADSI extension, especially when the remote machine names that come from an ADSI query are accessed because the current security context is used to perform the WMI connection. This implies that the user running the script must have the rights to access the remote machines.

In Sample 5.15, the script retrieves the *Win32_Service* instances available, but it can be any other instances available from this computer. To demonstrate the power of the WMI and ADSI integration, Sample 5.16 implements logic directly applicable for your day-to-day management tasks. Imagine a script that queries Active Directory for a list of computers and, based on that list, reboots the computers. If you use a naming convention in your company that allows the identification of a computer role based on its name, it is quite easy to create an LDAP query filter to retrieve a list of all the print servers in the company or any other server type. Once the LDAP query completes, the script binds to the corresponding ADSI **Computer** object (supposing that you have the necessary rights), from the ADSI object retrieves a WMI connection, and reboots the system. Let's see how Sample 5.16 works.

Sample 5.16   *Using the WMI ADSI extension to reboot computers retrieved from an LDAP query*

```
 1:<?xml version="1.0"?>
 .:
 8:<package>
 9:  <job>
..:
13:    <runtime>
14:      <unnamed name="LDAPFilter" helpstring="enter a list of computers as follow
               '(name=DCUK056)(name=DCBE017)(name=syst*)'" required="true" type="string" />
15:    </runtime>
16:
17:    <reference object="WbemScripting.SWbemLocator"/>
18:
19:    <script language="VBScript" src="..\Functions\ADSearchFunction2.vbs"/>
20:
21:    <script language="VBscript">
22:    <![CDATA[
..:
26:    ' -------------------------------------------------------------------------------
27:    ' Defaults used when only a LDAP filter is given for the query
28:    Const cLDAPClassFilter       = "(objectCategory=computer)"
29:    Const cLDAPPropertiesToReturn = "ADsPath"
30:    Const cHowDeepToSearch       = "subTree"
..:
45:    On Error Resume Next
46:
```

```
47:    ' -----------------------------------------------------------------------------
48:    ' Parse the command line parameters
49:    If WScript.Arguments.Unnamed.Count = 0 Then
50:      WScript.Arguments.ShowUsage()
51:      WScript.Quit
52:    End If
53:
54:    strLDAPNameFilter = WScript.Arguments.Unnamed.Item(0)
55:    strLDAPNameFilter = "(&" & cLDAPClassFilter & "(|" & strLDAPNameFilter & "))"
56:
57:    ' -------------------------------------------------------------------------------
58:    Set objRoot = GetObject("LDAP://RootDSE")
59:    strDefaultDomainNC = objRoot.Get("DefaultNamingContext")
60:    Set objRoot = Nothing
61:
62:    WScript.Echo "Applied LDAP filter is:"
63:    WScript.Echo "  (&" & cLDAPClassFilter & strLDAPNameFilter & ")"
64:
65:    WScript.Echo "Querying 'computer' class in Active Directory ..."
66:
67:    Set objResultList = ADSearch ("LDAP://" & strDefaultDomainNC, _
68:                                  strLDAPNameFilter, _
69:                                  cLDAPPropertiesToReturn, _
70:                                  cHowDeepToSearch, _
71:                                  False, _
72:                                          False)
73:
74:    WScript.Echo "Number of 'computer' class objects found is " & _
75:                 objResultList.Item ("RecordCount")
76:    WScript.Echo
77:
78:    intSuccess = 0
79:
80:    For Each objResult in objResultList
81:        intColumnPosition = InStr (objResult, ":")
82:        If intColumnPosition Then
83:           ' Query Active Directory for your computer.
84:           Set objComputer = GetObject(objResultList.Item (objResult))
85:
86:           intIndice = intIndice + 1
87:
88:           ' Use the GetWMIServices method on the DS computer object to
89:           ' retrieve the WMI services object for this computer.
90:           Set objWMIServices = objComputer.GetWMIServices
91:           If Err.Number Then
92:              Wscript.Echo intIndice & _
93:                           ": Failed to get WMI Service object " & _
94:                           "for 'computer' class object : '" & _
95:                           objComputer.Name & "'."
96:              Err.Clear
97:           Else
98:              Wscript.Echo intIndice & _
99:                           ": Getting 'Win32_OperatingSystem' instance " & _
100:                          "for 'computer' class object : '" & _
101:                          objComputer.Name & "'."
102:
103:             Set objWMIInstances = objWMIServices.InstancesOf("Win32_OperatingSystem")
104:             If Err.Number Then
105:                Wscript.Echo intIndice & _
106:                             ": Failed to get 'Win32_OperatingSystem' " & _
107:                             "instance for 'computer' class object : '" & _
108:                             objComputer.Name & "'."
109:                Err.Clear
```

```
110:                Else
111:                    Wscript.Echo intIndice & _
112:                                ": Creation of Win32_OperatingSystem instance successful."
113:                    intSuccess = intSuccess + 1
114:                End If
115:            End If
116:
117:            ' Add the necessary WMI privileges to reboot.
118:            objWMIServices.Security_.Privileges.Add wbemPrivilegeShutdown, True
119:            For Each objWMIInstance in objWMIInstances
120:                objWMIInstance.Reboot
121:                If Err.Number Then
122:                    WScript.Echo intIndice & _
123:                                ": Failed to reboot '" & _
124:                                objWMIInstance.CSName & _
125:                                "' running " & objWMIInstance.Caption & _
126:                                " - Build " & objWMIInstance.BuildNumber & _
127:                                " (" & objWMIInstance.CSDVersion & ")."
128:                        Err.Clear
129:                Else
130:                    WScript.Echo intIndice & _
131:                                ": Successfully rebooted '" & _
132:                                objWMIInstance.CSName & _
133:                                "' running " & objWMIInstance.Caption & _
134:                                " - Build " & objWMIInstance.BuildNumber & _
135:                                " (" & objWMIInstance.CSDVersion & ")."
136:                End If
137:            Next
...:
143:        End If
144:    Next
145:
146:    Wscript.Echo
147:    Wscript.Echo intSuccess & " sucessful reboot on a total of " & intIndice & " computers."
148:    Wscript.Echo
149:
150:    ]]>
151:    </script>
152: </job>
153:</package>
```

The script uses an ADSI function (line 19) performing the LDAP query and the Windows Script File facilities to read the parameters on the command line (lines 13 to 15 and lines 49 to 52). The command-line parameters are nothing more than the LDAP name of the computers to search in Active Directory. For instance, the script can be used with the following command line:

```
C:\>QueryAndReboot "(name=MyServer01)(name=MyServer02)(name=MyServer03)(name=MyExchange*)"
```

The script reads this line as one parameter and concatenates it with Active Directory *computer* class to create a valid LDAP filter (lines 54 and 55). Since the LDAP filter considers the computer list with an OR logical operator, every Active Directory computer name matching the LDAP name list returns a computer *distinguishedName*. After reading Active Directory default naming context (lines 58 to 60), the script performs the LDAP query (line 67) with the help of the ADSI function included at line 19.

Once the query completes, the script enumerates the results in a "For Each" loop (lines 80 to 144). For each **Computer** object matching the selection criteria, the script binds to Active Directory object (line 84) and retrieves the **SWbemServices** object (line 90). Next, the script performs the instantiation of the *Win32_OperatingSystem* class for the connected computer (line 103) by using the *InstancesOf* method. This method returns a collection that contains one instance of the operating system currently running in the system. Note that it is possible to reference the *Key* property of the *Win32_OperatingSystem* instance. The *Key* is a *Win32_OperatingSystem* class property called *name*, and it contains the name of the booted operating system, the path of the Windows NT directory, and the location of the partition hosting the operating system. Basically, these are the parameters contained in the **BOOT.ini** file of the operating system booted. For instance, the key may contain something like:

```
Microsoft Windows .NET Enterprise Server|J:\WINDOWS|\Device\Harddisk2\Partition3
```

Since this kind of string can make it quite difficult to determine whether all systems in the enterprise are installed in the same way, the script uses the enumeration technique to find the operating system booted. In any case, the enumeration contains only one instance of the operating system, as there is only one operating system running at the time. Doing so, it makes the code more independent of the Windows platforms setup. If this operation is successfully completed, the required privileges to reboot a computer are added to the **SWbemServices** object (line 118). As soon as the code enters the operating system enumeration loop (lines 119 to 137), the considered computer is rebooted (line 120). The rest of the code (lines 121 to 136) contains some error handling and counters to determine the number of rebooted computers of the total found by the LDAP query. This information can be useful as computers found in Active Directory are not necessarily up and running to perform the WMI connection.

5.6   Representing WMI data in XML

Many times throughout this chapter, the WMI instance data is represented from the properties exposed by the WMI instance. This forces us to use a coding technique that lists all properties available to extract the data. As we know, a WMI instance is contained in an **SWbemObject**. Under Windows XP and Windows.NET Server, it is possible to use an **SWbemObject** method called *GetText_* that extracts the data instance in XML. This object is not available under Windows 2000 and before. Sample 5.17 shows how to proceed.

Sample 5.17   *Representing WMI data in XML*

```
1:<?xml version="1.0"?>
 .:
8:<package>
9:  <job>
..:
13:     <script language="VBScript" src="..\Functions\WriteData.vbs" />
14:
15:     <object progid="WbemScripting.SWbemLocator" id="objWMILocator" reference="true"/>
16:     <object progid="WbemScripting.SWbemNamedValueSet" id="objWMINamedValueSet" />
17:     <object progid="Microsoft.XMLDom" id="objXML" />
18:
19:     <script language="VBscript">
20:     <![CDATA[
..:
24:     Const cComputerName = "LocalHost"
25:     Const cWMINameSpace = "root/cimv2"
26:     Const cWMIClass = "Win32_Service"
27:     Const cWMIInstance = "SNMP"
..:
33:     objWMILocator.Security_.AuthenticationLevel = wbemAuthenticationLevelDefault
34:     objWMILocator.Security_.ImpersonationLevel = wbemImpersonationLevelImpersonate
35:     Set objWMIServices = objWMILocator.ConnectServer(cComputerName, cWMINameSpace, "", "")
36:     Set objWMIInstance = objWMIServices.Get (cWMIClass & "='" & cWMIInstance & "'")
37:
38:     objWMINamedValueSet.Add "LocalOnly", False
39:     objWMINamedValueSet.Add "PathLevel", 0
40:     objWMINamedValueSet.Add "IncludeQualifiers", False
41:     objWMINamedValueSet.Add "ExcludeSystemProperties", True
42:
43:     ' wbemObjectTextFormatCIMDTD20 or wbemObjectTextFormatWMIDTD20
44:     strXMLText = objWMIInstance.GetText_(wbemObjectTextFormatWMIDTD20, , objWMINamedValueSet)
45:
46:     WriteData "WMI.XML", strXMLText
47:
48:     objXML.Async = False
49:     objXML.LoadXML strXMLText
50:
51:     WScript.Echo strXMLText
52:     WScript.Echo
53:     WScript.Echo objXML.XML
..:
58:     ]]>
59:
60:     </script>
61:  </job>
62:</package>
```

The script retrieves a single instance of the *Win32_Service* class (lines 33 to 36). As soon as the WMI instance is created, it is possible to extract the data in an XML format by invoking the *GetText_* method (line 44). To perform this operation several parameters can be specified. Some parameters are directly passed with the method invocation (line 44), some others via an **SWbemNamedValueSet** object (lines 38 to 41). The *GetText_* method requires one value that determines the type of Document Type Definition (DTD) to use for the XML representation. Under Windows XP and Windows.NET Server, WMI comes with two DTDs: one that contains a CIM DTD 2.0 definition and one that contains WMI DTD 2.0 definition. Using a WMI DTD 2.0 definition enables a few WMI-specific extensions, such as embedded objects (important when working with events; see Chapter 6) and scope (domain range of properties and methods declaration in a class; see Chapter 2). The DTD files (**cim20.dtd** and **wmi20.dtd**) are located in %SystemRoot%\System32\wbem\xml. For instance, to get a default representation of the WMI instance retrieved by Sample 5.17, line 44 can be coded as follows:

```
44:    strXMLText = objWMIInstance.GetText_(wbemObjectTextFormatWMIDTD20)
```

Executed this way, the XML representation contains the system properties, the class inheritance, and the values of all properties defined for the *Win32_Service* class. The XML data is assigned to a variable called *strXML-Text* (line 44). The content of this variable is saved to a file (line 46) by using a function included in the beginning of the script (line 13). The file created is called **WMI.xml** and can be viewed with any XML viewer. Figure 5.6 shows the created XML file with XML Spy 3.5.

Of course, it is likely that this information is not what is required in the XML representation. In this case, it is necessary to specify another set of parameters. These parameters must be passed to the *GetText_* method via the **SWbemNamedValueSet** object (lines 38 to 41). This object must contain four explicit parameters, listed in Table 5.8.

Table 5.8   *The Context Object Values for an XML Representation*

LocalOnly	When TRUE, only properties and methods locally defined in the class are present in the resulting XML. The default value is FALSE.
IncludeQualifiers	When TRUE, class, instance, properties, and method qualifiers are included in the resulting XML. The default value is FALSE.
ExcludeSystemProperties	When TRUE, WMI system properties are filtered out of the output. The default value is FALSE.
PathLevel	0 = A <CLASS> or <INSTANCE> element is generated.
	1 = A <VALUE.NAMEDOBJECT> element is generated.
	2 = A <VALUE.OBJECTWITHLOCALPATH> element is generated.
	3 = A <VALUE.OBJECTWITHPATH> is generated.
	The default is 0.

Based on the parameters provided in the script (line 44), the XML file contains only the data of the *Win32_Service* instance: no qualifiers (line 40), no system properties (line 41). The XML representation contains all properties available from the instance. We previously showed that properties can be inherited from a superclass; line 38 specifies that all properties (not only the locally defined) must be included in the XML representation. Because it uses a *PathLevel* equal to zero (line 39), the instance is included without its object path. In this case, the produced XML file looks as follows:

```
 1:<INSTANCE CLASSNAME="Win32_Service">
 2: <PROPERTY NAME="AcceptPause" CLASSORIGIN="Win32_BaseService" TYPE="boolean">
 3:  <VALUE>FALSE</VALUE>
 4: </PROPERTY>
 5: <PROPERTY NAME="AcceptStop" CLASSORIGIN="Win32_BaseService" TYPE="boolean">
 6:  <VALUE>FALSE</VALUE>
 7: </PROPERTY>
 8: <PROPERTY NAME="Caption" CLASSORIGIN="CIM_ManagedSystemElement" TYPE="string">
 9:  <VALUE>SNMP</VALUE>
10: </PROPERTY>
11: <PROPERTY NAME="CheckPoint" CLASSORIGIN="Win32_Service" TYPE="uint32">
12:  <VALUE>0</VALUE>
13: </PROPERTY>
14: <PROPERTY NAME="CreationClassName" CLASSORIGIN="CIM_Service" TYPE="string">
15:  <VALUE>Win32_Service</VALUE>
16: </PROPERTY>
..:
..:
..:
61: <PROPERTY NAME="Status" CLASSORIGIN="CIM_ManagedSystemElement" TYPE="string">
62:  <VALUE>OK</VALUE>
63: </PROPERTY>
64: <PROPERTY NAME="SystemCreationClassName" CLASSORIGIN="CIM_Service" TYPE="string">
65:  <VALUE>Win32_ComputerSystem</VALUE>
66: </PROPERTY>
67: <PROPERTY NAME="SystemName" CLASSORIGIN="CIM_Service" TYPE="string">
68:  <VALUE>XP-DPEN6400</VALUE>
69: </PROPERTY>
70: <PROPERTY NAME="TagId" CLASSORIGIN="Win32_BaseService" TYPE="uint32">
71:  <VALUE>0</VALUE>
72: </PROPERTY>
73: <PROPERTY NAME="WaitHint" CLASSORIGIN="Win32_Service" TYPE="uint32">
74:  <VALUE>0</VALUE>
75: </PROPERTY>
76:</INSTANCE>
```

The XML Spy representation shown in Figure 5.6 differs considerably from the representation shown in Figure 5.7.

Other *PathLevel* values can be used to get different WMI object path information (line 39). The script loads the XML representation issued by WMI in a **document object model XML (DOMXML)** object at line 49. The **DOMXML** object is created at line 17. Once loaded in DOMXML, the scripts displays the XML representation contained in the *strXMLtext* variable (line 51) and in DOMXML (line 53). This validates the WMI

Figure 5.6
*An instance
representation in
XML.*

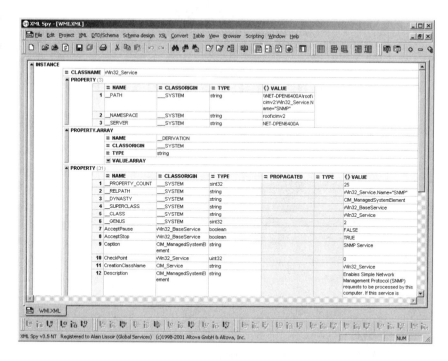

Figure 5.7
*Another instance
representation in
XML.*

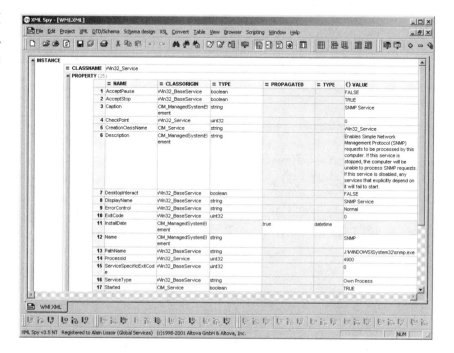

XML representation against DOMXML. From this point, any XML transformation is applicable (i.e., generating an HTML file of the WMI data with the help of an XML stylesheet).

5.7   Detecting changes with the Refresher object

Given the problem where a WMI script must monitor modifications on a real-world manageable entity, the first idea that may come to mind is to detect modifications by polling the monitored instances. For instance, with our current WMI knowledge, we can imagine the script shown in Sample 5.18.

Sample 5.18   *Looping in a script to detect a change*

```
 1:<?xml version="1.0"?>
 .:
 8:<package>
 9:  <job>
..:
13:    <object progid="WbemScripting.SWbemLocator" id="objWMILocator" reference="true"/>
14:
15:    <script language="VBscript">
16:    <![CDATA[
..:
20:    Const cComputerName = "LocalHost"
21:    Const cWMINameSpace = "root/cimv2"
22:    Const cWMIClass = "Win32_Service"
23:    Const cWMIInstance = "SNMP"
..:
29:    Set objWMIInstance = GetObject("WinMgmts:{impersonationLevel=impersonate, " & _
30:                                   "AuthenticationLevel=default}!\\" & _
31:                                   cComputerName & "\" & cWMINameSpace).Get _
32:                                   (cWMIClass & "='" & cWMIInstance & "'")
33:
34:    WScript.Echo "Set the service start mode to 'Disable' to stop the script ..."
35:    WScript.Echo "Watching '" & objWMIInstance.Name & "' service." & vbCRLF
36:
37:    strCurrentState = objWMIInstance.State
38:
39:    For intIndice = 0 To 1000
..:
49:        WScript.Echo Now & " - " & objWMIInstance.State
..:
57:        WScript.Sleep 2000
58:    Next
..:
62:    ]]>
63:    </script>
64:  </job>
65:</package>
```

Unfortunately, this script won't work because it instantiates the instance before the loop (lines 29 to 32). At no time during the loop (between lines

39 to 58) is the state of the instance refreshed. Of course, it is always possible to create the WMI instance inside the loop, but this is not a nice solution as it generates additional resource usage and useless network traffic. Creating or recreating the instance every loop is certainly not a best practice. To get an updated version of the created instance, the **SWbemObject** exposes a method called *Refresh_* (available only under Windows XP and Windows.NET Server). Sample 5.19 shows how to use this method.

Sample 5.19   *Looping in a script to detect a change with the SWbemObject Refresh_ method*

```
 1:<?xml version="1.0"?>
 .:
 8:<package>
 9:  <job>
..:
13:     <object progid="WbemScripting.SWbemLocator" id="objWMILocator" reference="true"/>
14:
15:     <script language="VBscript">
16:     <![CDATA[
..:
20:     Const cComputerName = "LocalHost"
21:     Const cWMINameSpace = "root/cimv2"
22:     Const cWMIClass = "Win32_Service"
23:     Const cWMIInstance = "SNMP"
..:
29:     Set objWMIInstance = GetObject("WinMgmts:{impersonationLevel=impersonate, " & _
30:                                    "AuthenticationLevel=default}!\\" & _
31:                                    cComputerName & "\" & cWMINameSpace).Get _
32:                                    (cWMIClass & "='" & cWMIInstance & "'")
33:
34:     WScript.Echo "Set the service start mode to 'Disable' to stop the script ..."
35:     WScript.Echo "Watching '" & objWMIInstance.Name & "' service." & vbCRLF
36:
37:     strCurrentState = objWMIInstance.State
38:
39:     For intIndice = 0 To 1000
40:         objWMIInstance.Refresh_
41:
42:         If strCurrentState <> objWMIInstance.State Then
43:             WScript.Echo "'" & objWMIInstance.Name & "' service state has change from '" & _
44:                          strCurrentState & "' to '" & objWMIInstance.State & "'."
45:         End If
46:
47:         strCurrentState = objWMIInstance.State
48:
49:         WScript.Echo Now & " - " & objWMIInstance.State
50:
51:         If objWMIInstance.StartMode = "Disabled" Then
52:             WScript.Echo "Ending the script because the '" & _
53:                          objWMIInstance.Name & "' service is 'Disabled'."
54:             Exit For
55:         End If
56:
57:         WScript.Sleep 2000
58:     Next
..:
```

```
62:    ]]>
63:    </script>
64:    </job>
65:</package>
```

Basically, it uses the same logic as Sample 5.18. The most important modification concerns the addition of line 40. This line invokes the *Refresh_* method. Beside this new line, some extra logic is added to do the following:

- Display a message when a service state change is detected (lines 37 and 42 to 45)

- Terminate the script if the startup mode of the monitored service is disabled (lines 51 to 55)

This method simply refreshes the created instance (line 40) without the need to reinstantiate the object. If the state of the service instance is modified (i.e., by using the Services snap-in), the script compares the current service state with the previous one (line 42). If there is a difference between the two states, the script shows the difference (lines 43 to 44). Next, the script verifies the service current startup mode and terminates if it is disabled (lines 51 to 55). If the service instance is not disabled, the script continues its loop to repeat the same process. Below is a sample output of the script execution that occurs when the SNMP service is started and stopped.

```
C:\>WatchInstanceStateWithRefreshMethod.wsf
Microsoft (R) Windows Script Host Version 5.6
Copyright (C) Microsoft Corporation 1996-2000. All rights reserved.

Set the service start mode to 'Disable' to stop the script ...
Watching 'SNMP' service.

19-07-2001 13:49:09 - Stopped
19-07-2001 13:49:11 - Stopped
'SNMP' service state has change from 'Stopped' to 'Start Pending'.
19-07-2001 13:49:13 - Start Pending
'SNMP' service state has change from 'Start Pending' to 'Running'.
19-07-2001 13:49:15 - Running
19-07-2001 13:49:17 - Running
19-07-2001 13:49:19 - Running
'SNMP' service state has change from 'Running' to 'Stop Pending'.
19-07-2001 13:49:21 - Stop Pending
19-07-2001 13:49:23 - Stop Pending
'SNMP' service state has change from 'Stop Pending' to 'Stopped'.
19-07-2001 13:49:25 - Stopped
19-07-2001 13:49:27 - Stopped
19-07-2001 13:49:29 - Stopped
19-07-2001 13:49:31 - Stopped
19-07-2001 13:49:33 - Stopped
19-07-2001 13:49:35 - Stopped
Ending the script because the 'SNMP' service is 'Disabled'.
```

In Sample 5.19, we poll only one instance. How can we poll several instances? Of course, an easy way would be to create all required instances and refresh each of them in the loop. However, WMI offers a better way to perform this by using an **SWbemRefresher** object. Basically, it is possible to encapsulate different object instances or object collections to refresh in an **SWbemRefresher** object. At a certain point of the script execution, it is necessary only to refresh the **SWbemRefresher** object with its *Refresh* method to refresh all objects that it contains. Sample 5.20 shows how to use the **SWbemRefresher** object.

Sample 5.20   *Refreshing different instances or a collection of instances with the SWbemRefresher object*

```
 1:<?xml version="1.0"?>
 .:
 8:<package>
 9:  <job>
..:
13:    <object progid="WbemScripting.SWbemRefresher" id="objWMIRefresher" />
14:
15:    <script language="VBscript">
16:    <![CDATA[
..:
20:    Const cComputerName = "LocalHost"
21:
22:    Const cWMINameSpaceItem1 = "Root/CIMv2"
23:    Const cWMIClassItem1  = "Win32_WMISetting"
24:    Const cWMIInstanceItem1 = "@"
25:
26:    Const cWMINameSpaceItem2 = "Root/CIMv2"
27:    Const cWMIClassItem2 = "Win32_Service"
..:
40:    Set objWMIServices1 = GetObject("WinMgmts:{impersonationLevel=impersonate, " & _
41:                                "AuthenticationLevel=default}!\\" & _
42:                                cComputerName & "\" & cWMINameSpaceItem1)
43:
44:    Set objWMIServices2 = GetObject("WinMgmts:{impersonationLevel=impersonate, " & _
45:                                "AuthenticationLevel=default}!\\" & _
46:                                cComputerName & "\" & cWMINameSpaceItem2)
47:
48:    Set objWMIRefresherItem1 = objWMIRefresher.Add _
49:            (objWMIServices1, cWMIClassItem1 & "=" & cWMIInstanceItem1)
50:    Set objWMIInstance = objWMIRefresherItem1.Object
51:
52:    Set objWMIRefresherItem2 = objWMIRefresher.AddEnum _
53:            (objWMIServices2, cWMIClassItem2)
54:    Set objWMIInstances = objWMIRefresherItem2.ObjectSet
55:
56:    WScript.Echo "Number of items in the refresher is " & objWMIRefresher.Count & "."
57:
58:    objWMIRefresher.AutoReconnect = True
59:
60:    For Each objWMIRefreshableItem In objWMIRefresher
61:        If objWMIRefreshableItem.IsSet Then
```

```
62:            WScript.Echo "   Item" & objWMIRefreshableItem.Index & " is a collection."
63:        Else
64:            WScript.Echo "   Item" & objWMIRefreshableItem.Index & " is a single object."
65:        End if
66:    Next
..:
70:    For intIndice = 0 to 1000
71:        objWMIRefresher.Refresh
72:        WScript.Echo vbCRLF & "--------- Pass " & intIndice & ":"
73:
74:        Wscript.Echo "Currently WMI Logging level is " & objWMIInstance.LoggingLevel
75:        WScript.Echo
76:
77:        For Each objItem In objWMIInstances
78:            WScript.Echo "'" & objItem.DisplayName & "' is " & objItem.State & "."
79:
80:            If objItem.StartMode = "Disabled" And objItem.Name = "SNMP" Then
81:                WScript.Echo vbCRLF & "Ending the script because the '" & _
82:                            objItem.Name & "' service is 'Disabled'."
83:                boolExitFlag = True
84:                Exit For
85:            End If
86:        Next
87:
88:        If boolExitFlag Then
89:            Exit For
90:        End If
91:
92:        WScript.Sleep (2000)
93:    Next
...:
103:    ]]>
104:    </script>
105:    </job>
106:</package>
```

Compared with Sample 5.19, Sample 5.20 works differently. The first part performs the connections to the WMI namespaces where classes of the monitored instance reside (lines 40 to 46). The two created objects are **SWbemServices** objects (lines 40 and 44).

To make the script more generic, the script creates the WMI connection twice: once for each class instance or instance collection to monitor. Although not mandatory when the classes are in the same namespace, this makes the script easier to reuse for classes spread among different namespaces (lines 40 to 42 and 44 to 46). It is possible that the two classes are not located in the same WMI namespace, in which case it is necessary to establish the connection to each specific namespace. Once connected to the different namespaces, the **SWbemRefresher** object created at line 13 is initialized with the *Win32_WMISetting* instance (lines 48 and 49) and the *Win32_Service* collection instances (lines 52 and 53). To add *Win32_WMISetting* instance in the **SWbemRefresher**, the *Add* method is used. To add the *Win32_Service* collection of instances in the **SWbem-Refresher**, the *AddEnum* method is used. Note that to initialize the **SWBemRefresher** object, the **SWbemServices** objects representing the connection to the WMI namespaces are also referenced (line 49 and 53). Once initialization is complete, the **SWbemRefresher** object contains a collection of items. Each item is an **SWbemRefreshableItem** object (lines 48 and 52), which may contain a single instance or a collection of instances.

From each **SWbemRefreshableItem** object, it is possible to retrieve the instance or the collection of instances stored in the **SWbemRefresher** object:

- The instance of the *Win32_WMISetting* class can be retrieved from the first **SWbBemRefreshableItem** object with the *Object* property (line 50). This instance is stored in an **SWbemObject** object represented by the *objWMIInstance* variable, as it is a single object instance.

- The instances of the *Win32_Service* class can be retrieved from the second **SWbemRefreshableItem** object with the *ObjectSet* property (line 54). This collection of instances is stored in an **SWbemObjectset** object represented by the *objWMIInstances* variable, as it is a collection of instances.

These two variables are used later in the script to reference the refreshed version of the instances contained in the **SWbemRefreshableItem** objects. To ensure that the WMI connection is reestablished at refresh time if the WMI connection is broken, the **SWbemRefresher** object property *AutoReconnect* is set to True (line 58).

The script shows the nature of the **SWbemRefreshableItem** objects contained in the **SWbemRefresher** object (lines 62 and 64). The script enumerates each item (lines 60 to 66) and tests whether the examined item is a collection by using the *IsSet* property of the **SWbemRefreshableItem**.

Next, the script performs a loop (lines 70 to 86) to show the state of the instances to be refreshed. Line 74 shows the *Win32_WMISetting* instance, and line 78 displays the *Win32_Service* collection instances states in a loop (lines 77 to 86). The script performs one thousand loops (lines 70 to 93) and exits immediately from the loops as soon as the startup mode of the SNMP service instance is disabled (lines 80 to 85 and 88 to 90). Sample output of the script execution while the logging level of WMI is modified (i.e., with the WMI Control MMC) and the SNMP service is started and stopped (i.e., with the Services MMC) is as follows:

```
C:\>WatchInstanceCollectionStateWithRefresher.wsf
Microsoft (R) Windows Script Host Version 5.6
Copyright (C) Microsoft Corporation 1996-2000. All rights reserved.

Number of items in the refresher is 2.
  Item1 is a single object.
  Item2 is a collection.


--------- Pass 0:
Currently WMI Logging level is 1

'Alerter' is Running.
'Application Management' is Stopped.
...
'SNMP' is Stopped.
...
'WMI Performance Adapter' is Stopped.
'Automatic Updates' is Running.
'Wireless Zero Configuration service' is Running.

--------- Pass 1:
Currently WMI Logging level is 2

'Alerter' is Running.
'Application Management' is Stopped.
...
'SNMP' is Running.
...
'WMI Performance Adapter' is Stopped.
'Automatic Updates' is Running.
'Wireless Zero Configuration service' is Running.

--------- Pass 2:
Currently WMI Logging level is 2

'Alerter' is Running.
'Application Management' is Stopped.
...
'SNMP' is Running.
...
'WMI Performance Adapter' is Stopped.
'Automatic Updates' is Running.
'Wireless Zero Configuration service' is Running.

--------- Pass 3:
Currently WMI Logging level is 1

'Alerter' is Running.
'Application Management' is Stopped.
...
'SNMP' is Running.
...
```

```
'WMI Performance Adapter' is Stopped.
'Automatic Updates' is Running.
'Wireless Zero Configuration service' is Running.

--------- Pass 4:
Currently WMI Logging level is 1

'Alerter' is Running.
'Application Management' is Stopped.
...
'SNMP' is Stopped.
...
'WMI Performance Adapter' is Stopped.
'Automatic Updates' is Running.
'Wireless Zero Configuration service' is Running.

Ending the script because the 'SNMP' service is 'Disabled'.
```

Table 5.9 shows the **SWbemRefresher** object properties and methods. Table 5.10 shows the **SWbemRefresherableItem** object properties and methods.

Although the polling techniques of the *Refresh_* method or the **SWbem-Refresher** and **SWbemRefresherableItem** objects are technically valid from a scripting point of view, they do not represent the most versatile means to watch system modifications. The objects are refreshed from the created instances, which means that the systems hosting these instances are contacted during each loop. This generates some unnecessary network traffic. Moreover, another inconvenience is the impossibility of executing the monitoring in parallel with other tasks. And last but not least, the script uses some CPU cycles regardless of whether an interesting change occurs. We clearly see the need for another technique to monitor changes. This is where the WMI event notification becomes really interesting. We will see that the **SWbemRefresher** object is useful in such a context too, but before

Table 5.9   *The SWBemRefresherableItem Object Properties and Methods*

Properties	Index	Index of the item in the refresher object.
	IsSet	The SWbemRefresher object in which this item resides.
	Object	Indicates whether the item is a single object or an object set.
	ObjectSet	The SWbemObject that represents the items.
	Refresher	The SWbemObjectSet that represents the items.
Methods	Remove	Removes the item from the refresher object.

Table 5.10   *The SWbemRefresher Object Properties and Methods*

Properties	AutoReconnect	Indicates whether the refresher automatically attemps to reconnect to a remote provider if the connection is broken.
	Count	Number of items in the refresher object.
Methods	Add	Adds a new refreshable object to the refresher object.
	AddEnum	Adds a new enumerator to the refresher.
	DeleteAll	Removes all items from the refresher.
	Item	Returns a specified item from the collection in the Refresher.
	Refresh	Refreshs all items in the refresher.
	Remove	Removes object or object set with a specified index from the refresher.

discussing the WMI event notification scripting, we must learn what WMI event notification is. This is covered in the following chapter.

5.8   Summary

The WMI scripting API offers many possibilities for performing various operations. Its versatility adds to its complexity in the sense that there are so many ways to perform an operation that it can sometimes be confusing. As we have said throughout this chapter, we recommend that you practice this technology to get a better working knowledge of the WMI scripting API.

Throughout our examination of WMI scripting, we have seen that it is possible to instantiate CIM classes or real-world manageable entities (mapped on defined CIM classes) by using a moniker or a series of WMI scripting APIs. Moreover, the security can be set at different object levels of the WMI scripting API. In addition to these two aspects, it is also possible to combine the WMI scripting API with WQL queries. Last but not least, the execution of the WMI operation can be performed synchronously or asynchronously. This provides many features and possibilities that can work together or separately. The ability to execute some WMI scripting API operations asynchronously is an important WMI features because it enhances the responsiveness of a script (or any application using the asynchronous calls). Conceptually, asynchronous operations are a big step in WMI event monitoring. The event monitoring makes extensive usage of the asynchronous features discussed here in combination with the WQL queries. In the following chapter, through different script samples, we combine the power of WQL with WMI asynchronous operations.

6

The WMI Events Scripting

6.1   Objective

At this stage of the discussion, with the knowledge acquired from previous chapters about WQL and the WMI scripting API, we are ready to explore the WMI event scripting techniques. Up to now, each time we developed a script that runs on top of WMI, the code performed some actions with the manageable entities. The script did not perform monitoring functions. Some monitoring was performed using the permanent *SMTP* event consumer (see Chapter 2), but this did not involve scripting. Moreover, only one event type was used from the collection proposed by WMI. As WMI is designed to support event notifications, it makes sense that the event notification capabilities are also part of the WMI scripting API. The event scripting technique relies on the WMI event architecture, and some aspects of its usage are very similar to the asynchronous scripting techniques described in the previous chapter. The WMI event technology is probably one of the most powerful features offered by WMI. It offers different event types to trigger any action in an application. In this chapter, we examine the various event types available, how they are organized, and how to take full advantage of this technology from the scripting world.

6.2   Event notification

Managing an environment means more than simply performing tasks with the manageable entities; it also means being able to respond to situation changes. This implies that the technology used to perform the management tasks is able to detect changes. These changes are considered by WMI as events. WMI supports event detections and their delivery to WMI clients. Of course, since many changes may occur in a manageable environment, it is clear that only occurrences of interest must be reported. Moreover, if an event is detected, WMI must know where to deliver the event. And last but not least, once the event is delivered, some actions must be taken regarding the detected change. These steps involve the presence of several mechanisms to support event detections.

WMI is able to detect changes by itself, such as changes in the CIM repository. Besides changes performed in the CIM repository, the real-world manageable entities are also subject to change. To help with these detection tasks, WMI uses some specific providers called event providers. For instance, the *SNMP* event provider, the *NT Event Log* event provider, and the *Registry* event provider are some typical WMI event providers.

To receive events, WMI clients must subscribe to WMI events. A WMI client can be an application such as **WBEMTEST.exe**, a script developed on top of the WMI scripting API, or any other applications developed on top of the WMI API. The WMI client, which creates the subscription, is called the subscription builder and provides two elements: the events in which the subscriber is interested and the WMI client request to be processed when the events occur. The subscription builder describes which event is of interest using a WQL event query. The WQL event query acts as a filter for events. For instance, in Chapter 3 we used an event query like

```
SELECT * FROM __InstanceModificationEvent WITHIN 2 Where
                              TargetInstance ISA 'Win32_Service' And
                              TargetInstance.Name='SNMP' And
                              TargetInstance.State='Stopped'
```

6.2.1   Event subscriptions

When a client submits a WQL event query, it performs an event subscription. There are two subscription types: temporary subscriptions and permanent subscriptions. The subscription type determines the type of consumer used to perform an action triggered by a WMI event. So, let's examine the differences between the two existing subscriptions.

6.2.1.1   *Temporary subscription*

Temporary subscriptions are created by an application interested in receiving certain events. In the context of a temporary subscription, the application will receive events only if the application is running. If the application stops, the application will stop receiving events. When the application terminates, it must cancel its subscription to finish the event notification smoothly and properly with regard to WMI. A script written on top of the WMI scripting API is a typical example of an application performing a temporary subscription. Of course, it can be any other application type; tempo-

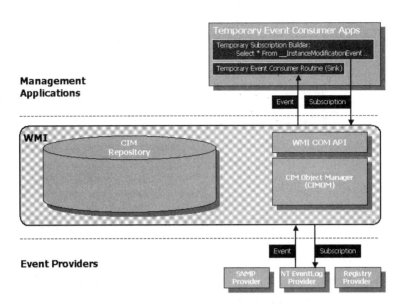

Figure 6.1
*The temporary
event consumer
and its relation to
the CIM repository
and WMI.*

rary subscriptions are not dedicated to scripts. Later, we see that an application can receive events synchronously, semisynchronously, or asynchronously. For instance, with an asynchronous notification, a temporary subscription includes a pointer to the application containing the sink that receives the events (with an **SWbemSink** object such as used in the previous chapter). This allows applications to handle received events and perform the related actions in parallel processing. Figure 6.1 represents a logical organization of the various items participating in a temporary event subscription using an asynchronous notification.

It is important to note that Figure 6.1 does not represent what happens when the event occurs. The figure logically differentiates the items to clarify their roles. The subscription builder contains the sink routine that receives events. The sink routine can be executed asynchronously and represents the temporary event consumer. In case of a synchronous or semisynchronous event, there is no explicit sink routine as with an asynchronous event notification. In this case the consumer waits for an event to occur. We consider the differences between these scripting techniques later in this chapter in Sections 6.5.1 and 6.5.2. In any case, regardless of the notification type, the consumer receives the WMI event. The consumer logic coding and WMI scripting API used determine the technique used to perform the action and how the consumer manages the received event.

Since the temporary subscription has a lifetime equal to the lifetime of the application, nothing related to the subscription is permanently or temporarily stored in the CIM repository. A subscription filter (WQL event query) is passed to WMI with the *ExecNotificationQuery* method (for synchronous and semisynchronous notifications) and the *ExecNotificationQueryAsync* method (for the asynchronous notifications) of the **SWbemServices** object. A temporary subscription is stored in memory.

6.2.1.2 *Permanent subscription*

A subscription builder performing a permanent subscription is interested in performing a specific action each time an event occurs. When the application supposed to perform the action is not running, WMI launches the application. To make the subscription permanent, WMI stores the subscription in the CIM repository. This means that the subscription is effective until the subscription builder removes the subscription explicitly, which means removing instances created in the CIM repository. This is an important difference from the temporary subscription. Figure 6.2 shows the logical organization of a permanent event subscription. With a permanent subscription, the sink routine must be a COM component (called a permanent event consumer).

Because this type of subscription is permanent, two types of instances are created in the CIM repository as follows:

1.   **An instance of the event filter**: As with the temporary subscription, the set of events that trigger the action of a permanent subscriber is specified with a WQL event query. This query uses the

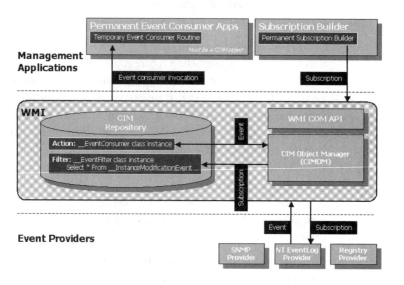

Figure 6.2
The permanent event consumer and its relation to the CIM repository and WMI.

same syntax and statements as a temporary subscription, but it is stored in an instance of the *__EventFilter* system class.

2. **An instance of the event consumer class**: Because the subscription is permanent, it uses a permanent event consumer. Each permanent event consumer defines its specific classes in the CIM repository. This is part of a registration process made during its installation. Usually, an event consumer comes with its MOF file containing the registration data and its exposed classes. The event consumer classes are subclasses of the *__EventConsumer* system class. A permanent subscription uses one instance of the permanent event consumer classes.

It is important to note that the subscription builder and the permanent event consumer can be two totally different things. For instance, the subscription builder can be a compiled MOF file or a script creating the required instances, (i.e., an event query filter instance with the event consumer instance) where the permanent consumer can be a .dll provided with WMI (i.e., *SMTP* event consumer).

Note that the CIM repository contains some WMI system classes especially designed to support permanent subscriptions. In addition to the *__EventFilter* and the *__EventConsumer* system classes, WMI implements other system classes related to the event notifications. Let's see what these classes are.

6.2.2   **Event system classes**

Before going further into the event notification, we must briefly examine a set of classes especially created for WMI to support the event instrumentation with its related components. Figure 6.3 shows a tree view of the system classes used by WMI events.

The most important system classes related to the WMI event notifications are as follows:

- *__Event:* This system class is used as a superclass to create all intrinsic event system classes (*__Intrinsic*), extrinsic event system classes (*__Extrinsic*), and timer system class (*__TimerEvent*) proposed by WMI. In Section 6.2.5 we examine the differences between the intrinsic, extrinsic, and timer event notifications.

- *__AggregateEvent:* This system class is used as a class template to represent the aggregated events. In Chapter 3, when we talked about the

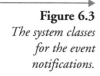

Figure 6.3
*The system classes
for the event
notifications.*

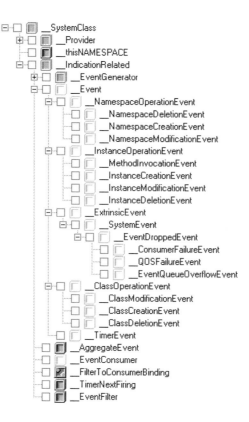

WQL event queries, we used the **GROUP** statement to get a single notification to represent a group of events. This type of query typically creates an aggregated event using the *__AggregateEvent* system class.

■   *__EventConsumer:* This system class is a superclass for the classes exposed by the permanent event consumers. A permanent event consumer registered in the CIM repository has its own set of classes. This set of classes is derived from the *__EventConsumer* class. Each time a

Figure 6.4
*The classes
supported by some
event consumers.*

```
⊟··☐ 🔲 __EventConsumer
      ┄☐ 📑 MSFT_ForwardingConsumer
      ┄☐ 📑 CommandLineEventConsumer
      ┄☐ 📑 LogFileEventConsumer
      ┄☐ 📑 ActiveScriptEventConsumer
      ┄☐ 📑 MSFT_UCScenarioControl
      ┄☐ 📑 MSFT_UpdatingConsumer
      ┄☐ 📑 SMTPEventConsumer
      ┄☐ 📑 NTEventLogEventConsumer
```

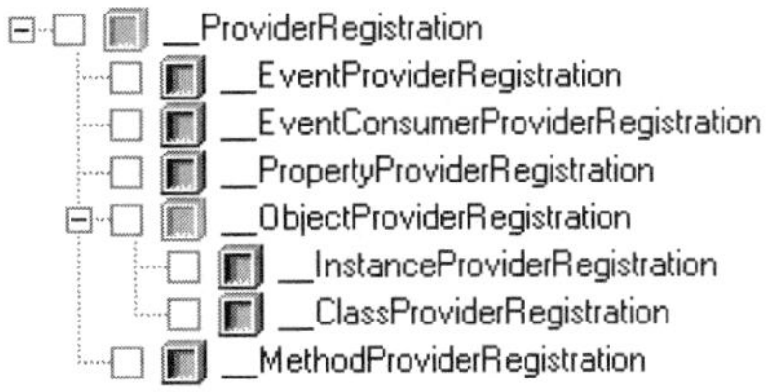

Figure 6.5

The system classes for the provider registrations.

permanent event consumer is subscribed to a WMI event, an instance of the class derived from the __*EventConsumer* system class is created.

- __*EventFilter:* This system class is a superclass for the class representing the WQL event query filter made by the subscription builders. This class is associated with the __*EventConsumer* class with the association class __*FilterToConsumerBinding*. So, every instance of an event filter should be associated to an instance of a permanent event consumer, which represents the action to be executed. The __*FilterToConsumerBinding* association class is the link between an event and the corresponding action.

- __*EventGenerator:* This system class is a superclass creating specific classes used to trigger timer events.

To summarize, these system classes are used to support event notifications. Each time an event is detected by WMI or reported to WMI, an instance of a class derived from __*Event* system class is created.

The last class to mention is the __*ProviderRegistration* system class. This class is not an event system class; however, it is a superclass template used to register the different type of WMI providers. Figure 6.5 shows the list of subclasses created from the __*ProviderRegistration* system class. For example, the registration of an event provider creates an instance made from the __*EventProviderRegistration* subclass. In the same way, the registration of an event consumer provider creates an instance made from the __*EventConsumerProviderRegistration* subclass. Each registered WMI provider creates an instance from one of these system classes in the CIM repository. Moreover, in addition to this created instance, each provider registration also creates an instance of the __*Win32Provider* system class.

6.2.3   Event consumers

Having both temporary and permanent subscriptions implies that we have two types of event consumers: temporary event consumers and permanent event consumers.

6.2.3.1   *Temporary event consumers*

As previously mentioned, the temporary consumer is nothing more than a routine that receives an event notification that matches the temporary subscription filter submitted by the subscription builder (see Figure 6.1). In the case of an asynchronous notification, an **SWbemSink** object contains a pointer to the sink routine. It is passed as a parameter when performing the subscription with the *ExecNotificationQueryAsync* method of the **SWbem-Services** object. Because the notification query can also be executed synchronously, semisynchronously, or asynchronously, this has a direct impact on the logic and the structure used by the temporary event consumer. In any case, as long as the application hosting the sink routine is running, each matching event is forwarded to the temporary event consumer.

6.2.3.2   *Permanent event consumers*

A permanent event consumer must be implemented as a COM object. It can be an in-process .dll, a local server, or a remote server. Permanent consumers implemented as local and remote servers require the distributed COM protocol. Under Windows Millennium, Windows NT 4.0, Windows 2000, and Windows.NET Server, DCOM runs by default. For the Windows 95 and 98 platforms, DCOM must be installed as a separated component from the Microsoft Web site (http://www.microsoft.com/com/dcom/dcom95/download.asp for Windows 95 and http://www.microsoft.com/com/dcom/dcom98/download.asp for Windows 98).

By default, WMI comes with a set of permanent event consumers, some of which are mentioned in Chapter 2:

- The *WMI Event Viewer* event consumer

- The *SMTP* event consumer

- The *Log File* event consumer

- The *NT Event Log* event consumer

- The *Command-Line* event consumer

- The *Active Script* event consumer

In Chapter 2, we used the *WMI Event Viewer* event consumer and the *SMTP* event consumer. Because the event registrations of these permanent consumers are stored in the CIM repository with two associated instances (one made from the *__EventConsumer* system class and the other made from *__EventFilter* system class), the even registrations persist through restarting the operating system. When an event matching the WQL filter occurs, WMI determines whether the consumer is active. If the consumer is not already active because the consumer is registered in the CIM repository with instances made from the *__EventConsumerProviderRegistration* and *__Win32Provider* system classes, or in the system registry as a COM object, WMI locates the consumer and loads it to deliver the event notification.

The permanent event consumers are registered in the CIM repository by creating an instance of the *__EventConsumerProviderRegistration* system class (see Figure 6.5). We can locate the permanent event consumers with the script written in Chapter 4 to locate instances of a given class across namespaces (see Sample 4.30, "A generic routine to display the SWbem-PropertySet object"). The script must be started with the class name of the instances to find. In this case, the class must be the *__EventConsumer-ProviderRegistration* system class. Started on a Windows.NET Server system, the output is as follows:

```
C:\>BrowseNameSpaceForInstancesWithAPI.wsf __EventConsumerProviderRegistration
Microsoft (R) Windows Script Host Version 5.6
Copyright (C) Microsoft Corporation 1996-2001. All rights reserved.

Root
Root/SECURITY
Root/MSAPPS
Root/RSOP
Root/RSOP/User
Root/RSOP/User/ms_409
Root/RSOP/User/S_1_5_21_1454471165_1647877149_725345543_1008
Root/RSOP/User/S_1_5_21_1454471165_1647877149_725345543_500
Root/RSOP/Computer
Root/RSOP/Computer/ms_409
Root/Cli
Root/snmp
Root/snmp/localhost
Root/MSCluster
Root/WMI
Root/WMI/ms_409
Root/CIMV2
  ConsumerClassNames (wbemCimtypeString) = Microsoft_SA_AlertEmailConsumer
  *provider (wbemCimtypeReference) =
          \\.\Root\cimv2:__Win32Provider.Name="Microsoft_SA_AlertEmailConsumerProvider"
  ConsumerClassNames (wbemCimtypeString) = EventViewerConsumer
  *provider (wbemCimtypeReference) = \\.\root\cimv2:__Win32Provider.Name="EventViewerConsumer"
  ConsumerClassNames (wbemCimtypeString) = ClearClientConfigAlertEventConsumerClass
  *provider (wbemCimtypeReference) =
          \\.\ROOT\CIMV2:__Win32Provider.Name="ClearClientConfigAlertConsumer"
  ConsumerClassNames (wbemCimtypeString) = ActiveScriptEventConsumer
  *provider (wbemCimtypeReference) = \\.\Root\CIMv2:__Win32Provider.Name="ActiveScriptEventConsumer"
  ConsumerClassNames (wbemCimtypeString) = CmdTriggerConsumer
  *provider (wbemCimtypeReference) = \\.\Root\CIMv2:__Win32Provider.Name="CmdTriggerConsumer"
  ConsumerClassNames (wbemCimtypeString) = SMTPEventConsumer
  *provider (wbemCimtypeReference) = \\.\Root\CIMv2:__Win32Provider.Name="SMTPEventConsumer"
  ConsumerClassNames (wbemCimtypeString) = LogFileEventConsumer
  *provider (wbemCimtypeReference) = \\.\Root\CIMv2:__Win32Provider.Name="LogFileEventConsumer"
  ConsumerClassNames (wbemCimtypeString) = CommandLineEventConsumer
  *provider (wbemCimtypeReference) = \\.\Root\CIMv2:__Win32Provider.Name="CommandLineEventConsumer"
  ConsumerClassNames (wbemCimtypeString) = SANTEventLogFilterEventConsumer
```

```
*provider (wbemCimtypeReference) =
         \\.\root\cimv2:__Win32Provider.Name="SANTEventLogFilterEventConsumerProvider"
  ConsumerClassNames (wbemCimtypeString) = NTEventLogEventConsumer
  *provider (wbemCimtypeReference) = \\.\Root\CIMv2:__Win32Provider.Name="NTEventLogEventConsumer"
Root/CIMV2/ms_409
Root/CIMV2/Applications
Root/CIMV2/Applications/MicrosoftIE
Root/MicrosoftActiveDirectory
Root/MicrosoftIISv2
Root/Policy
Root/Policy/ms_409
Root/MicrosoftDNS
Root/MicrosoftNLB
Root/Microsoft
Root/Microsoft/HomeNet
Root/DEFAULT
Root/DEFAULT/ms_409
Root/directory
Root/directory/LDAP
Root/directory/LDAP/ms_409
Root/subscription
  ConsumerClassNames (wbemCimtypeString) = NTEventLogEventConsumer
  *provider (wbemCimtypeReference) =
         \\.\root\subscription:__Win32Provider.Name="NTEventLogEventConsumer"
  ConsumerClassNames (wbemCimtypeString) = LogFileEventConsumer
  *provider (wbemCimtypeReference) =
         \\.\root\subscription:__Win32Provider.Name="LogFileEventConsumer"
  ConsumerClassNames (wbemCimtypeString) = MSFT_UpdatingConsumer
  ConsumerClassNames (wbemCimtypeString) = MSFT_UCScenarioControl
  *provider (wbemCimtypeReference) =
         \\.\root\subscription:__Win32Provider.Name="Microsoft WMI Updating Consumer Provider"
  ConsumerClassNames (wbemCimtypeString) = SMTPEventConsumer
  *provider (wbemCimtypeReference) = \\.\root\subscription:__Win32Provider.Name="SMTPEventConsumer"
  ConsumerClassNames (wbemCimtypeString) = CommandLineEventConsumer
  *provider (wbemCimtypeReference) =
         \\.\root\subscription:__Win32Provider.Name="CommandLineEventConsumer"
  ConsumerClassNames (wbemCimtypeString) = MSFT_ForwardingConsumer
  *provider (wbemCimtypeReference) =
         \\.\root\subscription:__Win32Provider.Name="Microsoft WMI Forwarding Consumer Provider"
  ConsumerClassNames (wbemCimtypeString) = ActiveScriptEventConsumer
  *provider (wbemCimtypeReference) =
         \\.\root\subscription:__Win32Provider.Name="ActiveScriptEventConsumer"
Root/subscription/ms_409
Root/registry
Root/NetFrameworkv1
Root/NetFrameworkv1/ms_409
```

Across all namespaces available in the CIM repository under Windows.NET Server, we find a collection of permanent event consumers. The most interesting ones are summarized in Table 6.1.

6.2.4   Event providers

Chapter 2 shows that WMI providers are components that act between CIMOM and the manageable entities. Since WMI providers allow access to the manageable entities, the CIM repository contains their registration and

Table 6.1 *The Most Common Permanent Event Consumers*

Namespace	Event Consumer Provider	Consumer Class Name
Root/CIMV2	EventConsumerProvider	TriggerEventConsumer
Root/subscription	NTEventLogEventConsumer	NTEventLogEventConsumer
	LogFileEventConsumer	LogFileEventConsumer
	SMTPEventConsumer	SMTPEventConsumer
	CommandLineEventConsumer	CommandLineEventConsumer
	ActiveScriptEventConsumer	ActiveScriptEventConsumer

the classes they support. WMI classifies the providers in several categories with regard to the type of request they service. For instance, in the previous section we talked about permanent event consumer providers. Regardless of whether they are event consumers, they are providers first! Each provider has its own particularities and determines the management capabilities of a real-world entity. Because the nature of the providers available is determinant, it has a direct impact on WMI scripting possibilities (classes they support, update operations they support, events supported, etc.).

For now, let's concentrate on the event providers. Event providers deliver events to WMI, and event consumer providers consume events delivered by WMI. An event provider is nothing other than a COM component providing an event notification to WMI when the submitted subscription matches the WQL event query. In turn, WMI forwards the notification to the event subscriber. As previously mentioned, the *SNMP* event provider, the NT *Event Log* event provider, and the *Registry* event provider are some typical event providers. Where is WMI offering other event providers? Let's try to answer this question by examining the CIM repository.

Event providers are registered in the CIM repository with an instance of the *__EventProviderRegistration* system class. The *__EventProviderRegistration* is a subclass of the *__ProviderRegistration* system class as shown in Figure 6.5. The registration is made per WMI namespace. Therefore, each instance of the *__EventProviderRegistration* class we find corresponds to an event provider registration made in a particular namespace. The same tactic used to locate the permanent event consumers across all namespaces is used to locate event providers. When the script runs on Windows.NET Server to retrieve instances of the *__EventProviderRegistration* system class, the script output is as follows:

```
C:\ >BrowseNameSpaceForInstancesWithAPI.Wsf __EventProviderRegistration
Microsoft (R) Windows Script Host Version 5.6
Copyright (C) Microsoft Corporation 1996-2001. All rights reserved.
```

```
Root
Root/SECURITY
Root/MSAPPS
Root/RSOP
Root/RSOP/User
Root/RSOP/User/ms_409
Root/RSOP/User/S_1_5_21_1454471165_1647877149_725345543_1008
Root/RSOP/User/S_1_5_21_1454471165_1647877149_725345543_500
Root/RSOP/Computer
Root/RSOP/Computer/ms_409
Root/Cli
Root/snmp
Root/snmp/localhost
   EventQueryList (wbemCimtypeString) = select * from SnmpExtendedNotification
   *provider (wbemCimtypeReference) =
            \\.\root\snmp\localhost:__Win32Provider.Name="MS_SNMP_REFERENT_EVENT_PROVIDER"
   EventQueryList (wbemCimtypeString) = select * from SnmpNotification
   *provider (wbemCimtypeReference) =
            \\.\root\snmp\localhost:__Win32Provider.Name="MS_SNMP_ENCAPSULATED_EVENT_PROVIDER"
Root/MSCluster
   EventQueryList (wbemCimtypeString) = select * from MSCluster_Event
   *provider (wbemCimtypeReference) = \\.\Root\MSCluster:__Win32Provider.Name="Cluster Event Provider"
Root/WMI
   EventQueryList (wbemCimtypeString) = select * from WMIEvent
   *provider (wbemCimtypeReference) = \\.\Root\WMI:__Win32Provider.Name="WMIEventProv"
Root/WMI/ms_409
Root/CIMV2
   EventQueryList (wbemCimtypeString) = select * from Msft_WmiProvider_OperationEvent
   *provider (wbemCimtypeReference) = \\.\root\cimv2:__Win32Provider.Name="ProviderSubSystem"
   EventQueryList (wbemCimtypeString) = select * from MSFT_WMI_GenericNonCOMEvent
   EventQueryList (wbemCimtypeString) = select * from MSFT_NcProvEvent
   *provider (wbemCimtypeReference) = \\.\root\cimv2:__Win32Provider.Name="Standard Non-COM Event Provider"
   EventQueryList (wbemCimtypeString) = select * from Win32_PowerManagementEvent
   *provider (wbemCimtypeReference) =
            \\.\Root\CIMV2:__Win32Provider.Name="MS_Power_Management_Event_Provider"
   EventQueryList (wbemCimtypeString) = select * from Win32_SystemConfigurationChangeEvent
   *provider (wbemCimtypeReference) = \\.\Root\CIMV2:__Win32Provider.Name="SystemConfigurationChangeEvents"
   EventQueryList (wbemCimtypeString) = select * from Win32_ComputerShutdownEvent
   *provider (wbemCimtypeReference) = \\.\Root\CIMV2:__Win32Provider.Name="MS_Shutdown_Event_Provider"
   EventQueryList (wbemCimtypeString) = select * from Win32_VolumeChangeEvent
   *provider (wbemCimtypeReference) = \\.\Root\CIMV2:__Win32Provider.Name="VolumeChangeEvents"
   EventQueryList (wbemCimtypeString) = select * from MSFT_ForwardedEvent
   *provider (wbemCimtypeReference) =
            \\.\root\cimv2:__Win32Provider.Name="Microsoft WMI Forwarding Event Provider"
   EventQueryList (wbemCimtypeString) = select * from Win32_IP4RouteTableEvent
   *provider (wbemCimtypeReference) = \\.\Root\CIMV2:__Win32Provider.Name="RouteEventProvider"
   EventQueryList (wbemCimtypeString) = select * from Win32_ProcessStartTrace
   EventQueryList (wbemCimtypeString) = select * from Win32_ProcessStopTrace
   EventQueryList (wbemCimtypeString) = select * from Win32_ThreadStartTrace
   EventQueryList (wbemCimtypeString) = select * from Win32_ThreadStopTrace
   EventQueryList (wbemCimtypeString) = select * from Win32_ModuleLoadTrace
   *provider (wbemCimtypeReference) = \\.\Root\CIMV2:__Win32Provider.Name="WMI Kernel Trace Event Provider"
   EventQueryList (wbemCimtypeString) = select * from MSFT_WmiEssEvent
   *provider (wbemCimtypeReference) =
            \\.\root\cimv2:__Win32Provider.Name="WMI Self-Instrumentation Event Provider"
   EventQueryList (wbemCimtypeString) = select * from __InstanceCreationEvent where TargetInstance isa
"Win32_NTLogEvent"
   *provider (wbemCimtypeReference) = \\.\Root\CIMV2:__Win32Provider.Name="MS_NT_EVENTLOG_EVENT_PROVIDER"
   EventQueryList (wbemCimtypeString) = select * from __InstanceModificationEvent where TargetInstance isa
```

```
"Win32_LocalTime"
  EventQueryList (wbemCimtypeString) =
          select * from __InstanceModificationEvent where TargetInstance isa "Win32_UTCTime"
  *provider (wbemCimtypeReference) = __Win32Provider="Win32ClockProvider"
  EventQueryList (wbemCimtypeString) = select * from Microsoft_SA_AlertEvent
  *provider (wbemCimtypeReference) = \\.\ROOT\CIMV2:__Win32Provider.Name="ApplianceManager"
  EventQueryList (wbemCimtypeString) = select * from MSFT_SCMEvent
  *provider (wbemCimtypeReference) = \\.\root\cimv2:__Win32Provider.Name="SCM Event Provider"
Root/CIMV2/ms_409
Root/CIMV2/Applications
Root/CIMV2/Applications/MicrosoftIE
Root/MicrosoftActiveDirectory
Root/MicrosoftIISv2
Root/Policy
Root/Policy/ms_409
Root/MicrosoftDNS
Root/MicrosoftNLB
  EventQueryList (wbemCimtypeString) = select * from WMIEvent
  *provider (wbemCimtypeReference) = \\.\Root\MicrosoftNLB:__Win32Provider.Name="WMIEventProv"
Root/Microsoft
Root/Microsoft/HomeNet
Root/DEFAULT
  EventQueryList (wbemCimtypeString) = select * from RegistryEvent
  *provider (wbemCimtypeReference) = \\.\Root\Default:__Win32Provider.Name="RegistryEventProvider"
Root/DEFAULT/ms_409
Root/directory
Root/directory/LDAP
Root/directory/LDAP/ms_409
Root/subscription
  EventQueryList (wbemCimtypeString) =
          SELECT * FROM __InstanceOperationEvent WHERE TargetInstance ISA "MSFT_TemplateBase"
  *provider (wbemCimtypeReference) =
          \\.\root\subscription:__Win32Provider.Name="Microsoft WMI Template Event Provider"
  EventQueryList (wbemCimtypeString) = select * from MSFT_TransientEggTimerEvent
  EventQueryList (wbemCimtypeString) =
          select * from __InstanceOperationEvent where TargetInstance isa "MSFT_TransientStateBase"
  *provider (wbemCimtypeReference) =
          \\.\root\subscription:__Win32Provider.Name="Microsoft WMI Transient Event Provider"
  EventQueryList (wbemCimtypeString) = SELECT * FROM MSFT_FCTraceEventBase
  *provider (wbemCimtypeReference) = \\.\root\subscription:__Win32Provider.Name="Microsoft WMI
Forwarding Consumer Trace Event Provider"
  EventQueryList (wbemCimtypeString) = select * from MSFT_TransientRebootEvent
  *provider (wbemCimtypeReference) = \\.\root\subscription:__Win32Provider.Name="Microsoft WMI Transient
Reboot Event Provider"
  EventQueryList (wbemCimtypeString) = SELECT * FROM MSFT_UCTraceEventBase
  EventQueryList (wbemCimtypeString) = SELECT * FROM MSFT_UCEventBase
  *provider (wbemCimtypeReference) = \\.\root\subscription:__Win32Provider.Name="Microsoft WMI Updating
Consumer Event Provider"
Root/subscription/ms_409
Root/registry
Root/NetFrameworkv1
Root/NetFrameworkv1/ms_409
```

The most interesting event providers are summarized in Table 6.2.

Each event provider has an associated WQL event query stored in a property called *EventQueryList*, which is the WQL event query supported by the provider. Before going into detail, let's see what notification types are

Table 6.2 *The Event Providers*

Namespace	Event Provider	Event Query list
Root/CIMV2	MS_Power_Management_Event_Provider	select * from Win32_PowerManagementEvent
	SystemConfigurationChangeEvents	select * from Win32_SystemConfigurationChangeEvent
	MS_Shutdown_Event_Provider	select * from Win32_ComputerShutdownEvent
	VolumeChangeEvents	select * from Win32_VolumeChangeEvent
	Microsoft WMI Forwarding Event Provider	select * from MSFT_ForwardedEvent
	RouteEventProvider	select * from Win32_IP4RouteTableEvent
	WMI Kernel Trace Event Provider	select * from Win32_ProcessStartTrace
		select * from Win32_ProcessStopTrace
		select * from Win32_ThreadStartTrace
		select * from Win32_ThreadStopTrace
		select * from Win32_ModuleLoadTrace
	MS_NT_EVENTLOG_EVENT_PROVIDER	select * from __InstanceCreationEvent where TargetInstance isa "Win32_NTLogEvent"
	Win32ClockProvider	select * from __InstanceModificationEvent where TargetInstance isa "Win32_CurrentTime"
Root/DEFAULT	RegistryEventProvider	select * from RegistryEvent
Root/MicrosoftCluster	Cluster Event Provider	select * from MicrosoftCluster_Event
Root/snmp/localhost	MS_SNMP_REFERENT_EVENT_PROVIDER	select * from SnmpExtendedNotification
	MS_SNMP_ENCAPSULATED_EVENT_PROVIDER	select * from SnmpNotification

Table 6.2 *The Event Providers (continued)*

Namespace	Event Provider	Event Query list
Root/subscription	Microsoft WMI Template Event Provider	select * from __InstanceOperationEvent WHERE TargetInstance ISA "MSFT_TemplateBase"
	Microsoft WMI Transient Event Provider	select * from MSFT_TransientEggTimerEvent
		select * from __InstanceOperationEvent where TargetInstance isa "MSFT_TransientStateBase"
	Microsoft WMI Forwarding Consumer Trace Event Provider	select * from MSFT_FCTraceEventBase
	Microsoft WMI Transient Reboot Event Provider	select * from MSFT_TransientRebootEvent
	Microsoft WMI Updating Consumer Event Provider	select * from MSFT_UCTraceEventBase
		select * from MSFT_UCEventBase
Root/WMI	WMIEventProv	select * from WMIEvent

available from WMI. Each event provider must conform to the different natures of notification available from WMI.

6.2.5 Event notification types

The events are reported to WMI in different ways and are classified as intrinsic events or extrinsic events. In addition to this classification, WMI offers another type of event not related to the CIM repository or the real-world manageable entities. These events are timer events and behave differently.

Intrinsic events are related to creation, modification, or deletion made in the CIM repository in regard to a namespace, a class, or a class instance. Extrinsic events are defined by the event provider designer and correspond to events that are not already described by an intrinsic event. For instance, a change to a registry key or an SNMP trap arrival is a typical extrinsic event. Timer events are events that occur at a particular time and day or repeatedly at regular intervals. Let's start with the intrinsic events.

6.2.5.1 Intrinsic events

WMI creates intrinsic events for data stored statically in the CIM repository and acquires information by inspecting the repository. There are different event types represented by a set of system classes derived from the __IntrinsicEvent system class. There is a set of system classes for classes, instances, and namespace creation, modification, and deletion (see Figure 6.6). Each time an intrinsic event is delivered by WMI, it corresponds to one instance of the event classes listed in Table 6.3. Based on the WQL event filter, this event instance will be delivered to the consumer.

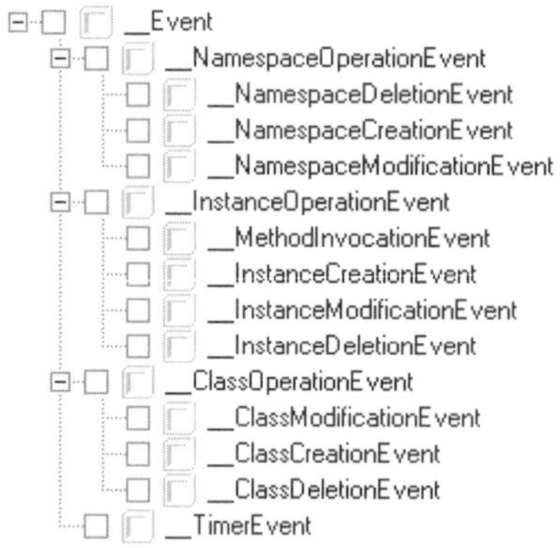

Figure 6.6
The intrinsic events.

```
□─□  □  __Event
   □─□  □  __NamespaceOperationEvent
         □  □  __NamespaceDeletionEvent
         □  □  __NamespaceCreationEvent
         □  □  __NamespaceModificationEvent
   □─□  □  __InstanceOperationEvent
         □  □  __MethodInvocationEvent
         □  □  __InstanceCreationEvent
         □  □  __InstanceModificationEvent
         □  □  __InstanceDeletionEvent
   □─□  □  __ClassOperationEvent
         □  □  __ClassModificationEvent
         □  □  __ClassCreationEvent
         □  □  __ClassDeletionEvent
      □  □  __TimerEvent
```

Table 6.3   *The Intrinsic Events*

__NamespaceCreationEvent	Notifies the consumer when a namespace is created
TargetNamespace	Contains a copy of the __Namespace instance that was created. The Name property of the __Namespace instance indicates which namespace was created.
__NamespaceDeletionEvent	Notifies the consumer when a namespace is deleted
TargetNamespace	Contains a copy of the __Namespace instance that was deleted. The Name property of the __Namespace instance indicates which namespace was deleted.
__NamespaceModificationEvent	Notifies the consumer when a namespace is modified
PreviousNamespace	Contains a copy of the original version of the __Namespace instance. The Name property of this instance indicates which namespace was modified.
TargetNamespace	Contains a copy of the __Namespace instance that was modified. The Name property of the __Namespace instance indicates which namespace was modified.
__ClassCreationEvent	Notifies the consumer when a class is created
TargetClass	Contains a copy of the newly-created class reported by the class creation event.
__ClassDeletionEvent	Notifies the consumer when a class is deleted
TargetClass	Contains a copy of the newly-deleted class reported by the class deletion event.
__ClassModificationEvent	Notifies the consumer when a class is modified
PreviousClass	Contains a copy of the original version of the class.
TargetClass	Contains a copy of the newly-modified class reported by the class modification event.
__InstanceCreationEvent	Notifies the consumer when a instance is created
TargetInstance	Contains a copy of the instance that was created.
__InstanceDeletionEvent	Notifies the consumer when a instance is deleted
TargetInstance	Contains a copy of the instance that was deleted.
__InstanceModificationEvent	Notifies the consumer when a instance is modified
PreviousInstance	Contains a copy of the instance prior to modification.
TargetInstance	Contains the new version of the changed instance.

Each of these instances represents the specific events with one or more properties embedding the object that is subject to the event (*Target* or *PreviousInstance*, *Class* or *Namespace*). We described this object encapsulation in Chapter 3 when discussing the WQL event queries.

A real-world manageable entity is represented in CIM by a dynamic instance provided by a WMI provider. If a dynamic instance is subject to

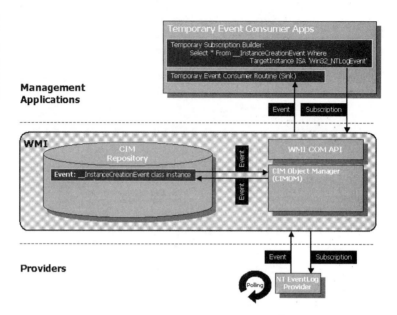

change, the WMI provider creates the intrinsic events for dynamic data.
To perform this, a WMI event provider must be available, and the polling
is executed at the level of the provider itself. This logic is represented in
Figure 6.7

Having a WMI event provider for dynamic instances provides the best
performance because it allows WMI to delegate the polling tasks to the provider. A typical case of an event provider delivering intrinsic events is the
NT Event Log event provider. It uses the intrinsic event system class
__InstanceCreationEvent for the notification creation. The WQL event
query to use is

```
Select * From __InstanceCreationEvent Where TargetInstance ISA 'Win32_NTLogEvent'
```

There are two important things to note:

1.   The *NT Event Log* is an event provider; there is no need to specify
      the **WITHIN** WQL statement.

2.   The event notification is classified as an intrinsic event because the
      event provider delivers an event already defined in the CIM repos-
      itory as a subclass of *__IntrinsicEvent* (*__InstanceCreationEvent*).

Figure 6.8 shows sample output of a temporary event consumer
(**WBEMTEST.exe**) using the *NT Event Log* event provider and an instance
of the intrinsic event system class *__InstanceCreationEvent*.

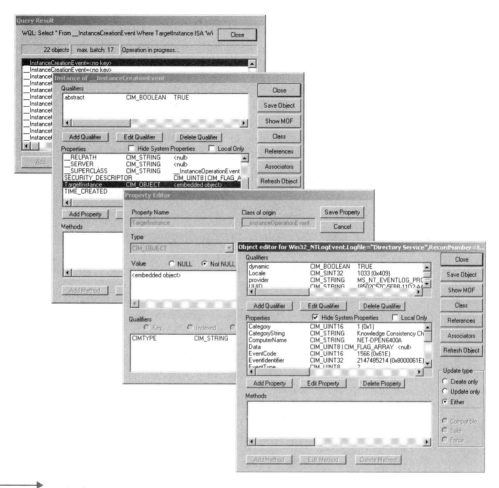

Figure 6.8 *An example of an intrinsic event with the NT Event Log event provider.*

For the facility, the event is created with a small WSH script using the *LogEvent* method of the **WshShell** object. Of course, any other means can be used to create an NT Event Log entry.

Sample 6.1 *A WSH script to create to generate a WMI event by creating an event log entry*

```
 .:
 6:Option Explicit
 .:
10:Set WshShell = Wscript.CreateObject("Wscript.Shell")
11:
12:WshShell.LogEvent 0, "Event Log entry for TEST."
13:
14:Set WshShell = Nothing
```

It is possible that a dynamic instance has no event provider; in such a case, the event consumer must register its WQL event query for polling with WMI by using the **WITHIN** statement. In such a case, WMI monitors the dynamic instance at a regular time interval for changes and delivers the intrinsic event. A typical case is when an application wants to monitor a dynamic class provided by the *Win32* providers. When discovering the WQL event queries discussed in Chapter 3, the WQL event query samples monitored the Windows services status changes. The *Win32* provider supporting this class is not implemented as an event provider, and the polling technique with the **WITHIN** statement was used. As a reminder, the WQL event query used was

```
Select * From __InstanceModificationEvent Within 30 Where TargetInstance ISA 'Win32_Service'
```

This query tracks the creation of an *__InstanceModificationEvent* instance embedding the *Win32_Service* instance modified. There are two important things to note in this query:

1.   The *Win32* provider is not an event provider; it is mandatory to specify the **WITHIN** statement.

2.   The event notification is classified as an intrinsic event because WMI delivers a predefined event of the CIM repository as a subclass of *__IntrinsicEvent* (*__InstanceModificationEvent*).

This logic is represented in Figure 6.9.

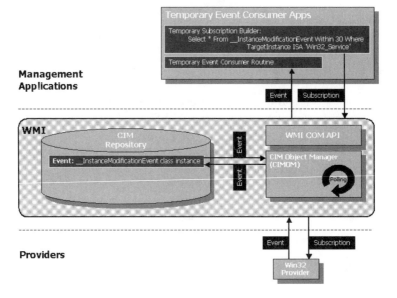

Figure 6.9
The temporary event consumer and its relation to the CIM repository and WMI.

If you need more information about intrinsic classes (such as the properties exposed by the classes), you can use the **LoadCIMinXL.wsf** script developed in Chapter 4. This script has been especially developed for this purpose. It self-documents the definition of every class created in the CIM repository. Of course, you can also use the **WMI CIM Studio** to examine the class content.

6.2.5.2 *Extrinsic events*

Extrinsic events are not represented by a fixed set of classes like intrinsic events. The classes representing extrinsic events are determined by the event provider capabilities and may correspond to a wide range of changes that can occur. It is the responsibility of the event provider developer to define the set of classes that best represent the changes monitored. Also, as opposed to intrinsic events, extrinsic events imply the presence of an event provider. By default, when WMI is installed, several event providers delivering extrinsic events are available. In the **Root\ CIMv2** namespace, for instance, there is one extrinsic event class, called *Win32_PowerManagementEvent* class, supported by the *Power Management* event provider (see Figure 6.10).

In the **Root\WMI** namespace, Microsoft implements some event classes from the WMI provider mainly related to the NDIS interface (see Figure 6.11).

In the **Root\SNMP\SMIR** namespace, the *SNMP* event provider offers an important set of event classes related to SNMP events (see Figure 6.12).

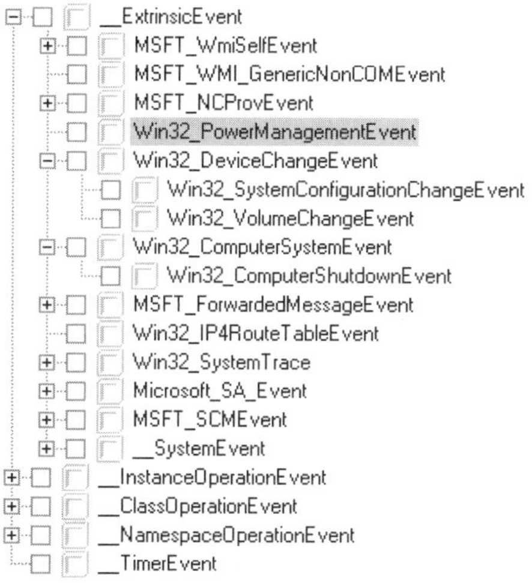

Figure 6.10

The extrinsic events in the Root\CIMv2 namespace.

```
__ExtrinsicEvent
    MSFT_WmiSelfEvent
    MSFT_WMI_GenericNonCOMEvent
    MSFT_NCProvEvent
    Win32_PowerManagementEvent
    Win32_DeviceChangeEvent
        Win32_SystemConfigurationChangeEvent
        Win32_VolumeChangeEvent
    Win32_ComputerSystemEvent
        Win32_ComputerShutdownEvent
    MSFT_ForwardedMessageEvent
    Win32_IP4RouteTableEvent
    Win32_SystemTrace
    Microsoft_SA_Event
    MSFT_SCMEvent
    __SystemEvent
__InstanceOperationEvent
__ClassOperationEvent
__NamespaceOperationEvent
__TimerEvent
```

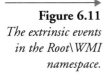

Figure 6.11

The extrinsic events in the Root\WMI namespace.

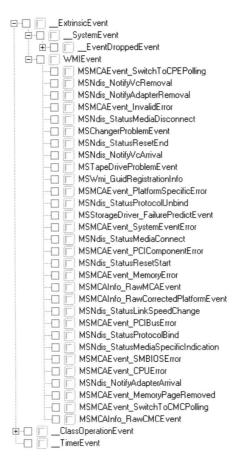

Last but not least, in the **Root\Default** namespace, the *Registry* event provider exposes three event classes as shown in Figure 6.13. As we see in Figure 6.13, the *Registry* event provider delivers an event called *RegistryTreeChangeEvent*. For instance, the formulation of the WQL event query using this class is as follows:

```
Select * FROM RegistryTreeChangeEvent Where Hive='HKEY_LOCAL_MACHINE' AND Rootpath='Software'
```

There are two important things to note in this WQL query:

1.   The *Registry* provider does not require the **WITHIN** statement to detect events because it is an event provider.

2.   The event notification is classified as an extrinsic event because it provides a set of event classes different from the standard intrinsic event classes supported by WMI. The event provider delivers specific events to WMI as a subclass of *__ExtrinsicEvent* (i.e.,

Figure 6.12

The extrinsic events in the Root\ SNMP\SMIR namespace.

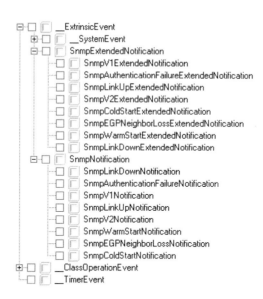

RegistryTreeChangeEvent), which is a subclass of the __Event system class. Actually, it is impossible to have a specific set of defined extrinsic event classes without an event provider.

As for intrinsic events, instances of leaf classes are delivered to consumers.

Figure 6.14 shows the sample output of a temporary event consumer (**WBEMTEST.exe**) using the *Registry* event provider and an instance of the extrinsic event system class *RegistryTreeChangeEvent*. To make this work with **WBEMTEST.exe**, do not forget to connect to the **Root\Default** namespace and select "Notification Query." Any change in the registry hive HKEY_LOCAL_MACHINE under the subkey "software" will create an event.

In Figure 6.14, the *LegalNoticeCaption* key is modified with the **REG-EDIT.exe** tool. As soon as the value is modified, the event consumer (**WBEMTEST.exe**) receives the extrinsic event notification.

All extrinsic event providers expose their sets of classes for event notifications. Independent of the nature of the WMI providers, each provider is

Figure 6.13

The extrinsic events in the Root\Default namespace.

```
□─□  □  __ExtrinsicEvent
   ⊞─□  □  __SystemEvent
   □─□  □  RegistryEvent
        □  □  RegistryValueChangeEvent
        □  □  RegistryKeyChangeEvent
        □  □  RegistryTreeChangeEvent
⊞─□  □  __ClassOperationEvent
   □  □  __TimerEvent
```

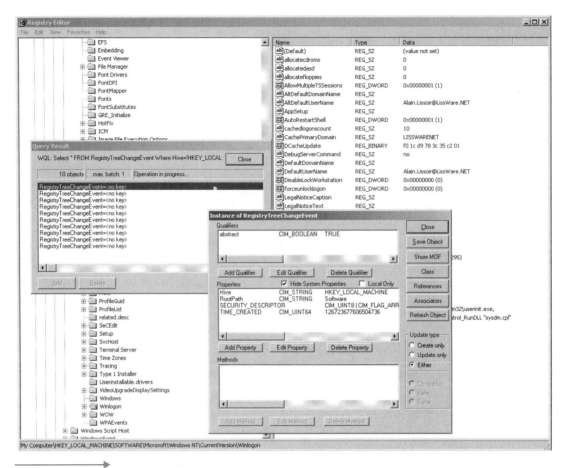

Figure 6.14   *An example of an extrinsic event with the Registry event provider.*

unique and brings its own set of classes. You can examine these classes using the **LoadCIMinXL.wsf** script (developed in Chapter 4) or with **WMI CIM Studio**.

6.2.5.3   *Timer events*

Timer events are totally different from intrinsic or extrinsic events because they are not related to a class, instance, or namespace creation, deletion, or modification. Timer events are events that occur in two situations:

1.   At a particular time and day

2.   Repeatedly at regular intervals

Figure 6.15
The timer events.

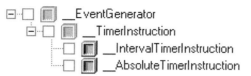

A subscription builder must explicitly configure timer events in order for them to occur. These events use two system classes derived from the *__TimerInstruction* system class (see Figure 6.15):

1. *__AbsoluteTimerInstruction:* This system class represents events that occur at a particular time and day.

2. *__IntervalTimerInstruction:* This system class represents event that occur repeatedly at regular intervals.

As soon as an instance of one of these classes is created, the corresponding timer event occurs, and the registered consumer receives an instance of the *__TimerEvent* system class from WMI. The *__TimerEvent* system class is derived from the *__Event* system class.

6.2.5.3.1 Interval timer event

To create an instance of a timer event, the WMI scripting API or a simple MOF file can be used. First, we use a MOF file for simplicity and the **WEBMTEST.exe** tool as an event consumer of the event. The MOF file used to create an instance of the *__IntervalTimerInstruction* is as follows:

```
instance of __IntervalTimerInstruction
{
  TimerId = "MyIntervalTimerEvent";
  IntervalBetweenEvents = 5000;
};
```

The *__IntervalTimerInstruction* class exposes two properties: the *TimerID* and the *IntervalBetweenEvents*. The *TimerID* is the key of the class and must use a unique name for the instance. The *IntervalBetweenEvents* expresses a delay in milliseconds, which is the time interval to use for the timer event. Next, the MOF file must be compiled with **MOFCOMP.exe**:

```
C:\>MOFCOMP -N:ROOT\CIMv2 IntervalTimerEvent.mof
```

The WQL event query to formulate with **WBEMTEST.exe** is

```
Select * From __TimerEvent Where TimerID = 'MyIntervalTimerEvent'
```

Figure 6.16
*The timer event
properties.*

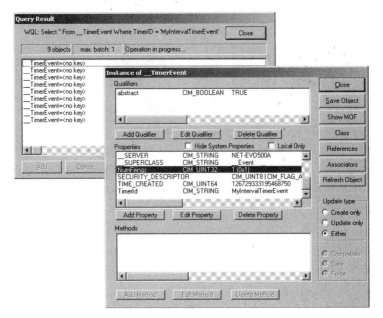

Because all timer events return an instance of the __*TimerEvent* system
class, the query performs the selection on this class. To narrow the scope of
the query (in case of several timer events), the WQL query uses the
TimerID specified in the MOF file. Figure 6.16 shows the output of the
timer event captured with the temporary consumer **WBEMTEST.exe**.

Instead of using a MOF file to create an instance of the __*Interval-
TimerInstruction* class, it is possible to use the WMI scripting API. The
script uses the set of WMI objects seen throughout Chapter 4.

Sample 6.2   *Creating an __IntervalTimerInstruction instance with a script*

```
1:<?xml version="1.0"?>
.:
8:<package>
9:   <job>
..:
13:     <object progid="WbemScripting.SWbemLocator" id="objWMILocator" reference="true"/>
14:
15:     <script language="VBscript">
16:     <![CDATA[
..:
20:     Const cComputerName = "LocalHost"
21:     Const cWMINameSpace = "root/cimv2"
22:     Const cWMIClass = "__IntervalTimerInstruction"
23:     Const cTimerID = "MyIntervalTimerEvent"
24:     Const cIntervalBetweenEvents = 5000
..:
30:     objWMILocator.Security_.AuthenticationLevel = wbemAuthenticationLevelDefault
```

```
31:     objWMILocator.Security_.ImpersonationLevel = wbemImpersonationLevelImpersonate
32:     Set objWMIServices = objWMILocator.ConnectServer(cComputerName, cWMINameSpace, "", "")
33:     Set objWMIClass = objWMIServices.Get (cWMIClass)   34:
35:     Set objWMIInstance = objWMIClass.SpawnInstance_
36:     objWMIInstance.TimerID = cTimerID
37:     objWMIInstance.IntervalBetweenEvents = cIntervalBetweenEvents
38:     objWMIInstance.Put_ (wbemChangeFlagCreateOrUpdate Or wbemFlagReturnWhenComplete)
39:
40:     WScript.Echo cWMIClass & " instance created."
..:
46:     ]]>
47:     </script>
48:   </job>
49:</package>
```

Lines 30 to 32 perform the usual WMI namespace connection. Next, the script creates an instance of the *__IntervalTimerInstruction* system class (lines 33 and 35). Once the instance is available, the script sets the miscellaneous parameters (lines 36 and 37). Before terminating the script, the created instance is committed in the CIM repository (line 38). From now on, every 5,000 ms (5 sec), a *__TimerEvent* notification is triggered by WMI to any registered subscriber for this event. WMI stops generating this event as soon as the *__IntervalTimerInstruction* instance is deleted. The way to proceed is shown in Sample 6.3.

Sample 6.3   *Deleting an __IntervalTimerInstruction instance with a script*

```
 1:<?xml version="1.0"?>
 .:
 8:<package>
 9:  <job>
..:
13:     <object progid="WbemScripting.SWbemLocator" id="objWMILocator" reference="true"/>
14:
15:     <script language="VBscript">
16:     <![CDATA[
..:
20:     Const cComputerName = "LocalHost"
21:     Const cWMINameSpace = "root/cimv2"
22:     Const cWMIClass = "__IntervalTimerInstruction"
23:     Const cTimerID = "MyIntervalTimerEvent"
..:
28:     objWMILocator.Security_.AuthenticationLevel = wbemAuthenticationLevelDefault
29:     objWMILocator.Security_.ImpersonationLevel = wbemImpersonationLevelImpersonate
30:     Set objWMIServices = objWMILocator.ConnectServer(cComputerName, cWMINameSpace, "", "")
31:     Set objWMIInstance = objWMIServices.Get (cWMIClass & "='" & cTimerID & "'")
32:
33:     objWMIInstance.Delete_
34:
35:     WScript.Echo cWMIClass & " instance deleted."
..:
40:     ]]>
41:     </script>
42:   </job>
43:</package>
```

This script is pretty easy to understand. The script gets the *__IntervalTimerInstruction* instance of the corresponding *TimerID* (line 31) and then deletes that instance with the *Delete_* method exposed by the **SWbemObject** representing the *__IntervalTimerInstruction* instance (line 33).

You can perform a simple test. First, subscribe to the event using the **WBEMTEST.exe** tool, and then run the script shown in Sample 6.2 to create the *__IntervalTimerInstruction* instance. As soon as the instance is created, **WBEMTEST.exe** receives the *__TimerEvent* instances at regular intervals. Next, execute the script shown in Sample 6.3 to delete the *__IntervalTimerInstruction* instance; you now see that **WBEMTEST.exe** no longer receives *__TimerEvent* instances from WMI.

6.2.5.3.2   Absolute timer event

The second timer event available from WMI is the absolute timer event. Like the *__IntervalTimerInstruction*, an instance of the *__AbsoluteTimerInstruction* class is created. The *__AbsoluteTimerInstruction* exposes two properties: the *TimerID* and the *EventDateTime*. The *TimerID* is the key property of this class and works as the *TimerID* property of the *__IntervalTimerInstruction* class. The event *EventDateTime* property allows the configuration of a precise date and time when the timer event has to occur. The date and time uses a DMTF format, as discussed in the previous chapter:

```
yyyymmddHHMMSS.mmmmmmsUUU
```

As soon as the date and time match, a *__TimerEvent* notification is triggered by WMI to the subscribed consumers. We can create the *__AbsoluteTimerInstruction* instance using a MOF file, but we can also create the *__AbsoluteTimerInstruction* instance with a script. Sample 6.4 performs this task. The script uses a date equal to 20020804135000.000000+060, which means that WMI will forward an event to the subscribed consumers on August 04, 2002 at 13:50 - GMT+1. Keep in mind that if daylight saving time is active, the hour to specify must be adapted accordingly. For instance, in Central Europe, some countries located in GMT+1 during the winter use a time moved forward by one hour during the summer. To receive an event at 13:50 during the summer, the *EventDateTime* value must be set to August 04, 2002 at 13:50 - GMT+2 (20020804135000.000000+120).

Sample 6.4   *Creating an __AbsoluteTimerInstruction instance with a script*

```
1:<?xml version="1.0"?>
 .:
8:<package>
9:  <job>
 ..:
```

```
13:     <object progid="WbemScripting.SWbemLocator" id="objWMILocator" reference="true"/>
14:
15:     <script language="VBscript">
16:     <![CDATA[
..:
20:     Const cComputerName = "LocalHost"
21:     Const cWMINameSpace = "root/cimv2"
22:     Const cWMIClass = "__AbsoluteTimerInstruction"
23:     Const cTimerId = "MyAbsoluteTimerEvent"
24:     Const cSkipIfPassed = False
25:     Const cEventDateTime = "20020804135000.000000+060"
..:
31:     WScript.Echo "Absolute timer scheduled for " & cEventDateTime
32:
33:     objWMILocator.Security_.AuthenticationLevel = wbemAuthenticationLevelDefault
34:     objWMILocator.Security_.ImpersonationLevel = wbemImpersonationLevelImpersonate
35:     Set objWMIServices = objWMILocator.ConnectServer(cComputerName, cWMINameSpace, "", "")
36:     Set objWMIClass = objWMIServices.Get (cWMIClass)
37:
38:     Set objWMIInstance = objWMIClass.SpawnInstance_
39:     objWMIInstance.TimerID = cTimerID
40:     objWMIInstance.SkipIfPassed = cSkipIfPassed
41:     objWMIInstance.EventDateTime = cEventDateTime
42:     objWMIInstance.Put_ (wbemChangeFlagCreateOrUpdate Or wbemFlagReturnWhenComplete)
43:
44:     WScript.Echo cWMIClass & " instance created."
..:
50:     ]]>
51:     </script>
52:   </job>
53:</package>
```

In Sample 6.4, the date and time are specified in the DMTF format. With the help of the **SWbemDateTime** helper object (see Chapter 5), it is possible to specify the date and time in another format. Sample 6.5 shows this modification.

Sample 6.5   *Creating an __AbsoluteTimerInstruction instance using the SWBemDateTime object*

```
1:<?xml version="1.0"?>
.:
8:<package>
9:   <job>
..:
13:     <object progid="WbemScripting.SWbemLocator" id="objWMILocator" reference="true"/>
14:     <object progid="WbemScripting.SWbemDateTime" id="objWMIDateTime" reference="true"/>
15:
16:     <script language="VBscript">
17:     <![CDATA[
..:
21:     Const cComputerName = "LocalHost"
22:     Const cWMINameSpace = "root/cimv2"
23:     Const cWMIClass = "__AbsoluteTimerInstruction"
24:     Const cTimerId = "MyAbsoluteTimerEvent"
25:     Const cSkipIfPassed = False
26:     Const cTriggerDateTime = "June 16 2002 15:20:00"
..:
```

```
32:    objWMIDateTime.SetVarDate CDate (cTriggerDateTime), True
33:    WScript.Echo "Absolute timer scheduled for " & objWMIDateTime.GetVarDate (True)
34:    WScript.Echo "                              " & objWMIDateTime.Value
35:
36:    objWMILocator.Security_.AuthenticationLevel = wbemAuthenticationLevelDefault
37:    objWMILocator.Security_.ImpersonationLevel = wbemImpersonationLevelImpersonate
38:    Set objWMIServices = objWMILocator.ConnectServer(cComputerName, cWMINameSpace, "", "")
39:    Set objWMIClass = objWMIServices.Get (cWMIClass)
40:
41:    Set objWMIInstance = objWMIClass.SpawnInstance_
42:    objWMIInstance.TimerID = cTimerID
43:    objWMIInstance.SkipIfPassed = cSkipIfPassed
44:    objWMIInstance.EventDateTime = objWMIDateTime.Value
45:    objWMIInstance.Put_ (wbemChangeFlagCreateOrUpdate Or wbemFlagReturnWhenComplete)
46:
47:    WScript.Echo cWMIClass & " instance created."
..:
53:    ]]>
54:    </script>
55:   </job>
56:</package>
```

Both scripts use exactly the same logic to create the timer instance. It is important to note that each script creates the _*AbsoluteTimerInstruction*_ only! They don't act as consumers of the timer event. For the moment, we continue to use the **WBEMTEST.exe** tool as a consumer. Writing a script acting as a consumer of a WMI event is discussed later in Section 6.5. To subscribe to the event, the WQL event query to formulate in **WBEM-TEST.exe** is:

```
Select * From __TimerEvent Where TimerID = 'MyAbsoluteTimerEvent'
```

Now, if you want to delete the _*AbsoluteTimerInstruction*_ instance previously created, you can run a script similar to Sample 6.6.

Sample 6.6   *Deleting an _AbsoluteTimerInstruction instance with a script*

```
1:<?xml version="1.0"?>
.:
8:<package>
9:  <job>
..:
13:    <object progid="WbemScripting.SWbemLocator" id="objWMILocator" reference="true"/>
14:
15:    <script language="VBscript">
16:    <![CDATA[
..:
20:    Const cComputerName = "LocalHost"
21:    Const cWMINameSpace = "root/cimv2"
22:    Const cWMIClass = "__AbsoluteTimerInstruction"
23:    Const cTimerID = "MyAbsoluteTimerEvent"
..:
28:    objWMILocator.Security_.AuthenticationLevel = wbemAuthenticationLevelDefault
29:    objWMILocator.Security_.ImpersonationLevel = wbemImpersonationLevelImpersonate
30:    Set objWMIServices = objWMILocator.ConnectServer(cComputerName, cWMINameSpace, "", "")
```

```
31:    Set objWMIInstance = objWMIServices.Get (cWMIClass & "='" & cTimerID & "'")
32:
33:    objWMIInstance.Delete_
34:
35:    WScript.Echo cWMIClass & " instance deleted."
..:
40:    ]]>
41:    </script>
42:  </job>
43:</package>
```

6.2.5.3.3   The *Win32_CurrentTime* alternative

The *Win32_CurrentTime* class represents the current time in the system and can be used as an alternate method to trigger events at regular time intervals. However, the *Win32_CurrentTime* class is not part of the WMI core event instrumentation. This class is supported by the *Clock* provider, which is implemented as an event provider. We examine this class and its usage in detail when exploring the *Clock* provider in Chapter 3 of the second book, *Leveraging Windows Management Instrumentation (WMI) Scripting* (ISBN 1555582990).

6.3   Using the permanent event consumers

Beside the permanent *SMTP* event consumer and the permanent *WMI Event Viewer* event consumer used in Chapter 2, we saw that WMI also includes some other interesting event consumers. In this section, we review how to use these consumers and the pitfalls or restrictions of using them. These permanent WMI event consumers are used in the same event context as the previous exercise with the permanent *SMTP* event consumer. In Chapter 2, the consumers were registered to receive an event when a change in a *Win32_Service* instance modification occurs. For simplicity, we will use the same event condition here.

6.3.1   Log File event consumer

The *Log File* event consumer writes a string in a flat file used as a log. The string and flat file name are defined in the event consumer class instance. The consumer allows the definition of a maximum size for the log file. Each time a new log file is created, it generates log files numbered from 001 to 999, when the maximum size of the current file is reached. If the log does not exist, the consumer creates the file. If the file is located in a subdirectory, the subdirectory must exist; otherwise, no log file will be created. This consumer has a few parameters. This event consumer is registered in the CIM repository with the **WbemCons.mof** file located in %SystemRoot%\

System32\Wbem. Under Windows 2000 and Windows.NET Server, it is registered in the **Root\Subscription** namespace. To use the event consumer from the **Root\CIMv2** namespace, it must be registered under that namespace with the following command line:

```
C:\>mofcomp -N:Root\CIMv2 %SystemRoot%\System32\Wbem\WbemCons.Mof
Microsoft (R) 32-bit MOF Compiler Version 5.1.3590.0
Copyright (c) Microsoft Corp. 1997-2001. All rights reserved.
Parsing MOF file: J:\WINDOWS\System32\Wbem\WbemCons.Mof
MOF file has been successfully parsed
Storing data in the repository...
Done!
```

Because the *Command-Line* event consumer and the *NT Event Log* event consumer are also defined in the MOF file, it is not necessary to perform this registration to use the two next consumers. For reference purposes, the section of the MOF file regarding the *Log File* event consumer is as follows:

```
 1:class LogFileEventConsumer : __EventConsumer
 2:{
 3:    [key]
 4:    string Name;
 5:    [Not_Null,
 6:     Description("Fully qualified path name for the log file."
 7:                 "If file does not exist, it will be created."
 8:                 "If directory does not exist, file will not be created.")]
 9:    string Filename;
10:    string Text;
11:    [Description("Maximum size to which file is allowed to grow.  It will "
12:                 "be archived when it exceeds this size.  Archived files "
13:                 "have an extension of .001 through .999.  A value of zero "
14:                 "will be interpreted to mean 'do not archive.' ")]
15:    uint64 MaximumFileSize = 65535;
16:    [Description("If FALSE or NULL, file will not be Unicode.")]
17:    boolean IsUnicode;
18:};
..:
66:instance of __Win32Provider as $P1
67:{
68:    Name = "LogFileEventConsumer";
69:    Clsid = "{266c72d4-62e8-11d1-ad89-00c04fd8fdff}";
70:};
71:
72:instance of __EventConsumerProviderRegistration
73:{
74:    Provider = $P1;
75:    ConsumerClassNames = {"LogFileEventConsumer"};
76:};
..:
..:
```

To use the consumer, it is necessary to create an instance of the consumer with its associated filter by using the following MOF file shown in Sample 6.7.

Sample 6.7   *A MOF file to associate the permanent log file event consumer and any change notification coming from the Win32_Service instances (LogFileConsumerInstanceReg.mof)*

```
 1://-----------------------------------
 2://   Sample for LOGFileEventConsumer
 3://-----------------------------------
 4:
 5:// Create the Event Filter
 6:instance of __EventFilter as $ef
 7:{
 8:   Name = "FilterForWIN32_Services";
 9:   Query = "SELECT * FROM __InstanceModificationEvent WITHIN 10 Where "
10:           "TargetInstance ISA 'Win32_Service'";
11:   QueryLanguage = "WQL";
12:};
13:
14:// create the consumer
15:instance of LOGFileEventConsumer as $LOGFileec
16:{
17:   Name = "LOGFileForSvc";
18:   Filename = "C:\\WMIServiceWatcher.LOG";
19:   Text = "Service %TargetInstance.DisplayName% is %TargetInstance.State%.";
20:   MaximumFileSize = 1024;
21:   IsUnicode = False;
22:};
23:
24:// bind the filter and the consumer
25:instance of __FilterToConsumerBinding
26:{
27:   Filter = $ef;
28:   Consumer = $LOGFileec;
29:};
```

From lines 6 to 12 we recognize the filter instance definition; from lines 15 to 22 we have the *Log File* event consumer instance definition with its parameters. At lines 25 to 29, we have the link between the filter and the associated *Log File* event consumer instance. Once the MOF file is loaded in the CIM repository, nothing else is needed. As soon as a Windows service modification occurs, the event is triggered and the *Log File* event consumer creates a log file called **WMIServiceWatcher.log** in the root of the C disk:. The file contains a string as defined in the *text* property (line 19), and a new log file is created every 1,024 bytes. Table 6.4 summarizes the parameters available from the log file event consumer.

The *Log File* permanent event consumer subscription can also be achieved with a script on top of the WMI scripting API. In this case, the script must create the three required instances for the *__EventFilter* class,

---

Table 6.4   *The Log File Permanent Event Consumer Class Properties*

Name	Qualifiers: Key
	String containing the unique name for this consumer.
Filename	Access type: Read/write
	String naming the file, including the path, to which the log entries are appended.
Text	Access type: Read/write
	Qualifiers: Template
	Template string for the text of the log entry.
MaximumFileSize	Access type: Read/write
	Unsigned 64-bit integer which sets the maximum size of the log file (in bytes). If the primary file exceeds its maximum size, the contents are moved to another file and the primary file is emptied. A value of zero (0) is interpreted as meaning no size limit, and NULL as meaning a 65,535 byte limit. The size of the file is checked before a write operation; therefore, you can have a file that is slightly larger than the specified size limit. The next write operation catches it and starts a new file.
	The naming structure for the backup file is as follows:
	If the original filename is 8.3, the extension is replaces by a string of the format "001", "002", and so on with the smallest number larger than all those previously used chosen. If "999" has been used, then the number chosen is the smallest unused number.
	if the original filename is not 8.3, the suffix described above is appended to the filename.
IsUnicode	Access type: Read/write
	Boolean indicating whether the log file is a unicode or a Multi Byte Code (MBC) text file.

---

the *LOGFileEventConsumer* class, and the *__FilterToConsumerBinding* class. This is the purpose of Sample 6.8.

Sample 6.8   *Creating a subscription for a permanent event consumer*

```
 1:<?xml version="1.0"?>
 .:
 8:<package>
 9:  <job>
 ..:
13:     <script language="VBScript" src="..\Functions\TinyErrorHandler.vbs" />
14:
15:     <object progid="WbemScripting.SWbemLocator" id="objWMILocator" reference="true"/>
16:
17:     <script language="VBscript">
18:     <![CDATA[
..:
22:     Const cComputerName = "LocalHost"
23:     Const cWMINameSpace = "root/cimv2"
24:     Const cWMIEventFilterClass = "__EventFilter"
25:     Const cConsumerClass = "LogFileEventConsumer"
26:     Const cWMIFilterToConsumerBindingClass = "__FilterToConsumerBinding"
27:
```

```
 28:    ' Consumer Instance data ---------------------------------------------------
 29:    Const cConsumerName = "LOGFileForSvc"
 30:    Const cLOGFileName = "C:\WMIServiceWatcher.LOG"
 31:    Const cLOGText = "Service %TargetInstance.DisplayName% is %TargetInstance.State%."
 32:    Const cLOGMaximumFileSize = 1024
 33:    Const cLOGIsUnicode = False
 34:
 35:    ' __EventFilter Instance data -----------------------------------------------
 36:    Const cWMIEventFilterName = "FilterForWIN32_Services"
 37:    Const cWMIEventFilterQuery = "SELECT * FROM __InstanceModificationEvent WITHIN 10 Where
                                     TargetInstance ISA 'Win32_Service'"
 ..:
 47:    objWMILocator.Security_.AuthenticationLevel = wbemAuthenticationLevelDefault
 48:    objWMILocator.Security_.ImpersonationLevel = wbemImpersonationLevelImpersonate
 49:    Set objWMIServices = objWMILocator.ConnectServer(cComputerName, cWMINameSpace, "", "")
 ..:
 52:    ' Create the Consumer instance ----------------------------------------------
 53:    Set objWMIClass = objWMIServices.Get (cConsumerClass)
 ..:
 56:    Set objWMIInstance = objWMIClass.SpawnInstance_
 57:    objWMIInstance.Name = cConsumerName
 58:    objWMIInstance.FileName = cLOGFileName
 59:    objWMIInstance.Text = cLOGText
 60:    objWMIInstance.MaximumFileSize = cLOGMaximumFileSize
 61:    objWMIInstance.IsUnicode = cLOGIsUnicode
 62:    objWMIInstance.Put_ (wbemChangeFlagCreateOrUpdate Or wbemFlagReturnWhenComplete)
 ..:
 65:    Set objWMIInstance = objWMIServices.Get (cConsumerClass & "='" & cConsumerName & "'")
 66:    strConsumerRef = objWMIInstance.Path_.Path
 67:
 68:    WScript.Echo "WMI Consumer Instance instance created."
 69:
 70:    ' Create the __EventFilter instance -----------------------------------------
 71:    Set objWMIClass = objWMIServices.Get (cWMIEventFilterClass)
 ..:
 74:    Set objWMIInstance = objWMIClass.SpawnInstance_
 75:    objWMIInstance.Name = cWMIEventFilterName
 76:    objWMIInstance.Query = cWMIEventFilterQuery
 77:    objWMIInstance.QueryLanguage = "WQL"
 78:    objWMIInstance.Put_ (wbemChangeFlagCreateOrUpdate Or wbemFlagReturnWhenComplete)
 ..:
 81:    Set objWMIInstance = objWMIServices.Get (cWMIEventFilterClass & "='" & cWMIEventFilterName & "'")
 82:    strEventFilterRef = objWMIInstance.Path_.Path
 83:
 84:    WScript.Echo "WMI __EventFilter instance created."
 85:
 86:    ' Create the __FilterToConsumerBinding instance -----------------------------
 87:    Set objWMIClass = objWMIServices.Get (cWMIFilterToConsumerBindingClass)
 ..:
 90:    Set objWMIInstance = objWMIClass.SpawnInstance_
 91:    objWMIInstance.Filter = strEventFilterRef
 92:    objWMIInstance.Consumer = strConsumerRef
 93:    objWMIInstance.Put_ (wbemChangeFlagCreateOrUpdate Or wbemFlagReturnWhenComplete)
 ..:
 96:    WScript.Echo "WMI __FilterToConsumerBinding instance created."
 ..:
102:    ]]>
103:    </script>
104:  </job>
105:</package>
```

The script creates the necessary instances to allow the notification to a particular consumer. Before, the consumer was a temporary consumer, and we used the **WBEMTEST.exe** tool. Now, we use a permanent event consumer, and the three required instances must be created accordingly: the consumer instance (lines 52 to 68), the _EventFilter_ instance (lines 70 to 84), and the _FilterToConsumerBinding_ instance (lines 86 to 96). The interesting particularity resides in the _FilterToConsumerBinding_ instance creation. Because this instance is an association instance that contains references, its references must be initialized with the complete object path of the consumer instance (lines 66 and 92) and the _EventFilter_ instance (lines 89 and 91). Except for this specific required information to create each instance, there is nothing new. This script can be used to create the required instance for any type of event consumer. Only the parameters must be reviewed (lines 29 to 33 and lines 57 to 61).

6.3.2   NT Event Log event consumer

In the same philosophy as before, instead of creating text lines in a flat file, WMI provides a permanent event consumer to log information in the NT application event log. By default, this consumer is also registered in the **Root\Subscription** name space. The section of the **WbemCons.mof** defining the class for the _NT Event Log_ permanent event consumer is shown below:

```
..:
..:
53:[description("Logs events into NT event log")]
54:class NTEventLogEventConsumer : __EventConsumer
55:{
56:    [key] string Name;
57:    string UNCServerName;
58:    string SourceName;
59:    [not_null] uint32 EventID;
60:    uint32 EventType = 1;
61:    uint32 Category;
62:    uint32 NumberOfInsertionStrings = 0;
63:    string InsertionStringTemplates[] = {""};
64:};
..:
90:instance of __Win32Provider as $P3
91:{
92:    Name = "NTEventLogEventConsumer";
93:    Clsid = "{266c72e6-62e8-11d1-ad89-00c04fd8fdff}";
94:};
95:
96:instance of __EventConsumerProviderRegistration
97:{
```

```
98:      Provider = $P3;
99:      ConsumerClassNames = {"NTEventLogEventConsumer"};
100:};
```

As before, an instance of the consumer class associated with an event filter must be created with the help of a MOF file as shown in Sample 6.9.

Sample 6.9   *A MOF file to associate the permanent NT event log event consumer and any change notification coming from the Win32_Service instances (NTEventLogConsumerInstanceReg.mof)*

```
1://----------------------------------------
2://   Sample for NTEventLogEventConsumer
3://----------------------------------------
4:
5:// Create the Event Filter
6:instance of __EventFilter as $ef
7:{
8:  Name = "FilterForWIN32_Services";
9:  Query = "SELECT * FROM __InstanceModificationEvent WITHIN 10 Where "
10:         "TargetInstance ISA 'Win32_Service'";
11: QueryLanguage = "WQL";
12:};
13:
14:// create the consumer
15:instance of NTEventLogEventConsumer as $NTEventLogec
16:{
17: Name = "NTEventLogForSvc";
18: UNCServerName = "";
19: SourceName = "WMI NTEventLog event consumer";
20: EventID = 100;
21: EventType = 2; // 0=Information, 1=Error, 2=Warning
22: Category = 0;
23: NumberOfInsertionStrings = 2;
24: InsertionStringTemplates = {"This is a WMI NTEventLog permanent event consumer action.",
25:                             "Service %TargetInstance.DisplayName% is %TargetInstance.State%."};
26:};
27:
28:// bind the filter and the consumer
29:instance of __FilterToConsumerBinding
30:{
31: Filter = $ef;
32: Consumer = $NTEventLogec;
33:};
```

Like any of the other MOF files registering the permanent event consumer class, the three traditional sections are defined. The only change is in the section defining the consumer instance (lines 15 to 26). Once registered, any change to a Windows service creates a warning (line 21) event record in the application event log with a source name "WMI NTEventLog event consumer" (line 19) and an event ID equal to 100 (line 20). Two insertion strings are also associated with the event log trace as defined in lines 23 to 24. Note that in line 18 no server name is given. This implies that the message is logged on the local machine. If the message must be logged on a remote machine, rights must be configured accordingly, and the server name must be provided in UNC notation. Table 6.5 summarizes the parameters available from the *NT Event Log* event consumer.

Table 6.5   *The NT Event Log Permanent Event Consumer Class Properties*

Name	Access type: Read/write
	Qualifiers: Key
	String containing the unique name of this consumer.
UNCServerName	Access type: Read/write
	String naming the computer on which to log the event, or NULL if the event is to be logged on the local server.
SourceName	Access type: Read/write
	String naming the source in which the message is to be found. The customer is assumed to have registered a DLL with the necessary messages.
EventID	Access type: Read/write
	Qualifiers: Not null
	Unsigned 32-bit integer identifying the event message in the message DLL. This property cannot be NULL.
EventType	Access type: Read/write
	Unsigned 32-bit integer specifying the type of event being raised. This parameter can have one of the following values which are defined in Winnt.h and Ntelfapi.h.
	EVENTLOG_SUCCESS Successful event
	EVENTLOG_ERROR_TPYE Error event
	EVENTLOG_WARNING_TYPE Warning event
	EVENTLOG_INFORMATION_TYPE Information event
	EVENTLOG_AUDIT_SUCCESS Success audit type
	EVENTLOG_AUDIT_FAILURE Failure audit type
Category	Access type: Read/write
	Unsigned 32-bit integer specifying the event category. This is source-specific information and can have any value.
NumberOfInsertionStrings	Access type: Read/write
	Unsigned 32-bit integer specifying the number of elements in the InsertionStringTemplates array.
InsertionStringTemplates	Access type: Read/write
	Qualifiers: Template
	Array of string templates used as the insertion strings for the event log record.

6.3.3 **Command-Line event consumer**

The *Command-Line* event consumer allows the startup of any Win32 application. It can be a command line (a new command prompt session) or any other Win32 application. The consumer also exposes some parameters to define the window style or the lifetime of the started process. This consumer is also defined in the **WbemCons.mof** file and registered, by default, in the **Root\Subscription** namespace. Here is the section related to its class registration in the CIM repository:

```
..:
..:
20:class CommandLineEventConsumer : __EventConsumer
21:{
22:    [key]
23:    string Name;
24:    string ExecutablePath;
25:    [Template]
26:    string CommandLineTemplate;
27:    boolean UseDefaultErrorMode = FALSE;
28:    boolean CreateNewConsole = FALSE;
29:    boolean CreateNewProcessGroup = FALSE;
30:    boolean CreateSeparateWowVdm = FALSE;
31:    boolean CreateSharedWowVdm = FALSE;
32:    sint32 Priority = 32;
33:    string WorkingDirectory;
34:    string DesktopName;
35:    [Template]
36:    string WindowTitle;
37:    uint32 XCoordinate;
38:    uint32 YCoordinate;
39:    uint32 XSize;
40:    uint32 YSize;
41:    uint32 XNumCharacters;
42:    uint32 YNumCharacters;
43:    uint32 FillAttribute;
44:    uint32 ShowWindowCommand;
45:    boolean ForceOnFeedback = FALSE;
46:    boolean ForceOffFeedback = FALSE;
47:    boolean RunInteractively = FALSE;
48:    [description("Number of seconds that child process is allowed to run"
49:                 "if zero, process will not be terminated")]
50:    uint32 KillTimeout = 0;
..:
78:instance of __Win32Provider as $P2
79:{
80:    Name = "CommandLineEventConsumer";
81:    Clsid = "{266c72e5-62e8-11d1-ad89-00c04fd8fdff}";
82:};
83:
84:instance of __EventConsumerProviderRegistration
85:{
86:    Provider = $P2;
87:    ConsumerClassNames = {"CommandLineEventConsumer"};
88:};
..:
..:
```

To create an instance of this permanent event consumer, the following MOF file can be used as shown in Sample 6.10.

Sample 6.10   *A MOF file to associate the permanent command-line event consumer and any change notification coming from the Win32_Service instances (CommandLineConsumerInstanceReg.mof)*

```
1://----------------------------------------
2://   Sample for CommandLineEventConsumer
3://----------------------------------------
4:
5:// Create the Event Filter
6:instance of __EventFilter as $ef
7:{
8:   Name = "FilterForWIN32_Services";
9:   Query = "SELECT * FROM __InstanceModificationEvent WITHIN 10 Where "
10:          "TargetInstance ISA 'Win32_Service'";
11:   QueryLanguage = "WQL";
12:};
13:
14:// create the consumer
15:instance of CommandLineEventConsumer as $CommandLineec
16:{
17:   Name = "CommandLineForSvc";
18:   ExecutablePath = "Cmd.exe";
19:   WindowTitle = "Started for 10 seconds (Service "
20:                "%TargetInstance.DisplayName% is %TargetInstance.State%) ...";
21:   KillTimeout = 10;
22:   WorkingDirectory = "C:\\";
23:   FillAttribute = 144;
24:   RunInteractively = true;
25:};
26:
27:// bind the filter and the consumer
28:instance of __FilterToConsumerBinding
29:{
30:   Filter = $ef;
31:   Consumer = $CommandLineec;
32:};
```

The MOF continues to use the same structure as before. The only change resides in the permanent consumer instance definition to define the parameters related to this particular consumer. Once registered, when a Windows service change occurs, the command-line consumer starts a new command prompt (line 18) with a default directory of C:\ (line 22) and with a window title defined in lines 19 and 20. The lifetime of the command prompt is 10 seconds as defined in line 21. The foreground and the background color is a value combination as defined in Table 6.6. The process is set to run interactively (line 24). Nothing else is needed except to

Table 6.6   *The Command-Line Permanent Event Consumer Class Properties*

Name	Access type: Read/write
	Qualifiers: Key
	String property that specifies the unique name of this consumer.
ExecutablePath	Access type: Read-only
	Qualifiers: Key
	String specifying the module to execute. The string can specify the full path and file name of the module to execute or it can specify a partial name. In the case of a partial name, the current drive and current directory will be assumed.
	The ExecutablePath parameter can be NULL. In that case, the module name must be the first white space-delimited token in the CommandLine-Template string. If you are using a long file name that contains a space, use quoted strings to indicate where the file name ends and the arguments begin; otherwise, the file name is ambiguous.
CommandLineTemplate	Access type: Read/write
	Qualifiers: Template
	Template string specifying the process to be launched. This parameter can be NULL. In that case, the method uses ExecutablePath as the command line.
UseDefaultErrorMode	Access type: Read/write
	Boolean indicating the error mode.
CreateNewConsole	Access type: Read/write
	Boolean indicating that the new process has a new console, instead of inheriting the parent's console.
CreateNewProcessGroup	Access type: Read/write
	Boolean indicating that the new process is the root process of a new process group. The process group includes all processes that are descendants of this root process. The process identifier of the new process group is the same as this process identifier. Process groups are used by the GenerateCon-soleCtrlEvent method to enable sending a Ctrl+C or Ctrl+Break signal to a group of console processes.
CreateSeparateWowVdm	Access type: Read/write
	Windows_NT/Windows_2000 only. Boolean indicating whether the new process runs in a private Virtual DOS Machine (VDM). This is only valid when starting a 16-bit Windows-based application. If set to false, all 16-bit Windows-based applications run as threads in a single, shared VDM. See Remarks.
CreateSharedWowVdm	Access type: Read/write
	Windows_NT/Windows_2000 only. Boolean indicating whether the CreateProcess method is to run the new process in the shared Virtual DOS Machine (VDM). This property is able to override the DefaultSeparateVDM switch in the Windows section of Win.ini if it is set to true.
Priority	Access type: Read/write
	Signed 32-bit integer that determines the scheduling priorities of the process's threads. The following table lists the priority levels available.

Table 6.6   *The Command-Line Permanent Event Consumer Class Properties (continued)*

Priority	0x00000020
	Indicates a normal process with no special scheduling needs.
	0x00000040
	Indicates a process whose threads run only when the system is idle and which are preempted by the threads of any process running in a higher priority class. An example is a screen saver. The idle priority class is inherited by child processes.
	0x00000080
	Indicates a process that performs high priority, time-critical tasks. The threads of a high-priority class process preempt the threads of normal-priority or idle-priority class processes. An example is the Task List, which must respond quickly when called by the user, regardless of the load on the system. Use extreme care when using the high-priority class, as a CPU-bound application with a high-priority class can use nearly all available cycles.
	0x00000100
	Indicates a process that has the highest possible priority. The threads of a real-time priority class process preempt the threads of all other processes, including operating system processes performing important tasks. For
WorkingDirectory	Access type: Read/write
	String specifying the working directory for this process.
DesktopName	Access type: Read/write
	String specifying the name of the desktop.
WindowTitle	Access type: Read/write
	Qualifiers: Template
	String specifying the title that appears on the title bar of the process.
XCoordinate	Access type: Read/write
	Unsigned 32-bit integer which specifies the x-offset (pixels) from the left edge of the screen to the left edge of the window, if a new window is created.
YCoordinate	Access type: Read/write
	Unsigned 32-bit integer which indicates the y-offset (pixels) from the top edge of the screen to the top edge of the window, if a new window is created.
XSize	Access type: Read/write
	Unsigned 32-bit integer which indicates the width (pixels) of the new window, if a new window is created.
YSize	Access type: Read/write
	Unsigned 32-bit integer which indicates the height (pixels) of the new window, if a new window is created.

Table 6.6 *The Command-Line Permanent Event Consumer Class Properties (continued)*

Property	Description
XNumCharacters	Access type: Read/write Unsigned 32-bit integer which specifies the screen buffer width in character columns, if a new console window is created. This property is ignored in a GUI process.
YNumCharacters	Access type: Read/write Unsigned 32-bit integer which specifies the screen buffer height in characters rows, if a new console window is created. This property is ignored in a GUI process.
FillAttributes	Access type: Read/write Unsigned 32-bit integer which specifies the initial text and background colors, if a new console window is created in a console application. This property is ignored in a GUI application. The value can be any combination of the following values: 0x00000001 blue foreground 0x00000002 green foreground 0x00000004 red foreground 0x00000008 foreground intensity 0x00000010 background blue 0x00000020 background green 0X00000040 background red 0X00000080 background intensity
ShowWindowCommand	Access type: Read/write Unsigned 32-bit integer which specifies the default value the first time ShowWindow is called, for GUI processes.
ForceOnFeedback	Access type: Read/write Boolean indicating that the cursor is in feedback mode for two seconds after CreateProcess is called. If during those two seconds, the process makes the first GUI call, the system gives five additional seconds to the process. If during those five seconds, the process shows a window, the system give another five seconds to the process to finish drawing the window.
ForceOffFeedback	Access type: Read/write Boolean indicating that the feedback cursor is forced off while the process is starting. The normal cursor is displayed.
RunInteractively	Access type: Read/write Boolean indicating whether the process is to be launched in the interactive winstation (true) or in the default service winstation (false). This property overrides the DesktopName property.
KillTimeout	Access type: Read/write Unsigned 32-bit integer specifying the number of seconds the WinMgmt service is to wait before killing the process. Zero (0) indicates the process is to not be killed. Killing the process is intended as a fail-safe to prevent a process from running indefinitely.

Figure 6.17
*The command-line
permanent event
consumer.*

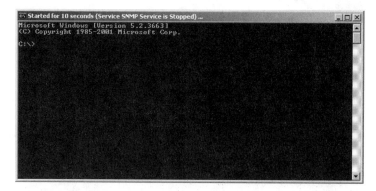

perform the registration of the consumer instance in the CIM repository with MOFCOMP.exe. Table 6.6 summarizes the parameters available from the *Command-Line* event consumer.

As a result, Figure 6.17 shows the created command line window.

Of course, for the exercise we used the **CMD.EXE** executable, but any other Win32 program can be used.

6.3.4   Active Script event consumer

Similar to the *Command-Line* event consumer, the permanent *Active Script* event consumer allows starting a VBScript or a JScript. This event consumer is registered in the **Root\Subscription** namespace with the **SCRCONS.mof** file located in %SystemRoot%\System32\Wbem.

```
C:\>mofcomp -N:Root\CIMv2 %SystemRoot%\System32\Wbem\SCRCONS.MOF
Microsoft (R) 32-bit MOF Compiler Version 5.1.3590.0
Copyright (c) Microsoft Corp. 1997-2001. All rights reserved.
Parsing MOF file: J:\WINDOWS\System32\Wbem\SCRCONS.MOF
MOF file has been successfully parsed
Storing data in the repository...
Done!
```

As usual, to use the consumer, an instance of its class must be created. Sample 6.11 shows the MOF file used to create the consumer instance.

Sample 6.11   *A MOF file to associate the permanent active script event consumer with a JScript and any change notification coming from the Win32_Service instances (ActiveScriptConsumerInstanceReg.mof)*

```
1://---------------------------------------
2://  Sample for ActiveScriptEventConsumer
3://---------------------------------------
4:
```

```
 5:// Create the Event Filter
 6:instance of __EventFilter as $ef
 7:{
 8:   Name = "FilterForWIN32_Services";
 9:   Query = "SELECT * FROM __InstanceModificationEvent WITHIN 10 Where "
10:            "TargetInstance ISA 'Win32_Service'";
11:   QueryLanguage = "WQL";
12:};
13:
14:// create the consumer
15:instance of ActiveScriptEventConsumer as $ActiveScriptec
16:{
17:   Name = "ActiveScriptForSvc";
18:   ScriptingEngine = "JScript";
19:   ScriptText = "var ForReading = 1, ForWriting = 2, ForAppending = 8;"
20:            "var TristateFalse = 0, TristateTrue = -1, TristateUseDefault = -2;"
21:            "var strFileName = \"c:\\\\ActiveScriptEventConsumer.txt\";"
22:            "var objFileSystem = new ActiveXObject(\"Scripting.FileSystemObject\");"
23:            "var objfile = objFileSystem.OpenTextFile"
24:            "                (strFileName, ForAppending, true, TristateFalse);"
25:            "objfile.WriteLine(new Date);"
26:            "objfile.WriteLine(\"Service %TargetInstance.DisplayName%"
27:            " is %TargetInstance.State%\");"
28:            "objfile.Close();";
29:   KillTimeout = 30;
30:};
31:
32:// bind the filter and the consumer
33:instance of __FilterToConsumerBinding
34:{
35:   Filter = $ef;
36:   Consumer = $ActiveScriptec;
37:};
```

Besides the traditional sections to define every instance type, the use of this consumer requires some particular attention. For security reasons, only an administrator may configure the active script consumer. Moreover, the started script runs in the LocalSystemSecurity context as a separate process from WMI. Next, the script is executed with the Windows Script Interfaces. This implies that the script environment is not Windows Script Host (WSH) and that no WSH feature is available. The script language is determined with a specific parameter (line 18). The script itself can be specified in two different ways. The first method, as shown in Sample 6.11, uses the *ScriptText* parameter. This parameter accepts the direct encoding of the script in the MOF file. Although this can be useful, some care must be taken to respect the MOF file syntax. Sample 6.11 uses a JScript already used in Chapter 1 for the remote script execution. The script simply creates a file with a UTC timestamp in it. The active script consumer MOF file starting the same script written in VBScript as shown in Sample 6.12.

Sample 6.12   *A MOF file to associate the permanent active script event consumer with a VBScript*
                  and any change notification coming from the Win32_Service instances
                  (ActiveScriptConsumerInstanceReg2.mof)

```
 1://---------------------------------------
 2:// Sample for ActiveScriptEventConsumer
 3://---------------------------------------
 4:
 5:// Create the Event Filter
 6:instance of __EventFilter as $ef
 7:{
 8:  Name = "FilterForWIN32_Services";
 9:  Query = "SELECT * FROM __InstanceModificationEvent WITHIN 10 Where "
10:          "TargetInstance ISA 'Win32_Service'";
11:  QueryLanguage = "WQL";
12:};
13:
14:// create the consumer
15:instance of ActiveScriptEventConsumer as $ActiveScriptec
16:{
17:  Name = "ActiveScriptForSvc2";
18:  ScriptingEngine = "VBScript";
19:  ScriptText = "Option Explicit\n"
20:               "Const ForReading = 1\n"
21:               "Const ForWriting = 2\n"
22:               "Const ForAppending = 8\n"
23:               "Const TristateFalse = 0\n"
24:               "Const TristateTrue = -1\n"
25:               "Const TristateUseDefault = -2\n"
26:               "Dim strFileName\n"
27:               "Dim objFileSystem\n"
28:               "Dim objfile\n"
29:               "strFileName = \"c:\\ActiveScriptEventConsumer2.txt\"\n"
30:               "Set objFileSystem = CreateObject(\"Scripting.FileSystemObject\")\n"
31:               "Set objfile = objFileSystem.OpenTextFile"
32:               "                (strFileName, ForAppending, true, TristateFalse)\n"
33:               "objfile.WriteLine(Date & \" - \" & Time)\n"
34:               "objfile.WriteLine(\"Service %TargetInstance.DisplayName%"
35:               " is %TargetInstance.State%\")\n"
36:               "objfile.Close()\n";
37:  KillTimeout = 30;
38:};
39:
40:// bind the filter and the consumer
41:instance of __FilterToConsumerBinding
42:{
43:  Filter = $ef;
44:  Consumer = $ActiveScriptec;
45:};
```

Once included in a MOF file, some characters (such as the backslash
and the quote) must be escaped to respect the MOF file syntax requirements (see Samples 6.11 and 6.12). If these modifications are not made, the
MOF complier will complain during the MOF file parsing. When the
JScript script is not included in a MOF file, it looks like this:

```
 1:var ForReading = 1, ForWriting = 2, ForAppending = 8;
 2:var TristateFalse = 0, TristateTrue = -1, TristateUseDefault = -2;
 3:
 4:var strFileName = "c:\\ActiveScriptEventConsumer.txt";
 5:var objFileSystem = new ActiveXObject("Scripting.FileSystemObject");
 6:var objfile = objFileSystem.OpenTextFile(strFileName, ForAppending, true, TristateFalse);
 7:
 8:objfile.WriteLine(new Date);
 9:
10:objfile.Close();
```

The second method consists of specifying the script file name itself. In this case, the script is no longer included in the MOF file but is stored on the file system as a standard JScript or VBScript. The ability to kill the script after a certain period (line 27 of Sample 6.11 and line 37 of Sample 6.12) is supported only if the script is started with the *ScriptText* parameter, not with the *ScriptFileName* parameter.

As WMI runs as a service, any script started by the permanent *Active Script* event consumer does not generate output. Running the WMI service **WinMgmt.exe** as an executable is not supported, but it allows any script to display popup messages by using the Msgbox function. But again, as mentioned before, no WSH function is available as the script is not started in the WSH context. Although the permanent active script consumer has some restrictions, such a consumer can be useful in some circumstances, especially when an administrator already has a script performing some tasks and wants to integrate the code with WMI quickly without having to rewrite the complete script logic on top of the WMI scripting API. In this case, it is a quick-and-dirty solution, but like any quick-and-dirty solution, it comes with restrictions (such as accessing remote systems from the started script and displaying output) and advantages (such as a quick WMI integration). Table 6.7 summarizes the parameters available from the *Active Script* event consumer.

6.3.5   The SMTP event consumer

The permanent *SMTP* event consumer was used in Chapter 2 when introducing the capabilities of WMI. Please refer to Chapter 2 for more information about this permanent event consumer provider.

6.3.6   The Forwarding consumer provider

The *Microsoft WMI Forwarding* consumer provider is available under Windows XP. However, before examining this consumer, it is necessary to gather more knowledge about WMI. Therefore, this consumer is discussed in

Table 6.7   *The Active Script Permanent Event Consumer Class Properties*

Name	Access type: Read-only
	Qualifiers: Key
	String that uniquely identifies the event consumer.
ScriptingEngine	Access type: Read-only
	Qualifiers: Not_Null
	String naming the scripting engine to use. For example: "VBScript" or "JScript". This property cannot be NULL.
ScriptText	Access type: Read-only
	Qualifiers: Template
	Template string containing the text of the script to execute. If NULL, the ScriptFileName property is used.
ScriptFileName	Access type: Read-only
	String naming the file from which the script text is read. Must be NULL if ScriptText is non-NULL.
KillTimeout	Access type: Read-only
	Unsigned 32-bit integer specifying the number of seconds after which the script will be terminated if it isn't already finished. If zero, the script will not be terminated. This property applies only to scripts specified in the ScriptText property.

Chapter 3 of the second book, *Leveraging Windows Management Instrumentation (WMI) Scripting* (ISBN 1555582990).

6.4   The permanent consumer registrations in the CIM repository

In using the permanent event consumers, we created several associations of an event filter with particular instances of the permanent event consumers. By using the WMI event registration tool, it is possible to see these instances (see Figure 6.18).

Because each of these instances is associated with the same event filter, changing the view to see the filters gives the permanent event consumers associated with the event filter (see Figure 6.19).

If you look using the **WMI CIM Studio**, you will see the class template of each permanent event consumer used to create the instances associated with the event filter (see Figure 6.20).

Figure 6.18   *The WMI event registration consumer instances.*

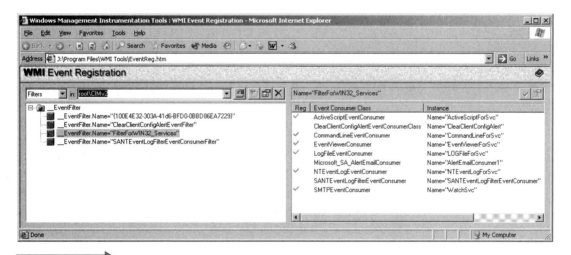

Figure 6.19   *The WMI event filter instances.*

Figure 6.20
*Some WMI
permanent event
consumers classes.*

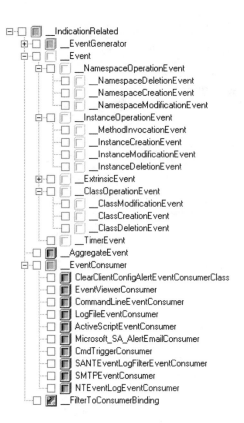

6.5   Scripting temporary event consumers

At this point, we have seen many things about the WMI event notifications, but we haven't learned how to script with WMI event notification. All the material we have examined is helpful to position WMI event scripting among all WMI features and to understand how this scripting technique works. Briefly, we have covered the following:

- **Temporary and the permanent subscriptions:** We know that the WMI event scripting uses only temporary subscription. This also helped us to understand the difference between a temporary event consumer and a permanent event consumer.

- **The typical event providers available:** It is possible to know the type of real-world entity that can be monitored without using the polling feature (**WITHIN** statement) of WQL and the type of event class that these event providers provide (extrinsic) or use (intrinsic).

■ **The WQL event query:** As soon as we know which event class to use
to track events related to instances, the formulation of the WQL
event query is key. The query is used as a filter to determine events
that are relevant for the consumer. We saw how to formulate WQL
queries in Chapter 3.

With this background in mind, we are ready to dive in the WMI event
scripting techniques.

When we ended the previous chapter with Sample 5.18 ("Looping in a
script to detect a change") by using the *Refresh_* method of the **SWbem-
Object** and the For Next polling technique, we created a form of monitoring. Note that this technique performs synchronous monitoring of an
instance (or collection of instances), but it does not represent a synchronous
event-monitoring technique! Sample 5.18 polled an instance to show its
current state regardless of whether there was a modification. The big difference with the WMI event notification is that the script is notified as soon as
a modification occurs. In this case, the script receives an instance representing the event type.

In Chapter 4, we saw two major scripting techniques: synchronous
scripting and asynchronous scripting. We will proceed exactly in the same
way here. Let's start with the synchronous scripting technique first.

6.5.1   **Synchronous events**

In the case of a synchronous event notification, the script execution is in an
idle state until a notification is received from WMI. To catch the event notification synchronously, we use the *ExecNotificationQuery* method of the
SWbemServices object. This method requires a WQL event query in input.
This tactic is implemented in Sample 6.13.

Sample 6.13   *Synchronous event notification*

```
 1:<?xml version="1.0"?>
 .:
 8:<package>
 9:  <job>
..:
13:    <object progid="WbemScripting.SWbemLocator" id="objWMILocator" reference="true"/>
14:
15:    <script language="VBscript">
16:    <![CDATA[
..:
20:    ' -------------------------------------------------------------------------------
21:    Const cComputerName = "LocalHost"
22:    Const cWMINameSpace = "root/cimv2"
23:    Const cWMIQuery = "Select * from __InstanceModificationEvent Within 10
```

```
                                               Where TargetInstance ISA 'Win32_Service'"
..:
29:    On Error Resume Next
30:
31:    objWMILocator.Security_.AuthenticationLevel = wbemAuthenticationLevelDefault
32:    objWMILocator.Security_.ImpersonationLevel = wbemImpersonationLevelImpersonate
33:    Set objWMIServices = objWMILocator.ConnectServer(cComputerName, cWMINameSpace, "", "")
34:
35:    Set objWMIEvent = objWMIServices.ExecNotificationQuery (cWMIQuery)
36:
37:    WScript.Echo "Waiting for events ..."
38:
39:    Set objWMIEventInstance = objWMIEvent.NextEvent
40:    If Err.Number then
41:       WScript.Echo "0x" & Hex(Err.Number) & " - " & Err.Description & " (" & Err.Source & ")"
42:    Else
43:       WScript.Echo
44:       WScript.Echo FormatDateTime(Date, vbLongDate) & " at " & _
45:                    FormatDateTime(Time, vbLongTime) & ": '" & _
46:                    objWMIEventInstance.Path_.Class & "' has been triggered."
47:       WScript.Echo ">The '" & objWMIEventInstance.TargetInstance.DisplayName & _
48:                    "' instance is currently " & _
49:                    LCase (objWMIEventInstance.TargetInstance.State) & "."
50:       WScript.Echo ">Before modification the '" & _
51:                    objWMIEventInstance.PreviousInstance.DisplayName & _
52:                    "' instance was " & _
53:                    LCase (objWMIEventInstance.PreviousInstance.State) & "."
54:    End If
..:
61:    WScript.Echo "Finished."
62:
63:    ]]>
64:    </script>
65:  </job>
66:</package>
```

As in previous scripts, Sample 6.13 establishes the connection with WMI by creating an **SWbemServices** object (line 31 to 33). Next, the script executes the *ExecNotificationQuery* method exposed by the **SWbemServices** object (line 35). The *ExecNotificationQuery* method takes the WQL event query, defined at line 23, as a parameter. This WQL event query requests to watch modifications to any *Win32_Service* instances. Once the *ExecNotificationQuery* method executed, it immediately returns an **SWbemEventSource** object (line 35). This object is part of the WMI scripting object model in Figure 4.3 (object number 9). The **SWbemEventSource** object exposes only one method called *NextEvent*.

If no event occurs, the script waits indefinitely (line 39). Because the script is in an idle state until an event occurs, this technique refers to synchronous event notification. When the *NextEvent* method invocation returns successfully, it means that an event occurred. In such a case, an **SWbemObject** is returned (line 39). This **SWbemObject** represents an instance of the event itself. In Sample 6.13, it is an instance of the

InstanceModificationEvent class (line 23). We know that the *InstanceModificationEvent* class exposes two properties that encapsulate an **SWbemObject** representing the instance subject to the modification. It is a *Win32_Service* instance; one property (*PreviousInstance*) shows the *Win32_Service* instance in its previous state (lines 47 to 49), and the other property (*TargetInstance*) shows the *Win32_Service* instance in its new state (lines 50 to 53). We have these two properties available because the WQL query refers to the *InstanceModificationEvent* intrinsic event class. Refer to Table 6.3 to get a list of the properties available from the intrinsic event classes. Below, you will find sample output when the Windows SNMP Service is stopped.

```
C:\>EventSyncConsumer.wsf
Microsoft (R) Windows Script Host Version 5.6
Copyright (C) Microsoft Corporation 1996-2000. All rights reserved.

Waiting for events ...

Sunday, 01 July, 2002 at 10:36: '__InstanceModificationEvent' has been
triggered.
>The 'SNMP' instance is currently stopped.
>Before modification the 'SNMP' instance was running.
Finished.
```

The WQL event query influences the returned objects in two ways: the type of event instance contained in the **SWbemObject** returned from the *NextEvent* method and the type of instance subject to the event (and contained in the properties of the **SWbemObject** returned from the *NextEvent* method). Basically, the WQL event query has two variables: the event itself and the real-world object entity subject to the event.

By using Sample 6.13 as a base and with the knowledge acquired before, we can develop a script that is much more generic. This gives us the facility to formulate any WQL event query type from the command line and get the result displayed accordingly. Once done, we can use this script instead of using **WBEMTEST.exe** as temporary consumer. This generic script can be easily created by combining the XML WSH features to parse the command line and by reusing the DisplayProperties() function created in Chapter 4 (see Sample 4.30). The logic is implemented in Sample 6.14.

Sample 6.14 *A generic script for synchronous event notification*

```
1:<?xml version="1.0"?>
.:
8:<package>
9:  <job>
.:
```

```
13:    <runtime>
14:      <unnamed name="WQLQuery" helpstring="the WQL Event query to execute (between quotes)."
                 required="true" type="string" />
15:      <named name="Machine" helpstring="determine the WMI system to connect to.
                   (default=LocalHost)" required="false" type="string"/>
16:      <named name="User" helpstring="determine the UserID to perform the remote connection.
                   (default=none)" required="false" type="string"/>
17:      <named name="Password" helpstring="determine the password to perform the remote
                   connection. (default=none)" required="false" type="string"/>
18:      <named name="NameSpace" helpstring="determine the WMI namespace to connect to.
                   (default=Root\CIMv2)" required="false" type="string"/>
19:    </runtime>
20:
21:    <script language="VBScript" src="..\Functions\TinyErrorHandler.vbs" />
22:    <script language="VBScript" src="..\Functions\DisplayInstanceProperties.vbs" />
23:
24:    <object progid="WbemScripting.SWbemLocator" id="objWMILocator" reference="true"/>
25:    <object progid="WbemScripting.SWbemDateTime" id="objWMIDateTime"/>
26:
27:    <script language="VBscript">
28:    <![CDATA[
..:
32:    ' -----------------------------------------------------------------------------------
33:    Const cComputerName = "LocalHost"
34:    Const cWMINameSpace = "root/cimv2"
..:
48:    ' -----------------------------------------------------------------------------------
49:    ' Parse the command line parameters
50:    If WScript.Arguments.Unnamed.Count < 1 Then
51:      WScript.Arguments.ShowUsage()
52:      WScript.Quit
53:    Else
54:      strWQLQuery = WScript.Arguments.Unnamed.Item(0)
55:    End If
56:
57:    strUserID = WScript.Arguments.Named("User")
58:    If Len(strUserID) = 0 Then strUserID = ""
59:
60:    strPassword = WScript.Arguments.Named("strPassword")
61:    If Len(strPassword) = 0 Then strPassword = ""
62:
63:    strComputerName = WScript.Arguments.Named("Machine")
64:    If Len(strComputerName) = 0 Then strComputerName = cComputerName
65:
66:    strWMINameSpace = WScript.Arguments.Named("NameSpace")
67:    If Len(strWMINameSpace) = 0 Then strWMINameSpace = cWMINameSpace
68:    strWMINameSpace = UCase (strWMINameSpace)
69:
70:    objWMILocator.Security_.ImpersonationLevel = wbemImpersonationLevelImpersonate
71:    objWMILocator.Security_.Privileges.Add wbemPrivilegeSecurity
72:    Set objWMIServices = objWMILocator.ConnectServer(strComputerName, strWMINameSpace, _
73:                                                     strUserID, strPassword)
74:    If Err.Number Then ErrorHandler (Err)
75:
76:    Set objWMIEvent = objWMIServices.ExecNotificationQuery (strWQLQuery)
77:    If Err.Number Then ErrorHandler (Err)
78:
79:    WScript.Echo "Waiting for events ..."
80:
81:    Set objWMIEventInstance = objWMIEvent.NextEvent
```

```
 82:      If Err.Number then
 83:         WScript.Echo "0x" & Hex(Err.Number) & " - " & Err.Description & " (" & Err.Source & ")"
 84:      Else
 85:         WScript.Echo
 86:         WScript.Echo FormatDateTime(Date, vbLongDate) & " at " & _
 87:                      FormatDateTime(Time, vbLongTime) & ": '" & _
 88:                      objWMIEventInstance.Path_.Class & "' has been triggered."
 89:         DisplayProperties objWMIEventInstance, 2
 90:      End If
 ..:
 97:      WScript.Echo "Finished."
 98:
 99:      ]]>
100:     </script>
101:    </job>
102:</package>
```

Except that the script is generic, the logic of Sample 6.14 is not different from that of Sample 6.13. Because any type of WQL event query can be provided from the command line, the script grants a particular privilege required when examining the NT Event Log (line 71). Doing so, if such a query is provided on the command line, access is not denied. Of course, it is possible to add more parameters to include the security requirements from the command line, but as we focus on the WMI event notification scripting techniques, we will try to keep the script as simple as possible.

Lines 13 to 19 define the XML structure used to parse the command line. Lines 50 to 68 extract the information available from the command line. The second adaptation concerns the DisplayProperties() function call (line 89), which displays all properties related to the **SWbemObject** returned from the *NextEvent* method invocation (line 81). To execute the script in the same conditions as Sample 6.13, the following command line must be used:

```
  1:    C:\>GenericEventSyncConsumer.wsf "Select * From __InstanceModificationEvent Within 10
  2:                                      Where TargetInstance ISA 'Win32_Service'"
  3:    Microsoft (R) Windows Script Host Version 5.6
  4:    Copyright (C) Microsoft Corporation 1996-2000. All rights reserved.
  5:
  6:    Waiting for events ...
  7:
  8:    Sunday, 17 June, 2002 at 15:33: '__InstanceModificationEvent' has been triggered.
  9:      PreviousInstance (wbemCimtypeObject)
 10:         AcceptPause (wbemCimtypeBoolean) = False
 11:         AcceptStop (wbemCimtypeBoolean) = True
 12:         Caption (wbemCimtypeString) = SNMP Service
 13:         CheckPoint (wbemCimtypeUint32) = 0
 14:         CreationClassName (wbemCimtypeString) = Win32_Service
 15:         Description (wbemCimtypeString) = Includes agents that monitor the activity ...
 16:         DesktopInteract (wbemCimtypeBoolean) = False
 17:         DisplayName (wbemCimtypeString) = SNMP Service
 18:         ErrorControl (wbemCimtypeString) = Normal
 19:         ExitCode (wbemCimtypeUint32) = 0
 20:         InstallDate (wbemCimtypeDatetime) = (null)
```

```
21:        Name (wbemCimtypeString) = SNMP
22:        PathName (wbemCimtypeString) = J:\WINDOWS\System32\snmp.exe
23:        ProcessId (wbemCimtypeUint32) = 2208
24:        ServiceSpecificExitCode (wbemCimtypeUint32) = 0
25:        ServiceType (wbemCimtypeString) = Own Process
26:        Started (wbemCimtypeBoolean) = True
27:        StartMode (wbemCimtypeString) = Auto
28:        StartName (wbemCimtypeString) = LocalSystem
29:        State (wbemCimtypeString) = Running
30:        Status (wbemCimtypeString) = OK
31:        SystemCreationClassName (wbemCimtypeString) = Win32_ComputerSystem
32:        SystemName (wbemCimtypeString) = XP-DPEN6400
33:        TagId (wbemCimtypeUint32) = 0
34:        WaitHint (wbemCimtypeUint32) = 0
35:    SECURITY_DESCRIPTOR (wbemCimtypeUint8) = (null)
36:    TargetInstance (wbemCimtypeObject)
37:        AcceptPause (wbemCimtypeBoolean) = False
38:        AcceptStop (wbemCimtypeBoolean) = False
39:        Caption (wbemCimtypeString) = SNMP Service
40:        CheckPoint (wbemCimtypeUint32) = 0
41:        CreationClassName (wbemCimtypeString) = Win32_Service
42:        Description (wbemCimtypeString) = Includes agents that monitor the activity ...
43:        DesktopInteract (wbemCimtypeBoolean) = False
44:        DisplayName (wbemCimtypeString) = SNMP Service
45:        ErrorControl (wbemCimtypeString) = Normal
46:        ExitCode (wbemCimtypeUint32) = 0
47:        InstallDate (wbemCimtypeDatetime) = (null)
48:        Name (wbemCimtypeString) = SNMP
49:        PathName (wbemCimtypeString) = J:\WINDOWS\System32\snmp.exe
50:        ProcessId (wbemCimtypeUint32) = 0
51:        ServiceSpecificExitCode (wbemCimtypeUint32) = 0
52:        ServiceType (wbemCimtypeString) = Own Process
53:        Started (wbemCimtypeBoolean) = False
54:        StartMode (wbemCimtypeString) = Auto
55:        StartName (wbemCimtypeString) = LocalSystem
56:        State (wbemCimtypeString) = Stopped
57:        Status (wbemCimtypeString) = OK
58:        SystemCreationClassName (wbemCimtypeString) = Win32_ComputerSystem
59:        SystemName (wbemCimtypeString) = XP-DPEN6400
60:        TagId (wbemCimtypeUint32) = 0
61:        WaitHint (wbemCimtypeUint32) = 0
62:    TIME_CREATED (wbemCimtypeUint64) = (null)
63:    Finished.
```

In boldface, at the first indentation level (lines 9, 35, 36, and 62), we have the properties of the event instance itself (which is an **SWbemObject** returned from the *NextEvent* method invocation of the **SWbemEvent-Source** object). We can clearly see the *PreviousInstance* and the *TargetInstance* properties with its **wbemCimtypeObject** type (lines 9 and 36). This type specifies that another **SWbemObject** is encapsulated in these properties. Because the DisplayProperties() function executes recursively when an object is encapsulated in a property, the script displays the properties of the instance subject to the modification (the *Win32_Service* SNMP instance). *PreviousInstance* (lines 10 to 34) contains the instance before modification, and *TargetInstance* (lines 37 to 61) contains the object after modification.

Sample 6.14 displays all items related to an event independently of its nature. Now we have an easy tool to see what we obtain with each event type available from WMI.

6.5.2   Semisynchronous events

The major inconvenience of Samples 6.13 and 6.14 is that the scripts are idle until an event matching the WQL event query occurs. If we slightly modify the logic used in these scripts, it is possible to perform other tasks while we check to see whether a matching event occurred. Sample 6.15 is a modified version of the synchronous generic event consumer script (Sample 6.14).

Sample 6.15   *A generic script for semisynchronous event notification*

```
1:<?xml version="1.0"?>
 .:
8:<package>
9:  <job>
..:
13:    <runtime>
14:      <unnamed name="WQLQuery" helpstring="the WQL Event query to execute (between quotes)."
                       required="true" type="string" />
15:      <unnamed name="EventWaitDelay" helpstring="The number of millseconds to wait for the
                       event (-1=Infinite)." required="true" type="string" />
16:      <named name="Machine" helpstring="determine the WMI system to connect to.
                       (default=LocalHost)" required="false" type="string"/>
17:      <named name="User" helpstring="determine the UserID to perform the remote connection.
                       (default=none)" required="false" type="string"/>
18:      <named name="Password" helpstring="determine the password to perform the remote
                       connection. (default=none)" required="false" type="string"/>
19:      <named name="NameSpace" helpstring="determine the WMI namespace to connect to.
                       (default=Root\CIMv2)" required="false" type="string"/>
20:    </runtime>
21:
22:    <script language="VBScript" src="..\Functions\TinyErrorHandler.vbs" />
23:    <script language="VBScript" src="..\Functions\DisplayInstanceProperties.vbs" />
24:
25:    <object progid="WbemScripting.SWbemLocator" id="objWMILocator" reference="true"/>
26:    <object progid="WbemScripting.SWbemDateTime" id="objWMIDateTime" />
27:
28:    <script language="VBscript">
29:    <![CDATA[
..:
33:    ' ------------------------------------------------------------------------------
34:    Const cComputerName = "LocalHost"
35:    Const cWMINameSpace = "root/cimv2"
..:
50:    ' ------------------------------------------------------------------------------
51:    ' Parse the command line parameters
52:    If WScript.Arguments.Unnamed.Count < 2 Then
53:      WScript.Arguments.ShowUsage()
54:      WScript.Quit
55:    Else
56:      strWQLQuery = WScript.Arguments.Unnamed.Item(0)
```

```
57:        intEventWaitDelay = WScript.Arguments.Unnamed.Item(1)
58:     End If
59:
60:     strUserID = WScript.Arguments.Named("User")
61:     If Len(strUserID) = 0 Then strUserID = ""
62:
63:     strPassword = WScript.Arguments.Named("strPassword")
64:     If Len(strPassword) = 0 Then strPassword = ""
65:
66:     strComputerName = WScript.Arguments.Named("Machine")
67:     If Len(strComputerName) = 0 Then strComputerName = cComputerName
68:
69:     strWMINameSpace = WScript.Arguments.Named("NameSpace")
70:     If Len(strWMINameSpace) = 0 Then strWMINameSpace = cWMINameSpace
71:     strWMINameSpace = UCase (strWMINameSpace)
72:
73:     objWMILocator.Security_.ImpersonationLevel = wbemImpersonationLevelImpersonate
74:     objWMILocator.Security_.Privileges.AddAsString "SeSecurityPrivilege", True
75:     Set objWMIServices = objWMILocator.ConnectServer(strComputerName, strWMINameSpace, _
76:                                                       strUserID, strPassword)
77:     If Err.Number Then ErrorHandler (Err)
78:
79:     objWMIServices.Security_.Privileges.AddAsString "SeSecurityPrivilege", True
80:     Set objWMIEvent = objWMIServices.ExecNotificationQuery (strWQLQuery)
81:     If Err.Number Then ErrorHandler (Err)
82:
83:     WScript.Echo "Waiting events for " & intEventWaitDelay & " ms ..."
84:
85:     Do
86:        Set objWMIEventInstance = objWMIEvent.NextEvent (intEventWaitDelay)
87:        If Err.Number then
88:           WScript.Echo "0x" & Hex(Err.Number) & "-" & Err.Description & " (" & Err.Source & ")"
89:           Exit Do
90:        Else
91:           WScript.Echo
92:           WScript.Echo FormatDateTime(Date, vbLongDate) & " at " & _
93:                        FormatDateTime(Time, vbLongTime) & ": '" & _
94:                        objWMIEventInstance.Path_.Class & "' has been triggered."
95:           DisplayProperties objWMIEventInstance, 2
96:        End If
97:
98:        WScript.Echo "Performing other tasks ..."
99:        WScript.Sleep (10000)
100:
101:        WScript.Echo "Waiting the next events for a new period of " & _
102:                     intEventWaitDelay & " ms ..."
103:
104:     Loop While True
105:
106:     Set objWMIEventInstance = Nothing
107:     Set objWMIEvent = Nothing
108:
109:     Set objWMIServices = Nothing
110:
111:     WScript.Echo "Finished."
112:
113:     ]]>
114:   </script>
115:  </job>
116:</package>
```

Because we continue to use the *ExecNotificationQuery* synchronous method of the **SWbemServices** object (line 80) and because the script no longer waits until an event occurs, this technique is referred to as a semisynchronous technique. The trick resides in the way the *NextEvent* method of the **SWbemEventSource** object is called (line 86). This method accepts one parameter value defining the amount of time to wait for an event. Previously, no time was specified. Now the same method is called, but a time is specified. This causes the script to stay idle only for the specified period of time because the *NextEvent* method returns from invocation when the period of time expires. If no event occurred in this delay, a timeout error is returned (lines 87 to 89).

The second particularity of the coding is that the portion of code checking for events is enclosed in a "Do Loop" to keep the script from terminating immediately (lines 85 to 104). Because the script is executing a "Do Loop" while checking for events (line 86) during a limited period of time, it is possible to execute any other required tasks in between. If an event occurs, the script displays all objects related to the event with the help of the DisplayProperties() function (lines 91 to 95). If a timeout occurs (lines 87 to 89), the script terminates its execution.

There are two important remarks regarding this script:

1.   If the provided WQL event query uses the **WITHIN** statement, it must be clear that the polling interval specified with the **WITHIN** statement must be shorter than the timeout period specified with the *NextEvent* method. Otherwise, a timeout will occur every time, as WMI will never return an event notification matching the WQL event query before the timeout expires. Of course, for any other queries not using the **WITHIN** statement, this is not an issue.

2.   The script continues to run if it receives a WMI event notification in the period of time defined by the timeout. If no event occurs, the script terminates its execution (as a timeout occurs).

The last point could be annoying in some situations if we want to perform continuous semisynchronous monitoring regardless of whether a timeout has occurred. In this case, Sample 6.15 is modified, but only at line 89, to clear the error generated by the timeout. This modification is shown in Sample 6.16.

Sample 6.16 *A generic script for continuous semisynchronous event notification*

```
..:
..:
..:
84:
85:    Do
86:        Set objWMIEventInstance = objWMIEvent.NextEvent (intEventWaitDelay)
87:        If Err.Number then
88:            WScript.Echo "0x" & Hex(Err.Number) & "-" & Err.Description & " (" & Err.Source & ")"
89:            Err.Clear
90:        Else
91:            WScript.Echo
92:            WScript.Echo FormatDateTime(Date, vbLongDate) & " at " & _
93:                         FormatDateTime(Time, vbLongTime) & ": '" & _
94:                         objWMIEventInstance.Path_.Class & "' has been triggered."
95:            DisplayProperties objWMIEventInstance, 2
96:        End If
97:
98:        WScript.Echo "Performing other tasks ..."
99:        WScript.Sleep (10000)
100:
101:       WScript.Echo "Waiting the next events for a new period of " & _
102:                    intEventWaitDelay & " ms ..."
103:
104:   Loop While True
...:
...:
...:
```

Although this semisynchronous method works well, it is not applicable in all situations. If many tasks must be performed between the check of the WMI event notifications, it could be that the response time is not fast enough. In the same way, if event notifications of a different type must be handled, waiting a predefined timeout period can introduce some delays with regard to response time. The problem comes from the fact that all tasks executed in a semisynchronous event notification scripting logic are serialized by the nature of the coding logic used. To avoid this limitation, the asynchronous scripting technique must be used.

6.5.3 Asynchronous events

Asynchronous event notifications use the *ExecNotificationQueryAsync* method of the **SWbemServices** object. The first part is exactly the same as previous script samples, but the delivery of the instance representing the WMI event is made to a sink routine. In the previous chapter, we worked with the asynchronous scripting techniques. Asynchronous WMI event notification uses the same principle. This implies the use of the **SWbem-Sink** object and the use of some of the four sink routines: OnCompleted, OnObjectPut, OnObjectReady, and OnProgress. As we work in the context

of a WMI asynchronous event notification, only the sink routines OnCompleted, OnObjectReady, and OnProgress are used. The OnObjectReady is
the sink routine receiving the instance representing the event. Sample 6.17
implements this logic. Basically, it combines some of the logic developed in
the previous WMI event scripts and some of the logic used in Chapter 4
when we worked with other asynchronous scripting methods.

Sample 6.17 *A generic script for asynchronous event notification*

```
 1:<?xml version="1.0"?>
 .:
 8:<package>
 9:  <job>
..:
13:    <runtime>
14:      <unnamed name="WQLQuery" helpstring="the WQL Event query to execute (between quotes)."
                             required="true" type="string" />
15:      <named name="Machine" helpstring="determine the WMI system to connect to.
                             (default=LocalHost)" required="false" type="string"/>
16:      <named name="User" helpstring="determine the UserID to perform the remote connection.
                             (default=none)" required="false" type="string"/>
17:      <named name="Password" helpstring="determine the password to perform the remote
                             connection. (default=none)" required="false" type="string"/>
18:      <named name="NameSpace" helpstring="determine the WMI namespace to connect to.
                             (default=Root\CIMv2)" required="false" type="string"/>
19:    </runtime>
20:
21:    <script language="VBScript" src="..\Functions\TinyErrorHandler.vbs" />
22:    <script language="VBScript" src="..\Functions\DisplayInstanceProperties.vbs" />
23:    <script language="VBScript" src="..\Functions\PauseScript.vbs" />
24:
25:    <object progid="WbemScripting.SWbemLocator" id="objWMILocator" reference="true"/>
26:    <object progid="WbemScripting.SWbemDateTime" id="objWMIDateTime" />
27:
28:    <script language="VBscript">
29:    <![CDATA[
..:
33:    ' -----------------------------------------------------------------------
34:    Const cComputerName = "LocalHost"
35:    Const cWMINameSpace = "root/cimv2"
..:
49:    ' -------------------------------------------------------------------------------
50:    ' Parse the command line parameters
51:    If WScript.Arguments.Unnamed.Count = 0 Then
52:       WScript.Arguments.ShowUsage()
53:       WScript.Quit
54:    Else
55:       strWQLQuery = WScript.Arguments.Unnamed.Item(0)
56:    End If
57:
58:    strUserID = WScript.Arguments.Named("User")
59:    If Len(strUserID) = 0 Then strUserID = ""
60:
61:    strPassword = WScript.Arguments.Named("strPassword")
62:    If Len(strPassword) = 0 Then strPassword = ""
63:
```

```
64:    strComputerName = WScript.Arguments.Named("Machine")
65:    If Len(strComputerName) = 0 Then strComputerName = cComputerName
66:
67:    strWMINameSpace = WScript.Arguments.Named("NameSpace")
68:    If Len(strWMINameSpace) = 0 Then strWMINameSpace = cWMINameSpace
69:    strWMINameSpace = UCase (strWMINameSpace)
70:
71:    Set objWMISink = WScript.CreateObject ("WbemScripting.SWbemSink", "SINK_")
72:
73:    objWMILocator.Security_.ImpersonationLevel = wbemImpersonationLevelImpersonate
74:    objWMILocator.Security_.Privileges.AddAsString "SeSecurityPrivilege", True
75:    Set objWMIServices = objWMILocator.ConnectServer(strComputerName, strWMINameSpace, _
76:                                          strUserID, strPassword)
77:    If Err.Number Then ErrorHandler (Err)
78:
79:    objWMIServices.ExecNotificationQueryAsync objWMISink, strWQLQuery,, wbemFlagSendStatus
80:    If Err.Number Then ErrorHandler (Err)
81:
82:    WScript.Echo "Waiting for events..."
83:
84:    PauseScript "Click on 'Ok' to terminate the script ..."
85:
86:    WScript.Echo vbCRLF & "Cancelling event subscription ..."
87:    objWMISink.Cancel
..:
92:    WScript.Echo "Finished."
93:
94:    ' ------------------------------------------------------------------------------
95:    Sub SINK_OnCompleted (iHResult, objWBemErrorObject, objWBemAsyncContext)
96:
97:        Wscript.Echo
98:        Wscript.Echo "BEGIN - OnCompleted."
99:        Wscript.Echo "END   - OnCompleted."
100:
101:    End Sub
102:
103:    ' ------------------------------------------------------------------------------
104:    Sub SINK_OnObjectReady (objWbemObject, objWbemAsyncContext)
105:
106:        Wscript.Echo
107:        Wscript.Echo "BEGIN - OnObjectReady."
108:        WScript.Echo FormatDateTime(Date, vbLongDate) & " at " & _
109:                     FormatDateTime(Time, vbLongTime) & ": '" & _
110:                     objWbemObject.Path_.Class & "' has been triggered."
111:
112:        DisplayProperties objWbemObject, 2
113:
114:        Wscript.Echo "END - OnObjectReady."
115:
116:    End Sub
117:
118:    ' ------------------------------------------------------------------------------
119:    Sub SINK_OnProgress (iUpperBound, iCurrent, strMessage, objWbemAsyncContext)
120:
121:        Wscript.Echo
122:        Wscript.Echo "BEGIN - OnProgress."
123:        Wscript.Echo "END   - OnProgress."
124:
125:    End Sub
126:
```

```
127:    ]]>
128:    </script>
129:    </job>
130:</package>
```

The script is exactly the same as Sample 6.16 until line 71. At line 71 the **SWbemSink** object is created and initialized with a name corresponding to the first part of the sink routine name (SINK_). Next, the script performs the WMI connection as before. At line 79, the asynchronous method *Exec-NotificationQueryAsync* is executed with the specified WQL event query and the corresponding **SWbemSink** object. As we have seen in previous chapters with asynchronous scripting, the script sample pauses (line 84) to avoid its termination. We have seen that a script is a temporary event consumer, so it is important to keep the script running to receive events. In a production environment, it is likely that some other tasks will be executed while receiving WMI events. Once the script starts and registers for events, the received event is displayed in the OnObjectReady sink (lines 104 to 116) by using the DisplayProperties() function, as before (line 112).

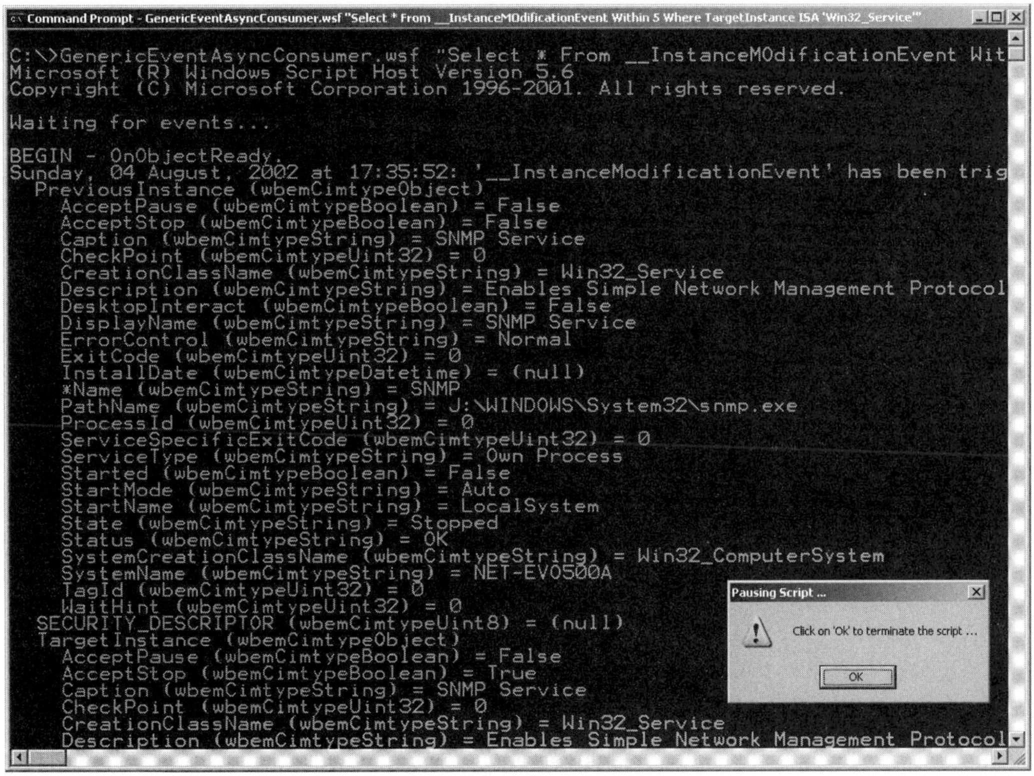

Figure 6.21   *The GenericEventAsyncConsumer.wsf script execution.*

The asynchronous event scripting technique is a powerful one. Of course, the script we discovered during this section is an academic script as it shows the mechanism that must be in place. Besides the event scripting technique, it is possible to code any type of management logic in a script. Let's see how we can use the power of the asynchronous event scripting technique to manage a Windows environment.

6.6   Going further with event scripting

Regarding the number of classes (and behind the scenes, the number of providers), it is almost impossible to give one sample for each class and each event type that exists with WMI. Although we review the WMI providers one by one in the second book, *Leveraging Windows Management Instrumentation (WMI) Scripting* (ISBN 1555582990), in this section we give three script samples that use most of the things we have discovered about WMI. In addition to showing other script samples of event scripting, they also provide a good synthesis of what we have already learned before discussing the WMI providers and their capabilities.

6.6.1   Monitoring, managing, and alerting script for the Windows services

The purpose of the script is to monitor a series of Windows services specified by the administrator to minimize the number of interventions when a Windows service is stopped. As soon as one of the specified services is stopped, the script restarts the service. If there is a problem, it is likely that the service won't be able to be restarted. In such a case, the script attempts to restart the service a certain number of times. For this, it maintains a sanity counter per service monitored. The script sends an alert once the number of trials has been reached. The alert is sent by e-mail, which is built on top of Collaboration Data Object (CDO) for Windows. Although, we don't focus on CDO in this book, we provide a brief explanation of how this works. The e-mail contains the status of the *PreviousInstance* and the *TargetInstance* of the concerned service. To make the WMI information easier to read, the script formats the message in HTML.

The script can monitor several services and maintains a sanity counter per service. To help achieve this, the script uses the notion of context. We used WMI contexts in the previous chapter when we examined asynchronous scripting. Samples 6.18 and 6.19 implement the logic described. Sample 6.18 is the initialization section of the script. Sample 6.19 is the sink routine handling the WMI asynchronous notifications.

Sample 6.18   *Monitoring, managing, and alerting script for the Windows services (Part I)*

```
 1:<?xml version="1.0"?>
 .:
 8:<package>
 9:  <job>
 ..:
13:    <runtime>
14:      <unnamed name="ServiceName" helpstring="the Windows Service list to monitor."
                 required="true" type="string" />
15:      <named name="Machine" helpstring="determine the WMI system to connect to."
                 required="false" type="string"/>
16:      <named name="User" helpstring="determine the UserID to perform the remote connection."
                 required="false" type="string"/>
17:      <named name="Password" helpstring="determine the password to perform the remote
                 connection. (default=none)" required="false" type="string"/>
18:    </runtime>
19:
20:    <script language="VBScript" src="..\Functions\TinyErrorHandler.vbs" />
21:    <script language="VBScript" src="..\Functions\PauseScript.vbs" />
22:    <script language="VBScript" src="..\Functions\LoopSvcStartupRetry.vbs" />
23:    <script language="VBScript" src="..\Functions\GenerateHTML.vbs" />
24:    <script language="VBScript" src="..\Functions\SendMessageExtendedFunction.vbs" />
25:
26:    <object progid="WbemScripting.SWbemLocator" id="objWMILocator" reference="true"/>
27:    <object progid="WbemScripting.SWbemNamedValueSet" id="objWMIInstanceSinkContext"/>
28:    <object progid="WbemScripting.SWbemDateTime" id="objWMIDateTime" />
29:
30:    <script language="VBscript">
31:    <![CDATA[
..:
35:    ' --------------------------------------------------------------------------------
36:    Const cComputerName = "LocalHost"
37:    Const cWMINameSpace = "root/cimv2"
38:    Const cWMIClass = "Win32_Service"
39:    Const cWMIQuery = "Select * from __InstanceModificationEvent Within 10
                              Where TargetInstance ISA 'Win32_Service'"
40:
41:    Const cPauseBetweenRestart = 2
42:    Const cRestartLimit = 3
43:
44:    Const cTargetRecipient = Alain.Lissoir@LissWare.NET
45:    Const cSourceRecipient = WMISystem@LissWare.NET
46:
47:    Const cSMTPServer = "10.10.10.202"
48:    Const cSMTPPort = 25
49:    Const cSMTPAccountName = ""
50:    Const cSMTPSendEmailAddress = ""
51:    Const cSMTPAuthenticate = 0' 0=Anonymous, 1=Basic, 2=NTLM
52:    Const cSMTPUserName = ""
53:    Const cSMTPPassword = ""
54:    Const cSMTPSSL = False
55:    Const cSMTPSendUsing = 2                ' 1=Pickup, 2=Port, 3=Exchange WebDAV
..:
61:    Class clsMonitoredService
62:          Public strServiceName
```

```
63:          Public intServiceRetryCounter
64:      End Class
..:
78:      ' ----------------------------------------------------------------------------
79:      ' Parse the command line parameters
80:      If WScript.Arguments.Unnamed.Count = 0 Then
81:          WScript.Arguments.ShowUsage()
82:          WScript.Quit
83:      Else
84:          For intIndice = 0 To WScript.Arguments.Unnamed.Count - 1
85:              ReDim Preserve clsService(intIndice)
86:              Set clsService(intIndice) = New clsMonitoredService
87:              clsService(intIndice).strServiceName = _
                                 Ucase (WScript.Arguments.Unnamed.Item(intIndice))
88:              clsService(intIndice).intServiceRetryCounter = 0
89:          Next
90:      End If
91:
92:      strUserID = WScript.Arguments.Named("User")
93:      If Len(strUserID) = 0 Then strUserID = ""
...:
101:     Set objWMISink = WScript.CreateObject ("WbemScripting.SWbemSink", "SINK_")
102:
103:     objWMILocator.Security_.AuthenticationLevel = wbemAuthenticationLevelDefault
104:     objWMILocator.Security_.ImpersonationLevel = wbemImpersonationLevelImpersonate
105:     Set objWMIServices = objWMILocator.ConnectServer(strComputerName, cWMINameSpace, _
106:                                                 strUserID, strPassword)
...:
109:     For intIndice = 0 To UBound (clsService)
110:
111:         Set objWMIInstance = objWMIServices.Get (cWMIClass & "='" & _
112:                                 clsService(intIndice).strServiceName & "'")
113:
114:         boolSvcStatus = LoopServiceStartupRetry (objWMIInstance, intIndice)
115:         If boolSvcStatus = False Then
116:             WScript.Quit
117:         End If
118:
119:         If Len(strWMIQuery) = 0 Then
120:             strWMIQuery = "TargetInstance.Name='" & clsService(intIndice).strServiceName & "'"
121:         Else
122:             strWMIQuery = strWMIQuery & " Or " & _
123:                         "TargetInstance.Name='" & _
124:                         clsService(intIndice).strServiceName & "'"
125:         End If
126:
127:         WScript.Echo "Adding '" & clsService(intIndice).strServiceName & _
128:                     "' to subscription to monitor '" & cWMIClass & "'." & vbCRLF
129:
130:         objWMIInstanceSinkContext.Add Cstr(clsService(intIndice).strServiceName), intIndice
131:     Next
132:
133:     strWMIQuery = cWMIQuery & " And TargetInstance.State='Stopped' And (" & strWMIQuery & ")"
134:
135:     objWMIServices.ExecNotificationQueryAsync objWMISink, _
136:                                         strWMIQuery, _
137:                                         ' _
138:                                         ' _
139:                                         ' _
140:                                         objWMIInstanceSinkContext
```

```
...:
143:      WScript.Echo "Waiting for events..."
144:
145:      PauseScript "Click on 'Ok' to terminate the script ..."
146:
147:      WScript.Echo vbCRLF & "Cancelling event subscription ..."
148:      objWMISink.Cancel
...:
153:      WScript.Echo "Finished."
154:
...:
...:
...:
```

As we can see, the initialization part of the script is quite a bit more complex than in previous samples. Because the alert notification is made by e-mail, the script includes some parameters required to send e-mails (lines 44 to 55).

The script needs to specify at least one Windows service on the command line. Several Windows services can also be specified. For instance, the command line could be as follows:

```
C:\>ServiceMonitor.Wsf SNMP SNMPTRAP
```

With this command line, the script monitors the SNMP and the SNMPTRAP services. Therefore, the command line accepts a collection of services where at least one service must be given. This is why the script tests the presence of some unnamed parameters (line 80). The unnamed parameters represent a collection that is enumerated (lines 84 to 89) and stored in an array (line 87). Each service has its associated counter initialized to zero (line 88). This is why a VBScript class is used to associate the counter to the service name (lines 61 to 64 and line 86). Next, the script examines any optional parameters (lines 92 to 100) provided on the command line. As the script uses an asynchronous event notification, it creates an **SWbem-Sink** object (line 101). Once created, it connects to the system where the service list must be monitored (lines 111 and 112).

Because we may have several services, the script creates one event subscription combining all services to watch. The WQL query is constructed from the service list. To construct this WQL query, the script enumerates the collection of services (lines 109 to 131). During this loop, several operations are performed. Because the script monitors services that are stopped, the script ensures that all monitored services are already started. For this, it uses a function called LoopServiceStartupRetry() (line 114). We revisit this function later, but basically, the function starts a service when it is not started. If the startup of one of the monitored services fails, the script terminates its execution (line 116). If a monitored service can't be started, there is no reason to perform its monitoring. The problem must be fixed first.

Next, the WQL event query is constructed for each service in the service list (lines 119 to 125). For further help in the sink routine, the script initializes an **SWbemNamedValueSet** object to add the notion of context to the subscription (line 130). This eases the retrieval of the counter for the corresponding service when an event occurs. We revisit the context usage later; for now, just note that the service name is used as a key in the **SWbem-NamedValueSet** and that the corresponding index is associated with it.

Once the service list enumeration completes, the script finalizes the WQL query construction by adding the **Select** statement (defined in line 39) and the condition stating that the service must be stopped (line 133). Last but not least, the subscription is executed by invoking the *ExecNotificationQueryAsync* method of the **SWbemServices** object (lines 135 to 140). That's it for the initialization part.

Why use one subscription for all monitored services instead of using one subscription per service? Currently, the WQL event query used for the subscription is as follows:

```
Select * from __InstanceModificationEvent Within 10 Where
                        TargetInstance ISA 'Win32_Service' And
                        TargetInstance.State='Stopped' And
                        (TargetInstance.Name='SNMP' Or
                        TargetInstance.Name='SNMPTRAP')
```

Now, it is possible to create a subscription per service listed on the command line. In this case, for the SNMP and the SNMPTRAP services, the WQL event queries are as follows:

```
Select * from __InstanceModificationEvent Within 10 Where
                        TargetInstance ISA 'Win32_Service' And
                        TargetInstance.Name='SNMP' And
                        TargetInstance.State='Stopped'"
```

and

```
Select * from __InstanceModificationEvent Within 10 Where
                        TargetInstance ISA 'Win32_Service' And
                        TargetInstance.Name='SNMPTRAP' And
                        TargetInstance.State='Stopped'"
```

If the script uses this subscription type, the number of resources requested of the system is higher, as we end up with one subscription per service. Because the event instance to watch is the same for all services (*__InstanceModificationEvent*), it is not necessary to use different subscriptions. When the event nature is the same, it is always best to use the same subscription if possible, which minimizes the number of resources requested.

Now, let's examine WMI asynchronous event management. Sample 6.19 shows the code logic. Like any other WMI event script, the event is delivered to the sink routine called OnObjectReady (lines 167 to 213).

Sample 6.19   *Monitoring, managing, and alerting script for the Windows services (Part II)*

```
...:
...:
...:
154:
155:      ' -------------------------------------------------------------------------------
156:      Sub SINK_OnCompleted (iHResult, objWBemErrorObject, objWBemAsyncContext)
...:
160:          Wscript.Echo
161:          Wscript.Echo "BEGIN - OnCompleted."
162:          Wscript.Echo "END   - OnCompleted."
163:
164:      End Sub
165:
166:      ' -------------------------------------------------------------------------------
167:      Sub SINK_OnObjectReady (objWbemObject, objWbemAsyncContext)
...:
175:          Wscript.Echo
176:          Wscript.Echo "BEGIN - OnObjectReady."
177:          WScript.Echo FormatDateTime(Date, vbLongDate) & " at " & _
178:                       FormatDateTime(Time, vbLongTime) & ": '" & _
179:                       objWbemObject.Path_.Class & "' has been triggered."
180:
181:          Select Case objWbemObject.Path_.Class
182:                 Case "__InstanceModificationEvent"
183:                     Set objWMIInstance = objWbemObject
184:                 Case "__AggregateEvent"
185:                     Set objWMIInstance = objWbemObject.Representative
186:                 Case Else
187:                     Set objWMIInstance = Null
188:          End Select
189:
190:          If Not IsNull (objWMIInstance) Then
191:            boolSvcStatus = LoopServiceStartupRetry (objWMIInstance.TargetInstance, _
192:                           objWbemAsyncContext.Item (objWMIInstance.TargetInstance.Name).Value)
193:
194:            If boolSvcStatus =  False Then
195:               If SendMessage (cTargetRecipient, _
196:                               cSourceRecipient, _
197:                               objWMIInstance.TargetInstance.SystemName & " - " & _
198:                                  FormatDateTime(Date, vbLongDate) & _
199:                                  " at " & _
200:                                  FormatDateTime(Time, vbLongTime), _
201:                               GenerateHTML (objWMIInstance.PreviousInstance, _
202:                                          objWMIInstance.TargetInstance) , _
203:                               "") Then
204:                  WScript.Echo "Failed to send email to '" & cTargetRecipient & "' ..."
205:               End If
206:            End If
```

```
207:          End If
...:
211:          Wscript.Echo "END - OnObjectReady."
212:
213:      End Sub
214:
215:      ' --------------------------------------------------------------------------
216:      Sub SINK_OnProgress (iUpperBound, iCurrent, strMessage, objWbemAsyncContext)
...:
220:          Wscript.Echo
221:          Wscript.Echo "BEGIN - OnProgress."
222:          Wscript.Echo "END   - OnProgress."
223:
224:      End Sub
225:
226:      ]]>
227:      </script>
228:    </job>
229:</package>
```

As soon as the event is retrieved in the sink routine, it displays the event class received (line 179). Currently, the WQL query uses the *__InstanceModificationEvent* intrinsic class (see Sample 6.18, line 39). The WQL query can be modified while continuing to use the *__InstanceModificationEvent* intrinsic class. For instance, the usage of the **GROUP** statement (see Chapter 3) in the query creates an aggregated event (using a class *__AggregateEvent*). This is why the script verifies the event class type provided through a **Select Case** statement to make sure that the examined instance always represents an instance modification event (lines 181 to 188).

Next, the script tries to restart the stopped service (lines 191 to 192). The sink routine tries to restart the service immediately because only a stopped service invokes the sink routine; this is because the WQL query clearly states that only stopped services can trigger an event (see Sample 6.18, line 133). To restart the service, we recognize the LoopServiceStartupRetry() function already used in the initialization of the script (see Sample 6.18, line 114). This function requires two parameters: the **SWbemObject** object that contains the instance of the service to be restarted and the index corresponding to the service instance examined in the sink routine. This is where the notion of context is used. The index is used to retrieve the service counter in the LoopServiceStartupRetry() function. Line 192 retrieves this index.

```
192:          objWbemAsyncContext.Item (objWMIInstance.TargetInstance.Name).Value)
```

The examined service name is contained in

```
objWMIInstance.TargetInstance.Name
```

Using the service name as a key in the **SWbemNamedValueSet** object retrieves the corresponding index value. Without the notion of context, it is necessary to perform a loop in the array containing the service list (see Sample 6.18, line 87) until the name of the examined service matches one in the service list. Using the notion of context is a much more elegant approach.

The LoopServiceStartupRetry() function contains the logic to continue to restart the service until the maximum number of retries is reached. Depending on the result, the function returns a value of True if it succeeds in restarting the service or of False if it fails. Let's take a look at Sample 6.20, which shows the LoopServiceStartupRetry() function.

Sample 6.20   *Restarting a service for a fixed number of times*

```
 .:
 .:
 6:' -------------------------------------------------------------------------------------
 7:Function LoopServiceStartupRetry (objWMIInstance, intIndice)
 ..:
13:    clsService(intIndice).intServiceRetryCounter = 0
14:
15:    Do
16:        WScript.Echo "Service '" & objWMIInstance.DisplayName & _
17:                     "' is '" & UCase(objWMIInstance.State) & _
18:                     "' (Startup mode is '" & objWMIInstance.StartMode & "')."
19:
20:        boolSvcStatus = GetServiceStatus (objWMIInstance)
21:
22:        If boolSvcStatus Then
23:           LoopServiceStartupRetry = True
24:           Exit Do
25:        End If
26:
27:        If clsService(intIndice).intServiceRetryCounter >= cRestartLimit Then
28:           WScript.Echo "Retry limit reached (" & _
29:                        clsService(intIndice).intServiceRetryCounter & "/" & cRestartLimit & _
30:                        ") for service '" & objWMIInstance.DisplayName & "'."
31:           LoopServiceStartupRetry = False
32:           Exit Do
33:        Else
34:           clsService(intIndice).intServiceRetryCounter = _
35:                                      clsService(intIndice).intServiceRetryCounter + 1
36:
37:           ' Pause x milliseconds between status checkings and restart tentatives.
38:           WScript.Echo "Waiting " & cPauseBetweenRestart & _
39:                        " second(s) before rechecking status and retrying."
40:           WScript.Sleep (cPauseBetweenRestart * 1000)
41:
42:           WScript.Echo "Retry " & _
43:                        clsService(intIndice).intServiceRetryCounter & "/" & cRestartLimit & _
44:                        " for service '" & objWMIInstance.DisplayName & "."
45:        End If
46:
47:        WScript.Echo "Starting service '" & objWMIInstance.DisplayName & "' ..."
48:
```

```
49:            If objWMIInstance.StartService Then
50:                WScript.Echo "Service '" & objWMIInstance.DisplayName & _
51:                             "' startup failed!'"
52:            End If
53:
54:            ' Refresh the service instance since its restart.
55:            objWMIInstance.Refresh_
56:        Loop
57:
58:End Function
59:
60:' --------------------------------------------------------------------------------------------
61:Function GetServiceStatus (objWMIInstance)
62:
63:        Select Case UCase(objWMIInstance.State)
64:            Case "RUNNING"
65:                GetServiceStatus = True
66:            Case "STOPPED"
67:                GetServiceStatus = False
68:            Case "START PENDING"
69:                GetServiceStatus = True
70:            Case "STOP PENDING"
71:                ' Returns True because it is impossible to restart a
72:                ' service while it is in 'STOP PENDING' state.
73:                ' WMI trigger another event when the service will be in 'STOPPED' state.
74:                GetServiceStatus = True
75:            Case Else
76:                GetServiceStatus = False
77:        End Select
78:
79:End Function
```

This routine starts by resetting the counter to zero. We will see further that the removal of this line changes the script behavior. But first, we must understand how the LoopServiceStartupRetry() function works.

After displaying the current state of the service (lines 16 to 18), the function calls a subfunction called GetServiceStatus() (line 20). This function (lines 61 to 79) returns a Boolean value based on the service state. Basically, if the service is stopped, the function returns False (line 20). If the service is started, the function returns True. In this case, there is no need to restart the service, and we exit from the LoopServiceStartupRetry() function (lines 22 to 25). The LoopServiceStartupRetry() and GetServiceStatus() functions are not written for situations where the service is only stopped. This is why the GetServiceStatus() function returns True in most of the services states, even when the service is in a STOP PENDING state. This will avoid an attempt to restart the service while it is in a STOP PENDING state, as it is impossible to restart a service until the state is STOPPED. As soon as the service is in a STOPPED state, WMI triggers another event (based on the WQL query), and the script can process the stopped service accordingly. Although it is not needed to test all service states because the actual WQL query ensures that only STOPPED services are passed to the sink routine, the function has been written for general purposes and not only in the context of this WQL query. As an exercise, you can change the submitted WQL event query by removing the statement that ensures that the service is stopped; you will see that the code behaves accordingly.

So, if the service is stopped, the LoopServiceStartupRetry() routine checks to see whether the maximum limit for the counter has been reached (line 27). If the limit was reached, the routine shows the current state of the counter and returns a False Boolean value to indicate that the service has not been restarted (lines 28 to 32). If the limit was not reached, the routine increments the counter by one, makes a pause, and displays the new counter value (lines 34 to 44).

Next, the service is restarted (line 49). If the startup fails, a message is displayed (lines 50 and 51). Because it is likely that the service instance has changed (due to the *StartService* method invocation), the routine refreshes the instance to get its new status (line 55) by using the *Refresh_* method of the **SWbemObject** object. This is a typical application of the *Refresh_* method. This is exactly the purpose for which it was designed. Keep in mind that this method is available only under Windows XP and Windows.NET Server. For instance, under Windows 2000, it is necessary to get a new instance of the service to know its new status.

Finally, the routine performs a loop to re-execute the process from the beginning (line 56). If the service instance has been restarted, the GetServiceStatus() returns a True Boolean value (line 20), which allows the routine to exit (lines 22 to 25). If not, the same logic is executed, and the counter is increased by one again (line 34). This is repeated until the limit is reached.

Now, let's revisit the counter itself. Because, the LoopServiceStartupRetry() function resets the counter every time the routine is called, there is no need to save the counter state. If there is no need to keep the counter state, there is no need to use the notion of context during the asynchronous sink calls. If the script resets the counter to zero each time the LoopServiceStartupRetry() is called, it limits the number of attempts to restart a service. In this case, a service can be stopped 10 times; as soon as it is restarted by the LoopServiceStartupRetry() function, there is no problem and no one will receive an alert. Keep in mind that an alert is sent only if the service restart fails in the LoopServiceStartupRetry() function.

If the line resetting the counter is commented out (line 13) each time a service is stopped, the counter starts at the value it had during the previous call. In this case, the number of times that a service can be stopped will be limited as the code remembers the value along the different calls. The script will restart a service until the maximum counter value is reached. Once reached, the script does not start the service any more and an alert is sent. The script keeps the counter value by using the notion of context. Note that by removing a single line (line 13), we have totally changed the script logic; we limit the number of attempts to restart a service, but we also limit the number of times it can be detected as stopped.

To send an alert, the script sends an e-mail. The e-mail is an SMTP mail formatted in MIME. To perform this, the script uses CDO for Windows. Before sending the mail, the script must prepare the mail content. The script prepares an HTML body with the help of the function Generate-HTML() (lines 201 to 202 of Sample 6.19). The GenerateHTML() function is a quite complex string manipulation function that enumerates the **SWbemObject** properties and encapsulates them with their syntax and values between HTML tags. It is nothing more that an enhanced version of the DisplayProperties() function developed in Chapter 4. Note that we can use the *GetText_* method to generate an XML representation of an instance. Transforming this XML representation with the extensible styleheet language (XSL) offers another way to generate the HTML representation. Because the XML instance representation is available only under Windows XP and Windows.NET Server, using the GenerateHTML() function allows the creation of an HTML instance representation under Windows 2000 and previous platform versions. The returned result is a string that contains the HTML stream (lines 201 to 202).

Once the HTML body is ready, the script invokes the SendMessage() function shown in Sample 6.21. The function constructs and sends an e-mail with CDO for Windows. The first four parameters are mandatory: the To field, the From field, the Subject, and the HTML body. Only the attachment field is optional.

Sample 6.21   *Sending an e-mail with CDO for Windows*

```
..:
10:' ----------------------------------------------------------------------------
11:Function SendMessage (strTO, strFROM, strSubject, strHTMLBody, strAttachment)
..:
18:        strTO = Trim (strTO)
19:        strFrom = Trim (strFrom)
20:        strSubject = Trim (strSubject)
21:        strHTMLBody = Trim (strHTMLBody)
22:
23:        If Not (CBool(Len (strTO)) And _
24:                CBool(Len(strFrom)) And _
25:                CBool(Len(strSubject)) And _
26:                CBool(Len(strHTMLBody))) Then
27:           SendMessage = True
```

```
28:        Exit Function
29:      End If
30:
31:      Set objMessage = CreateObject("CDO.Message")
32:      Set objConfiguration = CreateObject ("CDO.Configuration")
33:
34:      objConfiguration.Fields
     ("http://schemas.microsoft.com/cdo/configuration/smtpserver") = cSMTPServer
35:      objConfiguration.Fields
     ("http://schemas.microsoft.com/cdo/configuration/smtpserverport") = cSMTPPort
36:      objConfiguration.Fields
     ("http://schemas.microsoft.com/cdo/configuration/smtpaccountname") = cSMTPAccountName
37:      objConfiguration.Fields
     ("http://schemas.microsoft.com/cdo/configuration/sendemailaddress") = cSMTPSendEmailAddress
38:      objConfiguration.Fields
     ("http://schemas.microsoft.com/cdo/configuration/smtpauthenticate") = cSMTPAuthenticate
39:      objConfiguration.Fields
     ("http://schemas.microsoft.com/cdo/configuration/sendusername") = cSMTPUserName
40:      objConfiguration.Fields
     ("http://schemas.microsoft.com/cdo/configuration/sendpassword") = cSMTPPassword
41:      objConfiguration.Fields
     ("http://schemas.microsoft.com/cdo/configuration/smtpusessl") = cSMTPSSL
42:      objConfiguration.Fields
     ("http://schemas.microsoft.com/cdo/configuration/sendusing") = cSMTPSendUsing
43:      objConfiguration.Fields.Update
44:
45:      objMessage.Configuration = objConfiguration
46:      objMessage.To = strTO
47:      objMessage.From = strFrom
48:      objMessage.Subject = strSubject
49:      objMessage.HTMLBody = strHTMLBody
50:
51:      If Len(Trim (strAttachment)) Then
52:         objMessage.AddAttachment strAttachment
53:      End If
54:
55:      objMessage.Send
56:      If Err.Number Then
57:         SendMessage = True
58:      Else
59:         SendMessage = False
60:      End If
..:
68:End Function
```

The function checks whether these parameters are specified (lines 23 to 29). Next, the miscellaneous parameters to send an SMTP mail are set (lines 34 to 43). The function uses a **CDO.Configuration** object created at line 32. Next, the configuration parameters are associated with the **CDO.Message** object created at line 31. The **CDO.Message** object represents the MIME message. The various fields required for an e-mail are set before it is sent (line 55). In case of failure, the script returns a True Boolean value (line 57).

This returned value is used in Sample 6.19 (line 195) to display an error message (line 204). Once the SendMessage() function completes (line 195), the sink routine terminates, and the script returns to an idle state until another WMI event matching the WQL event query occurs.

When executed, the script displays the following output if a stopped service is restarted successfully:

```
1:C:\>ServiceMonitor.wsf SNMP SNMPTRAP
2:Microsoft (R) Windows Script Host Version 5.6
3:Copyright (C) Microsoft Corporation 1996-2000. All rights reserved.
4:
5:Service 'SNMP' is 'STOPPED' (Startup mode is 'Manual').
6:Waiting 2 second(s) before rechecking status and retrying.
7:Retry 1/3 for service 'SNMP.
8:Starting service 'SNMP' ...
9:Service 'SNMP' is 'RUNNING' (Startup mode is 'Manual').
10:Adding 'SNMP' to subscription to monitor Win32_Service 'SNMP'.
11:
12:Service 'SNMP Trap Service' is 'RUNNING' (Startup mode is 'Manual').
13:Adding 'SNMPTRAP' to subscription to monitor Win32_Service 'SNMPTRAP'.
14:
15:Waiting for events...
16:
17:BEGIN - OnObjectReady.
18:Sunday, 01 July, 2002 at 16:02: '__InstanceModificationEvent' has been triggered.
19:Service 'SNMP' is 'STOPPED' (Startup mode is 'Manual').
20:Waiting 2 second(s) before rechecking status and retrying.
21:Retry 1/3 for service 'SNMP.
22:Starting service 'SNMP' ...
23:Service 'SNMP' is 'START PENDING' (Startup mode is 'Manual').
24:END - OnObjectReady.
25:
..:
..:
```

As we can see before monitoring the services, the script starts the services that are not yet started (lines 5 to 9). Once started (lines 8 and 9) or if already started (line 12), the service list is added in a WQL event query (lines 10 and 13). Next, the script waits for any events matching the event subscription (line 15). Once a service is stopped, the script processes the implemented logic in the LoopServiceStartupRetry() function and tries to start the service while counting the number of attempts (lines 17 to 24).

When the stopped service can't be restarted, the output looks like the following:

```
..:
..:
25:
26:BEGIN - OnObjectReady.
27:Sunday, 01 July, 2002 at 16:04: '__InstanceModificationEvent' has been triggere
28:Service 'SNMP' is 'STOPPED' (Startup mode is 'Disabled').
29:Waiting 2 second(s) before rechecking status and retrying.
30:Retry 1/3 for service 'SNMP.
31:Starting service 'SNMP' ...
32:Service 'SNMP' startup failed!'
33:Service 'SNMP' is 'STOPPED' (Startup mode is 'Disabled').
```

```
34:Waiting 2 second(s) before rechecking status and retrying.
35:Retry 2/3 for service 'SNMP.
36:Starting service 'SNMP' ...
37:Service 'SNMP' startup failed!'
38:Service 'SNMP' is 'STOPPED' (Startup mode is 'Disabled').
39:Waiting 2 second(s) before rechecking status and retrying.
40:Retry 3/3 for service 'SNMP.
41:Starting service 'SNMP' ...
42:Service 'SNMP' startup failed!'
43:Service 'SNMP' is 'STOPPED' (Startup mode is 'Disabled').
44:Retry limit reached (3/3) for service 'SNMP'.
45:END - OnObjectReady.
..:
..:
```

The process is exactly the same as before, but here the script retries up to three times to restart the service (lines 30, 35, and 40). Because, the service is disabled (lines 28, 33, 38, and 43), the service restart fails and an e-mail alert is sent. The received mail is shown in Figure 6.22, which shows the state of the service before (*PreviousInstance*) and after the (*TargetInstance*) modification.

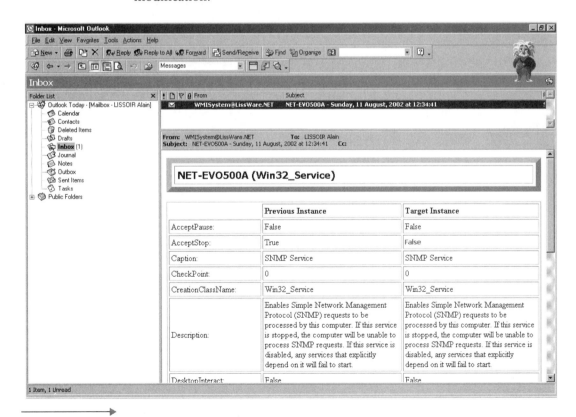

Figure 6.22   *The HTML e-mail viewed in Outlook.*

6.6.2 Calculating delay between two events

As we have seen throughout this chapter, when something occurs in a system, it is possible to receive a notification. But in some situations, it would be interesting to receive an alert when an executed operation takes longer than expected. For instance, if a server is executing some jobs in the background, there is no problem if the job takes 5 or 10 minutes. However, if the job takes more than 10 minutes, it would be nice to receive an alert. Two approaches can be taken here:

1. **Send an alert as soon as the job is completed and only if the execution time is longer than expected.** In this case, we wait for the job to complete and alert the administrator if it took longer than desired. This supposes that the job completes.

2. **Send an alert once the expected delay expires regardless of whether the job has completed.** In this case, we don't wait for the job to complete; the alert is sent as soon as the expected delay expires.

Although both methods are valid, they don't address the same type of problem. In some situations, the first approach would be good enough, and for some others, the second approach would be more suitable. As it is the easiest one, let's start with the first approach. In the next section, we illustrate the second approach by using the elements developed for the first.

A nice case of application for the first approach is related to the Knowledge Consistency Checker topology calculation time. When Active Directory is up and running, it starts a process called the Knowledge Consistency Checker (KCC) every 15 minutes. Among other things, this process calculates where connection objects that establish the link between the different DCs must be created. This allows Active Directory to replicate between DCs while respecting the rules defined by the architect. During its calculation, the KCC takes into consideration a certain number of elements defined by the architect, such as the DC locations, the number of domains, the number of sites created, the site links created, etc. In a large enterprise, when Active Directory deployment starts, the KCC calculation time is never an issue as the number of DCs and sites is quite small. If Active Directory design plans to have a huge number of Sites (more than 200 or more than 500 based on some design assumptions), the topology in place becomes bigger and bigger as the deployment moves forward. At a certain point, it is likely that the KCC calculation time will be an issue since it uses a lot of CPU time (close to 100 percent) during the calculation period. Although, some actions can be taken to avoid such a situation (mostly during Active Directory design phase), there are always practical limits. Active Directory design is a complex matter and is not covered in this book. For more information on this subject, refer to *Mission-Critical Active Directory* by Mickey Balladelli and Jan de Clercq (ISBN 1555582400).

Back to our initial question: How to monitor the KCC calculation time? The KCC is a process, and a first solution could be the use of WMI to monitor the CPU utilization time made by this process. However, there is an easier solution. By changing a registry key in each Active Directory domain controller, it is possible to get an NT Event Log trace of the KCC's starting time and ending time. The timestamp difference between the two traces will determine the KCC calculation time. For this, the following system registry entry must be set to a value of 3:

Key:	HKEY_LOCAL_MACHINE\System\CurrentControlSet\Services\NTDS\Diagnostics
Value Name:	1 Knowledge Consistency Checker
Value Data:	KCC diagnostic levels.
Default:	0

Now, each time the KCC starts and stops its topology calculation, the NT Event Log will at least contain the two messages shown in Figure 6.23.

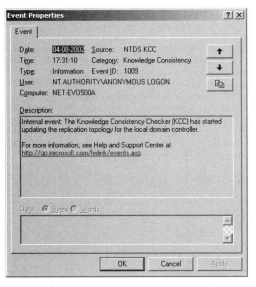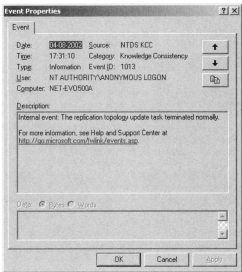

Figure 6.23   *The KCC start and stop events.*

The problem can be summarized as detecting the presence of two NT Event Log messages (1009 and 1013). When the second message appears (1013), the script logic calculates the amount of time between the two events. In order to make the script reusable in other circumstances, the event source name, the starting event code, the ending event code, and the maximum amount of time between the two events will be exposed as command-line parameters. If the amount of time is longer than expected, the script sends an e-mail alert as in the previous sample. Instead of generating an HTML stream for the e-mail body with the GenerateHTML() function seen before, the script will use the WMI XML representation discussed in the previous chapter. Sample 6.22 implements this logic in JScript.

Sample 6.22   *Sending alert when delay between two events reaches a fixed limit (Part I)*

```
 1:<?xml version="1.0"?>
 .:
 8:<package>
 9:  <job>
..:
13:    <runtime>
14:      <named name="SourceName" helpstring="Source event name. (i.e., NTDS KCC)"
                            required="true" type="string"/>
15:      <named name="EventCodeBegin" helpstring="Event code begining. (i.e., 1009)"
                            required="true" type="string"/>
16:      <named name="EventCodeEnd" helpstring="Event code ending. (i.e., 1013)"
                            required="true" type="string"/>
17:      <named name="MaxDelayBetweenEvents" helpstring="Maximum delay between Begin event and
                            Ending event. (in seconds)" required="true" type="string"/>
18:      <named name="Machine" helpstring="determine the WMI system to connect to.
                            (default=LocalHost)" required="false" type="string"/>
19:      <named name="User" helpstring="determine the UserID to perform the remote connection.
                            (default=none)" required="false" type="string"/>
20:      <named name="Password" helpstring="determine the password to perform the remote
                            connection. (default=none)" required="false" type="string"/>
21:      <named name="NameSpace" helpstring="determine the WMI namespace to connect to.
                            (default=Root\CIMv2)" required="false" type="string"/>
22:    </runtime>
23:
24:    <script language="VBScript" src="..\Functions\TinyErrorHandler.vbs" />
25:    <script language="VBScript" src="..\Functions\PauseScript.vbs" />
26:    <script language="VBScript" src="..\Functions\SendMessageExtendedFunction.vbs" />
27:    <script language="VBScript" src="..\Functions\SendAlertFunction.vbs" />
28:
29:    <object progid="WbemScripting.SWbemLocator" id="objWMILocator" reference="true"/>
30:    <object progid="WbemScripting.SWbemDateTime" id="objWMIDateTime" />
31:    <object progid="Microsoft.XMLDom" id="objXML" />
32:    <object progid="Microsoft.XMLDom" id="objXSL" />
33:
34:    <script language="Jscript">
35:    <![CDATA[
36:
37:    // ----------------------------------------------------------------------------
38:    var cComputerName = "LocalHost"
39:    var cWMINameSpace = "root/cimv2"
```

```
40:
41:     var cWMIQuery = "Select * from __InstanceCreationEvent
                                         Where TargetInstance ISA 'Win32_NTLogEvent'"
42:
43:     var cXSLFile = "PathLevel0Win32_NTLogEvent.XSL"
44:
45:     var cTargetRecipient = Alain.Lissoir@LissWare.NET
46:     var cSourceRecipient = WMISystem@LissWare.NET
47:
48:     var cSMTPServer = "relay.LissWare.NET "
..
76:     // -----------------------------------------------------------------------------
77:     // Parse the command line parameters
78:     if (WScript.Arguments.named.Count < 4)
79:        {
80:        WScript.Arguments.ShowUsage();
81:        WScript.Quit();
82:        }
83:
84:     strSourceName = WScript.Arguments.Named("SourceName");
85:     intEventCodeBegin = new Number (WScript.Arguments.Named("EventCodeBegin")).valueOf();
86:     intEventCodeEnd =
                  new Number (WScript.Arguments.Named("EventCodeEnd")).valueOf();
87:     intMaxDelayBetweenEvents =
                  new Number (WScript.Arguments.Named("MaxDelayBetweenEvents")).valueOf();
88:     strUserID = WScript.Arguments.Named("User");
...:
106:    strWMINameSpace = WScript.Arguments.Named("NameSpace");
...:
111:    strWMINameSpace = strWMINameSpace.toUpperCase();
112:
113:    objWMIEventSink = WScript.CreateObject ("WbemScripting.SWbemSink", "EventSINK_");
114:
115:    objWMILocator.Security_.ImpersonationLevel = wbemImpersonationLevelImpersonate;
116:    objWMILocator.Security_.Privileges.AddAsString ("SeSecurityPrivilege", true);
117:    try
118:       {
119:       objWMIServices = objWMILocator.ConnectServer(strComputerName, strWMINameSpace,
120:                                               strUserID, strPassword);
121:       }
122:    catch (Err)
123:       {
124:       ErrorHandler (Err);
125:       }
126:
127:    strWMIQuery = cWMIQuery +
128:                    " And TargetInstance.SourceName='" + strSourceName + "'" +
129:                    " And (TargetInstance.EventCode='" + intEventCodeBegin + "' Or " +
130:                    "TargetInstance.EventCode='" + intEventCodeEnd + "')";
131:
132:    WScript.Echo ("Creating subscription to monitor delay between event log events '" +
133:                    intEventCodeBegin + "' and '"  + intEventCodeEnd + "' for event source '" +
134:                    strSourceName + "'.");
135:    WScript.Echo ();
136:
137:    try
138:       {
139:       objWMIServices.ExecNotificationQueryAsync (objWMIEventSink, strWMIQuery);
140:       }
```

```
141:      catch (Err)
142:        {
143:        ErrorHandler (Err);
144:        }
145:
146:      WScript.Echo ("Waiting for events...");
147:
148:      PauseScript ("Click on 'Ok' to terminate the script ...");
149:
150:      WScript.Echo ();
151:      WScript.Echo ("Cancelling event subscription ...");
152:      objWMIEventSink.cancel();
153:
154:      WScript.Echo ("Finished.");
...:
```

As usual, the first part of the script is the initialization part. This part respects a structure used along all samples we have seen before. Lines 13 to 22 contain the XML structure that defines the command-line parameters. Lines 24 to 27 include some external functions and define some constants used later in the script. Next, the script parses the command line parameters (lines 78 to 111) and creates the WMI connection (lines 115 and 125). Once the WQL event query constructed with the information coming from the command line (lines 127 to 130), the script processes the WMI event subscription (lines 137 and 144). If the command line used is

```
C:\>EventLogTimeDiffMonitor.wsf /SourceName:"NTDS KCC"
                    /EventCodeBegin:1009
                    /EventCodeEnd:1013
                    /MaxDelayBetweenEvents:600
```

The produced WQL event query at line 127 is

```
Select * from __InstanceCreationEvent Where
            TargetInstance ISA 'Win32_NTLogEvent' And
            TargetInstance.SourceName='NTDS KCC' And
            (TargetInstance.EventCode='1009' Or TargetInstance.EventCode='1013')
```

Notice that there is no **WITHIN** statement because the *Win32_NTLogEvent* class is provided by the *NT Event Log* provider, which is an event provider. Next, the WQL event query ensures that the event source is the KCC and that only event code numbers 1009 and 1013 can trigger a WMI event. This means that we have one WQL query for both NT Event Log messages. As with Sample 6.19, many different approaches can be taken. It is also possible to perform a subscription for each message. In this case, it means that we create two subscriptions. Although technically valid, it is easier to combine the events in the same WQL event query as they relate to the same intrinsic event type. Moreover, this uses fewer system resources. If we had a situation in which two different types of event must be monitored (e.g., creation and modification of instances), then it is necessary to create two different subscriptions. Once the WQL query is submitted, the script pauses at line 148.

When the WMI event matching the WQL event query occurs, the OnObjectReady sink routine is called. This sink routine is available in Sample 6.23.

Sample 6.23   *Sending alert when delay between two events reaches a fixed limit (Part II)*

```
...:
156:    // ------------------------------------------------------------------------------
157:    function EventSINK_OnObjectReady (objWbemObject, objWbemAsyncContext)
158:        {
...:
166:        WScript.Echo ();
167:        WScript.Echo ("EventBEGIN - OnObjectReady.");
168:        WScript.Echo (objDate.toLocaleDateString() + " at " +
169:                      objDate.toLocaleTimeString() + ": '" +
170:                      objWbemObject.Path_.Class + "' has been triggered.");
171:
172:        switch (objWbemObject.Path_.Class)
173:              {
174:              case "__InstanceCreationEvent":
175:                   objWMIInstance = objWbemObject.TargetInstance;
176:                   break;
177:              default:
178:                   objWMIInstance = null;
179:                   break;
180:              }
181:
182:        if (objWMIInstance != null)
183:           {
184:           objWMIDateTime.Value = objWMIInstance.TimeGenerated;
185:
186:           switch (objWMIInstance.EventCode)
187:                 {
188:                 case intEventCodeBegin:
189:                      strBeginEventCodeTime = objWMIDateTime.GetVarDate (false);
190:                      WScript.Echo ("Saving '" + strSourceName + "' event '" +
191:                                    intEventCodeBegin +
192:                                    "' startup time (" + strBeginEventCodeTime + ").");
193:                      break;
194:                 case intEventCodeEnd:
195:                      if (strBeginEventCodeTime != null)
196:                         {
197:                         strStopEventCodeTime = objWMIDateTime.GetVarDate (false);
198:                         WScript.Echo ("Saving '" + strSourceName + "' event '" +
199:                                       intEventCodeEnd +
200:                                       "' ending time (" + strStopEventCodeTime + ").");
201:
202:                         objBeginEventCodeTime = new Date(strBeginEventCodeTime);
203:                         objStopEventCodeTime = new Date (strStopEventCodeTime);
204:
205:                         intDelayBetweenEvents =
206:                                 (objStopEventCodeTime-objBeginEventCodeTime)/1000;
                         strBeginEventCodeTime = null;
```

```
207:
208:                              WScript.Echo ("Delay between events is " +
209:                                      intDelayBetweenEvents + " seconds.");
210:
211:                      if (intDelayBetweenEvents >= intMaxDelayBetweenEvents)
212:                          {
213:                          SendAlert (objWMIInstance,
214:                                  "'" + strSourceName + "' event interval (" +
215:                                      intEventCodeBegin + "/" + intEventCodeEnd +
216:                                      ") is " + intDelayBetweenEvents + " seconds. " +
217:                                      objDate.toLocaleDateString() + " at " +
218:                                      objDate.toLocaleTimeString());
219:                          }
220:                      }
221:                  break;
222:              }
223:          }
224:
225:      WScript.Echo ("EventEND - OnObjectReady.");
226:
227:          }
228:
229:      ]]>
230:    </script>
231:   </job>
232:</package>
```

This sink routine is a bit more complex than previous sink routines. Although we do not use the notion of WMI context during the submissions (see Sample 6.22, line 139), there is a kind of context in presence. Why? The script must behave differently depending on whether the event received is the starting event or the ending event. For this reason the majority of the sink code is embraced in a **Switch Case** statement (lines 186 to 223). The **Switch Case** statement considers two cases: one for the starting event (lines 188 to 193) and one for the ending event (lines 194 to 221).

Let's start with the first event—the starting event. As soon as an event occurs, the sink routine saves the time when the event was generated in an **SWbemDateTime** object (line 184). Note that the script takes the time when the event is generated (line 184) and not the time when the WMI event is triggered in the script (line 169). This is important because if WMI has a lot of events in the queue, it is likely that the time when the event is submitted to the sink will be delayed in relation to the time when the event occurred. Because we are in the starting event case, this time is saved in a variable for further use (line 189). Once this is completed, the sink routine terminates normally.

After a while (from a few seconds up to a few minutes or hours), the ending event occurs. At this time, the sink routine branches to the other case of the **Switch Case** (lines 194 to 221).

This case is a bit more complex. First, the sink routine verifies whether the variable containing the starting time has been initialized (line 195). If not, this means that there was no starting event or the script missed the starting event (i.e., the script was started after the starting event). In such a case, there is no way to calculate the period of time between the two events. The triggered ending event is skipped. If the starting time is initialized, the ending time is captured with the help of an **SWbemDateTime** object and stored in a variable (line 197). Next, the sink routine calculates the difference between the two times in seconds with the help of two JScript **Date** objects (lines 202 to 205). This is where the saved time during the starting event is reused (line 202). Once the calculation completes, the starting time variable is reset (line 206).

The amount of time between the two events is evaluated against the maximum time expected (line 211). If the time is smaller than the maximum, the sink routine terminates silently. If the time is greater than or equal to the maximum, some more processing is made to send an alert. The alert creation is written with a VBScript function available in Sample 6.24.

Sample 6.24   *Sending alert when delay between two events reaches a fixed limit (Part III)*

```
 .:
 .:
 .:
6:' -------------------------------------------------------------------------------
7:
8:Function SendAlert (objWMIInstance, strTitle)
..:
17:    Set objWMINamedValueSet = CreateObject ("WbemScripting.SWbemNamedValueSet")
18:
19:    objWMINamedValueSet.Add "LocalOnly", False
20:    objWMINamedValueSet.Add "PathLevel", 0
21:    objWMINamedValueSet.Add "IncludeQualifiers", False
22:    objWMINamedValueSet.Add "ExcludeSystemProperties", True
23:
24:    strXMLText = objWMIInstance.GetText_(wbemObjectTextFormatWMIDTD20, _
25:                                        , _
26:                                        objWMINamedValueSet)
..:
30:    objXML.Async = False
31:    objXML.LoadXML strXMLText
32:
33:    objXSL.Async = False
34:    objXSL.Load (cXSLFile)
35:
36:    strHTMLText = objXML.TransformNode(objXSL)
37:    WScript.Echo "Sending an email alert."
38:
39:    If SendMessage (cTargetRecipient, _
40:                    cSourceRecipient, _
41:                    strTitle, _
```

```
42:                     strHTMLText, _
43:                     "") Then
44:       WScript.Echo "Failed to send email alert to '" & cTargetRecipient & "' ..."
45:    End If
46:
47:End Function
```

The script sends an e-mail alert (lines 39 to 43). In the previous sample, we used a VBScript function to generate the HTML output to send the mail. However, in the previous chapter, we saw that it is possible to obtain an XML representation of a **SWbemObject** by invoking its *GetText_* method, which is precisely what this function is doing (only supported under Windows XP and Windows.NET Server). With the help of the **SWbemNamedValueSet** object, the script passes the parameters desired for the XML generation (lines 19 to 22). Next, the XML representation is retrieved (lines 24 to 26). Instead of using a VBScript function to generate the HTML output, the sink routine takes advantage of the XML features offered by WMI. By referencing the XSL file defined at line 43 in Sample 6.22 and using some object methods provided by the Microsoft DOMXML object model, it is possible to generate the desired HTML output (line 36). Of course, an XSL file must be created for this purpose. Here is the content of the XSL file:

```
 1:<?xml version='1.0'?>
 2:
 3:<xsl:stylesheet xmlns:xsl="http://www.w3.org/TR/WD-xsl">
 4: <xsl:template match="/">
 5:
 6:  <html>
 7:   <TABLE ID="TBL" BORDER="10" WIDTH="100%" CELLSPACING="5" CELLPADDING="5">
 8:    <TR>
 9:     <TD>
10:      <B>
11:       <FONT color="black">
12:        <SPAN style="COLOR: black; FONT-FAMILY: Tahoma; FONT-SIZE: 14pt">
13:         <xsl:value-of select="/INSTANCE/PROPERTY[@NAME = 'ComputerName']/VALUE"/>
14:         (<xsl:value-of select="/INSTANCE/@CLASSNAME"/>)
15:        </SPAN>
16:       </FONT>
17:      </B>
18:     </TD>
19:    </TR>
20:   </TABLE>
21:
22:  <BR></BR>
23:   <TABLE ID="TBL" BORDER="1" WIDTH="100%" CELLSPACING="2" CELLPADDING="2">
24:    <TR>
25:    <TD>
26:     <b>Properties</b>
27:    </TD>
28:    <TD>
29:     <b>Values</b>
30:    </TD>
```

```
31:    </TR>
32:    <xsl:for-each select="/INSTANCE/PROPERTY">
33:     <TR>
34:      <TD>
35:       <xsl:value-of select="@NAME"/>
36:       (<xsl:value-of select="@TYPE"/>)
37:      </TD>
38:      <TD>
39:       <xsl:value-of select="VALUE"/>
40:      </TD>
41:     </TR>
42:    </xsl:for-each>
43:    </TABLE>
44:
45:    <FONT color="red">
46:     <SPAN style="COLOR:red; FONT-FAMILY: Tahoma; FONT-SIZE: 10pt; FONT-WEIGHT: bold">
47:
48:     </SPAN>
49:    </FONT>
50:
51:    <FONT color="black">
52:     <SPAN style="COLOR:black; FONT-FAMILY: Tahoma; FONT-SIZE: 10pt">
53:
54:     </SPAN>
55:    </FONT>
56:
57:   </html>
58:
59: </xsl:template>
60:</xsl:stylesheet>
```

For the sake of completeness, the XML representation of an instance delivered during the ending event is as follows:

```
 1:<INSTANCE CLASSNAME="Win32_NTLogEvent">
 2: <PROPERTY NAME="Category" CLASSORIGIN="Win32_NTLogEvent" TYPE="uint16">
 3:  <VALUE>1</VALUE>
 4: </PROPERTY>
 5: <PROPERTY NAME="CategoryString" CLASSORIGIN="Win32_NTLogEvent" TYPE="string">
 6:  <VALUE>Knowledge Consistency Checker</VALUE>
 7: </PROPERTY>
 8: <PROPERTY NAME="ComputerName" CLASSORIGIN="Win32_NTLogEvent" TYPE="string">
 9:  <VALUE>XP-DPEN6400</VALUE>
10: </PROPERTY>
11: <PROPERTY.ARRAY NAME="Data" CLASSORIGIN="Win32_NTLogEvent" PROPAGATED="true" TYPE="uint8">
12: </PROPERTY.ARRAY>
13: <PROPERTY NAME="EventCode" CLASSORIGIN="Win32_NTLogEvent" TYPE="uint16">
14:  <VALUE>1013</VALUE>
15: </PROPERTY>
..:
..:
..:
33: <PROPERTY NAME="SourceName" CLASSORIGIN="Win32_NTLogEvent" TYPE="string">
34:  <VALUE>NTDS KCC</VALUE>
35: </PROPERTY>
36: <PROPERTY NAME="TimeGenerated" CLASSORIGIN="Win32_NTLogEvent" TYPE="datetime">
37:  <VALUE>20020623103934.000000+120</VALUE>
38: </PROPERTY>
```

```
39: <PROPERTY NAME="TimeWritten" CLASSORIGIN="Win32_NTLogEvent" TYPE="datetime">
40:  <VALUE>20020623103934.000000+120</VALUE>
41: </PROPERTY>
42: <PROPERTY NAME="Type" CLASSORIGIN="Win32_NTLogEvent" TYPE="string">
43:  <VALUE>information</VALUE>
44: </PROPERTY>
45: <PROPERTY NAME="User" CLASSORIGIN="Win32_NTLogEvent" TYPE="string">
46:  <VALUE>NT AUTHORITY\ANONYMOUS LOGON</VALUE>
47: </PROPERTY>
48:</INSTANCE>
```

The script loads the XML and XSL files in two DOM XML objects created in the XML header of the script (lines 30 and 31 in Sample 6.22). Once both XML files are loaded (lines 31 and 34 in Sample 6.24), the sink routine performs the XSL transformation to obtain the HTML representation (line 36). Next, the sink routine sends the mail as seen before in Sample 6.21. The mail received is almost the same as the one shown in Figure 6.22, but the output is adapted to match the requirements of an NT Event Log entry instance.

6.6.3   Calculating delay between one event and one nonevent

The previous script works perfectly as long as the ending event occurs. But what happens if the ending event never occurs? The answer is quite easy: The script will never send an alert. This can be unfortunate in some situations. In the previous scenario, if the process takes an extremely long time to complete, it is clear that the alert will be sent, but will it be too late? Moreover, if the process crashes after the starting event, the alert will never be sent, which is worse! This is why the script must also be able to support situations where the ending event doesn't occur in an expected delay. If we combine the previous script with some of the features we learned about the timer events (see Sample 6.2), it is possible to solve this problem using the same command-line parameters. This logic is implemented in Sample 6.25 and reuses, as a base, the code developed in the previous section (Samples 6.22 to 6.24).

Sample 6.25   *Sending an alert if the expired time from one event reaches a fixed limit (Part I)*

```
...:
...:
...:
119:    objWMIEventSink = WScript.CreateObject ("WbemScripting.SWbemSink", "EventSINK_");
120:    objWMINonEventSink = WScript.CreateObject ("WbemScripting.SWbemSink", "NonEventSINK_");
121:
122:    objWMILocator.Security_.ImpersonationLevel = wbemImpersonationLevelImpersonate;
123:    objWMILocator.Security_.Privileges.AddAsString ("SeSecurityPrivilege", true);
```

```
124:    try
125:      {
126:      objWMIServices = objWMILocator.ConnectServer(strComputerName, strWMINameSpace,
127:                                             strUserID, strPassword);
128:      }
129:    catch (Err)
130:      {
131:      ErrorHandler (Err);
132:      }
133:
134:    strWMIQuery = cWMIQuery +
135:                  " And TargetInstance.SourceName='" + strSourceName + "'" +
136:                  " And (TargetInstance.EventCode='" + intEventCodeBegin + "' Or " +
137:                  "TargetInstance.EventCode='" + intEventCodeEnd + "')";
138:
139:    WScript.Echo ("Creating subscription to monitor delay between event log events '" +
140:                  intEventCodeBegin + "' and '" + intEventCodeEnd + "' for event source '" +
141:                  strSourceName + "'.");
142:    WScript.Echo ();
143:
144:    try
145:      {
146:      objWMIServices.ExecNotificationQueryAsync (objWMIEventSink, strWMIQuery);
147:      }
148:    catch (Err)
149:      {
150:      ErrorHandler (Err);
151:      }
152:
153:    WScript.Echo ("Waiting for events...");
154:
155:    PauseScript ("Click on 'Ok' to terminate the script ...");
156:
157:    WScript.Echo ();
158:    WScript.Echo ("Cancelling event subscription ...");
159:    objWMINonEventSink.cancel();
160:    objWMIEventSink.cancel();
161:
162:    WScript.Echo ("Finished.");
...:
...:
...:
```

The startup section of the script is the same as before. The only addition is the creation of two **SWbemSink** objects instead of one. Here, we use two sink routines: a first sink routine to catch the starting and ending events as before (line 119) and a second sink routine to catch a timeout event (line 120). The sink routine catching the starting and ending events is referenced as before during the WQL query submission (line 146). The second **SWbemSink** object is used during the execution of the sink routine catching the starting and ending events. As it is the only change in the script startup section, let's take a look at the new sink routines. These routines are shown in Sample 6.26.

Sample 6.26   *Sending an alert if the expired time from one event reaches a fixed limit (Part II)*

```
...:
...:
...:
164:      // -------------------------------------------------------------------------------
165:      function EventSINK_OnObjectReady (objWbemObject, objWbemAsyncContext)
166:          {
...:
176:
177:          WScript.Echo ();
178:          WScript.Echo ("EventBEGIN - OnObjectReady.");
179:          WScript.Echo (objDate.toLocaleDateString() + " at " +
180:                        objDate.toLocaleTimeString() + ": '" +
181:                        objWbemObject.Path_.Class + "' has been triggered.");
182:
183:          switch (objWbemObject.Path_.Class)
184:                {
185:                case "__InstanceCreationEvent":
186:                    objWMIInstance = objWbemObject.TargetInstance;
187:                    break;
188:                default:
189:                    objWMIInstance = null;
190:                    break;
191:                }
192:
193:          if (objWMIInstance != null)
194:             {
195:             objWMIDateTime.Value = objWMIInstance.TimeGenerated;
196:
197:             switch (objWMIInstance.EventCode)
198:                    {
199:                    case intEventCodeBegin:
200:                        objWMIBeginEventInstance = objWMIInstance;
201:                        strBeginEventCodeTime = objWMIDateTime.GetVarDate (false);
202:                        WScript.Echo ("Saving '" + strSourceName + "' event '" +
203:                              intEventCodeBegin +
204:                              "' startup time (" + strBeginEventCodeTime + ").");
205:
206:                        objWMINonEventClass = objWMIServices.Get (cWMIClass);
207:
208:                        objWMINonEventInstance = objWMINonEventClass.SpawnInstance_();
209:                        objWMINonEventInstance.TimerID = cTimerID;
210:                        objWMINonEventInstance.SkipifPassed = true;
211:
212:                        objWMINonEventInstance.IntervalBetweenEvents =
                                                    (intMaxDelayBetweenEvents) * 1000;
213:                        objWMINonEventInstance.Put_
                                (wbemChangeFlagCreateOrUpdate | wbemFlagReturnWhenComplete);
214:
215:                        WScript.Echo ("'" + cTimerID + "' instance created.");
216:
217:                        objWMIServices.ExecNotificationQueryAsync (objWMINonEventSink,
218:                                                    cWMINonEventQuery);
219:                        break;
220:                    case intEventCodeEnd:
221:                        if (strBeginEventCodeTime != null)
222:
```

```
223:                             strStopEventCodeTime = objWMIDateTime.GetVarDate (false);
224:                             WScript.Echo ("Saving '" + strSourceName + "' event '" +
225:                                           intEventCodeEnd +
226:                                           "' ending time (" + strStopEventCodeTime + ").");
227:
228:                             objBeginEventCodeTime = new Date(strBeginEventCodeTime);
229:                             objStopEventCodeTime = new Date (strStopEventCodeTime);
230:
231:                             intDelayBetweenEvents =
232:                                     (objStopEventCodeTime - objBeginEventCodeTime) / 1000;
232:                             strBeginEventCodeTime = null;
233:
234:                             WScript.Echo ("Delay between events is " +
235:                                           intDelayBetweenEvents + " seconds.");
236:
237:                             if (intDelayBetweenEvents >= intMaxDelayBetweenEvents)
238:                                 {
239:                                 SendAlert (objWMIInstance,
240:                                            "'" + strSourceName + "' event interval (" +
241:                                            intEventCodeBegin + "/" + intEventCodeEnd +
242:                                            ") is " + intDelayBetweenEvents + " seconds. " +
243:                                            objDate.toLocaleDateString() + " at " +
244:                                            objDate.toLocaleTimeString());
245:                                 }
246:                             else
247:                                 {
248:                                 try
249:                                     {
250:                                     objWMINonEventInstance = objWMIServices.Get
251:                                                    (cWMIClass + "='" + cTimerID + "'");
251:                                     objWMINonEventSink.Cancel();
252:                                     objWMINonEventInstance.Delete_();
253:                                     WScript.Echo ("'" + cTimerID + "' instance deleted.");
254:                                     }
255:                                 catch(Err) {}
256:                                 }
257:                             }
258:                         break;
259:                         }
260:                     }
261:
262:        WScript.Echo ("EventEND - OnObjectReady.");
263:
264:        }
...:
...:
...:
```

The EventSINK_OnObjectReady() sink routine receiving the starting and ending events is exactly the same as the one presented in Sample 6.23. All previous comments about this sink remain valid. Of course, to address the nonevent problem described, some extra logic is added. This code is represented in boldface in lines 206 to 218 and lines 246 to 256. This extra logic is executed in two phases. The first phase executes when the starting event occurs (lines 199 to 219). This phase starts by saving the instance representing the starting event (line 200). Previously, only the event generation time was saved (line 195 and 201), but now, because we may not have an ending event, it is useful to show the instance corresponding to the starting event when the expected period of time for the ending event has expired. This starting instance is used during the execution of the sink corresponding to the timeout event.

Next, the EventSINK_OnObjectReady() sink during a starting event creates a __IntervalTimerInstruction instance (lines 206 to 215). This piece of code simply reuses the code we discovered when examining the interval timer events. The code comes from Sample 6.2 (lines 35 to 40). Once the __IntervalTimerInstruction instance is created, the script proceeds to an asynchronous subscription for this interval timer event and references the second **SWbemSINK** object (line 217 and 218) created during the startup phase of the script (line 120). This sends all interval timer events to the dedicated timer sink. Note that this timer event is using a pulse corresponding to the maximum allowed time specified on the command line (line 212).

Now, the script is registered to receive two event types to two different sinks: (1) an event type corresponding to any starting or ending events and redirected to the EventSINK_OnObjectReady() sink and (2) an event type corresponding to the timer event and redirected to the NonEvent-SINK_OnObjectReady() sink. In such a situation, two cases must be considered:

1.   **The ending event occurs before the timeout.** This situation corresponds to the second phase of the EventSINK_OnObjectReady() execution. This is the phase corresponding to the ending event. In the code, it corresponds to the second part of the **Switch Case** (lines 220 to 258 in Sample 6.26). This part of the script executes the same logic as that used in Sample 6.23 (lines 195 to 219). The extra code added to this part of the **Switch Case** is visible in boldface in Sample 6.26 (lines 246 to 256). Because the ending event occurs before the timer event, it is not necessary to keep the timer event running, as it is created to alert in case of nonevent of the ending event. This is why the lines 246 to 256 delete the created timer event. These lines of code are extracted from Sample 6.3 (lines 31 to 33) when we saw how to proceed to the deletion of an interval timer event.

       You can see that the ending event case continues to compare the expired time with the maximum allowed time (line 237). This allows the script to send an alert when the ending event occurs after the timeout.

2.   **The timeout occurs before the ending event.** This situation occurs only when the ending event is not raised in the expected delay specified on the command line. In this case, the second sink, NonEventSINK_OnObjectReady(), is called (see Sample 6.27). Because the interval timer event has been triggered, it is no longer necessary to execute it, and the script deletes the interval timer event created during the starting event phase (lines 278 to 284). Because the interval timer occurred, it means that the maximum allowed time for the ending event has expired. In this case, the script sends an alert with the help of the SendAlert() function (lines 287 to 291). Notice that the SendAlert() function uses the starting instance as parameter. Doing so, the operator receives the timeout message with a view of the corresponding starting instance. When the ending event occurs, the EventSINK_OnOjbectReady() sink is invoked. Because the ending event is out of delay, the conditions at line 237 (see Sample 6.26) are True, and the script sends a second alert containing the ending event instance.

Sample 6.27   *Sending an alert if the expired time from one event reaches a fixed limit (Part III)*

```
...:
...:
...:
266:      // -----------------------------------------------------------------------------
267:      function NonEventSINK_OnObjectReady (objWbemObject, objWbemAsyncContext)
268:          {
...:
272:          WScript.Echo ();
273:          WScript.Echo ("NonEventBEGIN - OnObjectReady.");
274:          WScript.Echo (objDate.toLocaleDateString() + " at " +
275:                        objDate.toLocaleTimeString() + ": '" +
276:                        objWbemObject.Path_.Class + "' has been triggered.");
277:
278:          try
279:            {
280:            objWMINonEventInstance = objWMIServices.Get(cWMIClass + "='" + cTimerID + "'");
281:            objWMINonEventSink.Cancel();
282:            objWMINonEventInstance.Delete_();
283:            WScript.Echo ("'" + cTimerID + "' instance deleted.");
284:            }
285:          catch (Err) {}
286:
287:          SendAlert (objWMIBeginEventInstance,
288:                     "'" + strSourceName + "' event '" + intEventCodeEnd +
289:                        "' didn't occur within " + intMaxDelayBetweenEvents + " seconds. " +
290:                        objDate.toLocaleDateString() + " at " +
291:                        objDate.toLocaleTimeString());
292:
293:          WScript.Echo ("NonEventEND - OnObjectReady.");
```

```
294:
295:        }
296:
297:    ]]>
298:    </script>
299:    </job>
300:</package>
```

This script (from Samples 6.25 to 6.27) shows how the interaction of an intrinsic event (_*InstanceCreationEvent*) and an interval timer event (_*IntervalTimerInstruction*) can be combined to implement a powerful monitoring. In the code, we use only the *Win32_NTLogEvent* class, but this logic can be easily adapted to any class available in WMI. However, the properties and the conditions to trigger the desired event must be adapted.

6.7   Summary

This chapter examined WMI events by explaining the different event types available from WMI and the type of system classes they use. Beside the WMI scripting API used in a script managing WMI events, WMI events can be received only by formulating the right WQL event query. This is why the knowledge we acquired about WQL in Chapter 3 is very important. Without being able to formulate a WQL event query, it is impossible to work with the WMI events. In this chapter, we also saw that the event providers and the classes that they implement have an influence at three levels:

1.   The way the WQL query is formulated

2.   The retrieved properties from the event

3.   The instance subject to the event

6.8   What's next?

A good knowledge of the provider capabilities is key in retrieving the expected information. Up to now, we have worked with a very small number of providers. Because the WMI scripting capabilities are closely related to the WMI providers' capabilities, it is important to discover the WMI providers available under Windows.NET Server and their capabilities. Gathering such knowledge enhances our scripting capabilities. This is the purpose of the second book, *Leveraging Windows Management Instrumentation (WMI) Scripting* (ISBN 1555582990).

6.9   **Useful Internet URLs**

Patch for Windows 2000 SP2: Q306274 (Corrected in SP3): WMI Inadvertently Cancels Intrinsic Event Queries:

`http://support.microsoft.com/default.aspx?scid=kb;en-us;Q306274`

`http://www.microsoft.com/downloads/release.asp?releaseid=37814`

Index